Contents

AUSTRALIA

– SECTION 1 –
LIVING IN AUSTRALIA

DAILY LIFE

RETIREMENT

– SECTION II –
WORKING IN AUSTRALIA

EMPLOYMENT

NEW ZEALAND

– SECTION 1 –
LIVING IN NEW ZEALAND

– SECTION II –
WORKING IN NEW ZEALAND

ACKNOWLEDGEMENTS

This is the third edition of Live and Work in Australia and New Zealand. The first was written by Fiona McGregor and Charlotte Denny, the second edition by Elisabeth Roberts and Susan McIntosh and the third has been fully revised and up-dated by Dan Boothby and Susan Kelly. The book owes its origins to all of these people who have over the years contributed to the content.

The authors and publishers would like to thank the many other people who provided information and assistance in compiling this book. In particular, thanks are due to Geraint Davies of Montfort International for his contributions, the staff of Oxford University Computing Services for unfailing technical assistance. Thanks are also due to Nathan Males, Danny Jones, and Lucy Fahy at Australia and New Zealand Chamber of Commerce UK, Joanne Perry at the New Zealand High Commission in London, as well as Pete Plimmer and Laurence Moss for their contributions. Also Ron Mair, Information Analyst at Statistics New Zealand.

TELEPHONE NUMBERS

Please note that the telephone numbers in this book are written as needed to call that number from inside the same country. To call these numbers from outside the country you will need to know the relevant international access code; these are currently 00 from the UK and France and 011 from the USA

To call Australia: dial the international access code +61 and the number given in this book minus the first 0.

To call New Zealand: dial the international access code +64 and the number in this book minus the first 0.

To call the UK: international access code +44 then the number given in this book minus the first 0.

To call the USA: international access code +1 then the complete number as given in this book.

FOREWORD

This third edition of *Live and Work in Australia and New Zealand* has been revised throughout to aid anyone planning a prolonged trip to the lands down under in order to experience a way of life verging on the legendary. *Live & Work in Australia and New Zealand* provides information on all aspects of making the move to the Antipodes: from the first step of making an application and being granted the right visa to suit your needs, to arranging accommodation and work once (and even before) you have arrived in either Australia or New Zealand. This book contains many useful addresses and websites of companies that can smooth your way, and gives details of work and business opportunities in the various regions of Australia and New Zealand.

Australia has long been seen as a place where the laid back lifestyle and the unpretentiousness of a people with a 'give 'em a fair go' attitude makes for a great place to spend as long as possible. Add to this the incredible diversity of landscapes of the two countries, and the high standard of living, and you'll probably end up asking yourself why you didn't emigrate years ago.

Australia has vast areas of desert and bushland that give way to tropical rainforests, high-tech cities and beautiful coastlines; New Zealand has a hint of Victorian Englishness about it combined with the strongly felt influences of Polynesia and the Maori culture. The film epic *Lord of the Rings*, made on location in New Zealand in 2001, has helped to introduce millions more people to the beauty of the country and the next tourist seasons are looking to become the most successful yet.

There is scope for embarking on a successful new life in both countries, with many business opportunities available to the entrepreneur and jobseeker. Funding and tax incentives are also often offered to those wishing to invest in new or existing businesses. With the current low exchange rate on the Australian and New Zealand dollar many visitors to the region find that they are better off than they were back home. Australia has long been a country where long-term 'career' expats, who may have spent much of their working lives living in rather more austere countries, have decided to finally settle down and start a small business. New Zealand, although quieter than Australia, and definitely more remote, nevertheless can be the right place for many people looking for a high quality, outdoor, less stressful lifestyle.

Australia celebrated its centenary as a Federation in 2001, and for the time being remains part of the Commonwealth. The Republican movement failed to persuade the nation that it should sever its bonds with the UK. A referendum held in 1999 found narrowly in favour of the monarchists; but the battle of the Republic is far from over.

During the 1990s Australia recorded the second-fastest annual economic growth rate in the developed world (behind that of Ireland) and prospects remain promising. The Australian economy is in its best shape in thirty years and if ever there was a time to consider settling there, then it is now; New Zealand is a modern, stable, and strong democracy with a forward-looking and environmentally-conscious government. New Zealand and Australian immigration departments continue to favour young, educated and/or skilled migrants, while still allowing family-linked and a small amount of humanitarian immigration to take place. Working Holiday visas for both countries remain very popular and give those aged 18-30 a year's grace to live, work and holiday, and perhaps to discover whether they would like to commit themselves for longer and take the bigger step of emigrating.

The popularity of the earlier editions of *Live & Work in Australia and New Zealand* has proved that both Australia and New Zealand exert a strong pull on those who wish to escape the dreary winters of northern Europe, find a sunnier climate and make a new start in life.

Dan Boothby
Susan Kelly
April 2002

Australia

SECTION 1

LIVING IN AUSTRALIA

GENERAL INTRODUCTION

RESIDENCE AND ENTRY REGULATIONS

SETTING UP HOME

DAILY LIFE

RETIREMENT

GENERAL INTRODUCTION

CHAPTER SUMMARY

○ **Beginnings.** The first convicts to be transported to Australia landed at Jackson Harbour (now Sydney) in 1788.

   ○ The first free settlers arrived in 1793, lured by promises of unlimited land and free convict labour.

○ **Economy.** During the 1990s, Australia averaged an annual growth rate of 4%.

   ○ The countries of the Pacific Rim are Australia's biggest export market.

○ **Republic or Monarchy?** Despite growing republicanism, 55% of the Australian electorate voted in a 1999 referendum to remain a constitutional monarchy.

○ **Sheep and Cattle.** Australia leads the world in wool production.

   ○ 120 million sheep and 26 million cattle graze the plains of Australia.

   ○ Livestock farms are known as stations and the largest is the size of Belgium, or Maryland.

○ **Minerals.** Over 60 different kinds of metals and minerals are mined in Australia.

○ **Aboriginals.** Three years after the arrival of Europeans, two-thirds of aboriginals had been wiped out by European diseases and a deliberate policy of annihilation.

   ○ Today, about 1% of Australians have aboriginal blood and of these 10,000 are pure blooded aboriginals.

○ **Creatures that Bite.** Australia is notorious for its deadly insects, life-threatening snakes and many species of sharks.

   ○ Don't bathe at dawn or dusk as these are the usual shark feeding times.

○ **Sun Warning.** Australians have the highest rate of skin cancer in the world.

○ Children in Australia wear total body, zip-up swimsuits against the sun.

Destination Australia

For several generations, Australia has been one of the world's most popular migration destinations. The promises of eternal sunshine and prosperity, and of freedom from the class-bound traditions of the Old World have proved a magnet both for young, independent travellers and for families seeking a new life. In some cases, they have been disappointed. Australia is not a utopia and, although it is fiercely loved and defended by its citizens, it would not claim to be. Like any other country in the industrialised world, it experiences its share of contemporary social malaise: recession, unemployment, crime and public corruption have all made their mark in recent decades. Nonetheless, the attractions of good weather (but not *every* day!) and a high standard of living remain as strong as ever, and there has been no decline in the numbers of people seeking to emigrate from Europe and, increasingly, from South east Asia and other regions.

The days of the 'ten pound pom', though, are long gone. Australia no longer needs to offer inducements to build up its population and skill base, and immigration quotas are now strictly regulated. The application procedure is lengthy, complex and expensive, with an emphasis on the net gain to Australian society. Whilst the country actively pursues a programme of humanitarian immigration most applicants will need to be able to demonstrate financial security and significant professional experience.

The Pacific Rim is Australia's biggest export market and for more than a decade the country has pursued a policy of 'asianisation', forging close political, cultural, and economic ties with its near neighbours. Although the Australian dollar is relatively weak (good news for 'poms' who currently get about $3 to the £1) the Australian economy is in its best shape in thirty years, enjoying a sustained convergence of steady growth, low inflation, low interest rates, and a falling external deficit. During the 1990s Australia recorded an average annual economic growth rate of nearly 4% a year, the second-fastest rate in the developed world (behind Ireland) and Australia looks set to remain 'comfortably off' well into the 21st century.

Australia's greatest attractions remain unchanged whatever the state of her economy. The expansive landscape with its infinite variety, the oceans and waterways which are at the heart of the Australian way of life, and the spacious and attractive cities are all valued and enjoyed. Australian society is refreshingly open and vigorous, the people are friendly, and the ethical cornerstones of equality and freedom are championed in a kind of congenital anti-authoritarianism. Whether you are considering a short holiday or a lifetime's move, you will find that Australians will always be prepared to give you a 'fair go'.

Pros and Cons of Moving to Australia

Australia's climate has always been a motivating factor in the decision of many European migrants to leave their home shores. The warm, sunny weather in most coastal regions allows people to enjoy an outdoor lifestyle with an emphasis on leisure. Even hardship seems better when the sun shines; there are acknowledged health and psychological benefits to living in a favourable climate.

Fruit and vegetables are abundant, fresh, and almost invariably locally grown. There is a huge variety available, including many tropical and exotic fruits rarely seen in Europe, and prices are significantly lower. Meat is particularly cheap and of excellent quality, and there is no risk of BSE infection in Australian beef.

Most Australians live in large, modern cities, which compete successfully in the

global economy. Australian scientific and technical research lead the world in many areas, and technology, engineering, commerce and banking are now as important to the economy as its agricultural and mining industries. Salaries are not as high as in the UK when converted dollar-to-pound, but with a much lower cost of living an average wage goes much further. Real estate is very much cheaper and most Australians own their own home, which will be large by European standards. Sydney and Melbourne are the most expensive cities in which to purchase property, and although these cities have a higher population density than others in Australia, residents retain the expectation of a large, detached house with a garden and garage, even in central city areas. Relatively few people live in flats.

In spite of these and other advantages, many immigrants do find certain aspects of Australian life difficult at first. In particular, new arrivals are sometimes painfully aware of their geographical isolation in Australia. Homesickness and the prohibitive cost of international air travel occasionally promote a sense of exile. Many are overwhelmed and it is not uncommon for immigrants to return permanently to their home country within a couple of years.

Although the cost of living is, in general, low, imported goods carry a substantial luxury tax, which may place familiar or favourite brands and items outside financial reach. Local alternatives are always available, but there are those migrants for whom no amount of sun, sea and sand can compensate for an over-priced tin of mushy peas.

CREEPY CRAWLIES AND WORSE

Australia is also notorious for its unpleasant insects, life-threatening snakes and its many species of shark. With the warm weather come flies – swarms of them – and if you live near freshwater, probably mosquitoes too. It is wise to assume that any spider you encounter is probably venomous until you learn to recognise those which pose an actual danger. Red-back, funnel web, and trapdoor spiders are all potentially fatal to adults as well as children, and Australians learn from an early age where these are likely to lurk. Even local bushland parks may harbour snakes such as dugites, whose bite will be lethal unless treated immediately. Most Australians know how to apply a tourniquet and suck out venom from a snakebite (though most *never* need to use this knowledge), and it may be reassuring to take a first aid course when you arrive, especially if you have a young family. Sharks live in Australia's coastal waters and most beaches have an aerial shark patrol, as well as lifesavers on duty. Shark attacks are extremely rare and their possibility does not discourage Australians from beachlife. Once again, however, it is important to be alert and born-and-bred Australians do not swim at dawn or dusk, which is known to be the sharks' feeding time.

In spite of these disadvantages, Australia has a cultural vitality and diversity which is invigorating. The population is very cosmopolitan and this is reflected in the enormous choice of restaurants, and the range of entertainment available in every city.

From the European perspective, the main pros and cons of living in Australia can be summarised as follows:

Pros
Warm, sunny climate
High standard of living, including better pay
Better work conditions
Low cost of real estate
First class educational standards and facilities
Excellent medical facilities
Multicultural diversity
Low cost of living and high quality produce

Cons
Geographical isolation
Expensive national and international travel
High cost of imported goods
Annoying and dangerous insects and animals

POLITICAL AND ECONOMIC STRUCTURE

Australia is divided into six states – New South Wales (NSW), Victoria (Vic), Queensland (Qld), South Australia (SA), Western Australia (WA), and Tasmania (TAS) – and two territories, the Northern Territory (NT), and the Australian Capital Territory (ACT). The states and territories of Australia each have their own parliaments, capital city, flag, and emblems depicting regional flora and fauna. Australian mapmakers, atlases, and educationalists use cartographic projections which show Australia and the Southeast Asian region at the centre of the world map, with Europe to the extreme left and the American continents to the right.

Historical Background

Although archaeological and historical evidence suggests that Australia was first settled over 50,000 years ago by Aborigines, and later mapped by Dutch and Portuguese galleons in the 16th century, Australia's founding myths centre on the 'discovery' of the east coast by Captain James Cook in 1770. It was Cook who claimed the 'Great South Land' for the Crown. Eighteen years later, in response to a crisis in English jails and a shortage of natural resources following the American Declaration of Independence, the First Fleet arrived in Port Jackson (now known as Sydney Harbour) with 11 ships, 736 convicts and a contingent of guards. The majority of convicts came from the cities of London, Manchester, Liverpool, Dublin and Glasgow and were transported for what now seem petty offences. A total of 160,000 convicts were brought to Australia over the next 70 years, and many of those who survived their sentences, chose to stay on in the country as farmers.

Free Settlement. The first free settlers, lured by the promise of cheap land and convict labour, began to arrive in 1793, whilst explorers gradually opened up new country, discovering rich grazing land to the west. Wool soon became one of Australia's most important industries and remains so to the present. The discovery of gold in the 1850s brought a fresh influx of immigrants from Europe, China and America, and rich gold seams were found at Ballarat, north of Melbourne, and in central Western Australia, at Kalgoorlie. Large copper deposits were found in the York Peninsula in South Australia. Settlements were established in Hobart, Tasmania in 1803; on the Brisbane River, Queensland, in 1824; on the Swan River, in Western Australia in 1829; on Port Phillip Bay, Victoria in 1835; and on Gulf St Vincent, South Australia in 1836. The capital cities of each state have grown from these sites. In 1900 the colonies, which were previously independent entities, united in order to encourage economic expansion, regulate the postal system and build a military defence force. The constitution was presented to the House of Commons in London in 1900 and was signed by Queen Victoria. Australia became the Commonwealth of Australia on 1 January 1901, and this date is known as Federation Day. Australia Day is celebrated on 26 January every year and commemorates the arrival of the First Fleet at Port Jackson.

Government

Australia is governed by three levels of elected government – local, state, and federal – and has been called the most over-governed country in the world. Local government operates through city and shire councils who have responsibility for local amenities, town planning, parks and pet and vermin control. State governments fund and administer roads, vehicle licensing, the police force, education and health care (amongst many other departments) while the Government of Australia (the Federal or Commonwealth government) takes care of international trade, foreign affairs and the national treasury. State governments are located in the capital city of each state and the national parliament is in Canberra, the administrative capital of Australia. Although there are both state and federal taxes, income earners fill out only one tax return per year, remitted to the Australian Taxation Office, which then distributes revenue to the various states to fund their public services.

State and federal governments are run according to the British Westminster system, with two key differences. Firstly, unlike Britain, Australia has a written constitution, inspired by the constitution of the United States; and secondly, Australia's upper house, the Senate (equivalent in function to the British House of Lords) is a democratically elected body. The lower house is known as the House of Representatives, and its parliamentarians as Members of the House of Representatives (MHR). The legislative power of the Commonwealth of Australia is vested in the Parliament of the Commonwealth. Queen Elizabeth II is Australia's Head of State (under the Australian *Royal Styles and Titles Act* of 1973 her title is 'Queen of Australia and Her Other Realms and Territories, Head of the Commonwealth') and her representative in Australia is the Governor-General, who has the powers to prorogue Parliament and to dissolve the House of Representatives, and to assent in the Queen's name to any proposed law passed by both the Houses of the Parliament. The Governor-General is Commander-in-Chief of the Australian Defence Forces. In practice, the Governor-General's role is largely ceremonial and there has been only one occasion in recent memory where he has interfered in the democratic government of the nation. This incident, widely considered by Australians to have been an insupportable intrusion of monarchical power in Australian affairs, occurred in 1975 when the then Governor-General, Sir John Kerr, dismissed the democratically elected Prime Minister, Gough Whitlam, after backroom manoeuvring by opposition parties. Australia's real political power is held by the Prime Minister, currently John Howard, and the elected representatives of the upper and lower houses. Howard is head of the Liberal party and governs in coalition with the conservative National party and has been prime minister since

1996. He was re-elected in 1998 and in November 2001, when his conservative coalition won 43.1 per cent of the vote. The House of Representatives formulates and debates proposed legislation which is then passed on to the Senate for further reading and eventual ratification. A cabinet of ministers with responsibilities for various portfolios, such as trade and foreign affairs, is appointed by the Prime Minister on election, and is subject to frequent reshuffles during the lifetime of a parliament.

State Governments. State governments are constituted under the same bicameral system as the federal parliament, except in Queensland, which abolished its Upper House in 1992. The lower house of the state parliaments of New South Wales, Victoria and Western Australia is known as the Legislative Assembly, and in South Australia and Tasmania as the House of Assembly. The governments of Queensland, the Northern Territory and the Australian Capital Territory are known as the Legislative Assembly. In each state a Governor acts as the representative of the Queen, exercising prerogative powers conferred by Letters Patent issued under the Great Seal of the United Kingdom, as well as various statutory functions defined by the state constitution and by the Commonwealth *Australia Act 1986*. A Governor of a State assents in the Queen's name to bills passed by the Parliament of the State but acts on the advice of state cabinet ministers.

Suffrage. Australia has universal adult suffrage, and electoral registration and voting in both state and federal elections is compulsory for all eligible persons. In order to qualify to vote, you must be either an Australian citizen (or a British subject who was on the Commonwealth Roll on 25 January 1984), over 18 years of age, and resident in Australia. People who fail to vote in an election may be charged and fined (currently $50 for a first offence).

Political Parties

There are six mainstream political parties in Australia: the Australian Labour Party (ALP), the Liberal Party (LP), the Country Party (CP), the National Party of Australia (NPA), the Australian Democrats (AD), and the Green Party. The ALP is traditionally a left-wing party but has become increasingly centrist so that it now embraces such previously right-wing policies as privatisation. The Liberal Party is conservative in orientation and is currently the party of government. The Country Party and National Party are also conservative organisations whose power base lies in rural areas, and although they are never likely to hold power in their own right, they inevitably enter into a coalition with the Liberal Party when that party is in government. In many cases, including the current parliament, the Liberal Party holds power only by the consent and co-operation of the NCP. The Greens are active in environmental issues, particularly in states such as Tasmania where development threatens natural wildernesses, and they, together with the Australian Democrats, are usually successful in gaining seats in the Senate rather than in the House of Representatives.

A recent ugly development in Australian politics is the foundation and expansion of the One Nation Party, which espouses overtly racist policies. Sadly, the platform of this party appeals to redneck communities in highly conservative outback areas, particularly in Queensland. It is, however, reviled by the majority of Australians, and its leader, Pauline Hanson, is generally considered an embarrassment to the country. The antics of the One Nation Party have caused several diplomatic incidents between

Australia and its Southeast Asian neighbours, and the government is at pains to stifle its sphere of influence as far as democratically possible. At the time of writing One Nation has six state parliamentarians and a Federal Senator, as well as local government councillors. In January 2002 Pauline Hanson resigned from the National Executive as National President of One Nation. She remains a member of the Party and continues to play an active role in it.

Republicanism

Support for a republican Australia has been growing steadily since the 1970s, taking centre stage in national debate in the 1990s. In 1993, the Prime Minister of the day, Paul Keating, established a Republican Advisory Committee, which founded its enquiries on the premise of 'when and how' rather than 'if', enraging pro-monarchy factions. Although traditionally the conservative Liberal Party has opposed the formation of a republic (in the 1960s, Liberal PM Sir Robert Menzies was an arch-monarchist), the Liberal government, under John Howard, has been forced to bow to the public clamour for independence, and a referendum was held in 1999. In February 1998, a Constitutional Convention, comprising democratically nominated delegates from all areas of Australian society, was held in Canberra to consider firstly, whether or not Australia should become a republic and secondly, which republican model of government should be adopted. The Convention found in favour of the formation of a republic under the 'Bipartisan Appointment of President' model, and subject to a successful referendum outcome in 1999, it had been likely that the new republic would come into effect on 1 January 2001. However, although public support for a republic was high, on 6 November 1999 the majority of Australians – around 55 per cent – voted to keep the Constitutional Monarchy. The only state to return a vote of 'yes' to a Republic was Victoria, and that by the narrowest of margins – 49.6 per cent for a republic and 49.4 per cent against.

If, and when Australia does become a republic (and it is very likely that this will occur at some point in the future), it may be initiated by Australia, or by Britain itself. A new flag without the Union Jack inset will have to be invented. It is likely that it will be designed, probably by public competition, and will be placed before the voters in a referendum before being formally adopted. The Australian national anthem, 'Advance Australia Fair', which replaced 'God Save the Queen' in 1984, will be retained.

The Economy

Australia has a free-market economy, which is subject to extensive regulation and tariff controls. Government policy, however, currently favours privatisation and deregulation, and has embarked on the process of reducing the role of government in the national economy over the long term. Many of Australia's industries have already been deregulated and government monopolies in domestic airlines, banking and telecommunications have been opened up to private competition.

Australia's major trading partners are the USA, Japan, the EU, ASEAN (the Association of Southeast Asian Nations), New Zealand, Hong Kong, China, Taiwan and Korea. It is one of the world's largest suppliers of coal, iron ore, bauxite, alumina, petroleum, natural gas, gold, wool, beef, cotton and sugar. However, traditional trading patterns are changing, with manufactured goods now accounting for over a quarter of all exports. Around 53 per cent of Australian exports have gone to East Asian countries in recent years. Exports of goods and services account for around 19% of Australia's national income. Manufactures make up the largest sector of merchandise imports, especially capital goods, transport equipment and consumer goods.

Manufacturing industry accounts for around 13.3% of Australia's GDP, and has developed behind high tariff walls. Protection is now being reduced to make Australian industry more competitive and export-orientated. Approximately 98% of all manufacturing firms are small businesses. The main industries are chemicals, aerospace engineering, food processing, motor vehicles, iron and steel, paper, wood-chipping and forestry.

Australia's enormous natural resource base has allowed it to develop an efficient and competitive agricultural industry, which contributes around 3% to the GDP. Australia leads the world in wool production and is a major supplier of cereals, dairy produce, meat, sugar and fruit. Over 120 million sheep and over 26.7 million cattle are grazed on the nations plains and farms (known as stations), which are of a size undreamed of in Europe. The world's largest cattle station, Strangeray Springs in South Australia, comprises 30,029 square kilometres – about the same size as Belgium or Maryland! The export market for Australian wines has grown exponentially in recent years and fisheries products, especially crustaceans, are exported in large number to East Asia and the USA.

Australia is also a major producer and exporter of energy resources, and is one of the world's biggest producers of minerals and metals. More than 60 different minerals are mined, including bauxite, mineral sands, diamonds & black and brown coal. Mineral ores containing gold, silver, lead, zinc, iron, copper, nickel, tin, manganese and uranium are also mined in various locations all around Australia. Australia imports its heavy crude oil but exports light crude and liquefied natural gas. It is also an important producer of precious and semi-precious stones, most notably diamonds, sapphires, opals and pearls. Most electricity is produced using coal-fired power stations and Australia's large coal deposits allow it to produce its electricity at relatively low cost. Hydroelectricity is another important source of power and is generated in the Snowy Mountains and in Tasmania. The Australian government has become very environmentally-conscious in recent decades, and strict regulations govern the disposal of industrial waste. Flouting these regulations can result in the forced closure of a business as well as heavily punitive fines. Major mining companies, such as ALCOA, have for many years replanted and landscaped exhausted bauxite mining sites to a level where they are, in many instances, indistinguishable from native wilderness.

Australian science and technology has effected many advances in manufacturing, mining and agricultural industries, and private sector research and development has achieved an increasingly high profile in the last decade. The government has sought to discourage the traditional view of Australia as the 'Lucky Country', replacing it with a new ethos – the 'Clever Country'. The CSIRO (Commonwealth Scientific and Industrial Research Organisation) is Australia's main scientific body, and its work focuses on industry, the natural environment, minerals, energy and construction industries. Australia has bilateral agreements on technical co-operation with India, Russia, Germany, China, Japan, Mexico, France, the European Union and Indonesia.

Trade unionism in Australia is declining rapidly as new information-led industries arise to replace traditional blue-collar ones. Only around 30 per cent of the Australian workforce belongs to a union, and in recent years many unions have amalgamated into coalitions in order to remain viable.

GEOGRAPHICAL INFORMATION

Geography and Topographical Features

Australia is one of the world's biggest islands, which is referred to by some as a continent. It has a landmass of 7,682,300 square kilometres, and is the sixth largest country in the world after Russia, Canada, China, the USA and Brazil, and is 31 times larger than the United Kingdom. The coastline, which stretches over 36,735 km, encompasses a wide variety of coastal seascapes from the wild surf and dramatic cliffs of the Australian Bight, to the tranquil bays of the Southwest. It is bounded by the Pacific Ocean to the east, the Indian Ocean to the west, the Arafura Sea to the north, and the Southern Ocean to the south. The Great Barrier Reef, the largest natural reef in the world, runs almost parallel to the Great Dividing Range from the northernmost tip of Queensland at Cape York down to Fraser Island, approximately 200 km north of Brisbane. Australia's marine conservation reserves cover more than 380,000 sq. km.

Australia is characterised by the flatness of its topography and much of central Australia is a giant plateau; its highest mountain, Mount Kosiusko (2,228m), is only half as high as the tallest peak on any other continent. The coastal strip is fertile, but it is insignificant in size compared to the vast inland deserts at the dry heart of the continent. This inland region, known as the Outback, is broken by salt lakes, starkly beautiful mountain ranges such as the MacDonnell Ranges near Alice Springs and the Kimberly Ranges in WA, and by mysterious rock formations such as Uluru (Ayers Rock) and Mount Olga (Kata Tjuta). Deserts such as the Great Sandy Desert, the Gibson Desert and the Great Victoria Desert are barren, unpopulated wastes of red dust, low scrub and spinifex (hardy tufts of spiny grass) and are extremely hot by day, freezing by night. The harshness of this land is sometimes reflected in the names given to geographical features, such as Lake Disappointment in Western Australia.

The Murray River and the Darling River are the main internal waterways of Australia and form the Murray-Darling River Basin. This drainage basin comprises the major part of the interior lowlands of Australia, and covers more than one million square kilometres (around 14 per cent of the country). The headwaters of the Darling, Australia's longest river, are found in the Great Dividing Range between Queensland and NSW, and finally reach the coast southwest of Adelaide some 3,370 km later. Australia's three largest lakes, Eyre, Torrens and Gairdner, are located in the interior lowlands of South Australia and are fed by the rare run-off of heavy rains in the desert. Lake Eyre was filled only three times during the 20th century, and Lake Torrens only once.

Around 524,000 square kilometres of public land in Australia has been designated as nature conservation reserves, and a further 1.1 million sq. km. is preserved as aboriginal and Torres Strait Islander land.

Other Territories

Australia is responsible for administering seven external territories: Norfolk Island, Cocos (Keeling) Island, Christmas Island, Ashmore and Cartier Island Territories, the Territory of Heard Island, Coral Sea Islands Territory, the sub-Antarctic McDonald Islands, and the Australian Antarctic Territories.

Neighbouring Countries

Australia's nearest neighbour is Papua New Guinea, which lies less than 200 km across the Torres Strait to the north of Cape York. To the north west of Australia lies the Indonesian archipelago and further away to the north east are the Solomon Islands, the French Island of New Caledonia, Fiji, Western Samoa and Tonga. Australia's nearest neighbour in a cultural sense is New Zealand, lying approximately 1,700 km east of Sydney. Beyond Tasmania to the south, there is nothing but ocean until Antarctica, and to the west beyond Perth nothing before the islands of the Seychelles, Mauritius and Madagascar, near the African coast.

Population

The population of Australia is currently around 19.5 million. Most of this population is concentrated in cities situated in coastal areas, and although population density figures are as low as two people per square kilometre, this figure averages population over the vast inland areas of Australia and does not reflect Australia's urban environment. Population growth is between 1.0 and 1.5% per annum, and the projected population for the year 2010 lies in the region of 22 million. Around 92% of Australia's population are of Caucasian descent, a further seven per cent are Asian, and a mere one per cent are of Aboriginal extraction. Approximately 76 per cent of Australians are Christians (mainly Roman Catholic and Anglican). Australia's official language is English and 100 per cent of Australians are functionally literate.

Australia prides itself on its multicultural composition. Its multicultural policies enshrine the right to individual cultural identity and to social justice regardless of race, ethnicity, culture, religion, language, birthplace or gender. All Australians, whatever their background, are expected to have an overriding commitment to Australia and its interests and to accept the basic structures and principles of Australian society. Australia's multicultural policies have gone through three main phases over the decades. Until the 1960s, a policy of assimilation was in place, which drew its rationale from the long-discredited and disbanded 'White Australia Policy'. This policy effectively excluded non-European immigration but was weakened by attitudinal changes after the Second World War and is now regarded with shame by younger generations of Australians. From the mid-1960s through to 1972, the government adopted a policy of integration, recognising that large numbers of migrants, especially those whose first language was not English, required direct assistance and intervention to help them become integrated into Australian society. Finally, multiculturalism became established as government policy in 1973, and today minority groups are assisted in promoting the survival of their language and heritage within mainstream institutions.

In 1978 a comprehensive review of immigration in Australia led to the adoption of new policies and programmes as a framework for Australia's population development. Three-year rolling programmes were implemented to replace annual immigration targets, as well as developing a more consistent and structured approach to migrant selection, emphasising the need for skilled people who would represent a positive gain to the nation. Today, nearly one in four of Australia's population were born overseas, and in 1999/2000 (latest available figures from Australian Immigration), the number of new settlers totalled 92,272. Of these, 23.7 per cent came from New Zealand, 10 per cent from the UK, 7.4 per cent from China, and 6.2 per cent from South Africa. There are around one million British-born permanent residents and citizens in Australia, more than in any other country except the UK.

The Aboriginal People and Reconciliation

The native Australian and Torres Strait Islander people are the custodians of one of the world's oldest cultural traditions. This tradition is an oral one, in which legal, social and religious structures and customs are transmitted through story, dance and song. Art plays a central functional, rather than solely aesthetic role, in aboriginal culture; mapping out the Dreamtime (or creational mythology), explaining tribal law and describing ceremonies and events or historical happenings. Aborigines have traditionally subsisted as hunters and gatherers in small, tribally based communities and their unique relationship with the land has enabled them to survive for millennia in one of the harshest environments on earth.

The arrival of British settlers in Australia presaged the beginning of the end for traditional aboriginal culture and today their population, which was never huge, has been decimated. In the early years of settlement, the British sanctioned the deliberate destruction of the Aboriginal population; and a policy of genocide in Tasmania was effective in murdering every last indigenous inhabitant. Systematic campaigns of extermination, in the form of 'hunting parties', pursued their human quarry in every early settlement and within a mere three years of the arrival of the First Fleet in Sydney the Aboriginal population was reduced by two-thirds through imported diseases, accidents and violent death. Aborigines were considered by British settlers to be a sub-human species and were treated as animals, scientific specimens, or the subjects of social experimentation. Such attitudes prevailed, to some extent, into the 1970s and it was not until then that Aborigines were released from curfew restrictions or entitled to the rights of citizenship. The Aboriginal people now suffer from high rates of alcohol dependency, infant mortality, suicide, death in custody and criminal involvement. Their life expectancy is shorter than other Australians and they are four times as likely to suffer unemployment. There are very few pureblood Aboriginal people in Australia today, and aboriginality is defined by ancestry and identification, rather than racial purity. The population of pureblood Aborigines stands at approximately 10,000 – reduced from an estimated 100,000 at the time of the arrival of the first settlers. Although those who remain are now struggling to regain their cultural and historical heritage, many feel a sense of fragmentation, isolation, displacement, as well as a deep bitterness towards the successive governments responsible for their near-destruction.

Today, Aborigines have found a new voice and are actively defending and reinstating their rights within society and on their traditional lands. Reconciliation is now the cornerstone of public policy and seeks to foster co-existence, respecting the different rights of people in the same land. In May 1998, a National Sorry Day was held to allow all Australians, regardless of racial origin, to express their regret for the tragic past treatment of the nation's indigenous people. In particular, National Sorry Day sought to raise awareness of the distressing truths behind the forced removal of aboriginal children from their families well into the 1970s. It highlighted the consequences of this policy in terms of broken families, physical and mental abuse and the loss of language, culture and connection to traditional lands.

Land Rights. In 1992 the High Court of Australia handed down the Mabo Decision, which recognised that under Australian law indigenous people had land rights. This right was called 'native title', and reversed the long-standing legal fiction that the continent of Australia was *terra nullius*, land belonging to no one, at the time of British settlement. As a result of the Mabo Decision, in 1993 the Commonwealth

Government passed the Native Title Act after extensive consultation between the Australian government and indigenous Australians. Past grants of land away from indigenous ownership (for example, to pastoralists) were made valid, in return for the reinstatement of the common law rights of indigenous people according to their traditions, laws and customs. In particular, Aboriginal and Torres Strait Islander people sought the right to contribute to, if not control, future planning and development on native title land. Native title rights still exist on much Crown land and in national parks, where the traditional owners have maintained their cultural and religious connections. In 1997 the Wik Decision, which was handed down by the High Court following a case brought by the Wik people of Northern Queensland, enlarged native title rights by permitting the right of access to land held under pastoral leases for ceremonial and traditional activities. Mining companies wishing to operate on land held under a pastoral lease were also obliged to negotiate directly with the native titleholders. Although the rights of indigenous people under native title are still limited (native title is extinguished on land held under freehold or ordinary leases), the issue has become a controversial one in Australia, and is generally clouded by fear and misinformation.

CLIMATE

Australia's size means that it encompasses several climatic zones. The more southerly regions have a temperate, Mediterranean climate with hot, dry summers and mild, wet winters while areas nearer the equator are sub-tropical. Northern Queensland and parts of the Northern Territory experience heavy rainfall between January and March ('the wet'). The seasons in the southern hemisphere are inverted: the summer months are from December to February, autumn is from March to May, winter from June to August, and spring from September to November.

Sun Protection

Australians these days are highly aware of the dangers of their climate. The hole in the ozone layer, which is concentrated over the southern hemisphere, means that more and more ultra-violet rays are penetrating the atmosphere, with an increased risk of skin cancer. The greatest damage is done in childhood, and today everyone is prepared to cover up to an extent undreamed of by British holidaymakers. Factor 15-plus sunscreen should be worn at all times, and many people choose to wear the impenetrable zinc cream on their faces (often in fluorescent colours). Most adults and all children wear hats every time they step outside, and clothing often comes with a protection rating, depending on sleeve length, colour and fabric. Sunglasses are not a fashion accessory but an essential item, and you should choose a pair with high quality lenses, such as Raybans. All sunglasses are sold with a removable sticker on the lens indicating the level of ultra-violent rays against which they offer protection, and you should only buy those which screen 100 per cent of these dangerous rays. Sunglasses are available for all ages, from babies upwards; baby glasses come with colourful elasticated straps to keep them in place. All of the above points apply in winter as well as summer. On the beach, throw away those ideas of a mini bikini and a great tan. Today, tanning is out, and no one wears bikinis. Young women generally choose a one-piece swimsuit, and both men and women cover up with t-shirts and hats. Children *all*, without exception, wear swimsuits reminiscent of the Victorian era neck-to-knee bathing costume. These sunsuits are made of UV-resistant lycra and come in fluorescent colours. They have wrist or elbow length sleeves, cover the whole body, and extend to the knees or even the ankles, zipping up at the front like a diver's wetsuit. They are quick drying, designed for speed in the water and are generally thought 'cool' by children. Should you let your children on the beach in a European-style swimming costume the under-the-breath tut-tutting all around you will probably drown out the sound of the waves. Australian-style children's swimsuits are available in all surf shops and department stores as well as, and more cheaply, from Cancer Foundation Shops in most cities.

WEATHER CHART

Average temperature (Celcius), rainfall (mm), sunshine in hours per day

	Jan	Feb	Mar	Apr	May	Jun	Jul	Aug	Sep	Oct	Nov	Dec
Adelaide												
Max	29	29	26	22	19	16	15	16	19	22	25	27
Min	17	17	15	12	10	8	7	8	9	11	14	15
Rainfall	21	11	25	38	58	79	82	69	62	43	29	29
Rainydays	4	4	6	8	12	15	17	17	14	10	8	7
Sunshine	10	10	9	7	5	4	5	6	7	8	9	9
Brisbane												
Max	29	29	28	26	23	21	21	22	24	26	27	29
Min	21	21	20	17	14	11	9	10	12	16	18	20
Rainfall	160	173	140	89	98	70	62	41	33	93	96	126
Rainy days	13	14	14	11	10	7	7	6	7	10	10	11
Sunshine	8	8	8	7	6	7	8	8	9	9	9	9
Canberra												
Max	28	27	24	20	15	12	11	13	16	29	22	26
Min	13	13	11	7	3	1	0	1	3	6	9	11
Rainfall	62	55	53	50	49	39	42	46	51	66	64	53
Rainy days	8	7	7	8	8	9	10	11	10	11	10	8
Sunshine	9	9	8	7	6	5	6	7	7	9	9	9
Darwin												
Max	32	31	32	33	32	31	30	31	32	33	33	33
Min	25	25	24	24	20	19	21	23	25	25	25	25
Rainfall	431	344	316	98	22	1	1	6	16	72	141	234
Rainy days	21	20	19	9	2	1	0	1	2	6	12	16
Sunshine	6	6	7	9	10	10	10	10	10	9	8	7
Hobart												
Max	22	22	21	18	15	13	12	13	15	17	19	20
Min	12	12	11	9	6	4	4	5	6	7	9	11
Rainfall	42	36	37	46	37	29	47	49	41	49	45	58

| Rainy days | 9 | 8 | 10 | 11 | 12 | 11 | 14 | 14 | 14 | 14 | 14 | 12 |
| Sunshine | 8 | 8 | 7 | 6 | 5 | 4 | 5 | 5 | 6 | 7 | 7 | 8 |

Melbourne

Max	26	26	24	20	17	14	13	15	17	19	22	24
Min	14	14	13	11	9	7	6	7	8	9	11	13
Rainfall	49	47	52	58	57	50	48	51	59	68	60	60
Rainy days	8	7	9	12	14	14	15	16	15	14	12	11
Sunshine	9	8	7	6	4	4	4	5	6	7	7	8

Perth

Max	32	32	29	25	21	19	18	18	20	22	25	29
Min	17	17	16	13	10	9	8	8	9	10	13	15
Rainfall	7	16	15	42	106	174	163	118	70	47	27	12
Rainy days	2	3	4	8	13	17	18	16	13	10	7	4
Sunshine	12	11	9	8	7	6	6	7	8	9	10	12

Sydney

Max	26	26	25	22	19	17	16	18	20	22	24	25
Min	19	19	17	15	11	9	8	9	11	13	16	17
Rainfall	7	16	15	42	106	174	163	118	70	47	27	12
Rainy days	2	3	4	8	13	17	18	16	13	10	7	4
Sunshine	12	11	9	8	7	6	6	7	8	9	10	12

A GUIDE TO THE STATES AND TERRITORIES

Information Facilities

Tourism is one of Australia's most important industries and enjoys an increasingly high profile in the domestic economy. Every capital city has a large and well-supplied Tourist Bureau, and most regional towns have a smaller Tourist Information Office providing specialist and local information. Isolated regions and national parks which are not served by an office will usually have a tourist information point with maps, general information and points of interest displayed for reference. Most railway and bus stations also have counters where you can obtain information on your journey as well as advice on accommodation, facilities and attractions in the area you are visiting.

The Australian Tourist Commission has an office in London (open Monday to Friday from 9am-5.30pm) which will answer your travel queries and assist with itineraries. They also stock an extensive range of pamphlets, maps and guides, and will forward free literature to you on request. The Australian Tourist Commission has an excellent website at **www.australia.com**. The Australia Centre at the Australian High Commission in London provides information supplied by all the states except Queensland (which maintains its own office at Queensland House in the Strand,

London), including an extensive range of booklets. This office also has a reading room where you can consult up-to-date newspapers from each capital city, including the classifieds pages.

There are many guidebooks available covering every region of Australia, for every type of traveller. The specialist travel bookshop, Stanfords (12-14 Long Acre, London, WC2E 9LP; ☎020-7836 1321; fax 020-7836 0189) has a particularly extensive range, and publishes an Australian and New Zealand Book List on the internet at **www.stanfords.co.uk**.

Useful Addresses

Australian Tourist Commission (UK), 1st Floor, Gemini House, 10-18 Putney Hill, London SW15 6AA; ☎020-8780 2229; fax 020-8780 1496; www.australia.com.
Australian Tourist Commission (USA), 2049 Century Park East, Suite 1920, Los Angeles, CA 90067, USA; ☎(310) 229 4870; fax (310) 552 1215; www.australia.com.
Queensland Tourism, Queensland House, 392-393, Strand, London WC2R 0LZ; ☎020-7836 1333; fax 020-7420 8770; www.qld.gov.au.

WESTERN AUSTRALIA (WA)

Capital: Perth.
Area: 2,525,500 sq. km (1,515,300 sq. miles) = over 10 times the size of the UK.
Total area of Australia: 32.87%.
Coastline: 12,500 km (7,813 miles).
Climate: Average Perth daily maximum temperature in January (Summer) 27°C; in July (Winter) 15°C. Note that there is significant variation in temperatures throughout the state from the temperate South to the tropical North.

Western Australia's huge size (the whole of Western Europe can easily fit into Western Australia and still leave room for more) encompasses the whole range of climatic and geographical zones. From the endless white sands and crystal waters the tropical north to the arid zones of the Nullarbor Plain, through to the vineyards of the southwest, WA is the Australian landscape encapsulated. Its features include the spectacular Ningaloo Reef, a marine reserve less well-known than the Great Barrier Reef but equally impressive, majestic Karri forests, ancient and massive gorges, and geological formations such as Wave Rock and the Pinnacles (an ancient fossilised forest now standing in a desert landscape). The Stirling and Porongorup Ranges very occasionally see snow in winter.

The State is rich in a wide variety of natural resources and is a leading producer of iron ore, gold, industrial diamonds, alumina, mineral sands, wool, wheat, salt and forest products. Whilst wheat and wool account for around two-thirds of the state's income from primary industry, Western Australia is also developing more unusual primary industries; farming cashmere and angora goats, emu and deer. Western Australia's fishing industry produces rock lobster, prawns, shrimp and scampi, which are mainly exported to the USA and Japan. Mineral and petroleum production adds a further $8 billion per annum to the State's economy, and comprises 84 per cent of the value of the State's overseas exports and about 50 per cent of Australia's total mineral and energy exports. The minerals and petroleum industry in WA contribute about 30 per cent of the Gross State Product.

Since the 1960s, the Western Australian economy has grown faster than that of any other State, with an average real Gross State Product growth of 4.9 per cent. The state's economy is export-based and its overseas trade surplus is more than double that of the rest of Australia. Its major export markets are Japan and the Southeast Asian nations as well as the USA and the EU. It has the second lowest levels of unemployment in the country. Western Australia is second to New South Wales as the most popular destination for business migrants. More than a quarter of Western Australia's population was born overseas, and it consequently enjoys a broad and cosmopolitan lifestyle. It also has a young population, second only to the Northern Territory, with an average age of 30.4 years. Western Australian medical and health services are considered amongst the best in the world. At a doctor-patient ration of 1:288, the state now ranks with Norway, Sweden, Finland, Denmark, France and the Netherlands, and is considerably ahead of the USA, UK and Japan. The average life expectancy in Western Australia is high, and currently stands at 76 years for men and 82 for women.

Western Australian education is of a very high standard, both in the public and private sector. With five universities and over a thousand schools and colleges throughout the State, Western Australia has world-class education facilities, and is a world-leader in certain areas of research, such as wave technology.

Real estate costs are among the lowest in the country, and Western Australians enjoy a high rate of home ownership with more than two-thirds of all residences being privately owned.

Perth: Perth is the most geographically isolated capital city in the world and has a population of 1.38 million people (WA has a total population of 1.9 million). The city is stunning, situated along the banks of the Swan River, and has a relaxed and friendly atmosphere and easy-going lifestyle. The most popular residential areas are built along the river and coastal strip, with suburban sprawl extending inland to the edge of the escarpment of the coastal plateau. Perth summers are very hot, and although the average temperature is only 27°C, the mercury frequently hovers around 40°C for days at a time. The heat is very dry and as it is not sticky or cloying can easily be dealt with by staying in the shade. In the afternoons, the sea breeze comes in off the Indian Ocean and by sunset the weather is usually extremely pleasant. This breeze is known affectionately as 'The Fremantle Doctor', for its remedying effect on the wilting population. Perth is, in fact, Australia's windiest city, and the third windiest city in the world. It enjoys more sunshine and clear days than any other Australian capital and while it also has one of the wettest winters, rains are usually short and sharp, interspersed with cool, sunny periods.

The centre of Perth is dominated by King's Park, which consists of approximately 1,000 acres of natural bushland, wildflowers and landscaped gardens. This park is a focus for family life and its various cycle tracks, nature walks, adventure playgrounds and water features are popular with all sections of the community. King's Park is the home of the state botanical gardens, which features the full array of native flora, and hosts the Wildflower Festival in September.

Perth has an active cultural scene, with a permanent symphony orchestra, ballet company and opera company performing year-round at the city's two main arts venues: the Perth Concert Hall and His Majesty's Theatre. The enormous Entertainment Centre hosts large-scale popular events and commercial productions such as the Moscow Circus and ice shows. The Festival of Perth is held every year and is centred on the venues of the University of Western Australia. Major national and international performing artists in the fields of music, dance and theatre are brought in for the four week event, so that every year, the world's best can be seen on the local stages. In addition, the Festival Fringe offers cutting-edge comedy and experimental theatre and music, and the concurrent film festival screens art movies from around the world. Musica Viva operates a national and international chamber music touring scheme, the largest of its kind in the world.

Perth has an efficient public transport system made up of ferries, electric trains and buses, all run by Transperth. In Perth, travel on the Central Area Transport (CAT) system is free throughout the central business district. City planners are actively seeking to improve public transport to alleviate congestion in the city centre. Long distance commuting is rare in Perth, and most people live within about 20 minutes of their place of work.

The beaches and the Swan River provide a perfect water-playground for Perth's population, and the swimming, water-skiing, windsurfing, surfing and sailing are the cornerstone of Perth leisure activities. There are more boats per capita in Perth than in any other Australian city. The other major sports played in Perth include cricket (the Western Australian Cricket Association, affectionately known as the WACA, often hosts One-Day International and Test matches), various codes of football (Aussie rules, soccer, rugby), horseracing, tennis, hockey, lawn bowls and golf. Basketball and baseball are also increasingly popular.

Western Australia's healthy economy, its growing population, developing industries and technology, outdoor lifestyle, cheap real estate and prime facilities contribute to a general feeling of well-being, which occasionally borders on smugness, and most locals consider themselves lucky to live there.

Useful Addresses

Online WA, Portal website for the Government of Western Australia: www.wa.gov.au

Real Estate Institute of Western Australia, REIWA House, 215 Hay Street, Subiaco, Western Australia 6008; ☎08-9380 8222; fax 08-9381 9260; www.reiwa.com.au. REIWA produces an illustrated weekly property guide, 'The Homebuyer', available free every Friday from REIWA and local REIWA Agents.

Education Department of WA, 151 Royal Street, East Perth, Western Australia 6004; ☎08-9264 4111; fax 08-9264 5005; www.eddept.wa.edu.au.

Department of Industry and Technology, Dumas House, 2 Havelock Street, West Perth, Western Australia 6005; ☎08-9222 5555; fax 08-9222 5055; www.indtech.wa.gov.au. The DoIT produces a quarterly economic briefing on Western Australian economy.

Business Assistance Gateway. A single, initial point of contact, for all inquiries about business assistance in Western Australia (☎08-9481 2525; email gatewaywa@indtech.wa.gov.au).

NORTHERN TERRITORY (NT)

Capital: Darwin.
Area: 1,346,200 sq. km (807,720 sq. miles) = 5.5 times the size of the UK.
Total area of Australia: 17.52%.

Coastline: 6,200 km (3720 miles).
Climate: Average daily maximum temperature in January 31°C; in July 31°C. In Alice Springs temperatures vary more widely, as the town lies in the semi-arid central region rather than the tropics. The average daily maximum summer and winter temperatures for Alice Springs are 35.2°C and 20.5°C.

The Northern Territory (also known as 'The Top End') is situated in central northern Australia, to the east of Western Australia. It is bordered by South Australia in the south and Queensland to the east. The Northern Territory's history of development is closely linked with that of South Australia, as in 1863 the British Government handed over control of the Northern Territory to the Colony of South Australia. Within a year, the first sale of land in the Territory was held in Adelaide. In 1869 an expedition led by the Surveyor-General George Goyder resulted in the establishment of a permanent settlement, now known as Darwin. South Australia's control was relinquished in 1901 after Federation, and control over the Northern Territory was held by the Commonwealth Government until 1 July 1978, when the Territory was granted self-government. The powers of government differ from those of other states in the title only. Its assembly consists of a single lower house, and its leader is known as the Chief Minister. For inter-governmental financial purposes the Northern Territory has been regarded as a State by the Commonwealth since July 1988.

The remoteness and harshness of the Northern Territory has made it unique in many ways, not the least of which is its relatively tiny population. Its 192,882 residents (June 1999) comprise 0.75 per cent of Australia's population and it has a population density of only one person per nine sq. km. The population of Darwin is around 80,000 and of Alice Springs, 27,000. The annual population growth rate is 1.3 per cent. This rate has slowed recently due to changing patterns of interstate migration, but the Northern Territory continues to have the youngest population in Australia, with an average age of 29 years, compared with the Australian average of 34.7 years. Almost 28 per cent of the population are Aboriginal, although overall Aboriginal and Torres Straits account for only 1.5 per cent of the Australian population. More than 50 different ethnic groups are represented in Darwin, and 24 per cent of people speak a language other than English.

Although the Territory is hampered by its distance from major Australian economic and political centres, and by restricted transport and communication links, its economy has experienced a growth rate in Gross Domestic Product (GDP) which has generally exceeded that of Australia as a whole. Its rapid growth can be attributed mainly to developments in mining, to tourism, and especially to oil. The abundance of natural resources such as alumina, manganese, gold, bauxite and uranium, as well as oil and gas, has enabled the Northern Territory to participate substantially in the international market, and the value of exports for the Northern Territory per capita is almost double the national figure.

There are three main interstate highway links in the Northern Territory: the Stuart Highway from Darwin to the South Australian border, the Barkly Highway from Tennant Creek to the Queensland border, and the Victoria Highway from Katherine to the Western Australian border. Although there are roadhouses along these highways, there are stretches of road which are not serviced for over 280 km. It is always advisable to notify the Automobile Association of the Northern Territory before embarking on an unfamiliar road (especially in the wet season), or before undertaking long journeys over unsealed or unserviced roads. You should ensure that you take supplies of petrol, water and food, and if possible a CB radio. In the case of breakdown or emergency, stay with your vehicle at all times.

The cost of housing varies widely within the Northern Territory. Rented accommodation in Darwin is amongst the most expensive of all Australian capital cities, and suitable properties may be scarce.

Education has been the responsibility of the Northern Territory government since 1979, and in recent years it has modified its schools' curriculum to reflect the multicultural nature of its classrooms, promoting intercultural understanding and literacy. There are also correspondence schools, known as 'Schools of the Air', which use two-way radio, video and computers, to bring the classroom to isolated students. The Northern Territory Secondary Correspondence School offers an excellent range of secondary courses up to university entrance level for those who do not have access to normal school facilities. Tertiary education in the Northern Territory is usually undertaken through either the Northern Territory University or the University's Institute of Technical and Further Education which specialises in trade and technical courses. In 1985, the postgraduate research institution, the Menzies School of Health Research, was established at the Royal Darwin Hospital and it is currently enjoying a reputation as a centre of scientific excellence in its field. One of its primary objectives is to assist in improving the health of people in tropical and central Australia. The School has an academic link with the Northern Territory University and its students may qualify for the higher degrees of that university.

The Northern Territory Health Services are remarkable, considering the distance and difficult terrain that must be covered. There are modern, well-equipped hospitals in Darwin, Alice Springs, Katherine, Tennant Creek and Nhulunbuy. All hospitals provide general in- and out-patient, accident and emergency services. The Royal Darwin and Alice Springs Hospitals offer a wide range of specialist services and are both special teaching hospitals affiliated with the University of Sydney. A private hospital is also available in Darwin. Mobile services are also provided in remote areas and the Northern Territory government subsidises missions and Aboriginal organisations in the provision of health services. While there are health centres in all major towns and settlements, in extremely remote regions the Royal Flying Doctor Service (RFDS) and the Aerial Medical Service operate in cases of serious injury or illness. The Patient Assisted Travel Scheme (PATS) provides financial assistance to people from isolated areas that have had to travel for specialist consultation and treatment. The Northern Territory government also provides mental health services, blood banks, services for the aged, family, youth and children's services, services for the disabled and women's information services as well as women's refuges and shelters, a Sexual Assault Reference Centre, and the Ruby Gaea Darwin Centre Against Rape which provides counselling, support services and emergency accommodation.

The Northern Territory lies within the torrid zone of the Tropic of Capricorn and much of its area is semi-arid. Although its landscape contains Australia's great 'dead heart' of claypan desert, which covers an area 805 km long and 322 km wide, the tropical northern part of the Territory is luxuriantly verdant. These two climatic regions result in a diversity of vegetation within the Territory, ranging from mangrove and freshwater swamps and billabongs (pool or backwater), rainforest, eucalyptus and mulga woodlands, to spinifex grasslands, gibber plains and sandy deserts. There are no major rivers in the Northern Territory's interior, and rivers and creeks flow only after rains in the wet season (October-April). The Todd River, on which Alice Springs is located, is usually dry. 'The wet' is a period of high humidity, and torrential rain and thunderstorms occur in the transition from 'the dry' to the wet season. These rains often cause flooding, and transport and communications in the Northern Territory can be difficult or even disrupted at times. All of the Territory's major rivers are on the coastal fringe. The Roper River which flows into the Gulf of Carpentaria, is the Territory's largest. Amongst other smaller rivers are the Daly, Victoria, Adelaide, Mary, South and North Alligator rivers. The Northern Territory is prone to cylones or hurricanes, the most famous of which, Cyclone Tracy, destroyed Darwin on 24 December 1974. The city has subsequently been rebuilt and is now a modern showcase of urban planning. Houses are constructed to withstand cyclone conditions, and government authorities maintain crisis plans against future disasters.

Although the Northern Territory is best known to non-Territorians as one of the world's great wilderness, the capital, Darwin, is a modern city which provides the services and lifestyle expected of any Australian city. Like any other Australian state, the Northern Territory offers a huge range of outdoor activities, including a wide variety of sports, as well as diverse cultural events, including theatre and festivals. In general, the towns are small, sparsely populated, have a relaxed atmosphere and a strong sense of community.

Useful Addresses

The Territory. Portal website for the Northern Territory Government: www.nt.gov.au
Department of Business, Industry and Resource Development, 2nd Floor, Development House, 76 The Esplanade, Darwin, Northern Territory 0800; ☎08-8999 5153; fax 08-8999 5106; www.dbird.nt.gov.au

SOUTH AUSTRALIA (SA)

Capital: Adelaide.
Area: 984,377 sq. km (380,070 sq miles) = four times the size of the UK.
Total area of Australia: 12.81%.
Coastline: 3,700 km (2,300 miles).
Climate: Average daily maximum temperature in January 29°C; in July 15°C.

South Australia is situated in the middle of the southern coast of Australia along the Great Australian Bight. It is bordered by Western Australia to the west, the Northern Territory to the north and Victoria to the east. It has a Mediterranean climate, ideally suited to the production of wine, and vineyards established by early European settlers are prolific throughout the Barossa Valley. South Australia produces more wines that any other state or territory in the country and has a population of 1.5 million, or around 8.5 per cent of the total population of Australia. Most of South Australia's population lives in Adelaide, the capital, which has a population of just over one million. Adelaide is situated on the River Torrens, between the waters of the gulf and a range of low hills on the coastal plateau and the city stretches 90 km from its southernmost to northernmost suburbs. The rest of the state's population is scattered throughout the major regional centres of Whyalla, Mount Gambier, Port Augusta, Murray Bridge, Port Pirie and Port Lincoln.

Adelaide. Adelaide's transport system is a well-oiled machine that rarely experiences breakdown or congestion. This is largely due to the city's first planner, Colonel

William Light, who planned Adelaide with such geometric symmetry that all major city roads are straight and wide. Adelaide enjoys a unique bus service called the *O-Bahn*, which is a right-of-way guided transport system on which commuters are shuttled to and from the city at speeds of up to 100 km/h.

Most of the housing follows the pattern of single-storey houses on spacious blocks, ensuring off-street parking and a private back garden. The standard of homes in South Australia is amongst the highest in the country, and rented accommodation is cheaper than most other states. Industrial property rental is on average 35 per cent cheaper than in other Australian capitals.

South Australia is an important industrial and scientific centre, and is home to a rapidly expanding electronics industry. The Advanced Engineering, Electronic Research and Electronic Surveillance laboratories at the Defence Science Technology Centre are world-leaders in laser research, and the academic centres of the Adelaide and Flinders Universities support this research, as well as enjoying a fine reputation in many other disciplines. The University of Adelaide is one of Australia's premier universities, and consistently ranks high among the top universities in the Asia-Pacific region in winning research funds. Australia's first planned centre for high-technology development and manufacture, Technology Park Adelaide, is integrated with the campus of the University of South Australia. South Australia's industrial base is supported by vast mineral resources in the form of oil, gas and other hydrocarbons which are tapped in the Cooper Basin area. Brown coal is mined at Leigh Creek, and copper, uranium and gold are extracted at Roxby Downs. Australia's biggest opal fields are at Andamooka.

South Australia has a warm, friendly ambience, and Adelaide is a rapidly developing city. The capital has the highest ratio of health professionals per capita in Australia and has 173 public and private hospitals. It has excellent sporting and entertainment facilities and a highly regarded education system. The city has a permanent symphony orchestra, ballet company and opera company, and hosts the world-famous Adelaide Festival every summer. Adelaide offers a very attractive environment with some fine architectural features and is known as the 'City of Churches'. The cost of living and real estate is generally low in South Australia, making it an appealing place in which to live.

Useful Addresses

South Australia Central. Portal website for the Government of South Australia: www.sa.gov.au

Department of Industry and Trade, Level 10, Terrace Towers, 178 North Terrace, Adelaide, SA 5000; ☎ 08-8303 2252; fax 08-8303 2266; www.dit.sa.gov.au

International SA. Department of Industry and Trade, Level 8, Terrace Towers, 178 North Terrace, Adelaide, SA 500o; ☎ 08-8303 2197; fax 08-8303 2277; Investment Website www.business.sa.gov.au; Migration Website www.immigration.sa.gov.au

Department of Immigration and Multicultural and Indigenous Affairs, 4th Floor, 55 Currie Street, Adelaide, SA 5000; ☎ 013-1881; fax 08-8237 6699; www.immigration.sa.gov.au

TASMANIA (TAS)

Capital: Hobart.
Area: 68,331 sq. km (26,375 sq. miles) = 0.22 times the size of the UK.
Total area of Australia: 0.88%.
Coastline: 3,200 km (1,920 miles).
Climate: January 22°C; July 11°C.

Tasmania is Australia's smallest state. It is an island separated from the south east corner of the mainland by the Bass Strait, a shallow body of water with an average width of 240 km. Tasmania's coastline is bounded by the Southern Ocean to the south and west, and the Tasman Sea to the east. Tasmania spans 296 km from north to south and 315 km from east to west. Despite the fact that it is Australia's smallest state it is, nonetheless, still twice the size of Wales. Tasmania is the only Australian state, which does not have a desert region and it is fertile throughout. It is the most mountainous state and one of the almost completely mountainous islands in the world. It has the largest rural population in relation to its size of all the Australian states, and is one of the world's most richly mineralised areas. Tasmania is the leading Australian state in terms of the production of minerals in point of value of output per capita, and almost all of Australia's tungsten is extracted from King Island, situated in the Bass Strait.

Orchard and berry fruits are grown in the south of the state and due to its high production of apples and because of its shape, Tasmania is often referred to as the Apple Isle. Industries in the southern region include the Cadbury Schweppes cocoa and confectionery factory, the Electrolytic Zinc Company, the Australian Newsprint Mills, Stanley Works (manufacturers of hand tools such as the Stanley knife), Sheridan Textiles, International Catamarans and the Cascade Brewery, which was established in 1824 and is the oldest brewery still in operation in Australia.

Fishing is the major industry on the east coast of Tasmania and is based in the ports of St. Helens and Bicheno. Catches include crayfish and abalone. Tasmania has a rapidly developing fisheries industry and now farms salmon and oysters for the international market.

In the north east of the state, the fertile soil provides ideal farming land. Beef and dairy cattle, wool sheep and prime lambs are all farmed in this region. Market gardening is also important, as it is in the northwest of the state, where vegetable and dairy farming predominate. Other types of farming in the northwest include pig, sheep and also poppy farming (to provide oil for pharmaceutical preparations). Manufacturing here is dominated by forest-based industries, whereas in the central northern region of the state industries include the knitting yarn producers Coats Patons, the automotive parts manufacturers ACL Bearing Company, and the aluminium smelter and refinery Comalco. Central and northern Tasmania has developed a viticulture industry, and is the home of the Ben Lomond Ski Fields.

The west of the state is a region of dense forests and mountain ranges, raging rivers and rugged hills, and has a treacherous coastline and wild, inaccessible beaches. Mining is the predominant industry in the west, and metal ores such as copper, zinc, tin and iron are extracted here. Much of the southwest region is inaccessible and uninhabited, containing some of the most spectacular scenery in the world. The southwest wilderness area has been listed by the World Heritage Commission and consists of dense rain forests, scrub, wild rivers, rapids, ravines and harsh mountains, which can only be tackled by experienced bush-walkers.

Approximately 20 per cent of Tasmania is World Heritage Area, and there are extensive cave systems, many of which are Ice Age aboriginal cave art sites.

The central lakes area is dominated by the hydroelectric schemes which produce the state's electricity. Trout-fishing is also popular. In the flatter midland area sheep farming, particularly for wool, and beef cattle grazing are also popular.

Many parts of Tasmania are reminiscent of the green but windswept landscapes of some parts of Scotland, and over the decades a large number of British and other European immigrants have settled on the island. The population of Tasmania is currently around half a million, of which two-fifths were born outside Australia, mostly in England, Scotland and Germany and approximately 23% of whom are under the age of 15. Tasmania's climate and farming conditions are most comparable to those of northern European countries such as France and the UK, which also helps new British settlers feel more 'at home' than they might in the harsh dry regions of the Northern Territory or the tropical areas of Queensland.

Hobart. Hobart is Tasmania's capital city. It was founded in 1804 and is situated in the southwest of the state, 20 km from the mouth of the Derwent River. It is Australia's second oldest city, with a population of around 180,000, and extends over both sides of the river. To the west of the city lies Mount Wellington (1,269 m), which is usually snow-capped in winter. The city was founded as a penal colony and was reputed to be one of the harshest prison settlements. Transportation to Van Diemen's Land (as Tasmania was originally called) was as good as a death sentence, and many convicts did not survive. Despite its ruthless beginnings, the city flourished in the mid-nineteenth century thanks to its shipbuilding, whaling and port facilities. Today, Hobart is more likely to make the shipping news during the famous Sydney-Hobart yacht race held every year commencing on Boxing Day.

In 1869 Tasmania became the first colony in the British Empire to make education compulsory and in 1898 school attendance was made obligatory between the ages of seven and thirteen, expanding to between six and fourteen years in 1912. In 1946 Tasmania became the only Australian state to make attendance up to the age of sixteen compulsory. It has its own university, the University of Tasmania, as well as numerous colleges of advanced education and conservatorium of music. Tasmania's main employment sectors are retailing and manufacturing, however, employment is depressed and the outlook for young people is considered poor. Unemployment continues to rise in Tasmania, and it currently has the highest unemployment rate of all states.

Tasmania is becoming increasingly popular as a migration destination. The high standard of education, modern health facilities and cheap housing are all strong attractions. However, the cost of living can be slightly higher than in other states due to freight costs. Although some love the small-community feel of the state, others feel that the sense of isolation that almost inevitably affects new settlers is exacerbated by Tasmania's separation from mainland Australia.

Tasmania's geographical isolation has meant that the state has developed a unique flora and fauna. Tasmania has ten species of mammal not found elsewhere, including the Tasmanian Devil (a carnivorous, nocturnal marsupial) and the 'Tasmanian Tiger', generally believed to be extinct although occasional sightings are claimed, fourteen indigenous species of birds and two species of indigenous reptiles. The duck-billed platypus is more common in Tasmania than elsewhere and the Tasmanian mountain shrimp which is only known outside Tasmania as a fossil has remained obstinately unaltered and very much alive.

In terms of natural environment, Tasmania is breathtaking, and perhaps feels a little more familiar to the European settler than the harsh, sandy, sun baked land of mainland Australia.

Useful Addresses

Tasmania Online. Portal website for the Government of Tasmania: www.tas.gov.au
Tasmanian Department of State Development, 22 Elizabeth Street, Hobart, Tasmania; ☎03-6233 5888; www.dsd.tas.gov.au

VICTORIA (VIC)

Capital: Melbourne.
Area: 227 600 sq. km (136,560 sq miles) = 0.93 times the size of the UK.
Total area of Australia: 2.96%.
Coastline: 1,800 km (1,080 miles).
Climate: January 25.1°C; July 14°C, but the weather in Victoria, particularly in Melbourne, is notoriously unpredictable. Victoria's exposure to frequent cold fronts and southerly winds results in changeable weather patterns, popularly known as the 'Four Seasons in One Day' phenomenon.

Victoria is situated in the southeastern corner of Australia, bordered by South Australia to the west and New South Wales to the north. Even though Victoria is the smallest of all Australian States, it still offers a wide geographical diversity ranging from the Victorian Alps, which lie on the shared border with New South Wales, fertile wine-growing regions in the Murray and Yarra River Valleys, rainforest in the Gippsland region in the southeast corner of Victoria on the Errinundra Plateau, and desert beauty in the northwest inland Mallee region. Victoria has the world's third largest volcanic plain, situated in the Western District. The Great Dividing Range, which forms a spine down the inland 'back' of Victoria and New South Wales, is known as the 'High Country'.

The land on which Melbourne was built was purchased in 1835 from Aborigines of the local Dutigalla clan. The Aborigines had no concept of land as a commodity at that time, and in exchange for their ancestral home they received articles of clothing, 50 pounds of flour, handkerchiefs, knives, tomahawks, looking glasses and blankets. The driving force behind the founding of Melbourne was John Pascoe Fawkner, the son of a convict. A self-educated bush lawyer who also established several newspapers, Fawkner sat on the Legislative Council of Victoria for 15 years, where he was an energetic campaigner for the rights of small settlers and convicts, and instrumental in ending the transportation of convicts from Great Britain to Australia. His energy was drawn from his own personal experience of the harsh penal code – he received 500 lashes when he was 22 for assisting seven convicts to escape and he bore the scars for the rest of his life.

The population of Victoria (the most densely populated state in Australia) is currently estimated at 4.5 million, and consists of immigrants from the UK and EU as well as the Middle East and Southeast Asia. There are approximately 12,000 Aborigines in Victoria. All of these different ethnic groups give the state a real cultural diversity and have a positive influence on Victorian culture. Melbourne has a population of around 3 million, and other major regional centres include Geelong, Bendigo, Ballarat, Horsham, Mildura, Warrnambool, Castlemaine and Shepparton.

Victoria's economy has suffered in the past from industrial unrest and from poor economic government. In an attempt to boost the State's economy, the Victorian Government sponsors successful overseas entrepreneurs and senior executives intending to live permanently in Victoria through the Australian Government's State/Territory Nominated Independent Scheme Migration Category. Victoria is the site of research and development in the areas of food, paper, chemicals and petroleum, transport equipment, electrical equipment and biotechnology.

The standard of tertiary education in Victoria is particularly high. There are eight universities in the State, three of which specialise in technology, as well as numerous technical and further education institutions. The Commonwealth Scientific and Industrial Research Organisation is based in Victoria.

Melbourne. In 1990 the Population Crisis Committee, based in Washington DC, rated Melbourne the world's most liveable city in terms of safety, health, and air quality. Melbourne's location on the coastal plain between the Pacific Ocean and the beautiful Dandenong hills provides a superb living environment, and its cultural and sporting facilities are unequalled elsewhere in Australia.

Melbourne flourished during the great gold rush of the 1850s and as a consequence it became the Australian centre of business and commerce. Today, 16 of Australia's top 50 innovative companies have their headquarters in Melbourne. In the 1880s Melbourne was known as 'The Paris of the Antipodes', and it was the capital of Australia from 1901 (Federation) until 1927, when the capital was moved to Canberra (to avoid in-fighting between Melbourne and Sydney).

Melbourne is one of Australia's leading exporters of computers, engines and pharmaceuticals, and it is the location of eight major medical research institutes, including the Walter and Eliza Hall Institute, the home of modern immunology and one of the world's best known medical research centres. Australia's main telecommunications research and development facilities are based in Melbourne, and Victoria accounts for over 30 per cent of Australia's information and telecommunications technology turnover. Melbourne is a popular destination in the Asian region for conventions, meetings and exhibitions.

The 3.4 million population of Melbourne is a cosmopolitan one and, with nearly 200 different nationalities represented, it is one of the most multicultural cities in the world. It has the world's third largest Greek community, behind Athens and Thessalonia.

Melbourne is widely considered to be the cultural capital of Australia, and it enjoys the facilities of a world-standard Arts Centre. The Australian Ballet Company is based in the city. Melbourne is also the home of the Australian film industry and of much of Australian television output (including *Neighbours* and *Home and Away*). The city is Australia's premier shopping location, with an unlimited selection of designer shops and other stores. Melbourne also hosts the Melbourne Cup, the nation's richest horse race, the Australian Rules Football Grand Final, and the Australian Open at the impressive Koorong Tennis Centre.

Useful Addresses

State of Victoria Website, www.vic.gov.au
Business Victoria, 55 Collins Street, Melbourne, VIC 3001; ☎13 22 15 (within Aus.) or

+61 3 9651 9387 (International); www.business.vic.gov.au
Investment Centre Victoria, Level 46, 55 Collins Street, Melbourne, VIC 3000; ☎03-
9651 9066; fax 03 9650 2248; www.dsrd.vic.gov.au

AUSTRALIAN CAPITAL TERRITORY (ACT)

Capital: Canberra.
Area: 2,400 sq. km (1,440 sq. miles) = 0.01 times the size of the UK.
Total area of Australia: 0.0003%.
Coastline: 0 (except 35 km in Jervis Bay Territory).
Climate: January 28°C; July 11°C.

Canberra was established in 1901 (at Federation) to provide a 'neutral' headquarters for the new seat of government. Sydney had threatened to refuse to join the Federation unless the capital was in New South Wales; Melbourne, for its part, considered it had the greater claim. As a compromise, the Australian Capital Territory was established mid-way between the two states in a move which was, as it was said, 'acceptable to everyone, but satisfactory to nobody'. The American architect, Walter Burley Griffin, won the international competition to design the new capital city, resulting in a completely planned city where even the sites of trees have been carefully selected. The effect can appear sterile, and this sterility is reinforced by the fact that 60 per cent of Canberra's residents are civil servants. The weekend sees an evacuation of politicians back to their state of origin, giving Canberra the reputation for city without a soul. During the week, however, Capital Hill, through which the artificial Lake Burley Griffin cuts, is the hub of the nation's political activity. Canberra is a derivative of an Aboriginal word *kamberra* which means 'meeting place'. The city is home to the Australian National University, the Australian Institute of Sport, the Australian National Gallery and the Australian War Memorial and Museum. Canberra does not have a commercial centre and its big shopping centres are all located in suburban areas. Instead, the city has many parks and recreational areas, and traffic congestion is virtually unknown.

Canberra, with a population of 3 million, is an attractive city, although it is much derided by most Australians who find its planned and highly ordered environment less than easy to appreciate. Nonetheless, it has a friendly atmosphere, and is not inferior to other Australian cities, merely different.

Useful Addresses

Australian Capital Territory Website, www.act.gov.au
ACT Business Gateway, ☎1800 244 650; www.business.gateway.act.gov.au

NEW SOUTH WALES (NSW)

Capital: Sydney.
Area: 802,000 sq. km (309,572 sq miles) = 3.25 times the size of the UK.
Total area of Australia: 10%.

Climate: The mean January temperatures along the coast are usually between 8°C and 21°C, but 22°C at Sydney. The plateaux are about 4°C cooler and the temperatures in the plains increase in direct relation to the distance from the sea. Temperatures at the Queensland border are about 27°C to 31°C. The maximum temperature in July is 17°C and the minimum is 8°C.

New South Wales is probably the Australian state most visited by tourists and business people, and is the state which receives most international publicity. This is largely due to its spectacular capital city, Sydney, which played host to the Olympic Games in 2000. There is, however, so much more to New South Wales than Sydney, and it is well worth venturing beyond the city limits to explore its diverse regions.

New South Wales is bordered to the north by Queensland, to the east by South Australia and to the south by Victoria. The Australian Capital Territory lies wholly contained in the southeast corner of New South Wales. From Sydney, it is 1,157 km west to Broken Hill, almost on the South Australian border, 908 km north to Tweed Heads which borders Queensland, and 498 km south to Eden, the last sizeable town before Victoria. Within these extremes lie mountain ranges, beaches, fertile farmland, rainforests and arid desert.

The Blue Mountains, 100 km west of Sydney, is a national park containing some of the most breathtaking scenery in the world. Standing at one of the numerous lookouts it is possible to survey hundreds of miles of unbroken, uninhabited bush and to view the immense unusual rock formations at Echo Point known as 'The Three Sisters'. The area was home to Aboriginal people at least 14,000 years ago and they have left their mark in the numerous rock carvings and cave paintings. The rugged 250,000 hectare park is composed mainly of sandstone which has been eroded over the ages by rivers and creeks, to form dramatic valleys and sheer escarpments.

Approximately 150 km north of Sydney lies the main wine producing region of New South Wales, Hunter Valley. The Valley is divided into two distinct regions, the Lower and the Upper Hunter areas. Cessnock, 183 km from Sydney, is the centre of the Lower Hunter region and was originally founded on the coal-mining industry. The area produces some of the state's best wines and famous wineries include McWilliams, Mount Pleasant, Lindemans, Hungerford Hill, Tyrells and Brokenwood. One hundred km further to the northwest is the smaller and less well-known Lower Hunter, home of the renowned Rosemount Estate. Muswellbrook is the centre of this region and is known for its coal and agriculture.

To the southeast of the state lie the Snowy Mountains, less than a three-hour drive from Canberra in the ACT. Thredbo is a popular ski resort which has hosted various World Cup Ski events, and it is possible to take a chair lift to the top of Crackenback and then hike up Australia's highest mountain, Mount Kosciusko which, at 7,328 feet (2241 metres), is less than half the height of Mont Blanc in France. On the northern side of Mt. Kosciusko, in Perisher Valley, lie two of the most popular ski resorts, Perisher and Smiggins Holes. This is Australia's 'alpine country' that, surprisingly, contains more snow-covered area than Switzerland. Instead of pine trees and alpine scenes be prepared for ghostly eucalypts silhouetted against the snow. The Australian ski season runs from June to October and the snow is usually best between late July and mid-September. Mount Kosciusko is located at the heart of the Kosckiusko National Park, which contains 629,000 hectares of rugged moorland, glacial lakes, caves and the source of the Murray River, Australia's largest waterway. There are more than 200 species of birds here, and an abundance of wildlife including kangaroos, possums and wombats. The Snowy Mountains support seven hydroelectric stations which supply a large proportion of the state's power grid.

The Murray River rises in the Great Dividing Range and flows for over 2,500 km, forming the border between Victoria and New South Wales. From Wentworth, in the far west of New South Wales, the Murray continues through South Australia and veers south, flowing into Lake Alexandrina and to the ocean. The river is used extensively for irrigation and is crucial to the region's agricultural industries. One of the state's most important agricultural districts is the Riverina which lies along the northern borderlands of the Murray River. Crops as diverse as rice, vegetables and citrus fruits are grown here, and cattle and merino sheep are also important. Albury is at the heart of this fertile region and its population is approximately 42,000. It is a National Growth Centre, the aim of which has been to encourage the decentralisation of industry from major state capitals. Wentworth is important as the heart of the region's irrigation scheme and both the citrus and avocado growing areas.

Broken Hill is one of the state's most easterly settlements, lying almost on the border with South Australia. It is isolated and remote, but nearly 25,000 people live here and it is famous for its silver mines and the Royal Flying Doctor Services. The mining industry has survived, and silver, lead and zinc are still mined in significant quantities. In the northern desert region of the state, along the border with Queensland, lies the town of Lightning Ridge, famous for its opal mines. Over 1,000 people from 30 different nations are based at Lightning Ridge, and manage to survive the extreme weather conditions and limited water supply (artesian bore water is the only kind available here) to mine the fields for the highly prized black opals. Visitors are allowed to tour various mines and to *fossick* (prospect) for the gems.

New South Wales' north coastal region is one of the state's favourite holiday destinations, and the region contains spectacular surf beaches, lakes, rivers, small coastal towns and beautiful inland scenery. Byron Bay, Australia's most easterly point, is considered to be the unspoilt gem of the New South Wales coast. Cape Byron is home to many people who prefer an alternative lifestyle away from the rat-race of the busy cities. Coffs Harbour, closer to Sydney, is a popular harbour and port town, with many top-class tourist resorts. There is plenty of good surf, and it is also a famous yachting centre. Bananas are grown in this semi-tropical area and the nearby Dorrigo National Park contains rainforest, waterfalls and lush vegetation. Inland from Coffs is the Nymboida River, a popular spot for white-water rafting. Grafton is situated in this area, some 65 km inland, and is at the centre of a region which specialises in both dairy and sugarcane industries.

New South Wales also controls Lord Howe Island and originally owned Norfolk Island, although this is now a Territory of Australia. Lord Howe Island is a tiny island, 11 km long and 2.8 km at its widest point, some 700 km northeast of Sydney. It has a population of around 300 and was listed as a World Heritage area in 1982 because of its soaring volcanic peaks, the world's most southerly coral reef, exceptional bird life and scenic beauty. Lord Howe Island was first sighted in 1788 and was named after the first Lord of the Admiralty. The numbers of visitors to the island is strictly controlled to protect it from becoming overrun by crowds, and the island's 37 km coastline provides plenty of opportunity for fishing, coral reef viewing and relaxation. Norfolk Island is a much larger and more isolated island, 1,600 km to the east of Sydney. It was first discovered by Captain Cook in 1774 and later became a penal settlement for the colony of New South Wales between 1788 and 1855. Norfolk Island was the home of the Pitcairn Islanders who included descendants of the *Bounty* mutineers. There are still many Pitcairn descendants on the island who speak 'Norfolk', a curious mixture of Tahitian and English. The island has a population of about 2,000, most of whom are involved in either tourism or agriculture.

Sydney. Sydney has a population of nearly 3.8 million people, around 60 per cent of the state's total population of 6.2 million. The second largest city in New South Wales is Newcastle, on the northern coast 170 km from Sydney, with a population of 350,000, and Wollongong, some 82 km south of Sydney, is the third urban area. The city of Sydney is open and spacious, surrounded on three sides by national parks and on the fourth by 60 km of beautiful and quite spectacular coastline. Sydney Harbour, on which the city is built, has 240 km of foreshore, much of which remains as it was when the First Fleet made its initial investigative journey up the waterway in 1788. Sydney has been described as 'the best address on earth', and although Sydney has its share of the problems associated with big cities, such as pollution, ugly industrial areas, traffic congestion, homelessness, unemployment, drugs and crime, one still cannot help but feel that Sydney is perhaps even more beautiful now than it was over 100 years ago. The Sydney Harbour Bridge and the Opera House, which are the most dramatic features of the Harbour, were opened in 1932 and 1973 respectively.

Sydney is one of Australia's most historical cities, as it was into Botany Bay, just south of Sydney, that Captain Cook sailed in the *Endeavour* in 1770. In May 1787 the First Fleet of 1,044 people, including 759 convicts (191 of whom were women) set sail from Portsmouth and arrived in Australia eight months later. Unimpressed with Botany Bay's windswept barrenness, the Fleet moved north in search of a more suitable site and six days later the ships arrived at what became Port Jackson, described by Captain Phillip as 'the finest harbour in the world'. Even though Port Jackson was superior to Botany Bay, the first years of the colony were harsh, as crops failed and the anticipated supply ships failed to arrive. However, the colony managed to survive and slowly, began to grow. Captain Phillip was replaced by Governor Macquarie, known as the 'Father of Australia', in 1810 and over the next 11 years streets were laid down and fine new buildings erected. Convict transportation to New South Wales continued until 1840, but free settlers began to arrive from 1819. From 1831 to 1850 more than 200,000 government-assisted migrants streamed into the colony to begin a new life as far away as possible from the urban nightmare of Victorian Britain. During the 1850s, a gold rush brought a new influx of settlers which continued until the end of the nineteenth century, and by 1925 the area around Sydney had a population in excess of one million.

Sydney today boasts Australia's most influential Central Business District (CBD) and most national and international businesses choose to have their major Australian offices in Sydney. Darling Harbour houses the Sydney Aquarium, Chinese Gardens, Powerhouse Museum and the National Maritime Museum, and is linked to the CBD by monorail. The Rocks is Sydney's most historic area, and much of it has been restored to its former glory. Doyle's Restaurant at the foot of the Rocks is a haven for the seafood connoisseur, with fresh fish a house speciality. There are many beaches around the Sydney area, the most famous of which are, perhaps, Bondi (grossly overrated) and Manly (slightly overrated). The most beautiful, unspoilt and uncrowded beaches lie further north and south of the city. The northern coastal suburbs are particularly beautiful as the coastline is made up of rugged headlands interspersed with long sandy beaches. Most beaches have seawater swimming pools naturally carved out of the rocky headland, which provide safe, sheltered swimming areas. The beaches of Dee Why, Long Reef, Collaroy, Narrabeen, Newport, Avalon, Whale Beach and Palm Beach are among the most beautiful Sydney beaches.

Sydney is a cultural centre and is home to the Australian Opera and the Sydney Symphony Orchestra, both based at the Opera House. Standing tickets for the opera can be bought for as little as $25, and many agents sell last-minute tickets at half price. Sydney is also home to the Museum of Contemporary Art and the Sydney Observatory. The city's Gay and Lesbian Mardi Gras is an international crowd-puller, as the country's gay, bisexual and transvestite population take to the streets in bizarre and outlandish costumes. The Queen Victoria Building houses many chic boutiques and plenty of bargain shops, but better bargains can be found at Paddy's Markets in Paddington.

In 1988 a re-enactment of the First Fleet entering Sydney Harbour was staged as part of the bicentennial celebrations and the view included a bank-to-bank flotilla of small pleasure boats, the old 'Coathanger' and Centrepoint Tower in the background, in front of which stood the Sydney Opera House, the sun gleaming off the millions of highly polished white tiles that make up its shell. There is no doubt that Sydney Harbour is stunning and the city is an exciting place in which to live. Some Australians do, however, tire of the bright lights and relatively fast pace and prefer to move to quieter, calmer and perhaps safer cities.

New South Wales has many special events during the calendar year. The Festival of Sydney usually takes place in January, as does the New South Wales Tennis Open and the Country Music Festival. The Sydney Royal Easter Show usually occurs between March and April, and the Sydney Film Festival takes place in June, as does the Darling Harbour Jazz Festival. The Rugby League Grand Final is held in Sydney in September. Other major state sporting events include the Tooheys 1000 Bathurst Touring Car Race at Bathurst in October, and the Sydney to Hobart yacht race which commences on Boxing Day every year.

Sydney is one of the most expensive areas in Australia in which to live, but many of the outer suburbs and regional areas are less expensive. Rent in Sydney is very high by Australian standards, but is still markedly lower than current rental rates in London or New York for comparable properties. The state's unemployment rate is the lowest in Australia. Major employment sectors in the city are commerce (banking, insurance and finance), retail, manufacturing, hospitality and tourism. Agriculture and tourism are the biggest employment sectors in regional areas.

Education and health services are exceptionally good in New South Wales, which is home to many large and excellent tertiary educational institutions. New South Wales currently attracts more new settlers than any other state/territory.

Useful Addresses

New South Wales Government website, www.nsw.gov.au

Department of State and Regional Development, Level 44, Grosvenor Place, 225 George Street, PO Box N818, Sydney, NSW 1220; ☎02-9228 3111; fax 02-9228 3626; www.business.nsw.gov.au

QUEENSLAND (QLD)

Capital: Brisbane.
Area: 1,725,000 sq. km (1,035,000 sq. miles) = seven times the size of the UK.
Total area of Australia: 22.48%.

Coastline: 7,400 km (4,440 miles).
Climate: In Brisbane, the average daily maximum in January is 29°C and in June is 21°C. In Cairns, the average daily maximums for the same months are 31°C and 26°C.

Queensland is Australia's second largest state, but has the largest habitable area defined by rainfall. Queensland's habitable area is a staggering 1,554,000 sq. km. By contrast, a mere 57 per cent of Western Australia is considered habitable (1,440,000 sq km). Queensland is situated in the northeastern corner of Australia and it is bounded by the Northern Territory to the west, South Australia to the southwest and New South Wales to the south. It stretches from the temperate and densely populated southeast to the tropical and sparsely populated Cape York Peninsula in the north.

Queensland epitomises the marketed image of Australia overseas. With the Great Barrier Reef, the Whitsunday Islands, World Heritage areas such as the Daintree Rainforest and Fraser Island, and a beautiful climate, it is not surprising that Queensland is one of the most popular tourist destinations in Australia. Queensland is known as the 'Sunshine State' and Queenslanders are affectionately called 'banana-benders'. They are also considered to be the rednecks of Australia, and as such are renowned for their very conservative political outlook.

Like most of Australia, Queensland is rich in natural resources. Its four major products are sugar, meat, grains and wool, and the growing areas are spread throughout the state. Australia is the world's second largest exporter of raw cane sugar, and 95 per cent of Australia's production comes from Queensland. The State also contains vast mineral deposits, including coal, bauxite, gold, copper, lead, zinc, silver and magnesite. Besides agricultural and mining industries, Queensland's biggest industries are manufacturing and tourism. Queensland's economic growth is significantly higher than the national average, and tourism accounts for ten per cent of Gross State Product.

For more than 20 years, Queensland has experienced a consistently higher rate of population growth than the national average. Queensland's population growth can be attributed to overseas immigration, natural increase, and most importantly, to interstate migration. Queensland, it seems, is the place where most Australians want to live, and more Australians are moving to Queensland than to any other state or territory. Popular opinion has it that more and more Australians are moving to Queensland to retire. Census figures from the Australian Bureau of Statistics show that 31 per cent of Queensland's population lies in the 25-44 year age range, however, it is predicted that by 2021 at least 43 per cent of the population will be over 45.

Queensland's population is much more decentralised than that of any other state. The population of around three million is scattered over major regional centres such as the Gold Coast, Bundaberg, Toowoomba, Rockhampton, Longreach, Townsville, Cairns and Mount Isa, as well as Brisbane, which is home to 1.1 million people.

The Queensland Government has for many years had a reputation for ultra-conservativism. For most of those years the state was under the leadership of the Premier, Sir Joh Bjelke-Peterson, and became notorious for its repressive and racist attitudes. Vestiges of this xenophobia remain, and Queensland is the seedbed of the racist One Nation Party, until recently led by Pauline Hanson. Antipathy is particularly directed towards the Japanese who have invested large sums in Queensland property, however, most Queenslanders recognise that Japanese investments are tourists play a significant part in promoting Queensland's healthy economy. The Queensland Government has suffered from allegations of corruption at the highest levels. When the Labour Party was elected in September 1992, its leader, the Hon. W K Goss, became the first Labour Premier in Queensland since 1957. The new government represented the desire of Queenslanders to end the corruption and hypocritical moralising of the old government, and stood for a fresh start.

Queensland's health and education services are broadly comparable with the national standard. Brisbane is home to the University of Queensland and to Australia's first private university, Bond University, established by entrepreneur Alan Bond. The multi-millionaire Western Australian, after whom it is named, served a three-year prison sentence for illegal business ventures and was released in March 2000; however, the university that bears his name is none the less regarded as a centre of excellence.

Most Queensland residents own their own home, and the high standard of living combined with an extraordinary natural environment makes Queensland a popular choice for settlement.

Useful Addresses

Queensland Government Website, www.qld.gov.au

The Department of State Development, Business Migration, Floor 3, Executive Building, 100 George Street, Brisbane, Qld 4002; ☎07-3224 8576; fax 07-3224 9410; www.sd.qld.gov.au

Queensland Government Trade and Investment Office (Europe), Queensland House, 392 Strand, London WC2R OLZ, England; ☎020-7836 1333; fax 020-7240 7667.

GETTING THERE

These days, if you want to get to Australia, you have to fly. QANTAS is Australia's national carrier, and is legendary for its outstanding safety record, although its reputation for quality and service allows it to charge premium fares. Over 30 international airlines fly direct to Australia, usually to Perth or Sydney from destinations all round the world. The flight time from Europe to Australia, depending on your route, point of departure, and destination, is likely to be between 19 and 26 hours. From the United States' west coast the flight to Australia takes around 14 hours.

Fares to Australia vary dramatically according to the seasons, and are also affected by special events, such as Christmas. Prices skyrocket in early December, for example, but drop dramatically on the 26th of December, so delaying your departure by a few days may save you the cost of a couple of internal flights once you arrive in Australia. The cheapest time to fly to Australia is during the Low Season, from March to June (precise dates differ from airline to airline). Mid Season (or Shoulder), from July to November, and during February, is somewhat more expensive; and Peak Season, from December to January, is really best avoided from a financial point of view, unless you can only travel at that time. Once you have decided when to travel, you should try and book as early as possible – seats fill up very fast, and flights during the Australian summer may be fully booked as early as July.

Scheduled flights by various national carriers will usually offer the possibility of a stopover in their home country, which allows a welcome break in the arduous journey at the same time as providing a cheap exotic holiday. If flying with Malaysian Airlines, for example, you may be offered a stopover in Kuala Lumpur as well as a free internal flight, so that if you choose, you can fly to the resorts of Penang or Langkawi for a few days. Return fares are usually valid for 12 months, and travel agents are required to request proof of residency if you wish to purchase a one-way ticket. An open-jaw return ticket will allow you to enter Australia via one port and leave from another, however, this type of ticket is likely to be more expensive.

Charter flights, operated by tour companies rather than airlines, are usually the cheapest way to travel to Australia. They won't get you there in much style, but they are ideal for travellers on a budget. There are a number of websites (www.cheapflights.com; www.deckchair.com; www.expedia.com to name just a few) that provide details on last minute and budget flight deals from locations worldwide. In the UK bargains can also be found on teletext.

Currently, you can expect to pay around £500+ for a London to Sydney return flight; and around US$1,000 for a return flight from Los Angeles (add another US$300 if you are starting your journey in New York). The disadvantage of charter flights is that they generally operate on a short-term return basis, so that you are likely to have to return two weeks after arrival. Flights book out very early, and stopovers are not permitted. Many airlines also offer savings on Australian internal flights once you have booked with them.

Insurance

Working travellers and those on speculative job finding trips to Australia are strongly advised to take out comprehensive travel insurance. Insurers offering reasonable and flexible premiums include:

Atlas Direct Travel Insurance Ltd, 37 King's Exchange, Tileyard Road, London N7 9AH; ☎020-7609 5000; fax 020-7609 5011; www.atlasdirect.net

Columbus Direct Travel Insurance, 17 Devonshire Square, London EC2M 4SQ; ☎020-7422 5505; fax 020-7375 0274; www.columbusdirect.net.

John Mahon, Visas Australia, PO. box 1, Nantwich, Cheshire CW5 7PB; ☎01270-626626; fax 01270-626226;

www.visas-australia.com; john@visas-australia.com. Also in Dublin: 2nd Floor, 13 Aston Quay, Dublin 2; ☎01-6795452; fax 01-6795459. Offers very competitive long-stay insurance that allows you to work.

The Travel Insurance Agency, Suite 2, Percy Mews, 755B High Road, North Finchley, London N12 8JY; ☎020-8446 5414; fax 020-8446 5417; www.travelinsurers.com

Worldwide Travel Insurance Services Ltd, The Business Centre, 1-7 Commercial Road, Paddock Wood, Tonbridge, Kent TN12 6YT; ☎01892-833338; fax 01892-837744; www.worldwideinsure.com

Discount Fare Specialists for Australia & New Zealand
STA Travel, 86 Old Brompton Road, London SW7 3LQ; ☎020-7581 4132; www.statravel.co.uk. STA Travel specialises in student travel and discount fares for the under-35 market. It is particularly helpful in arranging nonstandard travel. STA has 45 branches in the UK and 300 worldwide, particularly in areas with large student populations.
Austravel, 152 Brompton Road, Knightsbridge, London, SW3 1HX; ☎0870-055 0212; www.austravel.net. Austravel also has several other offices in Manchester, Leeds, Edinburgh, Bristol, Bournemouth and Birmingham, and produces a fares guide which gives price comparisons between all the major airlines.

Bridge the World, 4 Regent Place, Regent Street, London W1R 5F; ☎0870-444 7474; www.bridgetheworld.com
Cresta World Travel, Cresta House, 32 Victoria Street, Altrincham, Cheshire WA14 1ET; ☎0161-927 7177; fax 0161-928 7551.
Platinum Travel Centre, 52 Earls Court Road, Kensington, London, W8 6EJ; ☎020-7937 5122.
Travelbag plc., 3-5 High Street, Alton, Hampshire, GU34 1TL; ☎0870-900 1352 or 0870-902 0152; www.travelbag.co.uk. Also at 373-375, Strand, London WC2R OJE; ☎0870-900 1351. Travelbag also has offices in other parts of the UK including Nottingham, Cheshire and Leeds.
The Australian Youth Hostels Association, Level 3, 10 Mallett St, Camperdown, NSW 2050; ☎02-9565 1699; fax 02-9565 1325; www.yha.org.au. Offers complete travel packages including accommodation and 12 months coach travel.

RESIDENCE AND
ENTRY REGULATIONS

CHAPTER SUMMARY

○ **Immigration Programme.** Australia's immigration programme is managed with quotas and categories regularly changed to adapt to the needs of the nation.

  ◑ In 1999-2000, 92,272 immigrants entered Australia on a long-term basis of which 7,267 were in the Humanitarian category.

  ◑ Immigration has been reduced considerably since the 1980s when the yearly total was 140,000.

  ◑ In 2001-2, 79,000 migrants were accepted in the immigration programme.

  ◑ Applying to live in Australia can be a time-consuming and expensive exercise.

  ◑ It is possible to use a migration consultancy to help you through the procedures.

○ **Tourist Visa.** This is free for three months. 12-month visas cost $60.

  ◑ You can apply for a Visitor's visa on the internet or at some travel agents.

  ◑ Aged parents and relatives of Australian residents may be eligible for permanent entry into Australia under certain conditions.

The Current Position

Immigration has recently become a contentious policy area in Australia with many people reacting to economic stringencies by calling for an end to Australia's migration programmes. The rationale for this position (that 'foreigners take our jobs') has been proved to be completely erroneous. This has not prevented anti-migration activists, generally operating from a distinctly racist platform, from continuing to dominate debate on the issue in the media. In response, the government has stressed its commitment to Australia as a 'deeply tolerant, fair-minded and generous society' and outlined the benefits of immigration in a recent booklet, *Dispelling the myths about immigration* (available from the Department of Immigration and Multicultural and Indigenous Affairs, or in electronic form, on their website at www.immi.gov.au/package/booklet.htm). The current government recognises that migrants have made, and continue to make, an enormous contribution to Australian society, bringing new ideas, technologies and skills to the nation's economy and skill base. In the context of the globalisation of Australia's economy, migrants' awareness of the nuances of international cultures provides an important asset for its international and domestic competitiveness.

Australia's migration programme is carefully managed, with annual quotas imposed on each area of temporary and permanent residency category after extensive assessment of the current economic circumstances. For 1999-2000, 92,272 people were granted entry to Australia on a long-term basis: 68,000 in the Migration programme (family and skilled streams) and 7,267 in the Humanitarian programme,

which offers entry to refugees of civil war and human rights abuse. The government's intention is that migration should become more focused on the intake of skilled migrants, although it retains a commitment to bona fide immediate family migrants. The overall intake is small compared to the high levels of the 1980s, when around 140,000 people a year were successful in gaining entry to Australia as permanent residents.

Although racist polemics in the popular press would suggest otherwise, Australia operates an entirely non-discriminatory immigration programme. It is selective on the basis of skills, age and language ability, but is open to anyone in any part of the world, regardless of their country of birth, ethnic origin, race, sex or religion. Figures from the Australian Bureau of Statistics show that 11 per cent of the population were born in the UK, the lowest per centage in 30 years. Between 1965 and 1970, 47% of settler arrivals to Australia were born in the United Kingdom and Ireland; however, in the five years to June 2000, the United Kingdom and Ireland contributed 12 per cent of settlers to Australia. Applying to live in Australia can be a time-consuming and expensive exercise, and a number of migration consultancies offer services which can help prospective applicants with the procedures. The Australian consular service advises prospective visa applicants that although such consultancies cannot 'get round the system' and guarantee success, a reputable firm may ease the pressure and provide valuable advice to those unfamiliar with the migration application process.

Useful Addresses

AAA Australian Migration, Westside House, 5th Floor, 72 Kings Park Road, West Perth, WA 6005, Australia; ☎(08) 9486 1533; fax (08) 9486 1544; www.australian-migration.com.au. The UK representative of AAA can be contacted on 07890-759449

Australian Migration Associates Ltd, Carrington Business Park, Carrington, Manchester, M31 4DD; ☎0161-776 9839; fax 0161-776 9841; e-mail enquiries@australiamigrate.co.uk; www.australiamigrate.co.uk; A professional agency that handles both migration applications in full and offers a checking service for those who wish to handle their own application.

CLB, Aldwych House, 81 Aldwych, London WC2B 4HP; ☎020-7242 2444; fax 020-7242 1117; e-mail hburnard@compuserve.com; www.clb.co.uk. Helen Burnard is a registered migration agent with 28 years experience. Full advice offered to those wishing to emigrate to Australia, with a free initial interview. Member Migration Institute Australia.

Concept Australia, www.conceptaustralia. co.uk. Grahame Igglesden and Partners (Registered Migration Agent Number 9901024) are professional migration consultants specialising in Australia with a code of conduct that ensures that they will only accept a case if they believe the applicants are eligible. Visit the above website for a copy of their brochure.

The Emigration Group Ltd., 7 Heritage Court, Lower Bridge Street, Chester, Cheshire CH1 1RD; ☎01244-321414; fax 01244-342288; e-mail info@TEGltd.co.uk; www.jobfastrack.co.nz. Provides full assistance with applications for residence and/or work visas. Sister company, Taylor and Associates matches job seekers with employers; together they provide an effective and total emigration service.

Four Corners Emigration, Strathblane House, Ashfield Road, Cheadle SK8 1BB; ☎0161-608 1608; fax 0161-608 1616; e-mail info@4-corners.com; www.4-corners.com. Specialists in assisting with immigration and visas to

Australia; full support with relocation and resettlement also given.

Global 9, The Limes, No. 24 Greengate, Swanton Morely, Dereham, Norfolk; ☎01362-6371260. Also 7 Sheahon Way, Marmion, Western Australia; ☎08 9246 7588; fax 08-9246 7588; e-mail uk:global9.org; www.global9.org. A firm of professional migration consultants offering integrated advice and assistance to those wanting temporary or permanent residence in Australia. Reg. No. ma90194.

Go Matilda, Enterprise House, Ocean Village, Southampton, Hampshire SO14 3XB; ☎02380-488777; fax 02380-488787. Australian office at Level 5, 11 Queens Road, Melbourne, VIC 3004, Australia; ☎(03) 8530 7030; fax (03) 9820 5834; www.gomatilda.com; info@gomatilda.com. A visa, tax and migration consultancy for those intending

to move or set up business in Australia.
Ian Harrop & Associates, Endeavour House, The Old Brewery, Priory Lane, Burford, Oxfordshire OX18 4SG; ☎01993-824111; fax 01933-824112; e-mail ihaburford@aol.com. London office: 232 Merton Road, South Wimbledon, London SW19 1EQ; ☎020-8540 8448; fax 020-8540 5811; e-mail ihalondon@aol.com. Australian emigration consultants with 28 years experience; free initial telephone assessments.

New Zealand and Australia Migration Bureau, Argyll House, All Saints Passage, London SW18 1EP; ☎020-8875 5442; fax 020-8875 5443; For a free eligibility assessment visit www.migrationbureau.com or contact the office nearest you: *Europe* Migration Bureau: Oranje Nassaulaan 25, 1075 AJ Amsterdam, The Netherlands; ☎+31 (0)20-6717017.
South Africa Migration Bureau: Sandton

Square, 2nd Floor, West Tower, Maude Street, P.O. Box 785553, Sandton, 2146 Johannesburg, South Africa; ☎+27 (0)11-881 5421;
Asia, The Americas & Australia Migration Bureau: Level 39, Citigroup Centre, 2 Park Street, Sydney, NSW 2000, Australia; ☎02-9004 7807;
New Zealand Migration Bureau, 366 Montreal Street, Christchurch 8001, New Zealand; ☎(+64) 03-3 77 44 11; fax (+64) 03 - 3 77 44 12.

OE Visas. 16 Forth Street, Edinburgh EH1 32H; ☎0131-625 6900; fax 0131-626 6907; www.overseas-emigration.co.uk. Scotland and the North's only Registered Migration Agent. Helping hundreds of people every day emigrate to Australia, New Zealand, Canada and the USA. Offices also in Cardiff, Ireland and London. Reg No. 990 5168

All migration agents and consultants charge for their services.

Useful Publication

Australian Outlook, published monthly by Consyl Publishing Ltd. (3 Buckhurst Road, Bexhill-on-Sea, East Sussex TN40 1QF; ☎01424-223111; fax 01424-224992; internet: www.consylpublishing.co.uk). Aimed specifically at migrants, this publication is a useful way of keeping up with Australian migration policy and entry regulations. In the UK six issues cost £12.00 and twelve issues £16.50; in Europe six issues cost £15.00 and twelve issues £21.20; elsewhere six issues cost £18.00 and twelve cost £29.90.

Entry for Australian Citizens

Travellers holding an Australian passport, a New Zealand passport, or a British passport with Australian permanent residency are exempted from the requirement to obtain a visa prior to entry into Australia. All other travellers, whether making a short-term visit as a tourist or for business purposes, or anticipating a longer stay on a working holiday or as a migrant, must obtain the appropriate visa from their nearest Australian mission before leaving their home country. Visitors who arrive in Australia without a visa are immediately deported and are held responsible for any costs arising from their deportation. If you are in doubt over whether you are an Australian or New Zealand citizen, or whether you have an entitlement to permanent residency, the Australian High Commission, which is responsible for all visa and migration queries, will be able to advise you. In general, if you wish to visit Australia as a tourist you will need a Visitor's Visa; if you are planning to go on a working holiday or to retire, you will need a Temporary Residence Visa in the appropriate category; and if you are hoping to settle permanently in Australia, you will need to be accepted as an immigrant and be granted permanent residence.

Visitor's Visa

To visit Australia as a tourist, you will require a Visitor's visa, for which you will need Form 48/48R obtainable from the Australian High Commission and many travel agents. This form can also now be downloaded as a pdf.file from the Internet at www.immi.gov.au/allforms/formlist.htm. Visitors' visas are classed as either 'short-stay' (3 months) or 'long-stay' (more than 3 months), are multiple entry visas and are valid for 12 months from the date of issue. There is no application fee for a short-stay visitor's visa, however, a non-refundable fee of $60 is charged for the longer visa. Travellers visiting Australia to conduct business of a short-term nature which is deemed not to disadvantage local residents, should also apply for a Visitor's visa on Form 48/48R. Retired parents of Australian residents are entitled to a Visitor's visa valid for a period of 12 months. In order to be eligible for this extended visa, you need to provide proof of funds sufficient to support yourself during the entire period of the visit. If you intend staying with family or friends for any or all of this time, the level of funds required will be assessed at a lower level than that for a tourist.

The three-month Visitor visa can be applied for by post, with a processing time of approximately three weeks. Enclose a large, stamped, self-addressed envelope for the return of your documents. Applications can be made in person at the Australian High Commission in London, the Australian Embassy in Dublin and from Australian Government offices elsewhere. The Australian High Commission in London can be very busy, especially from September to February, and you should expect a long wait;

Mondays to Wednesdays are generally the busiest days.

It is possible to extend a three-month visitor's visa to one of six months duration whilst in Australia, however, if you wish to stay longer in Australia, it is most important to extend the visa before it expires. The Department of Immigration and Multicultural and Indigenous Affairs will deport immediately any applicant who holds an expired visa. You must leave the country on a valid visa and renew it overseas before returning, although some travellers following this procedure have been refused re-entry into Australia despite leaving Australia on a valid visa and renewing their visas in New Zealand or Singapore.

Electronic Travel Authority. The Visitor's visa has now been pretty much superseded by Australia's state-of-the-art 'Electronic Travel Authority' (ETA) system, which is currently available to passport holders from 32 nationalities including British and US citizens, and most citizens of EU countries. The ETA system was introduced in 1996 and is an 'invisible', electronically-stored authority for short-term travel to Australia which can be issued in less than ten seconds at the time of making travel bookings. It is claimed that the ETA is currently the most advanced and streamlined travel authorisation system in the world, permitting visitors to be processed in seconds on arrival at their destination. At this end, the advantages include an end to form-filling, queues and embassy visits: the whole process is completed on the spot. The ETA system can be accessed by over 300,000 travel agents worldwide, and more than 75 airlines. In June 2001, over 96 per cent of ETA-eligible visitors and short-term business travellers were issued with ETAs. A worldwide trial of Internet access to the ETA system was announced in May 2001 which enables tourists and business travellers intending to visit Australia for three months or less to apply on-line at www.eta.immi.gov.au at a cost of $20. Over 10 million travellers have chosen to visit Australia on ETAs, which now account for around 85 per cent of all tourist and short-term business visas issued worldwide. There are three different types of ETA and travellers should make sure that they obtain the one appropriate to their needs: tourists and those visiting family or friends for a period of 3 months or less need a Visitor ETA, whilst business visitors need a Long Validity Business ETA, or a Short Validity Business ETA. It has recently been reported that some British travel agents are charging their clients to issue an ETA. The amount of work involved in supplying this visa can in no way justify this charge, and travellers should be alert to this potential rip-off.

TEMPORARY RESIDENCE

Visitors intending to enter Australia temporarily for the purpose of work or otherwise need to obtain a temporary residence visa. There are currently 20 different temporary residence visa sub-classes which are issued according to the type of activity the applicant will undertake in Australia. The temporary residence programme is designed to allow people from overseas to come to Australia for specific purposes, which are expected to provide some benefit to Australia. The focus is on the areas of skilled employment, social, cultural and international relations.

The categories for temporary residence visas are as follows:

Retirement Category (410). Allows for an extended temporary stay for those who want to retire in Australia. Working during your stay is not permitted.

Exchange (411). Allows visitors to come to Australia to broaden their work experience and skills under reciprocal arrangements by which Australian residents are granted similar opportunities abroad. A letter of invitation is required from the organisation offering the position.

Foreign Government Agency Staff (415). Intended for foreign government officials conducting official business on behalf of their government, where that government has diplomatic status in Australia. This visa category includes staff of the British Council, Alliance Franc[ceaise, Goethe Institute, and the Italian Cultural Institute.

Special Program (416). Intended for people visiting under approved programmes for the purpose of broadening their experience and skills. It is generally used for youth exchanges and programmes such as the Churchill Fellowship. A letter of support is required from the organisation.

Working Holiday (417). The Working Holiday Maker Visa aims to promote international understanding by giving young people the opportunity to holiday in Australia, whilst working to supplement their funds. The WHM visa has numerous conditions attached which are explained in the section **Working Holiday** below.

Educational (418). Allows entry of staff to fill academic, teaching and research positions in Australian educational institutions, which cannot be filled from within the Australian labour market. A letter of appointment is required.

Visiting Academic (419). Allows entry of people as Visiting Academics at Australian educational and research institutions, with the intention that their presence will contribute to the sharing of research knowledge. A letter of invitation is required and you may not receive a salary from the host institution.

Entertainment (420). Allows entry of actors, entertainers, models and their associated personnel for specific engagements or events in Australia. Visa assessment will take into account the need to protect the employment of Australians in the industry.

Sport (421). Allows entry of amateur and professional sportspeople, including officials and their support staff, to engage in competition with Australian residents and to improve general sporting standards through high calibre competition and training.

Medical Practitioner (422). Allows entry of suitably qualified medical practitioners. The relevant State or Territory Medical Board must recognise the applicant's medical qualifications as acceptable for practise in that State or Territory. There must be a demonstrated need to employ a practitioner from overseas.

Media and Film Staff (423). Allows entry of foreign correspondents to represent overseas news media organisations in Australia, and television or film crew members or photographers, including actors and support staff, involved in the production of films, documentaries or advertising commercials in Australia which are not being produced for the Australian market.

Public Lecturer (424). Allows entry of specialists and recognised experts to deliver public lectures in Australia.

Family Relationship (425). Allows a temporary stay of unmarried people under 18 for an extended holiday with relatives or close family friends who are Australian citizens or residents. A letter of invitation is required and you must not do any work while in Australia.

Domestic Worker (Diplomatic/Consular) (426). Allows entry of private domestic staff for work in the households of diplomatic and consular staff posted to Australia where Australian Department of Foreign Affairs and Trade (DFAT) supports the entry.

Domestic Worker (Overseas Executive) (427). Allows the entry of domestic staff of certain holders of visas in class 457 long-stay temporary business entry. A visa of this category will only be granted where it can be shown that the entry of such staff is necessary for the proper discharge of representational duties.

Religious Worker (428). Allows entry of religious workers, including ministers, priests and spiritual leaders to serve the spiritual needs of people of their faith in Australia.

Supported Dependent (430). Allows a temporary stay of dependents of either an Australian citizen or a holder of a permanent residence visa who is usually resident outside Australia and intends to remain temporarily in Australia. A letter of support is required from the Australian citizen/permanent residence visa holder.

Expatriate (432). Allows a temporary stay of certain spouses or dependents of persons employed by international companies in remote locations in Southeast Asia, the South Pacific or Papua New Guinea.

Occupational Trainees (442). Allows entry of persons for occupational training appropriate to their background and/or employment history, for the acquisition or up-grading of skills useful to their home country. A nomination must be provided unless the training is to be given by the Commonwealth of Australia.

New Zealand Citizen Family Relationship (461). Allows a temporary stay of family unit members of New Zealand citizen Special Category Visa holders.

Health and Character Check. People who wish to enter Australia on the temporary residence visas listed above must meet the normal health and character requirements for entry. Some applicants may be asked to have a medical examination before a visa will be granted. In most cases, if you have your application for temporary residence approved, you will then be granted a multiple entry visa for the period of the approved stay.

Re-entry Visa. If you need a further re-entry visa, you will need to apply to an office of the Department of Immigration and Multicultural and Indigenous Affairs (DIMIA). Fees for temporary residence visas are currently £155 and you will need to complete form 147. Temporary residence visa processing times are currently around three to six weeks.

Students

Australia's student visa programme provides for the entry of overseas students who wish to undertake full-time study in registered courses in Australia. Students have the right to work up to 20 hours per week while their course is in session, however, the intention is that income derived from working in Australia should be a supplement to the main source of funding, and applicants will need to produce evidence of their financial resources when applying for a visa. There are seven subclasses of student visa:

Independent ELICOS (Subclass 570). For overseas students undertaking an ELICOS (English Language Intensive Courses for Overseas Students) as a stand-alone course, and not as a prerequisite to commencing another course (for example, a degree course).

Schools (571). For overseas students undertaking a course of study at a primary school or a secondary school. This subclass is also for overseas school students participating in a formal registered secondary exchange program. The period of exchange may vary from one month to one year.

Vocational Education and Training-VET (572). Covers certificate I, II, III and IV, Diploma, Advanced diploma and Advanced certificate.

Higher Education (573). Covers a Bachelor degree, Associate degree, Graduate certificate, and Graduate diploma.

Masters and Doctorate (574). Covers a Masters degree by coursework or by research, and a Doctoral degree.

Non-award Foundation Studies/Other (575). Covers foundation, bridging or other courses that do not lead to the award of a degree, diploma or other formal award.

AusAID or Defence (576). Covers full-time study undertaken by AusAID- or Defence-sponsored students for the whole or part of an education or training course offered by an Australian education provider.

Student visas do not automatically provide for the holder to be granted permission to work in Australia. Students and their dependents are only able to apply for work rights once they arrive in Australia and the student has commenced their course of study. There is a charge of $50 made for this. Students may work full-time during holiday periods. Dependents of Masters and Doctorate students have unlimited work rights after the principal student visa holder has commenced his or her course in Australia. Note that student visas are subject to cancellation if a student works in excess of his or her entitlements. Currently student visas take four weeks to process and cost $290. For more information see form 1160i, available from DIMIA.

Working Holiday Maker

The Working Holiday Maker scheme aims to promote international understanding by giving young people the opportunity to experience the culture of another country.

It allows working holidaymakers to enjoy an extended holiday by supplementing their travel funds through incidental employment, thus experiencing closer contact with local communities. Australia has reciprocal working holiday arrangements with Canada, Denmark, Germany, Hong Kong Special Administrative Region of the People's Republic of China, Norway, Eire, Japan, Republic of Korea, Malta, the Netherlands, Sweden and the United Kingdom. Although there are specific arrangements with these countries, the Australian working holiday scheme is applied globally, and applicants from other countries are considered where there might be a benefit both to the applicant and to Australia.

The Working Holiday visa is available to applicants between the ages of 18 and 30. Applicants may be either single or married, but must not have any dependent children. You must not have previously entered Australia on a Working Holiday visa and you will also need to meet health and character requirements and be outside Australia at the time of the visa being granted. The visa is valid for 12 months from the day of issue, and allows a stay of 12 months from date of entry into Australia.

When you apply for a Working Holiday visa, you must demonstrate that your main purpose in visiting Australia is to holiday, and that any work you expect to undertake will be solely to assist in supporting you whilst on vacation. You must have a good chance of finding temporary work, and may not enrol in formal studies of any kind. You must also have a return ticket or sufficient funds for a return airfare, in addition to being able to demonstrate $5,000 in funds for your travels (or a parental guarantee for the same amount). A Working Holiday visa usually allows for multiple entry, which means that you may leave and re-enter the country as many times as you like (within the time restriction of your visa). When visa is granted, ensure that it has been stamped 'multiple entry'. You cannot get an extension on a Working Holiday visa under any circumstances (though you can apply to change your visa status if you meet requirements), and must leave the country on or before the expiry date of your visa.

A limit (reviewed annually) may be imposed on the number of Australian Working Holiday visas granted. A number of factors influence the volume of applications for Working Holiday visas, such as the strength of various economies around the world, and the popularity of certain kinds of tourism. Some prospective working holiday makers have suffered under the new 'capping' rules, and have had their application for a visa refused after paying for their travel. Travel agents who specialise in Australian travel suggest that one way of avoiding this is to plan to commence the working holiday shortly after the beginning of July, which is the beginning of the annual visa allocation period. Applications made at this time have a good chance of succeeding. In the period 200-2001, 76,570 working holiday visas were granted. Of these 39,554 were granted to British citizens, 11,426 to Irish citizens and 5,498 to Canadians.

Once in Australia, surveys show that most working holidaymakers find temporary or casual employment in farming, clerical and hospitality industries. Fruit picking, bartending, secretarial and clerical work obtained through temp agencies, and labouring are all popular options for travellers, and this work tends to be widely available on a seasonal basis. Most travellers, on average, experience three or four different jobs over the period of their visit, holding each for 6 to 8 weeks at a time. The Working Holiday Maker scheme permits you to work for a maximum of three months for any one employer. If you are found to be working beyond the approved time limit you may have your visa cancelled. At present, Working Holiday visas cost $155 and processing takes about four to five weeks. Form 1150 available from DIMIA contains additional information on the scheme.

Useful Address

John Mahon: Visas Australia, P.O. Box 1, Nantwich, Cheshire CW5 7PB; ☎01270-626626; fax 01270-626226; john@visas-australia.com. Also in Dublin: 2nd Floor, 13 Aston Quay, Dublin 2; ☎01- 6795452; fax 01-6795459. Also has an on-line site (www.visas-australia.com) that arranges a working holiday for a service charge of £15; also a site www.etavisas.com that will issue and e-mail a copy of the Australian tourist visa for £5

Retirement

Retiring to Australia is a popular option for many people, particularly those with family connections there. It is possible to retire to Australia permanently, but initially you must apply for the Temporary Residence Retirement visa (category 410). This visa does not officially entitle the applicant to permanent residence but in effect does allow you to stay indefinitely. If your visa is approved it will initially be granted for a period of four years, which may then be extended in two-year increments whilst in Australia. You will not have to demonstrate that you meet health and financial prerequisites on your subsequent applications for extension.

The Retirement visa is available both to single applicants, and to couples in a married or de facto relationship. You must be at least 55 years of age, have no intention of entering the workforce, have no dependents other than your spouse, and be of good health and character. You must also be able to meet 'Funds transfer requirements' on the day you lodge your application. This means that you should have sufficient funds to maintain yourself (and your spouse/partner, if applicable) in Australia. You need to prove that you have capital for transfer of at least $650,000, or that you have a combination of capital for transfer of at least $200,000 and a pension or income, or further capital providing an income of at least $45,000 per annum. If you need to sell a house to meet the funds transfer requirements, the Immigration Department requires that the sale be completed within 12 months of the date of your application. In the period 1999-2000, 1,622 temporary residence retirement visas were issued. Approval of the visa takes approximately three to six months and costs $155.

Aged parents and relatives of Australian residents may also be eligible for entry under the Family Stream of Australia's migration programme. For more detailed coverage of visa and other issues relating to retirement in Australia, see the section on Retirement later in this book.

PERMANENT RESIDENCE (MIGRATION)

Most applications for permanent residency in Australia are dealt with under one of several categories. These are: Family Stream Migration, which entails sponsorship by a relative resident in Australia; General Skilled Migration, requiring skills or outstanding abilities that will contribute to Australia's economy; Employer Sponsored Migration; Business Skills Migration, which encourages entrepreneurs to develop business in Australia; and migration under the Humanitarian Programme. Generally, a successful applicant for migration to Australia must meet the personal and occupational requirements of the category for which he or she is applying, be able to settle in Australia without undue cost or difficulty to the Australian community, and be of good health and character. In addition, successful applicants will need enough money to travel to and settle in Australia. In 2001-02, 79,000 migrants were selected in the Migration Program.

Family Stream Migration

Approximately fifty per cent of the migrants entering Australia each year do so under the Family Stream of the Migration Programme. In 2001-02, this amounted to some 37,900 successful applications for entry, all of whom were sponsored by a close family member or fiancée with the right of permanent residence in Australia. Family Stream migrants are selected on the basis of their family relationship with their sponsor in Australia, and there is no test for skills or language ability as there is for Skilled Stream migrants; they are still required, however, to meet the requirements of health and character which are applied to all migrants.

Family Stream applicants can be sponsored for migration (permanent residence) in one of the following visa categories:

Spouse. Issued to a husband, wife or de facto partner of the Australian sponsor. Since May 1997, it has been required that a de facto or interdependent partner of an Australian citizen or permanent resident must be able to demonstrate one year of co-habitation with the sponsor. The co-habitation requirement also applies to gay and lesbian partners of Australian sponsors, who should apply for an interdependency visa, but who otherwise are assessed in the same way as those applying for a spouse visa. In compelling cases, such as where a child of the relationship exists, the co-habitation requirement may be waived.

Prospective Spouse. Fiancées overseas must apply for a 'prospective marriage' visa which is valid for nine months from the date of issue. They must travel to Australia, marry their sponsor, and apply to remain permanently during that period. It is a requirement that the parties to a prospective marriage have met and be known to each other in person. If all requirements are met, applicants will be granted a temporary visa, followed by a permanent visa if the relationship is still continuing at the end of two years.

Interdependent Partner. Interdependency visas are for people who have an interdependent relationship with an Australian citizen or permanent resident which demonstrates a genuine, continuing and mutual commitment to a shared life together. The application process is the same as for the spouse visa.

Dependent Child. Parents are able to sponsor for migration their natural child or, in certain cases, their adopted dependent child. The granting of a dependent child visa must not prejudice the rights and interests of any person who has custody or guardianship or access to the child.

Orphan Relative. This visa permits the migration of orphans (as defined in the Migration Regulations), who are under 18 years old, unmarried and a relative of the sponsor.

Carer. To apply for a carer visa you must be willing and able to give substantial, continuing assistance to an Australian relative (or a member of their family) who has a medical condition that is causing physical, intellectual or sensory impairment of their ability to attend to the practical aspects of daily life. The need for assistance must be likely to continue for at least two years. You must be sponsored or nominated by the relative requiring care in Australia, who must be an Australian citizen, Australian permanent resident or eligible New Zealand citizen.

Aged Dependent Relative. To apply for an aged dependent relative visa you must be old enough to be granted an Australian age pension (for males 65, for females the qualifying age is between 60 and 65 depending on your date of birth), be single, having never married, or is widowed, divorced or formally separated from your spouse and have been dependent, and remain dependent, on your Australian relative for a reasonable period (normally three years).

Last Remaining Relative. This visa allows for entry of the last remaining brother, sister or non-dependent child outside Australia. You or your spouse must not have a parent, sibling or non-dependent child or step-relative (within the same degree of relationship) living outside Australia, and again your sponsor must have lived in Australia for at least two years prior to the sponsorship being lodged.

Any Family Stream applicant who is assessed by DIMIA as at risk of becoming a charge on the Australian social welfare budget is required to obtain an assurance of support. This is a legal commitment by the sponsor to repay to the Commonwealth of Australia any social security benefits paid to those covered by the assurance within the first two years after migration to Australia. There is a limit on the number of sponsorships any sponsor may make and on the timeframe in which they may be made.

Skilled Stream Migration

The skilled stream of Australia's migration programme is especially designed to target migrants who have skills or outstanding abilities which will contribute to the Australian economy. Current government policy is committed to increasing migration in the skilled stream, and seeks to address specific skill shortages in the Australian labour market, as well as to enhance the size and skill-level of the Australian labour force. There are five main categories of skilled migration:

Independent. Independent migrants are people selected on the basis of their education, skills and work experience, who are likely to contribute to the Australian economy. They are not sponsored by an employer or relative in Australia. This group is the largest sector of the skilled migration programme. In November 1997, a new component of the Independent migrant category was announced, known as the State/Territory Nominated Independent Scheme (STNI). This scheme enables State and Territory Governments to sponsor skilled migrants and their families on the condition that the selected migrants live and work in nominated regional areas. Regions and skills are identified through a skill-matching scheme, providing a resource for potential employers who are considering nominating overseas workers to fill their requirements.

Employer Sponsored. Employers may nominate personnel from overseas for migration under the Employer Sponsorship Scheme. This option is available only when the position cannot be filled from the Australian labour market. They may also sponsor skilled workers under a Labour Agreement, which was negotiated to allow the recruitment of an agreed number of personnel subject to various conditions. Labour Agreements provide for the permanent entry of workers with skills in demand in certain industries.

Distinguished Talent. This category permits distinguished individuals with special or unique talents to enter Australia, and is generally reserved for outstanding sportspeople, musicians, artists and designers who are internationally recognised in their field. It is open to very few applicants.

General Skilled Migration. Migrants in this category are selected on the basis of skills, age and English language ability. Chances of success in this category are improved if the candidate is sponsored by a relative already living in Australia or intends to live in a designated area of Australia.

Business Skills Migration. The Business Skills programme is designed to encourage successful entrepreneurs and other business people to settle in Australia and develop new businesses of benefit to the Australian economy. The current government has a strong commitment to increasing the entry of high quality business migrants, with numbers of visas granted almost doubling every year since 1994. You may be eligible for a Business Skills visa if you have net business assets of at least $200,000 with management responsibilities; if you are a senior executive employed in top-tier management of a company with an annual turnover of at least $50 million; or if you have a history of successful investment activity and agree to make an investment of at least $750,000 into a State or Territory government security for a period of three years. The expectation is that a business migrant will establish a new business or become an owner or part owner of an existing business, and participate in the management of that business. The progress of business migrants is monitored after arrival in Australia, and where no significant steps are taken towards these goals within three years, the visa may be revoked.

The Points Test

The Department of Immigration and Multicultural and Indigenous Affairs operates a 'points system' for international immigration applications under the Skilled Migration programme. Applicants must meet certain criteria, based on their skills, experience, age and language ability. Points are awarded for each criterion, and applicants must gain sufficient point to reach the Pass Mark. The Pass Mark currently stands at 110 points, but changes frequently. Applicants who score close to the Pass Mark are held in a reserve Pool for up to two years following assessment, however, if you do hit the pool mark your chances of making it to Australia as a migrant are considered to be slim. There are a number of consultancies, advertised in *Overseas Job Express* or *Australian Outlook*, which provide assistance in preparing for the points test by advising applicants on how to maximise the number of points they can accrue.

Generally, the baseline requirements for success in the points test are that you must be under 45 years old at the time your application is lodged, you must reach either the pool or pass mark in force at the time of assessment of your application (which may not necessarily be the same as the marks at the time your application was lodged), and you must be proficient in English. Points for skill are awarded on the basis of your usual occupation, which is determined by the migration officer. Normally, you will have worked in this occupation continuously for at least six months of the last two years. If you have held more than one job which fits this description, you will be assessed against both of your usual occupations, and will be allocated the one which provides you with the best score. The Australian authorities will also assess your qualifications and experience, and the resulting 'skill level' of your occupation will affect how many points you can score.

The occupation that you nominate as fitting your skills and qualifications must be on the 'Skilled Occupations List' at the time of assessment. You receive points allocated for your nominated occupation; for most occupations where training is specific to the occupation you will earn 60 points; for more general professional occupations 50 points, and for other general skilled occupations you will earn 40 points. Points are awarded for the amount of time you have worked in your nominated occupation and also if that occupation is in demand in Australia. Further points can be earned if you have gained an Australian qualification from an Australian educational institutional, studied for at least one academic year in Australia, or have Australian work experience (you must have legally worked in Australia in any occupation on the Skilled Occupations List for at least six months in the four years before you apply). You may earn extra points depending on the skills of your spouse; if you have capital investment in Australia (a minimum of $100,000) or fluency in one of Australia's Community Languages (other than English). For Skilled – Australian Sponsored applicants you may receive points if you have or your spouse has a relative who is an Australian citizen or permanent resident and willing to sponsor you. The costs of applying to migrate to Australia are as follows:

TABLE 1   MIGRATION APPLICATION PACKAGES AND CHARGES

Application for Migration to Australia Forms Package	$10
Application for Migration Visa Charge (1st instalment)	$1,125
Application for Business Migration (1st instalment)	$3,240
Application for Migration (2nd instalment)	$2,380
Application for Business Migration (2nd instalment)	$4,770
Additional Charge for Dependent Spouse (or other dependent adult)	$2,380
Employer Nominated Sponsorship	$4,770
Application for Temporary Residence Visa (most categories)	$155
Application for Working Holiday Maker Visa	$155
Application for Student Visa	$290
Application for Prospective Marriage Visa	$1,125
Application for Long-Stay Visitor's Visa (more than 3 months)	$60

Note that the second instalment of charges for permanent residency is payable only after the application has been accepted. Religious workers are fee-exempt in the Employer Nominated category. These costs are quoted in Australian dollars and will vary according to the exchange rate. The Australian High Commission will be able to advise of the current cost in local currency. Applicants for permanent residency should also allow for the cost of a medical examination by an approved practitioner, which will include screening for tuberculosis (chest X-ray), HIV and hepatitis.

Visa processing times vary according to the type of visa, and according to current demand. As a general guide, a spouse visa will take around 6 months, while family and skill stream migration visas can take up to 20 months. DIMIA has decided that priority is to be given to applications sponsored by Australian citizens; those sponsored by non-citizens will now go to the back of the queue, and it is expected that waiting time on such applications will become even longer. Visitor's visas can be issued the same day, or instantly if applying for an ETA.

Becoming an Australian Citizen

Many migrants, once they have completed all the requirements of permanent residency and feel settled in their new home, decide to show a commitment to Australia by becoming a citizen. Approximately 62 per cent of migrants take up citizenship within five years of arrival and 76.7 per cent do so after 15 years of residence. In recent years the Australian government has strongly encouraged immigrants to take up citizenship, and now offers various incentives for them to do so. There are, of course, various rights that come with Australian citizenship: you will have the right to vote; the right to apply for any public office; the right to apply for an Australian passport and to leave and re-enter the country without a resident return visa; the right to seek assistance from Australian diplomatic representatives while abroad; the right to enlist in the Australian armed forces as well as the right to apply for government jobs; and the right to register your child as an Australian Citizen by descent.

Many public sector jobs, especially in areas of national security, are now also open only to Australian citizens. A booklet, *What it Means to be an Australian Citizen* is available from the Department of Immigration and Multicultural and Indigenous Affairs and there is a dedicated Australian Citizenship website at www.citizenship.gov.au.

As a migrant, you will become eligible for Australian citizenship when you have lived in Australia as a permanent resident for a total of two out of the previous five years. You must be over the age of 18 to apply, though children may be included on their parents' application, and must expect to live permanently in Australia or maintain a close and continuing link with it. There is a fee of $120 to apply for the grant of citizenship, which is reduced to $20 for those on certain social security benefits.

Useful Addresses

UK Passport Service: London Passport Office, Globe House, 89 Eccleston Square, London SW1V 1PN; ☎0870-521 0410 (UKPS Adviceline); www.ukpa.gov.uk. There are also offices in Belfast, Glasgow, Liverpool, Newport, Durham and Peterborough.

Australian High Commission: Australia House, The Strand, London WC2B 4LA, ☎020-7379 4334; fax (DIMIA) 020-7465 8218; Recorded Information Line (24 hours) 09001-600 333. Open: Monday to Friday 9am-1pm (Office hours); 9am to 11am Monday to Friday (Migration/Visas); telephone service hours 2-4pm Monday to Friday.

Australian Consulate: First Floor, Century House, 11 St Peter's Square, Manchester M2 3DN; ☎0161-237-9440; fax 0161-237 9135; Open: Monday to Friday 10am-1pm. Telephone service open 8.30am-1pm, 2pm-4pm (migration).

Australian Embassy: 2nd floor, Fitzwilton House, Wilton Terrace, Dublin 2, Ireland, ☎+353 1 676 1517; fax (DIMIA) +353 1 661 3576; www.australianemba ssy.ie. Open: Monday to Friday 11am-12noon. Working Holiday Visa applications can be downloaded from the website obtained from the Embassy by sending a stamped self-addressed envelope to PO Box 6558 Dublin 2.

Information from the Department of Immigration and Multicultural and Indigenous Affairs is available on-line at www.immi.gov.au.

SETTING UP HOME

CHAPTER SUMMARY

○ It is a legal requirement for a house to have a laundry room separate from the kitchen in Australia.

○ **Home Ownership.** 71% of householders are owner-occupiers

○ By 2016 childless households will be in the majority.

○ **Hazards.** Apart from the climate, bushfires etc. the greatest threat to buildings with structural timbers is white ants (termites).

  ○ All homes have fly-screens over the doors and windows for fresh air without insect access.

○ **Prices.** Property prices generally are much lower than in the UK or USA.

○ **Mortgages.** Almost half the home loans in Australia are arranged through a broker.

○ **Project Homes.** Very popular are 'off-the-peg' architectural designs which can be customised to suit individual tastes and built on the purchaser's own land or the developer's.

○ **Home Open.** This is the preferred method of selling property. The owner agrees a regular time slot where the estate agent can show prospective buyers around while the owners are out.

  ○ Estate agents give far fewer details, dimensions and descriptions than British ones which is why the Home Open system is vital.

○ **Auctions.** Buying at auction can lead to a high price if it's a competitive sale, or a bargain if it's a distress sale.

The Australian Way of Life

The demography of Australia is rapidly changing, in line with trends in other industrialised nations. The traditional family unit no longer dominates Australian society, and the Australian Bureau of Statistics expects the number of households of childless couples to outstrip the number of couples with children and will be the most common family type by 2016. One parent families are also on the increase and are expected to increase by 30-66 percent over the next 20 years. The 'greying' of the population is well documented; as Australia's baby-boomers move into late middle age and their own children abstain longer and longer from establishing families of their own. The northern NSW/Queensland coastline is the premier 'grey spot' of Australia with dozens of retirement communities although statistically South Australia has the oldest population of all the states. Areas with a high proportion of children are generally located outside major towns and cities, especially in outback Queensland and the Northern Territory.

Australia has one of the highest levels of home-ownership in the world, with over 71% of Australian households either mortgaged or owner-occupied. Most Australians live in single-storey houses with a garden at both the front and the back of the house. Gardens are usually designed to take advantage of the weather and will generally have at least one shaded patio to create an external living area. Most will have a semi-detached lockable garage, or at the very least, a 'car-port' (covered hard-standing). A basic family home is expected to comprise three bedrooms, an open-plan living and dining area, fitted kitchen, at least one bathroom, and a separate laundry (including a large sink known as a trough, and fitted plumbing for a washing machine). Every home without exception (indeed, by law) will have a laundry, and it is unheard of to install a washing machine in a kitchen. Four-bedroom houses are also very common, but there are very few, if any, recently built two bedroom houses. Most houses are likely to have a family room (informal living area) in addition to the usual 2 reception rooms and will generally have 2 bathrooms, one of which is usually en suite. The focus of the bathroom is always the shower, which is *never* located over the bath. Australian showers come on hot and strong from the mains, and electric showers and booster pumps are not required; bathrooms are always tiled, thus a carpeted bathroom is a source of amusement to Australians visiting Britain. Kitchens always include a cooker (known as a stove) and fitted cupboards, which in modern houses will include a large pantry cupboard. Carpets, curtains and light fittings are always included in the price unless stated otherwise.

A very large number of homes in Australia have a swimming pool and these must be secured with childproof fences and gates. Local councils inspect swimming pools annually to ensure that they comply with legal requirements in terms of safety and security, and regulations are strictly enforced: fences must be unclimbable and over 1.5m in height, and pool gates must be locked and on a self-closing spring. Pool cleaning equipment (vacuum, hoses, and leaf rake) should be included amongst the house fixtures and fittings. Most home pools are chlorinated, which means that you will need to add chemicals daily, however, increasingly people are choosing either to install salt-water pools or to convert existing pools to saltwater technology. If you are lucky enough to have a salt-water pool you will only need to add salt once a year, and then leave the converter to do the rest. Saltwater pools also maintain a higher water temperature than chlorinated pools.

Australian houses are usually built either of double brick or of brick veneer (an external brick 'skin' over a timber-framed dwelling). Building regulations in

Western Australia require double brick construction, however, in the eastern states, where the topography is more inclined towards earth movement, brick veneer is more structurally sound. Roofs are generally tiled with terracotta or, in cheaper construction, (indistinguishable) coloured cement tiles, but colour bonded steel sheeting is currently fashionable, mimicking the traditional Australian tin-roof. Most Australian homes are fitted with insulation in the roof space and, often, the walls. This insulation, made from fibreglass or wool fibre compacted to the size of a hay bale, helps to keep the house cool in summer and warm in winter. All homes are fitted with fly-screens over the doors and windows, so that doors and windows can be left open without admitting insects.

Buying a Home or Land

Properties and vacant land are advertised for sale in the Real Estate supplements of all capital city newspapers, often on Wednesdays and Saturdays. Most local papers, including weekly freesheets, also carry extensive advertisements and are a good place to start if you have decided on a particular area. Government or 'Crown' land is also occasionally advertised for sale, especially in outer suburban areas undergoing new development. If you are interested in building a new home at an economical cost (that is, *not* by subcontracting your own architect and builder), you should look at the newspaper section headed 'Display Homes' or 'Project Homes'. A project home is an off-the-peg architectural design offered by a builder and built especially for you, either on your own land, or on land supplied by the builder and offered as part of a package. Once you have selected a suitable design, you are free to customise it to a certain extent, choosing internal finishes, bricks, tiles, and landscaping. Many people choose to have the ceiling heights raised in project homes (they are usually designed to the legal minimum of eight courses of brickwork), and this will add a few thousand dollars per course to the cost of the design. Project homes are an extremely popular choice in Australia, and rather than simply buying a new home in a development, most people prefer this more individual option. A project home package for a home comprising 4 bedrooms, 2 bathrooms, and 2 or 3 reception rooms, including plans, building and land, in an outer suburban area of Perth can cost as little as $90,000. If you choose to build on your own land, your new home can be built for around $60,000. Examples of builders' project homes, known as 'display homes', can be viewed at various 'display villages', the locations of which are advertised alongside the relevant floor plans.

A guide to the sort of price you can expect to pay for an average family home around Australia is given below. For the price listed, you are likely to get a 3-bedroom, 2-bathroom residence on about a third of an acre of land in a low/mid-range suburban area.

TABLE 2   PROPERTY PRICES IN THE PROVINCIAL CAPITALS

Property Values by Capital City ($'000)

	Sydney	Melbourne	Brisbane	Adelaide	Perth	Hobart	Canberra
House	316.0	291.0	180.0	148.2	165.7	120.0	203.0
Townhouse/ terrace/duplex	233.3	205.2	139.2	116.7	128.2	99.2	119.8
Flat	256.1	148.3	166.6	115.4	128.5	N/A	252.6

(Source: Australian Bureau of Statistics/REIA, 2002)

If you are moving to the ACT, you should note that there is no freehold land available in Canberra. Instead, the Commonwealth Government grants 99-year leases on blocks of land for residential purposes, and these are released for sale to keep pace with demand. All residential land is sold at public auction, and unsold sites are available after auction at the Land Sales Office. Reserve prices are set at 80 per cent of the assessed market value. Leaseholders are obliged to commence construction within twelve months and to complete construction in 24 months. All land released for sale under this system is within 30 km of the city centre, and all sites are fully serviced, with social amenities added as the suburb develops.

Rent or Buy?

In the late 1980s Australia witnessed a massive property boom. Prices escalated by 60-100% within two years. Home loan rates were at around 18%. It's no wonder that this market was unsustainable. The early 1990s saw a slump and prices remained low until about 1994. The prospect of the Olympic Games coming to Sydney in 2000 led to a fall in interest rates and the rise of the property market. Prices have increased steadily, especially in beachside and inner city suburbs, since the late 1990s. The Australian property market has seen controlled, sustainable growth and home loan rates are the lowest they've been for 40 years. However, the events of September 11, a faltering US economy and the Australian government's introduction of the Goods and Services Tax (GST) in July 2000 went some way to upsetting the boom. To compensate for the potential negative effect of the GST on the property market (it was feared that the new GST to add another 10% on to the price of property), the Government introduced the *First Home Owner Grant* of $7,000 Grant (later increased to $14,000). Interest rates have continued to drop, Australia's economy has remained buoyant and because of the low rate of exchange on the Australian dollar expats continue to buy property as an investment.

So the cost of property in Australia remains at an affordable level; interest rates are low, banking is highly competitive, and prices are relatively stable. Financial experts agree that buying your own home is the best step that you can take towards financial security, offering both the peace of mind of a secure roof over your head as well as significant tax benefits on your investment. It is currently very easy to obtain mortgage finance, and with low interest rates, paying off a property is likely to cost you less than renting one of an equivalent standard. Initial establishment costs can be high, however (see below), and it is likely to take several years before you can offset these against any gain on your investment. Residential property prices are affected by a number of variables, including migration, interest rates, government policy, consumer confidence and general economic conditions. There is an observable cycle in the property market, and if you arrive at the peak of a particular cycle, you may be well advised to rent and invest your money elsewhere until a downturn occurs. *The Real Estate Institute of Australia* monitors property cycles, and publishes bulletins and statistics which can help you assess where the market currently stands. Market analysts currently forecast an 11.8% per annum increase in property values in all Australian capitals, except Hobart, which should remain static, and Sydney, where demand is expected to fuel a property boom.

FINANCE

The home loan market in Australia has been highly competitive in recent years with a number of new players entering the fray and a myriad of options available. Having negotiated the maze, however, borrowers can currently enjoy exceptional value for money in their choice of investment. Non-bank lenders are now offering more flexible features, including the option to redraw on extra payments, and loans are being offered at competitive rates by established banks, credit unions, building societies, and new-style mortgage originators. Lenders will consider loans of up to 95 percent of the property value, and mortgage eligibility is calculated on a formula based on the income level of the applicant, or of the applicant and partner in combination (usually 3 times one salary or 2.5 times both salaries). There are an increasing number of lenders offering no-deposit home loan packages to encourage potential buyers into the market, including builders who will supply no-deposit finance for buyers to purchase their project homes. Usually such offers will have hidden (or not-so-hidden) costs – such as higher interest rates.

Application or establishment fees are charged by both banks and other lenders to cover the cost of setting up a loan agreement, including legal and valuation fees, and disbursements such as mortgage registration and stamp duty. The amount of these initial fees varies widely between lenders: some simply pass on their costs, others absorb them (a no-fees mortgage), while some of the bigger players, who have less to fear from competition, may charge as much as $800.

Lending terms and conditions can vary considerably between lenders, but in early-2002 the interest rate stands at around 5.95% per annum for standard variable home loans. The maximum term for a standard home loan is 25 years, with a few lenders offering 30-year terms, depending on the age of the applicant. Fixed loans are popular as they provide security against interest rate rises, and such loans are now more flexible than they have been with lenders offering the facility of extra repayments without penalty.

Australia's four largest banks are the Commonwealth, the ANZ, Westpac, and the National Australia Bank. All offer mortgage products and applications for a home loan can be lodged at any branch. Increasingly, suburban branches operate as little more than shop-fronts, with management and lending decisions taken at head office, so you need not necessarily approach your own branch for information. The Commonwealth Bank and the ANZ both have excellent websites, which describe their full range of products, and by entering your details online, you can receive an instant assessment of your eligibility for a mortgage. You can access the Commonwealth on *www.commbank.com.au* and the ANZ on *www.anz.com.au*.

Non-bank lenders are playing an increasingly important role in the mortgage market and are known as mortgage originators or mortgage managers. Such lenders, who include insurance companies and credit unions, act as intermediaries between borrowers and larger institutions. These big institutions are the real lenders behind mortgage originator loans, and are usually organisations which do not wish to participate in the market directly. Other funds are obtained from securitisers, who raise funds on the financial markets and then redistribute them to originators. Industry standards require that independent trustees oversee originators and the loan monies that they collect to protect the interests of the borrower. Aussie Home Loans (www.aussiehomeloans.com.au) is the most aggressive of the mortgage originators and advertises extensively on radio and in newspapers. Other major originators include Macquarie Mortgages, Mortgage Masters and AMP Home Loans.

In such a complex environment, borrowers are increasingly seeking the services of mortgage brokers, who are able to source the most suitable and cheapest loan for your needs. A good broker will be able to find you the best loan, explain it in detail, help complete the loan documents, and guide the application through to acceptance. Brokers make their money on commission from the lender, and there are no fees charged to the borrower. Almost half the home loans in Western Australia are now written by brokers and the trend is steadily increasing in the eastern states. Mortgage brokers advertise widely in the press and yellow pages, and some of the franchise real estate chains, such as Ray White Real Estate and LJ Hooker also offer broking services. 1st Australian Mortgage (www.1stam.com.au) is an independent mortgage broker, associated with a national network of mortgage lenders and claim to be able to provide you with the finance that suits best depending on your needs.

Useful Addresses

Australian and New Zealand Banking Group, Minerva House, Montague Close, London SE1 9DH; ☎020-7378 2121; www.anz.com

The Commonwealth Bank of Australia, Financial & Migrant Information Service, Senator House, 85 Queen Victoria Street, London EC4V 4HA; ☎020-7710 3999; fax 020-7710 3939; www.commbank.com.au

Westpac Banking Corporation, 63 St Mary's Annexe, London, EC3A 8LE; ☎020-7621 7000; www.westpac.com.au

PURCHASING & CONVEYANCING PROCEDURES

Every state in Australia has its own laws pertaining to real estate transactions, and its own licensing laws for real estate agents. In general, you should expect your real estate agent to hold certification from the appropriate state government authority, and preferably, that they or their agency should be a member of the Real Estate Institute of Australia (or state-affiliated branch). If your agent is a member of the REIA or its affiliates, such as REIWA (the Real Estate Institute of Western Australia), you will be protected in the case of any malpractice. Estate agents who are the Principals (proprietors) of an agency must be certified at a higher level, and any agent intending to conduct a sale by auction must hold a separate licence to do so.

There are five types of fees for which you must budget when purchasing a property in Australia:

- **Solicitors'/Settlement Agents' Professional Fees**. These are fees charged by a solicitor or settlement agent for conducting the legal business of the purchase on your behalf.

- **Search Fees and Outlays**. These fees cover the cost of the searches undertaken to ensure that the property is free from encumbrances.

- **Stamp Duty**. Stamp duty is a state government tax on the purchase price of the property. It is calculated as a percentage of the value of the transaction, and is affected by the area of land purchased and whether the purchasers intend to reside in the property. Concessions apply in some states (for example, Queensland) to first time buyers who will reside in the property. Stamp duty varies considerably and is calculated on *ad valorem*, nominal or concessional rates of duty depending on the state or territory.

○ **Registration Fees**. Fees are charged by the state department of land management or natural resources to effect the registration of transfer of ownership and related mortgage documents.

○ **Lender Fees**. It is common practice for lenders to charge administration fees for setting up a mortgage. As the home loan market becomes increasingly competitive, however, such fees (which can be as high as $800) have become more negotiable, and can be avoided completely if you shop around.

Settlement

The process of exchanging contracts to complete a property transaction is known in Australia as 'settlement'. Settlement is a far easier process in Australia than at home and the concept of the 'chain' does not exist. Once a vendor agrees to an offer on a property, a contract is signed stipulating a date for settlement, which will usually be 30 days from the date of offer. During this period, the purchaser arranges finance and completes all the legal formalities. Settlement MUST take place on the nominated date, and if it cannot, the party at fault becomes liable for the payment of penalty interest.

Conveyancing

The conveyancing market has been deregulated in recent years and is no longer the exclusive province of solicitors. Most people now turn to specialist 'settlement agents' instead, who are trained in conveyancing and property law, but who are not lawyers. Settlement agents' fees are almost always much lower than those charged by solicitors for an identical service, and are generally in the region of $400-$1,000, depending on the value of the property and the state in which you reside. In South Australia the legal legwork on most property transactions is handled by a land broker. It is possible to do your own conveyancing, but it is not recommended: the risk of steep penalty interest payments in the case of delay through error or lack of expertise can outweigh the saving of a few hundred dollars.

Buying Without Residency Status

If you have not been granted permanent residency in Australia, any property purchase will require the prior approval of the Foreign Investment Review Board. Generally speaking, the Board will *not* approve the purchase of residential real estate by non-residents; however, each case is considered on its merits, and if you are a temporary resident or overseas investor hoping to buy in Australia, you should seek advice from a solicitor specialising in Australian property law. You can write to *Foreign Investment Review Board*, The Executive Member, C/o Department of the Treasury, Canberra ACT 2600, Australia (☎ 02-6263 3795; fax 02-6263 2940; www.firb.gov.au).

Real Estate Agencies

Most people buy and sell their property with the services of a local real estate agent, and few owners market their own properties. Agents act on behalf of the vendor and not the purchaser, and their responsibilities include advertising and contract negotiation to obtain the best possible price for their client (who, you should always bear in mind when you are buying, is *not* you). Homes for sale will be advertised in the local press, and the larger state-wide newspapers will generally publish a property section at the weekend (often on Saturday). In addition, most agents will have extensive photo displays in their office window. The distribution of detailed description sheets giving measurements of each room, location of power points and other features is not an Australian practice, although top-of-the-range homes are often marketed through glossy, descriptive brochures. Instead, when you approach an agent regarding a property, you can expect to be told only the price (or, increasingly, an acceptable price range), the number and types of rooms and any other facilities, swimming pool, reticulation, air conditioning etc. If the property is still of interest, the agent will arrange to accompany you on a private inspection, or you may be asked to attend the next 'Home Open'. The Home Open is a standard property marketing tool in Australia and involves opening the property to all-comers at a specified, advertised time, usually for an hour or two every weekend. During this time the agent is in attendance and the owners are absent. Prospective purchasers, who are most likely to have seen the property advertised in that morning's paper, are free to walk around the house and garden and examine its suitability in privacy. The agent will take your name and address, and will chat a little to determine your bona fides. The Home Open is generally considered to be a convenient and low-key way of finding a property, and if you are house hunting it is an easy way of lining up four or five likely places to view in one morning.

LISTING A PROPERTY WITH AN ESTATE AGENT

There are three different methods of listing a property with an estate agent, and you will often see one of the following terms somewhere in an advertisement:

Sole/Exclusive Agency. This means that the property is being offered by one agent only, and can be viewed only by contacting the specified office. Advertisements for sole agency properties will carry the name of the particular agent (for example, Mike Jones of Smith White Realty) who has obtained the listing. All contact and requests for information must be directed to the named agent.

Open Listing. Under an 'open listing', any number of agencies can offer the property to buyers. This method is common in some states (Queensland) and unusual in others, or in some states (e.g. Western Australia), common for more down-market properties or areas, and unusual at the middle and upper end of the market. It is not generally considered to be an effective way to sell, as there is no single agent with a keen incentive to make the sale.

Multilisting. Multilisting is very similar to the American 'Multiple Listing Service' (MLS), and means that a property is listed by a number of specified agencies. Multilisting is the least common method of marketing a property.

If you are looking for a property to buy, you can approach an agent to act on your behalf in the search. The agent will then obtain lists of all the properties for sale in your price range and desired area, and will arrange for you to view them. There is no fee to the purchaser for this service; it can be a good way for a newcomer to find a suitable property, as the agent will have detailed local knowledge about shops, schools and amenities, which you may lack. Your agent makes his or her money, once you decide on a property, by negotiating a *conjunctional sale*: the vendor's agent splits the sale commission 50/50 with the introducing agent. Conjunctional sales apply to properties marketed under sole agency as well as by other methods, and there are very few agents who will refuse to conjunct.

Buying at Auction

Many Australian properties at every level of the market are sold by auction. Auctions, and attitudes to sale by auction, vary from state to state. Some franchise groups push vendors to sell by auction, but they are not universally popular: some agents consider them to be most suitable for distress sales (in which case, they can result in bargains), while others use them only in a competitive, rising market (in which case, you can end up paying too much). Vendors who sell by auction are responsible for the advertising costs of the agent.

Buying at auction can be an intimidating experience, and it is advisable to attend a few as a kind of 'dry run', to get the feel for what you will be up against. In Western Australia, auctions are conducted in the front garden of the property for sale, so it is easy to wander up and listen. In other states they are usually held in auction rooms. Success at auction depends on doing your homework: first, know your financial limits by visiting your bank manager beforehand, and *never* bid above that limit, no matter how persuasive the auctioneer's patter; secondly, know the market, so that you have a clear idea of the true worth of the property; shop around, comparing prices of similar houses. Once you have identified the house you want, spend several weeks before the auction date visiting other auctions in the area to evaluate the level of bidding; thirdly, make prior enquiries about the contract, establishing what the property includes, and making sure it is free from any important defects. Examine the building report and pest certificates, and ascertain the level of deposit which will be required in cash on the fall of the hammer (it is likely to be ten percent).

On auction day, you should check the contracts again, to ensure that no changes have been made. Arrive early, and have a last look around if possible. At this point you should introduce yourself to the auctioneer and let them know that you are interested in buying. Sit in easy view of the auctioneer, preferably near the front or at the sides, where you can observe competing bidders. The auctioneer will then commence the patter and ask if there are any questions: bidders who play tough like to take this opportunity to unsettle the opposition by fielding queries about six-lane highways or high-rise tower blocks. Try and ignore such strategies and bid with confidence; bid low and bid often is the approach recommended by experienced agents. When bidding is slow, a common tactic of the auctioneer is to pull out 'phantom bids' or bids on behalf of the vendor, but if you suspect this, you are within your rights to stop the auction and demand to know against whom you are bidding. Properties are always auctioned with an undisclosed reserve price, and if it is eventually passed in, you will be able to try and negotiate privately after the auction.

Finally, some agents advise that if you really want the house, you could try making an offer in advance: the vendor may be as nervous as you are, and only too glad to tie it up without going through with the whole ordeal.

Contracts

Most property sales are concluded through the exchange of a simple standard contract issued by the state Real Estate Institute. This contract will specify the sale price and deposit (notionally 10%, but in practice, highly negotiable), the date of settlement, and the fixtures and fittings to be included in the sale. You should note that it is expected that fixtures and fittings will be included in a sale and, if you are selling, you will be in breach of contract if you so much as remove a light bulb without specifying your intentions. Cookers and dishwashers are considered fixtures and must remain in the property. The contract will also require that all appliances are in good working order, and this includes external plant such as swimming pool filters, air conditioning, and ducted vacuum systems. At the time of making an offer, certain conditions are usually appended to the standard contract, and the failure of either party to meet the stated conditions will invalidate the sale. Usually a contract is signed subject to two main conditions: firstly, that the purchaser provide proof of mortgage finance or cash resources within 48 hours; and secondly, that the vendor provide a current white ant certificate within one week. White ants are a type of termite, which can cause havoc with a building's structural timbers; they are a serious concern and their control is monitored by law. A white ant inspection certificate ensures that your property is free from infestation or, if white ants have been found, that they have been destroyed by chemical treatment. Evidence of previous, treated white ant infestation is not an impediment to the sale of a property. A white ant inspection certificate costs around $200 and this cost is born by the vendor. If these conditions and any others particular to your property are met, the contract becomes binding. Should you change your mind for any reason, you will forfeit your deposit. Similarly, should the vendor break the contract, your deposit will be refunded plus the same amount again as a penalty payment.

Useful Addresses

Foreign Investment Review Board, The Executive Member, C/o Department of the Treasury, Canberra ACT 2600; ☎02-6263 3795; fax 02-6263 2940; www.firb.gov.au

L.J. Hooker is one of Australia's largest real estate groups with offices throughout the country. Their customer service centre (freephone 1800 621 212) will be able to recommend an office in your intended area as well as provide local information. They also have an excellent website at *www.ljhooker.com.au,* which provides useful advice on all aspects of buying and selling, and on-line property information.

Realestate.com.au Ltd, Suite 1, 733 Whitehorse Road, Mont Albert, VIC 3127, Australia; ☎03-9897 1121 (Freecall 1300 134 174); fax 03-9897 1114; Postal address: PO Box 197, Surrey Hills, VIC 3127; www.realestate.com.au. Realestate.com.au, exclusively endorsed by the Real Estate Institute of New South Wales (REINSW) and the Real Estate Institute of Tasmania (REIT), provides a medium for real estate agents to advertise their listings and for potential buyers to search for properties.

Useful Publications

Consyl Publishing Ltd., 3 Buckhurst Road, Bexhill-on-Sea, East Sussex, TN40 1QF distributes the Australian magazines, *Real Estate Weekly* and *The Homebuyer,* which contain illustrated for-sale advertisements for property around Australia. These can be ordered by mail from the above address or by phone on 01424-223 111; 01424-223 161 (24-hour); www.consylpublishing.co.uk

RENTING PROPERTY

Australians have a strong home-owning ethos. Most people prefer not to rent if at all possible and those who do rent in general occupy their rented property for less than a year. Rented housing in Australia is very much less expensive than in Europe, and both tenant and landlord rights are well protected. Amongst other things, tenancies are always covered by leases and there is no indefinite security of tenure. Renting out a property is not a risky venture for a landlord, who can easily have unsuitable tenants evicted so people are very willing to place their investment properties and homes on the rental market. Changes in taxation law have meant that it is no longer as financially advantageous as it once was to buy property for the purposes of renting it out, and as a result the amount of property available to rent has declined, with a concomitant rise in rentals. Nonetheless, the average weekly rental for a 3 bedroom house in Melbourne, which is generally considered an expensive city in terms of property prices, is $195, clearly far less than in most major European cities.

Rents are not subject to state control in Australia, but are set by the lease agreement signed by both tenant and landlord. Usually, such an agreement will set the rent for a six-month period, with a reassessment at the end of the lease period. In some states residential rents may be controlled, but only on properties which were tenanted prior to changes in the law. The Federal Discrimination Act prohibits discrimination by landlords against prospective tenants, and it is illegal to refuse a tenant on the grounds of sex or marital status, pregnancy, or ethnic origin. If you suspect that a landlord or agent has made an illegal refusal of your application to rent his or her property, you should contact the nearest Office of Consumer Affairs, which will be able to advise you further. In general, however, landlords are interested in having their property occupied by rent-paying tenants, and you are unlikely to have your application for tenancy turned down if you can provide good references and evidence of sufficient financial means.

Properties for rent are advertised in the 'To Let' section of the property pages in city and state newspapers and in weekly, free community newspapers. Real estate agents also usually have a specialist property management division, which will also have listings of available properties, and you can approach agents directly in the areas in which you hope to find accommodation.

Tenancy Agreements

Very short term rented accommodation can be difficult to find in Australia as most property owners will only accept tenants prepared to sign a tenancy agreement valid for six months. It is occasionally possible to find an owner who is prepared to make a short-term lease available, and in such cases the lease may later be extended by private agreement, allowing you to remain on a weekly or monthly basis after the expiry of the lease. Although this can be convenient for travellers, it does not give much security to longer-term visitors, and you will need to be willing to move at short notice should the owner decide to make other arrangements. In general, a first lease is given for six months and can be extended, provided that you and the owner both agree to any change of conditions, including a rent rise (most landlords do *not* automatically raise the rent every six months). Properties are almost invariably let unfurnished, but will include a cooker and, often, a fridge. Lease agreements in Australia usually conform to a standard format, and the contract can be purchased for a couple of dollars at any newsagent. They are simple to understand and offer fair and equal protection to both landlord and tenant. The underlying assumption in Australian rent law, however, is that the property belongs to the landlord, who has greater rights in terms of protecting and enjoying the benefits of his or her investment. There is, therefore, no concept of the 'sitting tenant' or of 'squatting', and unruly, destructive or non-paying tenants can be swiftly and effectively evicted.

Letting agents or property owners generally require tenants to pay a bond or deposit of four weeks rental, in addition to a month's rent in advance. The bond can sometimes be as much as six weeks rent, and owners may occasionally ask for up to two months rent in advance. You should, therefore, allow several thousand dollars to establish yourself in a rented property. The bond can be entirely or partly forfeited if the tenant defaults on payment or conditions of the lease. If you leave the premises and any provided furniture and fittings in a good condition, allowing for reasonable wear and tear, your landlord will refund your bond at the end of your tenancy. Most landlords will provide an inventory of the property, particularly if it is let furnished, and this will detail the condition of the house at the start of the lease (it might list, for example, existing scuff marks or cigarette burns). You should read and assess this inventory before you sign your lease, as signing will imply your agreement with its contents. The property will be inspected at the end of your lease, and may be inspected at any time during the period of the tenancy, providing the owner or agent gives 48 hours notice of their intention to enter. They must, however, by law, have good cause to effect entry, for example, if neighbours report obvious signs of neglect; and you have the right to be present during any inspection. End-of-lease inspections are usually very thorough indeed: expect to have extractor fan covers removed and inspected for dirt and grease, pictures moved, and carpets lifted. You will need to seek permission under the terms of a standard lease to effect any change to the fabric of the property, even if it is just to put up a picture hook.

The owner of a rented property is responsible for all council and water rates, as well as strata and management fees, but the tenant pays costs for all utilities such as electricity, gas and telephone.

Rental Costs

In Australia there is very little 'social housing' of the type provided by councils and district authorities in Europe. Traditionally, the 'Great Australian Dream' has meant that even in the lowest socio-economic groups there has been a high expectation of home ownership, and concomitantly, that to be housed by the state 'Housing Commission' has been an object of shame. In addition, rent laws, as outlined above, have kept the private rental sector competitive and stable, so that few people have needed to fall back on the state to provide them with accommodation. Most commonly, state housing is available to socially marginalised groups, such as Aborigines and refugees. The criterion for eligibility is that the applicant must demonstrate an inability to secure decent accommodation in the private sector at a rent, which is within their capacity to pay. However, given that rent assistance for private tenants, whether unemployed or on a low income, is available from Centrelink (the government agency responsible for social security payments), there are very few people to whom this might apply.

In the private sector, there is almost always a good variety of properties to available to rent, although it is usually easier to find flats (known as 'units') than houses. A rough guide to current weekly rental values for unfurnished property around Australia is given below:

TABLE 3 — RENTAL VALUES BY CAPITAL CITY($/WEEK)

	Sydney	Melbourne	Brisbane	Adelaide	Perth	Canberra	Hobart	Darwin
3-bedroom houses	235	195	190	185	162	230	160	240
Townhouses/ 2-bedroom flats/units	265	185	175	130	133	195	125	180

(Source: Real Estate Institute of Australia, 2002)

TABLE 4 — PROPERTY GLOSSARY

Duplex/Triplex. Property development in which two or three compact, single-storey houses in a unified architectural style are built on a large suburban block.

Freehold. Most Australian houses and land are held on a freehold title.

House. In Australia, a house is usually of the 'bungalow' type, i.e., it is likely to be single-storeyed, unless stated otherwise.

Strata Title. Flats, townhouses, villas, duplexes and triplexes are usually held on a strata title. Under this system a property owner owns absolutely all the space enclosed by the exterior walls of the property, as well as a pro-rata percentage share of all the communal space of the development in its entirety. Strata fees are payable quarterly to a 'body corporate', which is a democratically-constituted management authority, and cover the maintenance of the fabric of the structure and communal garden areas.

Terrace. A terraced house, with party walls on both sides. This type of housing is only found in old, inner-city areas and is often sought after for its 'character and charm'.

Town House. A compact house of two or more stories in a small development. It will usually share one or more party walls with neighbouring townhouses.

Unit. A term in common use to describe a flat or apartment. A unit can be located either in a high- or low-rise development.

Villa. A compact bungalow-style house in a small, unified development, usually with one or more party walls and a shared driveway.

RELOCATION

Relocation Companies

Although there are many relocation service companies offering assistance with intra-European and transatlantic moves, the antipodean sector of the market is poorly served. Relocators can assist corporate and domestic migrants with establishing the basis for life in a new home abroad, including finding accommodation, schools and employment. However, many of those that operate between Europe and Australia concentrate almost entirely on the corporate market. The cost of using such services can be prohibitive for the individual, and in many cases removal companies may be more helpful for people undertaking a domestic move. Many of the larger removal companies offer more than a shipping service, and may be able to advise and assist in many other aspects of your relocation. There are a number of relocation companies in Australia, and these will usually be better able to act on your behalf in organising the essentials for your arrival.

Useful Addresses

Carroll Dardis & Associates, 19 Grainger Drive, Claremont WA 6010, ☎08-9383 2677. Offers a meet and greet service at the airport upon arrival, introductions to reputable real estate agents, bank managers, accountants, solicitors, insurance brokers, motor car dealers, as well as information on education and health care in Western Australia.

Expat International Pty Ltd offer expatriate consultancy to corporations worldwide, visa documentation, international and interstate relocations, and cultural awareness courses. They are affiliated with the Migration Institute of Australia and the Employee Relocation Council (USA) and have offices worldwide: check the white pages telephone directory of your capital city, or contact them in Australia at 423 Bourke Street, Level 2, Melbourne, VIC 3000; ☎03-9670 7555; fax 03-9670 7799; www.expat.com.au

Four Winds International Relocations, Unit 20, Slough Business Park, Holker Street, Silverwater, Sydney, NSW 2128; tel/fax 02-9748 4840; www.fourwindsaus.com

Nuss, Sydney Head Office: 708 Mowbray Road West, Lane Cove, NSW 2066; ☎02-9428 1166; fax 02-9427 2956. Nuss also has offices in Melbourne: 29 Edward Street, Oakleigh, VIC 3166; ☎03-9569 6277; fax 03-9569 6377; www.nuss.com.au. Nuss belongs to the Federation Internationale des Demenageurs Internationaux, the British Association of Removers, the Household Goods and Forwarders Association of America and is an accredited IATA (International Air Transport Association) agent.

Relocation Resources International, 1st Floor, 56 Buckingham Gate, London SW1E 6AE ☎020-7802 2500; www.rriworld.com. One of the largest relocation firms in the world.

Assistance from Religious Organisations

Many people find that the common bond of faith is an excellent opening to new friendships, and that their co-parishioners are a useful source of assistance in settling in to a new environment. The Council of Christian Unity forms part of the World Division of the Archbishops' Council of the Church of England and helps those looking to explore ways of working with other Christian churches. For further details, write to the Assistant Secretary, Council of Christian Unity, Church House, Great Smith Street, Westminster, London SW1P 3NZ; www.cofe.anglican.org/ccu/.

The World Council of Churches is an international fellowship of Christian churches, formed to serve and advance the ecumenical movement. The World Council of Churches can be contacted at PO Box 2100, 1211 Geneva 2, Switzerland;

☎+41 22 791 6111; fax +41 22 791 0361; www.wcc-coe.org. While in Australia, the General Secretary of Anglican Church of Australia can be contacted by writing to PO Box Q190, QVB Post Office, Sydney, NSW 1230. The Church has a website at www.anglican.org.au.

Other Denominations. Members of other denominations or religions should contact the organisational headquarters of their religious group in their present country in order to obtain a list of religious contacts in Australia. The National Council of Churches in Australia is a council of 15 member churches and further information can be obtained from their office at Level 6, 379 Kent Street, Sydney NSW 2001; ☎02-9229 2215; www.ncca.org.au.

INSURANCE AND WILLS

Home Insurance

An increasingly competitive insurance market in Australia has meant that in recent years both the number of policies available to the consumer, and their variety, is widening all the time. Buying the right insurance for your particular needs can be confusing, and many Australians now use brokers to help them negotiate the maze of options. Noel Pettersen, executive director of the National Insurance Brokers Association, advises that selective purchasing in the key to proper coverage, rather than purchasing new insurance every time a new need arises. Buildings and contents policies are very long and involved, and when shopping around you should ensure that you obtain a copy of any contract you are seriously considering and assess it before you sign. The most important section is found under 'Exclusions', that is, what is *not* covered. This list can be long, and should be thoroughly checked against your own requirements. In particular, note which *fixtures* are covered: hot water systems, air conditioners, carports, pergolas, fences, and outside blinds may or may not be included. Bushfires, landslides and riot damage may also be excluded, and should be weighed up against your likely need. Anyone living in a well-timbered bushland suburb *must* ensure that they have bushfire cover. Most policies cover damage by fire and explosion, but not flood; once again, assess this according to your proximity to water sources or the climate and topography. Note, however, that some policies may include bushfire or flood damage cover, but the small print may specifically exclude homes situated in high-risk areas. You should also consider whether the sum insured includes cover for demolition costs, clean-up, temporary accommodation, and architect's fees, in the case of major damage to the fabric of your home.

Home insurance premiums, like car insurance, vary according to assessable risk factors. The insurers will take into account factors such as the age of the house, the type of construction (brick, brick veneer, or weatherboard), the value of the house, its size and location. Home insurance is usually payable on a yearly or half-yearly basis (although for a small credit charge, some companies will even allow monthly payments); a typical 4 bedroom, 2 bathroom Australian family home in a suburban location is likely to cost around $400-$500 per year to insure. Excess levels vary markedly from company to company, and generally by electing a higher excess level of, say, $500, the premium can be significantly reduced. The Insurance Council of Australia considers under-insurance to be the biggest trap in the insurance industry, with at least 40 percent of homes under-insured.

Under-insurance is the biggest cause of dispute between insurance companies and their clients, and you must be aware that if you are under-insured by a certain amount, any claim you make will be reduced by a pro-rata percentage by the insurance assessor. This could have serious consequences in the case of the destruction of a family home, and may mean that you are unable to rebuild in spite of being insured. You should make sure that your level of insurance keeps pace with inflation in the building industry.

Contents Insurance. Home contents insurance provides cover for personal effects kept in and around the home. Most contents insurance is of the 'new for old' replacement type; there are very few indemnity policies (which pay out only the current second-hand value of the insured items) available. Replacement policies should be read closely for restrictions. The best policies will replace new for old unconditionally, however, others will impose an age limit on items so covered (generally 10 to 12 years), and some exclude soft furnishings. To discourage fraudulent claims, many insurers offer a voucher system for replacement in the case of theft or destruction; instead of receiving a cheque for the sum involved, you will be sent a voucher for the amount which must be 'spent' at an appropriate shop (for example, an electrical retailer, if your television has been stolen). Such a policy can be irksome, as you, the customer, are not given any choice of retailer, and so may be limited in your choice of replacement item.

The level of premium payable varies quite widely from company to company, and depends to a large extend on the amount of cover that you require. Good home security will attract lower premiums, and before you start shopping around you can take a few simple steps by fitting deadlocks to external doors, keyed locks to windows, and becoming part of your Neighbourhood Watch Scheme. A replacement policy on contents valued at $30,000 is likely to cost around $350 per annum, however, if you take out a contents policy in conjunction with buildings insurance through the same company, you will generally receive a discount of between five and ten per cent on both policies. If you are aged over 55, you make fire or safety improvements to your home, you don't make a claim for a certain period or you take out multiple policies with an insurance company you may also be entitled to discounts.

Life Insurance

Personal, or life, insurance, is also available through all major insurance companies, as well as through many smaller specialist insurers. There are an ever-increasing number of different types of life insurance policies available, and most people turn to a financial advisor to choose a suitable one for their own particular needs and level of income. Combined savings/insurance policies are popular, providing for both life cover and medium term investment. Basic life insurance policies, in general, attract lower premiums, but are less financially advantageous during the lifetime of the policyholder. Most insurers will offer free (though not necessarily unbiased) consultation services. In addition, you should note that if you are employed and therefore paying into a superannuation fund, you are likely to have automatic life insurance (death benefits) which will be paid to your nominated beneficiary in the event of your accidental or natural death.

If you already hold life/personal insurance before you enter Australia, you must consult your insurers regarding your relocation. You should also discuss your policy with a tax accountant experienced in overseas investments, as any capital growth and income derived from your policy is likely to be taxed at the maximum rate in Australia. It is often possible to have your policy and funds transferred to an Australian company without incurring any costs or sacrificing any bonuses, and this may be financially advantageous in the long term.

Wills

If you die without having made a will, your estate will be distributed to your next of kin according to the various statutes of the state which provide for intestacy. These statutes vary from state to state, and distribution of the estate will vary according to the number and relationship of any immediate kin; in cases where there is no traceable family, the estate usually passes to the State Treasury. Clearly, it is preferable to make a will, especially if you have a de facto partner: the state of Victoria, for example, does not recognise the automatic right of inheritance of de facto spouses. Estate duties and State death duties have been abolished in Australia, and under the present law no such taxes are payable on any deceased estate, regardless of its size.

Proper estate planning can be complex, especially where large assets are involved, and in many cases can be complicated by the usefulness of family trusts. Professional assistance is highly recommended in order to maximise an estate's freedom from capital gains tax for the beneficiaries. A will must also fulfil certain formal and legal requirements in order to be valid and thus it is advisable to seek professional legal advice. Solicitors' costs for this service are likely to be high (around $150 per hour), although some solicitors now offer will making 'kits' which guide clients through the process for a much reduced fee. There are a number of kits available, and you can now even access these online, however, you should make sure that a kit satisfactory covers all aspects of will making, including family provision and capital gains tax. The 'Legal Kits of Victoria Will Kit' is recommended for its coverage of all such essential matters. Lawyers are permitted to advertise in Australia, and testamentary services are frequently advertised in newspapers. Most Australian states have, in recent years, relaxed many of will-making formalities in an attempt to protect the true intentions of testators, but there are still important obligations which must be followed to ensure the validity of your will. A will must be in writing and must be signed by the testator in the presence of two witnesses. If a witness is a beneficiary, or married to a beneficiary of that will, the gift to that beneficiary will fail (although the whole will may not necessarily fail). It is of the utmost importance that beneficiaries are not requested to witness the will. Wills may be revoked by the testator at any time after execution, by destruction, by a later will, or by marriage. Divorce, however, does not automatically revoke a will.

A will made overseas which is valid according to the law of the country where it was made, will be accepted for probate in Australia (a probate is an order or grant by the Supreme Court in favour of the executor authorising him/her to collect the assets of the deceased and deal with those assets according to the terms of the will), even though that will may not be valid according to the law of the particular state in which the deceased lived. A testator who has already made a valid will overseas can deal with assets acquired in Australia by means of a separate ancillary will.

Useful information on will making and other financial planning matters can be found on the 'Money Manager' website at *www.moneymanager.com.au*.

UTILITIES

Electricity, gas and water supplies are controlled throughout Australia by regional state authorities and costs vary to some extent between states, and between urban and rural areas. Remote outback areas may attract particularly high charges, especially for water.

Electricity and Gas

Most new homes in Australia are connected to both gas and electricity supplies. Australia's plentiful supplies of Natural Gas mean that this energy source is relatively cheap, and savings are passed on to domestic consumers; most people thus choose to use gas in preference to electricity wherever possible. Many older homes, however, are not connected to the gas supply, and although this can easily be arranged by contacting the local state gas authority, it is likely to cost several hundred dollars for the service to be installed. Some remote areas do not have a natural gas supply, and in these regions, LPG (liquid petroleum gas) is commonly used, obtained in bottled form, usually from the local garage.

Electricity is the most important source of domestic energy, but is considerably more expensive than gas. In an effort to make electricity more competitive, state authorities such as Western Power (in Western Australia) have introduced 'SmartPower'. SmartPower is a demand management system which relates the price paid for electricity to the cost of producing it, which is greater at times of peak demand. In order to take advantage of this system, a SmartPower Meter must be installed (at a cost, currently, of $199 to be installed into a new home and $329 to be installed into an existing home). The SmartMeter records the amount of electricity used in your home during different charging periods, enabling you to monitor your appliance usage and thus shift the times you run your appliances (washing machines and swimming pool filters, for example) in order to lower your electricity costs. In general, a family with a swimming pool will recoup the cost of the SmartMeter within a short time, and will make ongoing savings of at least 30 per cent on their previous power bills.

The voltage in Australia is 240/250V and the current is alternating at 50 Hz. The power points take three-pin plugs which have two diagonally slanting pins above one straight pin. Appliances brought from the UK will work throughout Australia, after changing the plugs, but those brought from the USA will not.

Solar Power. Australia is a world leader in solar technology, and Australian homes first began using solar power back in 1953. Today, many homes in areas with enough sunshine (most areas!) use solar power to heat water. A solar hot water heater provides around 95 per cent of hot water energy needs (for washing and home heating) free from the sun, resulting in enormous savings on traditional energy costs. The capital cost of a solar hot water heater is high, but once installed, they are maintenance-free and have a very long lifetime, so that the initial high cost is soon outweighed by the benefits. A solar hot water system looks like a large, flat, black rectangle, with a cylinder at the top; it is installed on the roof, usually on the western side of the house where it will receive the most sun, and is aesthetically unobtrusive. Solahart, Australia's largest supplier of solar hot water systems, has an informative website at *www.solahart.com.au.*

Domestic Climate Control

Australian homes are very seldom centrally heated, except in those few areas where the climate is sufficiently cold to require it. Instead, most homes are heated on a fairly ad hoc basis, usually by a combination of portable electric fan heaters or radiators, reverse-cycle air conditioning, and slow combustion stoves. Pot-belly stoves or other solid fuel enclosed fires are becoming increasingly popular as a means of heating the main living areas of the home, and can even be installed so that they heat the water supply as well. Coal fires are banned by law, and coal-substitute fires are extremely unusual; open fires and slow combustion stoves are wood-fuelled, though in Adelaide mallee roots (very dense knots of gnarled wood which do not need chopping), which can be bought by the tonne, dominate the fuel market. Wood suppliers (who are often farmers clearing their fields) advertise in the classifieds columns of local newspapers. Only about 50 percent of residents using firewood for heating actually buy their wood and thousands of Australians (the majority of them in metropolitan areas) collect their wood from roadsides, stock routes, private property and reserves. Of the 6 million tonnes of wood consumed in Australia each year, two thirds is used for domestic heating.

Home cooling rather than heating is the focus of most Australian climate control, and almost every home will have some method of lowering the internal temperature. Electric ceiling fans are popular and very effective, as well as being cheap to run and to install. There are several different types of air conditioning in common use: the evaporative type is the cheapest and is generally portable, but requires an open window to work effectively; reverse-cycle is more effective, and can also be used to heat the room in winter. The unit for reverse-cycle air conditioning is installed in an external wall. Homes in the upper end of the market will often have ducted air conditioning, which is run from a central plant in the roof or garage, distributing cold air through vents to every room. Air conditioning is essential in the northern regions of Australia, both in the home and the car, and all offices and shops throughout Australia are air conditioned.

Keeping Cool on the Cheap. Australian architects are very aware of the need to design for the climate and new houses will, for example, have few or very small windows on the hot, western side. Large windows and patio doors will always be shaded by a pergola, often covered with UV resistant plastic. Solar films, which allow in light but not heat, can be applied to windows, and are a cost effective way of keeping homes cool. Climate management in Australia is second nature to locals, but methods may surprise those brought up in a cooler climate. The British response to the sun is to throw open all the windows and enjoy; in Australia, this would be considered eccentric, if not completely mad. If you want to keep your home cooling costs down, you should do as the locals do:

- At sunrise, get up and close every single window in the house. Pull down all blinds and close all curtains; if there are awnings or shutters on outside windows, pull them into place. Close any vent that allows the entry of external air.
- When entering and leaving your home during the day, make sure that any door is open for as brief a time as possible. The aim at all times should be to prevent the hot external air from coming inside.
- When the exterior temperature drops below the interior temperature (usually at sunset), it is time to open up. Throw open everything that has been closed;

windows and doors will have lockable screens which will allow you to do this in safety. Leave everything open all night, to allow the house to cool down before the next day's onslaught.

○ On really extreme days, try 'hosing down' (but not if there are water restrictions in operation). This method involves soaking the exterior walls and patio areas with water from the garden hose, and should be done after dark to avoid instant evaporation.

Water

Water is a scarce and valuable commodity in Australia, and is treated with respect by most people. All urban areas are well served by high quality, clean water supplies from reservoirs, but extreme summer conditions and drought can mean the frequent imposition of water restrictions on non-essential water use. Public education campaigns encourage water-saving measures, such as shorter showers and water recycling (using washing-up water on the garden, for example). Garden watering is generally done after dusk to avoid evaporation.

Water is supplied to homes and businesses by state authorities who build and maintain reservoirs, and ensure the safety and management of the water supply. Water provision charges are imposed to fund these services and are paid annually or quarterly by consumers. Water and Sewerage Service Charges apply to every connected residential property, along with a metered Water Usage Charge currently 71 cents per kilolitre (1,000 litres) in Melbourne, and 93 cents per kilolitre in Sydney). A Sewerage Disposal Charge is also levied, and takes into account seasonal factors affecting water usage. Other charges may be applied depending on the state water authority, for example, in Melbourne a Parks Charge and a Water Drainage Charge is levied on all rateable properties. Depending on your circumstances rebates and concessions on water charges may be available and families suffering financial hardship can apply to make payments under pre-payment budget schemes.

High water charges mean that it is expensive to keep domestic gardens green during the summer months using mains water. Many Australian homes, therefore, have irrigation/sprinkler systems, known as 'reticulation', which water the garden automatically from a private artesian bore. Homeowners frequently pay to have a bore sunk in their garden, sometimes to a depth of up to 150 metres, to tap into the water table. The cost of the bore can be very high (around $4,000) and is determined by its depth and the geographical structure of the land, however, in the long term, a bore enables enormous savings on water bills. Bore water can *only* be used for gardening, as it is unsuitable for drinking and its high mineral content means that it will stain swimming pool surfaces. During periods of water restriction, bore owners are the only people who are able to water their gardens sufficiently to maintain them. All mains garden watering must be done before dawn or after dusk to reduce wastage due to evaporation (and, in fact, even homes with bore reticulation usually follow this method to avoid scorching leaves and grass). Most newer Australian gardens have moved away from the traditional British garden towards gardens in which native Australian plants predominate. Native plants have adapted to dry conditions over the millennia and require very little water to stay alive; their cultivation also encourages native bird life. Wood chips and extensive patio areas are also popular, reducing the area of garden devoted to lawn, which is expensive and time consuming to maintain in Australia.

In rural areas, domestic rainwater tanks are frequently used to collect precipitation for drinking, washing, and gardening. If your home or holiday cottage has a rainwater tank, make sure that it has a cover to prevent rodents and native marsupials drowning in it and contaminating the water.

Australian mains water is completely safe, and the taste is generally good. In most areas the supply is fluoridated to promote dental health. Unlike the water supply in most British areas, Australian water is 'soft', that is, it does not contain lime-scale. This means that soaps lather easily, tap fittings and appliances do not require the same maintenance, and dishwashers do not need the addition of salt. During the summer months, however, garden hoses and domestic swimming pools can be the site of the bacteria which cause amoebic meningitis, and it is extremely important to maintain chemical levels in pools, and to let the water run for a while before allowing children to play with or drink from garden hoses.

Residential Rates and Other Charges

Council rates are levied annually and are the responsibility of the property owner. They are a tax on property and not on the individual. Tenants do not have to meet any council rates charges, which include a Refuse Charge for the collection of domestic rubbish, and charges for amenities provided by the council. Council rates are determined by the location and size of the property, and are calculated by the Valuer-General on its gross rental value. Property valuations are made approximately every two years. Rates will be higher if you buy a house in a high demand area with excellent services and amenities. On an average, middle-class Australian suburban family home, you can expect a general rates charge of around $600 as well as an additional levy for refuse collection etc.

Rates and charges are payable to the local or shire council can be paid in two instalments, in which case an instalment surcharge applies. A discount is sometimes given for prompt payment, but more often prompt payers are rewarded by entry into a council draw which will offer a substantial prize, such as an international holiday or free rates for a year. Details of the council raffle will be published in the local newspaper in addition to being supplied with the rates notice.

Telecommunications

Until the late 1980s, Australia's telecommunications were controlled by a state monopoly, Telecom Australia. Since then, the market has gradually been deregulated, allowing at first just a single competitor, Optus. In 1997, however, full deregulation was achieved, and there are now a host of options in the telecommunications market, resulting in vastly reduced costs and, in general, a much more competitive service. Telstra (formerly known as Telecom Australia and 51 percent government owned) still dominates the local and domestic market, although Optus has a significant share of the interstate and international long-distance market. Telephone lines are mostly land-based and reach about 96 percent of all households. There are about 8 million mobile phone subscribers (42% of the population and one of the highest user rates in the world) and over 7 million Internet users in Australia. International telecommunications links are provided by the Overseas Telecommunication Commission (OTC). Since deregulation, ISDN suppliers have multiplied exponentially, and it is now possible to call abroad very cheaply by subscribing to one of these services, such as Primus or DigiPlus. Services and special offers are advertised in daily newspapers, and after subscribing, you simply prefix a special call-code to the number you want to dial. You will receive a separate bill from your supplier, and the service can be run concurrently with your Telstra or Optus account. International call rates are falling almost daily due to competition among phone companies. Calls to the UK and the USA are currently around $0.16 per minute – compared to a charge of around $1.60 per minute ten years ago.

All Australian homes are fitted with a telephone line, and a second line with a different number can be installed for $190 from Telstra, but there are special deals and packages available from all suppliers and it is a good idea to shop around. Telephone bills are issued quarterly by each of the suppliers whose services you use. Telstra and Optus bills include local metered calls, STD (interstate/long distance national) calls, and IDD (international) calls, as well as service fees, equipment and any other charges. Service charges are around $20 a month, and customers can choose either to buy their own telephone handsets (in which case there are no equipment charges), or to rent handsets from Telstra or Optus for around $5 per quarter per phone. Fax machines operate via the standard phone line, and their use is charged in the same way as a phone call. Mobile phone services are run by various cellnet providers, such as Vodaphone, and offer much the same range of contract options as available in the UK and USA; once again, they are billed separately from the main phone number.

In Australia, local calls are charged at a *flat rate* of 25 cents from a domestic phone (on a payphone, 40 cents), regardless of the length of the call. Whether you are on the phone for three seconds or three hours, the cost of the call is always the same, and you never need to worry about running up your phone bill or calling during economy periods if you are phoning within the suburban boundaries of your city or town. Flat rate local calling is of particular significance in the electronic communications sector and is one reason why Australia leads the world in domestic internet access: for the cost of a 25 cent call to your internet service provider, you can surf the net for as long as you wish without incurring any further calling charges. Long distance national and international calls are, however, charged according to the distance and the length of the call, as well as by time zone: Day rate (8am-6pm) is the most expensive, Economy rate (7am-9am, 6pm-9pm) is somewhat cheaper, and Night rate (9pm-7am and all weekend) the most economical for national calls.

THE CODES FOR DIALLING AUSTRALIA DIRECT FROM ABROAD ARE:

Adelaide	00-61 8
Brisbane	00-61 7
Canberra	00-61 6
Darwin	00-61 8
Hobart	00-61 3
Perth	00-61 8
Melbourne	00-61 3
Sydney	00-61 2

The code should prefix the local number, which will be 8 digits long in most capital cities, and six digits long in more rural areas. If you are dialling a number within Australia you must place a zero before the area prefix above before dialling. International directory assistance (from the UK, call 155) can advise on changes should you have any out-of-date contact numbers. To dial overseas from Australia, prefix the number you require firstly with your international call supplier over-ride number, then add the international dialling code 0011. International faxes are sent using the code 0015.

REMOVALS

Most people making a long-term or permanent move abroad will want to arrange to take some or all of their personal effects with them. The costs involved in doing so can be high, but a carefully planned move will save you money by minimising setting-up expenses on arrival. Household items vary widely in replacement value from country to country; so a little research will pay off in deciding what to take and what to leave behind. In making your calculations you should consider the second-hand sale value of your effects in your home country against the both the cost of shipping and insurance, and the cost of replacement. Car boot sales are an excellent way to dispose of the accumulated junk that you will inevitably uncover when you start going through your cupboards with a major international move in mind, but don't underestimate the sentimental value of items: there are some things that will simply have to go with you, no matter how worthless or unlikely.

Household Goods

There are many removal companies specialising in international shipping. The large national firms advertise in the regional Yellow Pages telephone directories, along with smaller local firms, and any reputable firm will be able to outline their costs (charged per cubic meter) over the telephone. The quality of the service provided is an important consideration when undertaking an international move and you should make sure that the remover offers 'export-quality packing' and deals with every aspect of the customs and shipping process. Once you have established a short-list of remover, you should request a formal quote (which will be free of charge). An estimator will visit your home and examine the contents of every room to assess the cubic meterage to be packed and shipped. Antiques and other items of special value may be assessed at a different rate. Most removers also broker their own insurance packages, which are generally charged at around three per cent of the value of the consignment, and although this can amount to a considerable sum on an average family's effects, it is an indispensable expense. Your valued possessions will spend around three months going from store to ship to customs warehouse before finally being unpacked in your new home, and it is very rare for a consignment to arrive completely undamaged.

Professional removers are remarkably efficient and can pack an average family house in one or two days. For a move to Australia, they will use export-quality packing, which is much more time-consuming than packing for a local removal. The removals men will wrap all furniture items in paper blankets, dismantling them where possible, and will also individually wrap every item of kitchenware and any other small items. Everything else will be packed in specially designed heavy-duty cardboard cartons (such as book boxes, linen boxes and picture boxes). International shipping is costed by volume not weight, and a good remover will pack lightweight items, such as linen, inside empty furniture (for example, chests-of-drawers) to reduce volume. You should bear this in mind when considering what to take: it may mean that if you plan to take certain furniture items, you will in effect be able to take linen or children's stuffed toys for 'free'. It is possible to self-pack for an international move, but the small cost saving it permits is cancelled out by the higher insurance premiums you must then pay.

Extensive list making will probably play a large part in your daily life when organising a move on this scale, and it is important to consider carefully which items to take with you to Australia. The *British Association of Removers* (address below) provides a useful list which may help in planning. As a general rule, it is much cheaper and easier to ship furniture than to replace it with new items at your destination, with some exceptions. Beds do not travel well, as a mattress which is packed vertically for three months will generally arrive with sagging springs; pianos do not benefit from the sudden climate change, may warp in the moist sea air, and frequently cannot be properly retuned; and vinyl seating is inappropriate for hot-weather countries. All Australian homes, whether rented or bought, come with a cooker installed (which is never taken with you when you move) and it is therefore redundant to ship your own. You would also be well advised to buy a new refrigerator on arrival, as Australian fridges are much larger and have extra fan assistance to cope with the climate, as well as a new television and video. Televisions from home can be converted to work in Australia, but it is expensive and often less than successful. Fax machines and telephones cannot be imported unless they conform to the Australian telecommunications standards. Most modern Australian homes also have built-in wardrobes, and so you may also decide to leave these behind, especially as their large volume makes freestanding wardrobes expensive to ship.

Taking your Car

Most removal companies also offer the option of shipping your motor vehicle and will supply all the necessary information including lists of customs and port charges, as well as providing a quote for shipping a private motorcar to Australia. The services provided by the shipper should include full preparation for containerisation, for example, covering the interior with floor mats and seat covers, and inserting silica desiccant bags or pillows to help avoid the possibility of condensation damage in the car. The car will be packed into a 'sole use' twenty foot ISO Reefer Container and secured in accordance with manufacturers' recommendations at the removers' warehouse. The quote should include return haulage of the container to the export loading berth, all port and handling charges, all export and customs documentation, provision of Bills of Loading to a nominated address on arrival, and all freight charges through to the destination port. Insurance is calculated at around 1.5 per cent of the car's insured value, and Australian unpacking and quarantine inspection charges are payable on arrival. Shipping to Australia takes between four and eight weeks, depending on the final destination. In addition to meeting the costs involved in transporting your vehicle to Australia, you will also be liable on arrival for the cost of ensuring that your vehicle meets Australian safety standards under the Motor Vehicle Standards Act of 1989. This process, known as 'compliance', can be very expensive, and your car will not be able to receive temporary registration (and thus be driven) until it has been completed. The total amount of money involved in shipping a car to Australia including freight, taxes, insurance, compliance, and re-registration, means that unless your vehicle is a very special, rare or luxurious, it is very rarely worthwhile. For those who decide to proceed, further information is given below in the section on Australian Customs.

Taking Pets

Moving your pets to Australia is as complicated and expensive a process as moving yourself and your family. Australian quarantine rules are extremely strict in order to protect the disease-free status of Australian livestock afforded by the country's geographical isolation. Most commonly, new arrivals choose to import their family pets, generally cats or dogs, and for this an Import Permit must be obtained from Australian Quarantine and Inspection Service (AQIS) in the State or Territory into which you plan to bring your animal. Stringent health and certification requirements must be met, which include identifying your pet with a microchip number, vaccinating the animal against an extensive list of diseases as well as testing for the absence of certain viruses 21 days prior to export. All cats and dogs must be treated for internal parasites 14 days before export and must pass a clinical examination 48 hours before shipment. Each animal must be accompanied by a certificate of inspection issued by an Official Veterinarian of the country of export. The types of containers in which animals may be exported are also strictly specified by Australian law and an animal will not be permitted to enter the country if it arrives in a non-IATA approved container. Both dogs and cats are required to undergo a period of quarantine on arrival in Australia at one of three centres (in Victoria, New South Wales and Western Australia). If you are moving to another state, you will incur additional costs in freighting your animal to your new home after it completes its period of quarantine. Dogs and cats from approved rabies-free countries, which meet all the vaccination and certification requirements for import, are currently quarantined for a period of 30 days upon arrival in Australia.

Costs for importing pets are high: the cost of transportation depends on the size rather than the weight of the object shipped, so taking your cat to Australia with you will be far cheaper than shipping a dog the size of a labrador. The cost of the extensive veterinary treatment and testing required for import needs to be taken into account, and you must also allow for the quarantine costs payable in advance in Australia. Currently the cost of quarantine for a cat is $12 a day and for a dog $16 a day. If you add to this additional charges incurred during the quarantine and inspection process, transporting a pet will add at least another $1000 to your moving costs.

Useful Addresses

Air Pets Oceanic, Willowslea Farm Kennels, Spout Lane North, Stanwell Moor, Staines, Middlesex TW19 6BW; ☎01753-685571; fax 01753-681655; www.airpets.com

Allied Pickfords, Heritage House, 345 Southbury Road, Enfield, Middlesex, EN1 1UP; ☎020-8219 8000 (freephone 0800-289 229); fax 020-8219 8321; www.allied-pickfords.co.uk

British Association of Removers, 3 Churchill Court, 58 Station Road, North Harrow, Middlesex HA2 7SA; ☎020-8861 3331; 020-8861 3332; www.bar.co.uk

Crown Worldwide Ltd., Security House,

Abbey Wharf Ind. Estate, Kingsbridge Road, Barking, Essex IG11 OBD, UK; ☎020-8591 3388; fax 020-8594 4571; www.crownworldwide.com

Department of Environment, Food and Rural Affairs, Export of Cats and Dogs Section, 1A Page Street, London SW1P 4PQ; ☎020-7904 6347 (helpline 0870-241 1710); fax 020-7904 6428; www.defra.gov.uk. Information and application forms for DEFRA export health certificate; information on all aspects of importing and exporting animals.

Karman Shipping Services, (Motor Vehicle

Shipping Specialists), 44 Chestnut Hill, Leighton Buzzard, Bedfordshire LU7 7TR; ☎01525-851 545; fax 01525-850 996; www.karmanshipping.co.uk
Ladyhaye Livestock Shipping, Hare Lane, Blindley Heath, Lingfield, Surrey RH7 6JB; ☎01342-832161; fax 01342 834778; www.ladyhaye.co.uk.
Worldwide Animal Travel, 43 London Road, Brentwood, Essex CM14 4NN; ☎01277-231611.
The Australian Quarantine Information Service (AQIS), provides quarantine inspection services for the arrival of animals into Australia and inspection and certification of animals exported from Australia. AQIS has a very informative website at www.aqis.gov.au

Australian Customs Regulations

The Australian Customs Service is extremely stringent in order to protect Australian flora and fauna from the many diseases affecting plants animals, such as rabies, foot-and-mouth disease, and BSE, found elsewhere in the world. Any wood or wooden artefacts, including furniture, must be declared to Customs on arrival in the country, so that it can first be quarantined and fumigated. This provision extends to items such as straw hats and wooden kitchen utensils. Garden equipment, lawnmowers, and outdoor furniture will be specially inspected, fumigated and cleaned (at your expense). Products made from protected wildlife species, non-approved cordless phones, live animals and weapons and firearms (which are either prohibited or require a permit and safety testing) are also prohibited imports. You must also declare all goods of animal and plant origin, including all fresh, frozen or tinned food, fruit, vegetables and flowers. Penalties of $50,000 to $100,000 and jail terms of 5-10 years may be levied on people who contravene customs regulations, so it is important to take some care when filling out your customs declarations forms before shipping your personal effects, and when arriving in the country. International flights are fumigated before passengers are allowed to disembark to ensure that no diseases enter the country on your person, your clothing or luggage. Although the spray used can be slightly irritating (it is recommended that you cover your nose and mouth, although the chemicals have been declared perfectly safe), it is an important part of the process of making sure Australia stays disease-free.

Like most countries in the world today, illicit drugs, including marijuana, are strictly prohibited and Australian Customs are very efficient in policing the entry of drugs into Australia. Flights arriving from Asia are often very slow to clear customs as officials will be especially rigorous with checking passengers travelling from or through this region. Under *no* circumstances should you agree to carry illicit drugs or any other package for anyone else, as you will bear the responsibility for any prohibited substance found in your possession.

Personal effects shipped into Australia for your own use, and owned and used by you previously, do not attract duties or other taxes on arrival in port. If you are thinking about taking your vehicle with you to Australia you should take into account the costs (and hassle) involved in the process, i.e. freight costs, customs duties and entry processing charges, the cost of steam cleaning the vehicle for quarantine purposes, wharf and transport charges and costs involved in having the vehicle meet state or territory registration requirements. Tourists and temporary residents can take a motor vehicle or motorcycle into Australia for a period of up to 12 months without paying duty provided that the vehicles are re-exported from Australia at the end of that period. For this concession to apply, you will need a *Carnet de Passages en Douanes* issued by an overseas organisations which has a reciprocal arrangement with the

Australian Automobile Association, as well as a cash or bank security equal to the amount of duty and GST otherwise payable.

Since 1 July 2000 a 10% tax on goods and services (GST) has replaced the old sales tax which applied to the purchase of goods. The current duty-free allowance for travellers includes 1125 ml of alcohol, 250 cigarettes or 250 grams of cigars or tobacco products other than cigarettes and up to $400 of duty-free goods. It is your responsibility to declare anything else that may be liable for GST. Duty-free shops at Australian airports are often cheaper than those at home, and there are shops prior to Customs in the arrivals hall of most international airports, which means it may be better not to 'buy before you fly'.

The Australian Customs Service provides full information on all aspects of its operations on its website (www.customs.gov.au).

BUYING A CAR IN AUSTRALIA

Australian cars are right-hand-drive, as in the UK, and since 1989 the importation of left-hand-drive vehicles has been prohibited. Although there remain a small number of left-hand-drive cars imported before 1989, in general, these cars are not well suited to Australian driving conditions, and parts and servicing are expensive. For the UK immigrant, driving conditions and road regulations will be reassuringly familiar, although you will notice that cars tend to be larger than in Europe. Cheaper petrol, wider roads and easier parking all contribute to a preference for more spacious and powerful family vehicles. Australia has a well-established motor industry with Ford and General Motors Holden building a large proportion of cars on the road. Japanese cars also have a much stronger presence than in Europe, and Mitsubishi, Toyota and Nissan all produce cars in Australia to Japanese levels of quality control. The practice of 'rebadging' means that many models will be familiar in their appearance to visitors and new arrivals, although they are likely to have different names. European cars of any model are very expensive in Australia because of high importation costs, which now includes a prohibitive 'luxury car tax'. This tax applies not only to obviously up-market luxury vehicles, such as Mercedes, but also to cheaper makes such as Peugeots, Fiats and VWs; as a result there is a certain prestige value in driving such vehicles, although in many cases home-grown versions are superior in finish and performance. The luxury tax also applies to imported parts which can make servicing a car of European origin very expensive. As a general rule, you should expect to pay considerably more for a vehicle in Australia than you would back home, especially if you are considering a second-hand car.

The registration and taxing of vehicles is the responsibility of State Departments of Transport, and whilst some states (for example, NSW) have a system equivalent to the British MOT, others do not. As a result of this, and because of the high cost of new cars, there tend to be many more older cars on the road than you will find at home and people tend to hang on to their cars for a number of years before deciding to upgrade. It is important, especially if you buy an older vehicle, that you keep your car's registration (equivalent to a tax disk) current, as, once lapsed, renewal cannot be effected until the car has undergone an extremely thorough safety check at the police vehicle registration centre. Once headed for the pits because of expired registration, it is usually difficult and expensive to get the car back on the road. Police also have the power to stop any vehicle in an obvious state of disrepair, and will frequently issue a

'Yellow Sticker' which identifies the car as unroadworthy. The car must not be driven until it has been repaired and inspected by the vehicle licensing authority. Emissions control is also taken very seriously and other drivers may, and often do, report vehicles with dirty exhaust emissions; the driver of such a car will receive a letter requiring that the problem be remedied, and this may be followed up by an inspection.

Most newer Australian cars have automatic transmission in preference to manual, and many have air conditioning and tinted windows to reduce problems of heat and glare. Sunroofs are unusual, as extreme temperature conditions makes them impractical – Australians aim to keep heat out, not bask in it. All modern cars run on unleaded petrol, and for older cars a 'lead replacement petrol' is sold. Many larger cars, particularly of the popular off-road variety, run on diesel, which is significantly cheaper than petrol.

New Cars

Buying a new car in Australia is little different from doing so in the UK, USA or elsewhere. Manufacturers market their vehicles through licensed dealers who advertise in the daily press and in the local Yellow Pages. The new car market is currently very competitive and it is important to shop around widely. There is always room for negotiation on price or on bonus extras such as air conditioning, stereo, and additional safety features. Traditionally, new car prices are discounted significantly at the end of the Australian financial year which falls in late June, when dealers particularly aim to attract the business and fleet buying markets. Car models which are about to be superseded are also often very much reduced in price to enable dealers to clear their stock and can be excellent buys; look out, too, for ex-demonstration vehicles which may have no more than a few hundred kilometres on the clock. The daily newspapers in each capital city generally allocate one day of the week to a motoring section or motoring advertising (on Wednesday and Saturday in *The West Australian*, for example), and scouring these pages will generally reveal the best buys and allow you to compare dealer prices. A number of car buyers' guides and magazines are widely available in newsagents, providing detailed technical information and assessments of every car currently on the market. Note that there are a number of abbreviations in common use in car advertisements, including abs (anti-lock braking system), ac (air conditioning), at (automatic transmission), cc (cruise control), cl (central locking), ps (power steering), pw (power windows), srs (supplementary restraint system), and mags (alloy wheels).

A very high proportion of new cars bought in Australia are registered in company names and if you expect to use your car for business purposes, most dealers will have specially tailored schemes to maximise the tax benefits for your company. Popular manufacturers like Ford, Holden, Toyota and Mitsubishi also provide business versions of their mainstream models. Leasing, rather than buying, is frequently advantageous to the business car user and offers both tax efficiency and ease of replacement. Other schemes offer a guaranteed replacement value (if the car is bought with dealer finance and serviced by them throughout the period of the contract), allowing an upgrade to a new model after a designated number of years.

Used Cars

New cars tend to depreciate dramatically in value once in use, and given the high price of a new car in Australia, many people prefer to buy second hand models. These are available from both specialist second-hand dealers and through the used car division of licensed new car dealers, as well as by private sale. Cars offered for sale privately are usually advertised in the classifieds section of the main state and local newspapers, and in auto classifieds magazines. Many dealers of new cars also sell used cars obtained by them through part-exchange (known in Australia as a 'trade-in'); such cars are likely to be more expensive than an equivalent vehicle sold privately, but will usually have the advantage of a dealer's warranty. By law, used cars offered for sale above a certain benchmark price (which varies from state to state) may not be offered for sale by a dealer without the provision of a warranty, the minimum terms of which are also laid down by the state government.

Travellers and temporary residents may find it more convenient to purchase a vehicle under a guaranteed buy-back arrangement. A number of firms specialise in selling cars by this method, ensuring that the vehicle is legal and roadworthy at the time of purchase and guaranteeing to repurchase it at the end of the stay.

Car theft is prevalent in many cities in Australia, so if you choose to buy a car privately you should ensure that the vehicle is neither a stolen one nor otherwise financially encumbered; if you buy a car on which the vendor still owes money the vehicle can be repossessed if they default on any payment. Remember that the loan company has first call on its security, and you could lose a considerable amount of money. Vehicle registrations may be checked free of charge against the government registers of financially encumbered vehicles, listed below:

NSW/ACT/NT: Register of Encumbered Vehicles (REVS), Level 5, 1 Fitzwilliam Street, Parramatta, NSW 2150; ☎ 02-9633 6333; www.revs.nsw.gov.au

QLD: Motor Vehicles Securities Register, Office of Fair Trading, 40 Ann Street, Brisbane, QLD 4000, ☎ 07-3246 1595; www.fairtrading.qld.gov.au

SA: Vehicle Securities Register, Ground Floor, EDS Centre, 108 North Terrace, Adelaide, SA 5000; ☎ 131 084; www.transport.sa.gov.au/rls/.

TAS: Transport Division, Department of Infrastructure, Energy and Resources, GPO Box 936, Hobart, Tasmania 7001; ☎ 1300-135 513; www.transport.tas.gov.au/regstat/.

VIC: Vicroads, Vehicle Securities Register, PO Box 2446, Kew, VIC 3101; ☎ 13 1171 (within Victoria); 1800-814 762 (interstate callers); www.vicroads.vic.gov.au. There are also maxi kiosks situated at various locations across Victoria.

WA: Register of Encumbered Vehicles (REVS), 219 St. George's Terrace, Perth, WA 6000; ☎ 1800-198 333 (Free Call); 1300-304 024 (local call).

When buying a used car, it is usual to pay an authorised, qualified mechanic from one of the automobile associations to make a thorough mechanical examination. The cost of such an examination (between $100 and $150) could well save you thousands of dollars by warning you off a potential lemon. It is not necessary to be a member of an automobile association to use such a service, although members will receive a discounted rate. Federal regulations govern safety standards including seat belts, emissions, tyres and engine noise; and state governments may have additional legislation. A vehicle that fails to conform to safety standards will not be registered until modifications have been made.

Once you have found and purchased your new used car, you will need to fill out a form to transfer ownership into your name. These forms are available from the local vehicle-licensing centre, and it is usually the vendor's responsibility to supply them at the time of purchase, signing the appropriate sections. The value of the vehicle must be declared on the form, and from this a transfer tax or stamp duty is calculated, the amount ranging from tens to hundreds of dollars, and must be paid within 30 days to affect the transfer of ownership.

Motor Insurance

In Australia the vehicle, rather than the driver, is covered by any insurance. Thus, anyone who has your permission to do so may drive your car (providing that they have a full Australian or equivalent licence and the car is privately owned) and will be fully covered by your existing insurance. Motor vehicle insurance tends to be slightly cheaper in Australia than at home, but is subject to the same kinds of variables. Around 80 per cent of Australian car owners choose to take out extra private insurance. Factors affecting insurance costs include the make and model of the car, the location of your residence, and the age and experience of the usual driver. Sports cars and high performance cars attract higher premiums, as do 'modified' vehicles; and drivers resident in non-metropolitan areas are likely to pay less for their insurance, although this varies widely and may mean significant differences in quotes if you shop around. Young drivers under the age of 25 will invariably be charged more, however, most companies now offer scaled premiums for those over 25, as well as discounted policies for the over-55s. Drivers who borrow to finance the purchase of their vehicle will usually also pay more in premiums. Insurers are increasingly offering policyholders a choice of excess, ranging from $50 to $500: a lower excess will generally mean a higher premium, although this can be offset by your no-claims record. Drivers with a motor vehicle insurance history gained overseas are usually able to 'import' their no-claims bonus, up to its full value. It is important to bring a letter from your previous insurer confirming your no-claims status so that it can be immediately applied to your new policy.

A new development in Australian car insurance has been the introduction of 'agreed value' sum-insured options. In the past, most policies paid on the basis of the 'market value' of your car at the time of the claim, however, the agreed value type of policy enables you to agree a fixed value for the term of your policy. An agreed value policy is generally a little more expensive, but may be worthwhile especially for older vehicles. Some policies also offer added extras such as travel and medical insurance. Covering the cost of car hire and accommodation in case of accident may also be useful, as may be the use of a courtesy car while repairs are made, whilst some policies offer brand-new replacement vehicles for damaged cars less than one year old.

Compulsory Third Party Insurance. Third Party Insurance (CTP Greenslip) is compulsory in Australia and the cost of this insurance is included in the vehicle registration charge paid to the State or Territory government. Third Party Insurance covers the driver for injuries to any other person caused in the course of driving, however, insurance against third party property damage must be taken out separately, and is the responsibility of the car owner. Expect to pay upwards of $230.

Third Party Property Insurance. Third Party Property Insurance (TPPI) covers the cost of any damage done *by* your vehicle in the course of an accident, but does *not* cover the damage done *to* your own car. TPPI is a very economical insurance option, rarely exceeding $200, and is popular with owners of old cars with little resale value.

Comprehensive Insurance. Comprehensive cover costs considerably more than TTPI and ranges between $275-$600, with discounts of up to 60% available to holders of a full no-claims bonus. Comprehensive insurance covers your car for accidental damage, theft and fire and gives liability cover for damage you may cause to someone else's car or property. Insurance companies assess their premiums by the following criteria:

- Accident Record: Do you have one?
- Age: Of both you and your vehicle (if you are less 25 years old, you will pay more).
- Business or Private Use: Insurance premiums are higher for business vehicles.
- Experience: How long have you been driving?
- Finance: Unfinanced vehicles are cheaper to insure.
- Make and Model: Some models pose a higher risk of theft or are more expensive to repair.
- Residence: Do you live in a high risk area?
- Sex: In certain age groups females have fewer accident claims than males.
- Trailer/Caravan: You are likely to need a separate policy for these vehicles to cover against damage cause by side-swiping.
- Value: Of the vehicle.

The cost of comprehensive motor vehicle insurance varies widely according to the above criteria and other factors. The best policy is to shop around – through the Yellow Pages, or by using an insurance broker. Forty percent of policies are now placed through brokers, who have immediate access to a huge range of policies and are thus able to obtain the cheapest one for your needs with a minimum of difficulty. A broker is legally bound to operate in the interests of the policy buyer and not of the companies whose policies he represents. Nonetheless, it is important to ensure that a broker is reputable, and so you should check that the firm is registered with the NIBA (National Insurance Brokers Association). Brokers are paid either by commission from insurance companies, or by fees charged for their advice to the consumer. Most brokers, however, will not charge a fee when arranging simple domestic and motor vehicle insurance. If a broker does charge a fee it must be fully declared at the beginning of the transaction.

Insurance companies, automobile associations offering insurance, and insurance brokers can all be found in the Yellow Pages. In addition, some companies now allow customers to take out insurance over the Internet meaning that transactions can be undertaken 24 hours a day with the whole quote-confirmation-payment process conducted online in a secure environment. Australia's biggest and most reputable insurance companies include AMP, Allianz, AAMI, SGIC, GIO, and RAC.

Useful Contacts

Australia Associated Motor Insurers Ltd (AAMI), To find the location of the nearest AAMI branch telephone 132 244; or visit the website at www.aami.com.au

Allianz Australia Ltd, GPO Box 4049,

Sydney, NSW 2001; ☎132 664 (local call); www.allianz.com.au

AMP, To find the location of the nearest AMP insurance adviser ☎133 888 (within Australia); www.amp.com.au

SGIC General Insurance Limited , South Australian Main Office, 211 Victoria Square, Adelaide, SA 5000; ☎133 233; www.sgic.com.au

GIO Insurance, GIO branch telephone 13 1010; or visit the website at www.gio.com.au

National Insurance Brokers Association of Australia, (Head Office) Level 18, 111 Pacific Highway, North Sydney, NSW 2060; ☎02-9964 9400, or 1800-252 558; fax 02-9964 9332; www.niba.com.au

National Roads and Motorists' Association Limited (NRMA), Podium Level 3, Bankstown Square, North Terrace, Bankstown, NSW 2200; ☎132 132; www.nrma.com.au

DAILY LIFE

CHAPTER SUMMARY

○ **Population.** Nearly 90% of the Australian population lives in coastal cities.

○ The beach is the cornerstone of Australian life.

○ **Children and Education.** Distance education is vital for outback children of all ages living miles from anywhere.

    ○ Distance lessons are given by radio and Internet.

    ○ Factor 15 sunscreen is provided free to all primary school students.

○ **Motoring.** It is legal to overtake on the inside on a dual carriageway and is known as 'undertaking.'

    ○ On a three-lane highway you can overtake in any lane.

    ○ Hitch-hiking is illegal in Victoria.

    ○ Drink-driving is considered a serious issue and motorists can be stopped and tested at random.

○ **Railways.** Rail travel is expensive and is done for the experience, not convenience.

    ○ One of the great railway trips of the world is between Perth and Sydney.

○ **Banking.** Even those with bad credit records can open accounts easily, provided that they meet the criteria for proving identity and place of abode.

○ **Tax.** The Australian tax year runs from July 1st to June 30th.

○ **Health.** The perceived healthy lifestyle of the Australians is gainsaid by the fact that 56% of adults are overweight and cholesterol busting drugs cost the health service more than half a million dollars annually.

One of the great attractions of Australia for many immigrants and other new arrivals is the quality of life it offers. Cosmopolitan cities border a landscape of sometimes awe-inspiring beauty, and most people enjoy circumstances in which work and play combine to provide the sort of relaxed and comfortable lifestyle available only to the very wealthy in Europe. Public facilities of all types are generally good, and standards in health care and education are very high, relative to other industrialised nations. Housing is also generally more spacious and affordable than in the UK and other European countries although more expensive than in the USA, and most homes have gardens and outdoor living areas designed to take advantage of the climate, and opportunities for family and other entertaining. Australia is one of the world's most urbanised societies, and nearly 90% of the population live in coastal cities consisting of sprawling suburbs with a high-rise city centre or CBD (central business district). All of Australia's state capitals are built on or very near the water – even the inland city of Canberra has been designed around a giant artificial lake, allowing residents to partake in the water-based activities which are part of the Australian lifestyle. In the shadow of the cities' skyscrapers, labyrinths of interconnecting courtyards and arcades offer shopping, cafés and restaurants, and the country has in recent years become world-famous for its restaurant culture and cuisine. Leisure is important to Australians, and the weekend has become a sacred institution devoted to pottering in the garden, preparing the family barbecue, or sports. Parks and ovals are taken over with children playing cricket, football, or riding their bicycles; some families head for the bush, others for the beach, and national parks are busy with picnickers. There is still significant resistance to Sunday trading but changes to trading regulations mean that shops which previously closed at 1pm on Saturday are now open all day, and in the more touristy areas of Australia Sunday trading is permitted. Larger shops in the larger cities will generally open for at least a part of Sunday and more and more working people are using the weekend to catch up on their shopping. In the summer, beachlife rules. Called the 'great leveller', the beach is accessible to all ages and social classes and is the cornerstone of Australian life.

EDUCATION

Australian education is internationally regarded as being of a high standard, particularly in tertiary institutions. An Australian honours degree holds a higher status than a UK honours degree in the UK university system, and holders of such degrees on scholarships to premier universities, such as Oxford and Cambridge, are exempted from one year of study at postgraduate level. International surveys of educational standards recognise Australia scoring up at the top of the list, with Germany and Japan, in terms of science education. Early education practice in Australia is significantly different to that of the UK or USA and many experts attribute later academic success to the different emphasis in teaching methods of young children where emphasis is put on self discipline, on learning by finding out, by questioning and by encouraging a child's interest and enthusiasm for learning.

Education is the responsibility of state governments, and is compulsory between the ages of five and 15. Upper secondary schooling begins at 12 or 13 years old and continues on to age 17 or 18; these extra years are mandatory for students considering further education and school retention rates are very high, averaging around 70 percent. Around 70 percent of Australian children attend free, public state-funded schools, which are mostly co-educational and non-religious. A parallel fee-paying, private sector also exists, and most such schools are run by various religious institutions and are single sex institutions. Children who need to attend boarding school in their secondary school years because of rural isolation will usually attend schools of this type, and their boarding costs are subsidised by the government. In the primary years, children in the outback are educated by the 'School of the Air' which provides distance learning by radio and correspondence. There are now a number of schools offering the International Baccalaureate programme to those in their final years of schooling. For children of parents who might be on short-term work contracts in Australia, the International Baccalaureate programme allows them to gain entry into universities in their home country, and into some universities in the USA.

Two magazines for emigrants to Victoria and New South Wales, *Choosing a School for your Child in Victoria* and *Choosing a School for your Child in NSW,* are available by subscription from Consyl Publishing, details of which are given below. These publications give useful information regarding the kinds of schools available in these states and answer many of the questions which arise when choosing a new school in an unfamiliar country. The New South Wales version of the magazine also covers boarding schools in NSW, Victoria, Queensland and Canberra.

Australia's academic year of three or four terms, depending on the state, follows the calendar year, running from January to December, so that the long summer holidays of around seven weeks coincide with the Christmas period.

The Structure of the Education System

The educational system is uniform in Australia and both the private and state sectors operate on the same patterns and curricula. Primary education in Australia takes six or seven years, depending on the state, and secondary education either five or six years, depending on the state. Wherever you live in Australia, the combined length of primary and secondary education is twelve years, and school years are numbered Years 1 to 12.

Pre-School. Pre-schooling is available for children aged four and five years old, and provides educational programmes in which young children are encouraged to develop their abilities, skills and knowledge of the world. Preschool centres operate in association with local primary schools, and, where possible, are located in the same grounds. In Western Australia and some of the eastern states, there is an early learning continuum, which covers children aged 3 to 8 years (K-3). The principles of this system recognise the distinctive learning patterns of young children, the nature of children's growth and development, and the value of home and community in learning. Children are encouraged to learn through play, experimentation, and interaction with other children and adults, learning to explore, manipulate objects, materials and technologies. Early reading is neither required nor pushed, and most children enter school in the year they turn six without any reading skills. Current research suggests that this is in fact more effective in encouraging later literacy than enforced early reading in the nursery years, and Australian results bear this out. Instead, preschools focus heavily on creativity and thinking skills, which can be applied later to more academic purposes. Children attend preschool mornings only in their first year, and from 9am to 3pm in their second year.

Primary School Education. Children enter primary school in the year they turn six, and there is no concept of 'rising fives' or term-by-term age-group entry. There is very little multi-age teaching in primary classrooms, except where numbers and resources require combined classes (in some rural areas, and in suburbs with falling rolls). Classes in state schools have a maximum of 30 students and many are smaller, depending on area. State primary schools are almost invariably co-educational, however, many private schools offer single-sex education at this level. Each state sets its own curriculum, but all have common elements, emphasising English language, mathematics, social studies, health education, and physical education. Many primary schools offer foreign languages from year three and there is a much greater focus on languages of the region, for example, Mandarin Chinese, Japanese and Indonesian. It is less common for children to study French or German, and Latin is not a commonly taught subject. Philosophy and thinking skills are now taught in most schools from year five, and there is a strong emphasis on creative work from the earliest years. Oral communication skills are developed early, and children as young as five will be expected to speak to the class regularly on topics of interest. Sports are an important part of the school day, and in summer all children will have daily swimming lessons. School assemblies provide an opportunity for classes to make drama presentations and are largely the responsibility of the students. Parents are encouraged to attend these weekly occasions. The school day usually runs from 8.50am to 3.15pm, but this will vary slightly from state to state.

Secondary Education. After finishing either year six or seven, depending on the state, children progress on to secondary school, which is known as 'high school'. In the state sector these are usually of the comprehensive variety, although some states still run a streamed, grammar school system, and other offer special programmes to children gifted in certain fields. These specialist programmes in music, theatre studies, art or sport offer scholarships to talented students from all over the state or territory, and entry is highly competitive. High school students enjoy modern facilities, and are taught a variety of subjects, which include the core studies of English, maths, science and social studies (history and geography), as well as art, home economics and languages. In many high schools, students in the first year must take the whole range of subjects available despite personal preferences in order to try and help them develop wider interests or recognise previously undiscovered talents. This means that regardless of gender, all students will have to study cooking, sewing, woodwork, metalwork, art, music, drama and sport, as required by the school. As students progress through the high school system, they are allowed to specialise in subjects of their own choosing, until they reach the final two years of school, where subject choices will be determined by future career preferences.

Special Needs Children. Special schools are provided for physically and mentally disabled children. Within the state system, children with learning disabilities are provided with special tuition inside the regular primary or high school structure. Individualised programmes are delivered by specialist teachers or a team of special educators. Provision is made for children with dyslexia and dyspraxia in most schools.

Gifted and Talented Children. State education departments recognise the needs of gifted and talented children, and provide special programmes for them. All schools are responsible for the ongoing identification of gifted and talented children, and monitor their progress carefully. Such children are offered a 'differentiated curriculum', the guiding principles of which are: a stimulating and interactive environment, an acceptance of individual differences and potential, a willingness to provide appropriate teaching methods and materials to match those differences, and flexibility. Teachers must, by law, provide for gifted and talented children at all times.

Technology in Schools. The various state education systems place a high priority on educating students to take advantage of new technologies. The present government has promised $130 million over four years to government schools for the purposes of achieving better scientific and technological literacy, to develop school based innovation and build supportive school environments. It has also promised $34.1 million over five years towards the development of online curriculum resources, services and applications. Schools are well equipped with information technology facilities and offer teaching in this field to even the youngest students. Most schools are also on the Internet and provide every class or student with an email address. In many private schools students are provided with their own laptop.

Vocational Education. There has been significant change in post-compulsory schooling in recent years, with an increasing emphasis on work-based learning. Work experience has been an important part of school programmes for many years, and this has now been expanded into structured work-based learning programmes which combine school and industry-based learning. A number of initiatives have been introduced including VET (Vocational Education and Training in Schools Programme), school-based new apprenticeships, vocational programmes, fast track programmes, and several others. Approval and certification arrangements provide a means of recognising students' achievements in work-based programmes.

Distance Education. Australia's vast size means that many students in rural areas are hundreds of miles from the nearest schools. Every state, therefore, runs an active distance education programme, which caters not only for students who are unable to attend school by reason of their location, but also for ill or otherwise isolated children. State governments provide professional staff, resources, and support, as well as radio broadcasts and internet services, to children of all ages.

Post-Compulsory Education. The compulsory years of secondary education finish at the end of year 10 (age 16). Secondary Education Authorities in each state issue School Leaving Certificates of achievement, based on coursework and exams and roughly equivalent to the British GCSEs, to students leaving school at this stage. Students who leave after year 10 tend to be less academically inclined and will generally seek an apprenticeship or some other form of vocational training. Retention rates for years 11 and 12 are high, with between 70 and 90% of students staying on, depending on the state and prevailing economic conditions. Students who hope to enter tertiary education take public examinations at the end of year 12. These go by different names in each state (in WA, it is the TEE, or Tertiary Entrance Examination; in NSW and Victoria, the HSC, or Higher School Certificate). Students study between five and seven subjects at this level, and these grades are combined to form a tertiary entrance aggregate, which is the sole criterion for entry to university. If your children are likely to be transferring to an Australian University course at this crucial stage, it may be worth them considering the International Baccalaureate as a post high school qualification as this is accepted internationally as an appropriate level for entry by most universities.

The Academic Year. Most schools begin their academic year at either the end of January or the beginning of February, and the year ends before Christmas in December. The year is divided into four ten-week terms, with holidays of approximately two weeks interspersing the middle terms. There are no mid-term breaks or 'half-terms'. Public and religious holidays are observed – students and teachers are given the day off along with the rest of the workforce.

Uniforms. State school education is free from kindergarten to year 12. Parents do have to pay the costs of books and uniforms for state schools, but these are kept at a very low level. Uniform may or may not be compulsory, but is generally favoured by both pupils and parents. Schools try to keep it simple: in summer, shorts and a polo shirt for boys, a cotton dress for girls; in winter, a tracksuit in school colours with a crest on the sweat shirt is most common. Hats, usually of the legionnaire type, are compulsory in years one, two and four, and this policy is strictly enforced. The motto learnt by all small children is 'no hat, no play', and anyone who comes to school without a hat will be kept indoors. Uniform shops are run by most school Parents and Friends' Associations, and the cost of a complete uniform shouldn't break the bank. Trainers are usually worn with winter uniform, and sandals with summer uniform. Flip-flops (known in Australia as thongs) are forbidden. Secondary school students tend to prefer the Australian Akubra-style hats (wide-brimmed and made of felt) or straw hats. Factor 15+ sunscreen is provided free to all primary school students, and you should make sure your child goes to school with some on. It will be re-applied during the day by teachers.

Independent and Private Education. Australia's 900-odd independent, or private, schools account for over 300,000 pupils, approximately 10% of enrolments in Australia. Around two thirds of overseas students in Australian schools are enrolled in private schools. Such schools are becoming an increasingly popular choice, despite the often considerable expenses involved. Private school fees usually begin at around $4,000 per year per child, but may go up to as much as $15,000. Independent schools are usually associated with the various Christian denominations, especially the Catholic Church and the Church of England, and these Christian and Catholic schools tend to charge lower fees than the big independent schools. There are also a number of schools in each state associated with the Baptist Church and non-denominational churches, as well as Jewish and Islamic Schools. Australian Bureau of Statistics surveys have shown that between 1999 and 2000 there was an increase of around 11% in the numbers of children enrolled in independent rather than state schools, concurrent with the closure of a significant number of state schools deemed to be suffering from 'falling rolls'. Many parents believe that their children will receive an enhanced education at private school, as the teacher-student ratio is usually lower. Class sizes in Australian schools average 30 students, but may be higher or lower than this, depending on the state budget and resources. Upper-school classes also tend to be much smaller, and in private schools the upper-school class sizes are often as low as 15-20 students, while in state schools the size is more often around 18-25. There are, however, some outstanding state schools which consistently achieve standards of excellence in academic, sporting and creative fields. Information about special programmes is available from the local Education Authority, via the Department of

Education, Science and Training in your state or territory, and rankings of academic excellence are published annually in the press.

Extra Curricular Activities. Australian students generally participate in a number of extra curricular school activities, which typically include camps, excursions, environmental groups and sports. Most schools have a concert band or orchestra, a choir, a dance troupe and drama society, which rehearse and perform throughout the year. Government schools provide free music tuition to certain children who have been recognised as talented after testing in years 3,4, and 6. Once selected, children receive tuition and an instrument through to year 12, as well as specialist ensemble opportunities.

Entry of New Arrivals. If you have children currently enrolled in the education system at home, you should bring with you recent school reports, including a reference from their teacher or head teacher. Samples of their work will also help the school assess the appropriate grade for your child. Ordinarily, children are placed in a year commensurate with the age of their peer group. Children who are significantly in advance of or behind the level of work being done by other children of the same age may be placed according to their ability. It is rare for a child to be placed with children more than a year older or younger. The difference in the commencement of the academic year can create problems in choosing the right level – the Australian academic year beginning in January/February.

Parents' and Citizens' Committees in Schools. Parents can expect to be more involved in their children's education than they may have been previously. Every Australian school has its own Parents' & Citizens' Committee (P&C), sometimes known as Parents' and Friends', which consists of parents, teachers and student representatives. These committees raise funds for school excursions or tours, school equipment, and assist in the administration of some aspects of school life, such as the canteen. The Australian school canteen is quite different to the school canteen system back home, as hot lunches are rarely supplied. Australians do not eat a large meal in the middle of the day due to the heat. Instead, school canteens are more like subsidised sandwich shops, and sell sandwiches, rolls, salads, pies, some sweet items, and drinks. Many P&C committees have designed healthy, economical and tasty lunch menus which have seen chips and crisps banned in favour of less fattening alternatives. P&C committees also decide on issues such as school uniform, homework policies and behaviour management policies.

Student Councils. Most schools no longer operate a prefect system in which certain children are appointed to school office by the teachers or head. Instead, in primary schools, all year sevens are given special responsibilities, and heads of sporting houses are elected by the student body. In secondary school, there will usually be a school council, consisting of representatives elected by each year group at the end of the previous year, who meet and advise school staff of student needs and problems, and who carry designated responsibilities. In general, schools try and operate an open and democratic process in the appointment of student officers, who in turn take their responsibilities seriously.

Further Education

Universities. The university academic year follows the calendar year, and teaching usually takes place between March and November. The university year is 'semesterised', and both semesters are divided into two halves by a one-week 'study break'. Enrolments usually take place in December of the year prior to commencement, but application must be made through the student's school to the state tertiary admissions centre by the August before final public examinations are undertaken. Australia's tertiary education sector has been undergoing a process of overhaul during the last decade, mainly for budgetary reasons. The most significant change has been that institutions which were established as technical colleges or colleges of further education have now acquired university status. This has created a divided system, with a group of six universities – the universities of Sydney, Melbourne, Adelaide, Western Australia, Queensland and Tasmania – acquiring a kind of 'Ivy League' status; a prestigious second level of long established polytechnic-type universities, such as the University of NSW, Curtin and RMIT; thirdly, a group of respectable but lesser institutions such as Murdoch University and the University of New England; and lastly, the ex-technical colleges, like Edith Cowan University. There is a constant scrabble amongst the various institutions for research funding, and rankings are very important. Although officially all on a par, there is no doubt that in the perception of the public, employers, and overseas institutions considering students for postgraduate research, there remain clear differences in the levels of academic excellence attained by these institutions and competition for entry to the top two levels is always intense. Australian universities offer a wide choice of subjects and qualifications. Currently, for a population of 19.5 million, there are 42 universities. The vast majority of tertiary institutions are funded by a combination of state and federal grants, however, public investment in university teaching and learning on a per student basis, with the exception of a period in the early 1990's has been declining since 1983. Nevertheless, in spite of changes in the funding system, Australian tertiary education remains financially accessible to all.

A report by the Organisation for Economic Co-operation and Development (OECD) has ranked Australia fourth behind the USA, Finland and Japan for entry into full-time tertiary education and also fourth, behind Canada, Norway and the USA, in the percentage of graduates produced. The report also found that of all degrees awarded, engineering accounts for approximately 5.3 per cent of degrees conferred by Australian institutions compared with 22.8 per cent in Japan, 18.9 per cent in Germany and 7.1 per cent in the USA (the OECD average is 12.1 percent). In natural sciences, however, Australia is a world leader with 14.1 per cent compared with 9.1 per cent in Germany, 4.7 per cent in the USA and 2.9 per cent in Japan.

Fees and Other Costs. Until 1989, tertiary education for was absolutely free for all students regardless of means. By 1990, however, budgetary constraints had forced a rethink on this sacred cow of education policy, and the system was changed so that students became liable for fees under the Higher Education Contributions Scheme (HECS). Under HECS, students who are Australian citizens, New Zealand citizens, or Australian permanent residents must pay a *part* of the cost of their further education, with the Commonwealth meeting the balance. Merit-based 'equity scholarships' are available to students in every state, which exempt them from meeting this contribution. The HECS contribution is a nominal sum, the precise amount of which varies according to a very complex formula derived from the type and combination of units a student studies. Subjects such as medicine and engineering attract more HECS than humanities courses. The HECS contribution can be met in one of two ways: either by payment up-front at the start of each semester, which attracts a 25% discount; or by 'deferral', in which case the government pays the contribution on behalf of the student. If a student chooses the deferral option, the debt must eventually be repaid once the student is in full time employment. Graduates begin repaying their loans when their income reaches $22,346 (2000-01 figures), and payments are deducted in the form of a tax levy of between three and six percent. Compulsory repayments increase as the income increases, and the debt is usually painlessly paid off within a few years. Students who opt to complete an additional honours year on top of pass degree may be eligible for HECS exemption for that year, which is known as a HECS scholarship. There is no interest charged on HECS debts, but the debt is indexed annually to bring it in line with the cost of living. The adjustment is made on the first of June each year and applies to the portion of debt which remains unpaid.

In addition to tuition fees, students must meet the costs of their own textbooks, which may be between $200 and $1,000 per year depending on the course, however, most institutions have good second hand bookshops where texts may be purchased more cheaply. Students are also charged fees to join their student organisations, known as unions, associations or guilds. These organisations provide and are involved in the administration of a large number of benefits, including sporting facilities, discounts, the issuing of student identification cards, insurance cover, photocopying, bookshops, catering, social functions such as balls, and student newspapers. Membership costs range from $65-$300 per annum. Until recently, membership of a university's student union was compulsory (except for conscientious objectors, who could choose to have their dues paid to a charity instead); however, in 1995, government legislation, aimed at weakening a united student voice in the light of controversial changes in the higher education sector, made it illegal to require compulsory membership. As a result, student unions now battle to attract new members, and are able to provide fewer benefits to students because of their diminished income.

Choosing a University. Selecting a university can be difficult, and most capital cities have a number of different institutions from which to choose. Every institution and department publishes a prospectus, and university libraries will usually hold a number of these from a range of universities across the country, and careful consideration of these will give a good idea of what is on offer. Most universities have an officer who deals with enquiries from prospective students, and schools will always offer careful guidance on appropriate institutions and courses. The Australian Department of Education, Science and Training runs a website (www.dest.gov.au/ tenfields/) outlining all course and university options available in the country while the publication *The Good Universities Guide* (www.thegoodguides.com.au) covers all 42 universities in Australia, giving a brief summary of each, including breadth of course offerings, depth, flexibility of admissions policy, mature-age opportunities, student-staff ratios, gender balance, research track record, affluence, graduate salaries, employment prospects, library quality, popularity with fee paying students and tuition fees. Details of various courses run by the different institutions, the entry marks required for each course, and entry procedures for the various courses are also given as well as a rating of Australia's top ten universities and details of comparative graduate employment rates and starting salaries. Annual rankings of the nation's university are published in *The Australian*, as well as most city newspapers. Year after year, the top performing institutions include the Universities of Melbourne, Sydney, Western Australia, and NSW, Monash and Macquarie Universities, RMIT, and ANU (the Australian National University in Canberra).

Student Funding and Loans. Australian university students usually survive financially on scholarships, part-time jobs, their parents (about 50 per cent of all university students still live with their parents throughout their academic careers), the Youth Allowance, or a combination of all of these. Until July 1998, eligible students were funded by a national educational grant system known as Austudy. Only about 33% of students received Austudy, which was designed as an income support scheme rather than a full living allowance. Many students were not eligible for any Austudy allowance whatsoever on the basis of their parents' income, and relatively few were eligible for the full Austudy allowance. Austudy for students aged between 18 and 24 years has now been replaced by the Youth Allowance, a single payment made to all eligible young people and replacing not only Austudy but also the dole and other social security benefits. The Allowance is still subject to parental means test, but offers some advantages to students over the old system, insofar as they are now also eligible for rent assistance (up to the value of $90.60 per fortnight for a single adult with no dependents). An interest-free loan of $500 is also available.

A pared-down version of Austudy remains in force for students over the age of 25. Eligibility for Austudy, and the amount which a mature or independent student can receive under the scheme depends upon enrolment in an approved full-time course (almost all university courses are approved), and on the applicant's income and assets, and, if applicable, those of his or her spouse. If you receive Austudy, you are also allowed to earn an income of up to $6,136 per annum without affecting your allowance. If you earn above this amount, your Austudy payments will be reduced proportionately. The Austudy supplement provides further funding through a government-sponsored personal loan, the Student Financial Assistance Scheme. Note that while Austudy is a *grant*, the Austudy Supplement is a *loan*, and although it can help students in need, many choose not to take it up as repayment conditions are onerous.

TAFE. Tertiary education is also available at Technical and Further Education Centres (TAFEs) which offer vocationally orientated qualifications. There are approximately 250 TAFE institutions in Australia, but many of these have additional affiliated campuses, training centres and ancillary teaching centres. Every state and territory has a large number of TAFE colleges and centres, in both capital cities and major regional areas. More than a million students are enrolled in TAFE courses, though many of these are part-time students. Many school leavers who want to upgrade their skills or adults who wish to retrain or re-enter the workforce study at TAFEs either on a full-time or part-time basis. TAFEs specialise in training and pre-apprenticeships in a diverse range of trades, including building, the vehicle, metal, electrical and automotive trades, electronics, plumbing, printing, catering, gardening, dairy farming, hairdressing, textiles, jewellery and watch-making, and secretarial and business studies. Both evening and day classes are usually available for most courses. School Certificate and Higher School Certificate subjects are also available for mature students who may be aiming for university entrance. TAFEs also offer literacy and numeracy classes, as well as English as a Foreign Language for migrants and other new arrivals. There are also a number of short-term, part-time courses available in subjects like bar service, typing, commercial floristry and woolclassing. In a recent survey conducted by the National Centre for Vocational Education, nearly 87 percent of TAFE students rated their lecturer's knowledge of course content and teaching skills, and their general level of satisfaction, very highly.

The cost of attending a TAFE is significantly lower than university. Fee-exemptions are given to students in receipt of Youth Allowance or Austudy, and there are concession rates for low-income earners. TAFE students do not pay HECS. Usually TAFE colleges will allow you to pay fees in instalments.

Overseas Students at Australian Universities

Australian universities rely increasingly on overseas students for a proportion of their funding. Southeast Asian students make up a significant proportion of enrolments, and are concentrated in faculties offering business, commerce and economics, with some entering medicine and law. The latest figures from Australian Education International, the government agency promoting Australian education abroad, show that between 1999 and 2000 the number of international students studying within the higher education sector in Australia was around 107,622. Around half of these were studying at a secondary level, attending short intensive English language courses (ELICOS) in public or private institutions, enrolled on TAFE courses, or preparing for university on special bridging courses. The remainder were attending university courses. The number of overseas students attending Australian universities has grown incredibly in the over the years, and some universities now hold graduation ceremonies in Singapore and Kuala Lumpur to cater for their Southeast Asian alumni. The Australian government requires all institutions which accept overseas students to register with state authorities to assure continuing high standards of management and education.

If you wish to enter Australia to study, you will need to apply for a Student Visa, and this cannot be issued until you can provide evidence that you have been accepted for a course of study and have paid half the first year's annual fee for your course. It is important to note that you cannot change from Visitor status to Student status while you are in Australia, and that application for a Student Visa can only be made in your own country of residence. In order to retain your visa, you must have a satisfactory record of attendance at your institution, and achieve satisfactory academic results. Upon completion of your course, you must leave Australia before your Student Visa expires, and the Australian Government offers no leniency in this area.

Overseas students do not receive the privileges of government-funded education as offered to Australian citizens and permanent residents. Universities vary considerably in the fees that they charge overseas students, and costs are determined by the demand for the course, the location of the institution, and its level of prestige. The government sets a minimum fee structure for each course, but institutions are free to charge above this level, and frequently do. Fees vary considerably between disciplines and are subject to regular revision: as a general rule, you should expect a humanities degree to cost in the region of $14,000 per annum, a science degree to cost around $18,000, and professional courses like medicine and engineering, anything up to $40,000 a year. Various grants and scholarships may be available depending on your qualifications and circumstances. Individual institutions will have information about these.

Most universities have student accommodation associated with the campus, and overseas students will receive help in finding housing and settling in generally. Establishment costs have been estimated by the University of Sydney to be around $900, and annual living costs for a single student to be around $16,000 taking in rent, food, travel expenses and 'entertainment' costs. Australian universities are committed to equity policies, and seek to provide an environment of equal opportunity, free from discrimination, for all students and staff. They will make special arrangements for students with disabilities, and usually provide good childcare facilities for students with children.

Overseas Student Societies. Most universities have student-run societies which cater for overseas students from specific countries and regions. These associations organise camps, social functions, speakers and orientation programmes, and will also offer assistance if you contact them before you arrive at the institution. Your university will supply you with contact names for appropriate on-campus student organisations. Universities in Australia are completely free from religious discrimination, and those with large overseas student populations, like the University of Western Australia, provide worship facilities for most major religious groups.

Useful Addresses

Australian Education International, International, Analysis and Evaluation Division, Department of Education, Science and Training, GPO Box 9880, Canberra City ACT 2601, Australia; www.studyinaustralia.gov.au

EdNA Online, www.edna.edu.au. EdNA Online is funded by the Australian federal and state governments. It provides information about education and training in Australia and a database of Internet resources useful for teaching and learning.

Studylink, www.studylink.com.au. An internet based directory exploring higher and vocational educational courses in Australia.

The Commonwealth Department of Education, Science and Training,16-18 Mort Street, Canberra, ACT 2600; ☎02-6240 8111; www.dest.gov.au

State Tertiary Admissions Centres:

NSW & ACT. Universities Admissions Centre (UAC) Pty Ltd, Quad 2, Australia Centre, 8 Parkview Drive, Homebush Bay, NSW ; Postal address: UAC, Locked Bag 112, Silverwater NSW 2128; ☎02-9330 7200; www.uac.edu.au

NT. Students must apply direct to The Northern Territory University, Uni Info Shop, Darwin, NT 0909; ☎08-8946 7766 or 1-800 061 963 (Toll Free); www.ntu.edu.au

QLD. Queensland Tertiary Admissions Centre, Level 2, 33 Park Road, Milton QLD 4064; Postal address: QTAC, PO Box 1331, Milton QLD 4064; ☎07-3368 1166; www.qtac.edu.au

SA. South Australian Tertiary Admissions Centre (SATAC), 4th Floor,104 Frome Street, Adelaide SA 5000; Postal Address: SATAC, PO Box 2, Rundle Mall, Adelaide, SA 5000; ☎08-8224 4000; www.satac.edu.au

TAS. Students must apply directly to The Admissions Office, University of Tasmania, GPO Box 252-45, Hobart, TAS 7001; ☎03-6226 7151 or 1 800 030 955 (Toll Free); www.utas.edu.au

VIC. Victorian Tertiary Admissions Centre (VTAC), 40 Park Street, South Melbourne VIC 3205; ☎1300 364 133; www.vtac.edu.au

WA. Tertiary Institutions Service Centre (TISC), 39 Fairway, Nedlands WA 6009; ☎08-9347 8000; www.tisc.edu.au

TAFE:

NSW. TAFE Information Centre, 47 York Street, Sydney NSW 2000; ☎131 601; www.tafensw.edu.au

QLD/NT. There are no central information centres, but information can be obtained directly from your nearest college. College contact numbers are found in the government section at the

beginning of the telephone directory.
SA. TAFE Information Centre, Da
Costa Arcade, Shop 4, GHD Building
Adelaide SA; Postal Address: GPO
Box 819, Adelaide, SA 5001; ☎1800
882 661; www.tafe.sa.gov.au
Tas. Institute of TAFE Tasmania, GPO
Box 2015, Hobart TAS 7001; ☎1300
655 307; www.tafe.tas.edu.au
VIC. The TAFE Virtual Campus;

☎1800 896 122; www.tafevc.com.au.
Also available is the TAFE Course
Line; ☎131 823 (freecall within VIC
only) or 03-9637 2203.
WA. Training Info Centre, Ground
Floor, Albert Facey House, 469-489
Wellington Street, Perth WA 6000;
☎08-9325 9322 or 1-800 999 167
freecall).

Youth Allowance and Austudy: Telephone the enquires line on freecall 132 490 for
information.

International Schools

International Baccalaureate Schools are becoming increasingly common in Australia,
and most capitals have at least one. A regional list of the schools offering the IB
is given below. A complete list of such schools in Australia can be found on the
International Baccalaureate Organization's website (www.ibo.org).

NSW
S.C.E.C.G.S Redlands, 272 Military Road,
Cremorne, New South Wales 2090;
☎(02) 9909 3133; fax (02) 9909 3228;
www.redlands.nsw.edu.au

SA
Glenunga International High School,
L'Estrange Street, Gelnunga, South
Australia 5064; ☎(08) 8379 5629; fax
(08) 8338 2518; www.gihs.sa.edu.au
Mercedes College, 540 Fullarton Road,
Springfield, South Australia 5062;
☎(08) 8379 6844; fax (08) 8379 9540;
www.mercedes.adl.catholic.edu.au
Pembroke School ,18 Holden Street, Kensington Park, South Australia 5063;
☎(08) 8366 6245; fax (08) 8364 1525;
www.pembroke.sa.edu.au

VIC
Lauriston Girls' School, 38 Huntingtower
Road, Armadale, Victoria 3143;
☎(03) 9864 7555; fax (03) 9822 7950;
www.lauriston.vic.edu.au
Wesley College, 620 High Street Road, Glen
Waverley, Melbourne, Victoria 3150;

☎(03) 9881 5394; fax (03) 9886 3276;
www.wesleycollege.net
Presbyterian Ladies' College, 141 Burwood
Highway, Burwood, Victoria 3125;
☎(03) 9808 5811; fax (03) 9808 5998;
www.plc.vic.edu.au
St. Leonard's College, 163 South Road,
Brighton East, Victoria 3187;
☎(03) 9592 2266; fax (03) 9592
3439; www.stleonards.vic.edu.au
Tintern Anglican Girls' Grammar School, 90
Alexandra Road, Ringwood East, Victoria 3135; ☎(03) 9845 7820; fax (03)
9845 7713; www.tintern.vic.edu.au

WA
Montessori School Kingsley Inc., PO. Box 194,
Landsdale, Western Australia 6065;
☎(08) 9409 9151; fax (08) 9409 1682.

Useful Publication

Choosing a School (New South Wales,
or Victoria) magazines are available
from the Subscription Department,
Consyl Publishing, 3 Buckhurst
Road, Bexhill-on-Sea, East Sussex
TN40 1QF; ☎01424-223 111; www
.consylpublishing.co.uk

MEDIA AND COMMUNICATIONS

The Australian media provide much the same type of services as in the UK, Europe and the USA. Its film, television and radio output is highly regarded internationally and much of it is distributed overseas (including children's television and art films, along with *Neighbours, Home and Away* and *Mad Max* etc.). Each state has a range of local and regional newspapers, as well as access to the national press. Editorial content is considered to be mostly fair and unbiased, although media monopolies are under constant surveillance to maintain standards and to prevent the exercise of undue political influence. Australians are news-hungry, and newspaper and magazine readership per capita is one of the highest in the world. Most news providers offer a good balance of domestic and international news. In the communications sector, the monopoly of the state-owned Australian Telecom has now given way to a more open market with several providers competing to supply both domestic and business users. The government agency, Australia Post, provides mail and ancillary services to the whole country. Australia has one of the highest proportions of personal computer and mobile telephone ownership in the world and the Internet takeup rate is second only to the USA (consider: population of the USA 286,624,418 people; population of Australia 19.5 million people). As a result, Australian communications are heavily geared to the electronic environment – noticeably more so than in Europe – and most government agencies, schools, television channels, newspapers, and community services have websites on which they post constantly updated information. Even the telephone directories are online and at the touch of a button you can access and search Telstra's telephone databases for both business and residential numbers.

Newspapers

Australian newspapers are largely state, or indeed, capital city-based. There is one national daily newspaper, *The Australian*, owned by Rupert Murdoch's *News Corp*, and sometimes referred to as 'Murdoch's Australian charity'. This broadsheet newspaper is of a calibre equivalent to, say, *The Times* or *The Guardian* in Britain, but like most broadsheet newspapers, it fights a continuing battle for profitability. *The Australian*'s weekend sister publication, *The Weekend Australian*, is similar in style and, as with broadsheet weekend papers, comes groaning with additional arts, lifestyle, sports and business sections. Apart from the omnipresent Rupert Murdoch, the other big player in Australia's newspaper industry is Fairfax Holdings. This group publishes respected major titles including *The Sydney Morning Herald, The Age* (both broadsheets, from Sydney and Melbourne respectively), *The Sun-Herald*, and *Business Review Weekly* and *The Australian Financial Review*, the Australian equivalent of *The Financial Times*. Currently, Sydney, Melbourne and Brisbane all have at least three major daily newspapers, and other capitals and major regional centres have at least two. In addition, almost every area has a local community newspaper (usually weekly, and often of very high quality).

Expats can keep up with news from home which may not make the international new pages of the Australian press by subscribing to weekly news digests from home or by logging on to home newspaper websites. *The International Express*, sold throughout Australia and New Zealand, is the international sister paper of the *Express* and *Express on Sunday* and has the same tabloid format and human-interest focus. It is printed in Sydney, Melbourne and Perth, and is available in Australia from local newsagents. A six-month subscription costs $90 and is available by writing to:

International Publishing Group; PO Box 107, Sydney NSW 2001 or by e-mailing sub scriptions@theinternationalexpress.com. The *Guardian Weekly* is also widely available and offers a selection of higher-brow articles and features in English derived from the previous week's *Guardian, Washington Post* and *Le Monde*. Subscriptions are available from: The General Manager (The Guardian Weekly, 164 Deansgate, Manchester M3 3GG; ☎0870 066 0510; fax 0161 876 5362; www.guardianweekly.com). In Australia subscriptions to the *Guardian Weekly* can be taken out by writing to PO Box 70, Sydney, NSW 2001; ☎+612 9543 7616; fax +612 9543 8842 or by e-mailing australia @guardianweekly.com.

Addresses of the major Australian newspapers are given below:

NSW

Sydney Morning Herald, 201 Sussex Street, Sydney, NSW 2000; ☎02-9282 2833; www.smh.com.au

The Australian, 2 Holt Street, Surry Hills, NSW 2010; Postal address: GPO Box 4245 Sydney NSW 2001; ☎02-9288-3000; fax 02-9288-2250; www.theaust ralian.news.com.au

The Australian Financial Review, 201 Sussex Street, NSW 2007; ☎02-9282 2833; www.afr.com.au

The Daily Telegraph, 2 Holt Street, Surry Hills, NSW 2010; ☎02-9288 3000; fax 02-9288 2300; www.dailytelegraph.news.com.au

QLD

The Courier Mail, 41 Campbell Street, Bowen Hills, QLD 4006; ☎07-3666 8000; www.couriermail.news,com.au

VIC

The Age, 250 Spencer Street, Melbourne, VIC 3000; ☎03-9600 4211; www.theage.com.au

The Herald, 40 City Road, Southbank, VIC 3000; ☎03-9292 2000; fax 03-9292 2002.

The Weekly Times, 40 City Road, Southbank, VIC 3000; ☎03-9292 2000; fax 03-9292 2002; www.theweeklytimes.com.au

WA

Sunday Times, 34 Stirling Street, Perth, WA 6000; ☎08-9326 8326; www.sun daytimes.newsltd.com.au

The West Australian, Newspaper House, 50 Hasler Road, Osborne Park, WA, 6017; ☎08-9482 3111; www.thewest.com.au

Australian Magazines

IPC ACP Magazines Australia Pty Ltd, Stockland House Level 2, 181 Castlereagh Street, Sydney, NSW 2000; ☎02-9288 9600; fax 02-9283 4849; www.acp.com.au. The IPC-ACP produces Australian magazines such as *Women's Weekly, Street Machine* etc. and has a London office, IPC Media Ltd., King's Reach Tower, Stamford Street, London SE1 9LS; ☎0870-4445000; www.ipc.co.uk

Magazines

The Australian Woman's Weekly is the most popular Australian women's magazine. Don't be misled by the name; this is a *monthly* magazine. When this long-standing publication underwent a makeover, including name change, a couple of decades ago, they decided against 'The Australian Woman's Monthly' as a title – for obvious reasons! The quality of this magazine is unmatched and its readership and circulation make it the most widely read magazine in the history of Australian publishing. It is particularly famous for its outstanding cooking sections, and Australian Consolidated Press publish a continually updated range of cookbooks developed by the magazine staff. It is said that you can never go wrong with a *Woman's Weekly* recipe. The cover price of the *Woman's Weekly* is $4.95. Australian editions of *Woman's Day, New Idea, Vogue, Cosmopolitan* and *Marie Claire* are available in all newsagents and most supermarkets, and there are innumerable special interest publications, such as *Australian Gourmet Traveller* and *House and Garden*, which are also of very high quality. The *Business Review Weekly* is probably the most important financial magazine, roughly equivalent to the *Economist* (which is available in good newsagents), and the main domestic current affairs magazine is *The Bulletin*, which incorporates the American publication, *Newsweek*. *The Bulletin* is an old and prestigious publication, particularly well regarded for its efforts to foster new writing, especially poetry. Most international magazines with any significant level of circulation, such as *Time* and *National Geographic* are widely available, although their cover price may reflect import costs where special Australian editions are not printed.

Books and Bookshops

Books in Australia used to be expensive but are now pretty much equivalent in price to those in Britain and the USA. All major publishers distribute in Australia, although if you are looking for something unusual you may have to order. Scholarly publications and new hardcover releases tend, however, to be expensive in Australia. There is also a significant Australian publishing industry, and much highly regarded fiction is currently being written there, and meeting with international success. Peter Carey, for instance, has won the Booker Prize twice for *Oscar and Lucinda* (1988) and *True History of the Kelly Gang* (2001) and Thomas Keneally won the Booker Prize in 1982 for *Schindler's Ark*, which was later filmed as *Schindler's List*. Large bookshops are found in all Australian cities, including a number of chains, such as Dymocks, and Angus & Robertson; there are also many smaller independent booksellers. The 'book café' has recently arrived in Australia and proved a popular innovation. Book cafés, as the name suggests, incorporate a small, high quality café in amongst the books, where people can meet for coffee, or just enjoy a break while they browse.

Book clubs and reading groups are hugely popular, and most cities will have hundreds of these small, informal groups which meet monthly for friendship and literary discussion: book cafes provide both a venue for meetings, as well as a selection of new texts for the next get-together.

Some specialist bookstores are listed below:
All Arts Bookshop, Woollahra Antiques Centre, 160 Oxford Street, Woollahra, NSW 2025; ☎02-9328 6744; www.allarts.com.au. Collectors' reference books on antiques, Australian, Asian and tribal art. Phone and mail order.
Angus & Robertson Bookworld, 195 Murray Street, Perth, WA 6000; ☎08-9325 5622; www.angusrobertson.com.au. Stores Australia-wide.
Boffins Bookshop, 806 Hay St, Perth 6000; ☎(08) 9321 5755; fax (08) 9321 5744; www.boffinsbookshop.com.au. Technical and specialist books. Computer access to over one million USA, UK, NZ and Australian books in print. Local and overseas special orders.
Dymocks Booksellers, 705-707 Hay Street Mall, Perth 6000; ☎(08) 9321 3949; fax 481 1964; www.dymocks.com.au. Interstate franchise with comprehensive range of general, technical and education books. Computer access to over 100,000 titles. Will obtain any book in print.

Television

Many television watchers are probably as familiar with Australian television productions as Australians themselves. Series such as *Burke's Backyard*, *Neighbours*, *Home and Away*, *A Country Practice* and the *Flying Doctors* are all regularly broadcast at home, and indeed, the popular soaps *Neighbours* and *Home and Away* have a much higher profile in Britain than in their country of origin, so that Australians visiting the UK are often bemused by fervent requests for updates on the latest from downunder. Other famous TV exports include Clive James and Dame Edna Everage, and the majority of children will tell you about *Bananas in Pyjamas* or *The Ferals*.

There are four main channels broadcasting nationwide. The Australian Broadcasting Commission (ABC) operates Channel Two, and is equivalent to the BBC. The ABC is funded by the federal government and provides commercial-free television and radio throughout the country. Advertisements for forthcoming features are screened only at the end of programmes. The three other channels, Seven, Nine and Ten, are commercially owned and operated networks which broadcast around Australia and like commercial television elsewhere in the world they are funded by advertising, the airing of which tends to be fairly frequent.

Although the channels are operated by national networks both advertising and news output tends to be state-specific. In very remote areas, it may only be possible to receive Channel Two and perhaps one other commercial channel specifically aimed at country viewers such as, in Western Australia, GWN (Golden West Network).

The Special Broadcasting Service (SBS) provides multi-lingual and multicultural broadcasting (both television and radio) across the country. It is specifically designed for viewers of ethnic origins, and regularly broadcasts foreign language films. SBS is an optional channel for which you will require a special receiver or antennae. The SBS antennae can usually be installed cheaply enough but these days most houses will already have one fitted. Many people consider that the SBS news is the best available on Australian television, with a high international news content and in-depth analysis. SBS also broadcasts minority and international domestic sports coverage, and is a good way to keep up with your favourite teams back home. Weather forecasts on Australian television in general are more detailed and meteorologically sophisticated than those at home.

The best British and American television productions all come to Australian television, and you will not have to miss out on *Friends*, *The X-Files*, *Sex and the City* or any other favourites. Australian television is ratings-dominated, and during ratings periods the television programming is outstanding, with the best films and series from around the world competing for your attention and the advertising dollar. At other less crucial times, programming may be more mundane but sports coverage tends, in general, to be very good. The government requires a certain percentage of Australian-produced output (which must *not* be cheap-to-make games shows and the like), so that there is always a good flow of new and interesting local productions.

Cable and satellite television are available in Australia, with cable far more widespread than satellite. The channels available are exactly the same as in the UK or the USA: Nickelodeon, the Disney Channel, MTV, CNN, UK Gold, the Movie Channel, and so on. Cable networks are operated by Foxtel (another Murdoch venture), and Optus Vision. Subscription rates are around $40-$50 per month. There are also satellite stations available by subscription, which once again broadcast much the same international fare as the cable channels. The majority of Australians do not yet subscribe to pay channels but the takeup rate is growing all the time. Most do, however, own a video, and increasingly a DVD player, and video rental shops are found in every high street. Videos and DVDs are cheap to hire and many stores offer special rental deals. A new release video will cost approximately $7 to hire for 24 hours, and older movies can be rented for up to a week from as little as $3.

Television programmes are advertised daily in local newspapers, and a weekly lift-out programme guide, usually in magazine format, is available in the weekend papers. There is a TV listings guides, *TV Week*, which is produced in different editions for the different states (due to the time zones across Australia programme schedules differ throughout the country).

Probably the most important difference between Australian and British television is that there is no television licensing system. Naturally, you must pay for your own television sets and antennae, but you may have as many televisions in your home or business as you like and you do not have to pay for the privilege of watching them. The Australian Broadcasting Commission is funded from taxation revenue and no further charge is made for broadcasting services.

Radio

The Australian Broadcasting Commission owns and runs four national radio networks which can be received Australia-wide and one international radio service. They are renowned for their excellent news coverage. Radio National is the ABC's general current affairs and talk station, and is middle to highbrow in its orientation. It produces programmes such as *The Science Show*, *The Law Report*, and *The Book Programme*, as well as daily drama, book readings, interviews etc. It also has a classical music station, and supports an orchestra in each state. The Australian airwaves have been deregulated for decades and across Australia there are over 100 commercial stations on the AM band, more than 50 commercial FM stations, over 200 community radio stations, run by universities, ethnic groups etc., and Aborigine-run radio stations which service the outback regions. Radio stations are often advertised on car bumper stickers, on television and in the newspapers, so it is easy to find something to your taste and tune in. Australians own nearly 30 million radio receivers and most households own four or more radios.

Film Industry

The Australian film industry has been thriving for the last thirty years, and is one of Australia's major cultural exports. The Australian Film Commission assists in the growth of this industry by aiding project development through script, pre-production assistance grant giving, and international promotion. The government is keen to support a vigorous and diverse cultural environment, and this is reflected in Australian films, which find a big audience both at home and abroad. Recent hits have included Baz Luhrmann's *Moulin Rouge*, *Muriel's Wedding*, *The Castle* and *Shine* and Australian actors are a big feature of Hollywood these days. All the big international releases find their way to Australian cinemas, generally about six months before they hit the screens in Britain. Film-going is a popular pastime, and tickets cost about $10. In some cities, certain weeknights are 'concession nights', with all tickets costing under $6, and this has greatly boosted mid-week sales. In the summer months, the Festival of Perth hosts the *Lotteries Film Season* which shows art-house movies at the two outdoor venues of the Somerville Auditorium in Crawley and the Joondalup Pines Picture Garden at Edith Cowan University. It is one of the great pleasures of life in Perth to take a picnic to the Somerville at dusk and sit in a deck chair under the pine trees by the banks of the Swan River, sharing a bottle of wine and watching a movie.

Post

The Australia postal service is owned and run by the Australian Government, and in general provides excellent services. Post offices and PostShops are open from 9am to 5pm Monday to Friday, and 9-11 am on Saturdays, but are closed on Sundays and public holidays. Letters between Australia and the UK and the USA take between four-seven days to arrive, and parcels take between seven and ten days. The cost of postage for a letter to Britain or the USA is $1.50, and an aerogramme costs $1. Sea mail and Surface Air Lifted (SAL) mail services are also available at a significantly cheaper cost, but are, naturally, much slower services. Most people send parcels SAL or Sea mail, particularly Christmas parcels, and Australia Post issues a list of send-by dates for guaranteed pre-Christmas delivery all over the world. To send parcels back home in time for Christmas, the send-by date is usually at the beginning of October. Australia Post also offers a cheaper rate for Christmas cards, which should be in unsealed envelopes marked 'card only', and there is a different send-by date for international cards, usually four weeks before Christmas. There is no division between first and second-class services for local letters, but only one standard service and cost. Local letters cost 45 cents and it usually takes one working day to deliver letters posted within the same metropolitan area, or two working days if the letter is from outside the metropolitan region or from interstate. Mail is usually delivered once a day from Monday to Friday in metropolitan regions, but in remote and/or rural regions the mail may only be delivered once a week and can also often be delayed by adverse conditions such as flooding, torrential rain or even snow. There is no Saturday delivery. Mailboxes are located at the front of properties, and mail is never delivered through a slot in the front door. In the case of blocks of flats, there is usually a structure containing one letterbox for every flat, at the front entrance to the property. In some urban areas, it can be wise to lock your mailbox with a small padlock if it is in a communal block, as your mail is not otherwise secure.

Australia Post deals with around 4 billion letters per year and seeks to maintain a uniform standard letter service at a uniform price. It has a 'community service obligation' to fulfil this mandate. As well as letter services, Australia Post offers a telephone bill paying service. It has a website at **www.auspost.com.au** where you can assess your postage costs, locate postcode numbers, find out about services and special offers, and check the location of your nearest office or agency.

If you intend to travel extensively through Australia during your stay, it is possible to have letters and parcels sent to you at any office of Australia Post using the international postal convention of Poste Restante. Providing it is clearly addressed with your name and the words *Poste Restante*, followed by the name and address of the post office, the letter/parcel will be held for up to a month during which time you may, upon producing proof of your identity, collect it. If the letter or parcel is not claimed within a month, it will be returned to the sender. For travellers, there are also private mail holding and forwarding services available, which can be useful if you have no permanent address. These services work on a membership basis, so that after paying a joining fee you are then able to call the service from anywhere in Australia to check if there is any mail or messages for you. The service will then forward your mail/messages to your present address.

Useful Addresses

A privately owned travellers' mail service is operated by the *Travellers' Contact Point,* Level 7, 428 George Street, Sydney NSW 2000; ☎ 02-9221 8744; www.travellers.com.au

The main Australian post offices (known as GPOs) are at:

ACT   53-73 Alinga Street, Canberra, ACT 2601
NSW   1 Martin Place, Sydney NSW 2000
NT   31-33 Hartley Street, Alice Springs, NT 0870
          48 Cavenagh Street, Darwin, NT 0800
QLD   Shop A6,366-370 Shute Harbour Road, Airlie Beach, QLD 4802
          261 Queen Street, Brisbane QLD 4000
          13 Grafton Street, Cairns QLD 4870
          Paradise Centre Shop 112, 2-10 Cavill Avenue, Surfers Paradise, QLD 4217
          Shop 1, Shaws Arcade, Sturt Street, Townsville, QLD 4810
SA   141 King William Street, Adelaide SA 5000
TAS   9 Elizabeth Street, Hobart, TAS 7000
          68 Cameron Road, Launceston, TAS 7250
VIC   410 Elizabeth Street, Melbourne, VIC 3000
WA   Ground Floor, 3-7 Forest Place, Perth WA 6000

Telephones

The Australian telecommunications sector was deregulated in 1997 and the monopoly of Australian Telecom has now given way to a new era of competition. The national government-owned provider has been 'rebranded' as Telstra, and its major competitor is Optus. To have a telephone line connected to your new residence, you should contact either of these two providers, who will supply you with your new phone number. If you connect with Optus, you can still receive and make calls to Telstra numbers, and vice versa. New customers are not usually required to pay a deposit (unless they have a bad credit rating), and fully itemised bills are sent quarterly. There is a constant battle to provide the cheapest international calling rates, and if you expect to make a lot of overseas calls, it is worth watching the newspapers for special offers, such as Telstra's '0018 Easy Half Hours' package where customers pay for the first half hour block of a call and the next half hour block is free. Using this service calls to the USA or the UK will cost you $5.25 for an hour's chat. In addition, there is an ever-increasing number of international call providers, who offer exceptionally low rates, and these also advertise extensively in newspapers. If you see a special deal with, say, Telstra, and you are an Optus customer, you can still take advantage of it by prefixing your call with a special dialing code (which will be clearly stated in the advertisement). You will then receive a separate bill from the service you have been using at the end of each quarter.

Local calls in Australia are not charged on a timed basis – a single connection charge of around 25 cents on a domestic phone allows you to talk all day if you want to; similarly, phone calls made for the purpose of connecting to the internet are also charged on a connection-only basis, making web-time much more economical in Australia than in many other countries where you are charged for time spent on-line.

Telstra's most popular value-added products (and Optus offers very similar inducements), are call forwarding, call waiting and faxstream (multi-recipient fax sending), the Telstra telecard, which allows you to automatically charge calls made overseas to your home number, and messageBank, an answering service. The PhoneAway card is a prepaid international and domestic telephone card.

Public Telephones. Public telephones in Australia are very similar to those found in Europe. Local calls cost 40 cents, and STD and international calls are charged according to the rate (determined by the time of day at which you call), distance covered and the length of the call. The telephones accept 10 cent, 20 cent, 50 cent and $1 coins. Many telephones have the facility to accept major credit cards or automatic teller cards from the bigger Australian national banks. Phone cards are also available from newsagents and vending machines in denominations of $5, $10, $20 and $50. STD public telephones are available throughout metropolitan suburbs, outside post offices and in shopping centres. These phones accept all Australian coins, as well as Telstra's Telecard, allow uses to switch from coin to card in mid-phone call if necessary, and have an easy-to-read display providing instructions in four languages. They also feature an adjustable volume level and hearing aid coupler in the handset. The booths are accessible by wheelchair.

If you are British and resident in Australia temporarily or short-term, it may be useful for you to apply to British Telecom for a BT Chargecard. This card is free and means that all calls you make from Australia are charged to your own British account. Contact BT on 0800-345 144 or check the website at www.payphones.bt.com for an application form and further details.

To call the UK from Australia, you will need to dial 0011-44 and then the number, deleting the first 0 from the area code. To send faxes from Australia, the process is the same, except the international prefix is 0015 followed by the country code, area code (minus the 0) and the number. For example, to send a fax to Oxford, the code necessary would be 0015-44 1865 + number. To call Australia from the UK, dial 00-61 followed by the area code (omitting the initial 0 of the area code) and then the number. The procedure for sending a fax to Australia is exactly the same as telephoning. The area codes for major Australian cities are given in the previous section (*Setting Up Home, Utilities*).

The emergency number throughout Australia is 000.

CARS AND MOTORING

The wide roads in Australia and the low risk of hazards such as fog and snow make driving in Australian conditions reasonably easy. City traffic in Australia, as all over the world, is subject to the problems of congestion and tortuous one-way systems, but the suburban and country roads are usually excellent. In more remote areas the roads are often rough dirt or gravel surfaces best suited to rugged four-wheel drive vehicles. These are also the only vehicles suited to the tough conditions of the outback. Even in comparatively populated rural areas, apart from main roads and highways, most roads will be unmetalled. Generally, it is a good idea to keep your speed down on such roads as vehicles do not respond as quickly as they do on bitumen roads, and are likely to slide around a bit. On city and suburban roads, highways and freeways, driving is straightforward, and with many of the major interstate and intercity highways hugging the coast, you can often enjoy some outstanding scenery on your travels.

Fuel. Leaded petrol has been phased out in environmentally-friendly Australia, and the owners of old cars now use a 'lead replacement petrol' instead. Fuel costs vary from one area to another, and even within the metropolitan area, prices may vary considerably from suburb to suburb. Petrol tends to be more expensive in rural and remote areas due to freight costs. Petrol is comparatively cheap in Australia, and in 2002 prices hovered around the 85 cents to one dollar per litre mark (making it approximately half the price of petrol in Britain but similar in cost to the US). Regular (91 octane) and premium (96 octane) grades of unleaded petrol, and Diesel are readily available at petrol stations (often the cheapest petrol can be bought at supermarket garages), and two-stroke petrol is available for lawnmowers, boat engines etc. Most garages also sell LPG (liquefied petroleum gas) for taxis (many now run on LPG rather than petrol) and for topping up the boat and barbie.

Driving Regulations

Australians drive on the left of the road, as in Britain. There are, however, significant differences in speed limits, overtaking and other rules. Some of the basic differences between Australian and European driving are therefore worth noting.

Speed Limits. Speed is restricted to 60km/h in built-up areas (defined as those with kerbs and street lighting) and to 100 or 110km/h on freeways or in country areas.

Overtaking. It is legal to overtake in the left (or inside) lane of a dual carriageway/ freeway (this is known as undertaking). On a three or more lane freeway (motorway), it is legal to overtake in any lane. The extreme right lane is not established exclusively as a fast lane, but it is courteous to keep to the left. It is not, however, obligatory to do so, so the British custom of driving up behind a car in the right lane, sitting on its tail and flashing your lights until it moves over to let you pass, is completely inappropriate. This kind of driving is likely to be interpreted as aggressive and may be met by an angry response from Australian drivers.

Road Etiquette. It is imperative that you give way to your right when entering a freeway or dual carriageway from a slip road. It would be considered bad driving to come onto a freeway and expect cars in the left lane to move over to the right in order to let you enter the flow of traffic. Courteous drivers may do this, but it is not common practice, and drivers who do not change lanes to let you onto the freeway or dual carriageway are not considered rude.

The practice of flashing your lights also carries a different meaning in Australia. In Britain you may flash your lights to indicate to another car that it may enter your lane, that you wish to overtake them, or to warn another driver that their headlights are not on. In Australia, you may also flash your headlights to indicate to another driver that their headlights are not on, but most commonly drivers will flash their lights in order to warn oncoming drivers that there is a police speed trap ahead. It is, in some states, illegal to warn other cars that they are approaching a speed trap, but the tradition of Australian anti-authoritarianism lives on and most drivers derive satisfaction from helping others avoid a speeding fine.

Highway Code. You can check the rules of the road by obtaining a copy of the Highway Code from your local police station or traffic-licensing centre. The Highway Code varies in its details from state to state, often on minor points, but there are a number of differences on such crucial points as priority at intersections. If you wish to drive interstate, it would also be helpful to obtain the Highway Code relevant to your destination as each State/Territory writes its own road laws. It is compulsory to wear seat-belts, both in the front and back, and the practices of both hitch-hiking and picking up hitch-hikers is actively discouraged, and in Victoria, illegal.

Licence Penalty Points. For minor driving offences, most States have a system of penalty points. Every driver has 12 points, and a certain number of points are deducted according to the gravity of the traffic offence. Details of the points allocated to a particular offence are outlined in the Highway Code. If a driver loses all 12 points within a certain period of time, the driver loses his/her licence for a minimum of three months; this, however, can be much longer if there is serious damage to property or persons involved. Serious traffic offences may be punishable by a jail term.

Drinking and Driving. Penalties for drinking and driving in Australia are very severe, and may result in a criminal record. One Australian commentator has described the obsessive drives by the State and Territory governments to eradicate drink-driving as surpassed only by the similar fanatical endeavours of the Scandinavian governments. Random Breath Testing (RBT) is now legal and means that a driver can be pulled over at any time by the police, who will ask you to blow into a breathalyser in order to check the alcohol level of the blood. RBT vehicles are popularly known as Booze Buses and are found at all times of the day and night, on both major and suburban roads. The permitted blood alcohol level in Australia is much lower than at home, and is currently 0.02 per cent. You will reach 0.02 per cent after only one glass of wine or beer. Australian drivers take the risk of being caught extremely seriously. Do not drink and drive in Australia. You are almost certain to get caught, may get a criminal record, will definitely get a very large fine, and will definitely lose your licence for at least three months. These days, very few people, even the young and foolish, take the risk. The positive side of this draconian policy is that statistics now show that the RBT system is successful and the number of alcohol-related road deaths has fallen considerably.

Breakdowns and Accidents

Automobile Associations. There are a number of accident and breakdown services in Australia, but the biggest is the NRMA (National Roads and Motorists' Organisation). All companies offer varying levels of cover, but home-start is part of basic cover rather than an optional extra. Policies change and prices fluctuate, so you will need to contact the companies directly to obtain current details. On the whole, accident and breakdown cover is much cheaper than in Europe, and it is the car, not the driver, which is covered. In general, you can expect to pay around $50-$100 for a year's breakdown cover. If you need a breakdown service and you are not a member, you can join at the roadside, however, a premium is charged for this service. The bigger companies also offer national and international accident and/or breakdown cover free, or at a minimal rate, and will cover the cost of towing a car from remote areas, or, in the event of a fatality, the cost of flying a body home. The standard of cover is excellent and membership is well worth the fee, particularly if your car is over five years old. Up to 75 percent of Australian motorists are members of an automobile association, twice the European rate of membership. As on European motorways, there are telephones every kilometre on Australian freeways for the purpose of calling for roadside assistance. Automobile associations also offer other benefits such as tourist information, including hotel guides and maps, as well as the facility to have one of their qualified mechanics check over a used car that a member may wish to buy.

Accidents. If you are involved in a motor vehicle accident in Australia, whether as a passenger, pedestrian or driver, it is essential that you record the details of the other parties involved, including their full names, addresses, phone numbers, driver's licence numbers, the name of the insurance company of the other party or parties, the names, addresses and phone numbers of any witnesses, and a list of damage to the vehicles involved. This inventory should be made at the scene of the accident if at all possible. If the total cost of damage caused by the accident is thought to exceed $500-$1,000 (depending on the state/territory you are in) you must call the police, and in this case, it is helpful to record the name of any attending officers. If you sustain any physical injury, no matter how minor, you should attend your GP and describe how your injuries were caused, and their extent, in detail. Medical records will often affect any amount awarded as compensation in any personal injury claim.

Driving in the Outback. It is very important to never underestimate the danger that is ever present for wanderers in the outback. If you intend to drive in the outback, or undertake long distance trips, the Australian Tourist Commission can provide information detailing city-to-city links, motoring clubs, information on vehicle rental and accommodation, as well as essential rules for outback motoring. Drivers are advised to prepare thoroughly for a trip through the outback, to notify friends and relatives of expected times of arrival, and to inform them upon arrival, to check intended routes carefully, to refuel at every opportunity and to keep an additional week's supply of food, water and fuel in case of a breakdown in remote areas. Many people have died of exposure and dehydration after breaking down in the outback. You are advised *always* to remain with your car if it breaks down in the outback, as the vehicle will provide shelter from the sun and serves as an obvious point of reference for rescue teams. The Royal Flying Doctor Service of Australia (RFDS) offers a service for outback travellers which includes advice on touring and emergency procedures, as well as hire of transceiver sets with emergency call buttons. It is advisable to contact the RFDS for information before embarking on a trip into the outback.

Useful Addresses

Australian Council of the Royal Flying Doctor Service, Level 5, 15 Young Street, Sydney, NSW 2000; ☎ 02-9241 2411; fax 02-9247 3351; www.rfds.org.au. Contact this office for a list of RFDS bases Australia-wide.

Australian Automobile Association, 216 Northbourne Avenue, Braddon, ACT 2612; ☎ 02-6247 7311; fax 02-6257 5320; www.aaa.asn.au

Automobile Association of the Northern Territory (AANT), MLC Building, 78-81 Smith Street, Darwin NT 0800; ☎ 08-8 8981 3837

National Roads and Motorists' Association (NRMA), NRMA Centre, 388 George Street, Sydney, NSW 2000; ☎ 02-9292 9222; www.nrma.com.au

Royal Automobile Association of South Australia Inc., 41 Hindmarsh Square,

Adelaide, SA 5000; ☎08-8202 4600; www.raa.net
Royal Automobile Club of Queensland (RACQ), 300 St Pauls Terrace, Fortitude Valley QLD 4006, ☎131 905; www.racq.com.au
Royal Automobile Club of Tasmania (RACT), Cnr Patrick & Murray Streets, Hobart, TAS 7001; ☎13 2722;

www.ract.com.au
Royal Automobile Club of Victoria (RACV), 550 Princes Highway, Noble Park, VIC 3174; ☎131 955; www.racv.com.au
Royal Automobile Club of Western Australia Inc., 228 Adelaide Terrace, Perth, WA 6000; ☎08-9421 4444; www.rac.com.au

Driving Licences

Each of the states and territories has a separate authority responsible for the issuing of driving licences. The minimum age for holding a licence is either 17 or 18 years, depending on the State or Territory. A Learner's Permit may be obtained by a potential new driver three months before they reach driving age (i.e. at either 16 years 9 months or 17 years 9 months of age depending on state/territory), after first passing a written test on the Highway Code. A learner driver may only be accompanied or instructed by someone who has a clean driving licence and who has been driving for at least seven years. Learners are not permitted to drive on freeways or in the dark, and must always display 'L' plates attached to the car. Although in practice most learners get at least some driving experience in the presence of a suitably qualified friend or member of the family, it is nonetheless compulsory to have lessons with a qualified instructor before attempting the driving test. Once a learner feels confident with the basic driving skills, the driving instructor will make an appointment for the driving test with a police examiner. On passing the test, which is usually at the second attempt (unless you are very lucky or proficient), a driver is granted a 'probationary' licence and is required to display 'P' plates on the car every time they drive, for their first year as a licence holder. Probationary drivers are subject to restrictions on speed and blood alcohol limits, and face severe penalties if caught exceeding these limits. After one year, the probationary driver is considered to be sufficiently experienced to be awarded a full driving licence. Driving licences are not issued for an indefinite period (or until your 70th birthday) and must be renewed periodically, generally every five years.

If you arrive in Australia with a driving licence issued overseas, different regulations apply. If you are considered to be a visiting driver (i.e., you are temporarily in Australia and usually reside outside Australia), you may drive any vehicle, including a locally registered one, provided you hold a current full driving licence or International Driving Permit (issued in your home country) for the class of vehicle to be driven. In Britain, an International Driving Permit can be obtained from the AA, even if you are not a member, and from most main post offices.

Obtaining an Australian Driving Licence. If you intend to become a permanent resident of Australia, you must obtain a driving licence issued by the relevant state or territory authority. Although you may be given a period of grace, which varies from state to state but is usually three months, you will be required to obtain a driving licence as soon as you take up permanent residence. New settlers holding a current valid British driving licence must take a written test based upon knowledge of the State/Territory Motor Traffic Handbook (also known as the *Highway Code*) as well as a practical driving test. In addition, it is necessary in most states to undergo an eyesight test. A driver's licence issued in one particular Australian State or Territory is valid Australia-wide.

Car Registration

Registration fees are payable according to the type of vehicle and the expected wear and tear that vehicle will inflict on the State's or Territory's roads over the course of a year. In most states or territories, temporary residents and visitors are exempt from registration fees as long as the registration of the vehicle continues to be valid in the country of origin. A vehicle imported from abroad must be inspected on arrival by the nearest registration authority to ensure it is roadworthy immediately after its arrival in Australia. In addition, you will need to provide the following documents: a *Carnet de Passage* or other evidence that security has been lodged with Australian Customs, evidence that it is covered by Third Party Insurance in Australia, a current registration certificate from the country or origin, and a valid driver's licence from country of origin. Registration payments include Third Party Injury Insurance (CPI), and costs vary between States. The combined cost of registration and CTI of a popular 6-cylinder family sedan ranges from $400-$600. Fees differ depending on whether the vehicle is intended for business or commercial use (for which standard fees apply) or solely for family or personal purposes (for which family vehicle fees apply). A family vehicle will receive a discount of around $50 on the annual registration fee.

To register your vehicle, contact your local traffic authority (listed below). In New South Wales you must get an endorsed Compulsory Third Party Certificate (The Green Slip) from an insurance company in order to be able to register your vehicle. Payment of the combined vehicle registration and CPI can be made at any metropolitan Post Office or at the office of the relevant authority, although payment procedures are subject to change and you should check with the proper registration authority. In Western Australia payment of vehicle registration can only be done by cheque or via the metropolitan Post Office branches, and not at the Police Department. Once registered the vehicle will be fitted with Australian number (registration) plates.

Useful Addresses

ACT – *Road User Services*, Technical Standards Section, PO Box 582, Dickson, ACT 2602; ☎02-6207-7019.

NSW – *Roads Traffic Authority*, Centennial Plaza, 260 Elizabeth St, Surry Hills, NSW 2010,(Postal Address: PO. Box K198, Haymarket, NSW 1238); ☎02-9218 6888; fax 02-9218 6227; www.rta.nsw.gov.au

NT – *Motor Vehicle Registry*, Department of Transport and Infrastructure, PO Box 530, Darwin, NT 0801; ☎08-8999 3111; www.nt.gov.au

QLD – *Queensland Transport, Queensland Transport Customer Service Centre* , Service Centres are located throughout

Queensland. Telephone 07-3253 4500 to find nearest centre or check at www.transport.qld.gov.au

SA – Registration and Licensing Office, QBE Building, 7th Floor, 108 King William Street, Adelaide, SA 5000; ☎13 10 84; www.transport.sa.gov.au. Transport SA has 19 Customer Service Centres throughout South Australia which deliver Registration and Licensing services.

TAS – *Registrar of Motor Vehicles*, GPO Box 1002, Hobart 7001; ☎131 105 or 03-6233 5201; www.transport.tas.gov.au

VIC – *Victorian Roads, Vehicle Registration*, PO Box 1644N, Melbourne,

VIC   3001;   ☎03-9854   2666;   131 156 or 08-9427 6404 or check at
www.vicroads.vic.gov.au   www.transport.wa.gov.au/licensing/
WA – *Licensing Services*, Licensing centres   to find your local centre.
are located throughout WA. Telephone

TRANSPORT

Although Australia is a vast country, transport networks are very good and it is
relatively easy to explore it by air, rail and coach. Around 913,000 km of roads
and 9,458 km of rail networks span the continent, and several major airlines offer
a choice to travellers. Qantas was one of the world's first commercial airlines and
has an unrivalled safety record; its main competitor, Ansett, a subsidiary of Air
New Zealand was declared bankrupt in September 2001 and its future was still
uncertain at the time of writing. Scheduled domestic flights carry more than 18
million passengers a year. Trains operate in all states except Tasmania, and there are
interstate lines travelling deep into the outback and along the lush coastline of the
eastern seaboard. Rail Australia provides a nation-wide service linking the major
tourist orientated passenger rail operators Queensland Rail, Countrylink, and the
Great Southern Railway. In addition, Australia has about 70 ports of commercial
significance, used mainly for trade, although cruise ships are enjoying a prolonged
popularity and regularly call at the ports of Sydney and Fremantle.

Air

Domestic air travel in Australia isn't particularly cheap, due in part to the huge
distances which separate major cities, but also because of lack of competition among
the airlines. Tourists will find it is often cheaper to book internal flights from their
home country through a travel agent than arrange them in Australia, although clearly
this option is not available to anyone who has already taken up residence in Australia.
Many international airlines offer free or discounted internal flights with their tickets,
and there are also a number of air passes available which offer more economical
travel within Australia. If you fly to Australia with Qantas (www.qantas.com.au) the
Boomerang Pass allows you to explore Australia, New Zealand and the South West
Pacific by buying flight coupons (costing £100-125) before you leave home to travel
in or between various 'zones' of the region. Offers are constantly changing, but there
are consistently specials available for overseas visitors. Check with your travel agent
for the latest information.

Rail

Australia has an extensive rail network, although it is impossible to travel the whole
country by train. The remote outback of both the Northern Territory and Western
Australia is not served by railway lines at all (the intense heat can cause track to
buckle), and Tasmania, being both small and sea bound, has never developed a rail
system. The eastern coast of Australia, however, is well served by trains, and one of
the great railway lines of the world, *The Indian Pacific* runs between Perth and Sydney
and operates weekly. 4,348 km, 65 hours and two time zones after watching the sun
rise over the Pacific Ocean in Sydney, you can enjoy the Perth sunset over the Indian
Ocean. Other legendary train journeys include The Ghan (from Port Augusta to

Alice Springs), The Prospector (from Perth to Kalgoorlie), and The Overland (from Melbourne to Adelaide). Interstate rail travel is expensive, and most travellers will choose to undertake it for the experience rather than for the convenience.

There are several passes available for rail travel within Australia, which can be booked before departure. The *Austrailpass* allows you unlimited stops on most trains on the Rail Australia Network over a specified time period (determined by price). First and economy class passes are available, and an economy pass will cost between $660, for 14 days, to $1035, for 30 days. Alternatively, the *Flexipass* provides four passes for travel for eight, 15, 22, or 29 days within a six-month period, and costs between $550 and $1440. Several other passes, the *East Coast Discovery Pass*, *Queensland RoadRail Pass* and the *Countrylink Discovery Pass* all allow unlimited state-specific travel within a limited time for a fixed price. Further details of these passes can be obtained from the Rail Australia website (www.railaustralia.com.au) and Leisurail (details below).

As some long distance rail services operate on a weekly basis, you are well advised to book ahead, particularly if you have a limited travelling time or are travelling in peak season. Tickets may be booked up to six months in advance and there are often discounts on those tickets purchased in advance. Single tickets are valid for two months and return tickets must be used within six months of using the outbound section of the ticket.

Bookings can be made in the UK through local travel agents, or directly through Rail Australia's appointed agent, Leisurail (PO Box 5, Unit 12, Coningsby Road, Peterborough PE3 8XP; ☎0870 7500222; fax 0870 7500333; www.leisurail.co.uk). Leisurail have a free brochure available on request.

Bus

Travelling by coach around Australia, while time consuming, is actually one of the best ways to see the country, as well as one of the cheapest. Nearly 80% of independent travellers use coach services to get around Australia. There are a number of independent bus companies, and daily services travel to almost anywhere in the country from every major city. Prices are competitive and the standards are very high. Long-distance coaches are usually fitted with video and stereo facilities, and the bus drivers often consider themselves to be part of the entertainment, maintaining humour levels should they begin to flag in the middle of a long trip. Every bus is fitted with air conditioning, a toilet and drinking water fountains, and there are frequent stops at roadhouses for food, drinks, toilets and even showers. All coaches are strictly non-smoking.

Bus Companies. Greyhound Pioneer and McCaffertys are the two largest coach companies in the country and both provide services to over 900 destinations throughout Australia. Both of these companies have booking agents in the UK who can be contacted for further details or you can log onto their websites(www .greyhound.com.au; www.mccaffertys.com.au). In Tasmania the state bus company is Redline Coaches (www.tasredline.com).

For Greyhound Pioneer, contact Greyhound International (Kings Place, Wood Street, Kingston-upon-Thames KT1 1JY; ☎01342-317 317; fax 01342-328 519), and for McCaffertys and Greyhound Pioneer, contact Visit Australia (21 Norman Road, St Leonards-on-Sea, East Sussex, TN37 6NH; ☎01424-722 152 or fax 01424-722 304).

Bus and Combined Bus/Rail Passes. There is a range of bus passes available for travellers in Australia and information can be obtained from travel agents in Australia, or at home if you intend to travel with Greyhound Pioneer or McCaffertys. Greyhound Pioneer operates a number of passes with travel valid on both Pioneer and McCaffery coaches. For example the *Aussie Kilometre Pass* allows you to travel a certain amount of kilometres over a period of a year. A 2,000 kilometre pass costs $281 while a pass allowing a year's worth of travel up to 10,000 kilometres will cost $1,077. The *Aussie Explorer Pass* lets you choose a pre-set travel route and you can stop off as often as you like, travelling in one direction. Selected passes include free tours and transfers to destinations like Kakadu National Park and Ayers Rock. There are 17 pre-set routes and passes are valid for 1 to 12 months from the first date of travel depending on the pass. McCaffertys' *Princes Pass* allows unlimited stops between Melbourne and Sydney at a cost of $95, valid for 90 days.

In addition to the travel options given above, there are also a number of combined rail and road passes. New South Wales has a *Countrylink Discovery Pass* available for economy travel on all Countrylink rail and coach services (excluding national companies and the Indian Pacific train). A 14 day pass costs $165, while a 30 day pass costs $198. The *Queensland RoadRail Pass* is valid on any McCafferty's Express Coach services throughout Queensland and/or Queensland Rail's long distance Traveltrain services and costs $286 for travel on any 10 days over a 60-day period or $374 for travel on any 20 days over a 90 day period.

Urban Transport

Most Australian cities are well served by public transport. Within the city centre, there frequent and economical buses, and trains also service the central business district. In Melbourne, the city transport system also includes trams, which have become a feature and an attraction of the city, and which are now considered to point the way forward in public transport planning strategies. Trams on certain city routes are free. Sydney has an underground rail system (commonly referred to as the City Circle), and in Adelaide commuters use the O-Bahn, the world's longest and fastest guided busway. In Perth, the city council provides free bus services within a restricted area of the city. The Central Area Transit System (CATs for short) is a bus service which operates in the City Centre and also in Fremantle. Routes are colour-coded and you can catch one of the service buses at any point along its route and stay on as long as you like, without paying a cent. In both Perth and Melbourne, these free transport services are provided to encourage city workers to leave their cars at home thus reducing city traffic congestion, however, many tourists and shoppers also take advantage of the excellent services. In common with many European city transport systems in many Australian cities public transport tickets are valid for a certain length of time rather than for a single or return journey. If, for example, you buy a ticket (which is priced according to how many zones you need to cover), that ticket will be valid for a specific length of time, and will remain valid regardless of how many times you get on and off any buses or trains within that time period, and within the specified zones. Zones are set in concentric circles, so it is possible to travel the out again from the city centre to the other side of the city without purchasing extra zones. In addition, in Perth it is possible to use bus and train tickets interchangeably, so you can catch the bus into Perth and then use the same ticket to catch a train to another destination, or vice versa, within the zonal distance. You usually pay the driver for your ticket as you board, and at stations there are automatic ticket vending machines. Australian cities are very sprawling and there are often long distances to be crossed between various areas. In consequence, the public transport is perhaps not as frequent or as well established as in European cities. There is, however, considerable new investment in rail services, especially in Perth, which is constantly increasing its track miles. Most Australians still like to drive to work, although there are an increasing number of 'Park & Ride' schemes by which you drive to a convenient bus/rail depot and travel into the city centre by public transport.

BANKS AND FINANCE

Banking in Australia is straightforward and the tellers (cashiers) are generally courteous and helpful. All banks are open the same hours nation-wide: from 9.30am to 4.00pm Monday to Thursday, and from 9.30pm to 5.00pm on Fridays. Building societies and some banks may open on Saturday mornings from 9.00am-noon, but regional and remote branches may have more restricted opening hours. Australian banking has all the usual electronic facilities that a customer will expect, plus a few extras. ATM machine cards can be used in all supermarkets, and Electronic Funds Transfer at Point of Sale (EFTPOS) facilities are available in most stores, petrol stations, grocery stores and boutiques, with the larger outlets also allowing cash withdrawals. Australians are big on the idea of a cashless society. The four largest national banks (known as 'the big four') are Westpac, the National Australia Bank, the Commonwealth Bank of Australia, and the ANZ (which also has branches in New Zealand). Many building societies, including the St. George, have gone through the same demutualisation process as those in the UK and now operate as banks.

Bank Accounts

If you are going to Australia for more than six months, or to work, it is worth opening a bank account either before you leave your home country, or immediately upon arrival in Australia. It is much easier to open an account with an Australian bank when you are actually in Australia, but accounts can also be arranged through bank offices in the UK. The Commonwealth, ANZ and Westpac all have branches in London which offer services particularly geared to new arrivals and migrants. Their advisors are extremely helpful, and will guide you in choosing the best accounts to meet your requirements, as well as providing general advice about services. The Commonwealth Bank, for example, will establish a bank account for you with a convenient branch in Australia and transfer your funds prior to your departure so that when you arrive in Australia you have immediate and full access to their range of banking facilities (including automatic telling machines throughout the country). The Commonwealth Bank can only establish an account for you prior to your arrival if you intend to work in Australia, if you are migrating, or if you are a resident returning home after an extended period abroad. To qualify for their services in the UK branch you will need to be able to show them evidence that you have been given the relevant visa. Contact the Commonwealth Bank of Australia's Migrant Banking Services (details listed below) for further details or to speak with one of their consultants, 9am-5pm Monday to Friday.

The One Hundred Points System

Banking is relatively open and available in Australia and there are very few people who will be excluded from having an account, even with a bad credit record. References or proof of income are not required, however, proper identification is crucial and all banks must by law operate the '100 points system' of identification. Under this system you must conclusively demonstrate your identity and place of residence by providing various forms of identification, which are scored by the level of their official authority. A passport, for example, will provide you with 70 points, which you might back up with a Visa or Mastercard (25 points), a birth certificate (70 points), or a driver's licence (50 points). When you go to the bank to open an account, be sure to take a selection of appropriate documents with you, as you will be sent away empty-handed if you cannot comply with this government requirement. Note, however, that if you apply for a bank account within six weeks of arrival in Australia you will only need to show your passport as proof of identification.

International & Internal Money Transfers

If you wish to send an international money transfer to Australia, it will cost you a flat fee regardless of the amount of money sent and the transfer may only be sent through a bank, using the 'Swift' service. You can also send money through American Express and Western Union offices but these services, although quick, are expensive. In Australia, international money transfers are made either by bank draft, or electronically. Within the country, travellers without a cheque (current) account may send money within the country by bank cheque (costing approximately $5, although the charge varies from bank to bank), or by Australia Post Money Orders, which can be bought to a maximum value of $1,000 for a cost of around $2.50. Express Money Orders can be bought to a maximum value of $10,000 and cost around $20. Money Orders are generally the cheapest way to send money and can be cashed at any of Australia Post's 3900 post offices Australia-wide.

Other Banking Services

Credit Cards. All Australian banks offer a credit card facility, and all the usual international credit cards, including Mastercard, Visa, Diners Club and American Express, are available via your local bank branch. If you intend to stay in Australia for less than 12 months, you may prefer to apply for a credit card in your home country before you leave and then establish a standing order to pay off your monthly credit card bill. It is a good idea to deposit any savings in a high interest account whilst you are away, allowing the interest from this account to cover the approximate charge of 2% on cash advances made against your credit card in Australia.

Direct Debits. Australian banks offer direct debit facilities, known as standing orders for the payment of regular bills, and many now also offer telephone and Internet banking facilities which enable you to authorise and conduct transactions by telephone and online from your home or office.

Cheque Accounts. The chequebook facility only applies to specific accounts, and it is important to check whether the account you are considering offers this service. There is no cheque card system in Australia, so there is also no limit as to the amount of the cheque you are able to write. In order, however, to write a cheque, you will need to have your driver's licence or other acceptable form of identification showing your full name and address, with you, and this information will be noted on the reverse of the cheque. Not all shops will accept cheques as payment is not guaranteed, so with smaller shops, ask first if they are prepared to accept one. Almost every shop now prefers the cashless transaction, and even the smallest corner deli will accept your ATM card. Very few Australian bank accounts offer free cheques and as a result, Australians use cheques sparingly, prefer to use cash or credit cards. Cheques take three working days to clear, but foreign cheques may take up to four weeks and you are likely to be charged a commission on the exchange of cheques made out in a foreign currency.

Investment Advice. Many expatriates tend to seek advice on money related matters such as employee benefits, retirement income funding, personal investments and savings. Companies specialising in providing worldwide finacial services include *Brewin Dolphon Securities* of 5 Giltspur Street, London EC1A 9BD (☎ 020-7247 4400; fax 020-7236 2034; www.brewin.co.uk) and *Aon Consulting* of 15 Minories, London EC3N 1NJ (☎ 020-7767 2000; fax 020-7767 2001; www.aon.com/uk/en/).

Money

Australia has had a decimal currency for over 40 years, abandoning the archaic imperial pounds, shillings and pence system in 1965. The basic unit of currency is the Australian dollar, which is worth 100 cents. In 1993, 'coppers', or one and two cent pieces, were withdrawn from circulation, having become virtually worthless and more of a nuisance than an item of value. Their withdrawal has provided a certain complicating factor into Australian shopping, which will confuse the new arrival. Although coppers are no longer available to be given as small change, goods for sale are still marked up in terms of single cents (for example, $2.98). Your shopping will be rung up in these hypothetical numbers and the final total will be rounded off – always, by law, in favour of the customer. Thus, if your supermarket till total comes to $47.68, it will be rounded down to $47.65. Items paid for by cheque or cashcard, however, will cost the precise amount as stated, and not rounded off. This system sounds complicated but has been quickly accepted by Australians, and few people are nostalgic for the bad old days of a wallet full of dirty little coins. Australian coinage consists of the silver-coloured, cupronickel 5, 10, 20 and 50 cent pieces, and of gold-coloured $1 and $2 coins, which replaced notes of the same value in 1994. The 5 cent coin is very similar in size to an old sixpence, the 20 cent coin is easily confused with a UK 10 pence, and the 50 cent coin has the same hexagonal shape as its UK equivalent. The $1 coin is about the same size as the 20 cent piece, and has irregular milling which allows it to be easily distinguished by blind people. The $2 coin is smaller and thicker, and is much like a UK £1 in dimension. Australian notes are in denominations of $5, $10, $20, $50 and $100. In recent years, the Australian currency has been gradually redesigned to make it both counterfeit-proof and longer lasting. New $5, $10, $20, $50 and $100 notes have now been released, and are made of a kind of plastic, which mimics paper but cannot be torn. It is considered virtually indestructible. The plastic notes bear a forgery-proof transparent seal in the corner (i.e., you can see right through the note), and a hologram in the centre of the seal. All notes and coins bear the head of Queen Elizabeth II on the reverse side. Old paper notes have been quickly withdrawn from circulation and destroyed. Paper money is still legal tender, but will be returned to the mint for destruction on receipt. The Australian mint also coins gold bullion and coin, known as Australian Nuggets. Each coin has a set purchase price (from $15-$100), but the actual value is determined by the daily-fluctuating price of gold, and the demand for the coins. The Australian Nugget can be bought Australia-wide at banks as individual coins or as full sets. They are popular as souvenirs for wealthier visitors.

Visitors are permitted to import and export an unlimited amount of foreign currency into Australia, but if you intend to import or export more than $10,000 you need to contact customs or the *Australian Transaction Reports and Analysis Centre* (www.austrac.gov.au). Should you be lucky enough to clean up at that illegal Australian coin game, 'Two-up', you might have to leave your winnings behind or, if you've been really lucky, invest it in Australian business or property. Banks are also legally obliged to report deposits of more than $10,000 in cash made into Australian bank accounts, primarily to safeguard against money laundering activities.

Useful Addresses

Australian & New Zealand Banking Group (ANZ), Minerva House, Montague Close, London SE1 9DH; ☎020-7378 2121; fax 020-7378 2378; www.anz.com

National Australia Bank Ltd, 88 Wood Street, London EC2V 7QQ; ☎020-7710 2100; www.national.com.au

Reserve Bank of Australia, Basildon House, 7 Moorgate, London EC2R 6AQ;

☎020-7600 2244; www.rba.gov.au

The Commonwealth Bank of Australia, Financial & Migrant Information Service, Senator House, 85 Queen Victoria Street, London EC4V 4HA; ☎020-7710 3990; fax 020-7710 3939; www.commbank.com.au

Westpac Banking Corporation, 63 St Mary's Annexe, London, EC3A 8LE, ☎020-7621 7000; www.westpac.com.au

TAXATION

Income Tax

Australia revised its taxation laws a few years ago and on 1 July 2000 a new tax system was introduced, bringing in new measures such as the Goods and Services Tax (GST), Pay-As-You-Go (PAYG) taxation and some business tax reform measures. Australia's government structure means that each tier imposes its own taxes: The Commonwealth Government administers general taxes such as income tax, GST, customs and excise, fringe benefits tax, superannuation guarantee charge, and taxes on natural resources projects; State and Territory governments administer taxes such as payroll and workers' compensation taxes, stamp duties, bank account taxes and land tax, and the Municipal governments levy rates and charges on the owners of real estate. For more detailed information on the tax reforms the Australian Tax Office runs and additional website to their online homepages at www.taxreform.ato.gov.au.

Income Tax in Australia can be quite a complicated business and the completion and lodgement of a tax return is the responsibility of the individual. To help to demystify the taxation procedures Tax Packs containing forms and an information magazine, produced by the Australian Taxation Office, are available free from newsagents and Taxation Offices Australia-wide. The Tax Pack is reviewed annually, in an effort to make completing a tax return less difficult, but even so, the Tax Pack is a formidable publication with detailed information and instructions. Both format and terminology are quite daunting and for this reason, fewer and fewer Australians are choosing to complete their own taxation returns and are turning to chartered accountants or licensed tax agents to complete the forms for them.

The Australian financial year begins on 1 July and ends on 30 June, and tax returns must usually be lodged by the end of October. Even if you think you are not liable to pay any tax, you are generally required to lodge a tax return in Australia if you are normally resident there, or if you are a non-resident who has derived an income in Australia. Every taxpayer requires a Tax File Number (TFN). To apply for a TFN you will need to contact the Australian Tax Office upon arrival in Australia.

Although taxation rules and regulations are subject to continual re-assessment and change, clearly most Australian adults will fall somewhere within these categories and are therefore required to complete and lodge an annual taxation return. It is important to note that despite the necessity of completing a taxation return, most pensions and state allowances are tax-free and should not be included in your taxation return.

Completing a Tax Return

In order to complete a tax return, you need to attach official statements of the amount of tax you have paid over the year. These statements are known as PAYG Payment Summaries and are issued automatically by employers at the end of the financial year. If you do not receive a Payment Summary from your employer you must request one.

If either you or you employer have lost your PAYG Payment Summary, or they have gone missing in the post, you are usually able to get a copy from your employer. If your employer is unable to provide you with a copy, then he/she can give you a letter showing all the details of the original documents. In the unlikely event that you are not able to obtain a letter from your employer, you can fill in a Statutory Declaration of lost or missing Payment Summaries (available from your local Tax Office). If any information on your Payment Summary is wrong, your employer must provide a letter showing your correct income and tax details.

Self-Assessment. If you choose to complete your own tax return, the tax office will work out your refund or tax bill based on the information you have provided. The tax office assumes the information you have provided is true and correct but you should note that after they have calculated your rebate or bill and informed you of their calculations in your Notice of Assessment, their computers continue to check for missing or incorrect information. Your tax return may also be subject to an audit and, should the original assessment be judged incorrect, the tax office will change it and send you an amended assessment. In addition to extra tax, you may be liable for a penalty if you fail to show reasonable care in the preparation of your return. Knowing this, it is understandable why many Australians simply don't want to take the risk and so pay a professional to shoulder the responsibility.

Professional Assistance. If you would like assistance filling out your own taxation return, you will be able to find chartered accountants or other professional taxation assistance services in the Yellow Pages phone book. It is advisable to phone around as the cost of the service can vary greatly. The Tax Office recommends that if you

It is obligatory to lodge a tax return at the end of the financial year if any of the following are applicable:

- ○ You had tax deducted from your pay or other income (including Australian Government pensions, allowances or benefits);
- ○ You had tax deducted from interest, dividends or unit trust distributions (applicable only to residents) because you did not quote your TFN or Australian Business Number (ABN) to the investment body;
- ○ You were required to lodge an activity statement under the PAYG system and pay an instalment amount during the year;
- ○ Your taxable income for the previous year was more than $6,000 (residents) or $1 or more (non-residents);
- ○ You incurred a net taxable loss, or are entitled to a deduction for a prior year loss;
- ○ You were entitled to a distribution from a trust, or you had an interest in a partnership and the trust or partnership carried on a business of primary production;
- ○ You were an Australian resident for tax purposes and you had exempt overseas employment income and $1 or more of other income;
- ○ You are a special professional covered by income averaging provisions;
- ○ You received income from dividends or distributions exceeding $6,000 and you had imputation credits or amounts withheld because you did not quote your TFN or ABN to the investment body;
- ○ You conducted business in Australia;
- ○ You paid provisional tax on your previous year's assessment;
- ○ You were under 18 years of age as at 30 June and your total income was not from a salary or wages, and was more than $643;
- ○ You are the liable parent under a child support assessment;
- ○ You have a reportable fringe benefits amount on your PAYG payment summary;
- ○ You are entitled to a tax offset;
- ○ You received a pension, allowance or benefits and your assessable income was more than: $15,970 if you were single, widowed or separated at any time during the year; $15,164 if you had a spouse but either of you lived in a nursing home or you had to live apart due to illness; $13,305 if you lived with your spouse for the whole income year.

get someone (other than them) to help you complete your return, you should ensure that that person is a registered tax agent. Some agents offer a free initial assessment, and discounts to pensioners. Tax return fees charged by a registered tax agent are tax deductible against your *next* annual tax return. In addition, tax help is available for seniors, people from non-English speaking backgrounds, the disabled and those on low incomes who cannot afford assistance with completing their tax returns. Tax help centres are run by community volunteers, and you should contact your local tax office for details of your nearest one.

There is also a Translating and Interpreting Service (TIS) available specifically to help non English-speaking people with their tax returns. The TIS offers joint meetings with interpreters and tax officers, and you simply call the TIS to make an appointment. TIS phone numbers are found in the community information pages of your phone directory.

The postal addresses and phone numbers of the various state and regional Tax Offices are listed at the back of Tax Packs and in the government section of the telephone book.

E-Tax. During October 1998, the Australian Taxation Office (ATO) trialed a new electronic tax preparation and lodgement software package, *e-tax*, which was based on the hard-copy *TaxPack*. Following trials, the *e-tax* facility is now available to the public and in 2001, 117,000 Australians lodged a tax return through the *e-tax* service. It is expected that numbers will continue to increase dramatically, with an expected user-base of 400,000 in July 2002. The ATO has developed high levels of security to ensure that personal income tax information is secure. When you complete your return online, you sign it electronically using the in-built public key technology, and the *e-tax* software will encrypt your tax return file for transmission over the Internet using a secure link.

The Australian Taxation Office has a very comprehensive and informative website at **www.ato.gov.au**.

Claiming Back Tax on Expenses. If you are audited, you will usually receive written notification at the beginning of the audit, and you should follow the instructions contained in the letter. If audited, you will have to substantiate your work expenses claims, e.g. motor vehicle, travel, clothing, tertiary studies, tools of trade, reference books and other expenses. It is therefore necessary to keep records of any work-related expenses in order to avoid additional tax and a possible penalty.

If you are an employee and the total of your claims is $300 or less, you must keep a record of how you worked out each of your claims. If the total of your claims is more than $300, you must keep records of receipts, invoices and similar documentary evidence supported by or on behalf of the supplier of the goods or services. Cheque stubs are not considered acceptable as evidence. The receipt, invoice or documentary evidence must be in English or the language of the country where the expense was incurred, have the date on which the expense was incurred, name the person who (or business which) supplied the goods or services, show the amount of the expense in the currency in which the expense was incurred, give details of the nature of the goods or services, and show the date the document was made out.

A diary may be used to prove your claims for expenses that are no more than $10 each and which add up to no more than $200, or for which it was unreasonable to expect to get a receipt. The diary should contain all the details that would be required on a receipt or invoice. In addition, you must sign each entry in the diary.

The information outlined above should be kept for a period of five years after lodging your tax return. Records of other business-related expenses incurred by self-employed persons should also be retained for five years after lodging their tax return. If you appeal against an assessment, you must retain your records until the dispute has been finalised if that period exceeds the given record retention period.

You can claim for the cost of using your car for work or business purposes; for example travelling directly from one place of work to another, or from one job to another. You cannot, however, generally claim for the cost of travelling from home to work.

Table of Income Tax

The following table shows personal income tax thresholds and the reduced income tax rates as of July 2000. There is currently a tax threshold of $6,000 in Australia which means that the first $6,000 earned is tax-free. The tax rate applicable on earning over this amount is described below:

TABLE 5	INCOME TAX RATES
Taxable Income	**Tax rate %**
$0-$6,000	Nil
$6,001-$20,000	17
$20,001-$50,000	30
$50,001-$60,000	42
$60,00 and over	47

If you become a resident of Australia during the financial year you are entitled to a pro rata amount of the $6,000 tax threshold. For the tax year, you calculate this amount by adding up the number of months from when you became a resident of Australia up to the 30 June. This amount is then divided by twelve to give you the proportion of the year spent in Australia, then multiplied by $6,000 to give you your tax-free threshold. If, for example, you have only been resident in Australia for two months, your tax threshold is assessed as 2/12 x $6,000 = $1,000, but if you have been resident for eleven months, your tax threshold is 11/12 x $6,000 = $5,500. Your assessment can take up to eight weeks after lodging your tax return. If you are required to pay tax, you will be given thirty days notice. Tax can be paid by cheque or postal money orders made payable to the Deputy Commissioner of Taxation, in cash or cheque at any Post Office (you must take your Notice of Assessment with you), by mail (cheque or postal order only), at Tax Offices (take your Notice of Assessment), or by direct debit/refund. This last service is available from tax agents who lodge tax returns electronically.

If you cannot pay your tax by the due date, you may be given extra time to pay depending on your circumstances. You will have to provide details of your financial position including assets, liabilities, income and expenditure, and the steps you have taken to obtain funds to pay your debt. If granted additional time, you will be charged interest calculated on a daily basis. This rate is currently 11.89%.

Rebates

There are numerous tax offsets (formerly called tax rebates) which may be available to you, and it is certainly worth being aware of them even if you are not currently eligible. If your tax offsets are greater than the tax on your taxable income, they can only reduce the amount of tax you pay in that year to zero. There are three exceptions to this rule: the 30% private health insurance rebate, where any excess is refunded to you; the landcare and water facility tax offset, where any excess is refunded to you; and the franking tax offset, where any excess imputation credits on dividends paid to you on or after 1 July of the tax year are refunded to you. Generally, tax offsets do you reduce your Medicare levy. Where you have excess refundable tax offsets available, these can be applied to reduce your tax, including the Medicare levy. Being eligible to claim a tax offset depends on things like maintaining a dependant, or living in a remote area, or on how much taxable income you earned. A brief summary of some of the tax offsets available is given below:

SOME TAX OFFSETS

- You were involved with heritage conservation work.
- You were earning interest from government securities.
- You were earning interest from the land transport facilities tax offset scheme or infrastructure borrowings scheme.
- You were entitled to the landcare and water facility.
- You were living in a remote or isolated area of Australia.
- You were responsible for the maintenance of your parent, spouse's parent or invalid relative.
- Your net medical expenses were over $1,250 in the tax year.
- You were serving overseas as a member of the Defence Force or a United Nations armed force.
- You were responsible for superannuation contributions on behalf of your spouse.
- Low income tax payers - if you were an Australian resident for tax purposes and your taxable income was less than $24,450.
- You claimed family tax benefit.
- You are a low income, aged person.

Other Taxes

Capital Gains Tax

Australia has had a Capital Gains Tax (CGT) since 1985. You will be liable for this tax if you sell or otherwise dispose of any assets or receive any other capital amounts in a financial year. Examples of capital amounts include a forfeited deposit, premium received for granting a lease, or a capital gain distributed to a beneficiary of a trust. This includes any 'gifts' received, particularly those deemed as 'business' gifts, and the recipient is taxed on the gift at its fair market value. Any assets you may have acquired before 20 September 1985 are not subject to capital gains tax. CGT assets fall into three categories: collectables, personal use assets, and other assets:

Collectables. include items that are used or kept mainly for personal use including paintings: sculptures, drawings, engravings or photographs; reproductions of these items or property of a similar description or use, jewellery, antiques, coins or medallions, rare folios, manuscripts or books, and postage stamps or first day covers. A collectable can also be an interest in, a debt that arises from, or an option or right to acquire any of the above items. Any capital gain or capital loss you make from a collectable acquired for $500 or less is disregarded. A capital gain or capital loss you make from an interest in a collectable is disregarded if the market value of the collectable when you acquired the interest was $500 or less. However, if you acquired the interest for $500 or less before 16 December 1995, a capital gain or capital loss is disregarded. If you dispose of collectables individually that you would usually dispose of as a set, you are exempt from paying capital gains tax only if you acquired the set for $500 or less. This does not apply to collectables you acquired before 16 December 1995.

A **Personal Use Asset** is deemed to be a CGT asset, other than a collectable, that is used or kept mainly for personal use including: an option or a right to acquire a CGT asset of this type, a debt resulting from a CGT event involving a CGT asset kept mainly for your personal use and enjoyment, or a debt resulting from you doing something other than gaining or producing your assessable income or carrying on a business. Personal use assets also include such items as boats, furniture, electrical goods and household items. Land and buildings are not personal use assets. Any capital loss you make from a personal use asset is disregarded. If a CGT event happened to a personal use asset during or after the 1998-99 income year, any capital gain you make from the asset or part of the asset is disregarded if you acquired the asset for $10,000 or less. If you dispose of personal use assets individually that would usually be sold as a set, you obtain the exemption only if you acquired the set for $10,000 or less.

Assets that are not collectables or personal use assets include: land and buildings, shares in a company, rights and options, leases, units in a unit trust, instalment receipts, goodwill, licences, convertible notes, your home (with some exceptions), contractual rights, foreign currency, and any major capital improvement (above the improvement threshold) made to certain land or pre-CGT assets.

   A full explanation of Capital Gains Tax with all its separate clauses can be had from the Australian Taxation Office website at www.ato.gov.au.

Fringe Benefits Tax. The Fringe Benefits Tax (FBT) was introduced in July 1986 by the government in an effort to control the amount of non-cash (and therefore non-taxable) benefits offered by employers as part of a job package. Companies cannot claim expenses such as business lunches and entertainment costs on behalf of the company, and any fringe benefits are considered an assessable part of an individual's or a company's taxable income. Taxable fringe benefits include company cars, free or low-interest loans, free or subsidised accommodation or board, goods and services sold at a reduced rate or provided free, and expenses paid on behalf of an employee.

   Cars are probably the most common fringe benefit, and Fringe Benefits Tax is normally paid by an employer when a car is owned or leased by a company and made available to an employee (or family member) for private use. Fringe Benefits Tax on cars does not normally apply to self-employed people or to a partnership if the vehicle is used wholly and exclusively for business. It does not apply to cars owned or leased by an employee, even when the cost of operating the car for business use is claimed as an expense against the taxable income. When Fringe Benefits Tax is chargeable, it applies to all passenger cars, wagons, minibuses, panel vans and utilities designed to carry less than one tonne or a bus with fewer than nine seats. There are many variations and exemptions to the Fringe Benefits Tax (the FBT year also doesn't follow the regular tax year but runs from 1 April to 31 March) and probably the safest way of working out whether you are liable or not is to get a professional to do it for you.

Goods and Services Tax. The GST was introduced along with other tax reforms on 1 July 2000. Bearing some similarity to the system of VAT in the UK, the GST is a broad-based tax of 10 percent on the supply of most goods, services and anything else consumed in Australia. You must register for GST if the annual turnover of your business is $50,000 or more ($100,000 or more for non-profit organisations). You may choose to register if the annual turnover of your business is less than $50,000 (less than $100,000 for non-profit organisations). GST is charged on imported goods, but not on wages or salaries. The amount of GST payable on a taxable supply is 10 percent of its value. To work out how much GST is included in the price of a taxable supply, you need to divide the price of the goods by 11. Some supplies are not taxable and are called GST-free supplies. These include most food, some exports, most health and childcare services, educational supplies, and cars for use by disabled people. The GST has not been greeted too warmly by Australians.

Higher Education Contributions Scheme. HECS regulations are described in detail in the Higher Education section of this book. The rate of HECS tax varies from 3% to 6% of your taxable income. In addition, since 1994, the Australian government has instructed employers to deduct additional taxation instalments to cover any possible Higher Education Contributions Assessment Debt in future years. These deductions will only be made if you earn more than $441 per week. For further details on HECS and taxation, you should request a copy of the booklet *HECS; Your Questions Answered, available from your educational institution, or any Tax Office or at the HECS website (www.hecs.gov.au).*

Death Duties. Currently, there are no Death Duties in Australia, although Capital Gains Tax is widely considered to be death duty by another name and widely resented as such. If you are making a will, you should seek tax advice on the most effective method of disposal of assets.

HEALTH INSURANCE AND HOSPITALS

A report published in 1998 by the Australian Institute of Health and Welfare reveals that Australians born in the 1990s are expected to live 15 years longer than those born in the 1920s; boys born in 1994 can expect to live to an age of 75 while girls will live to an age of 80.9. In 1999 Australia's mortality rate was around 5.87 per 1,000 people per year, although Aboriginal people continued to have a mortality rate far higher than the national average. Interestingly, the report also compared the mortality rates of migrants and Australian-born residents and found that most migrant groups had death rates significantly lower than the Australian average. Greeks, Italians, Central and South Americans, Vietnamese and Yugoslavs had the lowest rate. In addition, among Australians aged 25-64, the death rate was 15% higher for men living in rural regions, and 9% higher for women in rural areas.

The report also noted an increase in the rate of multiple births with improving technology in the field of artificial conception, such as IVF treatment, and that dental health has improved dramatically over recent years to an extent where few people under 35 years of age have lost all their teeth. Despite the large number of people on hospital waiting lists, the report also indicated that trends showed a continued decline in basic and supplementary private hospital insurance, and government measures have been put in place to offset this decline, by offering incentives to insure privately.

The report also showed that the nation's health was dogged by a rising suicide rate, with more Australians dying by their own hands than in traffic accidents. For the most part, victims were males between 15 and 24 years old, but women of the same age were also at risk. The survey indicated strong links between suicide and the socially disadvantaged and the unemployed, particularly in the Aboriginal population. The number of Aboriginal deaths in custody in the 1990s, which were statistically disproportionate when compared to the average rate of suicides in prison were so alarming that the government ordered a Royal Commission to investigate. Despite the Royal Commission's findings (released in May 1991) and its 339 recommendations, indigenous people are still 14 times more likely to be imprisoned than non-Indigenous Australians; in the Northern Territory for instance, 72.8 percent of the prison population is indigenous.

High cholesterol levels are a major contributor to health problems in Australia, affecting nearly three million people nationwide and killing 50,000 each year. Public health concern over this issue is reflected in the amount spent on drugs. Between 1998 and 2000 the cost of the cholesterol lowering drug subsidy paid by the Federal Government rose by more than $110 million. The number of prescriptions for these drugs increased by nearly two million and now tops the Pharmaceutical Benefit Scheme (PBS) in cost, amounting to over half a billion dollars in 2000 and rising by around 25 per cent each year.

Cancer rates also appear to be on the increase, accounting for over 27 percent of Australian deaths, compared with 15 per cent in 1965. Breast, lung and skin cancers are the most common killers. As a result of increased public awareness of these health risks, most Australian buildings, including restaurants, are now completely smoke-free. Australians are highly educated about the risk of skin cancer and the dangers of the sun, and now almost universally take thorough protective measures when outdoors.

The perception that Australians have apparently healthy lifestyles has also been challenged by the 1995 National Nutrition Survey which showed that some 56 percent of the adult population (18 years and over) were overweight, with 19 percent of these classified as obese.

Currently six priority areas of concern have been endorsed by Australian Health Ministers. These are: cardiovascular health; cancer control; injury prevention and control; mental health; diabetes mellitus and asthma. A range of program initiatives has been established, aimed at improving health in these areas, which together account for approximately 70 percent of the burden of disease and cost in Australia – a high demand on the nation's health services.

The Health Care System

Using the General Practitioner. The first point of contact in obtaining health care in Australia is the local GP, whom you are free to choose yourself. Whilst most people will have a preferred doctor, it is not necessary to register with a doctor, and you are able to go to a different practice at every visit, should you so wish. Depending on the doctor, you will either be billed for the consultation, for which you will be reimbursed by Medicare, the Australian national health system, or the doctor will 'bulk-bill' which means they will claim reimbursement directly from Medicare. Doctors who practise in low-income areas generally bulk-bill in order to avoid asking their patients for payment, however, this is largely a gesture of goodwill on behalf of the GP. The benefits that you get from Medicare are based on a Schedule of fees (index linked) set by the Commonwealth Government. Medicare pays either 85 per cent of the Schedule fee for outpatient services or 75 per cent of the Schedule fee for inpatient services, or the Schedule fee less an amount of up to $52.50, whichever is greater. If the charge is less than 85 per cent of the Schedule fee, Medicare will only pay the amount equal to the charge. GPs are able to charge fees they consider suitable for the services they provide, however, any extra amount about the Schedule fee with not be included in the calculation of Medicare benefits and the patient is liable for any amount in excess, which is known as the 'gap'.

Should you wish to have a second medical opinion, you simply make an appointment with another doctor. Generally, appointments are made over the telephone, and you can usually see your GP within two days of your call.

If a GP refers you to a consultant or specialist, you will be given a letter and required to make the necessary arrangements yourself. Even specialists seeing public patients consult in their own rooms, and there is no system of attendance at hospital outpatients' clinics. There may be a waiting period before you are seen, although it is usually not long, and once again you will be billed and reimbursed through Medicare. You may choose to see a consultant on a private basis, without referral, for which you will be unable to obtain a refund either from Medicare or from your private insurer.

There are an increasing number of clinics and medical centres opening in suburban areas. Most large practices will provide a Well-Woman Clinic, minor surgery, and other services. There may also be a pharmacy housed within the centre, from which you can purchase your prescriptions immediately.

Prescriptions charges are subsidised under the Pharmaceutical Benefits Scheme (PBS). Patients pay the full cost of medication up to the value of approximately $22.40, and the PBS meets the balance up to the list price; patients on benefits of any kind pay only $3.60. Contraception is not free in Australia, but is covered by the PBS.

Using Hospitals. Patients who require hospital attention or surgery can also choose to be treated either publicly or privately. If you opt for private treatment, you can choose both your attending consultant and the hospital, but will pay a considerable amount for this privilege. On the other hand, you can expect a great deal of luxury for your money, including 5 star food chosen from a daily menu, as well as immediate treatment. If you choose to be treated under Medicare, you do not have a choice of hospital or doctor (although you will have had some say in choosing your specialist during discussions with your GP in the early stages), and you may face a long wait for a bed; on the other hand, your treatment will be completely free. In the event of an emergency, all patients will be taken directly to a public hospital, and may be transferred if they wish once their condition has stabilised. Ambulance transport is not free, and many people choose to pay a small insurance premium annually to the St. John's Ambulance Brigade to cover themselves in case they or their family need to call on this service.

Health Insurance Contributions

Every Australian is covered by Medicare, which is financed through progressive income tax and an income-related Medicare levy. There is no additional charge equivalent to National Insurance in the UK. The Medicare levy is paid at a rate of 1.5 per cent of taxable income above an earning threshold of around $13,807, or $23,299 for couples. In the 1996-97 budget the Federal Government announced that a 1 percent Medicare levy surcharge, in addition to the 1.5 per cent levy, would be introduced for higher income earners ($50,000 per year for single earners, $100,000 per year for couples) who do not have private patient hospital cover through private health insurance. This surcharge is part of a package of measures designed to encourage people to retain or take up private health insurance. People receiving state benefits fall below the earning threshold of the Medicare levy, and payments are made on their behalf by the government. If you choose to be privately insured, you are not exempt from the Medicare levy.

THE AUSTRALIAN NATIONAL HEALTH SYSTEM

Australia's national health system, Medicare, is outstandingly good (although nurses are generally considered to be underpaid), but its services are becoming increasingly oversubscribed with the increasing population of Australia and the fact that the population is a 'greying' one. Many Australians, however, do choose to take out additional private medical cover. There has been a recent surge in so-called 'medical tourism', whereby people in need of major treatment, such as a hip replacement or heart surgery, visit Australia specifically to take advantage of the good facilities, medical expertise and reasonable costs. Medicare is funded by the federal, state and territory governments, and administered by the Health Insurance Commission (www.hic.gov.au). Hospitals and other facilities are built and run by the various state health departments who are responsible by law for maintaining a uniform minimum standard of care.

In order to be eligible for Medicare, you must first register by completing an application form obtainable from a Medicare regional office (call 132 011 to find your nearest office). You need not necessarily have registered with Medicare before you receive any medical treatment, but will be required to do so before you can make any claim. After you have registered, you will be sent a Medicare card, which looks like a credit card, and this should be carried with you at all times. You will need to present this card on arriving at a hospital for treatment. Any children under 15 years old will be listed on the card of one or other of their parents. When you lodge a claim for a Medicare rebate, you will be required to quote your number or present your card; rebates can be made in cash over the counter, and the process is straightforward. You can also lodge claims by post, which takes considerably longer, and forms are available in chemists, doctors' surgeries and post offices.

All immigrants are covered by Medicare, provided they pay the Medicare levy (included in general taxes), and temporary residents who stay in the country longer than six months may be covered by Medicare without having to pay the levy. Medicare covers in-patient and outpatient treatment at public hospitals, as well as hospital accommodation costs in public hospitals. If you need regular, expensive treatment, Medicare will cover all of the scheduled fees incurred over the rest of the year once the gap has reached a total of $302.30 for any financial year. Most medicines available on prescription are subsidised under the Pharmaceutical Benefits Scheme (PBS). Most PBS-listed medicines cost the consumer a maximum of $22.40, or $3.60 for relevant concession cardholders. If you have a record of spending $686.40 on PBS medicines for yourself and your family in a calendar year you will be entitled to any further PBS medicines for only $3.60 for each item for the rest of the calendar year.

Medicare does not cover physiotherapy, chiropractic or dental treatment, although some orthodontic treatment is refundable, particularly if surgery is involved. Neither medical repatriation nor funeral costs are covered, and ambulance costs (including transport and treatment) cannot be refunded through Medicare.

Reciprocal Agreements

Visitors to Australia from the UK, New Zealand, Ireland, Malta, Italy, Finland, Sweden and the Netherlands are also covered by Medicare under reciprocal arrangements, and can receive treatment under Medicare for six months from the date of arrival in Australia. You are not, however, entitled to claim health benefits for a medical condition which existed before your arrival in Australia, including any illness caught on your journey to Australia, or for any on-going medication. Travellers from the countries listed above should enrol at a Medicare office, presenting a passport containing an appropriate visa, and proof that you are enrolled in the national healthcare scheme of your home country. If you are a short-term visitor and you do not come from a country which has reciprocal health agreements with Australia, it is advisable to take out private medical insurance, which is usually available through your travel agent and is likely to be included in any travel insurance policy.

Medicare Exclusions. There are two categories of new settler which are exempt from eligibility for Medicare. These are people entering Australia to retire, and those who have been granted permanent residence in the family stream migration category, who are the parents of their sponsor and are more than 55 years old (men) or 50 years old (women). Retirees need to take out travel insurance and private medical insurance (either in their country of origin or in Australia), as they are liable for all expenses incurred in the case of medical and hospital treatment, including the cost of hospital accommodation. In the case of migrants on a parent visa application, any medical or hospital expenses be incurred by the migrant parent (over the stipulated age limit) will be the responsibility of the sponsor, unless the migrant has private insurance. If only one of the sponsor's parents is over the age limit, then the sponsor is only responsible for the medical expenses incurred by that parent. In addition, if you enter Australia as a foreign diplomat or as a member of a foreign diplomat's family, you are not covered by Medicare. It is advisable to take out private medical insurance either before you leave your home country or take out a policy in Australia immediately upon your arrival.

Private Medical Insurance

Private health insurance is widespread in Australia, with around 70% of the population choosing to take out additional cover. Private health cover is much cheaper in Australia than in Britain, and premiums are not indexed for age or gender. Most people enjoy the security of knowing that they have the right to choose both the hospital where they will be treated and their specialist who will treat them. In addition, private cover offers refunds for medical services not covered by Medicare, such as physiotherapy, prescription glasses and sunglasses, and dental work. Different levels of cover are available, from basic table (shared-room) through to a fully comprehensive, deluxe table. Costs vary from around one dollar a week, up to around five dollars per week for the ultimate in hospital care. Premiums are usually payable in monthly, quarterly or annual instalments and discounts are sometimes given for prompt payment or for payments made annually. Children and dependants are normally covered by their parents' private medical insurance.

   The Private Health Insurance Incentives Scheme, developed to make private insurance a more attractive proposition, especially to the young and healthy, was replaced by the Federal Government 30% Rebate on 1 January 1999. The 30% Rebate means that for every dollar you contribute to your private health insurance premium, the Government will give you back 30 cents. All those who are eligible for Medicare and who are members of a registered health fund are eligible for the Rebate-no matter what their level of cover, income or type of membership. Further information on the Federal Government 30 Percent Rebate can be obtained by calling the Private Health Insurance Information Line (1800 676 296) or by visiting the Commonwealth

Department of Health and Aged Care web site at www.health.gov.au.
When choosing a health fund, points to consider should include whether there are any exemptions for previously known illness or for AIDS, what the waiting period is before you can make a claim, and what the benefit limits are for each service covered. Private health insurance companies advertise widely in the local newspapers and on radio and television, with some of the largest and best-known being Medibank Private (www.medibank.com.au), the Hospital Benefits Fund (www.hbf.com.au), and the Medical Benefits Fund (www.mbf.com.au). Some smaller funds now offer rebates for alternative medical treatments, such as homeopathy and acupuncture, so if you use these services, it will be worth shopping around quite carefully.

Useful Addresses

BUPA International, Russell Mews, Brighton BN1 2NR; ☎01273-208 181; fax 01273-866 583; www.bupa-intl.com

Columbus Travel Insurance, 17 Devonshire Square, London EC2M 4SQ, ☎020-7375 0011; www.columbusdirect.net

Department of Work and Pensions, Overseas Branch, Tyneview Park, Whitley Road, Benton, Newcastle Upon Tyne NE98 1BA; ☎0191-218 7777.

The Travel Insurance Agency, Suite 2, Percy Mews, 755B High Road, North Finchley, London N12 8JY; ☎020-8446 5414; fax 020-8446 5417; www.travelinsurers.com

CRIME AND POLICE

Australia has many of the crime problems associated with developed nations and urban life, but on the whole, residents and visitors report feeling relatively safe. In particular, compared with other western countries, Australia's homicide statistics are very low, and, in spite of popular opinion, which seems to indicate an escalation, they have remained fairly static over the last decade. The Australian Bureau of Statistics recently found that the most frequently reported crime is unlawful entry with intent, with motor vehicle theft the next most common crime, followed by robbery and sexual assault. The defining feature of Australian crime is the rarity with which firearms are employed. Australia has very stringent gun laws (which have become even more so since the tragic Port Arthur massacre), and only 20 to 25% of homicides in Australia involved the use of a gun, compared to around 70% in the USA.

Crime patterns differ throughout the states and territories: the Northern Territory, for example, has the highest per capita rate for homicide and sexual assaults, but the lowest for armed robberies. Western Australia has the highest number of motor vehicle thefts and burglaries, but its rate of murder and attempted murder are at or below the national average. New South Wales had the highest rate of armed robbery, which is attributed to the fact that it has the largest heroin-dependent population in Australia. Canberra had the highest rate of kidnapping, attributed to acrimonious marital disputes over custody of children, and South Australia has the highest incidence of robbery and blackmail. The International Crime Victims Survey has noted that urban dwellers in Australia are four times more likely to install security devices than their rural cousins, and 62 % more likely to feel the need for special locks on exterior doors and windows. These levels are exactly comparable to similar communities in other western industrial nations. Australian crime figures are, in general, much more closely in line with European ones, than with US figures, and Australian rates of motor vehicle theft are very low compared with those in the UK.

Police forces are the responsibility of state/territory governments, and are headed in each state by a Commissioner for Police. Regulations for each force vary, and some may carry guns on duty, depending on the state. There is also a Federal Police Force. This is Australia's international law enforcement and policing representative, and the chief source of advice to the Australian Government on policing issues. It enforces Commonwealth criminal law, and protects Commonwealth and national interests from crime in Australia and overseas. In recent years, allegations of police corruption in several Australian states have resulted in purges and high public accountability. In general, the police enjoy a good public profile and maintain open communications with the community.

LOCAL GOVERNMENT

Below the level of State government, the administration of local areas is undertaken by an elected town or shire council. This body is responsible for the provision and maintenance of public facilities and amenities, such as leisure centres, libraries, and rubbish collections. Payments for all housing rates, and even dog licensing, are made to the local government. Planning permission for new buildings, demolitions and extensions are also the responsibility of the local government, and vocal public meetings are frequently held to hear public discussion over topical local issues such as town planning and new developments. The local government level is the only one at which voting is not compulsory and, in general, most Australians are somewhat apathetic and avoid close involvement in local government decisions. Addresses and telephone numbers of local governments are available under the 'Local Government' section at the front of state telephone directories.

SOCIAL LIFE

Australians are generally friendly and outgoing people. They find the British extremely reserved and often find it difficult to establish relationships with them because of this cultural barrier. Most Australians will quickly invite you into their home, often on introduction, and a barbecue is the most likely first point of association for both neighbours and colleagues. Nothing, however, will repel this friendly approach more than polite formality. First names rule in Australia, from top to bottom, and people are likely to be insulted by any other form of address. So, how can you break the ice, meet the locals and both accept and be accepted by them? This section tries to give you a little insight into Australian social life and the kinds of people and attitudes you are most likely to meet.

Manners and Customs

On the whole, Australians are a lot more casual than their British or European cousins. You will find that people, while friendly and courteous, will be far more

direct in asking questions or in telling you what they think. You are much less likely
to experience the occasionally chilling British reserve, and are more likely to know
exactly where you stand. When you meet an Australian for the first time at a social
gathering you may find that you are asked a lot of questions which you may think
'forward' or even intrusive. This directness is the normal form of social discourse,
and a similar directness of response will be expected. It is generally considered to be
a time-saver, enabling friendships to develop to a deeper and more interesting level
more quickly. Titles are rarely used, and most people regardless of their position will
expect to be addressed in first name terms. It would be quite normal, for example,
for an undergraduate student to be comfortable calling the Vice-Chancellor of their
university, say, 'Fay' or 'Derek'; and the corollary of this is that it would be extremely
insulting for a person of senior position to address someone of lower status as Mr
or Mrs. Far from being respectful, it would be considered patronising. Australian
women will expect others to use the title Ms on occasions when a title is required,
and eyebrows will be raised if a woman chooses to indicate her marital status by the
use of Miss or Mrs.

One Australian custom which cuts across all social barriers is the use of 'mate' as a
form of address. The concept of mateship is a peculiarly Australian phenomenon and
has been much studied anthropologically. Mateship generally refers to a specifically
male bond, and constitutes a somewhat macho, but nonetheless powerful, kind of
friendship. Many Australian men consider their mates to be as important, or even
more important, than their female partner; and this bond often lasts to the grave. To
be described as someone's life-long mate is the highest of compliments. Conversely,
however, Australians also often use the term 'mate' ironically, or as an aggressive
indicator in potentially explosive situations. The tone of voice will clearly indicate the
level of use. Australian men, regardless of ethnic origin, will almost invariably use
this form of expression.

Australians have a great respect for people who get out there and try something
new or difficult. They love to support the underdog, and newcomers who really 'give
it a go' will readily win the admiration and friendship of their new acquaintances and
colleagues.

There are a number of associations of migrant communities in Australia, and all
major cities will have branches of the Chung-Wah Chinese Association, and Greek,
Italian, Yugoslav, and Irish Clubs. The United Kingdom Settlers' Association (First
Floor, 146 Toorak Road West, South Yarra, VIC 3141, ☎ 03-9787 3112) is specifically
intended to provide assistance and a point of contact for new migrants from Britain
and publishes a journal, 'Endeavour' every second month. Other clubs may be found
in the Yellow Pages or your telephone directory, or by contacting the Department of
Multicultural Affairs in your state.

Sport

Sport is popularly considered to be the Australian national pastime, and is central to
the social life of many Australians. Most Australian children are encouraged to play at
least one sport from a very early age. Little Athletics, an athletics training programme
for children from the age of five upwards, is held on Saturday mornings around the
country, and is very popular. Regional and national competitions are attended by club
scouts on the lookout for new talent. Similarly, cricket and football (Australian Rules)
are enormously popular at every age and skill level, and most Australian boys play at
some time or another for their local club. Cricket is becoming increasingly popular

with girls, but usually not until secondary school age or even later. Sporting centres all over the country also offer volleyball, netball and five-a-side soccer, and single-sex or mixed teams often have their own leagues. Many young working Australians will play in one such team at least one night per week as a way of keeping fit and meeting their friends.

Australian Rules Football. Australian football is the most popular winter game, and is a predominantly male sport. Aussie Rules football is a national institution, and the AFL Grand Final is comparable to the FA Cup Final in the UK in the level of interest it excites around the country. Every state has its own team or teams which play in the national league, with the West Coast Eagles, the Sydney Swans, Carlton, the Geelong Cats, and the Essendon Bombers amongst the big names. Aussie Rules is a fast and athletic game, with much handling of the ball and some impressive jumping and mid-air collisions. The game is played by two teams of 18 players who try to score goals against each other. The goal posts consist of four tall, evenly spaced poles, the two outer ones slightly shorter than the inner ones, and there is a goal at each end of the oval. The oval-shaped football field is about three times the size of a soccer pitch. If a player touches the ball over the line between the two middle posts, he has scored a goal, the team gains six points, and the goal umpire (always dressed in a white coat) will gesture and energetically wave two white flags. If the player touches the ball over the line between a middle and an outer pole, he will have only scored a single point, and the goal umpire will gesture with one of his index fingers, waving just one of the flags. The game consists of four quarters, each quarter lasting 45 minutes. Running with the ball is allowed, as long as it is bounced every three seconds; failure to do this means being 'caught with the ball'. Bouncing the ball while on the run is in fact not easy as the ball is oval-shaped, like a rugby ball. Although some of the players at the interstate level have started to wear head protection and gloves (to give them a better grip on the ball), Aussie Rules players pride themselves on their toughness and fitness. The game is gruelling and extremely hard on the players. It is long and very physical, but can also be intense and exciting. The best way to see a game is to go to an important interstate match, and catch the enthusiasm of the crowd.

Rugby and Football. In the eastern states, rugby (both league and union) is also known as football, and Queenslanders in particular take the game very seriously. Western Australia, the Northern Territory and Tasmania do not share the enthusiasm of the other states for rugby, but the nation as a whole is proud of its top-level international rugby team, the Wallabies. Football of the kind played in the UK is always known as soccer and has a small but enthusiastic following, particularly amongst European ethnic communities who often field their own teams in state soccer competitions.

Hockey. Hockey is very popular with men, women and children, and Western Australia prides itself on its exceptional facilities at Curtin University, and on its track record of providing most of the players in the national team. The Australian Institute of Sport trains its specially selected hockey stars of the future at these facilities. The Australian men's and women's hockey teams are respected and feared worldwide and they both compete at the very top of the international circuit.

Basketball and Tennis. These are widely played throughout the country, and Australia has produced many Wimbledon champions. Basketball is played at regional and interstate levels, and the national league is extremely well supported and avidly watched on television. Australian players have gone on to positions in America's NBL teams, and there is considerable interchange between the two countries. Obtaining a ticket for an interstate match can prove to be very difficult as they are snapped up as soon as they become available. Baseball is an even newer sport to Australia, but there is also a national league which is becoming increasingly popular.

Netball and Softball. Netball and softball also enjoy almost universal participation amongst young girls. Around 90% of Australian schoolgirls play in non-school netball teams during winter, and there are also summer competitive leagues, playing on weekday evenings, which are very popular. Most schoolgirls play softball in the summer.

Sport and Schools. The Australian school curriculum incorporates sport into the normal school day, and each school, whether private or state, usually participates in both an interschool swimming carnival and an interschool athletics carnival every year. In addition, there are interschool cricket, netball, football, and softball leagues with games scheduled during school time or immediately after school. Many private schools, however, hold their interschool sporting matches on Saturdays. In fact, Saturday mornings and afternoons are unofficially dedicated to sport around the country, and parents should resign themselves to the inevitability that for at least five years they will have to get out of bed early on a Saturday morning to deliver their offspring to the relevant sporting venue.

Modified Rules for Children. An important difference in Australian sport for children is the widespread use of 'modified rules' in almost every game. Under modified rules sports, even quite young children are able to compete in complete safety, whilst learning the basic skills of the sport. Primary schools will undertake careful coaching in every sport played, and there is a strong emphasis on skill development. Modified rules sports are known by names which differentiate them from their big brother sports: junior hockey is called minkey, a game based on baseball and softball for kids is called tee ball and is currently wildly popular, junior Aussie rules is touch football, and junior tennis, short tennis.

Water Sports. Above all, though, water sports are the cornerstone of Australian social and sporting life. Water-skiing, windsurfing, surfing, boating and diving are all common leisure activities, as well as highly competitive sports. Many Australians own their own pleasure boat, whether a yacht, power boat, or launch. Swimming is an essential part of every school's sporting curriculum at both primary and secondary levels, and in summer students will swim in either the school or local pool at least two or three times a week, if not every day. Pupils are divided into classes according to their age and swimming ability, and are rigorously coached by qualified instructors. Students are expected to attain swimming qualifications to a high level, and from the age of 13 are coached towards attainment of life-saving qualifications. Most students will leave high school with the Royal Life Saving Society's Bronze Medallion and Instructors Certificate. Every public swimming pool is home to a competitive swimming club, and many young Australians join these at an early age, often eventually swimming at a state or even national level. Almost every Australian child is a safe swimmer by the age of six, and school classes are focused on the development of refined technique and stamina. If you are moving to Australia with children, it would be advisable to have swimming coaching before you leave, so that they are not left high and dry at school. Once in Australia, do not allow your children to swim 'widths' in public swimming pools: this is considered highly anti-social and derisory, and even three year olds will be expected to tackle the length or keep to the baby pool. The Australian swimming, diving and water polo teams are amongst the world's best, and proved the point during the 2000 Olympic Games in Sydney.

Arts

Although Australians are famous for their love of sport, they are also enthusiastic supporters of the arts. Their expenditure on arts products ranks among the highest in developed countries, and research shows that they read more newspapers per head than any other nation. Australian cultural achievements are now well known internationally, through the awards gained by its many arts exports. The movie *Strictly Ballroom* won the Prix de la Jeunesse at Cannes in 1992, and *The Piano*, the Palme d'Or in 1993 and Australian actors such as Russell Crowe (originally from New Zealand), Nicole Kidman, Mel Gibson, Cate Blanchett and Geoffrey Rush are now big players in Hollywood. Thomas Kenneally and Peter Carey have both won the Booker Prize for Literature in Britain, and the Australian Ballet was described by the New York Times during one of its world tours as 'world class'. The Australian Youth Orchestra is widely regarded as one of the best in the world, and is the training ground for the country's finest musicians.

Government support has been an important factor in developing the arts, and funding currently totals about $3.5 billion per annum. Funding for the development of Australia's cultural heritage comes from all three levels (Federal, State/Territory and local) of government. The Arts are also heavily supported by corporate and business sponsorship. The Australian Broadcasting Commission supports orchestras in each capital city, and the Sydney and Melbourne orchestras are flagship ensembles which frequently tour internationally. There are two major organisations involved in ballet and opera on a national basis, the Australian Ballet, and the Australian Opera, and most states also have state opera and ballet companies of a high standard. Musica Viva, established in 1945 to promote chamber music in Australia, now co-ordinates one of the largest ensemble music concert networks in the worlds. It also organises overseas tours for Australian chamber music groups and commissions works by Australian composers. Youth Music Australia, formed in 1948, has helped the careers of thousands of young musicians, and the Australian Chamber Orchestra is at the cutting edge of early music performance.

Aboriginal Arts. Aboriginal art, indigenous dance and music have recently begun to be introduced to national and international audiences. Companies like Bangarra and the Tjapukai Dance Theatre now take their performances around Australia and around the world. Aboriginal art, once confined to the ethnographic sections of local museums, now takes its place in contemporary art galleries internationally. Aboriginal writers, such as Sally Morgan and Jack Davis, and the late Kevin Gilbert and Oodgeroo Nunuccal, are well known throughout Australia. Sally Morgan's *My Place* is a moving account of the discovery of her Aboriginal heritage, and provides a keen insight into some regrettable episodes in Australia's history.

SOME ANNUAL FESTIVALS AND OTHER IMPORTANT CULTURAL EVENTS

Artrage: The Festival of Perth Fringe
Moomba Festival (Melbourne)
Sydney Festival
Sydney Gay and Lesbian Mardi Gras
The Festival of Adelaide
The Festival of Perth
Wangaratta Jazz Festival (Victoria)

Every state has excellent library services both at the local and state level, and the National Library of Australia provides research facilities for scholars from all around the country. It is also home to the national archives. There are good art galleries in every state, and a strong commitment to bringing international touring exhibitions to Australia.

SHOPS AND SHOPPING

Shopping in Australia's metropolitan centres is generally excellent. In suburban areas, large shopping centres offer speciality shops for clothing and goods, as well as supermarkets. Bigger shopping centres often also have a 'food hall', offering a wide variety of economical cuisines from around the world. Many also have cinema complexes. Most of the older suburbs will have a 'high street' (although it will never be known by this name) very similar to a British high street, with smaller retailers, chain stores, and service outlets. Newer suburbs tend to be planned around a US-style shopping mall, and do not usually have the convenience of a 'corner shop' – known in Australia as a 'deli'. In areas with large immigrant populations, delis often stock a wide range of exotic foods in addition to essential items. Shops are generally open from 8.30am-5.30pm, Monday to Friday; 8.30am-4.40pm on Saturdays; with 'late night trading' until 9pm one night a week (usually a Thursday). Many shops now open on a Sunday, especially in tourist and city centre areas, but Sunday trading is frowned upon in some states. Delis are usually open from 8am-8pm and every city will have a number of chemists which are open 24 hours a day, 365 days a year. There are an increasing number of 24-hour shops in Australia, of the 7-ll type, and most cities have a handful of these scattered throughout the suburbs.

The quality of Australian produce and goods is generally good. Items bearing a green and gold kangaroo trade mark symbol have been manufactured in Australia, and these are generally more expensive than equivalent goods manufactured in Southeast Asia, due to the higher cost of Australian labour. The high quality of Australian-made products is also reflected in their higher prices. In general, however, Japanese, Taiwanese and Korean products, particularly vehicles and electrical goods, conform to Australia's strict quality standards and are usually very competitively priced. Australia is constantly seeking to improve its balance of trade by encouraging consumers to buy Australian, and in many cases appeals to loyalty and patriotism to counteract the imperative of the hip pocket.

Shopping in Australia can be an enjoyable experience, with a wide range of products available in modern, well-equipped shopping centres, as well as ample car parking. In the rural and more remote areas, however, the situation can be very different. Choice is much more likely to be limited as shopping centres service much smaller populations, and prices may be significantly higher because of freight costs. Most country dwellers prefer to wait until a trip to the city before shopping for electrical goods or clothing.

Supermarkets. All supermarkets use the barcode shopping system, and groceries are electronically scanned at the tills. Under the ruling of voluntary Code of Practice for Computerised Checkout Systems in Supermarkets, if an incorrect price registers on the supermarket scanner – and you are on-the-ball enough to spot the mistake – the price of the item is voided from your receipt and by law you are given the item for free. Supermarkets thus have a keen incentive to keep their barcodes accurate.

Loyalty cards have not been introduced in Australian supermarkets on a wholesale basis yet (although some small boutiques and restaurants operate similar schemes), however, many of the larger supermarkets, such as Coles and Woolworths, print vouchers on the back of their itemised receipts offering free meal deals (on a buy one, get one free basis) at local restaurants and chains, and discounts on anything from carpet cleaning to photo processing.

Edge-of-town superstores are rare, and most people shop in either a large supermarket located in a shopping mall, or in one of the many smaller franchised supermarkets, such as *Supa-Valu* or *Foodland*, in the local high street. Supermarkets large and small advertise pages of weekly 'specials' in the local papers, and prices are very competitive.

The vast majority of shops accept cheques and major credit and debit (EFTPOS) cards with adequate proof of identification.

Bottle Shops. By law, alcohol may not be sold in Australian supermarkets. Alcoholic drinks can only be bought from licensed liquor stores, also known as 'bottle shops'. Drive-in bottle shops are very common and provide the convenience of allowing you to drive up to a shop, roll down the car window and give your order and money to an attendant in exchange for cartons of beer or casks of wine. If availing yourself of a drive-in bottle shop, remember that in Australia you cannot drink and drive! Bottle shops are usually open from 10am-10pm, Monday to Saturday, and until 8pm on Sunday. They generally stock an extensive range of quality wines, as well as the usual beers and spirits. Most will have a giant walk-in coolroom, where all white wines are kept chilled so you need *never* visit a bottle shop in summer and come home with a warm bottle of white wine. Australians visiting the UK are incredulous at the lack of refrigeration in off-licences. Larger alcohol-retailing chains, such as Vintage Cellars, hold regular wine tastings, wine discussion evenings for regular customers, and publish monthly newsletters analysing the latest releases and the grape harvests. If you are having a party, most shops will accept the return of unopened bottles purchased from them in a bulk order (as long as labels and seals are not water-damaged from immersion in ice).

Clothes. Many European immigrants to Australia are of the opinion that the quality of clothing in Australian department stores is not as high as that found in equivalent stores in the EU. European clothes are usually made from better quality materials and to higher standards than the same kind of clothing in Australian stores, which are largely imported from Southeast Asia. Having said this, the cost of clothing from a budget-priced Australian store such as KMart or Target, as well as from other mid-range chain boutiques, is, depending on the current exchange rate, as much as 50 percent less than clothing from UK stores of a comparable standard. Classic Aussie 'clobber' such as moleskins, Driza-Bone coats, RM Williams boots, and Akubra hats are all going to be cheaper if bought in Australia. European designer label fashions can be bought in all the capital cities, but at a price, and Australia has some very highly regarded designers of its own. You will find, however, that the dress code, both at the office and at most social occasions, is informal by European standards, especially in summer. Leather goods, especially shoes and bags, tend to be expensive in Australia, to the extent that it may be worth investing in a few good quality items before you leave home; for women, the same applies to Marks and Spencers lingerie, which is always gleefully acquired by the bagful by Australians travelling through the UK.

FOOD AND WINE

Food

Australian food and eating habits have changed enormously in recent decades. The practically cuisine-less country has become one of the trendy food meccas of the world. As recently as the 1980s, Australian cooking was known only for its meat pies, slabs of steak, lamingtons, pavlovas, and pumpkin scones. In the post-war years, however, the gradual influx of waves of immigrants from Italy, Greece, Yugoslavia, Turkey, Lebanon, India, Thailand, China, Malaysia, Indonesia and Vietnam, meant the enrichment of the longer-standing Anglo-Irish eating style. The sunny climate and outstanding fresh produce and seafood provided the perfect seedbed for the cuisines of the Mediterranean and Southeast Asia, so that now chefs are renowned for their 'fusion food', mixing traditions from around the world.

Meat still plays an important part in the Australian diet, and the choice and quality is impressive by European standards. It is also largely inexpensive. Beef, lamb, pork and poultry of all cuts and types are available, as are more unusual 'bushmeat' options, such as kangaroo, emu and crocodile. These latter items are speciality fare, but are beginning to be farmed for both the export and domestic markets. In recent years 'bush tucker' has become popular, at least as a concept, and in each state there are a number of restaurants offering native aboriginal foods elevated from the campfire to the table. If you have a strong stomach, you may like to try witchetty grubs, usually served, tongue-in-cheek, poking out of a bush apple. More appetisingly, Australia has a superb range of delicious seafood, including prawns, lobsters, crayfish, octopus, oysters, mussels, mudcrabs and Balmain bugs (a type of crustacean). A huge variety of fresh fish, mostly unfamiliar to European visitors, is available: try dhufish in Western Australia, for example. If you buy fish from a fish and chip shop you are most likely to be served either shark or snapper; don't be put off by the idea of shark, as it is considered to be a good quality eating fish. The menu of the average fish and chip shop will also offer crab, prawns, squid (calamari), oysters or mussels, as well as a choice of homemade marinated pickles. Fruit and vegetables are all grown locally, and include many tropical varieties, such as lychees, avocados, and papayas.

Barbecues continue to be an integral part of Australian social life, but the menu has broadened. A respectable barbecue will be laden with tiger prawns, marinated rump steak and chicken fillets, or perhaps a whole fish garnished with ginger and spring onions. Even without the spectacular beaches, Finlays Fresh Fish BBQ in Kalbarri, Western Australia, would makes the six-hour drive north from Perth worthwhile. This little shack in the sand will cook you up unbelievable prawns fresh out of the water, as well as fish and enormous steaks, barbecued for you by Mr Finlay himself. Finlay's mum takes your cash (about $12-$14 depending on what you are having) and prepares a range of about six salads, and as many sauces, for your meal, from which you help yourself as you sit on the benches with a drink and watch the sun set the vast sky, your prawns sizzling next to you on the barbecue.

Whether you have a barbie prepared by professionals like the Finlays, or one in your own back yard, or you grill-up on coin-operated gas barbecues provided by the local council, the food is likely to be great and the company congenial.

Restaurants

Australian food is distinguished by the outstanding quality and freshness of the produce. You can expect to eat at a cheap-and-cheerful restaurant for between $15-$20 for a two course evening meal and coffee, excluding wine. Portions are usually generous. In cities with big multicultural populations (most of the capitals, and many larger regional towns), you will usually find family-run restaurants which offer great food at incredible prices: in Sydney, 'No Names' used to be famous for serving up giant plates of spaghetti with a hunk of ciabatta and olive oil for just $2, and in Perth, 'The Roma', run by the same Italian family for 30 years, still has queues outside on a Friday night for a plate of mama's pasta. You can eat at The Roma, and dozens of places like it, for a few dollars a head. The decor is basic, but the service is good, and children are welcomed. In Northbridge, there are very similar restaurants run by Vietnamese families, serving up dozens of hot and spicy specialties. The variety of restaurants available in all major Australian cities is enormous, and is at least as varied as in London or New York. Greek, Vietnamese, Mongolian, ethnic Chinese and Indian, Mexican, Lebanese, Portuguese, Italian, Russian, Thai and Polish are all available Australia-wide. Japanese food is very popular, and *ramen* shops and sushi bars are found in most suburban areas. Street markets, like shopping centres, will often have a food hall (in Perth, try Subiaco Markets), where you can buy a good Japanese, Thai, or Italian meal for as little as $8. Australians are generally very accommodating towards families who bring their children to eat in restaurants, probably because of the influence of child-loving Eastern European and Chinese immigrants, and you will be treated with consideration and respect if you choose to introduce your offspring to fine dining at an early age.

At the top end of the market, there are innumerable first class restaurants, offering the finest food and wines. Modern Australian cuisine emphasises the quality of the ingredients rather than fanciful techniques, and there is a horror of 'over-worked' food. Service is discreet, and there will usually be a qualified *sommelier* to advise on appropriate wines (which will be predominantly Australian). Expect to pay up to $150 a head in the best restaurants, but it will be worth it, especially if, as many do, the restaurant comes with spectacular views over a river, harbour or ocean.

Café culture is firmly established in Australia. You can be sure of a really good cup of coffee in most establishments. The *Dome*, a national franchise of coffee vendors, takes its coffee very seriously indeed, and even casual staff spend a week in training, learning how to make cappucino, macchiato, and espresso as they are made in Italy. If your preferred cuppa is of the type known as a *latte*, you should ask for a 'flat white' (or with low-fat milk, a 'skinny flat white'). Any decent café will sell all its various coffees in decaffeinated style as well.

Tipping is discretionary in Australia, however, if you should decide to tip your waiter, it is customary to leave between 10 and 15 per cent. Some restaurants include a service charge, but this is unusual.

Traditional Australian Food

Australians are particularly fond of fruit and vegetables, and an Australian fruit salad is likely to surpass anything you have previously eaten. Fruit salad is the traditional dessert to accompany a barbecue, and you may be asked to bring one if you are invited as a guest. Be imaginative and include all the various fresh and exotic fruits on display in your greengrocers. Another favourite, the pavlova, is an Australian invention, also most often seen at barbecues. It was created for the ballerina, Anna Pavlova, on an Australian tour, and consists of a meringue base covered with whipped cream and seasonal fruits.

The lamington is another Australian institution, and consists of a cube of extremely light sponge which has been dipped in a special chocolate sauce and then rolled in coconut. School Parents' Associations invariably have 'Lamington Drives' as a way of fund raising; school members take orders from students, parents, friends and relatives for at least one dozen lamingtons each, and then a battalion of parents get together to prepare this delicacy. A box of a dozen lamingtons usually sells for about $5. Everybody loves lamingtons, and there are few more effective fund-raising endeavours.

Many Australians grow passion fruit vines in their gardens, and passion fruit icing is very popular for sponge cakes. If you are lucky enough to have a passion fruit vine, make sure that you give it plenty of water and you will be rewarded with the world's most heavenly fruit right through the summer months.

The most famous Australian take-away food is the meat pie. This is traditionally eaten at Aussie Rules Football matches, and by school children (or at least by those with undeveloped taste buds) and they are always served with tomato sauce. Commercially mass-produced meat pies are pretty horrible, and you really have to be drunk or starving to eat one in these days of gastronomic variety. At a basic barbecue, perhaps one given by older Australians, expect the traditional fare of beef sausages and a big slab of steak.

Wine

Viticulture is one of Australia's leading primary industries, and wine drinking has enjoyed enormous growth over the years as wine production has become more sophisticated and eating habits have changed. Australia's climate and coastal fringe landscape is conducive to wine growing, and all states have extensive wine producing areas. The diverse climate, topography and soil types mean, however, that Australia is able to produce a wide range of wine styles, from delicate sparkling whites, to full-bodied reds, and exceptionally rich fortified wines. There are currently 44 regions of significance to the wine industry, each of which produces distinctive wine varieties. Australia has around 60 different varieties, although most wine drinkers will be familiar with around only 20 names, including Chardonnay, Semillon, Sauvignon, and Shiraz. Lesser-known types, such as Palomino and Pedro Ximenes, which do not appear on wine labels, are used for making sherry, and Pinot Meunier, is used in the production of sparkling wine. Every variety has a specific aroma and taste, known as the primary fruit characters, and many wines will use a blend of these different types. There are over 1,300 vineyards in Australia, and over 148,275 hectares of land under vines. The top export markets for Australian wines are the UK and USA, and exports today total around $1.76 billion annually – and rising; wine exports exceed wine imports by ten to one. The top six wine grape varieties currently under cultivation are Shiraz, Cabernet Sauvignon, Chardonnay, Semillon, Merlot and Colombard.

Regional Varieties. Most Australian wine production is located in the more highly inhabited south-eastern provinces of New South Wales, Victoria and South Australia – the latter produces approximately 70 per cent of Australian wine. The climate of much of South Australia is a lot like California, with a range of microclimates and a low to moderate rainfall. Inland, the weather gets hotter, and varieties of red wine can be made in almost all of the regions. Some of the best-known regional wine growing areas are described below:

Margaret River (WA). Western Australia produces about 3 percent of Australia's wine – but the grape harvests here account for approximately 20-30 per cent of Australia's premium bottled wines. The wine industry in Western Australia was founded even before those of South Australia and Victoria, and for the next 135 years commercial viticulture was confined to the Swan Valley, around Perth. In the mid-1960s, the wine industry began to move south, with the first plantings at Margaret River and Mount Barker. Margaret River has grown to be one of Australia's finest and most vibrant wine producing regions, known for its Chardonnay, Sauvignon Blanc and Cabernet Sauvignon.

The climate of the Margaret River area is strongly maritime, more so than any other Australian wine region, and is the most Mediterranean in style. Overall, the climate is similar to that of a Pomerol or St. Emilion in a dry vintage, which accounts for the quality of its Cabernet, Sauvignon, and Merlot varieties. Margaret River's reputation was founded on its Cabernet Sauvignon, and rests on it today. Virtually every winery produces one of these blends, and the style has evolved over the last few decades. The common threads of this wine are ripe grapes, which produce a sweet core, and a slightly earthy tannin. The Chardonnay variety was pioneered by the Leeuwin Estate, and is probably Australia's greatest example of the type. It tends towards a concentrated, complex, viscous and tangy taste, which does not cloy or become heavy. Permutations of Semillon and Sauvignon Blanc are combined to produce a regional speciality known as the Classic Dry White. This wine has a pleasantly herbal or grassy flavour.

There are many fine restaurants in the Margaret River region, a number of which are attached to vineyards: the most outstanding (and expensive) is without doubt the one on the Leeuwin Estate. Important regional events include the annual Leeuwin Concert, and the Porongorup Wine Festival.

Barossa Valley (SA). Vines arrived with the first settlers to South Australia and, in the early days, suburban Adelaide was the site of extensive vineyards. The Barossa Valley (including the Eden Valley), Clare Valley, and McLaren Vale were all established in the middle of the nineteenth century by German immigrants, and wine growing continues to play a central role in the state's economy. In 1996, South Australia produced half of all Australia's wine. The climate of the Barossa Valley is almost identical with that of Bordeaux, and is ideal for full-bodied red wines, excellent fortified wine, and robust whites. Shiraz is the most important local variety, and the Barossa Valley is the home of Penfolds Grange, the greatest Shiraz wine made outside the Rhone Valley. Almost every Barossa winery will include a Shiraz or Shiraz blend amongst its offerings. The style is full bodied, rich in colour, with a touch of chocolate, and a hint of roasted flavour; the wines are long lived. Old vine Grenache and Mourvedre are currently in as much demand as old vine Shiraz, with intense competition between fortified and table wine makers for the available harvest. The Barossa Valley Reisling has a quintessentially Australian style, with strong passion fruit/tropical fruit/lime flavours, which build beautifully with bottle age. Semillon has had a renaissance in recent years, and is frequently given a toasting of American oak; it develops quickly into a robust, full-bodied wine.

Important local events include 'Barossa Under the Stars' (attracting performers such as Julio Iglesias and Rod Stewart), the Barossa Vintage Festival, and the Barossa Wine Show.

Clare Valley (SA). The Clare Valley has a continuous history of wine making which dates back over 150 years. It is a high quality producer of long lived, intensely flavoured, and strongly structured table wines, which are all made in strictly limited quantities. The climate of the Clare Valley, in terms of its viticulture, is strongly dependent on its cool afternoon breezes which play an important role in slowing ripening on the vines. It is moderately continental, and irrigation is essential due to the winter-spring dominance of the rainfall.

Much of Australia's finest Riesling is grown in the Clare Valley; typically, it is an austere wine at first, with hints of passion fruit and lime, which quickly develops a touch of lightly browned toast. These wines are long lived and will improve in the bottle for up to 10 years. Cabernet Sauvignon is the other great wine of the region, and is always full-bodied, or even dense. Chardonnay, Semillon, Sauvignon Blanc and Grenache, either singly or in blends, contribute the other main wines of the region.

Important regional events include the Clare Valley Spring Garden Festival, and the Clare Valley Regional Wine Show.

Hunter Valley (NSW). The Hunter Valley, and particularly its upper region, was reborn in the 1960s and has become one of Australia's premier white wine areas. Typically, it produces soft, rich Chardonnays and quick maturing Semillons from its highly productive vineyards. Chardonnay is regarded as the outstanding wine of the region, with all wine makers produces examples of real merit. Rosemount Roxburgh is considered Australia's greatest example of the style, and is rich, complex, toasty and creamy, with a strong charred oak overlay. Hunter Valley Semillons are usually fleshy, soft, and likely to be oak-influenced, although in recent years there has been a strong move towards traditional, unwooded Semillon styles. These wines peak at around two to four years of age. In February, March and April annually, the Hunter Valley hosts the Hunter Valley Harvest Festival.

The Australian wine industry has an excellent website at **www.wineaustralia.com.au** which gives general information, the location of all vineyards, and events listings for the whole country. If you plan to sip your way around Australia, this is the place to start.

Brewing

A couple of decades ago adverts for the the 'amber nectar' declared it to be Australia's favourite drink; something that many Australians would not dispute. Every state has its own local beers, which are available nationally; the best known of these are Swan and Emu from WA, Tooheys and Fosters (NSW), Victorian Bitter, or VB, from Victoria, and Castlemaine XXXX from Queensland. Australians drink 'stubbies' 375ml bottles of beer a little shorter and fatter than the American 12 ounce beer. You will also find that most Australians also drink international lagers, and Mexican beers like Sol and Corona are particularly popular. Beer in pubs is always served ice-cold. Bitter beer or stout is not generally available on tap (draught) in pubs as Australia is an almost exclusively lager-drinking nation, and most Australians find the idea of 'warm beer' pretty disgusting. You should, however, be able to find Guinness on tap in most pubs. Ciders such as Strongbow (dry, sweet or draught) or Woodpeckers are also available. Boutique beers are now an important part of the market: Redback and Matilda Bay are major players in this field, but are expensive compared with homegrown ones. Ice-brewed beers such as Hahn Ice are also popular. There are plenty of pubs and bars all over Australia, and if you don't fancy these you can drink in wine bars, pleasant beer gardens, or with friends at home. Pubs often have a 'sundowner', or happy hour, with cheaper drinks and sometimes entertainment, usually around the hours of summer sunset. The 'Sunday Session' is a similar occasion, held on a Sunday afternoon. For older Australians, the sundowner or the Sunday session is an important part of leisure and social life.

PUBLIC HOLIDAYS

The long weekend has become an Australian institution, and is taken very seriously as an opportunity to get in some quality leisure time. On Friday afternoons at the start of a long weekend there is inevitably heavy traffic as people head out of the city to various beach and bush locations, something to be repeated on the following Monday evening as the traffic streams back. Every state legislates its own public holidays, however, there are also a number of country-wide holidays, which are usually occasions of national or religious significance.

TABLE 7   PUBLIC HOLIDAYS THROUGHOUT AUSTRALIA

New Year's Day, 1 January.
Australia Day, 26 January. This is the day on which Australia celebrates the anniversary of the landing of the first fleet at Port Philip in NSW, a date popularly considered to be Australia's birthday. All around the nation, local councils and authorities mount concerts and firework displays to help the celebrations get under way with a bang. Fireworks are considered a centrepiece of the occasion (especially as Guy Fawkes' Day is not commemorated and, after all, everyone needs an excuse to let off some rockets). In Perth, the 'Skyshow' is mounted from two barges moored in the Swan River. Hours before the show starts, the river is lined with families and friends carrying their torches (to switch on and wave about at the given signal), blankets, picnics and portable stereos. Two hours of music, lasers, fireworks and general goodwill follow, and a spirit of community dominates.
Good Friday March/April.

Easter Monday March/April.
ANZAC Day, 25 April. This national holiday commemorates the sacrifices of Australia's war heroes. Originally designed to recognise the soldiers of the Australian and New Zealand Army Corps who died at Gallipoli during WWI in a defining moment in Australian history, it now includes all Australian military personnel and commemorates their participation in campaigns in both world wars, Vietnam, and Korea. Every major city and town hosts marches by old soldiers and, these days, their descendants, wearing uniforms and medals. There are dawn ceremonies at war memorials around the country, and the day is considered to be a solemn one. Many citizens line the streets to watch the marches. These days there are also a significant number of people who believe that ANZAC day has become irrelevant to Australia's younger generation, and who resent the glorification and sentimentalising of war. *Armistice Day* (11 November) is not widely observed in Australia, and the tradition of poppy wearing is now quite rare.
Queen's Official Birthday. This is a movable holiday which always falls on the second Monday in June (except in WA where it falls on the last Monday of September).
Christmas Day 25 December.
Boxing Day 26 December.

TABLE 8   REGIONAL HOLIDAYS

The dates of some of these holidays may be variable.

Labour Day	7 March	(WA/TAS)
Labour Day	14 March	(VIC)
Canberra Day	21 March	(ACT)
Bank Holiday	5 April	(TAS)
Labour/May Day	2 May	(QLD/NT)
Adelaide Cup Day	16 May	(SA)
Foundation Day	6 June	(WA)
Alice Springs Show Day	1 July	(NT)
Darwin Show Day	22 July	(NT)
Bank Holiday	1 August	(NSW/ACT)
Picnic Day	1 August	(NT)
Labour Day	3 October	(NSW/ACT)
Queen's Birthday	26 September	(WA)
Labour Day	11 October	(SA)
Recreation Day	7 November	(TAS)
Melbourne Cup Day	1 November	(VIC)

TIME

Calculating the time difference between Australia and Europe or the USA can be confusing, especially in the southern hemisphere summer, when some states institute daylight saving and others don't. Queensland, the Northern Territory and Western Australia do *not* have daylight saving (it has been voted out in various referenda held in these states) and thus, their clocks do not move forward one hour between the last Sunday in October and the last Sunday in March. Below is a list of the time differences from GMT Greenwich Mean Time of the different states and territories:

Eastern Standard Time (EST) – 10 hours ahead of GMT: New South Wales, the Australian Capital Territory, Tasmania and Queensland.

Central Standard Time (CST) – 9.5 hours ahead of GMT: South Australia and the Northern Territory.

Western Standard Time (WST) – 8 hours ahead of GMT: Western Australia.

The time difference between WST and CST is 1.5 hours, between WST and EST is two hours, and between CST and EST is 30 minutes. An hour plus or minus should be added to account for daylight saving, according to the time of year.

METRICATION

Australia fully adopted the European metric system in the late 1970s and imperial measurements were dropped completely. Consumers were never given conversions on packaging, for example 1lb/454g, or alternative Fahrenheit and Celsius weather reports so people learnt new ways very quickly. If you ask for a pound of mince at the butcher you will not be understood. All street signs and road maps note distances in kilometres, as do speedometers; a freeway sign which reads 'Next exit 3.5', must be interpreted as a metric distance. Weights are calculated in grams and kilograms, and temperatures are given in degrees Celsius. Distances and measurements are invariably expressed as a decimal rather than as a fraction. If you have children at school, they will be expected to be conversant with the metric system, and no instruction will be given in calculating imperial measurement. The modern Australian child is unlikely to have any idea how many inches there are in a foot, ounces in a pound or yards in a mile; and, in fact, this probably applies to anyone under 40.

RETIREMENT

CHAPTER SUMMARY

○ People over 60 are known as 'seniors' in Australia.

○ The terms 'OAP' or 'pensioner' are considered derogatory and are not officially used.

○ Generally, the Australian policy towards seniors is to keep them lively and independent for as long as possible.

○ **Family Migration Programme.** Those with family living in Australia may be able to enter permanently as a retired person under this programme.

   ○ 510 Parent visas were issued in 2001-2 under the Family Migration programme.

   ○ Your relatives must agree to sponsor you financially for two years after your arrival.

○ **Retirement Visa.** If you enter Australia on this type of visa, you will not be able to stay permanently.

   ○ You will have to periodically renew your Retirement visa, which has to be continually approved by the authorities.

   ○ The authorities are not lenient with seniors found staying illegally.

○ **Retirement Villages.** All cities and large towns have purpose-built accommodation for seniors. Some are state-run and some private.

   ○ If you enter Australia on a Retirement visa you will not be entitled to a place in a state-run retirement village, and it will be more difficult to buy into a private one.

○ **Retirement Areas.** Favourites include Queensland, especially Cairns and the Gold Coast.

○ **Pensions.** Immigrant seniors are not entitled to an Australian pension until they have accrued 10 years' worths of contributions.

Introduction

Australia has traditionally been the destination of young people, and most new arrivals have generally been either backpackers travelling on Holiday Working visas or young immigrant families. Indeed, it is well known that applicants under 35 are far more likely to be granted residency in Australia, and the Points System of visa eligibility actively discriminates in favour of youth by docking points as the age of the applicant increases. In the past, the average age of the Australian population was relatively low in comparison with that of other developed countries, however, these days, in common with most industrialised nations, Australia is experiencing the 'greying' of its population. On the other hand, the elderly are perhaps not as noticeable in Australia as in Europe, as the climate allows and encourages them to remain healthy and active for much longer.

As Australia has become more accessible in terms of cost and ease of travel, there has been a marked increase in the number of older people both visiting Australia and choosing to retire there. The Australian government has introduced a visa and residence classification specifically for parents of new migrant settlers which allows any child who has gained permanent residency to sponsor their parents to enter the country on a long term basis (see the *Residence and Entry Regulations* chapter for details). In 1993-94 the number of retirement visas issued was 240; in 1999-00, this figure was 1,622. The warmer weather, cheaper housing and yearning for contact with children and grandchildren are all powerful factors influencing the decision to leave a lifetime's history behind to start a new life on the other side of the world.

Many older people moving to Australia feel that the journey itself is one of the most daunting considerations, as it is both expensive and physically gruelling. Travel agents, however, can recommend ways of breaking your journey without adding too much to the expense and enable you to recoup in stages and minimise jet lag. Alternatively, if you buy a cheap ticket, you are likely to find that it is cheap precisely because it is not a direct flight and will stop two or three times for up to four hours during the course of the journey. Many passengers take advantage of these stops to wander around the airports, helping to avoid stiffness, cramping and swollen ankles. Airlines can provide wheelchairs and support staff (who will, for example, help you collect your luggage) providing prior notice is given; you should also tell your travel agent or airline of any special medical conditions or dietary requirements at the time of booking your ticket. It is useful to know that if you order special meals for your flight, you are likely to be served first which, in a plane carrying around 300 passengers, can make a big difference to your personal comfort. In addition to practical tips and advice, this chapter provides information specifically for those wishing to retire to Australia, including the names and addresses of government support agencies.

The Decision to Emigrate

Many retired people will experience the 'empty-nest syndrome' most keenly if their offspring have moved not just away from home, but thousands of miles away to Australia. Although the warmer weather, hours of sunshine and lower cost of living are appealing factors in their own right, the deciding factor is likely to be the pull of the heart strings. The fact that many retirees who move to Australia have never previously visited the country suggests that it is the people, rather than the place, which provide the main reason. Although it takes enormous energy and motivation to move abroad when retired, it requires a significant extra input to pack up and transport yourself to the other side of the world. The images most Europeans have of Australia have been carefully packaged by marketing experts to encourage tourism, and as a consequence they are generally aimed at the young and mobile independent traveller. In order to make sure that Australia really is the place in which you wish to spend the rest of your days, it is highly advisable to take an extended holiday of up to six months in order to gain a more accurate impression of what life in Australia as a retiree might be like. A long stay in Australia to allow you to familiarise yourself with its people and way of life may, to a certain extent, prevent you from eventually suffering too intensely the inevitable homesickness.

There are distinct advantages to be gained by retiring to Australia. Firstly, you will not need to master a foreign language. Additionally, the weather in most inhabited parts of Australia is superb, with warm temperatures and glorious sunshine, and the coastal location of most Australian cities means that residents enjoy the benefits of fresh sea air. Senior Citizens are well looked after, and receive many special benefits and discounts for various facilities and services including public transport, holidays, utility bills, restaurants and hairdressing. Currently, the very favourable Australian dollar exchange rate, combined with the lower costs of living and property in the country, mean that moving to Australia from most European countries after retirement, particularly to join children who have already migrated, can also be very financially advantageous.

People over the age of 60 in Australia are always known as 'Seniors'. The rather derogatory terms 'old age pensioner', 'OAP', and 'pensioner' were removed from the official vocabulary years ago. Seniors are generally accorded a level of respect commensurate with their lifetime of experience.

Residence and Entry Regulations

The Residence and Entry requirements for retired people who wish to move to Australia are described in full in Chapter Two. Briefly, there are two ways in which it is possible to retire to Australia. The first method is only applicable if you do not have family already living in Australia. In this case, if you are at least 55 years of age and have no dependants other than your spouse, you may be able to enter Australia to retire providing you meet financial, health and character requirements. The Australian Government will only allow retired people who have no other connections with Australia to enter the country if they can support themselves and have the financial means to make Australian investments. In other words, you will be expected to contribute to, and not drain, Australian resources: you will need at least $650,000 capital, or a combination of at least $200,000 plus further income of at least $45,000 per annum.

If you do have family in Australia, you may be eligible to enter as a retiree under the family stream migration programme, which enables parents to join children already living in Australia. This is by far the more common way to enter the country to retire and within the 2000-01 Family Stream programme 510 parent visas were issued. Full details of this scheme are given in the *Residence and Entry* chapter. Basically, Category 103, Family Stream Migration, entitles the parent of any child, who must have been a permanent resident of Australia for a minimum of two years, to be granted residency in their own right. The potentially prohibitive financial requirements applying to non-family stream retirees do not apply in this case; however, your child must guarantee to sponsor you financially for two years after your arrival in the country.

Like all migrants, Family Stream applicants are assessed on an individual basis and against Australia's health and character requirements.

Obtaining a Residence Permit

If you enter Australia on a Retirement visa, you will never be granted permanent residency. You will enter the country on a six month multiple entry visa which you then need to transfer to a four-year Retirement visa. This visa is issued on a renewable basis, so your status as resident is more tenuous, perhaps, than for other categories of residency: applications for visa renewal can be refused if your circumstances have changed significantly or if you no longer meet the financial, health or character requirements.

If you enter the country on a Class 103 Family Stream Migration visa, you will automatically be granted permanent residency after you have been resident in Australia for two years.

You should note that Australia really takes a very strict line on visas and immigration, and the authorities will not hesitate to deport people who do not comply with regulations, regardless of considerations of age or compassionate circumstances. A cautionary tale is told of a British couple who, a few years ago, were deported after staying on illegally for 16 years. The couple, who had worked and paid taxes in Australia during this period, were given no leeway, and were required to leave the country immediately and permanently. They were discovered after making a pension claim.

Possible Retirement Areas

Almost every major city in Australia offers ideal retirement conditions, in terms of beautiful weather and reasonable housing costs. Darwin, Alice Springs and other cities and towns in Australia's interior or northern regions, however, often experience insufferably hot weather in summer, which many people (both old and young) find difficult to tolerate. The southern coastal regions have quite cool winters, but nowhere will conditions be as severe as a typical northern European winter. Many older people love the Mediterranean weather of Perth, Adelaide and Sydney, while others prefer the cooler temperatures of Tasmania or the unpredictable and varied Melbourne weather. A large number of Australians like to retire to Queensland, particularly favouring Cairns and the Gold coast, with its abundant tropical sunshine and cheap housing; others find the humidity oppressive and prefer a more temperate climate. In NSW, the Central Coast, particularly around Gosford, is a major retirement area, with many facilities for the elderly; and in WA, the regional towns of Safety Bay, Mandurah and Dunsborough have a special appeal for retirees.

Retirement Villages

All cities and major regional towns have special accommodation, known as retirement villages, available for seniors. The decision to enter a retirement village usually means a major financial commitment as well as a lifestyle change, and should be regarded as an investment in lifestyle rather than a financial arrangement: usually, any amount payable on refund will be considerably less than that originally contributed. By law, villages must consist of units for completely independent residents, units with assistance, including some nursing care and meals for less independent residents, and rooms with 24-hour nursing care available for the fully dependent residents. There are both government and privately owned and managed retirement villages, and many are run by church groups of different denominations.

Buying into a retirement village can be complex, and will involve a contract. Such contracts are usually lengthy and replete with legalese, and it is wise to obtain the advice of a solicitor or accountant with experience in this area. Not all legal professionals will be aware of important issues for ageing people, such as contracting incomes, and advocacy organisations such as the Council on the Ageing (addresses for each state are given below) can provide expert advice.

TABLE 9	QUESTIONS TO ASK BEFORE SIGNING A RETIREMENT VILLAGE CONTRACT

- Are there any conditions attached to changes of ownership?
- What are the annual charges?
- What are the ongoing costs? Look especially for items such as water levies, swimming pool maintenance, audit fees, and management.
- Who has decision-making powers? Are there resident panels or elected representatives?
- Are there deferred management fees?
- Is there an arbitration process available in case of disputes?

You should also note that it is not necessarily automatic that you will be moved from one tier of care to another as your circumstances change. Instead, you may be required to terminate the original agreement and buy in again. Buying a home in a retirement village is not an investment, and there is no guarantee of security: if the development has problems, there may be no protection for the money you have put in. Before you sign a contract to live in a retirement village, the retirement village administrators are required by law to provide you with the *Code of Fair Practice for Retirement Villages*. This ensures that prospective residents are given clear information about the facilities and charges, and terms and conditions of residence. The Code sets out the rights and responsibilities of both residents and the administering bodies of retirement villages. Additionally, a prospective resident is entitled to a copy of every contract required to be entered into in order to reside in the retirement village, and details of any costs associated with entering into such contracts. Using such information provided by the retirement village administrators will help you to compare villages and work out the likely costs of your preferred choice. The information should also help you decide if a village would really suit your lifestyle.

If you plan eventually to enter a retirement village, you should shop around before placing your name on a waiting list. Villages are generally modern, well equipped and are professionally managed with a high quality of care. They are often built close to shopping centres, public transport and police stations, and have contact with the community through local schools and churches. In general, the Australian attitude to seniors is to keep them active and independent as long as possible and the retirement villages, purpose-built according to strict legal guidelines, reflect this. Further information about retirement villages and other types of seniors accommodation is available from the organisations listed under *useful addresses* below.

Note that if you enter the country on the Retirement visa and you wish to buy a house in Australia, you will need to write to: The Executive Member, The Foreign Investment Review Board, c/o Department of the Treasury, Canberra, ACT 2600; ☎ 02-6263 3795; fax 02-6263 2940; www.firb.gov.au. As you will never be considered a permanent resident, you will not be eligible for a place in a government retirement village, and you may also find it more difficult to find a place in a private one.

TABLE 10   RETIREMENT VILLAGE TERMINOLOGY

Accommodation Unit. The part of the retirement village in which a resident has exclusive right to reside. This can be an independent living unit, a service apartment, or a hostel bed.

Body Corporate Manager. The manager of the body corporate (legally-constituted owners' association) of a freehold retirement village. The role of the retirement village manager is usually greater than that of the body corporate manager, especially where a range of services are provided.

Deferred Management Fee. A fee paid to the operators for their part in the operation of the scheme over the time a resident stays in the village. It is usually expressed as a percentage of the price of the unit, and increases over the years as a person stays in the village.

Ingoing Contribution. The price for the right to reside in a unit in a retirement village.

Nursing Homes. Most nursing homes are regulated by the Commonwealth Government under the Aged Care Act 1997.

Sinking Fund. A fund established to provide for irregular expenditure (for example, external painting or roof maintenance). Residents usually contribute to the sinking fund through service charges.

Statutory Charge. A means of protecting residents' ingoing contributions by registering a security similar to a mortgage on the title to the retirement village land.

Types of Ownership. Generally these are either leasehold (usually 99 years), freehold or strata title. Strata title gives you ownership of the living area and a share of any property held in common.

The Pension Rights of Immigrants from the UK

In March 2001 the Australian Government terminated the social security agreement that existed between Britain and Australia. Until that time, UK citizens emigrating to Australia were able to use their UK pension contributions to help qualify for an Australian pension. Prospective migrants should be aware that now that the Agreement has terminated there will be no early access to Australia's social security system for migrants from the UK. Instead they will have to accrue 10 years qualifying residence before being eligible to claim Australian Age Pension. This means that although you are fully entitled to and will receive your British pension if you live in Australia, the level of pension payments will be frozen from the date you leave Britain, and you will not receive any cost of living increases in pension payments made after this date. In Britain, pensions are indexed to the cost of living and are adjusted annually, but when you become resident of some countries (but not others) you forfeit this adjustment. Although this may seem a nominal sum to forfeit, over the years it may become a significant amount of money and your pension may cease to be adequate. This must be weighed up against the lower cost of living in Australia and the fact that there is no council tax or VAT on electricity and gas.

The Frozen UK Pensions Issue. The frozen pension issue affects the vast majority of British pensioners who live in 48 of the 54 Commonwealth countries. In September 1994 British expatriates in five of the largest Commonwealth countries including Australia, formed an organisation, the World Alliance of British Expatriate Pensioners (http://wabep.hypermart.net), as part of a continuing battle to improve the financial position of those pensioners residing in the countries where British State pensions are frozen. There are currently 224,000 people in such a position in Australia. Of the 932,000 British expatriate pensioners worldwide, 442,000 – mainly those residing in the European Union and the United States – *do* receive the same annual increments as pensioners in Britain.

Transferring a UK Pension to Australia. If you intend to become a permanent resident of Australia, the process of transferring your pension payments is surprisingly simple. All you need to do is go to your local social security office and inform them that you are leaving the country. They will then make arrangements upon your instructions to have your pension paid to you in Australia, or into a bank account in your home country if you prefer. They can also send a cheque (in sterling) at the end of every four or 13 weeks straight to you in Australia, to your overseas bank or to someone else outside the UK chosen by you. If you are away for less than 2 years they can pay your benefit as a lump sum when you return to the UK. For further information, you should contact the Pensions Info-Line on 0845-731 3233 or write to DSS Pensions, Freepost BS5555/1, Bristol, BS99 1BL (www.pensionguide.gov.uk), or Centrelink International Services (GPO Box 273C, Hobart, TAS 7001; ☎ 03-6222 3455; fax 03-6222 2799; www.centrelink.gov.au).

Taxation For British Immigrants

It is not often that one receives good news from the tax office, and therefore it perhaps comes as something of a pleasant surprise to learn that if you leave Britain and you are currently paid a pension, you will not have to pay any British tax on that pension when you leave the country. If you are not currently retired and therefore are not receiving a pension, it is advisable to have a Retirement Pension Forecast made by the Benefits Agency. This is a simple process which involves going to your local social security office and picking up a BR19 form. Upon its completion and return, the social security will be able to give you some idea of what kind of pension you can expect to receive when you retire and whether you will be paying any tax on it. You can request a pensions forecast by telephoning 0191-218 7777 and asking for the Pensions and Overseas Benefits Directorate. This kind of information may be extremely helpful to if you are considering the financial implications of moving to Australia, and may also help you with your taxation returns in Australia.

Tax on Pension Funds. Although you will not pay tax on income currently received from a state pension in the UK, British residents who settle in Australia can face taxes of up to 47% on any growth in their pension fund since leaving the UK. This developed from a ruling brought in by the Australian Taxation Office in 1994, which seeks to prevent tax avoidance through offshore funds. When British residents in Australia tap into their pension funds, any growth since the date they emigrated is now taxed as income – at the higher marginal rate of 47%. This rule, however, applies to money-purchase pensions only, and not to final salary schemes. They should also be aware that even if money is left in the UK fund, payments *will* be regarded as income by the Australian Taxation Office when it is finally drawn upon and will be taxed at the pensioner's marginal tax rate.

Anyone moving or retiring to Australia who holds an existing UK pension fund must seek professional advice. You should also be aware that UK life policies, unit trusts, personal equity plans and individual savings accounts do not necessarily carry the same tax advantages in Australia as in their country of origin, and that there may be tax implications depending on the particular product in which you have invested. Anyone in Australia in receipt of foreign source income is required by law to maintain comprehensive records of their overseas investment holdings, and penalties are in place for those failing to do so. Geraint Davies of Montfort International (☎01483-202 072; fax 01483-202073; email info@miplc.co.uk) is an acknowledged expert in this field, with experience of both UK and Australian tax laws, and can advise prospective emigrants of their potential tax liabilities and suggest ways of minimising them. Among many services they provide projections to see how migrants' current financial planning will be affected by a move to Australia.

Alan Collett of Collett and Co., Chartered Accountants (Enterprise House, Ocean Village, Southampton, Hampshire S014 3XB; ☎02380-488777; alan@gomatilda.com) provides tax and financial planning advice and services to people heading for Australia, and also gives free factsheets from www.collettandco.com.

Australian Pensions and Health Insurance

If you meet the requirements for a Retirement visa and are granted entry into Australia, you will not be covered by Medicare (because you will not have contributed towards its costs through the Medicare levy, paid via income taxes), and you will have to make arrangements in your country of origin or take out private health insurance in Australia.

If you enter the country as a Class 103 migrant, your permanent residency entitles you to full Medicare cover once you have been in the country for two years. Your sponsor (i.e. your child) is expected to meet any medical expenses you may incur the first two years, although some of this may be refunded. It is important to check with Medicare and/or your private health insurer as to the conditions which are attached. After two years, you will be entitled to full benefits as at that point you will be granted the rights of any other permanent resident. Full details on the health care system and private medical insurance are given in the *Daily Life* Chapter.

Pensions in Australia are administered by Centrelink. Formerly known as The Department of Social Services, Centrelink Customer Service Centres also provide services for various government departments including the departments of Family and Community Services (FaCS). The full rate of the basic pension for a couple is currently around $17,815 per annum, with further benefits accruing to most pensioners in the form of concessions. If you care for dependent children or students, you may be eligible for extra pension payments, as you are if you live in a remote area. If you rent privately, you may also be able to claim rent assistance. Rules and rates of payment and subject to change, and frequently reassessed by Centrelink.

Pension entitlements are calculated under two separate tests: the income test and the assets test. The test which calculates the lower pension rate is the one used.

The Income Test. A full pension must be paid if gross income is no more than $112 per fortnight for singles or $200 per fortnight per couple. Pensioners may earn up to $112 a fortnight without jeopardising any pension. If you are eligible for the pension but your spouse is ineligible, you will be paid half the combined married rate.

The Assets Test. Takes into account financial assets, excluding the family home. The full state pension will be paid if the total net market value of your assessable assets is no more than $141,000 (for a single home owner), or $242,000 (for a single, non home owner), $200,500 (for a home owner couple) and $301,500 for a non home-owning couple. A couple's combined assets must be less than $200,500 if they own their own home for them to qualify for the full pension. If you are on a pension and your spouse is not, you will be eligible for half the combined married rate of the pension. You should also note that there is a difference between pensions and allowances: for those on allowances, such as the Mature Age Allowance, Newstart Allowance, and Partner Allowances, the thresholds given above are all-or-nothing. Allowees will lose their entire entitlement as soon as assets rise above these levels.

Age, Disability, and Carer pensions, however, are phased out gradually, at a rate of $3 for every $1,000 in assets above the thresholds. The family home and superannuation are exempt from the Assets Tests.

Rebates. Single pensioners are permitted to earn non-pension taxable income up to $112 per fortnight, and couples, up to $200 per fortnight, on top of their pension. In addition, pensioners receive a tax rebate of $2,230 for singles, and $1,602 for each member of a couple. The rebate reduces to nil when taxable income is over $20,000 for singles, and $16,306 for each member of a couple.

Seniors' Benefits. Most of the benefits to which pensioners are entitled in Australia are claimed by presenting various cards issued by Centrelink and other agencies. These cards give concessions to low-income earners as well as to pensioners for a number of different services. *Pensioner Health and Concession Cards* are issued to pensioners who qualify for fringe benefits (check with Centrelink and state/territory governments for the current qualifications as they are continually under review). These cards entitle you to certain transport and medical services as well as the use of local amenities at a reduced cost. Holders of a Retirement visa are generally ineligible for any health and concession cards, and even Class 103 migrants only become eligible for certain cards after they have been resident in Australia for two years. Some concessions, however, do not depend on a particular Centrelink or other authorised card, but only on·age, so if you are able to produce any identification documents which state your date of birth, you may also be able to claim certain concessions. It is always worth checking before you pay for anything as to whether you are eligible for a concession on the basis of age. It is estimated that seniors who take advantage of all the concessions on offer will save around $2,000 per year. The most common cards and transport, amenities and health concessions are listed below.

Seniors Card. A Seniors Card is available to Australians aged 60 and over who are not working full time. The cards are issued free and enable holders to get a wide range of discounts on public and commercial activities. Businesses in one state will usually recognise cards from another and such business will display a Seniors Card Welcome sticker. Seniors Card Schemes are the responsibility of each State and Territory Government, not the Commonwealth Government and the eligibility criteria and the range of benefits vary.

The Commonwealth Seniors Health Card. The Commonwealth Seniors Health Card gives older Australians access to concessions on prescription medicines through the PBS (Pharmaceutical Benefits Scheme) as well as payment of a telephone allowance. Many self-funded retirees will be eligible for the Commonwealth Seniors Health Card.

The Health Care Card. The Health Care Card gives concessions on prescription medicines. Additional concessions may be offered to Health Care Card holders including health, household, educational, recreational and some transport concessions. These additional concessions vary widely within each State and Territory.

The Pensioner Concession Card. The Pensioner Concession Card gives access to concessions on prescription medicines, hearing services and, in conjunction with a Medicare card, basic hospital and medical treatment. Another benefit for cardholders is an $18 quarterly telephone allowance. The card also entitles holders to some concessions from state and local governments (such as reduction in council rates, water and electricity bills) and from some private organisations and businesses. Concessions vary from state to state.

Transport Concessions. All states and territories offer concession travel to people over 60 years of age regardless of whether or not they are in receipt of a pension. Concessions include reduced fares on public transport, reductions on motor vehicle registration and one or more free rail journeys within the state each year. Concessions differ from state to state and though you may b able to get discounts on some products and services while travelling interstate, others may be denied you. In Tasmania, interstate cards are accepted for local buses. In NSW holders of a Seniors Card are entitled to half fare travel within NSW on all State train and coach services, Sydney and Newcastle Government bus services and Sydney Harbour and Stockton ferry services. Seniors organisations are currently lobbying state governments to allow more interstate Seniors Card transport concessions.

Amenities. Seniors are generally also able to claim a reduction (the amount varies from state to state) for council rates, as well as some other services. Enquiries should be made at your local council. A rebate on water and sewage rates is also usually offered to qualifying pensioners, and your nearest water authority office will give you further information. If you are eligible for fringe benefits, you should contact your state or territory electricity and gas authorities for any concessions that may be applicable on your electricity and gas bills. You may also be eligible to take advantage of a free mail redirecting service from your local post office if you move house within Australia, and also of an $18.00 concession on each quarterly phone bill. Further details are available from Centrelink offices (Customer Relations: 1800 050 004) which publish Pensioner Concession Card brochures outlining the range of pensioner concessions offered by each state or territory. The brochures include information about concession eligibility and provide a useful contact. Most local councils also offer a rebate on the registration of seniors' dogs. The National Seniors Association (Level 3, 50 Market Street, Melbourne, VIC; ☎ 03-9620 1311; fax 03-9620 1399; www.nationalseniors.com.au) offers the over-50s discounts on literally thousands of products. You can join this Association for $21 ($28 for couples), and have access to guided tours and discounts on travel, members rooms in Melbourne, Brisbane, Perth and Sydney, discounts on insurance, a directory of benefits and services and a subscription to the bi-monthly *50 Something* Magazine. Under the NSA scheme, thousands of national traders offer discounts on nearly everything, from insurance, security systems, car tyres, carpets, motel accommodation, through to funeral services.

Health Benefits. The Pensioner Concession Card and the Commonwealth Seniors Health Card can help with doctors' bills, cut price pharmaceuticals, and ambulance services. The 1998 budget introduced new rulings which meant that for the first time wealthier seniors who were ineligible for a pension could receive the Commonwealth Seniors Health Card entitling the holder to concessions on prescription medicines through the PBS and payment of the Telephone Allowance. The income limit for eligibility is $50,000 for singles, and $80,000 for couples. You will never have to pay more than $3.60 for a prescription, and if you pay more than $187.20 in a year for any drugs, all further prescriptions are free. As a pensioner, you are fully entitled to Medicare benefits, but there are many different health services which are offered at reduced rates to holders of such cards. In addition, free dental treatment is offered at some hospitals and dental clinics to holders of a Pensioner Concession Card or a Health Care Card. It is worth contacting your local hospital to obtain information on the free treatment to which you are entitled and those treatments for which you would only have to pay a concessionary rate.

Assistance may also be given for the cost of spectacles from some state government health or community service departments. You should contact your local department for details but should also be aware that this assistance is determined by a strict means test.

Government subsidised hearing aids, maintenance, repairs and batteries are also available from hearing centres of Australian Hearing if you hold a Pensioner Health Benefits Card or a Sickness Benefits Card. For assistance, you should contact your nearest Australian Hearing Centre, listed under the Commonwealth Government departments section at the front of the white pages telephone directory.

There are a number of associations which have been established to address those health problems which particularly affect older rather than younger people. These organisations offer information, advice and assistance, and have branches in every state and territory, the addresses of which can be obtained from the national bodies listed below:

Useful Addresses

Arthritis Foundation of Australia, GPO Box 121, Sydney, NSW 2001; ☎02-9552 6085; www.arthritisfoundation.com.au

Australian Hearing, Australian Hearing has over 70 permanent centres operating 5 days a week. Visit the website www.hearing.com.au or call 131 797 to locate your nearest centre.

Diabetes Australia, 1st Floor Churchill House, 218 Northbourne Ave, Braddon, ACT 2612; ☎1800-640 862; www.diabetesaustralia.com.au

National Continence Helpline, Freecall 1800 33 00 66.

Stroke Recovery Association Inc., PO Box 673, Petersham, NSW 2049; ☎02-9550 0594; www.strokensw.org.au

If you move to Australia as a Class 103 migrant, there is a possibility that at some time your sponsoring child will have either to care or obtain care for you as you get older. There is a national body of carers which provides support in the form of counselling and advice, organises respite care or temporary relief, gives advice about benefits and other support services which may be helpful, and also puts your carer in touch with other carers. For further information, contact the *National Carers Association of Australia* (PO Box 73 Deakin West, ACT 2600; ☎02-6282 7886 or 1800 242 636; www.carers.asn.au).

Wills and Legal Considerations

This has been discussed in more detail in the *Setting up Home* chapter, but the clear message is that if you move to Australia, you should really make another will as there are variations in the law which may significantly and adversely affect your estate. If you wish to have a will drawn up for you in Australia, it is relatively easy to find assistance as solicitors advertise in telephone directories and also on television and the printed media. The Public Trustee Office of each state specialises in the drawing and storing of wills and it is reassuring to know that their funds are protected by an Act of Parliament. The Trustee's funds are guaranteed by the government and so the office of the Public Trustee can never die, go bankrupt or leave the state, ensuring the efficient and legal execution of the affairs of your estate. Some state Public Trustee Office's have a free will-drafting service and you should contact your state government office or website to find more details on this service. The free and independent financial information service of Centrelink (132 300; www.centrelink.gov.au) can also advise on wills and Estate planning.

If you intend to pass on substantial assets in your will, you may wish to consider establishing a Testamentary Trust. For pensioners, this means that when assets pass to the surviving spouse, those which are included in the Trust will not count against the assets test, ensuring that any pension is protected. Where child beneficiaries are involved, a testamentary trust will significantly reduce tax liability. However, since 1 January 2002 a source and control test operates for existing social security recipients and prospective recipients who have an interest in a family trust. This means that assets which in the past could be 'hidden' from assessment will now be counted if you are either the trustee or appointee of a Testamentary Trust or can influence the distribution of income or assets of the Trust. This is a highly technical area, however, and professional legal and financial planning advice is essential.

Prepaid Funerals. Although a subject most prefer not to think about, any discussion of wills and estates should include mention of funeral arrangements. Many seniors want to give their family the comfort of knowing that their funeral arrangements have already been made and paid for in advance. To serve this need, funeral directors now offer pre-paid funeral packages which involve making contributions today to offset future costs. If you enter into such an arrangement, you should ensure that the contract is covered under the Funerals (Pre-paid Money) Act, so that your contributions are paid into a trust fund. A contract should specify the amounts to be contributed, whether the amount will cover the full cost of the funeral, and any management, entry or surrender fees.

Funeral Bonds offer another alternative, and are a type of friendly society bond attracting tax and social security exemptions. The proceeds of funeral bonds must go towards the funeral expenses of the holder, but bonuses paid during the lifetime of the holder are tax-free. The capital value of any funeral bond is exempt from the Centrelink Income and Assets Tests up to $5,000.

Hobbies and Interests

Sporting Activities. In 1987 a report commissioned by the New South Wales Department of Health revealed that more than half of all physical decline in any age group aged over 65 can be attributed to boredom, inactivity and a fear that infirmity is inevitable. Since that report, there has been a widespread effort to promote continuing physical and social activities amongst seniors in the community. A 1999 report from the same source states that between 40% and 60% of older people live a regularly active lifestyle, and that compared to sedentary adults, those older adults who maintain an active lifestyle have a daily functioning comparable to people aged 15 years their junior.

In Australia, the favourable weather means that popular pursuits differ somewhat from those in the UK and Europe. Bingo, for example, is very much less popular in general, and many more seniors engage in outdoor activities. Bowls is especially popular, and in every suburb, seniors can be seen clad in white playing both competitive and friendly lawn bowls in the summer sun. You should contact your local shire or community centre for information on how to get involved in your local lawn bowls club. Golf and tennis are also widely played, and are not restricted to wealthy club members and most districts will have well-maintained public golf courses and tennis courts which can be used for a small daily fee. Most public swimming pools will have seniors' sessions, as well as hydrotherapy classes and seniors aquarobics. The very hardy amongst the senior community can also usually be seen at dawn, enjoying a communal early morning swim at their local beach; many veterans swear by this method of keeping fit, and enjoy it winter and summer. There are also a variety of associations and clubs which cater for older as well as younger members, some of which are listed below:

State Cycling Organisations. These provide organised rides as well as advice on what kind of bike to buy and maintenance.
Bicycle Federation of Australia Inc., PO Box 3222, Canberra, ACT 2601; ☎+61 3 9827 4453; www.bfa.asn.au
Bicycle NSW, Level 2, 209 Castlereagh Street, Sydney, 2000, ☎02-9283 5200; www.bicyclensw.org.au
Bicycle Queensland Inc., PO Box 8321, Woolloongabba, QLD 4102; ☎07-3844 1144; www.bq.org.au
Bicycle Tasmania, PO Box 1050, Sandy Bay, TAS 7006; ☎03-6266 4582.
Bicycle Victoria, Level 10, 446 Collins Street, Melbourne, VIC 3000; ☎03-8636 8888; www.bv.com.au

Walking for Pleasure (freecall 131 302) is an organisation which specialises in hiking and camping, and is a programme developed by the Department of Sport and Recreation(www.dsr.nsw.gov.au) in New South Wales. Walks are graded Very Easy (which means it is suitable for wheelchairs and prams), Easy, Medium, Medium/ Hard and Hard. The benefit of this programme is that you actually get to meet and talk to other people from every sector of society and every age group while you are exercising.
Federation of Victorian Walking Clubs, 332 Banyule Rd., Viewbank, Vic 3084; ☎03-9455 1876.

Cultural Activities. If you prefer to be challenged cerebrally rather than physically, most universities and colleges offer part-time courses for mature age students, and you should contact the relevant institution for details. The University of the Third Age runs short courses, for self-study or study in small groups, throughout Australia and there is a central U3A website at http://u3aonline.edna.edu.au which provides details covering a wide range of recreational interests. Local libraries are usually the best source of information on academic, cultural, and social activities for all age levels of the community.

Senior Citizens' Clubs and National Clubs. Senior Citizens' Clubs are very active throughout Australia and welcome new members. Most suburbs or districts will have an SCC, which will usually be affiliated with the National Seniors Association. These clubs organise a wide range of activities for their members, including talks and visits to places of interests as well as indoor activities such as regular bingo and chess afternoons, film screenings and community exchanges. Interaction between Seniors

Clubs and local primary schools is especially popular, with schools in particular valuing the input from older members of the community. Seniors with special expertise or knowledge of local history may be asked to talk to junior classes during the course of their studies in relevant fields.

The Older Women's Network (OWN) was established in 1991 to counteract the marginalisation of older women, and is committed to speaking out against ageist and sexist stereotyping. This group, which has an excellent website at www.zipworld.com.au/ownnsw/ publishes a newsletter and has its own theatre group, aboriginal studies group and health group. It also runs a consumer advocacy service. Contact details are given under *Useful Addresses* below.

If you would like to meet and socialise with other settlers from your country of origin, you should check your local telephone directory or with the Department of Immigration and Multicultural and Indigenous Affairs for information on national clubs such as the Italian Club or the Chung Wah Association. There are also Irish, Scottish, English and Welsh Clubs in most capital cities throughout Australia (check your white pages telephone directory), as well as a United Kingdom Settlers' Association in Victoria.

Religious Associations. Many churches and other religious groups also provide activities and coffee mornings during the week, as well as a welcoming service for people new to the area. Most churches advertise in their local newspaper, so you should check your local freesheet or the telephone directory for further details. In addition, members of the Anglican Church will find a very useful website at www.anglicansonline.org which has link to Anglican Dioceses and Parishes worldwide.

Seniors Travel. Many seniors like to take advantage of their increased leisure time to see something of Australia, and there are a number of travel options specially designed for this category of traveller. As mentioned above, in the section on Seniors Benefits, state governments provide subsidised coach and rail travel. Airlines frequently offer discounts, usually as part of a special promotion, and it is worth asking whether there are any new schemes or offers being launched in the near future before you book. A service called Seniors Home Exchange (www.seniorshomeexchange.com) charges US$60 for a three-year listing of your property on their listings service. As a member of the exchange scheme you will be able to take advantage of some 900 properties listed worldwide, cutting down considerably on the cost of holidays. Unfortunately a senior homestay service called 'Senior Citizens Stopovers Australia' which provides an economical accommodation option for travellers is now only available to those referred to the service by existing members. Under the scheme, seniors with a spare room in their home, or even a driveway suitable for a caravan, pay a small once-only membership fee, after which they are placed on a contact list. The list is circulated to all members, who must be available to host overnight visitors, as well as enjoying the opportunity to stay with other members on their travels. This service is web-based and it may be worth checking the website at http://users.chariot.net.au/annet/ to check on developments.

Useful Addresses

Clubs

Australian American Association, Level 1, 2 Eden Streeet, North Sydney, NSW 2060; ☎1300-550 920; www.aaafed.asn.au

Australia Britain Society, National Office, PO. Box 9088, Deakin, ACT 2600; ☎02-6273 2369; fax 02-6273 2364; www.aust-britsociety.org.au

Australian Irish Society, 52 Killeaton Street, St Ives, NSW 2075; ☎02-9440 0695.

Older Women's Network, 87 Lower Fort Street, Millers Point, Sydney, NSW 2000; ☎02-9247 7046; fax 02-9247 4202; www.zipworld.com.au/ownnsw/

The United Kingdom Settlers' Association, First Floor, 146 Toorak Road West, South Yarra, VIC 3141; ☎03-9787 3112; fax 03-9866 1799

Councils on the Ageing (COTA)

The Australian Council on the Ageing is a national non-profit organisation designed to provide assistance and independent advice to seniors on issues such as accommodation, financial management or health. COTA is also a major lobby group for older Australians. It has a national branch and branches in each state, many of which have a freecall number for enquiries.

Council on the Ageing (Australia), Level 2, 3 Bowen Crescent, Melbourne 3004; ☎03-9820 2655; fax 03-9820 9886; www.cota.org.au

Council on the Ageing (ACT) Inc., Hughes Community Centre, Wisdom Street, Hughes, ACT 2605; ☎02-6282 3777; fax 02-6285 3422; www.cota-act.org.au

Council on the Ageing (NSW) Inc., Level 4, 280 Pitt Street, Sydney, NSW 2000; ☎02-9286 3860; fax 02-9286 3872; freecall 1800 449 102; Seniors Information Service: 131 244; www.cotansw.com.au

Council on the Ageing (NT) Inc., 18 Bauhinia Street, Nightcliff, NT 0810; ☎08-8948 1511; fax 08-8948 1665; e-mail:execcotant@octa4.nt.au

Council on the Ageing Queensland Inc., Units 1-3, 82 Buckland Road, Nundah 4012; ☎07-3256 6766; fax 07-3256 6788; www.cotaq.org.au

Council on the Ageing (SA) Inc, 45 Flinders Street, Adelaide, SA 5000; ☎08-8232 0422; fax 08-8232 0433; freecall 1800 182 324; email: cotasa@cotasa.org.au

Council on the Ageing (Tasmania) Inc., 2 St John's Avenue, Newtown, TAS 7008; ☎03-6228 1897; fax 03-6228 0481; www.tased.edu.au/tasonline/cotatas/

Council on the Ageing (Victoria) Inc., Level 4, Block Arcade, 98 Elizabeth Street, Melbourne, VIC 3000; ☎03-9654 4443; fax 03-9654 4456; Seniors Info Service 1300 13 50 90; www.cotavic.org.au

Council on the Ageing (WA) Inc., 2nd floor, Wesley Centre, 93 William Street, Perth, WA 6850; ☎08-9321 2133; fax 08-9321 2707; www.cotawa.asn.au

Independent Living Centres. Independent Living Centres (www.ilc.asn.au) provide information for those with disabilities or limited mobility who live independently. They also demonstrate and develop products designed to help such people live more easily and retain their independence. Products include bathroom and toilet aids, as well as aids to help with communication, eating, drinking, walking and sitting. Transport and lifting equipment is also available. Information on where to hire such products, as well as their cost and availability, is available from these centres. The Independent Living Centres also produce a number of brochures providing information and updates. Visits to Independent Living Centres are by appointment only.

Australian Capital Territory: 24 Parkinson Street, Weston, ACT 2611; ☎02-6205 1900; e-mail ilcact@act.gov.au

New South Wales: 600 Victoria Road, Ryde, NSW 2112; ☎02-808 2233; www.ilcnsw.asn.au

Queensland: Cnr Goring St & Cavendish Road, Coorparoo, QLD 4151; ☎07-3397 1224; www.ilcqld.org.au

South Australia: 11 Blacks Road, Gilles Plains, SA 5086; ☎08-8266 5260; e-mail ilcsa@ilc.asn.au

Tasmania: 46 Canning Street, Launceston, TAS 7250; ☎03-6334 5899.

Victoria: Equipment Services, Yooralla Society of Victoria, 705 Geelong Road, Brooklyn, VIC 3025; ☎03-9362 6111; http://deis.vic.gov.au

Western Australia: 3 Lemnos Street, Shenton Park, WA 6008; ☎08-9381 0608; www.ilc.com.au

SECTION II

WORKING IN AUSTRALIA

EMPLOYMENT

TEMPORARY WORK

PERMANENT WORK

DIRECTORY OF MAJOR EMPLOYERS

STARTING A BUSINESS

EMPLOYMENT

CHAPTER SUMMARY

○ One of the biggest surges of employment opportunities in Australia has been in tourism.

○ **Job Prospects.** Engineers have the highest level of employment buoyancy followed by construction and property services.

○ There are currently 22 skilled occupations which are experiencing shortages including nursing.

○ **Part-time Work.** A government report predicts a leap in part-time workers by 2005.

○ **Working Illegally.** From November 2000 to June 2001 155 warning notices were issued to employers who had taken on illegal workers.

  ○ Every year 50,000 people stay on after their visa has expired.

  ○ Linkage of the computers of the Immigration, Tax and Medicare (Health) departments means it is almost impossible to flout the immigration regulations indefinitely.

○ **Casual Work.** The average harvest picker can expect to earn $300-$500 for a six-day week.

○ **Pay Increases.** The average annual pay increase is estimated at 5.2%; inflation is 4.4%.

○ **Fringe Benefits.** Only the most senior positions offer benefits, which are not generally popular because of the tax implications.

○ **Private Pension Plans.** PPPs (known as Superannuation in Australia) are compulsory.

○ The most common form of incentive is the employer's contribution of up to 10% towards employees' compulsory private pension plans.

○ **Holidays.** The statutory minimum is four weeks.

  ○ Holiday leave is sweetened with a bonus of 17.5% during the holiday period.

Overview

Australia is currently experiencing high levels of job optimism and enjoys low inflation, declining unemployment, and positive GDP growth. The most recent figures available from *tmp worldwide* show that nationally the government and social infrastructure sector is the most optimistic sector for permanent employment, while financial and professional services are also buoyant, followed by the consumer sector and information technology and telecommunications. The industrial sector shows the lowest levels of employment optimism. At present small- and medium-sized businesses show higher levels of growth and profitability than larger firms, especially small businesses that deal with the governmental and social infrastructure, and IT and telecommunications sectors. Medium-sized businesses in the financial and professional sector do best, followed by those that work in the government and social infrastructure sectors and IT and telecommunications. Large firms that deal with government and social infrastructure are most buoyant, followed by those dealing in the consumer and industrial sectors.

Within the various areas of employment the highest surges in employment in the consumer sector have been in the tourism industry, followed by advertising and the health, medical and pharmaceutical industries. Western Australia shows the biggest rise in consumer sector employment. In industry, engineers have the highest levels of employment buoyancy followed by those working in the construction and property services. Other areas where employees are increasingly being taken on are in utilities, resources, wholesale and distribution. Employment levels in the chemical and oil industry, transport and manufacturing, are all well below national expectations. Again Western Australia shows the best biggest rise in industrial industry employees. The education sector, followed by non-profit making organisations and government are most optimistic in terms of employee take up within the government and infrastructure sector. In the financial and professional services sector, the legal industry is best off, followed by service industry employees and finance and insurance service employees. The Information technology and telecommunications industries continue to show growth, but they are not growing as fast as expected. It is expected over 2002 that the greatest number of job vacancies will be found in sales, computing and IT, accounting, finance and engineering, marketing, law and other white-collar occupations. Opportunities for full-time staff are better at present than for contract or temporary workers.

State to state the financial and professional sector is the most optimistic in terms of employee take on in ACT, followed by the IT and telecoms sector, and government and social infrastructure. In New South Wales the finance and professional sector is also the most buoyant, followed by the industrial and consumer sectors. Queensland shows growth in the financial and professional sector, followed by IT, telecommunications and industry. In South Australia IT was the most buoyant sector of employment, followed by the government and social infrastructure sector, and the finance and professional sectors. Victoria showed most buoyancy in the government and social infrastructure sector, followed by the consumer, IT and telecommunications sectors. Western Australia shows the largest employee growth spread over the three sectors of industry, consumer services, and government and social infrastructure.

Current Skills Shortages. There are currently 22 skilled occupations which are experiencing labour shortages in Australia and are on the Migration Occupations in

Demand List (MODL) published by the Department of Immigration and Multicultural and Indigenous Affairs. These occupations include chefs (excluding commis chefs), nurse managers, nurse educators and researchers, registered nurses and midwives, registered mental health nurses, registered developmental disability nurses, hospital pharmacists, retail pharmacists, physiotherapists, medical diagnostic radiographers, radiation therapists and sonographers. Computer professionals in a number of specialisations including PowerBuilder, Unix, SAP, e-commerce etc., are also in high demand. Additionally there are shortages of accountants, electrical engineers, childcare co-ordinators and IT Managers. Tradespeople, especially refrigeration and air conditioning mechanics, cabinetmakers, hairdressers, and furniture upholsterers are also in demand in many areas of Australia.

Skill shortages are caused by many factors, including economic and demographic change, qualified workers deciding not to work in the field in which they trained, and variations in labour demand within the states and territories of Australia. Shortages often have more to do with the lack of available tradesmen than an increased demand on the trades themselves. Vocational education has increased the number of school leavers going out into the labour market with training and specific job-related skills but in some trades skill shortages are so severe that employers have applied for special permission from the Commonwealth Government to bring in overseas-trained personnel to fill skilled jobs. Many companies are now using labour hire contractors to fill jobs that would previously have been done by apprentices.

All states show the same pattern of skill shortages, with a few exceptions. In NSW, cadastral surveyors, actuaries, and concreters are in demand; and in Victoria, dentists, enrolled nurses, and bricklayers. In Queensland, extractive metallurgists, locksmiths, and cabinetmakers are needed; in South Australia, communications tradespersons, and printing machinists; and in Western Australia, petroleum/drilling/chemical/civil/mechanical engineers and associate professionals are all required, as well as cooks, in country areas.

The Future. The government report, *Australia's Workforce 2005: Jobs in the Future*, projects significant changes in the composition of the working population, with long-term trends towards more part-time work, a middle-ageing of the workforce, and an increased proportion of female employees. Prospects for employment vary according to industry sector and the skill level of the occupation. The employment prospects of highly skilled occupations such as managers, professionals and para-professionals are expected to enjoy continued growth, especially in those occupations which meet domestic consumer needs. Other professional groups, such as engineers, which are employed in export or import-competing industries, will also experience strong growth, and their services are expected to be increasingly in demand as these industries introduce new technologies. Production workers in manufacturing, including machine operators and labourers, will face declining or weak employment growth as industry strives to raise labour productivity to meet international competition. To offset decline in traditional industries, the government is strongly focused on the need for vocational education, skill building, and the multi-skilling of the workforce. It is seeking to build on emerging competitive strategies to take advantage of improved technologies, innovative marketing, better management, and organisational change, and more and more mature workers now accept the need to retrain or develop their skills.

Unemployment Rates for Migrants. Unemployment rates for migrants vary depending on skill levels and proficiency in the English language. In August 2001, the unemployment rate for those born in the main English speaking countries was 5.8 per cent, while the unemployment rate for those born in other countries (combined) was 7.7 per cent. Recent arrivals generally have a higher unemployment rate than those who have lived in Australia for some time. The Department of Employment and Workplace Relations (www.dewrsb.gov.au) publishes a quarterly magazine called the *Australian Jobs Review* which is intended to give migrants an overview of the prevailing labour market conditions. DEWRSB also publishes a monthly skilled vacancy survey available at *www.workplace.gov.au.*

On-line Employment Sources

Australian Governments' Entry Point (www.nla.gov.au/oz/gov/). Entry point to all Australian government websites.

Australian Taxation Office (www.ato.gov.au). Information on Australian tax laws.

Department of Employment and Workplace Relations (www.dewrsb.gov.au). Workplace relations in Australia, maritime transport, policy and legislation, government employment, and related sites. At the time of writing the Office of Small Business is moving from the Department of Employment and Workplace Relations to the Department of Industry, Tourism and Resources (www.industry.gov.au). Until this move is finalised, all information relating to the Office of Small Business is available at www.dewrsb.gov.au/smallbusiness/.

Melbourne City Council (www.melbourne.vic.gov.au). Includes information on products and services of Melbourne City Council as well as details of forthcoming events, maps and guides etc.

NSW Department of State and Regional Development, (www.srd.nsw.gov.au). Information for potential investors and business migrants to Sydney and New South Wales.

New South Wales Government (www.nsw.gov.au). Includes information on doing business with the NSW government, rural information, reports and papers, related links.

Queensland Government Online (www qld.gov.au). Includes information on business in Queensland, and government departments and agencies.

Tasmania Online (www.tas.gov.au). Includes information on investing in Tasmania and migrating to Tasmania.

Government of Victoria (www.vic.gov.au). Includes information on state projects, arts, business, education etc.

Australia White Pages (www.whitepages.com.au). Online access to over 8 million residential, business and government listings.

The Australian Yellow Pages Telephone Directory (www.yellowpages.com.au). National searchable database.

Residence and Work Regulations

In order to work in Australia, you must hold an appropriate temporary or permanent residency visa. The Australian immigration authorities are draconian in their treatment of illegal workers, and anyone caught working without a visa should expect to be deported immediately. Between November 2000 and June 2001 DIMIA issued 155 warning notices to employers who had taken on illegal workers, there were 9,054 enforced removals, 179 criminal removals and 290 repatriations. At the end of December 2000 there were an estimated 58,674 people who had stayed on after their visa had expired. To put these figures into context, during the period 2000-01 there were 17,679,474 arrivals to and departures from Australia. A data-matching programme operated by the Department of Immigration and Multicultural and Indigenous Affairs links the computers of the Australian Taxation Office, Centrelink, and the Health Insurance Commission (Medicare), making it almost impossible to get away with flouting immigration laws. DIMIA is focusing its efforts to locate illegal workers in industries which employ large numbers of casual workers, especially in rural areas, where cash payments have traditionally made it easier to work outside the purview of the eagle eye of the tax office.

The eligibility criteria, requirements and procedures for obtaining residency in Australia, whether on a short or long term basis, are described in detail in the *Residence and Entry Regulations* chapter. Those visas which allow foreigners to work legally or to seek employment in Australia are described in brief below.

Working Holiday Maker Visa. The purpose of the WHM visa is to allow young people the chance to tour extensively in Australia, with the option of working for up to three months in any one area. If you are granted this visa, you will only be able to consider employment of a temporary or casual nature. Applicants for a Working Holiday Maker visa must:

- be a citizen of Canada, Denmark, Japan, the Republic of Korea, the Republic of Ireland, Malta, the Netherlands, Germany, Sweden, Norway or the United Kingdom;
- be between the ages of 18 and 30;
- have no dependent children;
- have not previously entered Australia on a Working Holiday visa;
- meet health and character requirements;
- be outside Australia at the time of the visa grant;
- leave Australia before the expiry of the visa;
- be capable of finding temporary work as a means of supplementing holiday funds;
- have a return ticket and sufficient funds (approx. $5,000) to cover living expenses for initial stage of your holiday in Australia;
- have no intention of working for more than three months for any single employer.

Employer Nominations Scheme. This scheme allows employers to recruit highly skilled workers on a permanent basis from overseas, or temporary residents currently in Australia if they are unable to fill a vacancy in Australia. The Nominee must:

- be under 45 years of age;
- have qualifications and experience that match the vacancy requirements;
- have vocational level English;
- be able to satisfy any mandatory licensing, registration or professional membership requirements;
- meet mandatory health and character requirements.

The Employer must:
- prove that they have exhausted all possible avenues to employ an Australian citizen for the position;

○ prove that the position is a full time, fixed term appointment of at least three years, with the possibility of renewal;
○ demonstrate an excellent training record and commitment to training and up-grading skills of semi-skilled Australian workers.

Business Class Visas. There are many different types of business visas which permit professionals to work in Australia as temporary residents on a short- or long-term basis. The conditions and requirements of these visas are detailed in *Residence and Entry Regulations*, and include not only business fields, but also educators, entertainers, and others. The three main classes of business visa are:

○ Temporary Business Entry: A short-term business visa that allows multiple entry to Australia for three months at a time. The travel validity for this visa varies.
○ Business (Long-Stay) visa: Caters for people who intend to pursue business-related activities in Australia. This visa covers a variety of different circumstances, from foreign firms bringing employees out on overseas assignments, to overseas business people wanting to establish offshore operations in Australia. Educators, entertainers, and others are likely to be covered by this visa, which is valid for three months to four years.
○ Business Skills (Migrant) Class: Targets executives and investors who wish to establish themselves in Australia permanently (see below).

Medical practitioners wishing to work in Australia should note that applicants for a Medical Practitioner visa must be sponsored by an Australian organisation. For this to be approved by DIMIA there must be a demonstrated need to employ an overseas-trained doctor.

Permanent Residents. Migrants entering Australia on permanent residency visas are not subject to any restrictions or regulations, other than those which govern the working practices of all Australians. There may, however, be specific conditions attached to the class of visa granted, particularly if you are entering under a regionally sponsored migration scheme which may oblige you to work or settle in a remote area. The skilled stream of Australia's migration programme is designed to facilitate entry for people who have skills or outstanding abilities deemed to be valuable to Australia's economic advancement. If you have been accepted as a skill-stream migrant, you are, in effect, one step ahead in the job search process, insofar as you are likely to have been accepted on the basis that your particular experience and training are in demand. Current immigration policy addresses specific skills shortages in the Australian labour market, and this policy is applied to Skilled-Australian Linked migrants (sponsored by a family member already resident in the country), as well as to independent migrants (who are *not* sponsored by a relative or employer in Australia). For detailed information on permanent residency visa criteria and requirements see *Residence and Entry Regulations*.

Business Stream Migration. The Business Skills visa class of the migration programme is designed to encourage successful business people to settle permanently in Australia and develop new business opportunities. Business migration benefits the Australian economy by developing its international markets, creating employment, introducing new or improved technology, and by adding to commercial activity and to competitiveness in general. Business migrants are expected to contribute to these benefits by establishing and conducting new business, by transferring capital, and by investment. The following criteria apply for different types of applicants and visa categories under the Business Skills programme:

Business Owners. Business owners are required to demonstrate that they have had a successful business career and that for two of the previous four fiscal years have had net business assets of at least $200,000. In addition, they must have been involved in and responsible for the overall management of a business in which they have at least a 10 percent ownership share, and which has employed no fewer than five employees. Business owners must also pass a points test which assesses factors such as annual turnover, annual labour costs, total business assets, age, language ability, and net personal assets.

Senior Executives. Senior execs must demonstrate that they have had a successful business career and that for two of the previous four years they have been employed in the top three levels of management in a business with an annual turnover of not less than $50 million. They must also pass a points test which assesses factors such as age, English language ability, and net personal assets.

Investment-linked Applicants. These must demonstrate a history of successful ownership and management in business and/or investment activities, as well as make an investment into a State or Territory government security of between $750,000 and $2 million for a period of three years. They must also demonstrate assets worth at least 50 percent more than their proposed investment, and must pass a points test which assesses age and English language ability.

Established Business in Australia Applicants. These must demonstrate that they have managed a business in Australia in which they have at least 10% ownership for 18 months prior to application. They must have assets in Australia worth $250,000, of which $100,000 must be invested in their business, and they must have been resident in Australia for a total of nine out of the previous 12 months prior to application. Applicants can only apply for this visa while resident Australia, and while holding a temporary visa other than a Bridging visa or a Criminal Justice visa. As with other categories, applicants must pass a points test which takes into account such factors as turnover and exports, number of employees, net assets, age and English language ability.
    A sub-category of this visa class makes special concessions for applicants who have established businesses while holding a temporary business entry (long stay) visa in designated areas outside Sydney, Newcastle and Wollongong and the main urban centres of Melbourne, Perth and Brisbane. Under the 'Regional Established Business' category, asset and turnover criteria are slightly more lenient but applicants must be sponsored by a State/Territory Government business development agency.

Once a business migrant has arrived in Australia he or she must meet visa conditions and business obligations. The expectation is that he or she will establish a new business, or become an owner or part owner of an existing business and that they will take an active part in the management of that business. Having established a successful business initially as a temporary resident, a Business Skills migrant is expected to remain in Australia permanently to continue that business. The progress of business migrants is monitored after their arrival in Australia, and where no significant steps have been taking towards meeting these obligations within the first three years after arrival, the Minister for Immigration and Multicultural and Indigenous Affairs has the power to cancel the right of residence of the business immigrant and his or her family.

Skills and Qualifications

Successful applicants under the Skill Stream or the Skilled-Australian Linked Stream of the migration programme are required to have a prescribed level of professional experience and qualification. As explained more fully in *Residence and Entry*, these skills are assessed during the application process by means of the 'Points Test'. Points awarded for skill levels are based on your current occupation and the level of your qualifications, which must be of a standard recognised as industry-appropriate in Australia. Your current occupation is defined as the one which you have performed over the last twelve months and which you regard as your usual occupation. Thus, if you have obtained qualifications in one field (say, a degree in modern languages) but are currently working in a field which does not *directly* utilise those qualifications, you will, in effect, be assessed as unqualified. This clause creates difficulties for many applicants who are working in areas such as information technology or office management, where in many cases skills have been acquired on-the-job or through graduate programmes. Concessions are made for workplace training, however, and each case is assessed on its individual merits. Points are awarded for length of professional experience (usually three years is required) and for membership of professional or industrial associations. The table below shows the value at the time of writing of the different qualifications under the Points Test. Trade certificates, diplomas and degrees must be recognised as 'acceptable' (i.e., equivalent to an Australian qualification) in order to score any points. DIMIA has Migration Occupation in Demand and Skilled Occupations lists.

TABLE 11	GENERAL SKILLS POINTS
Assessed Category	**Points**
Skill	
Applicant has training specific to occupation (degree or trade certificate)	60
Applicant has a more general occupation (requiring non-specific degree level qualifications)	50
Applicant has an occupation which requires diploma or advanced diploma level qualifications	40
Age at time of application	
18-29	30
30-34	25
35-39	20
40-44	15
Language ability	
Vocational English	15

Competent English	20

Work experience
Applicant has been employed in an occupation on the skilled occupation list for 3 out of 4 years — 5
Applicant's occupation scores 60 points under the skill factor, and has worked in nominated occupation for 3 of 4 years — 10

Migrant Occupation in demand
Applicant's occupation is in demand — 5
Applicant's occupation is in demand *and* applicant has firm offer of employment — 10

Australian qualifications
Applicant has completed 1 academic year in full-time education at Australian institution (post secondary degree/diploma/trade qualification etc. — 5
Applicant has PhD from an Australian institution — 10

Spouse skills
Applicant's spouse satisfies basic requirements of age, English proficiency etc. — 5

Bonus points
Capital investment of $100,000 in an approved Government investment for a minimum period of 12 months *or* 6 months work experience in Australia *or* fluency in a community language — 5

NOOSR Bridging Courses for the Overseas Trained.
The National Office of Overseas Skills Recognition (PO Box 9880, Canberra, ACT 2601, Australia) can provide advice on the acceptability of any qualification which you hold. They also offer bridging courses for overseas-qualified professionals whose qualifications have not yet been recognised in Australia, enabling applicants to meet the academic and professional requirements for registration or entry to regulated professions. Government-regulated professions include: dentistry, veterinary science, medicine, law, radiography, pharmacy, architecture, physiotherapy, and nursing. Accountancy, dietetics, social work, engineering and surveying are self-regulating. You will be eligible for support on a NOOSR course if you have permanent residency in Australia, have overseas professional qualifications at Bachelor's degree level or above, and you have obtained details of the training you require from the professional body which assessed your qualifications. Contact NOOSR for information and advice (☎1800 020 086 (freecall); www.dest.gov.au/noosr).

SOURCES OF JOBS

On-line Resources

If you are job-hunting in Australia from overseas, by far the best, quickest, and most convenient resource is now the Internet. There are dozens of Australian recruitment agencies on the Internet, all of which advertise frequently up-dated lists of positions, as well as providing registration and CV lodgement services. Two major Australian media groups, Newscorp and Fairfax, which between them publish the greater part of Australia's mainstream newspapers, also put their classified recruitment sections on-line, and these are up-dated daily. The websites of these two corporations together carry around 20,000 job advertisements per week. In addition, the Australian Job Network (the government job-finding organisation, details below) has an excellent site searchable by location, job type, and interactive map. In most cases, jobs listed on the AJN site will detail conditions and pay, and although it may be difficult to apply for jobs listed on this site from overseas, it will give you a good idea of the kinds of work available in almost any field.

Useful Australia-specific Recruitment Websites

Australian Job Network: www.jobsearch.gov.au

CareerOne Services Pty Ltd: (www.careerone.com.au). This Newscorp site carries more than 30,000 jobs listed daily.

Employment.net.au: www.employment.net.au

Employment Opportunities Australia: www.employment.com.au

Fairfax Holdings: (www.mycareer.com.au). This site lists daily advertisements carried in a range of national papers. It carries around 10,000 advertisements per day, and is searchable by job type and location.

Jobnet: (www.jobnet.com.au). The largest IT jobsearch website in Australia. Thousands of permanent, contract and consulting positions available for IT Professionals.

Monster.com: (www.monster.com.au). Local portal for the leading global online careers network.

Willing Workers On Organic Farms Australia: (www.wwoof.com.au). Willing Workers On Organic Farms (WWOOF) is a form of cultural exchange in which WWOOFers live and work as family with host farms, and learn about the skills of organic growing as well as the area they are visiting.

Individual agencies can be quickly located on the Internet by using search engines such as Google, and the search terms 'Australia' in conjunction with 'recruitment' or 'employment'.

Newspapers

UK Newspapers and Directories.

The Directory of Jobs and Careers Abroad: Published by Vacation Work (£12.95) has a section on Australia including contact details and other sources of employment information. Vacation Work Publications also has a very useful links page on their website www.vacationwork.co.uk.

Overseas Jobs Express: A fortnightly publication which lists over 1,000 overseas jobs including professional, non-professional, seasonal, temporary, permanent, long- and short-term employment. A year's subscription costs around £120 and is available from OJE (20 New Road, Brighton, East Sussex BN1 1UK; ☎01273-699611; www.overseasjobsexpress.com).

TNT Planners: Produce a quarterly information booklet which carries advertisements for numerous Australian recruitment agencies. The magazine is available from travel agents or from TNT Planners (14-15 Child's Place, London,

SW5 9RX; ☎020-7373 3377). TNT also publish an Australian edition, TNT Magazine Australia (www.tntmagazine.com/au/). TNT have a useful website at www.tntmag.co.uk which has an international jobsearch facility and publish an annual guide to Australia; available by sending a stamped A5 self-addressed envelope to TNT Guides at the above address.

Australian Newspapers. Jobs are advertised in community, local, regional and national newspapers. Most major daily newspapers carry a large recruitment section on Saturdays, and many carry advertisements for specialist professional positions on certain days (for example, tertiary education sector jobs in *The Australian* on Wednesdays). Professionals and executives are advised to consult *The Australian* in additional to their state newspapers, as most high-status jobs will be advertised in this paper, regardless of location. A list of state and national newspapers is given in Chapter 4, *Media and Communications*.

Professional Associations and Specialist Publications

Most professions in Australia have a national association or governing body, which is also likely to have state chapters. In some cases, membership of an association is compulsory for practising members, and in such instances, membership fees are tax deductible. Most professional associations publish a journal, which, in specialist fields, may be the best source of employment information. Specialist publications provide another important source, and will usually report on developments in their field, as well as advertising job vacancies. Conferences and development courses will also be advertised in such publications.

Working Holiday Assistance Schemes

BUNAC. The British Universities North America Club (16 Bowling Green Lane, London, EC1R 0QH; ☎020-7251 3472; fax 020-7251 0215; www.bunac.org.uk) has a 'Work Australia' programme, which is designed to help those aged 18-30 deal with all the organisational aspects of a working holiday. The service helps with obtaining flights, insurance and a working visa, and includes comprehensive orientation sessions at home and on arrival in Australia, a group two-day stopover in Bangkok or Hong Kong en route, two free nights accommodation in Sydney. It also provides ongoing support through BUNAC's subsidiary, International Exchange Programs PTY Ltd, including a postal service, voicemail card and the help of the Sydney resource office for general advice throughout your stay.

John Mahon. Visas Australia (P.O. 1, Nantwich, Cheshire CW5 7PB; ☎01270-626626; fax 01270-626226; john@visas-australia.com: also in Dublin: 2nd Floor, 13 Aston Quay, Dublin 2; ☎01- 6795452; fax 01-6795459) operate an on-line site (www.visas-australia.com) that arranges a working holiday visa for for a service charge of £15; also a site www.etavisas.com that will issue and e-mail a copy of the Australian tourist visa for £5.

SWAP. The Student Work Abroad Programme (SWAP) runs programmes in Australia for those aged 18 to 30 on working holidays. SWAP has a website at www.swap.ca and is administered by IEP (International Exchange Programs PTY Ltd, PO. Box 13278, Law Courts Post Office, Melbourne, VIC 8010; ☎03-9329 3866; fax 03-9329

1592;www.iep-australia.com). Canadian students should contact any office of Travel CUTS/Voyages Campus, which is part of the Canadian Federation of Students (National Office, 170 Metcalfe Street, 5th Floor, Ottawa, Ontario K2P 1P3; ☎(613) 232-7394; fax (613) 232-0276; www.cfs-fcee.ca).

Employment Wanted Advertisements

Placing an advertisement in a local or community newspaper can be a useful way of finding casual work, but is unlikely to land you secure long-term employment. Most people using 'Situations Wanted' classifieds are looking for occasional cash jobs, such as gardening, baby-sitting, or cleaning. If you are on a working holiday, this may be one of the best ways of picking up occasional work to suit your travel schedule, and will probably pay at least $10 per hour. For graduates, short-term tutoring, particularly around exam time, can be quite remunerative, and most local papers will have a separate column for advertising services of this type.

The Australian Job Network

The Job Network is a national network of around 200 private, community and government organisations dedicated to finding jobs for unemployed people, particularly the long term unemployed. The Department of Employment and Workplace Relations provides a very comprehensive website detailing available jobs, and with links to other employers at www.workplace.gov.au.

Employment Agencies

UK-based Australian Employment Agency. *Bligh Appointments* is the largest employer of working holidaymakers in both Sydney and London, and can help in the search for temporary work before you even leave home. They specialise in secretarial, accounting and IT jobs, and offer good rates and an immediate start. Bligh have offices at: Level 7, Dymocks Building, 428 George Street, Sydney NSW 2000, ☎02-9235 3699; www.employment.com.au/bligh and in London at 70 North End Rd, London W14; ☎020-7603 6123.

Recruitment Consultancies. Recruitment consultancies generally specialise in placing staff in sales, marketing, finance, accounting, IT, engineering, office administration, and hospitality. While many employment agencies also cover these areas, recruitment consultants deal mainly with executive and upper and middle management placements. They advertise available jobs in major newspapers and usually offer a complete recruitment service. If you are seeking work of this kind, you can contact a recruitment consultancy 'on spec' to discuss your qualifications and experience, and any potentially suitable vacancies. A list of recruitment consultants and contact numbers can be found in the local Yellow Pages.

Employment Agencies. Employment agencies deal in both temporary and permanent work, usually in the secretarial, clerical, accounting and IT fields, or in hospitality or heavy industry. Most advertise in the Yellow Pages and are found in prominent locations in the Central Business Districts and other urban centres. The international firms Drake Personnel, Kelly Services, Centacom and Adecco all have agencies in Australia. In addition to the large, generalist agencies, there are many smaller, specialist firms, particularly in fields such as nursing, legal temping, banking, and IT. If you are a registered nurse or teacher looking to work in Australia, it is vital that you take proof of registration and qualifications with you. You can expect to earn around $12 an hour for clerical work, $14 for secretarial and $15 for computer work.

Useful Addresses

Adecco, Adecco is the world's leading employment services company, with over 5,000 offices in 58 countries. They have a dedicated Australia website at *www.adecco.com.au,* and can be contacted at their main Sydney office (Level 2, 280 George Street, Sydney, NSW 2000; ☎02-9244 3400; fax 02-9223 4626).For office locations in other areas call 132 993.

Au Pair Around the World, PO Box 157, Sanctuary Cove, Brisbane, Qld 4212; tel/fax 07-5530 1123; Level 1, 789 Botany Road, Roseberry, Sydney; ☎02-9557 6644; www.nanny.net.au. Australia's leading au pair agency with offices Australia-wide.

Australian Nanny and Au Pair Connection, 404 Glenferrie Road, Kooyong, Melbourne, VIC 3144; ☎03-9822 5296; www.nannycollection.com.au

Crowe Associates, Supply executive recruitment, temporary and contract placements of legal, IT and accountancy staff. The Sydney Head Office is located at Level 17, Town Hall House, 456 Kent Street, Sydney, NSW 2000; ☎02-9261 5100; fax 02-9261 5300; www.crowe.com.au

Goldstein and Martens Recruitment Consultants; Level 4, 285 George Street, Sydney; ☎02-9262 3088; www.goldsteinmartens.com.au. Pays $2-$3 above the average hourly wage.

Metro Personnel, Level 6, Thakral House, 301 George Street, Sydney, NSW 2000; ☎02-9299 5477; www.metropersonnel.com.au

Michael Page International, Level 19, 1 York Street, Sydney, 2000; ☎02-9254 0200; www.michaelpage.com.au. Temporary and contract work in finance & accounting, legal, sales & marketing, technology, human resources and engineering.

Select Appointments specialise in placing professional, motivated travellers. They have positions for receptionists, data entry operators, secretaries, accounts clerks, medical and legal secretaries, WPOs and warehousing staff. Select have offices in Sydney, ☎02-9206 2311; Perth, ☎08-9321 3133; Brisbane, ☎07-3406 3900; Melbourne, ☎03-9297 4700; www.selectappointments.com.au

Labour Hire Contractors. Labour hire contractors specialise in placing skilled manual workers and tradespeople, labourers, storepersons, process workers and factory staff. These agencies generally do not operate high street offices and are found in industrial areas. Most advertise in the Yellow Pages, and it is usually best to visit in person, taking with you any trade or City and Guild certificates you may have. Qualified tradespeople are paid well in Australia, and in states with booming construction industries there is usually a shortage of such people. Bricklayers are particularly in demand and can expect to earn a high wage, whilst mine workers can earn more than $1,000 per week. Mining work is very labour-intensive and unskilled workers are often needed; modern mine sites operate equal opportunities policies, and most employ women in a wide range of capacities. There is also strong demand for skilled mechanics.

Chambers of Commerce

The Australian Chamber of Commerce and affiliated state Chambers of Commerce advise and provide information on employment in Australia. They also produce detailed regional summaries of employment and economic growth, and are particularly useful as a point of contact for small businesspeople. The Australian-British Chamber of Commerce, for example, aims to promote business growth and development within Australia, and to encourage reciprocal trade between the UK and Australia.

Useful Addresses

Australian British Chamber of Commerce, Level 16, The Gateway Building, 1 Macquarie Place, Sydney, NSW 2000; ☎02-9247 6271; fax 02-9247 6671; www.britishchamber.com

Australia and New Zealand Chamber of Commerce UK, 393 Strand, London, WC2R 0JQ; ☎020-7379 0720; fax 020-7379 0721; www.anzcc.org.uk

Australian Industry Group, 20 Queens Road, Melbourne, VIC 3004; ☎03-9867 0111; fax 03-9867 0199; www.aigroup.asn.au. The Australian Industry Group is an independent organisation created to help Australian industry be more competitive domestically and internationally. Aspects of industry covered include the economy and related investment issues, taxation, industrial relations policy, environmental issues, education and training.

Company Transfers and Job Exchanges

If you are currently working for a company which has offices or branches in Australia, opportunities may exist for either permanent or temporary transfer. Outside the multinationals, it may be possible to find work in Australia under an exchange scheme. Such schemes are common in the teaching profession, and you should contact your local education authority for further information. Many exchanges provide not only a job swap, but also all the domestic necessities. You may find yourself minding your exchange colleague's pets for a year, but you'll probably also find yourself minding their pool too!

ASPECTS OF EMPLOYMENT

Salaries

Pay rates in Australia fall broadly into four bands: the lowest paid workers earn an average of $350 or less per week, mid-range salaries cluster firstly around $600 and then, in the upper-mid-range, around $850 per week, and finally, the highest paid employees can expect a weekly pay packet in excess of $1,257 per week. Rates of pay are differentiated between the public and private sector, and by gender and age. Men still tend to receive a higher weekly income than women in the same sector do (although this can be accounted for by gender divides within industry, rather than in terms of direct discrimination, which is, of course, illegal). Younger people are likely to be paid less than their seniors. Employees earning at the top end of the salary bands are likely to fall into one of two key industries – finance and insurance, and mining – whilst those at the bottom end are generally found in the retail trade and in the hospitality industry. The table below illustrates the current full-time adult average weekly wage in Australia:

TABLE 12	AVERAGE WEEKLY EARNINGS FOR FULL-TIME WORK ($)
Accommodation, cafes and restaurants	575.30
Communication services	857.40
Construction	738.00
Cultural and recreational services	720.30
Education	875.70
Electricity, gas and water supply	920.30
Finance and insurance	782.50
Government administration and defence	761.90
Health and community services	739.50
Mining	1,214.10
Manufacturing	668.70
Personal and other services	791.50
Property and business services	767.10
Retail trade	586.40
Transport and storage	746.40
Wholesale trade	672.70
Source: Australian Bureau of Statistics	

Earnings are related to skills obtained through education and work experience. Work experience is related to age, especially for those in their 20s and 30s and therefore wages tend to rise with age. Unskilled workers can expect to earn between $10-$20 an hour depending on location, level of skill, and whether they are paid hourly or are on piece work rates. The traditional working holiday stand-by, fruit picking, may be easy to find but is poorly paid. Workers are often paid not by the hour but by the quantity of produce harvested. The average harvest picker can expect to earn somewhere in the region of $300-$500 for a six-day week. Bear in mind that a dollar goes a long way in Australia and that although earnings may seem low the same standard of living that you are used to back home can be had for less in Australia.

The Australian Bureau of Statistics estimates an annual increase of 5.2% per annum on the rates of pay. The Australian economy currently has a CPI (Consumer Price Index) of around 3.1% and an average inflation rate of 4.4%. Industries with a shortage of skilled labour are expected to experience a greater increase in pay rates, while salaries in those areas where there is an oversupply of labour may see wages decline.

Award Rates – recommended minimum wages – are set by both the Federal and State governments for various trades and industries. Many, if not most, employers pay above the Award Rate, but you should find out if there is an Award in place before entering into negotiations with an employer. The appropriate union will be able to advise you on Award Rates and Conditions.

Benefits and Perks

Only the most senior positions attract additional benefits in Australia since changes in taxation laws made fringe benefits economically unattractive. Cars, health insurance plans, entertainment expenses, and even frequent flyer points are now all taxed as income, so that any benefit is offset by a commensurate loss of salary. Benefits earned under incentive schemes are also taxable. Childcare and workplace crèches, however, are not included in the fringe benefit tax, and indeed, employees using external childcare can claim a rebate on their expenses via the local Medicare office.

All employers pay superannuation (private pension contributions) for their employees at a basic rate of 9% of salary. Many employers also offer an additional percentage or two, up to around 10%, and this is now the most common form of employment incentive.

Most senior executives can still expect to receive a company car, but in general, benefits offered at any other level of employment are likely to be industry-linked. Thus, if you work for a major bank, you can expect to be eligible for subsidised borrowing, or in health insurance, for free or discounted health cover. Most Australian employees do not expect, or indeed want, any other fringe benefits which may cut into the cash in their pocket.

Superannuation

Superannuation is Australia's answer to the economic burden of state pensions in the context of an ageing population. In essence, it is a compulsory private pension planning scheme. All employees are required by law to pay a percentage of their salary into a superannuation fund designated by their employer, to which the employer also contributes an additional minimum percentage payment on the employee's behalf. If you move jobs, you are entitled to transfer your superannuation package to your new employer's chosen superannuation fund without incurring any penalty. The transfer of super from one fund to another is known as a 'roll-over'. Alternatively, if you wish to remain with your current fund, you can ask your employer to contribute to that fund instead, although they are not obliged to do so either by law or under any award. Contributions to 'super funds' are of two types: preserved and voluntary. Preserved contributions comprise the minimum compulsory contributions, described above, and these cannot be withdrawn or otherwise utilised until the age of 55. In addition, however, employees are entitled to make on-going voluntary contributions or occasional lump sum contributions to their fund, and this component is non-preserved, i.e., it can be withdrawn on leaving a job. Self-employed people are advised to take out a 'self-employed' superannuation policy available from banks and life insurance companies.

If you leave the country permanently, your superannuation will remain locked into a fund until you reach retirement age.

Working Hours, Overtime and Holidays

The Australian working week averages 35-40 hours over a five-day week, with government positions taking the middle road at precisely 37.5 hours. In most jobs, you can expect to work an eight-hour day with an hour for lunch, although some shift-work industries, such as nursing or hospitality, will usually require much greater flexibility. Flexi-time is common, and allows you to set your own working hours around a compulsory 'core time' (usually 10am to 4pm). Extra hours worked can be 'banked' against time off on full pay, which is in addition to statutory leave. Flexi-time is very popular, and is in place in almost all government jobs, tertiary education administration, and in many private companies. Minimum working pay and conditions are set by either the Commonwealth or State governments.

If you are required to work on a Sunday or a public holiday, you should be paid at twice the normal rate. At any other time, overtime is paid at 1.5 times the normal rate for the first three hours, then at double-time after that. Employees are entitled to a statutory minimum of four weeks paid leave per annum. Holiday leave is sweetened with a bonus known as 'holiday loading', which means that your salary is increased by an extra 17.5% during the period you are on leave. Many industries and professions offer increasing leave entitlements linked to length of service, and may, in some cases, offer as much as eight weeks' holiday per year. Untaken leave can usually be carried over from year to year, and many people choose to bank up holidays in order to take extended travel breaks.

After between seven and ten years consecutive service with a single employer (ten years in government positions), an employee is entitled to 'long service leave' of up to six months on full pay or twelve months on half pay. Long service leave conditions vary considerably between employers, and in many cases additional incentives such as a travel allowance may be offered.

In addition to annual leave, all employees are granted a period of paid sick leave, the length of which will be specified in their contract. Most employers give between two weeks and three months paid sick leave. Any absence of more than 48 hours generally requires a medical certificate from a GP in order to claim payment. Many employers also offer compassionate leave of several days per year, which can be used in times of personal emergency such as bereavement. Compassionate leave and sick leave cannot be carried over from year to year.

Trade Unions

The trade union movement in Australia has become much weakened over the past decade, with fewer Australian employees joining unions than ever before. To offset loss of membership, many unions have amalgamated with others in related trades and professions, forming super-unions with increased negotiating power. The unions that have remained strongest are those representing industries in which there is continued unrest, particularly in teaching, nursing, policing, and wharfside occupations. 'Closed shops' are illegal, but the powerful BLF (Builders Labourers Federation) is occasionally known to operate union-only sites. Most workplaces have a union representative, and if you choose to join, dues can be automatically deducted from your salary. Union dues are a tax-deductible expense. The Australian Council of Trade Unions (ACTU, Level 2, 393 Swanston Street, Melbourne, VIC 3000; ☎03-9663 5266; fax 03-9663 4051; www.actu.asn.au) is the national trade union organisation and can provide advice on the union most appropriate to your circumstances and occupation.

Employment Contracts

In Australia every employee is covered either by a contract or a 'workplace agreement'. Workplace agreements are signed by both employer and employee, and stipulate the agreed conditions of employment, including hours, leave arrangements, uniform or safety-wear requirements, and notice and termination procedures. Even casual workers must be covered by one of these contracts, which is then lodged with the State Commissioner for Workplace Agreements as a legally binding document. Workplace agreements have not entirely replaced employment contracts, though they are nearly identical in purpose and effect, however, it is usually only in more senior and permanent positions that employees are covered by a contract.

A contract should specify all leave entitlements (holiday, sick, parental, and compassionate leave), overtime conditions, benefits, superannuation contribution levels, hours (including flexi-time arrangements), long-service leave, uniform regulations, and health and safety observances. It should also clearly stipulate termination procedures, which will usually follow the form of a first and second verbal warning, written warning, and formal interview (which may be attended, at your request, by a union representative). If a contract is broken by either party, the injured party is able to sue the other party for breach of contract through an industrial tribunal. Temporary workers and travellers should particularly note that if you fail to give the contractually defined period of notice of resignation, your employer is legally entitled to withhold wages equivalent to that period.

Work Practices

Different industries have different codes of practice, and you should be made aware of these by your employer at your interview or when you commence work. Most industries which expose their employees to physical safety hazards require that appropriate safety gear be worn, and this will generally be supplied by the employer. Almost all workplaces, including many restaurants, are now smoke-free, and smokers are expected to take their 'smokoes' outside the building. Health and safety regulations are rigorously upheld in the workplace, and most offices and sites will appoint a member of staff as its 'H and S' representative. This representative will make sure that regulations are not breached by any management practice and that any new legislation is promptly enforced. Australian offices are generally far less authoritarian than British ones, especially in the corporate and public sectors. The dress code is likely to be more casual, and employer and employee are expected to be on first name terms, regardless of the extent of their difference in status.

Women in Work

Discrimination on the basis of gender is illegal in Australia and equal pay for women has been an accepted basic right for decades. Nonetheless, women in Australia, like their counterparts throughout western industrialised nations are still behind in the wages stakes, and their participation at the highest levels of management and industry is still low. With girls now easily outstripping boys in educational achievement, and with the gender balance tipping in favour of women in many university courses (women now outnumber men in medicine, for example), it is likely that this situation will change in coming years. Currently, a number of incentive schemes, such as WISE (Women in Science and Engineering), are in place to encourage women into male dominated professions, and some public employers, particularly in the tertiary sector, operate positive discrimination policies to draw highly qualified women back into the workforce after childrearing. For women in Australia, part-time work accounts for 24 percent of the total hours worked, in comparison to just 5 percent for men. The retail trades and health and community services are the largest employers of females, employing about 17 percent of the total female workforce. Women professionals outnumber men and more women than men work in intermediate clerical, sales and service work. 56% of females employed in Australia work on a full-time basis.

Women, in general, seek more flexible employment opportunities and are more likely to be found in part-time or freelance work. They are also likely to seek shorter hours, with statistics showing that single mothers work around 12 hours per week fewer than men with similar family responsibilities. In income terms, men continue to receive higher average earnings than women within the same occupation group. For example, women managers and administrators are likely to receive about 85 percent of a man's average weekly total earnings employed in the same profession. For tradespeople, women's earnings average out to be around 70% of men's.

Maternity Benefits, Parental Leave and Employment Rights

Maternity Benefits. Australia, along with New Zealand and the United States, is one of the few industrialised nations in which the state does not pay maternity leave benefits. Government sector employees are entitled to three months paid leave, however, few women employed in the private sector receive paid maternity leave. All women are entitled to unpaid maternity leave of not more than 52 weeks, taken either during or after their pregnancy. On the expiry of the leave, the employee is entitled to return to her previous position or an equivalent, if that position no longer exists. All new mothers who are legal residents of Australia are entitled to receive the Maternity Allowance, a one-off lump sum payment of $798.72 made by Centrelink. In cases of multiple birth, the Maternity Allowance payment is paid for each child born (including still-births). In addition, Centrelink offers an incentive payment for immunisation called the Maternity Immunisation Allowance. This allowance is designed to combat falling levels of immunisation and provides parents with a lump sum of $208 on presentation of proof of full immunisation in their 18-month-old child.

Paternity and Adoptive Leave. All Australian workers, and not just mothers, are entitled to parental leave, which in addition to maternity leave also comprises paternity and adoptive leave. Paternity leave may be taken in conjunction with the birth of a child to a spouse or *de facto* partner, whilst adoptive leave may be taken in conjunction with the adoption of a child under the age of five years. For both types of leave, ten weeks notice of intention must be given to the employer. Any employee who has completed at least 12 months continuous service, whether full or part time (but not casual), is eligible for parental leave, however, paternity leave cannot be taken simultaneously with maternity leave for the same child. Employees are entitled to take up to 52 weeks parental leave, which must be completed before the child's first birthday (or the first anniversary of an adoption). You cannot be dismissed for taking parental leave and your application for it cannot be legally refused by your employer. On your return to work, you are entitled to your old job back or, if it no longer exists, to one at an equivalent level, and your seniority and accumulated leave must be preserved in your absence.

Employment Rights. All employees have a basic right to a fair and reasonable working environment and conditions. Reasonable working conditions include the right to personal and physical safety. If you suffer injury at work due to your employer's negligence or unsatisfactory working conditions, you have the right to claim worker's compensation for any injury, discomfort, and loss of earnings you may incur as a result of that injury. Sexual harassment is also considered to be a fundamental denial of the right to a fair and reasonable working environment, and employers have been taken to court because they have allowed offensive or pornographic posters and pictures to be displayed in common staff areas. Most public employers and many larger corporate ones will have a sexual harassment officer on their staff who will provide confidential advice and liaison in the case of complaints.

As an employee, you have the right to a fair dismissal, and each trade and industry has its own rules regarding acceptable practice. It is illegal to breach the contractually stated dismissal procedure, and if you believe that you have been treated unfairly, you can take your employer to an industrial tribunal for unfair or constructive dismissal.

Discrimination in the workplace (or, indeed, anywhere) on the grounds of ethnic origin, gender, religious or political beliefs, or nationality is against the law, and if you have reason to believe that you are experiencing discrimination of any kind, you should contact your local Department of Education, Science and Training (DEST) office for advice on how to pursue a complaint.

Useful Addresses

The Australian Council of Trade Unions (ACTU): Represents 1,900,000 workers and provides information on legislated employment rights at www.actu.asn.au

Commonwealth Department of Education, Science and Training (DEST): Have an informative website at www.dest.gov.au

Department of Employment and Workplace Relations: The Department of Employment and Workplace Relations aims to support an efficient and equitable labour market that links people to jobs and promotes the transition from welfare to work, and fair and flexible workplace relations at the enterprise level. It has a website at www.dewr.gov.au

Department of Workplace Relations and Small Business: Federal awards; ☎02-6121 6000; www.dewrsb.gov.au/smallbusiness/. The Office of Small Business is in the process of moving to the Department of Industry, Tourism and Resources (www.industry.gov.au).

Social Security and Unemployment Benefits

Australia has a full cradle to grave state welfare system which has, in recent years, been significantly streamlined. Social security benefits, including unemployment and family benefits, are not, however, available to temporary residents, and migrants are also ineligible to claim any kind of benefit until they have been resident in Australia for a full two years. The two-year 'no-claim' period was introduced in 1997 by the government following public concern that migrants were taking advantage of Australia's social security system; previously, new settlers could start claiming benefits within 26 weeks of arrival. The Department of Family and Community Services (faCS) and Centrelink provides detailed information on all its available benefits, including pay rates (which are regularly updated), current policy, and discussion papers, on its website at (www.facs.gov.au). Within Australia, there is a Centrelink office in each capital city and in most major regional centres, where advisors will provide current information and discuss your eligibility for benefits.

Pensions

Australia is currently raising the retirement age for women to bring it in line with the male retirement age of 65 years. Currently, women can receive the pension from age 60, and this is being phased upwards in 6-monthly intervals, to bring it to the point where women born after 1 January 1949 will not be eligible for the pension until age 65. The pension is paid fortnightly at a maximum rate of $421.80 per fortnight for a single person and $352.10 each per fortnight for a married couple. In addition, a pharmaceutical allowance of $5.80 per fortnight may also be payable. To be eligible for an Australian pension, you must have been resident in Australia for at least 10 years, of which five of those years must have been in a single extended period. Australian age pensions are subject to income and assets tests and various other benefits and allowances may be claimable depending on circumstance.

UK Pensions in Australia

If you currently receive a pension paid by the UK government, it will be frozen from the time you leave Britain, so that you will no longer be eligible for any pension rate increases awarded after your departure from Britain. You will, however, be entitled to full payment of your current pension once you arrive in Australia, and this can be arranged through the Department of Work and Pensions in Britain prior to your departure.

If you are a UK migrant with permanent residency and reach pensionable age in Australia, you should make arrangements with the Department of Work and Pensions in Britain in order to claim your UK pension entitlement, together with your Australian pension if you are eligible for the latter. As with retirees, your UK pension will be frozen at the rate current when you reach pensionable age and you will not receive any pension rate increases awarded in the UK.

Other retirement and pension issues are discussed more fully in the *Retirement* chapter.

SHORT-TERM EMPLOYMENT

There are many opportunities in Australia for short-term and casual employment. The Australian government has never felt it necessary to restrict drastically its working holiday maker scheme, even in times of economic downturn, as it is clear that travellers are prepared to take on the kind of temporary jobs that locals seeking a career or job security shun. Some industries, especially in the primary sector, rely on itinerant casual workers to fill their labour needs, and the adventurous should find plenty of scope for some once-in-a-lifetime employment experiences.

Agriculture

Primary industry is the backbone of the Australian economy and there is a great variety of work available on farms and stations all year round. These opportunities are not just limited to working the land: mechanics, builders, tractor drivers, welders, domestics, cooks, and teachers are all needed. Horse riding skills or an HGV licence will improve your chances of finding work. If you have a farming background, preferably with experience in cereal crops, you will find it easy to get seasonal farm work, especially in heavy tractor soil tillage, drilling, single pass seeding, and combine harvesting. Pay varies between a flat rate of $90-$120 per day, or $9-$12 per hour before tax. You are likely to have to work between 50 and 80 hours per week, seven days a week, particularly during seeding.

Fruit farmers rely quite heavily on casual labour at harvest time and this kind of work is ideal for travellers as it is of brief duration and offers the opportunity to 'follow the crops' from region to region. The summer months, from October to April, are the prime time for harvest work around Australia. The work can be hard, but once you become proficient you can expect to earn around $300 per week after tax.

TABLE 13 HARVEST WORK OPPORTUNITIES

Month	Crop
Western Australia	
Feb-Mar	Grapes
Mar-May	Apples, pears
Mar-Jun	Crayfish
Mar-Jun	Oats, wheat, barley
Mar-Oct	Prawns, scallops
May-Sep	Squash, rockmelon
Apr-Nov	Melons
Jun-Dec	Peppers, tomatoes
Jul-Aug	Bananas
Jul-Dec	Wildflowers
Oct-Jan	Mangoes
Victoria	
Jan-Apr	Pears, peaches, apples, tomatoes, tobacco
Feb-Mar	Grapes
Sep-Nov	Asparagus
Oct-Dec	Strawberries
Nov-Feb	Cherries, berries
Nov-Dec	Tomato weeding
New South Wales	
Jan-Mar	Stone fruit, grapes, pears, prunes
Feb-Apr	Apples
Mar-Jun	Cotton picking
Sep-Dec	Asparagus
Sep-Apr	Oranges
Nov-Dec	Cherries
Nov-Apr	Oranges
Dec-Jan	Onions
Dec-Mar	Stone fruit
Dec-Apr	Blueberries
Queensland	
Feb-Mar	Pears, apples

Feb-Apr	Rock melon, ginger
Mar-Dec	Wide range of vegetables
Apr-Jun	Citrus fruit
Apr-Nov	Beans
Apr-Dec	Tomatoes
May-Oct	Broccoli
May-Dec	Sugar cane
Jul-Sep	Ginger
Jul-Dec	Onions
Sep-Nov	Tobacco
Nov-Jan	Plums, cotton, peaches
South Australia	
Jan-Mar	Dried fruits
Feb-Apr	Apples, pears, grapes, peaches
Feb-Aug	Brussels sprouts
Jun-Sep	Pruning
Sep-Jan	Oranges (juicing and packing)
Oct-Feb	Strawberries
Dec-Feb	Apricots
Tasmania	
Mar-May	Apples
Dec-Jan	Soft fruit
Feb-Apr	Grapes
Mar-Apr	Hops
Jan-Feb	Scallop splitting

Almost all harvest work is advertised through the Australian Job Network (AJN), and now that all Centrelink offices (under whom the Australian Job Network operates) are linked by the Internet, it is no longer necessary to go to the appropriate regional office to find out what work is available. Instead, you can visit the Centrelink office in the city or town where you are currently located and, using the computer terminal and interactive map, find out what opportunities are available throughout Australia. Alternatively you can search the online database (www.jobsearch.gov.au). Once you have found the kind of work you want, in an area that interests you, you will need to travel to that region to be interviewed by the local AJN officer, however, the on-line service does make co-ordinating your work and travel much easier.

If you intend to do harvest work, you will need to be fit and healthy, and capable of working long hours in hot, dry and dusty conditions. There is usually minimal accommodation available during harvest, however, most orchards have on-site camping facilities if you have your own tent or caravan. Farms can be located as much as 100 km from the nearest town, so this kind of work is most practical if you have your own transport.

Aquaculture

Aquaculture is a rapidly growing area of primary industry in Australia, and fishing work is available in many coastal areas. Crayfish, prawns, scallops, and abalone are all harvested according to very strict seasonal regulations, and work in these areas can be very highly paid. Many fishing trawlers, especially those with processing facilities, also take on workers. However, this kind of work often requires being at sea for extended periods and is not for the faint-hearted. The seas around Australia can be perilous.

Mining

Working in the mining industry in Australia can be both challenging and very rewarding financially. There is plenty of work available for unskilled labourers, and the best way to find such work is usually to visit the personnel offices of large mining companies at their city headquarters. If you strike lucky, you could find yourself on a plane within a few hours – finding mining work really is about being in the right place at the right time. There are mines and related mining activities all over Australia, from giant iron-ore projects in the northwest to small family-run gold and precious stone prospecting ventures in the south. Miners usually work a seven-day week, often from dawn to dusk, and sometimes for as many as six weeks straight. The pay is likely to be over $1,000 per week, and there is very little to spend it on on-site. If you work above the 26th parallel (the Tropic of Capricorn), you are entitled to extra pay, known as the 'tropical loading' or 'remote area allowance'. Most mining companies are now prepared to employ women on-site, and indeed many prefer to do so, as women are considered to respond less aggressively to the pressure-cooker atmosphere of isolated mine sites.

Nursing

There is a large demand for supply nurses in Australia, especially during the Australian autumn and winter months from April to December. Specialist nurses, particularly A&E, ICU and psychiatric, are always needed and any qualified and experienced nurse is likely to have no difficulty in obtaining work from a nursing agency.

Registering with the Nurses' Registration Board. To work as a nurse in Australia, even on a temporary basis, you will need to be registered with the Nurses' Registration Board of the state in which you hope to work, and many agencies will help you with this procedure. New South Wales is the least expensive state to register in – the fee is currently $50 for one year. Before you leave home you should apply for your Authority to Practice which will prevent any delays on arrival.

Bigger agencies will provide you with a pager so that you are not tied to the telephone – an important bonus for those who have better things to do. Information on nursing in Australia is provided by the Australian Nursing Council Incorporated (ANCI, First Floor, 20 Challis Street, Dickson, ACT 2602; Postal Address: PO Box 873, Dickson, ACT 2602; ☎02-6257 7960; fax 02-6257 7955; www.anci.org.au). ANCI also has a list of all Nurses' Registration Boards in Australia.

Useful Addresses

Heartbeat Nurses: 12 Pitt Street, Parramatta, Sydney, New South Wales 2150; ☎02-9891 2255; fax 02-9806 9731; www.heartbeatnursing.com.au. Agency that supplies

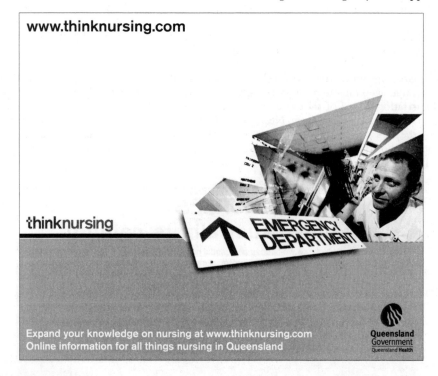

all leading public and private hospitals in Sydney; also jobs in Country and Inter-state hospitals. Day or three-month contracts, Nurse Work and Travel Programmes around Australia etc.

Nurseworldwide: Suite 111 (1), Business Design Centre, 52 Upper Street, London, N1 0QH; ☎020-7688 8250; fax 020-7688 8251; e-mail f.jones@select.co.uk. Established 1986. Provides comprehensive assistance package including help with registration, visa sponsorship (if required), accommodation and 'meet and greet' at main airports.

Queensland Health, Health Advisory Unit (Nursing) Level 6, GPO Box 48, Brisbane QLD 4001, Australia; ☎07-3234 0231; fax 07-3234 0062; www.thinknursing.com. Queensland Health is a Government department involved in all areas of health care across Queensland. For job opportunities for registered nurses please see the above website.

TEFL

Australia has a flourishing TEFL market which caters mainly to Southeast Asian students. There are large English language schools in every capital city, all of which require casual, short- and long-term teachers for their various courses. To teach English as a Foreign Language in Australia you will need a recognised TEFL qualification and some prior teaching experience, and many people on working holiday visas now choose to take an appropriate course before they leave home in order to have this remunerative option on their travel. Casual TEFL teachers can expect to earn between $15 and $25 per hour. Perth, Sydney and the Gold Coast have the largest and most active TEFL sectors.

Au Pair

Au pair work is another standby for working holidaymakers, and there is considerable work available for those with experience and good references. Once confined almost entirely to remote rural families who needed the services of a child-minder cum governess, changing work patterns have led more and more urban families to employ full- or part-time nannies or au pairs. Australian families generally will *not* expect anyone employed as a childminder to undertake household duties other than those required for the immediate well-being of their children. Extra work, such as ironing, should be specified by the employer in advance and agreed to by you, and you can negotiate extra pay for these additional duties.

Male Au Pairs: Australian anti-discrimination laws do permit employers to specify the gender of a childminder; many families prefer to employ women to care for their children, and male applicants can be legally rejected. However, some families might actually prefer a male au pair, especially if the children are boys and like playing sports. There are numerous domestic and specialist au pair agencies supplying staff in this field. References will be checked thoroughly and holding a driving licence will be an asset.

Tourism and Hospitality

Australia's tourist industry is one of the country's largest employers, and there are a wide variety of jobs available. Hotels require childminders, porters and kitchenhands, in addition to more qualified and experienced employees such as chefs, waiters, and bar staff. A silver service or bar attendant qualification acquired before you leave home will equip you to find well paid work in every city.

Croupiers are required by casinos (there are one or two very large ones in most states, but no Las Vegas-style gambling mecca) and this kind of work is very highly paid; you will, however, require training and experience to be considered.

There is work available for instructor level PADI-qualified divers at the major dive spots around the coast, especially on the Great Barrier Reef and off Exmouth, in northwest WA. Divers should note that PADI is the most common certification system in Australia; BSAC-qualified divers will find it easier to find work if they convert their qualifications before travelling.

Any working holidaymakers already very experienced in the Australian outback may find work as guides in some of the national parks, particularly Kakadu, and many coach companies also take on tour leaders and coach drivers with an appropriate licence and experience. Queensland offers the greatest opportunities in terms of resort work, however, most jobs are found by word of mouth: if you hope to work, say, on the Gold Coast, the most likely way of picking up work is to go there and ask around. The Australian Job Network, once again, is the best first port of call for work in the tourism and hospitality sector.

Office Work, Telemarketing and Sales

Office temps are particularly in demand during the Australian summer months and over major holiday periods such as Christmas and Easter. Most commonly, short-term work is available in secretarial, clerical, word-processing and data entry positions, all of which require some degree of skill and previous experience. The banking, finance, and stockbroking industries always require temps, especially during peak periods such as the end of the financial year (30 June). Unskilled casual work is often also available at this time when large supermarkets and department stores do their annual stocktake. There are innumerable employment agencies supplying both general and specialist short-term staff, and these are listed in the *Yellow Pages*. The Australian Job Network is generally less fruitful as a source of this kind of work, although temporary government and public sector positions will be advertised there.

Telemarketing does not appeal to everyone, but can be financially rewarding if you are successful. Turnover is unusually high in this industry, and telemarketing firms have no hesitation in employing backpackers as it is rare for any staff, whether itinerant or not, to stay the pace for more than a few weeks. Telemarketing jobs are usually advertised in the employment classifieds of local and major city newspapers.

Job seekers are advised to avoid sales jobs offering commission-only remuneration, and especially those which advertise 'travellers welcome'. In most cases, such jobs offer one-way transport to a remote location, from which you will be required to make enough sales to fund your own way back to civilisation.

Voluntary Work

Countless charitable organisations throughout Australia rely on volunteers to help run their many aid, development and conservation programmes. Becoming involved in such enterprises offers the working holidaymaker an opportunity to experience a different side of Australian life whilst gaining new skills and contributing to a worthwhile cause. If you are interested in volunteering in any capacity, contact the

Charities' Commission in your state (listed under Government Organisations in the White Pages) who will be able to supply you with a list of all the charities registered with them. Visitors to Australia who are interested in the country's unique landscape are often particularly attracted to conservation work, and the *Conservation Volunteers Australia*, (National Head office, 13-15 Lydiard Street North, Ballarat, VIC 3350; ☎ 03-5333 1483; fax 03-5333 2166; www.conservationvolunteers.com.au), can help with placements in this field. Volunteers are expected to raise at least $966 to contribute towards their food, lodging, and travel expenses.

Tax Notes for Casual Workers

Working holidaymakers pay tax on their earnings like any other Australian employee. However, as you will only be working for a short period it is likely that your earnings will fall below the tax threshold and that you will, therefore, be eligible for a tax refund at the end of your visit. Everyone who works in Australia must have a 'tax file number', and you will need to apply for one as soon as you start work or, preferably, even sooner. The tax file number can take up to six weeks to be issued, and until you receive your number and are able to pass it on to your employer, you will be taxed at the maximum rate of 49 per cent. Application forms for a tax file number are available from all Centrelink and tax offices. Non-residents with a tax file number pay tax at a rate of 29 cents in the dollar (29 per cent of all earnings up to $397 per week).

Before you leave Australia, you should lodge a tax return (also available from the Centrelink offices, and inside the 'Tax Pack'). Every employer for whom you have worked should have supplied you with a 'payment summary' on leaving; you will need to keep these and attach them to your tax return as proof of your total earnings. The taxation office will assess your return, usually within a couple of weeks of lodgement, and a refund cheque (if applicable) will be forwarded to your nominated address, either in Australia or overseas.

PERMANENT WORK

Agriculture and Food Processing

It is generally acknowledged that Australia got rich off the sheep's back, and today agriculture is still the backbone of the Australian economy. The traditional export products of wheat and wool, however, have long since ceded prominence to other sectors, including fisheries and viticulture, and exotic produce such as native bush meats and wildflowers.

The Australian agricultural sector is relatively stable at present, with grain and livestock farmers in a better market position than cotton and sugar producers. Wheat production is currently forecast at 21.7 million tons and live cattle exports have continued to increase. The wool industry is experiencing a rise in profitability due to the decline in sheep numbers and the increasing cost of competing fabrics. Wine exports have increased significantly and production is forecast to increase steadily until 2005 as new vineyards come into yield. Both cotton and sugar exports remain at high levels and both industries are expected to experience steady increases in production until 2005.

The food, beverage and tobacco processing industry is Australia's largest manufacturing sector and accounts for around 20% of Australian manufacturing. It is expected to experience continued growth of around 10% per annum. It is projected that employment growth areas in this industry will shift away from factory processing and into sales, research, development and marketing. This trend reflects both a move away from convenience foods by consumers towards high quality fresh produce, as well as a competitive imported food market.

Automotive

Australia has a strong automotive industry with Ford, Holden-General Motors, Mitsubishi and Toyota all producing cars in Australian factories. There are also over 200 component, tooling, design and engineering firms. In total the automotive industry employs over 51,000 people. Car sales are currently buoyant, reflecting the general economic situation in Australia, and sales of locally produced cars are strong as luxury taxes make imported cars expensive. All automotive manufacturers are investing heavily in robot technology, so that the employment outlook for factory floor workers is poor, whilst that for people skilled in computer technology is good. Since 1984 exports of automotive products (the majority going to Saudi Arabia, the USA, and the UAE have grown consistently. In 2000, total automotive vehicle exports to all markets grew by about 38 percent compared with the previous year. For automotive components, total exports grew by 20 percent. The automotive industry is experiencing a skill shortage and employment prospects in this industry are good.

Executive Employment

Executive employment prospects are generally good, particularly with smaller companies. After a period of rationalisation business has stabilised and most firms are experiencing reasonable growth. DEWR assess the employment outlook for generalist managers and administrators as average in both the short- and long-term, whilst those with specialist skills have above average prospects. Marketing personnel, sales reps, accountants, finance professionals and management all have good job prospects in Australia.

Finance and Property

The property and business services industry has seen a decline as both residential and non-dwelling building projects turn down sharply. Non-dwelling building has seen a downturn primarily due to the completion of a number of major projects and because of oversupply in some regions.

Finance has seen a small decrease in the number of jobs available although average weekly earnings remain very high in this sector, and are second only to mining. However, the downturn of the financial sector globally has seen a job cuts and cutbacks in banks and financial institutions. There is at present a national lack of accountants. Qualified graduates, with degrees in either business or finance, or with experience in a related field are most likely to succeed in finding work in this sector.

Information Technology

Information technology is a major growth sector in the Australian economy and is projected to continue to expand through to 2005. Australia has a vigorous, high-tech industry, particularly in the fields of information and medical technologies. Australians are keen to maintain a leading technological edge and are continually updating their technology. Twenty international IT firms have their regional headquarters in Australia and this is in many ways due to the sophistication of the Australian IT market; as well as the fact that Australia has the second highest number of computer owners, and one of the largest number of Internet users, in the world. Job prospects are strong for well-qualified and experienced professionals, and there is a particular need for people with Powerbuilder, Linux, Unis, and SAP skills among others. The government is keen to encourage the IT sector, particularly in areas where application of new technology will enhance Australia's competitiveness in the export market.

Medical

Medical practitioners hoping to work in Australia will need to prove that there are no Australian doctors qualified to do the same job. Overseas-qualified doctors already granted permission to work in Australia are required to pass stringent registration examinations before they are permitted to practice.

Both Registered nurses and Nurse educators and researchers are in demand throughout Australia, particularly those qualified in specialist fields such as accident and emergency, intensive care, and psychiatry. You will need to have your qualifications ratified by the Nurses Registration Board in the state in which you live and then register with this Board before you are able to apply for work.

Health therapists, such as physiotherapists, occupational therapists and speech therapists, also need to have their qualifications approved by Australian authorities before practising in Australia. In some cases, further study may be necessary before your registration can be accepted. There is currently an identified shortage of sonographers, midwives, pharmacists, radiographers and nurse managers in Australia.

Petrochemicals

There has been massive investment in oil and gas exploration, particularly in the North West Shelf Natural Gas Project off the coast of Western Australia and a record number of oil and gas discoveries were made in Australia in 2000. Engineers of all types are in demand in this industry, and petrochemical engineering is identified by DEWR as an area of particular employment shortage. In 2000/2001, Australia produced around 84% of its liquid petroleum needs and all of its gas needs. As a result, it makes a major contribution to national welfare in terms of output, employment, exports, tax revenue and energy self-sufficiency. There are twelve major players in the oil and gas exploration and production industries in Australia: Apache, BHP Billiton, BP, ChevronTexaco, ExxonMobil, Magellan, Nexen, OMV, EnCana, Santos, Shell and Woodside.

Retailing

The retail sector employs the largest number of employees in the Australian economy at around 15%. The health of the retail industry in Australia has seasonal highs and lows; the Australian Retailers Association estimated that Christmas 2001 sales had been around $2.1 billion, 4.5 per cent better than in 2000. Employment prospects in both retail sales and management are good, and increased by nearly 4 percent in the 12 months prior to May 1998. DEWR assesses both the short and long term outlook for employment in retail management as sound and in retail sales as good.

Steel and Non-ferrous Metals

Australia is one of the world's largest exporters of iron ore, although its steel-processing sector is much less developed. Mining is a major employment sector, and is the highest paid industry in the country, with average weekly earning in excess of $1,000 per week. Mining continue to employ large numbers and short- and long-term employment prospects are sound in professional, skilled, and semi-skilled occupations. The Australian mining industry is one of the most highly productive in the world and is a significant investor in capital equipment. British equipment suppliers enjoy a large share of the underground black coal mining market. Australia's aluminium industry is one of the major building blocks of Australia's economy and in 1999-2000, Australia produced nearly 40% of world bauxite, and almost 30% of world alumina, making it the world's largest producer of both. The Stanwell Magnesium Project will be the world's largest magnesium plant, creating 1 350 jobs during construction and 350 jobs once the plant is running. Metal production at the Australian Magnesium Corporation plant is expected to commence in October 2004 with the plant reaching full capacity by October 2006.

Australia is also rich in other natural resources including manganese, uranium, diamonds, zirconite, mineral sands, lead, zinc, copper, gold, silver, alumina and bauxite. These mining industries operate on a large scale across the country and are all significant employers of skilled and unskilled labour.

Teaching

To teach in Australia, you will be required to be four-year-qualified, that is, you must hold either a bachelor's degree plus a one year Graduate Diploma of Education (equivalent to a PGCE), or a four-year Bachelor of Education. Teachers in both the state and private education sector who are not qualified at this level are now required to upgrade their qualifications by means of external study and summer schools. Primary school teachers require a specialist degree in primary education while secondary school teachers normally teach in a subject area related to their degree major. Whereas once private schools were prepared to employ non teacher-trained graduates, this is now extremely rare and teachers arriving from overseas with experience but no qualification are unlikely to find work in either the state or private sector. Teaching, tutoring and lecturing posts in the tertiary sector are very oversubscribed and obtaining a position is highly competitive.

Education is the responsibility of the state government, and to obtain work as a teacher you will need to apply to the Ministry of Education in your state. Some states require new teachers on the permanent register to work for a period in a remote rural location before offering a choice of more convenient schools. If you are unable to do this, you may have to undertake work on a temporary or casual basis for some years before being offered permanency. Employment prospects for Primary School teachers are expected to remain low and employment has fallen slightly over the past five years. Employment of Secondary School Teachers has remained steady, while job prospects for music, dance and other extra-systemic teachers are average. Employment in this area has fallen over the last five years. Special Education teachers have good prospects of finding employment and number employed in this sector have risen in the past five years, however, job turnover for Special Education teachers remains low.

REGIONAL EMPLOYMENT GUIDE

This section summarises the employment opportunities and economic strengths of each state and territory, and should be read in conjunction with the analysis contained in the *Regional Guide* in *General Introduction*.

Western Australia

Permanent. Western Australia is a major exporter of a wide range of commodities worldwide and provides about 25% of Australia's exports. The state has a highly educated workforce of 850,000 and manufacturing and services are the state's fastest growing sectors of industry. The state government has identified and is promoting a group of key strategic industries in order to reduce dependence on raw materials export. These strategic industries include: building and construction, defence and aerospace, education and training services, health and medical services, information technology and telecommunications, marine industries, mining equipment and services, oil and gas equipment and services, processed foods and wine, and professional services. Asian markets play a significant role in Western Australian industry as state production is heavily export-focused. WA is also a global supplier of minerals and energy, with production totalling $21.3 billion in the period 1999/2000; in the same period oil, gas and liquefied natural gas (LNG), comprised 36% of output and Iron ore was the state's largest mineral export at $3.7 billion. WA produces 40 per cent of the world's diamonds; 44% of its zircon; 22% of its alumina; 13% of its iron ore and 9% of its gold, nickel and LNG.

WA has one of the world's largest and most technologically advanced mining sectors, and mineral and energy production is forecast to experience continued growth. Bulk commodity export is under some pressure, however, as a decreasing international scarcity of non-reproducible natural resources has made the market highly competitive. Reforms have been implemented within the industry to make it more competitive and these have included a decline in traditional award-type employment which has been replaced by staff-only operations. There is likely to be a sharp increase in contracting-out in the mining industry.

Western Australia has the world's largest zirconia plant. ALCOA, Worsley Alumina, and Dampier Salt are the three major investors in mineral extraction and processing, and between them employ around 4,000 people. Western Australia's goldfields are based inland around Kalgoorlie, 600 km east of Perth, and this area is experiencing renewed rapid growth after a period of recession. Only the diamond industry is expected to experience any decline in the short-term, with implications for the economic strength of the Kimberley region. The oil and gas industry is a major contributor to the state's economy and is centred on the North West Shelf, which contains one of the world's largest deposits of natural gas. Oil and gas exploration is ongoing in Western Australia, and further major finds are expected. Since 1994, numerous international companies associated with the petroleum industry, including Western Geophysical, Nopec, Drillex, WS Atkins, ESD Simulators, and Global Drilling, have all established Southeast Asian regional headquarters in Perth. Engineers, metallurgists, and other mineral extraction industry professionals are in demand in Western Australia, and employment prospects in both the short and long term are good. Over 90 percent of Australia's oil and gas resources are located off Western Australia. A steady increase has been forecast for the production of gas.

Western Australia has the largest marine industry in Australia. It has an international reputation for building quality ships and infrastructure for offshore oil and gas production and for providing a wide range of marine services. The state supplies about 20% of the world's lightweight high-speed ferries. A marine industry technology park is currently being developed at Lake Coogee. A State Government initiative, it aims to provide land and opportunities for marine-related high technology industries, such as ship design, maritime training and testing of naval defence systems.

Some 400 companies work in the IT and telecommunications industry manufacturing, developing and wholesaling equipment, software and services for information processing, multimedia or communications. Most of these companies are located in Perth.

There are around 3,000 different manufacturers in Western Australia. Food processing, base metal processing, wine production, and pharmaceuticals have experienced strong growth, with continued expansion forecast. The Government recognises the importance of the industry to the economy of the state and offers programs designed to assist companies in the food industry. Agriculture is increasingly focused on niche markets, such as emu, kangaroo, ostrich, deer and genetically modified animals; and on value-added crops, such as specialised noodle wheat. The raw grains market (wheat, oats, and barley) has a positive medium term outlook. In forestry, there has been rapid expansion in eucalypt plantations in the south west of the state. The fisheries industry is experiencing rapid growth, hampered only by the restrictions of wild harvesting. Mariculture (sea-based) and aquaculture (land-based) fish production is therefore being encouraged, and these industries have a strong economic outlook. Western Australia's major success in aquaculture has been the culture of pearl oysters. Based in the Kimberleys, in the far north of the state, the industry represents Australia's largest and most successful aquaculture venture, producing quality pearls worth around $150 million a year. WA is also the world's largest exporter of live animals and a major exporter of skins and hides.

The services sector of the Western Australian economy currently accounts for more than 70% of the state's GDP. The financial sector has expanded rapidly since deregulation in the 1980s and there are now more than 20 banking groups represented in the state. WA exports consultancy services in mining, engineering, forestry, agriculture and conservation, and the state's highly regarded medical research and hospital facilities have made Perth a centre for Australia's 'medical tourism' industry. The service sector's biggest growth area is currently tourism.

In 1999/2000, Western Australia's gross state product (GSP) totalled $66.5 billion and accounted for 11% percent of the national economy. Over the last decade, Western Australia's annual rate of growth has averaged 4.9%, compared to the national average of 4.1% over the same period. In 2000, WA attracted 12.5% of all new private capital investment in Australia. Perth has become a favoured location for international companies choosing a regional base for Southeast Asia, especially in industries servicing the oil and gas sectors. Retail trade, property and business services, health and community services, manufacturing and construction employ nearly half of the workforce and employment rates in these industries continue to grow.

Temporary. Harvest work is available throughout the year, mainly in the southwest of the state; casual work in the fishing industry around Carnarvon is available between March and October. General agricultural labouring can usually be found on cattle stations, and on sheep stations, particularly at shearing time. The hospitality industry always needs short-term employees, with work available year-round in Perth and during the tourist season in other major centres (May to September in Broome, and the summer months in other areas). Unskilled mine work is relatively easy to find in the northwest and can be highly paid. In Perth, all the usual temporary employment opportunities, including office work, teaching and nursing, are readily available.

Northern Territory

Permanent. The Northern Territory has a population of just 190,000, about 1% of the Australian total and produces 10% of the nation's exports. The Northern Territory is rich in natural resources, which are being developed by the private sector with the support of the state Government, which is presently half way through a five-year, $16 million geophysical survey of the Territory. This data is being produced mainly for mineral and hydrocarbon exploration companies. Unemployment in the state is currently around 5.5%. Gross State Product (GSP) growth for 2002 to 2006 is estimated at 7%, double the national rate and the NT is set to lead the country in economic growth over the next five years by an estimated 50%.

The Northern Territory continues to experience economic growth and has benefited from an increase in private capital expenditure in mining, capital investment and tourism. Advertised job vacancies are increasing steadily in the Territory and are generally stronger in the dry season, from May to October.

The mining industry is the Northern Territory's biggest earner, and is the state's major employer. There are 14 operating mines, and minerals, including alumina, manganese, gold, bauxite and uranium, dominate the territory's overseas exports. Zinc, lead and silver are mined at Woodcutters mine, McArthur River, and uranium is mined at Alligator River. Gold mines are located in the Adelaide River/Pine Creek region, the Tanami Desert and at Tennant Creek. Oil and gas production occurs onshore at Mereenie and Palm Valley in the Amadeus Basin, and offshore on the Jabiru and Challis fields in the Timor Sea. Natural gas production for export is being developed on the Petrel and Tern gas fields in the Bonaparte Gulf. Oil and gas account for approximately 35 percent of the state's exports.

In the East Arnhem region of the Northern Territory, which comprises the eastern half of Arnhem Land and Groote Eylandt in the Gulf of Carpentaria, bauxite and manganese are produced in two of the world's largest mines of their type. Gove Joint Venture mines bauxite on the Gove Peninsula, exporting it as alumina and aluminium hydroxide. The mine, which is managed by Nabalco, employs more than 1,000 people, of whom more than 260 are independent contractors. The mine is expected to be operational until 2035. Manganese is mined by the BHP subsidiary, Groote Eylandt Mining Company (GEMCO), which produces more than ten per cent of the world's manganese output. Mining support businesses in the region turnover around $45 million per annum. Apart from the mining industry, the East Arnhem region supports mainly small business, in particular retail and property services.

Growth industries in the Northern Territory include building and construction, and prawn fishing. More unusually, another growing industry services the need of farming, mining, and conservation sectors to harvest the 30,000 head of wild buffalo (feral cattle), which cause massive damage as they rampage across the fragile landscape. Additionally, the Northern Territory cattle industry is also booming and in 2000, 300,000 cattle were exported – mainly to the Philippines and Indonesia.

Traditional industries are continuing to show strong growth. The tourism industry has averaged 7% growth over the last seven years, experiencing 11% growth in 2000, and is projected to grow at least until 2005. Around 1.4 million tourists visit the eco-tourism region at Uluru (Ayers Rock), as well as Kakadu National Park. The Northern Territory Government is working towards developing Darwin as a transport hub between the markets of Australia and Asia and the first stage of the construction of the $100 million East Arm Port was completed in 1999. Work is underway on the second stage of this project, which is expected to be completed in late 2003. Work on the $1.3 billion, 1,500 kilometre Darwin to Alice Springs rail link started in May 2001 and should be completed by early 2004. The railway will eventually run from Darwin in the north of Australia to Adelaide in the south.

Oil and gas deposits in the Timor Sea has led to a shift in the focus of Australia's oil industry to the north and northwest of Australia. This has meant a continuing need for an oil and gas industry infrastructure, and services including engineering, transportation and communications continue to see growth. Timor Sea gas will be brought ashore at Darwin and this will mean the construction of about 500 kilometres of sub-marine pipeline and the establishment within the new East Arm Port industrial complex of a range of service and support companies to the offshore oil and gas industries.

Temporary. Most temporary jobs are provided by the tourist industry, especially during the tourist season from May to December (all year round at Alice Springs). Remote resorts have a high staff turnover and are frequently able to offer short-term employment. There is occasional station work available to those with good horse skills.

South Australia

Permanent. South Australia's major exports are road vehicles and automotive parts and accessories, followed by wine and wheat. The state's information technology development programme aims to make the state an internationally recognised centre in the five specialist areas of software development, multimedia, spatial information, electronic services, and education. Motorola, TechSouth, AWA Defence Industries, Telstra and Tandem have already made major investments, and SA hopes to attract more key investors. The global communications giant, Motorola, has established its Australian Software Development Centre in Adelaide and Technology Park in Adelaide is home to more than 35 technology organisations including British Aerospace Australia, Computer Science Corporation, and Celsiustech. There are a further six research centres, including the Signal Processing Research Institute, which undertakes research in mobile and defence communications. The electronics sector provides employment for nearly 10,000 scientists, engineers, technicians, production and support personnel and local industry output is currently $1.8 billion and growing at 14% per annum.

The motor vehicle sector is South Australia's largest single industry and is the state's largest employer, with Mitsubishi Motors Australia and General Motors Holden together employing over 9,000 people. Mitsubishi have invested $500 million at their Clovelly Park plant. The automotive components industry in SA provides over 20% of the national production, and directly employs a further 6,000 people.

South Australia is at the centre of Australia's defence industry and attracts around 40% of the nation's defence development budget. Facilities include the Defence Science and Technology Organization complex in Adelaide, the Port Adelaide construction site for conventionally powered submarines and the Woomera Rocket

Range test and evaluation facility. There are some 30 defence-related companies located in South Australia and research and development for the $5.3 billion Collins Class submarine project is currently underway in Adelaide.

The state is rich in natural resources, including coal, copper, gold, iron ore, lead, silver, uranium, crude oil, natural gas, dolomite and gypsum. The world's largest zinc smelter, owned by Pasminco and BHAS, is located at Port Pirie, and the Santos Moomba Field in Cooper Basin is Australia's largest producer of oil and gas.

South Australia is Australia's largest producer of wine, and grows around 40% of the national crop. It is also a leading producer of wheat and barley. There are over 180 small to medium-sized businesses involved in wine production spread throughout the six wine growing regions. The major producers, Penfolds, Orlando Wyndham, BRL Hardy, and Mildara Blass, have a national and international presence. Aquaculture is also thriving and incentives are in place to encourage development in this industry. Blue fin tuna, abalone, and Pacific oysters are farmed and exported on a large scale, and the farming of freshwater crayfish and barramundi is currently being developed. Agricultural products contribute around $3.3 billion to the South Australian economy each year.

In the minerals and energy sector, South Australia has one of the world's largest lead/zinc smelters. It also has one of the largest copper/uranium sites in the world, and its on-shore oil and gas resources are among the most significant in Australia. The state is also developing strengths in niche industries, such as water management and environmental services.

South Australia produces about $42 billion in Gross State Product, representing approximately 7 percent of Australia's Gross National Product (GNP). Unemployment in the state is decreasing and export figures are very healthy. New infrastructure projects such as the Adelaide to Darwin Railway and the Pelican Point Power Station are expected to improve the efficiency of South Australia's key industries and access to export markets. However, economic growth is not as healthy as it could be, mainly due to a pattern of interstate migration and a low rate of population growth, which began during the recession of the 1990s.

The South Australia government encourages new business, and the workforce is well educated and highly skilled. Government supported research and development in South Australian information industries is over $80 million a year, accounting for over one-third of all Research and Development expenditure in the state. In addition, real estate and office space is cheaper than in some of the other states. High productivity levels and low operational base costs combine to make the capital, Adelaide, more economical and responsive than other cities in Australia and significantly better than many overseas cities. Business opportunities are to be found in light and heavy industry, agriculture, IT, agribusiness, engineering (especially foundries and tool making), defence and aerospace, food and wine, aquaculture, and traded services, particularly health and tourism. SA also has well-developed links with markets in Asia, North America and Europe.

Temporary. Grape picking is available in the Barossa Valley and Adelaide Hills from February to April, as is other harvesting work throughout the rest of the year. Hospitality and office temporary work is available in Adelaide all year, particularly during the summer months.

Tasmania

Permanent. Tasmania has been the butt of 'would the last person to leave Tasmania...' jokes for so long that it hardly needs saying that this is a state gripped by considerable economic difficulties. Many Tasmanians are optimistic, however, despite an 8.5% unemployment rate and an economy that continues behind most other Australian states. The Tasmanian Government welcomes investment, but only on Tasmania's terms. Although the state is actively pursuing economic development, Tasmanians have not abandoned their environment-friendly sentiments and all sides have made it clear that investors will have to meet various environmental and quality of life standards before their projects will be given the go ahead in the State.

Tasmania is rich in mineral resources, especially iron, copper, lead, zinc, tin, and tungsten, and a recent geological data survey has revived interest in gold mining in the region. There are seven major mining operations at Henty, Savage River, Beaconsfield, Hellyer, Mt Lyell, Pasminco Roseberry, and Renison. After a long period during which the mineral resources industry was starved of investment, the Tasmanian Government is now committed to developing the infrastructure and investment conditions necessary to encourage the growth of multiple-stage mineral processing in the state. The Government is seeking to combine innovative agricultural and manufacturing techniques with Tasmania's natural beauty and environmental cleanliness.

Tasmania has a highly diversified rural sector, of which the major components are the vegetable, dairy, sheep, and beef cattle industries. Continuing problems in the wool market have meant that the sheep industry, once the mainstay of Tasmanian agriculture, is now the poor relative of vegetable and dairy farming, and recently, beef has experienced a similar downturn. Tasmanian agriculture is strongly export-orientated, both to mainland Australia and internationally.

Dairying is considered to have the best medium to long term prospects and is already the state's largest agricultural industry: in addition to 747 dairy farms, Tasmania has seven fresh milk processing plants, one UHT milk processing plant, seven manufacturing plants, ten farm cheese producers, and three cheese shredders. The industry employs 2,000 people at farm level and a further 1,600 people at factory and distribution level. Emerging rural industries include emus, poppies, lavender, and wine grapes, whilst apple farmers are experiencing renewed economic growth.

Sea fisheries are a rapidly growing industry; the most valuable sector of the fisheries market is Atlantic salmon, which is mainly grown in the marine farms of the state's southeast. Abalone and rock lobster account for half the total value of Tasmanian marine production, and the marine farming sector as a whole provided over 40%. Tasmania's wild fisheries have now reached the limits of their sustainable exploitation, however, intensification and expansion is projected for in the area of cultured fisheries. Around 2,000 people are employed in marine industries in the state.

The largest sectors of Tasmania's manufacturing industry are food, beverage and tobacco, which together contribute 30%. Tasmania is also the base for Incat, one of the world's largest manufacturers of high-speed ferries. Wood and wood products, textiles, clothing and footwear, paper and paper products, chemical and petroleum products, basic metal products, fabricated metal products and transport equipment industries also contribute to the state's economic base, however, there has been a marked decline in employment in these sectors in recent years. Retailing is experiencing slow to moderate growth but there is strong growth in the tourism sector, particularly in eco-tourism.

Ongoing economic developments include the production of pyrethrum, a plant which produces a natural pesticide; the booming aquaculture industry; and the Government's plan to increase its energy supply by building a gas pipeline and an electricity cable to mainland Australia, expected to be completed by mid-2002. Alternative technologies such as wind power are also being explored in Tasmania but due to the lack of sites outside of World Heritage areas Tasmania is no longer able to develop new hydroelectric power plants to offer low-cost power. Recently the Government announced a reduction in payroll tax rates so that employers with 50 employees now pay less in taxes than any other Australian State.

Temporary. Hospitality work is available in the Mount Field and Ben Lomond Ski Resorts during the ski season – from June to August. Fruit picking is available from December to April in the Huon Valley, Derwent Valley, Tasman Peninsula, and West Tamar. Scallop splitting work can be found in Bicheno in January and February.

Victoria

Permanent. The state of Victoria accounts for 34 percent of the Australia's manufacturing industry and produces 26 percent of the country's GDP. Many international corporations, including Saab, Kodak, General Motors, Ford, Ericsson, Mercedes Benz, BMW, Toyota, Kia, Hewlett-Packard, Olivetti, NEC, Oracle, Kraft, Heinz and Simplot have their Australian base in Victoria and the Australian headquarters of seven of the top twenty US Fortune 500 companies are based in Melbourne. The government of Victoria's strong commitment to encouraging international competitiveness in local business has lifted export growth, which is currently strongest in chemicals, the automotive industry, information technology, and medical and scientific equipment. Employment prospects are also strongest in these sectors. Over half of Australia's automotive industry production occurs in Victoria, with Ford, General Motors and Toyota all manufacturing in the state, together with more than 500 components producers.

Victoria's food processing industries account for around a third of the state's export earnings; agriculture and food provide over 35% of the State's export income. 40% of the nation's aluminium production occurs at the primary aluminium smelters at Portland and Point Henry. Victoria is also the centre of Australia's textiles, clothing and footwear industries, and continued growth is expected in niche and designer sectors.

Victoria has Australia's largest industrial concentration of information technology, scientific, and medical facilities, as well as a highly skilled workforce. Almost half of Australia's $2 billion telecommunications industry is based in Victoria; around a third of the country's software development companies are based in the state.

Traded services, such as the health and education sectors, are becoming highly competitive in the export market and are actively seeking new business overseas. The education sector currently generates around $500 million in annual exports and is experiencing continued growth.

Victoria boasts a significant and prosperous history in the finance and banking sectors. Two of Australia's largest banks: the National Australia Bank and ANZ have their headquarters in Melbourne, and Melbourne stockbrokers account for more than half of all capital raisings on the Australian Stock Exchange (ASX). Melbourne is one of Australia's leading industrial centres and is Australia's leading centre for biotechnology in the Asia-Pacific region.

Melbourne has Australia's largest throughput cargo airport and its largest container seaport; the Port of Melbourne handles 40 percent of Australia's container trade. The two terminal operators at Swanson dock, Australian Stevedores and Conaust, are committed to developing their facilities to operate at international best practice performance levels and investment in the redevelopment of these terminals over the next 20 years will exceed $300 million.

Geelong is Australia's eleventh largest city and plays a major role in the country's wool production and textile industries. In addition to these traditional industries, the city is now developing its economic base in high-technology industries, education and research. Geelong is home to manufacturers of textiles, clothing, footwear, petroleum and coal products, chemicals, basic metal products and transport equipment and is the centre of the Australian aerospace industry – at Avalon Airport, while major assembly and maintenance plants are operated by ASTA and Hawker de Havilland in Melbourne. Ford Motor Company, Shell Oil Company of Australia and the aluminium giant ALCOA are the largest among the many industries that have chosen to expand in the region.

As a result of the Victorian Government's approach to financial management Victoria has very low debt levels and is in a strong economic position. The 2001-02 state budget places Victoria as a world leader in innovation, science and technology. There has been a massive funding injection for science, technology, research, education, and skills development. The State government is committed to science, technology and innovation. The development of a biotechnology precinct in central Melbourne and the national Synchotron facility will make Victoria a global leader in biotechnology and scientific research with the aim of developing knowledge-based industries, professional services, design, advanced manufacturing and environmental management. The government has also committed funding for a high technology film and television studio facility at the Melbourne Docklands.

Victoria contains the largest concentration of research institutions in Australia and accounts for 35 percent of the country's total business research and development. Employment in rural and regional Victoria accounts for more than a third of the state total.

Temporary. Harvest work is available around Mildura and Shepperton from January to April, and around Echuca and Lilyfield from September through to February. The Northern Victoria Fruit-growers' Association in Shepperton, Victoria, and the Victorian Peach and Apricot Growers' Association in Cobram, Victoria, are both able to offer jobs during the harvesting season. Hospitality work is available during the ski season in the Snowy Mountains. Temporary secretarial, office and administration work, as well as hospitality work (including gaming), is widely available in Melbourne.

New South Wales

Permanent. The strength of the New South Wales' economy is due in its diverse range of industries. The state has one of the world's leading service economies, and also has a significant manufacturing and primary industry base. Its capital, Sydney, is a sophisticated, global city, and is the base for Australia's major financial institutions – the Reserve Bank of Australia, the Australian Stock Exchange and the Sydney Futures Exchange. It is a major financial centre in the Asia-Pacific region. The majority banks, both national and international, have their headquarters in Sydney.

New South Wales is the location of the regional headquarters of a number of multinational companies in Australia and 50% of the top 500 companies in Australia are located in the state. There are a number of industry sectors present in NSW including: information technology, telecommunications, aerospace, medical equipment, pharmaceuticals, environmental industries, industrial textiles, shipping and railways, construction and mining equipment, metal and minerals processing, processed foods, paper and pulp, banking, tourism, advertising, film, and audio products. European, US, and Japanese companies are all represented. NSW is the base for 45.8% of Australia's finance and insurance industry, 40.7% of its property and business services (including IT) industry, and 35% of its communications industry.

New South Wales is Australia's premier agribusiness state, accounting for around one third of the national primary industry output, and many leading agribusiness companies have their headquarters in Sydney. NSW agribusiness industry includes farming, processing, transport, distribution, export, and supply. The industry's strengths have traditionally been in bulk commodities and minimally processed products such as wool, grains, meat and sugar; however, recent innovation and new product development has made the sector increasingly market focused. In particular sector growth is focused on the Asian food market, with heavy demand projected for western foods over the next five years.

The state has a well-established chemical industry and is home to the country's largest petrochemical complex. Its mining and mineral processing industries generate an annual output of over $12 billion, of which coal production accounts for 80%. The major minerals derived from the state's rich mineral resources are black coal, copper, gold, silver, lead, zinc, mineral sands, and gemstones. NSW is also a major minerals processing state with established steel and aluminium production, and new copper smelting capacity currently coming into operation. The government of NSW is spending $35 million to expand the geological database of the state in order to attract new mineral and petroleum exploration and development. The Lithgow Minerals Processing Park has been located in the central west of the state to encourage development in that area.

The electricity sector dominates New South Wales' energy industry and employs over 4,000 people. The government monopoly has recently been restructured to form three independent power generators, Pacific Power, Delta Electricity, and Macquarie Generation. NSW gas sector is 95% controlled by Australian Gas Limited (AGL), a publicly listed company with 2,100 employees. Environmental management is a growth industry in the state, and is currently the largest in Australia.

The state is also a leading information technology and telecommunications centre, and the base for almost half of Australia's IT industry. This sector is forecast to grow rapidly over the next five years. The state is a significant producer of digital material content for multimedia, and has a strong film and television production sector. Fox Studios in Sydney will soon become the largest film and television studios in the southern hemisphere, and will offer many opportunities in the digital post-production industry.

NSW and Sydney are the major entry points to Australia, with Sydney Airport providing the bulk of airfreight and business air passenger activity. NSW is a major centre for aerospace, electronics and defence industries. These industries are among the fastest growing in the state with extremely strong investment growth expected over the next five years. The state is the base for over 30,000 defence personnel and Sydney Harbour is an important naval base and centre for marine repair activity. Airframe and systems support, sensors, processors, and defence aerospace training

systems are all under development in NSW, as is world-leading C2I technology.
Cultural industries generate an estimated $4.3 billion in turnover for NSW, and education is a growing market, with over 50,000 international students studying at various educational institutions. Food processing comprises 8% of the state's GDP and retail trade for 15 percent of the economic output. Both these sectors are significant employers. The state's largest service sector is tourism, which currently injects $15 billion a year into the economy. NSW also accounts for 38.6% of national output in the 'lifestyle' industries – accommodation and food outlets, and 36.3% of cultural and recreational services.

NSW accounts for almost a third of the total Australian workforce and more than 45% of all employees in the finance and insurance sectors. NSW also employs more than a third of the national workforce in the transport, communications, property and business services sectors. In 1999-2000, NSW received more than a third of Australia's new private investment.

Temporary. The full range of temporary work opportunities is available in NSW, ranging from harvest and seasonal farm work in almost every region, to hospitality and office work, particularly in Sydney.

Australian Capital Territory

Permanent. Employment opportunities in the ACT are concentrated in Canberra. Most permanent work available is either service-based, reflecting the city's political function, or in the extensive public service which supports the government and federal ministries. The Commonwealth Government is the territory's biggest employer.

There are over 13,000 businesses in the ACT. Canberra's workforce is more computer-literate and highly educated than any other workforce in Australia with 51 percent possessing university degrees. Several hundred national associations have their headquarters in Canberra and the city is home to a number of multinational companies including Hewlett-Packard, NEC, British Aerospace, Fujitsu, Unisys, Oracle and Intec. Companies dealing in IT & telecommunications, advanced technology manufacturing, defence related services, call centres, information and business services, light manufacturing and assembly, and agribusiness can all be found in Canberra.

Temporary. Temporary employment in Canberra, will be available in the IT and service industries and will include clerical and hospitality work.

Queensland

Permanent. The rapid growth experienced by Queensland in recent years slowed considerably during 2000/2001 although the state still benefits greatly from rich natural resources, diversified agriculture, and a vibrant tourist industry. The state government has allocated large sums towards maintaining Queensland's favourable economic position, including a $1.6 billion Infrastructure Rejuvenation Package. A further $4.8 billion is being spent in developing the state's regional road networks, and another $690 million on Queensland Rail. Queensland has Australia's lowest state taxes and debt levels, and welcomes foreign investors. Queensland's annual employment growth is currently one percent higher than the national average.

Queensland is Australia's most decentralized state, and has the largest rail network, and more deepwater ports, than the whole of the rest of Australia combined. Infrastructure developments to which the government has made a commitment include the installation of a water management system and new weir in the Atherton Tablelands, a new cruise liner port in Brisbane, expansion of the Dalrymple Bay Coal Export Terminal, and a ten-year development of the Port of Mackay. The Queensland Hospital Project will upgrade all the state's hospital facilities, and gas turbine power plants will be built at Yabulu and Mt Stuart. New wharf facilities are being built at Fisherman islands to handle large container vessels.

Agriculture is the cornerstone of Queensland's economy, with grains, beef and wool dominating rural industry. Tropical and citrus fruits, dairy products, vegetables, cotton, and tobacco are also important, and the state has the world's highest yielding sugar cane industry. Queensland's fishing industry is second only to Western Australia's, with nearly 5,000 commercial fishing vessels in operation, mainly fishing prawns, crustaceans and fin fish for export to Asia, Europe and the USA. Recently established food processing plants include a high technology piggery and integrated pork processing facility (DanPork Australia), and an upgraded Golden Circle Canned Fruit and Vegetable Plant. In 1999-00 exports of primary, semi-processed and processed food products contributed approximately $4.5 billion to the State's economy, representing 25 percent of Queensland's total exported merchandise.

Mount Isa Mine is one of the world's leading producers of lead and silver, and is ranked in the world's top ten for copper and zinc production. The state's high-grade coal and bauxite reserves are among the largest in the world, and magnesite, phosphate rock, and limestone are also mined. Queensland is the largest Australian producer and exporter of black coal. Large resources of magnesite, oil, shale, uranium, tin, mineral sands, clay and salt remain untapped, and continued development is projected. New mines are currently being developed at Cannington Base Metals Deposit (BHP), Century Base Metals Project (Century Zinc), Ely Mining Project (Alcan South Pacific), Ensham Coal Mine (Bligh/Idemitsu), and Enterprise Mine (MIM Holdings), amongst many others. Minerals mined in these projects include lead, zinc, bauxite, copper, gold, and predominantly, coal. In addition, a number of minerals processing plants are being brought online, such as the Sun Metals Corp Zinc Refinery in Townsville, and Dupont/Ticor Sodium Cyanide Plant, and the Boyne Island Aluminium Smelter. Coal seam methane gas is being recovered from productive coal along the western flank of the Bowen Basin, and a 27 km gas pipeline is under construction to connect coal seam methane supplies with the PG&E gas pipeline.

Manufacturing industries in Queensland have developed to support the state's mineral processing and agricultural industries. The manufacturing sector is dominated by food, beverage, and tobacco processing, fabricated metal products, and chemicals, petroleum and coal products. The processed food industry employs around 37,000 people, and is Queensland's largest manufacturing sector. The state's service industries include the construction, wholesale and retail trades, communications, business and financial services, and tourism.

The Environmental Management Industry is a new growth sector in Queensland and is concerned with creating sustainable development through pollution abatement and environmental protection and the monitoring, planning, management and rehabilitation of the environment. It is estimated that the global environment market is worth about $A100 billion a year with the Australian market worth at least 10 percent of that figure. The potential for growth and technological innovation in this sector is significant. At least 125 Queensland firms are already delivering environmental expertise and services overseas.

Queensland has Australia's most successful tourism market and this sector employs a significant proportion of the state's workforce. Recently four major tourist resorts have been developed at Coomera Waters, Cowan Cove, Port Hinchinbrook, and East Hill, an integrated urban/resort project, covering 245 hectares.

Japan is the major destination for Queensland merchandise exports, Major export earners for the state include coal, meat, non-ferrous metals and crude minerals. Business and investment opportunities occur in the traditional industries, and there has been recent growth in communications services, biotechnology, IT and leisure industries. The area surrounding Surfers Paradise on the Gold Coast has become Australia's third largest city, and is the fastest-growing area of Australia.

Temporary. Fruit and vegetable picking is available throughout the state, particularly at Stanthorpe, Bowen and Warwick. Employment in the hospitality sector is widely available at resorts during the tourist season, especially on the Gold Coast; and work on prawn trawlers can be found at Cairns and Karumba. Mining and cattle station work is available in the Mount Isa region.

DIRECTORY OF MAJOR EMPLOYERS

Major companies inevitably require staff from time to time in order to maintain their basic operations. Even though it may be more difficult to find companies that are advertising for additional staff, it is worth knowing who the big companies are so that you can approach them before they advertise. It is a good idea to approach their overseas office in your country (if applicable) before you depart.

Below is a list of the top one hundred fastest growing employers in Australia. It must be noted that recent economic reports show that small to medium sized companies are now the main creators of jobs in the private sector. Many of the larger companies are reducing instead of increasing their workforce, and this is partly due to the fact that once a company has reached a threshold level, it can avoid paying payroll tax, higher superannuation benefits and/or increased training levies if it does not hire more staff. If you choose to look for employment with a smaller company, try to choose one with less than 50 staff and one which produces high-value-added, high-technology products for export to Asia as such companies have experienced growth in excess of 30 percent in recent years.

Australia's 100 fastest growing companies (over three years to June 2001) are listed below. All the companies have fewer than 200 employees and include listed as well as privately owned companies. The 'Fast 100' is a list compiled by researchers at Monash University and is published by the *Business Review Weekly* (www.brw.com.au), Australia's leading business magazine, which also publishes league tables of Australia's top law and accountancy firms, the 'Australia Rich List', industry reports and the top 500 firms. The type of industries represented below will give you a good indication of those that are in demand in Australia at present and which may be worth investing in.

100 MAJOR EMPLOYERS

Agriculture, forestry and fish
Agrilink Holdings, Suite 7, 69 Sir Donald Bradman Drive, Hilton, SA 5033; ☎08-8416 9900; www.agrilink-int.com
Atlas Pacific Limited, 6 Rous Head Road, North Fremantle, WA 6159; ☎08-9336 7955 www.atlaspacific.com.au
Brian McGuigan Wines Ltd, Cnr Broke and McDonalds Road, Pokolbin, NSW 2320; ☎02-4998 7700; www.mcguiganwines.com.au
Goundrey Wines, PO Box 42, Mount Barker, WA 6324; ☎08-9851 1777; www.goundreywines.com.au
Manjimup Syndicate Coolstores Co. Ltd, Lot 689, Franklin Street, Manjimup, WA 6258; ☎08-9777 2576

Communications
20th Century Fox Home Entertainment, Level 3, Frank Hurley Grandstand, Fox Studios Australia, Driver Avenue, Moore Park, NSW 2021; ☎02-8353 2100; www.foxmovies.com.au
Fone Zone, 67 Links Ave., Eagle Farm, QLD 4009; ☎07-3868 6000; www.fonezone.com.au
Histar Invotek Group Pty Ltd, Port Melbourne, 198 Lorimer Street, VIC 3207; ☎03-9646 5144; www.hig.com.au
Hunter Watertech, Unit 5, 50 Derby Street, Silverwater, NSW 2128; ☎02-9648 6815; www.hunterwatertech.com.au
Integrity Data Systems Pty Ltd, 456 Cross Road, Glandore, SA 5037; ☎08-8351 1900; www.integritydata.com.au
M&C Saatchi Pty Ltd, 131 Macquarie Street, Sydney, NSW 2000; ☎02-9270 2700; www.saatchi.com.au
Nethead, 72 Campbell Street, Surry Hills, Sydney, NSW 2010; ☎02-9211 1311; www.nethead.com.au
PowerServe Pty Ltd, 575 Bourke Street, Melbourne, VIC 3000; ☎03-9618 1222; www.powerserve.com
Pretzel Logic, 11 Brown Street, East Perth, WA 6004; ☎08-9218 8588; www.pretzel.com.au

Rowland's Underground Technology Pty Ltd, Level 1, 129 Ogilvie Ave., Echuca, VIC 3564; ☎03-5480 7822; www.rut.com.au

Construction
Complete Scaffolding, Unit 2, 390 Victoria Road, Malaga, WA 6090; ☎08-9249 8299; www.completescaffolding.com.au
Grant Constructions Pty Ltd, Unit 5, Capital Business Centre Building, A/38 Brookhollow Avenue, Baulkham Hills, NSW 2153; ☎02-9899 7444
Total Concept Projects (Australia) Pty Ltd, 34-36 Adderley Street, Silverwater, NSW 2264; ☎02-9648 3444; www.tcpinternational.com
Walton Construction Pty Ltd, 37 Thistlethwaite Street, South Melbourne, VIC 3205; ☎03-9696 8866; www.waltonconstruction.com.au

Cultural and recreational services
Australian Outback Travel, Level 8, 420 St. Kilda Road, Melbourne, VIC 3000; ☎03-9867 7233; www.aot.com.au
Dial-A-Coach Group, Bronka Arcade, Shop 4, Oxford Street, Bondi Junction, NSW 2022; ☎0419-311 536
Intrepid Adventure Travel, 13 Spring Street, Fitzroy, VIC 3065; ☎03-9419 4426, www.intrepidtravel.com.au

Education
Performance Edge Systems Pty Ltd, Level 12, 220 George Street, Sydney, NSW 2000; ☎02-9251 9922; www.performanceedge.com.au
Phoenix Academy, 223 Vincent Street, West Perth, WA 6005; ☎08-9227 5538; www.phoenixela.com.au
The Pan Pacific Training Company, Suite 13, 40 Karalta Road, Erina, NSW 2250; ☎02-4365 6733; www.ato-l.com

Finance and insurance
Computer Fleet Management Pty Ltd, Level 11, 65 Berry Street, North Sydney, NSW 2060; ☎02-9957 3333;

www.computerfleet.com.au

Ezypay, 358 Pennant Hills Road, Pennant Hills, NSW 2120; ☎02-9980 9055; www.ezypay.com.au

Mortgage Choice, Head Office, Level 7, 182-186 Blues Point Road, North Sydney, NSW 2060; ☎02-8907 0444; www.mortgagechoice.com.au

Plan B Financial Services Ltd, Central Pk Level 28, 152 St. Georges Terrace, Perth, WA 6000; ☎08-9324 6000; www.planbonline.com

RentSmart Pty Ltd, The West Centre Level 1, 1260 Hay Street, West Perth, WA 6005; ☎1300-855 555; www.rentsmart.com.au

Terri Scheer Insurance Brokers, 313 Payneham Road, Royston Park, SA 5070; ☎08-8363 3800; www.terrischeer.com.au

Health and community services

IOR Health Benefits, Head Office, 26-28 Prospect Street, Box Hill, VIC 3128; ☎03-9843 4422; www.ior.org.au

Quality Occupational Health, Unit 2, 2-6 Gladstone Street, Merrylands, NSW 2160; ☎02-9897 7699

Staffing Australia, Level 1, 580 Church Street, Richmond, VIC; ☎03-9254 2000; www.staffingaustralia.com.au

Information technology

Adaptive International, Level 12, 50 Berry Street, North Sydney, NSW 2060; ☎02-9954 6822; www.adaptiveinternational.com

Eclipse Computing (Australia) Pty Ltd, Level 10, 191 Clarence Street, Sydney, NSW 2000; ☎02-9279 3000; www.eclipsecomputing.com

Invizage Technology, level 1, 21 Burwood Road, Hawthorn, Melbourne, VIC 3122; ☎03-9818 1222; www.invizage.com.au

IWL Pty Ltd, Level 5, 620 Bourke Street, Melbourne, VIC 3000; ☎03-9691 1600; www.iwl.com.au

Lochard Pty Ltd, 69 Kooyong Road, Caulfield North, VIC 3161; ☎03-9500 1017; www.lochard.com.au

Objective Corporation Objective Corporation,

Level 37, 100 Miller Street, North Sydney, NSW 2060; ☎02-9955 2288; www.objective.com

Rich Computing, Level 9, 123 Epping Road, North Ryde, NSW 2113; ☎02-8875 7979; www.rich.com.au

Southern Cross Computer Systems Pty Ltd, 27 Church Street, Richmond, VIC 3121; ☎03-9420 1700; www.sccs.com.au

Tower Software Engineering Pty Ltd, 10 Geils Court, Deakin, ACT 2600; ☎02-6282 4655; www.toersoft.com.au

Upstream Technology Pty Ltd, 234 Whitehorse Road, Blackburn, VIC 3130; ☎03-9875 3500; www.upstreamtech nology.com.au

Manufacturing

AJ Mayr Engineering Pty Ltd, 10 McIntyre Road, Tomago, NSW 2322; ☎02-4964 8181

Bagel House, Unit 29, 566 Gardeners Road, Alexandria, NSW 2015; ☎02-9313 5487

Cathay Pigments (Australasia) Pty Ltd, 70 Quantum Close, Dandenong South, VIC 3175; ☎03-8795 8088;www.colourmix.com.au

Clarity International, Level 42, 100 Miller Street, North Sydney, NSW 2060; ☎02-9925 5000; www.clarity-int.com

Combined Resource Engineering Pty Ltd, 13 Heath Street, Lonsdale, SA 5160; ☎08-8326 3955; www.cre.com.au

Drypac Pty Ltd,12 Lindy Court, Warragul, VIC 3820; ☎03-5622 3179; www.drypac.com.au

Livingstone International, 106 Epsom Road, Rosebery, NSW 2018; ☎02-9313 6111; www.livingstone.com.au

NAD'S, PO Box 161, Kenthurst, NSW 2156; ☎1800-352 626; www.nads.com.au

Orbis Australia, 81 Racecourse Road, Hamilton, QLD 4007; ☎07-3630 6400

Ramler Furniture Group, 33-35 Jack Road, Cheltenham, VIC 3192; ☎03-9584 7377; www.ramler.com.au

Redarc Electronics, Unit 1, 7 Lindsay Road, Lonsdale, SA 5160; ☎08-8322 4848;

www.redarc.com.au

Roma Food Products, 47-51 Aster Avenue, Carrum Downs, VIC 3201; ☎03-9776 9044

TNA Australia Pty Ltd, 7 Ferngrove Place, Chester Hill, NSW 2162;☎02-9743 8133; www.tnarobag.com

Touchstone Colour, 158 Fitzgerald Street, Perth, WA 6000; ☎08-9227 4888; www.touchstonecolour.com.au

Mining

Troy Resources, Ground Floor, 44 Ord Street, West Perth, WA 6005; ☎08-9481 1277; www.try.com.au

Personal and other services

Blue Rock Management Group, PO Box Q63, Sydney, NSW 2000; ☎02-9268 1115; www.bluerock.com.au

Cleanevent, 95 Buckhurst Street, South Melbourne, VIC 3205; ☎03-9684 9500; www.cleanevent.com.au

Ford & Doonan Air Conditioning, 5 Weatherburn Way, Kardinya, WA; ☎03-618 9331 8800; www.fordanddoonan.com.au

Nationwide Termite and Pest Management, 176 Bannister Road, Canning Vale, WA 6155; ☎08-9256 1177; www.nationwidetermites.com.au

Property and business services

Advertising Energy Pty Ltd, Level 10, 100 Arthur Street, North Sydney, NSW 2060; ☎02-9964 9000; www.adenergy.com.au

Bartercard, Level 2, 121 Scarborough Street, Cnr Welch Street, Southport, QLD 4215; ☎07-5561 9000; www.bartercard.com

BBX Management Limited, Level 4, 117 Pacific Highway, Hornsby, NSW 2077; ☎02-9476 6655; www.bbx.aust.com

Bensons Property Group Pty Ltd, 187-189 Peel Street, Melbourne North, VIC 3051; ☎03-9600 9003; www.bensonsproperty.com.au

Buildev Group, U2/1 Jacaranda Ave Raymond Terrace, NSW 2324; ☎02-4987 1590.

Coomes Consulting Group Pty Ltd, 24 Albert Road, South Melbourne, VIC 3205; 03-9690 1966; www.coomes.com.au

CPT Global, Level 1, 4 Riverside Quay, Southgate, VIC 3000; ☎03-9690 3911; www.cptglobal.com

Customcall (Blueprint Management Group), Level 3, 185 Macquarie Street, Sydney, NSW 2000; ☎09-216 4900; www.blueprintmg.com.au

Fastway Couriers, 51 Hill Road, Homebush, NSW 2140; ☎02-9737 8288; www.fastway.com.au

Igatech Consulting, Level 3, 86 Pirie Street, Adelaide, SA 5000; ☎08-8232 9622; www.igatech.com

Infocomp Holdings, Level 6, 48 Hunter Street, Sydney, NSW 2000; ☎02-4228 8599; www.infocomp.com.au

IT People, Level 9, 100 Walker Street, North Sydney, NSW 2060;☎02-9957 5838; www.it-people.com.au

JobNet WorldWide Pty Ltd, Level 4, 500 Pacific Highway, St. Leonards, NSW 2065; ☎02-8437 6388; www.jobnet.com.au

Kowalski Consulting, 222 City Walk, Canberra, ACT 2601; ☎(02) 6230 6636.

Lanteri Partners Group, Financial Advisers & Solicitors, Ground Floor, 1 Collins Street, Melbourne, VIC 3000; ☎03-9650 3722

Larkin Teys Consulting, Level 1, 19 Hope Street, Brisbane, QLD 4101; ☎07-3844 4431; www.larkinteys.com.au

Law Solutions/Career Solutions, Recruitment Consultants, Level 1, 99 Queen Street, Melbourne, VIC 3000; ☎03-9642 0777; www.solutions-group.com.au

Luken and May, Level 3, 1 Mitchell Road, Brookvale, NSW 2100; ☎02-9905 8100; www.lukenmay.com.au

McGrath Estate Agents, Head Office, Level 1, 191 New South Head Road, Edgecliff, NSW 2027; ☎02-9386 3333; www.mcgrath.com.au

Medland Mitropoulos Consulting Engineers, Level 3,47-49 Murray Street, Pyrmont, NSW 2027; ☎02-9552-2022;

www.medmitro.com.au
Prime Placements, 135 Waymouth Streey, Adelaide, SA 5000; ☎08-8110 5601; www.primeplacements.com.au

Rosch Group, 3 St. Kilda Road, St. Kilda, VIC 3182; ☎03-9534 0699; www.rosch.com.au

Specialised Business Solutions Pty Ltd, Level 1, 293 Queen Street, Brisbane, QLD 4000; ☎07-3221 1100

Whybin Lawrence TBWA, 80 Gipps Street, Pyrmont, NSW 2009; ☎02 8584 5500; www.wltbwa.com.au.

Retail trade

Len Wallis Audio, 64 Burns Bay Road, Lane Cove, NSW, 2066 ☎02 9427 6755 ; www.lenwallisaudio.com

Petals Network, 171 Cluny Road, Armidale, NSW 2350; ☎02-6774 9200; www.petals.com.au

Sydney Express Travel, Corporate Headquarters, Level 4, 2 Barrack Street, Sydney, NSW 2000; ☎02-92625511; www.sydneyexpresstravel.com

The Perfume Connection, PO Box 7883 GCMC, Bundall, QLD 4217; ☎07-955 315 299.

Wombat Enterprises Pty Ltd, Westfield Miranda Shop 2019, 600 Kingsway, Miranda, NSW 2228; ☎02-9542 7124

Transport and storage

Andrew's Airport Parking, 247 Mickelham Rd Tullamarine, VIC 3043; ☎03-9334 5777; www.andrewsairportpark.com.au

Great Northern Rail Services Pty Ltd, Level 2, West Tower, Cnr Dudley Street and Footscray Road, West Melbourne VIC 3003; ☎03-9619 6323; www.greatnorthernrail.com.au

Wholesale trade

Brighter Ideas Pty Ltd, 18 Moonbi Street, Brendale, Qld 4500, ☎07-3881 0037; fax 07-3881 0037

Enjo Australasia Pty Ltd, 11 Aldous Place, Booragoon, WA 6154; ☎1800-648 334

Interaust Foods Pty Ltd, 1/21 Stud Street, Bayswater, VIC 3153; ☎03-9720 4466.

Lighting Corporation Limited, 1/10 Bradford Street, Alexandria NSW 2015; ☎02-9353 9453; fax 02-9353 9494; www.lightcor.com.au

The National Liquor Company, 95 Bannister Road, Canning Vale, WA 6155; ☎08-9455 2477

TodayTech Distribution, Unit D2, 3-9 Birnie Avenue, Lidcombe Business Park, Lidcombe, NSW 2141; ☎02-9737 8118; www.todaytech.com.au

STARTING A BUSINESS

CHAPTER SUMMARY

○ Small businesses in Australia employ 3.2 million people.

○ **Business Immigration.** In 2000-2001, 7,364 Business Migration visas were issued for Australia.

    ○ Most business immigrants come from oriental countries, South Africa and the UK.

○ **Growth Areas.** Information and telecommunication industries are amongst the fastest growing sectors.

    ○ Between 1996-1999 the number of computer industries in Australia rose by 50%.

    ○ Service industries now make up 64% of the economy.

    ○ Buying an existing business is far less risky than starting your own.

○ **Women in Business.** Women in Australia start small businesses at twice the rate that men do.

○ **Company Tax.** Tax on company profits is 30% (compared with the highest rate of personal income tax 48.5%).

    ○ The Australian financial year ends on 30 June.

○ **Courses for Entrepreneurs.** TAFE (adult education) colleges run courses in managing your tax affairs as a small business owner.

Australia used to be considered the 'Lucky Country' or the 'Land of Opportunity' and businesses of all shapes and sizes blossomed across the country. Aspiring entrepreneurs have always been a part of the Australian social landscape, and small businesses such as plumbers, caterers, painters and decorators, landscapers, hairdressers, beauticians and potters have not only found space for themselves in the Australian market, but remained solvent and generated good incomes.

With the recession of the 1980's, however, came a much more depressed business climate, and large and small businesses collapsed in dramatic profusion. Although the Australian economy has recovered well it has in general become far more difficult for new businesses to survive their first year. However, business growth is now being encouraged and protected by legislation, government assistance, and an extensive network of government small business offices and advisors, to ensure that once off the ground, new enterprises stay airborne, while tax incentives are now offered in the recognition that the earlier tangle of red-tape and taxation was enough in itself to discourage new business. The small business sector in Australia employs almost 3.2 million people and accounts for 30 per cent of total wages and salaries generated by all Australian businesses. Small businesses produce some of Australia's best innovations. Their contribution to the Australian economy is critical.

The manufacturing and services industries are currently the most successful sectors of the market, largely due to the devaluation of the Australian dollar. The need to become more competitive internationally has forced small businesses to provide higher quality products and services at costs, which can challenge international businesses. Economic analysts believe that this trend is likely to continue for some time, and the government is particularly keen to encourage an export-based economy, offering many incentives to businesses to export both products and services.

The present Australian government is committed to selecting high quality business migrants, and both top-flight executives and well-heeled investors continue to head south to take advantage of the relatively stable economic conditions, highly qualified labour market, and the various incentive programmes available to help build new enterprises. Business migrants take with them to Australia a knowledge of overseas markets, business networks, cultural practices and languages other than English, as well as their specific business skills and experience. A recent survey by DIMIA of Business Skills migrants showed that three years after arrival, 77% were engaged in a business and that each new business employed an average of 4.3 staff. In 2000-01, the top ten source countries for business migrant visa grants were Indonesia, Taiwan, South Africa, Malaysia, China, the UK, Singapore, Hong Kong, Zimbabwe and Fiji. A two-year survey of Business Skills migrants showed that 38% had settled in NSW, 20% in Western Australia, 16% in Queensland, 16% per cent in Victoria, 1% in South Australia and less than 1% in Tasmania, Northern Territory and Australian Capital Territory. Demand for business migration has increased in recent times and in 2000-01, 7,364 business migration visas were granted to business people and their families. This compares with over 6,260 visas issued in 1999-00 and 6,080 visas issued in 1998-99.

This chapter aims to give practical advice about starting a new business as well as suggestions as to those businesses which are likely to succeed in Australia: careful research and preparation will help prevent your business from becoming one of the failures. It also provides preliminary information regarding the taxation rules and regulations relevant to creating a new business and also the procedures for buying an existing business. The *Useful Addresses* section at the end of the chapter may be particularly helpful in providing contact names and addresses of advisors and authorities to help you get your new business venture off the ground.

ESTABLISHING A NEW BUSINESS

If you have an idea for a new venture, you will need to do some careful market research and ask yourself some searching personal questions. Do you have the right background or qualifications to set up the sort of enterprise you are considering? Are you prepared to risk almost everything to achieve your goals? You will need to be completely familiar with your product or service, and have detailed technical knowledge of it. You must also ensure that there is a market for this product and you should identify the size, geographical and socio-economic distribution of that market. Research is the key to success and you would be well advised to find out as much as possible about both your target population and your competition. This kind of information can be gained from government statistics (the Australian Bureau of Statistics, www.abs.gov.au, is particularly helpful), universities and institutes of technology, small business agencies, advertisements, and telephone directories (both the yellow pages and the business directory). In addition, you should find out whether there is a trade association that deals with the product or service you are offering as this is likely to be a good source of information, advice and assistance. The Australia and New Zealand Chamber of Commerce UK (www.anzcc.org.uk) is a primary source of information (for other contact details see *Useful Addresses* below) and has an invaluable database, updated daily, of over 6,000 Australian and New Zealand businesses which provides a valuable research tool for anyone considering setting up a business in the region. This organisation also offers regular investment and business seminars, as well as a library of information on Australian and New Zealand business, taxation, and government regulations.

Intellectual Property Protection

Legally protecting your business image and the products which you have developed can be vital in maintaining your competitive advantage. Businesses built on innovation and design need to protect their intellectual property rights, which in commercial terms means your proprietary knowledge. There are several different types of intellectual property, and various methods of protecting them:

TABLE 14   INTELLECTUAL PROPERTY PROTECTION

Circuit Layout Rights. Are granted for three-dimensional configuration of electronic circuits or layout designs.

Copyrights. Are granted for original material in literary, artistic, dramatic or musical works, films, broadcasts, multimedia, and computer programmes.

Designs. Refer to the features of shape, configuration, pattern or ornamentation which can be judged by eye in finished articles. A new or original design may be registered for up to 16 years. Registration gives the owner the exclusive rights to make, use and sell articles incorporating the registered design.

Patents. Are for inventions which are recognised as new, novel, non-obvious and useful. Inventions that serve an illegal purpose or which are unrelated to manufacturing processes are not patentable. A patent lasts for up to 20 years and gives its owner exclusive rights to exploit the invention or to authorise others to exploit it.

Plant Breeder's Rights. Are also available and are granted for new varieties of plants. These are administered by the Plant Breeder's Rights Office, under the Department of Agriculture, Fisheries and Forestry-Australia (www.affa.gov.au).

Trade Marks. Are granted to protect words, symbols, pictures, sounds and smells, or a combination of these, distinguishing the goods and services of one trader from those of another. Initial registration of a trademark lasts for 10 years.

Trade Secrets. Protection covers know-how and other confidential information.

Intellectual property rights are administered in Australia by the government agency IP Australia (Central Office, Ground Floor, Discovery House, 47 Bowes Street, Woden, ACT 2606; ☎ 02-6283 2211; fax 02-6282 5810) which is division of the Department of Industry, Tourism and Resources. Formerly known as the APIO, IP Australia provides valid IP rights and related services, monitors the Australian IP system, and partakes in the development of international IP law. The agency also administers the Olympic Insignia Protection Amendment Act 2001. IP Australia has an informative website at (www.ipaustralia.gov.au).

The Patent Co-operation Treaty (PCT) allows companies to file an international patent application, protecting the product in all participating PCT countries. There are 89 countries participating in the PCT, including the USA, Canada, Mexico, the UK, Austria, Belgium, Switzerland, Germany, Denmark, Spain, France, Greece, Ireland, Italy, the Netherlands, Norway and Sweden. There are also many other participating countries from Eastern Europe, Africa and the Asian-Pacific region. The patent application consists of several forms and a detailed set of drawings, and the cost of submitting an application is dependent upon the complexity of the drawings. A schedule of fees is available from IP Australia and applications are submitted to that office. There are Patent Offices in every PCT country.

If your product is competing with others of a similar type, it may be advantageous to register a *trademark*. A trademark can be registered with IP Australia, and once registered will be protected indefinitely provided that renewal fees are paid ten years after the initial registration. Processing time for trademark applications is currently around six months, and this time lag should be incorporated into your business plan. On acceptance, your trademark will be published in the *Official Journal of Trade Marks*, after which objections may be filed within three months. If there is no opposition, or if opposition is unsuccessful, your trademark will be registered when you pay the registration fee (to be paid no later than 6 months from the date the acceptance was advertised). Your new trademark is then registered from the date you filed your application, recorded in the *Register of Trade Marks*, and you will be sent a Certificate of Registration.

New products can also be assessed by the Standards Australia International (www.standards.com.au) – formerly known as the Standards Association of Australia – which provides recognised specifications for a wide variety of items. If your product meets the strict standards of this organisation, you will be able to use the product certification mark and benefit from the associated product credibility.

Registering a Business

Establishing a new business means you must comply with numerous licensing laws and other regulations. You must register your business with the Australian Taxation Office and obtain a tax file number (TFN) and an Australian Business number (ABN). Depending on your business structure, you may also need to register with the Australian Securities and Investments Commission (www.asic.gov.au; info line 1300 300 630) and obtain an Australian Company Number (ACN). Business registration with the Australian Taxation Office and with the ASIC can now be completed electronically via the Australian Government Business Entry Point website at www.business.gov.au, and this site also provides electronic links to the Business Names Registration offices in each state and territory. Before you start a business, or if you are not sure which licences, permits or approvals your business needs, you should contact your local Business Licence Information Service (via the Australian Government Business Entry Point website or at www.bli.net.au), which will provide you with all the necessary application forms.

Forming a Company

Any new company may be registered either as a proprietary company or a public company. When a company is registered under the Corporations Law it is automatically registered as an Australian company and thus may conduct business as a company throughout Australia without needing to register in each individual state or territory jurisdiction. Most companies in Australia are registered as proprietary companies under the Corporations Law. Proprietary companies are generally cheaper and easier to register than a public company. A private company only needs to have a nominal share capital to commence operating. Directors and a company secretary must be appointed and as soon as is practically possible after incorporation, a public officer has to be appointed for taxation purposes. For proprietary companies, there must be at least two directors, one of whom must be an Australian resident. Public companies must have at least three directors, two of whom must be residents of Australia. There are several steps in the process of registering a company:

Choosing a Name. First, you must select a name, which may either be one of your choice, or the companies ACN (Australian Company Number). Before you decide on a name, you should consult the alphabetical listing of company and business names available by checking the National Name Index at the ASIC Internet site. The ASIC will reject your name if it is identical or similar to any other company name. A company name must indicate the company's legal status, with a proprietary company including the word 'proprietary' or its abbreviation Pty in the name. The liability of a company's members must also be indicated, so that where liability is limited, the name must end with the word 'limited' or its abbreviation. The British form, PLC, is not used in Australia (where it is usually Pty Ltd).

Registering a Company. Next, you will need to obtain the consent of proposed directors and a company secretary, and then formally appoint them via the application process. After your application has been received and successfully processed by ASIC, a certificate of registration will be posted to the registered office of your company, and only once you have received this can the directors officially commence operating as a company. Such operations include opening bank accounts, which cannot be done prior to the completion of registration. The law requires that the company's name be clearly displayed at the registered office and at each business address, and the Australian Company Number (ACN) must appear on the common seal, every public document issued, all documents required to be lodged with ASIC under Corporations Law, and on every eligible negotiable instrument issued.

Off-the-Shelf Companies. The formation of a company from scratch takes between one to two weeks from application and will cost around $1,000, not including professional fees (which are likely to be high). If you need to establish the company very quickly, agents and solicitors can also offer ready-made 'off-the-shelf' companies, which can be purchased more cheaply, as legal expenses are then kept to a minimum. Shelf companies are incorporated with names, which in most cases will be unsuitable, and amendments will then need to be made to the company's Memorandum and Articles of Association. A change of name usually takes approximately four weeks to be processed and approved, and the ASIC must issue a *Certificate of Incorporation on Change of Name*. The additional cost of changing the name of the company and the Memorandum and Articles is around $320. If you do choose to buy a shelf company, you should consult with your advisers to consider whether the Articles of Association need to be amended. You need to consider whether the existing constitution allows for: the rights of directors to decline to register a future share transfer; the requirements if a shareholder ceases to be a director or employee or dies; the chairperson's casting vote; the shareholder/director's voting rights; and who controls the company, as different levels of shareholding confer different rights and there may also be different classes of shares conferring different rights.

When you purchase a shelf company, you should receive a complete set of first board minutes and statutory books. If you do not receive these, it would be advisable to check with the previous owners as they can often contain important information and you are expected to hold them.

Partnership/Sole Trader Legalities. If you are starting the business as a partnership or sole trader (see *Business Structures* below), there are no legal formalities involved other than the notifications required for tax purposes. In the absence of a partnership agreement, the partnership will be governed by the Partnership Act of the relevant state or territory, which will specify how a partnership should administer its affairs. Most partnerships, however, prefer to draw up a tailor-made agreement to meet their own particular needs. Partnership agreements are usually drawn up by a solicitor and should include details of the arrangements for partners' capital, banking accounts, profit sharing, salaries (if relevant), drawings, change or termination of partnership, and voting rights. This agreement is particularly important if a dispute between partners arises, but business experts claim that the more important course of action is to avoid such potential disputes by choosing the right partner/s in the first place.

If you are planning on setting up a company, please note that this information is intended only as a guide. It is *essential* that you seek professional advice in the process of forming a company, and that you are fully aware of your obligations and commitments when registering a company.

Choosing an Area

If you choose to buy an existing business your area will generally be predetermined, but if you are starting your business from scratch, the decision of where to locate your business, including the type of premises you require, can be vitally important to its future. The needs of your business should determine its location. Various factors, such as whether you expect frequent deliveries from suppliers or visits from customers and whether you need to attract passing trade, can influence your decision as to the best location. You will also need to consider the likely needs of your staff, especially in terms of public transport and parking.

Renting Business Premises

The rental rates of commercial properties vary greatly across Australia. Melbourne and Perth currently offer low rents (calculated in dollars per square metre) compared to similar properties in Sydney or Canberra. Additionally, the rates of leasing commercial property in Darwin, Adelaide and Hobart are markedly lower than that of comparable properties in the central business districts of Sydney or Brisbane.

Whether leasing or purchasing, you need to make sure that the premises have adequate facilities such as security, access, essential services (including electricity, water, waste collection, energy efficiency, sound and thermal insulation), flexibility of design should you wish to expand at a later date, and that the dimensions in terms of height and floor space are sufficient. Furthermore, you need to ask your solicitor to check that your type of business will not breach any environmental laws if you conduct that business in those particular premises. The buildings must comply with fire and safety regulations, town planning and other regulations, the Health Act and Shops and Factories Act (obtainable from the Government Printer or various technical publishers) applicable in your state or territory.

If you choose to lease premises, ensure that the lease is checked by a solicitor and, if possible, by an accountant. The terms of the lease are always negotiable, and your solicitor or accountant will advise you on the negotiation of terms and conditions. You should attempt to negotiate a rent-free period, a lower initial rental, reduced annual escalations, payment by the landlord for any improvements or refurbishments to the property, and payment by the landlord of any outgoings associated with the property. You should identify who is responsible for insurance, property taxes and maintenance, what your rights are to make alterations or renovations, and whether the lease permits sub-letting of the premises. Your negotiating power will always depend on the state of the property market at the time. At present, this tends to be favourable to lessees.

The term of the lease can be important, as a long lease may reduce flexibility. A shorter lease with the option to renew can be preferable, depending on the current economic conditions and your choice of premises. When considering a lease, it is helpful to ask for a plan which clearly states the extent of the premises being let, and make sure that the proposed use of your building does not breach any terms of the lease. Before you sign, you should also compare the rent, rates and service charges (usually given on a dollar per square metre basis), annual escalations and rent review clauses with those of other premises. You should also be aware that a verbal lease, which is binding on both parties, is recognised by law but should be avoided as such agreements are fraught with difficulties.

Your choice of premises will also have tax implications, as payments for the rent of business premises are tax deductible; but the rate of such deductions will vary according to the age of the building. Moveable furnishings and equipment within the buildings are subject to higher rates of depreciation for taxation purposes.

Raising Finance

You can have the best ideas, products and service in the world, but if you cannot manage to raise the finance to put your plans into practice, your dreams (not to mention potential profits) will remain unrealised. Before you approach any potential source of finance, you will need to be fully prepared to explain your business concept and to answer any questions about your proposal. A thorough and careful business plan is the first key to success.

The Business Plan. A completed business plan is a summary and evaluation of your business idea. It is the written result of the planning process and a blueprint for your business operations. Your ability to make it work depends on checking your progress against the plan and reviewing that plan as your business evolves. In the early stages of development, when you are seeking finance, your business plan may well be the only tangible aspect of your intentions. The business plan, which you present to a bank or other money lender should contain a fully considered financial plan, including a budget for at least the first 18 months. You should make sure that you include an allowance for unexpected and intangible expenses, in particular taxes such as provisional tax (tax paid against estimated future earnings), as one of the most common reasons for business failure is the lack of planning for such contingencies.

There are many publications available which will help in preparing your business plan, and assistance is also available from your nearest Small Business Development Corporation, industry associations, chambers of commerce, and from business advisors and accountants. The Commonwealth Bank of Australia offers a guide in its *BetterBusiness Planner* available either as a software package or in hardcopy form. The software package includes a sample business plan, financial templates which automatically calculate budgets and cash flows, and follow-up software to keep track of your business plan's progress. You can obtain the *BetterBusiness Planner* from the Commonwealth Bank's Business Line, ☎131 998 (8am-8pm, week days) or through the business centre section of the bank's website www.commbank.com.au. There is also a very informative website covering all aspects of starting a business and supported by the Commonwealth government at www.homebusinessmanual.com.au.

Financing a Business

One of your first steps in drawing up a business plan is to consider the different sources of finance available to you. The Commonwealth Bank of Australia strongly recommends that business owners should look much more carefully at maximising the business's ability to generate internal funds in order to avoid relying too much on external sources for the funding of its operations. Although for the first three years a new business is hardly likely to be in the position to generate enough internal funds in order to become self-sufficient, you should think very carefully about trying to borrow as little as possible from outside sources in the long term, and incorporate self-sufficiency into your long-term business proposal. Once you have done this, you need to look very carefully at all the different financial institutions and the options available to you in order to choose one or a combination that is most appropriate to the needs and goals of your company, and your repayment capacity. Lenders will also expect a significant level of personal capital investment in your business. One of the most common reasons for finance refusal is that applicants have not allowed for sufficient personal contribution; this is seen, at best, as a demonstration of lack of commitment.

As discussed in the *Daily Life* chapter, there are many different financial institutions in Australia. Deregulation of banking has led to increased competition and, as a consequence, more innovative and sophisticated banking techniques have been introduced. In addition, opportunities to obtain loan funds have greatly increased and there are now many more options available in terms of structuring loan agreements. In an effort to encourage the growth and development of Australian industry and resources, a number of industrial banks have been established which provide development finance, equity funding and financial advisory services. Other methods of raising finance can include accessing venture capital, which may provide funding for high-risk projects, or floating a company on the stock exchange.

Types of Finance

Equity, long-term loan finance, and working capital finance are the three principal types of finance available for starting a new business in Australia. Equity is usually contributed by the owners of the business, and businesses with significant equity will find it easier to attract financial backing from other sources. If you are seeking finance for a major project, such as investment in plant and machinery for your business, long-term loan finance is likely to be the most appropriate option. In many cases the loan will be secured against the business or the equipment purchased. In addition, the financial institution will generally require personal guarantees from the business owners. There is usually a substantial difference between the amount of the loan and the value of the asset in order to allow for risk and for the costs involved should the business fail.

There are a variety of options available in obtaining long-term business finance. Firstly, it is important to calculate how much of your own personal contribution can be used as share capital and how much can be used as loan capital – this proportioning of capital can affect your taxation (see *Taxation* below for further details). Cash subscription from your family and friends can also be used as long term finance, as can cash received from any other sponsor or from venture capital. Most often, however, long-term business capital is raised through a bank or finance company loan, or through leasing or hire purchase finance. It must be noted, however that leasing or hire purchase finance generally have interest rates which are significantly higher than other sources.

In the present very competitive finance market, banks and other lenders are increasingly offering tailored loan packages, and the variety of types of finance is growing exponentially. Options are also changing almost every month, and the best advice is to start by approaching the major banks to discuss the available financing methods. Most larger bank branches now have specialist business advisors who will be only too happy to guide you – remember they are selling a product too.

Government-Backed Finance. The Australian government, at both Federal and State levels, is very keen to promote new business, and to ensure that such businesses are successful. Government agencies exist in every state to provide various kinds of assistance: technical as well as financial. Financial assistance can include direct cash grants, subsidies and tax concessions, while technical assistance will include both professional and technical advice, and research and development seminars. There are many opportunities for small business to benefit from government-backed schemes, with substantial incentives available to all kinds of enterprises. There are a number of different financial assistance schemes run by the state and federal governments, and by various industry agencies. *AusIndustry*. (Hotline 132 846; www.ausindustry.gov.au) is the best starting point for obtaining information on these schemes. Their database contains information on all Federal, State and Territory government support programmes, as well as programmes offered by industry associations and chambers of commerce around Australia. The AusIndustry Hotline can also put you in touch with sources of information in research and development, networking, management, strategic planning, benchmarking, diagnostic reviews, environmental management, marketing, export planning and business licensing.

Rebates and subsidies are also offered to employers as an incentive to provide employment and to encourage them to provide training for their employees (or to allow employees to attend trade or development courses). Such schemes, which are usually aimed either at the youth or long-term unemployed workforce, are administered by the Australian Job Network, which can provide further information. Employment incentive schemes are a favourite vote-winner for governments and tend to be restructured with each budget and change of government.

Most states and territories also provide financial assistance in the forms of loan funds or guarantees to businesses. However, this assistance is generally only provided as a final resort. Other assistance can include transportation and freight subsidies, and advice services in such areas as effective business operations, production processes, technological development and export market opportunities. State Government assistance is generally given to encourage the establishment of new businesses or the expansion of existing industries within the state or territory, and in order to receive such assistance businesses must demonstrate that they are viable, both in the short and long term, and that they can provide assessable benefits to the state. The government will be likely to favour business which will create new permanent jobs, provide new skills, increase the state's technology or production capacity, tap new markets outside the state, or offer diversification of the state's industrial base or range of products. For further details about State Government assistance, you should contact your state's Small Business Development Corporation or similar body, the Australian Job Network, or AusIndustry (see *Useful Addresses* below).

Importing/Exporting

Australia has a policy of gradually and systematically removing trade tariffs on imported products. However, in those industries still subject to protection, *bounties* are sometimes offered, which are direct cash payments to Australian manufacturers (operating within Australia) in lieu of, or supplementary to, assistance provided by means of tariff or customs duty. Bounties can assist manufacturers to compete more effectively with imported products. Many imported goods will also be liable to the Goods and Services Tax. You should contact the Australian Customs Information Centre on 1300 363 263 or look at their website (www.customs.gov.au) for further information.

If your business is involved in exporting goods from Australia, AUSTRADE (The Australian Trade Commission; ☎132 878; www.austrade.gov.au) will be able to provide marketing advice and assistance. Additionally, the R&D Start Program, available to non-tax-exempt Australian companies, is a merit-based program designed to assist the commercialisation of Australian industry and to undertake research and development (R&D) through a range of grants and loans. The Federal Government also offers a range of tax incentives.

Summary of Financing

Although a potential financier will want a thorough plan, they will not want a long report, so you should try to keep your proposal down to between ten and twelve pages. You must ensure that you describe your product, the premises from which you intend to operate, relevant information about each member of the management team, your marketing strategy, your competition, past performance (if any), financial projections and assumptions relating to them, the financial resources required and what changes will be necessary if your assumptions prove to be either pessimistic or optimistic, and your assessment of the risks involved in the project. A professional-looking presentation is important, as this is the document that will 'sell' your business to lenders. It is vitally important to obtain impartial professional advice when preparing a business plan, but you must also be fully involved; when you come face to face with the bank manager, you are the one who will have to answer all the questions.

Accountants

A good accountant is essential to the success of your business. You will find that the process of creating a new business or buying an existing one is so complex and involved that you will not be able to complete it without expert assistance. Your accountant should be registered with one of the industry associations, and it is essential that you confirm this. You should also shop around and obtain quotes in respect of hourly rates and estimated annual expenses. Your accountant will act as your financial and, on many occasions, as your legal adviser, and will often undertake duties which could also be done by a solicitor. If the advice you receive is false or misguided it could mean the failure of your business and possibly even fines and legal costs. For this reason, you will want to make sure that the accountant you decide to use is reliable and reputable. Large accountancy firms are likely to be considerably more expensive, but may be more reliable and offer backup guidance. Your accountant is really another business investment you will have to make, and so you will want to reduce the element of risk. It is advisable to consult your accountant on every initial business decision you make, as a good accountant will always give you more impartial advice than you may receive from a real estate agent, bank business advisor or business broker.

Useful Addresses

AusIndustry, ☎Hotline 132 846; www.ausindustry.gov.au
Department of Industry, Tourism and Resources, 20 Allara Street, Canberra, ACT 2601; ☎06-213 6000; fax 06-213 7000; www.industry.gov.au. ITR is based in Canberra with offices in all Australian State capitals, and representatives in North America, Europe and Asia.

Small Business Agencies

These provide advice and referral services for intending, starting and existing businesses in each state:
ACT: ACT & Region Chamber of Commerce and Industry, 12a Thesiger Court, Deakin, ACT 2600; ☎02-6283 5200; fax 02-6282 5045; www.actchamber.com.au
NSW: Small Business Advisory Services, State and Regional Development NSW, Level 35, Governor Macquarie Tower, 1 Farrer Place, Sydney, NSW 2000; ☎Hotline 131 145; fax 02-9228 3626; www.smallbiz.nsw.gov.au
NT: Business Services, Department of Business, Industry & Resource Development, 2nd Floor, Development House, 76 The Esplanade, Darwin, NT 0800; ☎08-8999 5153; fax 08-8999 5106; www.nt.gov.au
QLD: Department of State Development, Level 21, 111 George Street, Brisbane, QLD 4000; ☎07-3225 1915; www.sd.qld.gov.au
SA: Centre for Innovation, Business and Manufacturing, 145 South Terrace, Adelaide, SA 5001; ☎08-8463 3800; fax 08-8463 3840; www.cibm.sa.gov.au
TAS: Business Licence Information Service, 22 Elizabeth Street, Hobart, TAS 7000; ☎03-6233 5858; fax 03-6233 5800; www.bt.tas.gov.au
VIC: Small Business Victoria, level 5, 55 Collins Street, Melbourne, Vic 3000; ☎132 215 (local call cost); fax 03-9651 9725; www.sbv.vic.gov.au

WA: Small Business Development Corporation, 553 Hay Street, Perth, WA 6000; ☎08-9220 0222; fax 08-9325 3981; www.sbdc.com.au
Inventors' Association of Australia, has chapters in several states. In South Australia contact: Inventors Association of Australia (SA) Inc, PO Box 172, Kensington Park, SA 5068; www.inventors.asn.au
The Australia and New Zealand Chamber of Commerce (UK), 393 Strand, London WC2R 0JQ, ☎020-7379 0720; fax 020-7379 0721; www.anzcc.org.uk
The Australian Copyright Council, 245 Chalmers Street, Redfern, NSW 2016; ☎02-9318 1788; fax 02-9698 3536; www.copyright.org.au
The Institute of Patent and Trade Mark Attorneys of Australia, 711 High Street, East Kew, VIC 3102; ☎03-9857 0311; fax 03-9857 0411; www.ipta.com.au
United Kingdom Patent Office, Concept House, Cardiff Road, Newport NP10 8QQ, South Wales; ☎01633-813930; fax 01633-813600; www.patent.gov.uk, or filings by hand may be made at Harmsworth House, 13-15 Bouverie Street, London EC4Y 8DP

Accountants

Most accountants advertise in the Yellow Pages of their state telephone directory. The Institute of Chartered Accountants, the Australian Society of Accountants in your capital city, or the National Institute of Accountants can also provide lists of professionals associated with their organisation. A brief list of other contacts is given below:
Australian Accounting Group, 56 Neridah Road, Chatswood, NSW 2067; ☎02-9411 4866.
Collett & Co. Level 5, 11 Queens Road, Melbourne, VIC 3004, Australia; ☎03-8530 7030; also in UK at Enterprise House, Ocean Village, Southampton, Hants. SO14 3XB; ☎02380-488777;

alan@gomatilda.com. Provides tax and financial planning advice to businesses and individuals heading for Australia.

Deloitte Touche Tohmatsu, 225 George Street, Sydney, NSW 1217; ☎02-9322 7000; fax 02-9322 7001; www.deloitte.com.au

Ernst & Young, 321 Kent Street, Sydney, NSW 2000, ☎02-9248 5555; fax 02-9262 6565; www.ey.com/global/gcr.nsf/australia/home.

Institute of Chartered Accountants in Australia, level 9, 37 York Street, Sydney, NSW 2000; ☎02-9290 5674; fax 02-9262 4841; www.icaa.org.au

KPMG Australia, www.kpmg.com.au

PricewaterhouseCoopers, Darling Park Tower 2, 201 Sussex Street, Sydney, NSW 1171; ☎02-8266 0000; fax 02-8266 9999; www.pwcglobal.com/au/

Trading Banks

Australia and New Zealand Banking Group Ltd, 16/100 Queen Street, Melbourne, VIC 3000, ☎Small Business Hotline 1800 670 522; www.anz.com.au

Commonwealth Bank of Australia, 48 Martin Place, Sydney, NSW 2000; ☎02-9378 2000; fax 02-9378 3317; www.commbank.com.au

National Australia Bank Ltd, 500 Bourke Street, Melbourne, VIC 3000; ☎03-9641 3500; fax 03-9641 4916; www.national.com.au

Westpac Banking Corporation, 60 Martin Place, Sydney NSW 2000; ☎02-9226 3311; fax 02-9226 4128; www.westpac.com.au

See also the banking section of Chapter Four, *Daily Life* for the British branches of these banks.

Merchant Banks

BNP Paribas Australia, 60 Castlereagh Street, Sydney NSW 2000; ☎02-9216 8633; www.bnp.com.au. The 3rd largest foreign bank in Australia, in terms of assets, and the 12th largest bank in Australia overall.

BT (Bankers Trust) Financial Group , Level 15, The Chifley Tower, 2 Chifley Square, Sydney, NSW 2000, ☎02-9259 3555; www.btal.com.au

Deautsche Bank AG, Level 20, 225 George Street, Sydney, NSW 2000; ☎02- 9258 3666; fax 02-9241 2565; www.aus.deuba.com

JPMorgan , Head Office, Level 26, Grosvenor Place, 225 George Street, Sydney, NSW 2000; ☎02-9220 1333; www.jpmorgan.com.au

Macquarie Bank Ltd, 22 Floor, 20 Bond Street, Sydney, NSW 2000; ☎02-9237 3333; fax 02-9237 3350; www.macquarie.com.au

Finance Companies

Australian Guarantee Corporation (AGC) Ltd, 60 Carrington Street, Sydney, NSW 2000; ☎02-8234 4455; www.agc.com.au

Esanda Finance Corporation Ltd, 85 Spring Street, Melbourne, VIC 3000; ☎132 373; www.esanda.com.au. Australia's largest asset-based finance company.

Real Estate

There are countless real estate agencies in every area of Australia. To locate those in the area of Australia to which you are moving, try searching Telstra's on-line database at www.telstra.com.

Useful Publications

Books and Information Packs:

Vacation Work Publications, Other books in the *Live and Work* series may be useful if you are considering setting up an export business. Each book in the series contains a 'Starting a Business' section relevant to the particular country or area covered.

Australian Bureau of Statistics (Central Office), ABS House, 45 Benjamin Way, Belconnen, ACT 2617; ☎1300 135 070 or +61 2 9268 4909; www.abs.gov.au. The Australian Bureau of Statistics has offices in every Australian state/

territory and publish yearbooks containing the results of every recent survey and research project, which are useful when undertaking initial market research.

Doing Business in Australia, Published by Ernst & Young as part of their *International Business* series and is available from their Australian office listed above under *Accountants* and also online from www.ey.com. Copies are also held by their international branches, and you should consult the telephone directory in your country's capital city for further information.

Commonwealth Government Info Shops, are run and sell books published by the Department of Communications, Information Technology and the Arts (www.dcita.gov.au). There are outlets throughout Australia. In Sydney: 32 York Street, Sydney NSW 2000; ☎132 447; www.bookshop.gov.au

Periodicals

Australian Business for Sale News, A magazine produced every three months which gives information and details about franchising, business opportunities, distributorships, licenses etc., plus information on how to buy or sell a business. It is available from Australian Business for Sale News, PO BOX 586, Darlinghurst, Sydney NSW 1300; ☎02-9281 4599; fax 02-9212 6925; www.businessforsale.com.au. Alternatively, the periodical is available in the UK from the Subscription Department, Consyl Publishing, 3 Buckhurst Road, Bexhill-on-Sea, East

Sussex, TN40 1QF; ☎01424-223 111; www.consylpublishing.co.uk

The Australian Financial Review, 201 Sussex Street, Sydney NSW 2000, ☎09-282 2833; www.afr.com.au

Dynamic Small Business Magazine, a bi-monthly magazine, is regarded as essential reading for Australian small business. It is available by writing to PO Box 77, Cremorne, NSW 2090; ☎02-9949 8022; fax 02-9949 8033; www.dsbmag.com.au

Economic Outlook, 124 Sturt Street, Adelaide, SA 5000; ☎08-8231 0941; fax 08-8231 0949; www.econ-outlook.com.au

Franchising

Franchising & Own Your Own Business Magazine, is a bi-Monthly which gives the latest national and international news, discussion of key industry issues, and information from the Franchising Council of Australia. The magazine also includes information on how to choose the right franchise and how to franchise your existing business. It is available from Niche Media, PO Box 2135, St Kilda, VIC 3182; ☎03-9525 5566; fax 03-9525 5678; www.franchise.net.au

Franchisenet, is a very useful website with industry information, a links page and a franchise directory at www.franchise.net.au

The Franchising Council of Australia, National Office, PO. Box 1498N, Melbourne, VIC 3001; ☎03-9650 1667; fax 03-9650 1713; www.franchise.org.au

RELOCATION AGENCIES AND BUSINESS SERVICES

In addition to assisting with housing, education and employment arrangements on your behalf, many of the relocation companies also specialise in finding appropriate business premises and in relocating complete companies, including plant and machinery. These services tend to be very expensive and are best suited to large, international companies. Most large relocators have offices overseas or have reciprocal arrangements with certain firms in Australia. However, many relocators in the UK are established to provide services for those relocating to the UK from other countries. If you require the services of a business relocator it may be most appropriate to engage the assistance of a specialist Australian firm, of which some are listed below.

Useful Addresses

The following relocators specialise in the relocation of executives, company personnel and their families.

Allied Pickfords, has offices Australia-wide and can be contacted at 19 Rowood Road, Prospect NSW 2148; ☎02-9636 6333; www.allpick.com.au, or call 122 554 to find nearest office location.

Australiawide Relocations Pty Ltd, (Head Office), Abignano House, Suite 17, 19-23 Bridge Street, Pymble, NSW 2073; ☎02-9488 9444; fax 02-9488 8259; www.relocations.aust.com

Australian Way Corporate Relocation, 9 Lower Almora St., Balmoral Beach, NSW 2009, ☎02-9969 0171; fax 02-9969 0181;

www.australianrelocations.com.au

Expat International, Level 2, 423 Bourke Street, Melbourne, VIC 3000; ☎03-9670 7555; fax 03-9670 7799; www.expat.com.au

Grace Removals, Executive and Commercial Relocations, Head Office, 4 Tucks Rd, Seven Hills, Sydney, NSW 2147; ☎02-9838 5600; www.grace.com.au. Grace is Australia's largest mover of household goods internationally, both from and to Australia.

Relocations in Melbourne, Suite 112620, St Kilda Road, Melbourne, VIC 3004; ☎03-9533 6831; fax 03-9525 1477; www.relocations-melb.com.au

IDEAS FOR NEW BUSINESSES

The various state governments have all identified strategic industries in which the greatest opportunities for investment lie, and these are outlined in the *Regional Employment Guide* section of the preceding chapter. Most state governments can offer incentive packages to investors. In overview, Australia is currently a leading exporter of commodities such as coal, iron ore, wheat, beef and veal, petroleum and gas, and cotton. However, the export market in unprocessed foods, fuels, minerals and other primary products is declining.

Service industries now make up 64% of the economy, and Australia is becoming an information-based economy. Between 1996 and 1999 the number of computer service businesses grew by just over 50%. Australia is developing a new competitive edge in high-technology exports, such as scientific and medical equipment, telecommunications, software and aerospace products. Knowledge-based industries now contribute almost half of Australia's GDP and the information and communications technologies are Australia's fastest-growing sectors. The manufacture of components for mechanical and electronic equipment, and cars, has also recorded strong growth in the last decade. The shift from an economy based on manufacturing to services has been rapid; the growth rate of non-service industries has dropped, while service industries continue to grow. About 36.5 percent of Australians now work in professional, technical, managerial or administrative jobs and the service industries are Australia's biggest employers. In 1998, according to the OECD (Organisation for Economic Co-operation and Development), service industry employees accounted for almost 77% of total employment in Australia.

New businesses, which either compete directly in these sectors or which provide related services, are the most likely to succeed. Retailing is less buoyant and import businesses are suffering because of the relatively weak Australian dollar. Both federal and state governments are, however, strongly export-oriented, and any business which exports Australian goods and services is likely to be eligible for a variety of export subsidies and incentive schemes.

WOMEN IN BUSINESS

According to figures from the Australia Women's Network while nine out of ten businesses in Australia are small businesses, women are opening small businesses at twice the rate of men. Currently, 32% of all small businesses across Australia are owned and operated by women and every year, 37% of women leave salaried employment to open their own small business venture. Australian women are opening businesses at nearly twice the rate of men and their businesses have a higher success rate, particularly in the first five years. Women are considered to be more successful in business because they are willing to acquire formal business skills and to develop non-formal management skills such as networking and flexibility, which may give them a competitive advantage over men.

In many states today, women-centred business networks have been developed, and these are generally viewed as valuable resources by women entrepreneuses. A survey by *Yellow Pages Australia* found that both men and women believe that women business owners are more persuasive, more prepared to ask for advice, are better at dealing with customers, learn faster, are more hard-working, and are more pleasant to deal with. The trend in business ownership and operation by women is towards a far greater involvement in the services sector of the economy, with around 83% of businesses operating in this sector owned by women. Most states have specific programmes to encourage the development of women in business, and details of schemes can be found online at www.womensnetwork.com.au. The Australian Businesswomen's Network (www.abn.org.au) is an organisation seeking to help women in business by raising their profile and providing exposure to a range of business success models.

BUYING AN EXISTING BUSINESS

One of the options you may have when starting in business is to purchase an existing operation. Getting into business in this way can be much less risky and more quickly profitable than starting your own business from scratch, but it is not entirely risk free and your success will depend heavily on how wisely you choose and evaluate the business you buy.

Buying a business will include the purchase of plant and equipment, stock in trade and, usually, a goodwill component. Goodwill is represented in part by location, existing customers and reputation, but also by other factors which can influence the profitability of the business or its income-producing capacity. The correct assessment and identification of the value of a business is crucial in the process of buying a going concern, and it is highly recommended that you obtain professional assistance in making this assessment. When you investigate a prospective business purchase you should make sure that you examine the following: financial statements, payables and receivables, employees, customers, location, facilities, competitors, registration, zoning, and image. Financial figures should be accompanied by an audit letter from a CPA (certified practising accountancy) firm, and you should make sure that business licences and other legal documents can be easily transferred and determine the costs involved in doing so. Customers are your most important asset, however, and you should make sure that they are as solid as the other tangible assets that you will be acquiring. Check if the current clientele has a special relationship with the present owner (are they long-time friends, neighbours and relatives?). How long have these accounts been with the business, and what percentage of income do they represent? Will they leave when the business passes to new hands? Make sure, too, when you are buying a business that you understand the competitive environment in which it operates. Check whether local price wars are common, or whether any competitors have gone out of business recently. You can track down this information by contacting an industry association or by reading trade publications. Finally, look at how a business is perceived locally, and in general. This 'goodwill' factor cannot necessarily be established from a balance sheet, and you will need to evaluate everything from the way a company services customers to how employees answer the phone. To learn more about a firm's reputation talk to suppliers, competitors, customers, banks and owners of other businesses in the area, and remember that it can be very difficult to change a negative perception.

Transferring Ownership

Transferring the ownership of a business from one owner to the next requires a management plan to ensure a smooth transition of the business and its assets (including goodwill and the customer base). You will need to notify the Australian Taxation Office of the transfer and, in the case of an incorporated business, the Australian Securities and Investments Commission, and supply details of new directors and the transfer of trading name. You may also have to transfer ownership of any licences which are required to operate the business, for which you should contact your local Business Licence Information Service (locations available by contacting www.licence.sbdc.com.au; ☎ 08-9220 0234).

Franchising

Australia is the most franchised nation per head of population in the world and has at least three times as many franchise systems per head of population than the United States. Because many new business owners are attracted to the ready-made brand awareness and back up available to franchisees, each year franchising contributes over $77 billion to the Australian economy. There are over 747 different types of franchise available in Australia.

The Franchising Council of Australia (FCA) should be your first port of call if you are considering this type of business option. The FCA has a strict code of conduct which protects members from unscrupulous operators, and can also direct potential franchisees to accountants and lawyers who are members of the FCA and who understand the specialist field of franchising practice. The FCA publishes *The Franchisee's Guide: Everything you need to know as a Franchisee* for intending franchisees, available from the FCA Franchise Library for $16.50. They also have a very comprehensive website at www.franchise.org.au.

The position of the franchise in the market in which it trades should be carefully assessed. You should not only look at the particular franchised business in relation to its own activities, but also make an assessment of the prospects for the industry overall. The franchise will either be dealing in goods, products or services and you should consider whether these are new or have distinct advantages over their competitors. Check that the franchised business has been thoroughly proven in practice, or whether it is exploiting a fad or current fashion which may be transient or short-lived. If the product is strongly associated with a celebrity name, remember that a person's fame can fade as quickly as it came, and that your business, built on a name, may fade with it.

The basis of any franchise operation is the franchise agreement. This must be considered very carefully and it is advisable to consult your accountant/solicitor before signing anything. Before you enter into any franchise agreement, you need to consider whether you are technically able to deal with the product or service, as well as the extent of the competition. If the franchise involves evolving technology, you will also need to assess whether the franchiser also has the expertise and resources to be able to compete successfully in the market. If your product is manufactured overseas, or is composed of parts made elsewhere, you must identify delivery times and calculate the risk of delays and the potential for foreign currency losses. In addition, you will have to ascertain whether there are any import duties or regulations which have an impact on the price of the product. You should also be clear on how much assistance is given, and control exercised, by the franchiser, and you would be well advised to investigate the franchiser's financial credibility and stability. It can be beneficial to talk to other franchisees about the business and the franchiser's methods of operation. It is imperative that you understand what the duration of the franchise is, what costs and fees are involved, whether you have to pay a royalty to the franchiser (and if so, how much), and what the arrangements are for termination.

Franchising offers significant benefits to business owners, and can be considered as going into business with an experienced partner. A good franchiser will offer training and continuing assistance; and the franchisee will benefit from established brand recognition and a customer base. The franchisee will usually need less capital than they would if setting up business independently. Although business risk is significantly reduced because you are under the umbrella of a franchise, setting up your own business is still a risk.

Other Businesses

Most businesses for sale are advertised with real estate agents, business brokers, trading associations and in the national and local newspapers. A successful acquisition depends on a thorough study of the business or company from many different angles. Your accountant should check out the value of stock and the cash flow of the business. Profit should be calculated after the fair working salaries of proprietors or partners have been deducted. Your accountant should also advise you on the stamp duty and tax implications of the purchase of a particular business. The last three years' accounts of the company (audited if possible) should be examined, together with current management accounts and projections (if available), particularly in terms of the valuation of assets, contingent liabilities and the company's tax position. Finally, you need to ensure that you will be able to raise the finance required before committing yourself to the purchase, and this applies to the purchase of either a business or a company. Further details are given above in the section *Raising Finance.*

BUSINESS STRUCTURES

Companies

Most small businesses in Australia are embodied in some kind of legally recognised entity. Australian company law is mainly governed by the Corporations Law of individual states, which is basically the commonwealth legislation for the Australian Capital Territory with minor variations pertinent to that particular state. The Corporations Law contains the rules, procedures, accounting and reporting requirements for companies. This is administered by the Australian Securities and Investments Commission (ASIC) and detailed information regarding Corporations Law can be obtained upon request (see address below).

Public and Proprietary Companies. A company is a legal body distinct from its individual members. Generally, investors combine their capital to form a company and share its profits. Usually, this is without the risk of loss beyond their original investment or guarantee amount. Companies can buy, sell and hold property, sue and be sued, and enter into contracts. They have what is known as 'perpetual existence', which means that unless there are exceptional circumstances (such as in the case of default on payments to their creditors), they cannot be involuntarily terminated. Of the various types of companies which operate in Australia, two types of corporations have limited liability (public and proprietary/private), and there are also no-liability companies and foreign companies. Public companies can invite public subscription of their shares and be listed on the stock exchange, whereas proprietary companies cannot. A proprietary company must have at least two, but no more than fifty, members. It is not allowed to invite public subscription of its shares. A no-liability company is usually only used by specific mining companies and oil and gas ventures, and a foreign company is considered to be one which originated overseas but conducts business in Australia.

THE ADVANTAGES AND DISADVANTAGES OF A LIMITED (REGISTERED) COMPANY

Advantages
- The liabilities of the company are the responsibility of the company so that shareholders are liable to lose only the share capital they subscribed although directors may be personally liable for any debts incurred when the company is unable to pay its debts.
- After tax, profits of the business can be retained within the company to provide funds for future expansion.
- In some cases greater superannuation benefits can be secured; tax on company profits is currently 30% compared to the current maximum personal tax of 48.5% (excluding the Medicare levy).

- ○ It is easier to spread ownership of the company.
- ○ The company has an ongoing existence and does not need to be wound up in the event of death or permanent disability of any of the directors or shareholders.

Disadvantages
- ○ Financial and certain other information must be filed on public records (although in the case of a proprietary company accounts need not be lodged and only certain declarations and statements are required to be made).
- ○ Loans can be made to directors of proprietary companies.
- ○ However, in the case of other companies, the shareholders in the general meeting have to approve such loans as part of a scheme for making loans to full-time employees and disclosure of such loans must be made in the company's accounts.
- ○ There may be tax consequences of making loans to shareholders and/or directors.
- ○ Compliance with the extensive requirements of the Corporations Law can be time consuming and costly.
- ○ Lenders often seek personal guarantees from directors which tends to significantly reduce the value of limited liability.
- ○ Tax is payable when accumulated profits are withdrawn from the company as dividends or extra remuneration.
- ○ Auditors must be appointed unless all shareholders agree that this is not necessary; and losses in a company are not distributable to the shareholders and therefore cannot be offset against other income of the owners.

Partnership. As an alternative to the company structure, many small businesses choose to structure themselves as a partnership. A partnership is usually formed by two or more people (individuals or companies) in order to conduct business for profit as co-owners. It is governed by the Partnership Act of the relevant state and the terms of the partnership agreement, which should be in writing. This partnership agreement means that each partner has the same rights, liabilities and powers as any other partner, unless the agreement specifically states otherwise. As a member of a partnership, each partner is jointly responsible for partnership debts. In Western Australia, Tasmania and Queensland, limited liability partnerships can be used. A limited liability partnership allows some partners who are not as involved in the management of the partnership to have a limited liability. The Australian Taxation Office requires that partnerships maintain 'appropriate' accounting records, but they are not legally required to be audited. Unlike a company, a partnership is not usually considered as a separate legal body from its partners. This means that the partnership's profits are taxable to the individual partners, regardless of the distribution of those profits. Even so, partnerships must also file an annual tax return separate from and in addition to that of each partner.

Joint Venture. Another form of business structure is the unincorporated joint venture. This occurs when an Australian entity joins with either an Australian or foreign entity to create a venture for their mutual benefit. Examples of such joint ventures are most often found in various mining and exploration projects. A contractual relationship exists between the joint venture participants and this form of business entity has recently become increasingly popular. Unincorporated joint ventures are often considered to be partnerships for tax purposes if the income is jointly derived, which means that each 'partner' is required to file partnership tax returns. It is possible, however, to set up an unincorporated joint venture so that participants share in the production rather than the income. This kind of joint venture is not considered to be a partnership by Australian law, so each venturer is required to state its share of the income and expenditure from the joint venture project in the venturer's tax return. Incorporated joint ventures are considered to be the same as ordinary companies, and are treated and taxed accordingly.

Sole Trader. It is possible to be a sole proprietor if you individually own an unincorporated business and you receive all the business profits and incur all of its liabilities. On the whole, if you are the sole proprietor, you will be actively involved in the management and conduct of the business. You can form sole proprietorship without official approval and you need not have your financial statements audited. You do, however, need to supply the tax authorities with proper accounting records.

ADVANTAGES AND DISADVANTAGES OF SOLE TRADER PARTNERSHIP

Advantages
- ◐ Confidentiality is maintained since the public has no access to financial accounts.
- ◐ PAYG (income tax) and Medicare levy contributions do not need to be paid when proprietors or partners draw cash but is paid on a partner's share of the profits.
- ◐ Losses from the business can be offset against other income.
- ◐ It is relatively easy to transfer the business to another legal structure (e.g. a limited company) at a later stage.

Disadvantages
- ◐ The owner is personally liable for the business, which means that if one partner fails to meet his share of the partnership debts, other partners will have to settle them.
- ◐ There is less flexibility in transferring ownership (for example to other family members).
- ◐ In the event of death, permanent disablement or retirement of the sole trader/partner there may be difficulties in maintaining the business structure.

Trusts

Trusts are not normally used for a sizeable partnership or joint venture with Australian residents, but more for wholly owned projects or ventures. This is largely due to the fact that a trust is not considered to be a separate legal body to the beneficiary's property, and so it may not enter into contracts in its own right. As a result, creditors and bankers will not grant credit to the trust or allow it to open and use a bank account unless personal guarantees are obtained from the trust or beneficiaries. The advantages of a trading trust are:

ADVANTAGES AND DISADVANTAGES OF A TRADING TRUST

Advantages

- ○ Confidentiality is maintained since the public has no access to the trust's accounts, although certain information is disclosed in the trustee's accounts.
- ○ Income is distributed to beneficiaries who pay tax on their allocation of profits at their respective personal tax rates.
- ○ Trusts are not subject to income tax on their profits provided they are fully distributed to beneficiaries.
- ○ A discretionary trust is usually preferred because it provides flexibility to the trustee to allocate income amongst various classes of beneficiaries under the trust.
- ○ To some extent, limited liability can be achieved through the establishment of a trust with a company acting as a trustee.

Disadvantages

- ○ Generally banks and financiers require assurances from solicitors that the trust has been properly constituted.
- ○ In the case of corporate trustees, there is a necessity for compliance with the extensive requirements of the Corporations Law.
- ○ Losses derived in a trust are not distributable and therefore cannot be offset against other income of a beneficiary (owner) of the trust.

There are also subsidiary businesses, branches and representative offices, but these are usually owned by existing foreign companies that wish to operate in Australia.

Duties of Directors & Company Office-Bearers

Every company, whether public or private, must appoint directors and a company secretary. These company officials have clearly defined duties under law. The directors of a company are not necessarily actively involved in the daily management of the business, but they are responsible for the actions of the management of the business. In accordance with the Corporations Law, a director must act with the utmost good faith towards the company and its members, and must not obtain any benefit for him/herself from the activities of the company, other than remuneration. A director is expected to exercise skills, which reflect his or her qualifications and experience. Although a director is responsible for the keeping of the statutory records and the books of account, this duty is usually delegated to an appropriate professional, such as an accountant. The Corporations Law clearly specifies the kinds of books and records, which must be kept and it is important that you seek professional advice in these matters. A director may accept a loan from the company providing that loan has been approved by the shareholders. It must be noted that such loans must be shown in the accounts in accordance with statutory requirements. A director has the power to appoint an alternative director who has the full powers and duties of a director. If the business becomes insolvent, the directors become personally liable for any debts contracted by the company during the period of insolvency.

Within one month of the first and every annual general meeting, companies must provide the ASIC with their directors' names, ages, addresses, company share holding and details of other public company directorships. The appointment of additional or new directors, the company secretary, and an auditor (if required) should also be made at this time. Banking arrangements and the end of the company's financial year (normally 30th June) should also be determined. Shares should be allotted and transfers of subscribers' shares should be approved. Arrangements should also be made for keeping statutory books such as the Register of Members, Register of Directors and a Minute Book, and the company's registered office must be specified. A Public Officer must also be appointed for income tax purposes.

The company secretary is responsible for statutory duties and must be a resident of Australia. Public companies must have at least five members, while proprietary companies need only have two. Wholly owned subsidiaries, public or proprietary, have no minimum requirement. A proprietary company must have between two and fifty shareholders, whereas public companies must have a minimum of five shareholders and have no maximum limit. Shares may be sold for cash or otherwise issued, but details must be reported to the ASIC. For both public and proprietary companies, the minimum capital derived from shares is one share per subscriber. The minimum time required to establish a company is three to four days and ASIC fees must be paid during the process of registration.

RUNNING A BUSINESS

Once you have had your business plans approved, secured financial backing, established the business as a legal entity, chosen and registered its name and have obtained premises from which to operate your business, then it is time to consider the daily operations of your new livelihood. Here, the critical factors are staff and taxes. If you manage to get both of these areas right, it is likely that your business will run smoothly and be a success.

Taxation

Australian business taxation law is extremely complex and if you are starting a new business there are a certain number of things you will have to do and decisions you will have to make. Taxation issues are made even more complex if you have been employed in Australia prior to setting up your business. Furthermore, the structure you choose for your business may have significant tax consequences, so it is important to investigate taxation thoroughly when planning its structure. There is simply no avoiding the tax maze and it is vital that you get professional advice from the outset. Doing so is likely to mean considerable expense, but will save you costly mistakes in the long term.

Sole traders and partnerships are subject to very different taxes to either companies or trusts. Essentially, for a sole trader or partnership, any profit earned from the business is added to any other income that you have and you are taxed on the total. Your level of taxable income is determined by the financial statements you produce for the Tax Office, however there are some adjustments that are made to the income shown on the statements in order to arrive at a taxable income. You may, for example, be allowed to claim special deductions such as those available for research and development costs. Tax concessions and grants are available to cover research and development costs, and for businesses seeking to develop new export markets. Some of the income you receive may not be subject to tax such as the rebates paid to you under special youth employment schemes. Depreciation can be claimed on all of your plant equipment and other business fixed assets, and items valued at less than $300 or with an effective life of less than three years can be written off in the year of acquisition.

Companies are taxed differently because they are considered to be separate legal entities from their owners. A company is subject to income tax on its taxable income whereas the partners in a partnership are taxed on their share of partnership taxable income even though a tax return must be lodged for the partnership. An important difference to note is that there is no variation according to income of the tax rate for companies as there is for individuals. Both resident and non-resident companies are subject to corporate income tax of 30%.

The calculation of a company's or family trust's taxable income is roughly the same as that use to assess a partnership or sole trader, with some significant differences. Firstly, providing that it is at a reasonable level, the remuneration of the company's directors (or owners in the case of a family company) is a deductible expense in determining the company's taxable income. Secondly, there is a complicated system known as 'Dividend Imputation' which refers to the distribution of a company's dividend income. Dividend imputations distributed by Australian resident companies have a tax advantage attached to them if the dividends are paid from profits, which have been taxed in the company's hands at the company rate. Basically, this means that the system allows shareholders a tax rebate to the extent of the difference between personal and corporate income tax rates. Any excess rebate may be offset against any other income tax of the shareholder, including capital gains, and these dividends which have been relieved of tax are known as 'franked'. If the company holds on to its dividend, it will generally be subject to credit under the 'Dividend Imputation' system. Your taxation adviser will be able to explain the system of tax payment, as companies must pay instalments of tax by certain dates.

If you decide to take over an existing company, you should ask your accountant to help you draft taxation warranties and indemnities which should appear in the purchase agreement, as these will protect you from any unexpected tax liabilities that may arise as a result of the acquisition. The capital gains tax-exempt status of assets owned by a company may be lost when ownership of the company is changed.

As the owner of a business, whether new or already in existence, you will be expected to pay Goods and Services Tax, Fringe Benefits Tax and PAYG deductions. If you employ staff, you are responsible for deducting taxation instalments (PAYG) from your employees' wages and paying it to the Commissioner of Taxation. In order to do this, you must register as a group employer with the Commissioner of Taxation and each employee must submit to you their personal particulars, including a tax file number, on an income tax instalment declaration form. PAYG must be deducted from wages, overtime pay, commissions, fees, bonuses, gratuities, lump sum payments and any other allowances.

The Australian tax year ends on 30 June, and for companies that also end their financial year on this date, tax returns must be filed by the following 15 March or, in certain circumstances, 15 December of the end of the following tax year. If an alternative financial period has been adopted by the company, its tax returns must be filed at the earliest by the fifteenth day of the sixth month following the year-end, with a maximum extension to the earlier of the fifteenth day of the ninth month or

15 June following the end of the alternative financial year. Tax returns of individuals, partnerships and trusts must generally be filed by 31 October each year and an extension may be granted if the return is to be filed by a registered tax agent. It is important to note that penalties of up to 200% of tax underpayment may be imposed for filing an incorrect return, together with interest charges and penalties for the late filing of returns or payment of tax. These penalties are strictly enforced, and the sophisticated data-matching processes employed by the ATO make tax evasion nearly impossible and certainly foolish.

The Australian Taxation Office has a comprehensive website, which offers assistance to small business owners, including a wide range of electronic pamphlets to download. You can access the ATO site at *www.ato.gov.au*. Many TAFE colleges also now offer short courses and evening courses in managing your taxation affairs as a small business owner.

Fair-Trading

Fair-trading concerns the ethical environment in which you interact with other business and customers. The Federal Government announced a fair trading reform package for small business in 1997, which strengthened the Trade Practices Act. The new package protects small businesses against unconscionable conduct, and imposes a mandatory Code of Conduct for franchisers, to protect franchisees. It also offers support for alternative dispute resolution to provide businesses with quicker, less costly, and more efficient remedies; and has extended the banking Industry Ombudsman to small businesses. The Australian Competition and Consumer Commission (ACCC), on-line at *www.accc.gov.au*, and the Department of Employment and Workplace Relations (*www.dewrsb.gov.au*) can provide information on both your obligations as a trader and the laws which are designed to protect your business.

Useful Addresses

Australian British Chamber of Commerce, Level 16, The Gateway Building, 1 Macquarie Place, Sydney, NSW 2000; ☎02-9247 6271; fax 02-9247 6671; www.britishchamber.com

Australian Bureau of Statistics (Central Office), ABS House, 45 Benjamin Way, Belconnen, ACT 2617; ☎1300 135 070 or 02-9268 4909; www.abs.gov.au

Australian Business Economists, 251 Oxford Street, Bondi Junction, Sydney, NSW 2022; ☎02-9299 2610

Australian Business Research Pty Ltd , Level 10, 231 North Quay, Brisbane, QLD 4000; ☎07-3837 1333; fax 07-3236 3422; www.abr.com.au. Credit and Business Information Services.

Australian Customs Service, 3rd Floor, Tower Sydney Central Building, 477 Pitt St., Sydney, NSW 2000; ☎02-9213 2000; Infocentre ☎1300 363 263; www.customs.gov.au

Australian Industry Group, 20 Queens Road, Melbourne, VIC 3004; ☎03-9867 0111; fax 03-9867 0199; www.aigroup.asn.au

Australian Securities and Investment Commission (ASIC), Level 8, City Centre Tower, 55 Market Street, Sydney NSW 2000; ☎02-9911 2500 for general enquiries, document lodgement and searches. ASIC website: www.asic.gov.au

Australian Stock Exchange Ltd, 20 Bridge Street, Sydney NSW 2000, ☎02-9227 0000; www.asx.com.au

Australian Trade Commission (AUSTRADE), Level 24, Aon Tower,201 Kent Street, Sydney, NSW 2000; www.austrade.gov.au. The Australian Trade Commission has offices throughout Australia and the world. Telephone 132 878 or check the website to find the location of your nearest office. In London Austrade can be contacted at Australia House, Strand, London WC2B 4LA; ☎020-7836 4250

Department of Employment and Workplace Relations, Garema Court, 148-180 City Walk, Canberra, ACT 2600, ☎02-6121 6000; fax 02-6121 7542; www.dewrsb.gov.au

Department of Immigration, Multicultural and Indigenous Affairs, Benjamin Offices, Chan Street, Belconnen ACT 2617, ☎02-6265 1111; www.immi.gov.au

Department of Industry, Tourism and Resources, 20 Allara Street, Canberra, ACT 6001, ☎02-6213 6000; fax 02-6213 7000; www.industry.gov.au

Foreign Investment Review Board, The Executive Member, c/o Department of the Treasury, Canberra, ACT 2600, ☎02-6263 3795; fax 02-6263 2940; www.firb.gov.au

IP Australia (Patent, Trade Marks and Designs Office), Ground floor, Discovery House, 47 Bowes Street, Woden, ACT 2606; ☎02-6283 2211; fax 02-6282 5810; www.ipaustralia.gov.au. Trade marks helpline, ☎02-6283 2999.

Reserve Bank of Australia, Head Office, 65 Martin Place, Sydney NSW 2000, ☎02-9551 8111; fax 02-9551 8000; www.rba.gov.au

Securities Exchanges Guarantee Corporation Ltd, 20 Bridge Street, Sydney NSW 2000, ☎02-9227 0424; fax 02-9227 0436; www.segc.com.au

Standards Association of Australia, Head Office, 286 Sussex Street (cnr Bathurst Street), Sydney, NSW 2000; ☎02-8206 6000; fax 02-8206 6001, www.standards.com.au

Export

The Australian Institute of Export, Level 12, 83 Clarence Street, Sydney, NSW 2000; ☎02-9350 8170; fax 02-9262 3262; www.aiex.com.au

Business Brokers

Century 21 Real Estate, Level 12, 76-80 Clarence Street, Sydney, NSW 2000; ☎02-8295 0600; fax 02-8295 0601; www.century21.com.au

Chris Couper & Associates, Business Brokerage, 93 Surf Parade, Cnr Surf Parade and Victoria Avenue, Broadbeach, QLD 4218; ☎07-5592 0687; fax 07-5531 5978; www.chriscouper.com.au

Harry's and Waters Australiawide Realty, 335 Homer Steet, Earlwood, NSW 2206, ☎02-9558 2537.

Resort Brokers, Head Office, Level 4/49 Station Road, Indooroopilly, QLD 4068, ☎07-3878 3999; fax 07-3878 1199; www.resortbrokers.com.au. Licensed real estate agents

Talberg Pty Ltd, 115 Mary Street, Gympie, 4570 Qld; ☎07-5482 7708

Wilsons Business Brokers Pty Ltd, 59A Stewart Avenue, Hamilton South, NSW 2303; ☎02-4962 3388, fax 02-4969 5682; www.wilsons.com.au

Taxation

Australian Investment and Taxation Services, 25 Belmore Road, Randwick NSW 2031; ☎02-9399 8333; www.aitx.com.au

Australian Sales Tax Consultants Pty Ltd, Level 10, 1 Market Street, Sydney, NSW 2000; ☎02-9267 9344.

Australian Taxation Office, National Office, 2 Constitution Avenue Canberra, ACT 2600; ☎132 861; www.ato.gov.au

Australian Tax Planning Consultants, 122 Dutton Street, Yagoona NSW 2199; ☎02-9707 1833

Institute of Chartered Accountants in Australia, level 9, 37 York Street, Sydney, NSW 2000; ☎02-9290 5674; fax 02-9262 4841; www.icaa.org.au.

Employment

Employers First (formerly the Australian Employers' Federation), 313 Sussex Street, Sydney NSW 2000; ☎02-9264 2000; ww.employersfirst.org.au

Australian Industrial Relations Commission, Principal Registry, Level 35, Nauru House, 80 Collins Street, Melbourne, VIC 3000; ☎03-8661 7777; fax 03-96546812; www.airc.gov.au

New Zealand

Section I

LIVING IN NEW ZEALAND

GENERAL INTRODUCTION

RESIDENCE AND ENTRY REGULATIONS

SETTING UP HOME

DAILY LIFE

RETIREMENT

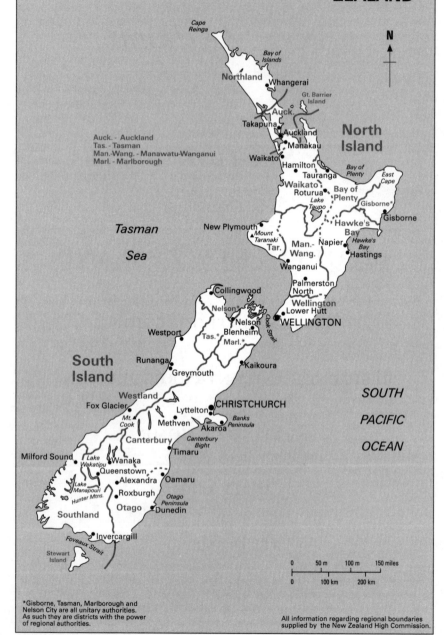

NEW
ZEALAND

N

*Cape
Reinga*

*Bay of
Islands*

Northland
● Whangerai

*Gt. Barrier
Island*

Auck. - Auckland
Tas. - Tasman
Man.-Wang. - Manawatu-Wanganui
Marl. - Marlborough

Auck.
Takapuna ●
● Auckland
● Manakau

North
Island

Waikato ●

Hamilton ●
● Tauranga

*Bay of
Plenty*

*East
Cape*

Waikato
Roturua ●
*Lake
Taupo*

Bay of
Plenty

Gisborne*
● Gisborne

New Plymouth ○
*Mount
Taranaki*
Tar.

Man.-
Wang.

Hawke's
Bay

Napier ●

*Hawke's
Bay*
● Hastings

Tasman

Sea

Wanganui ●

Palmerston
North ●

● Collingwood

Wellington
Lower Hutt ●
● WELLINGTON

Nelson*
● Nelson

Westport ●

Blenheim ●

Tas. *
Marl.*

Cook Strait

● Kaikoura

South
Island

Runanga ●

Greymouth ●

SOUTH

Fox Glacier ●

Westland
Lyttelton ●
● CHRISTCHURCH

PACIFIC

*Mt.
Cook*
● Methven

*Banks
Peninsula*

OCEAN

Milford Sound ●

*Lake
Wakatipu*
● Wanaka
● Queenstown

Akaroa ●

Canterbury

*Canterbury
Bight*
● Timaru

*Lake
Manapouri*
Hunter Mtns.

● Alexandra
● Roxburgh

Otago

Oamaru ●

*Otago
Peninsula*
● Dunedin

Southland

● Invercargill

Foveaux Strait

*Stewart
Island*

0		50 m	100 m	150 miles

0	100 km	200 km

All information regarding regional boundaries
supplied by the New Zealand High Commission.

GENERAL INTRODUCTION

CHAPTER SUMMARY

- 85% of New Zealanders live in urban areas.

- **The Maori.** The original Maori inhabitants have fared slightly better than the Australian aborigines.

  - The number of Maori descendants are increasing as a percentage (now nearly 10%) of the population.

  - The Maori name for New Zealand is Aotearoa.

- **History.** Among the first Europeans to set foot in New Zealand was the explorer Abel Tasman in 1642.

  - The country was named after Zeeland, an island in the Baltic Sea.

  - New Zealand was able to exploit its agricultural potential fully with the development of refrigeration in the 1880s.

- **Politics & Economy.** Britain was New Zealand's main source of income from exported goods until the UK's entry into the Common Market in 1973.

  - Unemployment rose to 10% by the 1990s but has since fallen to just over 5%.

  - Diversification of products and new trading areas have put NZ on the road to economic recovery.

  - The New Zealand economy is heavily influenced by events in South East Asia.

- **Women.** New Zealand has had two women prime ministers and one is currently in office.

  - Women were enfranchised in New Zealand in 1893, 25 years before the UK.

- **Population.** 230,050 people in New Zealand are of British origin and 11,625 of North American origin.

DESTINATION NEW ZEALAND

New Zealand has a reputation for being an unspoiled 'clean and green' haven in the South Pacific, a diverse landscape filled with uncrowded beaches, mountains, farms and sheep. Although the economy is still largely based on the land, over the last century the proportion of people living in towns and cities has doubled, and 85% of people now live in urban areas. Four-fifths of New Zealanders are of European descent, mostly from Britain but also from Germany, the Netherlands, Greece and the former Yugoslavia as well as other nations. A significant and growing proportion of New Zealanders are descended from the original Maori inhabitants, or are Polynesian or, more recently, immigrants from Asia.

New Zealand political traditions derive from Britain, but constitutionally it has often been several steps ahead. New Zealand gave women the vote in 1893, 25 years before they were enfranchised in the UK. New Zealand's first woman MP, Elizabeth McCombs, was elected in 1933. In 1938 New Zealand was one the first countries in the world to set up a comprehensive system of social security, from child care benefits through to old-age pensions.

Since European settlement first began in the early 1800s, links with Britain have been close. Early generations of settlers grew up regarding England as 'home'; strangely enough this attitude can sometimes still be found among older, more conservative New Zealanders, some of who have never even set foot outside New Zealand. New Zealand foreign policy was basically an extension of British policy and the idea that 'where England leads, we follow', as one New Zealand Prime Minister put it, led New Zealand into a number of wars as a British ally. When Britain joined the European Community in the early 1970s, New Zealand found its own path in the world and its own identity as a Pacific country, rather than an outpost of Europe located in the Antipodes. In general, visitors and immigrants from America and Britain are warmly welcomed. New Zealanders deserve their reputation as some of the friendliest people in the world; when they invite you to come and stay, or to 'drop in any time' it is genuinely meant.

Newcomers will find that while elements of the traditional culture owe something to Europe (the national obsession with sports revolves around cricket and rugby) and New Zealand youth culture is heavily indebted to America, New Zealand is carving its own identity as a Pacific nation. The old ties with Britain have been loosened, and new relationships with neighbours around the 'Pacific Rim' and other Asian countries are of growing importance. Polynesian, particularly Maori, culture is a growing influence. Auckland, the largest New Zealand city, has the largest Polynesian population in the world. There are new immigrant communities from various Asian countries as well as a long established Chinese community. The different groups make for an interesting cultural mix. New immigrants will find that it is important to respect the cultural traditions of various groups, most particularly the Maori as they were the first inhabitants of the islands. The Maori call themselves the *Tangata Whenua*, which means 'the people of the place'.

In many respects New Zealand will seem quite familiar to many immigrants. The main language is English, and the systems of government, schools and health care are similar to those in many European countries. A wide selection of arts and culture is on offer in the big cities. If you are looking for a country with fewer social problems than Europe or the USA, where the environment is cleaner, the standard of living higher and the pace of life is more relaxed, New Zealand could be the place for you.

Pros and Cons of Moving to New Zealand

Despite having a comparatively low GDP per capita compared to other developed countries, New Zealanders enjoy a high standard of living. While it is true that income per head of the population compares unfavourably, the upside is that both US dollars and pounds sterling go a long way in New Zealand. Other attractions for immigrants are the non-quantifiable factors that make for quality of life: clean air, clean water, miles of unspoiled and accessible beaches and native forest, and some of the most spectacular scenery in the world. If your idea of the good life is a city where rush hour lasts for ten minutes and the nearest beach is no more than 30 minutes away, then you will enjoy the New Zealand lifestyle. Many others obviously agree; currently living in New Zealand there are 230,052 people who were born in the UK and Ireland, as well as 11,625 people originally from the USA.

New Zealanders enjoy a wide range of outdoor activities in their spare time, including climbing, hiking, swimming, surfing, canoeing and mountain biking. Two great attractions of the country are the parks and reserves and the sea. Even New Zealand's biggest cities are within twenty or 30 minutes of hills and forest largely free from human habitation and all the major cities, apart from Hamilton, are on the coast. With a lifestyle revolving around outdoor pursuits, the nightlife in smaller towns is not exactly lively. In the big cities the scene is more interesting. European style cafés and bars have proliferated in the last decade and there is always the traditional Kiwi pub - watering holes more noted for the cheapness of the beer than the social ambience. Licensing laws are liberal and some pubs and cafés in the big cities are open almost 24 hours.

The standard working week is five days, 40 hours, although many people do work extra hours and overtime. Many employers no longer pay extra for overtime, although you can usually expect to be given time off in lieu of hours worked if you are required to put in a significant amounts of extra time. Professionals on salaries can expect to work quite long hours, particularly at the start of their careers. Wage workers used to enjoy a high level of employment protection; national pay rates and conditions were set down in awards, legal documents which bound employers. Unions at a national

Pros:
- Favourable exchange rate
- High quality of living
- Diverse ethnic mix
- Cheaper living costs
- Relaxed lifestyle
- Easy access to beautiful areas of countryside and coast
- Friendly locals
- No language problem

Cons:
- Small economy
- Remote; it takes around 13 hours to fly to the USA, and 26 to England
- Can be parochial and inward looking
- Unsettled climate in some parts
- Limited range of the arts and culture familiar to Europeans, except in big cities

level did most of the bargaining. Employment protection has been considerably weakened over the last decade and a half, and in some areas of the labour market (particularly casual work in catering, horticulture and agriculture) pay rates and conditions can be very poor. The social security system, once relatively generous, has also been trimmed back. On the other hand personal tax rates on high incomes are lower than in many European countries; there is no capital gains tax, GST (Goods and Services Tax) is 12.5% and the highest income tax rate is 39% (for incomes over $60,001 per annum). Unemployment has dropped by nearly half in the last decade.

Rented accommodation is not hard to find, although it can be expensive in Auckland and Wellington. Rental agreements can either be on a renewable basis where the tenancy continues until either side gives notice, or for a fixed term, usually one year. Houses are usually let unfurnished, while apartments and townhouses may be let either furnished or unfurnished. Furnished properties will usually be more expensive.

ECONOMIC AND POLITICAL STRUCTURE

History

The original inhabitants of New Zealand were the Maori, Polynesian settlers who arrived by canoe from the central Pacific in about the 10th century. They lived a nomadic lifestyle initially dependent on hunting a large flightless bird called the moa (now extinct), but by the 12th century there were settlements scattered along the coastline. Permanent settlements were based on cultivating the kumara, a type of sweet potato, and harvesting seafood. By the time the first Europeans arrived in the 18th and 19th centuries, the Maori had settled throughout the warmer North Island. The Maori are a tribal people, with 79 traditional tribal bases throughout New Zealand. Their family-based society has always had a complex oral tradition and maintains a strong spiritual attachment to their customs and the land. The Maori were skilled craftspeople, particularly in woodcarving and weaving (which some still practise), and also in warfare. War between tribes was common at this time, as part of the competition for status and authority.

Among the first European visitors to New Zealand were members of a Dutch East Indies Company ship led by the explorer Abel Tasman. They briefly anchored off the coast of the North Island in 1642, at a place they called Murderer's Bay because local Maori killed four of their crew there. Tasman named the country after Zeeland, an island in the Baltic Sea. The Maori name for the country is 'Aotearoa', meaning 'the Land of the Long White Cloud'. Other explorers followed Tasman's lead. Englishman James Cook arrived in 1769 and returned again twice in the 1770s. Members of his second expedition were the first Europeans to make landfall in New Zealand and to explore the coastline thoroughly. As with Tasman's first contact with local tribes, there were misunderstandings at first, the Maori interpreting the arrival of the strangers as a hostile force. Ten of Cook's men were killed in one incident. Other meetings were more favourable for the visitors, local Maori for the most part being curious to meet the strangers and keen to trade.

Trade and commerce provided the impetus for the first semi-permanent European settlements. Whalers and sealers arrived in the 1790s. They set up bases along the coasts but generally did not make permanent homes in the new country. Next to arrive, in the early 1800s, were Christian missionaries, who established stations around the Bay of Islands, on the north east of the North Island. They began preaching their faith amongst the tribes as well as introducing European cultivation techniques, literacy and other skills. They were the first to write down the Maori language so that they could translate the scriptures into Maori. Other settlers with more worldly ambitions soon arrived. They were interested in exploiting natural resources such as timber and flax. Local Maori tribes began cultivating wheat and maize to trade with the new arrivals. New Zealand's export trade in agricultural produce began in the 1840s with the export of potatoes, wheat and pigs to Australia. Maori farmers grew the bulk of the produce. Contact between Europeans and local tribes was confined to the small areas around the settlements, the whaling bases around the coasts of the South Island and the lower North Island, the mission stations in the north and the trading settlements at various points. For most of the first half of the 19th century, the balance of power between the settlers and the tribes was still very much in favour of the Maori, as the early settlements were dependent upon the goodwill of local tribes for their survival. However this was about to change. The Maori population was declining as a result of the spread of foreign diseases (such as influenza and smallpox) against which they had no immunity, and the introduction of firearms, which had transformed the formerly ritualised inter-tribal wars into massacres.

By 1840, a balance of firepower had led to a virtual halt in inter-tribal warfare, the cost in lives being too high. The legacy of the warring period was large-scale loss of life, disruption of land tenure and social dislocation. The decline in the Maori population alarmed the missionaries. They were also concerned about the rough, lawless lifestyle of the early settlements. Accordingly, back in Britain, the Church Missionary Society put pressure on the British Government to annex New Zealand as a Crown Colony, and to establish the rule of law.

In 1840, New Zealand was made a part of the British Empire. A treaty was signed at Waitangi, a little settlement in the Bay of Islands, between the new Lieutenant Governor Captain William Hobson and representatives of local Maori tribes. Hobson then sent copies of the Treaty around the country for other tribes to agree to, but some important chiefs refused or failed to sign. The terms, significance and validity of the Treaty of Waitangi have been a source of controversy ever since. Under the English text, the tribes ceded sovereignty to the British Crown and gained the rights of British citizens. The Maori text, hastily translated by local missionary, Henry Williams, is considerably vaguer in its terms. In particular, Williams used the unfamiliar term 'kawanatanga' a transliteration of the English word 'governorship', to express the concept of sovereignty. It is doubtful that the first signatories understood that they were handing over rule of the land to the newcomers.

During the late 1830s plans for widespread colonisation were developed under the auspices of Edward Gibbon Wakefield's New Zealand Company. Wakefield intended the settlements to mimic the pre-industrial class structure of England but the actual settlements bore little resemblance to his plans. Street plans formally laid out in Britain did not necessarily take into account the geographical vagaries of the mountainous land in New Zealand.

Prospective immigrants attracted by the promise of cheap land may not have been aware that the Company and its agents did not always acquire the land legitimately from the tribes, especially as the pressure to provide more land increased. Maori land tenure is complex as land is not owned by individuals but by the tribe as a whole. Company agents were not particularly scrupulous about whose signatures they obtained on sale documents and, as the increasing numbers of new settlers demanding land put pressure on them to provide it, their methods undoubtedly became more dubious.

New Zealand was directly governed by the British Crown between 1840 and 1852. After pressure from the settlers, self-government was granted in 1852. As European settlers increased in numbers and demand for land grew, conflicts occurred with the Maori people over land tenure. The tribes disputed a number of deals undertaken by New Zealand Company agents and resistance movements to further land sales developed.

The settler government ignored its responsibilities to protect Maori rights under the Treaty. Skirmishes between the government and the tribes began in the 1860s and full-scale war developed. It took nearly fifteen years for the forces of the government, reinforced by troops from Britain, to defeat Maori opposition. Even at the end of hostilities in the 1870s, Maori tribes in the centre of North Island still held out against government control. The wars exacerbated the decimation of the Maori population and resulted in the confiscation of the land of the 'rebellious' and 'loyal' tribes alike. The loss of land and the resulting social breakdown probably contributed more than any other factor to the decline in the Maori population at the end of the 19th century.

Meanwhile European settler numbers were increasing, spurred on by the discovery of gold in the South Island in the 1870s, and the invention of refrigerated shipping in the 1880s which made the export of meat and dairy products to Europe viable. The gold deposits were soon mined out but the agrarian economy founded in the late 19th century has remained the basis of New Zealand's economic prosperity. Economic security brought on social reform, at least for the European population. First the extension of the vote to women (1893), then a new system of industrial relations, based on minimum wage rates for every industry (1894) and one of the earliest pension schemes (1898). Maori were legally equally able to vote but the property owning rule (which was based on European patterns of individual tenure, rather than an understanding of Maori communal tenure) effectively disbarred many of them until its abolition in the late 19th century.

New Zealand was involved in both World Wars as a British ally. The disastrous Great War campaign at Gallipoli in Turkey in 1915 proved to be one of the defining moments in forming a separate national identity. New Zealand lost more soldiers as proportion of its population than any other allied country; nearly one in three men between the ages of 20 and 40 were killed or wounded. The interwar years brought the election of the first Labour government, which continued the tradition of pioneering social policy programmes started by the Liberals. The 1938 Social Security Act established a national health service and a universal social security system. Public education to secondary level was free to all. World War Two saw New Zealand participating again as a British ally, but in the post-war years it began to rely less on Britain for defence and to form closer relations with Australia and the United States. Britain's entry into the Common Market in the 1970s confirmed the loosening of colonial ties. At the same time closer links were being developed with other countries in the Asia-Pacific region.

Economic restructuring resulting from the increasingly poor performance of the economy since the late 1970s and race relations have been the major policy issues over the last three decades. The prevailing belief that relations between the races were harmonious was challenged by a number of Maori political movements during the last thirty years, ranging from radical groups calling for the restoration of Maori sovereignty to tribal leaders taking a more conciliatory stance. Two common concerns unite the diverse strands of Maori protest movements: a call upon the government to honour the terms of its original treaty with the Maori people and a concern with the inequality between Maori and European living standards. Income, life expectancy, health, and education standards differ markedly between the two groups. The Treaty has become central to government policy towards the Maori and in 1985 the Waitangi Tribunal was given power to hear grievances relating to Maori land. The government's obligations towards the Maori as an equal partner under the Treaty were acknowledged. Maori became an official language in 1987 (English being the other) and knowledge of Maori culture and language is increasingly a prerequisite for employment in areas of public service departments and is stressed as equally important as cultural heritage. Tensions remain between the Maori and the Government over historical injustices, particularly the large scale acquisition of Maori land by Europeans in the 19th century through confiscation, extortion, blackmail and theft, and the Government's neglect of its duty to protect Maori rights under the Treaty.

Economy

New Zealand has a worldwide reputation as an agricultural producer with increasingly efficient and innovative methods. Since 1984 the government has undertaken some major restructuring and transformed New Zealand from an agrarian economy largely dependent on Britain to a more industrialised and globally competitive free market economy. Technology and research have played a major part in this transformation. The temperate climate is ideal for growing grass suitable for rearing farm animals cheaply, but it took a century and a half of effort to cultivate the ten million hectares of arable land currently in production. Modern machinery and efficient soil, stock and pasture management have played an important role. Much of the land was initially unsuitable for agriculture, being heavily forested, while the mountainous terrain has provided a challenge to develop alternative cultivation techniques. Nearly two-thirds of farmland is too rugged to be fertilised and sown by tractor. Instead New Zealand farmers pioneered the use of light aircraft to spread fertiliser and seed.

New Zealand was able to exploit its agricultural potential with the development of refrigerated transportation in the 1880s. Meat and dairy products joined wool as the basis of exports to Europe. At the end of the 19th century, New Zealand was one of the richest countries in the world. As a former colony, it enjoyed close cultural and economic links with the UK. For most of the following century, three-quarters of New Zealand's exports went to the UK. Britain was also the major source of imports.

By the 1950s New Zealand was an efficient producer of wool, meat and dairy products and could compete successfully in Northern hemisphere markets. The success of the export industry allowed New Zealanders to enjoy a similar standard of living to the industrialised countries of Europe and America. The relatively high standard of living attracted a constant inflow of immigrants. In the early 1960s, as a result of a worldwide boom in commodity prices, it enjoyed amongst the highest living standards in the OECD. However, even during this relatively prosperous period, it was recognised that future economic security depended on diversifying the export base, both in terms of markets and of the range of goods being exported. New Zealand's traditional market, Britain, was not growing as fast as other countries and there was the possibility throughout the 1960s that it would eventually join the European Economic Community (now the EU).

The golden years ended in the 1970s. Several factors were influential such as the entry of Britain into the EEC in 1973 and the first oil price-shock in the same year. Britain's entry into the EEC led to the restriction of access for New Zealand exports and this coincided with the rise in the price of oil which had a severe effect on the New Zealand economy, as it was extremely dependent on importing oil to meet its energy needs. There was a sudden decline in economic performance. The cost of imports rose sharply while exports receipts dropped and the Balance of Payments deficit plummeted to 14% of GDP. Arguably however the effect of these two events only exposed the underlying weakness of New Zealand's economy rather than causing the economic decline. The government of the time decided that the best solution to the problem of New Zealand's dependency on fuel imports was to embark upon a series of major investment projects to develop domestic energy sources. Unfortunately the viability these projects was based on the price of oil continuing to rise more than it did. Most of the so-called 'Think Big' projects turned out to be expensive white elephants.

By the early 1980s, the economy was performing badly. Inflation was high, and at the same time, unemployment was rising rapidly. Subsidies protected inefficient sectors of the economy and discouraged innovation. Years of borrowing to cover the trade deficit and the cost of the 'Think Big' experiment had increased New Zealand's foreign debt. The National government tried to control inflation by imposing a price and wage freeze in 1982. The freeze succeeded in controlling inflation, but money supply continued to grow throughout the two and half years it was in place. In 1984 a Labour government was elected. At the time of the election there was no indication that the new administration would introduce a period of radical economic reform. The Labour party manifesto made no mention of many of the central policy changes they enacted. The programme of economic liberalisation included removal of price and wage controls, deregulation of financial markets, the floating of the dollar, the introduction of a sales tax, the reduction of agricultural and industrial subsidies, the removal of employment protection, and the weakening of the collective bargaining power of unions. This was accompanied by tight monetary policy and the selling of a number of state assets, including the railways, forests, the national airline and the telecommunications section of the post office.

Against these short-term swings in government economic policy, a longer-term process of economic adjustment has been occurring. New Zealand's export industry has diversified both in product and export markets. A free trade agreement was signed in 1982 with Australia, which is now New Zealand's main trading partner. The development of new markets in Asia has been a significant development during recent years. Japan is the third largest source of export income (13%) after Australia (22%) and the USA (14%). Europe, which in the late 1960s provided two-thirds of New Zealand's export revenue, now accounts for less than 20%. The range of exports has diversified to include forestry, horticulture, wine and manufactured goods, and fishing and tourism have become more significant. The dependence upon meat, wool and dairy exports has declined considerably as a result. In the 1960s, these three sectors accounted for over 80% of export revenue; they now make up less than 50%. Total exports are currently worth $14.6 billion to the economy. Although the range of products has diversified, the economy as a whole is still reliant upon exporting agricultural and horticultural commodities. This heavy dependence on trade leaves growth vulnerable to changes in economic performance, particularly in Asia, the USA and Europe. New Zealand's growth prospects are also vulnerable to climatic and environmental factors.

The adjustment process to the restructuring has been long and difficult. Unemployment rose from under 4% in 1985 to over 10% in 1990, levels not seen since the Depression years, as economic activity declined due to tight monetary policy. Farmers' gross incomes dropped by nearly half when government subsidies were removed. A large number of manufacturing industries went to the wall, unable to compete with cheap imports once tariffs were removed. The abolition of financial controls caused a brief speculative boom in the mid-1980s but the stock market crash in 1987 exposed much of the increased activity as paper wealth. The dollar rose as high interest rates attracted overseas investment, which reduced returns from exports, critical to the overall health of the economy.

Whether the social costs of economic restructuring outweigh the efficiency gains is still being debated. Some sectors of the economy have adjusted better to deregulation than others. Despite predictions that many farms would not survive the removal of agricultural price supports, there were only a few casualties. The agricultural sector has become more efficient. Manufacturing has not been as fortunate and the shedding of jobs in this sector along with the restructuring of previously inefficient government industries largely accounted for the rise in unemployment. Unemployment has now dropped again and is estimated to be around 5.2%. However, the gap between high and low income earners has grown and poverty has emerged for the first time since the war as a visible social problem. For a country that used to pride itself on its egalitarian ethos and comprehensive social welfare system, these developments have caused much public concern.

Future economic predictions are mixed, as the New Zealand economy is heavily influenced by the economic and political upheavals of Southeast Asia. Consumer confidence has picked up, although business confidence remains fairly low. Inflation remains among the lowest in the industrial world, and the GDP real growth rate is estimated at 3.6% at the time of print. The high exchange rate in favour of foreigners and falling house prices mean that this is a good time for immigrants to be buying property and investing in the country.

Government

New Zealand is an independent parliamentary democracy within the Commonwealth. Queen Elizabeth II is the titular head of state, represented in New Zealand by the Governor-General. The current inhabitant of Government House is Dame Silvia Cartwright. The Prime Minister is the head of government, supported by a Cabinet of Ministers chosen from the elected Members of Parliament. Government policy is implemented by 39 public service departments.

New Zealand has one of the most centralised systems of executive government in any western country. While levels of local government exist, they do not provide a countervailing force as their powers and responsibilities are comparatively weak. Local government bodies are funded largely by rates, and exist in the form of regional councils, community boards, special authorities and territorial authorities. Radical policy programmes can be introduced relatively quickly as was demonstrated by the fourth Labour government, which transformed the country between 1984 and 1990. The problem has been that the electorate has not universally welcomed change as was demonstrated by the electoral backlash against both the major parties in the 1993 election. Neither of the big parties gained the confidence of the electorate, and small parties got a record number of seats. The result on the night was a hung parliament, but a recount in some of the most marginal seats resulted in a narrow victory for the ruling National party.

All New Zealanders over the age of eighteen have the right to vote. Parliament is elected every three years by Mixed Member Proportional Representation (MMP), a system which was introduced in 1993 following a referendum. But the support for MMP seemed to stem from a reaction against conventional politics and the mainstream parties rather than from any widespread support or even understanding of the consequences of changing the electoral system.

Under the MMP system, voters have two votes; the first for the political party ('party vote') that enables the you to choose which party you would like to see in Parliament, and the second, an 'electorate vote' is for the MP you want to represent your electorate. As an almost fully proportional system, MMP is a system that makes it difficult for a party to win a majority of parliamentary seats and govern in its own right. This means that coalition or minority government is the most likely form of government. Parliament is made up of 120 MPs, and the proportion of each party is dependent upon the outcome of the party vote. A total of 67 electoral representatives are chosen from the 45 general electorates in the North Island and sixteen in the South Island, as well as the six Maori electorates that cover the whole country. Voters of Maori descent may choose whether to register on the general or the Maori electoral roll. The remaining 53 MPs are called 'Party list MPs', and win their places in Parliament by making up the proportion of their party according to the 'party vote'. Party lists are the pecking order of MPs for that party. As well as pitting MPs in the same party against each other in the undignified struggle for selection, MMP makes it much easier for small parties to gain representation than was previously the case. The MMP system has led to the increase in number of women MPs; about one third of MPs are now women, making New Zealand a country with an unusually high proportion of women politicians. MMP has also resulted in increased numbers of Maori and ethnic minority politicians in Parliament. Some rebel MPs who have struggled in the political wilderness for years also benefit from the MMP system. Two MPs in particular decided that the best way to get on the new world of MMP was leave the big parties to found a party in their own image. Former National MP Winston Peters created the New Zealand First party, and Jim Anderton, former Labour MP, established the Alliance party and is now Deputy Prime Minister. More information concerning MMP can be obtained from The Electoral Commission (Level 6, Greenock, 39 The Terrace, Wellington; ☎(04) 474 0670; fax: (04) 474 0674; e-mail: info@elections.govt.nz; internet: www.elections.org.nz).

Political Parties

For most of the second half of this century, the New Zealand political scene has been dominated by two major parties, National and Labour. National is a conservative party, traditionally the party of farmers and business people. It has been the dominant political party in New Zealand politics, holding office for the majority of the post-war period. The Labour party arose out of the labour movement, but has subsequently had relative independence from the trade unions. It has often been the innovator of radical social policies, even when these have gone against its own political traditions. The fourth Labour Government, which held power from 1984 to 1990, was responsible for introducing anti-nuclear legislation that stopped American warships from entering New Zealand ports. It also deregulated the economy, ran a tight monetary policy along Thatcherite lines and sold off a number of state assets - not exactly socialist policies. For those who like their political spectrum neatly divided into left and right, New Zealand politics now presents a confusing spectacle. Currently, Labour together with Alliance form the government coalition, with National as the opposition party. The current Prime Minister and leader of the Labour party, Helen Clark, has held the position since December of 1999. Jenny Shipley was New Zealand's first woman Prime Minister. She was sworn into office only five weeks after gaining the allegiance of the National Party power base whilst Jim Bolger was overseas on business. In a strange twist, she herself was recently ousted while out of the country, with Bill English replacing her as National's leader.

Until 1993, smaller parties were kept out of power by the First Past the Post electoral system. Parties were able to gain power holding less than a majority of votes, and small parties whose supporters were spread around the country would not even gain sufficient votes in any one electorate to elect an MP to Parliament, even though their overall share of the vote could be substantial. One of the results of MMP is that the minor party in the Government can now be quite an influence on governmental policy. Currently, Labour holds 49 of the 120 seats in Parliament, Alliance holds ten, and the National Party claims 39. Four smaller parties are also represented: ACT has nine seats, the Greens have seven, New Zealand First has five seats and United NZ has one. The next election will be called by November 2002.

GEOGRAPHICAL INFORMATION

Area

Located in the southwest Pacific Ocean, midway between the equator and the South Pole, New Zealand is an island chain on the south edge of the 'Pacific Rim of Fire', an area characterised by volcanic activity and frequent earthquakes. It is approximately 1600 km east of Australia and the closest countries to the north are Fiji, Tonga and New Caledonia. Consisting of two major islands (North and South) and a number of smaller ones, New Zealand has a total land area of 270,534 sq km (103,515 sq miles). This makes it about the size of Japan, Italy, or Colorado, and slightly larger than the United Kingdom. It is nearly 1600 km long, stretching across 13 degrees latitude from 34 degrees S to 47 degrees S, only 420 km wide at its widest point. The two main islands are separated by Cook Strait, which is 32 km across at its narrowest point. Most of the country is mountainous. The snow-capped Southern Alps form the backbone of the South Island, from one end to the other, dividing the land between the rainforests of the West Coast and the dry pasture lands of the Canterbury, Marlborough and Otago. The Alps include eighteen peaks reaching higher than 3000 metres, including Mt Cook which is the tallest at 3754 metres. The Maori name for Mt Cook is *Aoraki*, meaning 'cloud piercer'. Over 360 glaciers, which carry snow and ice down from the Alps, feed the major rivers on both sides of the island. Fiordland, the south-west corner of the South Island, is almost all national park and as its name suggests consists of deep sounds or fiords carved into the bush-covered mountains. Mountains in the North Island include several volcanic cones, such as Ruapehu, Tongariro, Taranaki and Ngauruhoe. The chain of occasionally active volcanoes runs from White Island (sending up clouds of steam off the East Coast) through the central volcanic zone (where snow exists alongside hot springs and steam vents) to Mt Taranaki on the West Coast. There are active thermal areas where mud pools literally bubble and geysers send up streams of boiling water. There are many lakes throughout the country. In the South

LIVING IN NEW ZEALAND

LIVING IN NEW ZEALAND

264 LIVING IN NEW ZEALAND

264   LIVING IN NEW ZEALAND

Island the major lakes originate from glaciers, while in the North Island the larger lakes lie on the central volcanic plateau. No point on either of the main islands is further than 120 km from the coast.

National Parks

Roughly 30% of New Zealand's land area is in protected conservation sites, in a network of national, maritime and forest parks. Many of these wilderness areas are untouched by human habitation, although unfortunately the effect of the animals introduced with the arrival of humans has been harder to control. The Department of Conservation which looks after the parks aims to preserve the flora and fauna as far as possible, while allowing people recreational access. They look after an extensive network of tracks and huts for hikers (known in New Zealand as trampers). There is usually a small fee for using the huts. The walking tracks vary in difficulty from family strolls of less than half a day to serious two or three day hikes. Most New Zealanders go tramping at some point in their lives, whether they are dragged reluctantly along on a school trip or are keen walkers every weekend.

Bear in mind, however, that although the New Zealand bush looks welcoming on a warm day, it can be a very hostile environment. The weather can change unexpectedly and, in some areas of New Zealand's national parks, you can be far away from any inhabited areas if something goes wrong. It is important to take precautions before venturing into the bush, such as bringing warm, waterproof clothing and emergency food and water supplies. It is always recommended that you inform someone of your plans, including your route and the approximate time you expect to return.

Regional Divisions and Main Towns

The following regions correspond to the territorial divisions of local government, with the exception of some of the smaller districts such as Gisborne which have been grouped with larger neighbours.

North Island: Northland, Auckland, Waikato, Bay of Plenty, Gisborne/Hawke's Bay, Taranaki, Manawatu/Wanganui, Wellington.

South Island: Nelson/Marlborough/Tasman, West Coast, Canterbury, Southland and Otago.

There are five main cities:

North Island: Auckland, Wellington and Hamilton

South Island: Christchurch and Dunedin

Population

By world standards, New Zealand is lightly populated; according to the final count of the 2001 census the population numbers 3,737,277. Growth rates have been declining since the mid-1970s as a result of downward trends in birth rates, as is the case in most Western countries, the current rate of increase is about 1.4%. The other major factor affecting population change is migration patterns, which have been particularly volatile over the last twenty years. New Zealand has a very low population density compared with European countries.

Despite New Zealand's reputation as a largely rural society, 85% live in cities. The number of people living in Auckland, the biggest city, is currently 1.1 million, nearly one-third of the country's total population. 74.5% of the population are New

Zealand Europeans, known as Pakeha (from the Maori word for non-Maori). New Zealand Maori make up the next largest group forming about 9.7% of the population. Other Europeans account for 4.6%. Pacific Islanders, such as Samoans, Tongans, and Fijians, form 3.8% of the population. Asian and other ethnic groups (including Chinese and Indian, and more recently, Korean and Japanese) now make up 7.4% of the population.

Climate

New Zealand has an oceanic climate, without extremes of hot or cold except for isolated areas of the central South Island. It is temperate, but with sharp regional contrasts. Most areas enjoy ample sunshine, wind and rainfall. The seasons are not as varied as in the USA and Britain, and are the opposite of the Northern hemisphere. January and February are the warmest months, and July is the coolest. New Zealand's long thin shape results in considerable climatic variation between regions. The far north of the country has an almost sub-tropical climate, with mild winters, hot summers and quite a lot of rain. In the south of the South Island, the country can be frozen over for three months during the winter and the summers are hot and dry. During the winter there is extensive snowfall on the Southern Alps, and the central North Island mountains. Snow does not often fall at lower levels, and when it does it is only in the southern parts of the South Island. The sun is strong in the Southern hemisphere, and unfortunately the ozone hole over the Antarctic has a tendency to drift north over New Zealand during December, which heightens the risk of burning even further. During the summer, a 'burn time' rating is included with television and radio weather reports to warn people of the time it takes to burn during the hottest hours of the day. This can sometimes take as few as twelve minutes. Fair-skinned people are advised to stay out of direct sun between 11am and 4pm from late October through to early April, as they will burn easily. Along with Australians, New Zealanders have one of the highest rates of skin cancer in the world.

TABLE 15	AVERAGE MAXIMUM TEMPERATURE, SUNSHINE AND RAINFALL			
City	Mean daily maximum		Bright sunshine hours	Mean annual rainfall (mm)
	Jan (C/F)	Jul (C/F)		
Auckland	23/73	14/57	1952	1046
Wellington	20/68	11/52	2172	994
Christchurch	22/72	11/52	2141	706
Dunedin	19/66	10/50	1513	926

Annual average. Source: National Institute of Water and Atmospheric Research Ltd.

REGIONAL GUIDE

Most New Zealanders live in the North Island, one third of them in the greater Auckland region. The two major North Island cities, Auckland, the largest city, and Wellington, the capital, provide the closest New Zealand equivalent to the culture and lifestyle of big cities in the rest of the world. There is amicable rivalry between the two cities, Auckland being bigger, brasher and more commercial, Sydney for beginners according to some people. Wellington takes itself more seriously as befits a capital city. It is the headquarters of most national cultural institutions, such as the Royal New Zealand Ballet and New Zealand Symphony Orchestra, and the seat of government. The South Island is more sparsely populated but attracts more visitors because of the splendours of the scenery. Christchurch, the biggest city in the south, is very English in appearance and has a rather staid, conservative feel, perhaps because of the architecture. In the south of the South Island, the influence of Scottish settlers is very strong. About the only distinctive regional accent in New Zealand is the rolled 'rr' of the Southlander. Groups of new immigrants often used to settle in particular regions. The area just of north of Auckland is full of family vineyards run by Dalmatian immigrants who arrived last century from what is now the country of Croatia. Danes settled in the Wairarapa, the area just north of Wellington.

Information Facilities

The New Zealand Tourism Board runs a network of Visitor Information Centres throughout the country, where you can obtain maps of the area, information, public transport timetables, and answers to your questions. Information Centres can be found in most large towns. The address of the National Office of the New Zealand Tourism Board is Level 16, 80 The Terrace, PO Box 95, Wellington; ☎(04) 917 5400; fax: (04) 915 3817; internet: www.tourisminfo.govt.nz. There are also offices in Christchurch and Auckland. Other useful websites for a general overview include the AA New Zealand Guide (www.aaguides.co.nz/index) and Pure New Zealand (www.purenz.com).

Northland

Visitor Information Centre: Whangarei Visitor's Bureau, Tarewa Park, 92 Otaika Rd; ☎(09) 438 1079; fax: (09) 438 2943; e-mail: tourism@whangarei.net.nz.
Main city: Whangarei ('wh' in Maori is pronounced as 'f').

Northland is one of the larger regions but is one of the least densely populated with 122,670 residents. It stretches from north of Auckland to the very tip of the North Island, Cape Reinga, where according to Maori legend, departing souls in the form of birds pause on the tree at the very end of the land before setting off for the oceans. Northland has a semi-tropical climate, miles of isolated beaches, and undisturbed rainforests. The Bay of Islands on the East Coast was one of the earliest sites of European settlement. The Treaty of Waitangi, under which the British Crown gained sovereignty over New Zealand, was signed at Waitangi on one side of the Bay of Islands. On the opposite side of the bay is Russell, which was the capital of New Zealand for the first twenty years of British rule. These days one of the main areas of economic activity is tourism. It is a popular destination for New Zealand and overseas visitors. Aside from the historical attractions, it is a centre for big game fishing enthusiasts, sailors and divers.

Auckland

Visitor Information: Auckland Travel and Information Centre, 287 Queen Street; ☎(09) 979 2333; fax: (09) 979 2334; e-mail: citysails@aucklandnz.com; also, New Zealand Tourism Board Auckland Office, 147 Victoria Street, PO Box 91893, Auckland; ☎(09) 914 4780; fax: (09) 914 4789. Useful websites: www.akcity.govt.nz and www.aucklandnz.com.
Main city: Auckland.

The Auckland region is dominated by the city from which it takes its name, the largest in the country with a population of 1.16 million people. It is the financial and manufacturing centre. Two natural harbours, one on the Pacific coast, the other on the Tasman, bite deep into the land forming an isthmus, and the island consequently is narrow at this point. The city covers the width of the island between the harbours. Although Auckland has the highest population concentration in the country, it is not densely populated by the standards of other cities around the world. Most Aucklanders live in detached single storey dwellings in the suburbs, which stretch further into the surrounding countryside each year. The city centre is situated beside the Waitemata Harbour and although it has a number of modestly tall high rise buildings, it's not exactly Manhattan. In fact one of Auckland's most attractive aspects is the parks and reserves that are dotted throughout the urban area. Many of these reserves are volcanic hills, such as Mt Eden. There are over 60 extinct volcanoes in the city area. Another attractive feature is the beaches within walking distance of the city centre. The remainder of the country sometimes resents Auckland as it dominates New Zealand through its size and concentration of economic activity. There is also a general feeling (sometimes justified, unfortunately) that Aucklanders don't think there is anything worthwhile 'south of the Bombay Hills', a cluster of hills marking the division between Auckland and Waikato. Nearly one third of New Zealand's population lives in the greater Auckland region and this is likely to be the fastest growing area of economic activity for some time to come.

Waikato

Visitor Information: Hamilton Visitor Information Centre, Transport Centre, Anglesea Street, Hamilton; ☎(07) 839 3580; fax: (07) 839 3127; e-mail: info@ waikato.tourism.co.nz. Useful website: www.waikatonz.co.nz/VisitorCentres.
Main city: Hamilton.

The Waikato region is home to 39,855 people. It stretches from the Bombay Hills south of Auckland to Lake Taupo in the centre of the North Island. The lake has an area of 60,606 hectares (234 sq miles) and is the source of the river for which the region is named. The Waikato River is the longest in New Zealand. Along its 425-km (264-mile) length there are nine hydro-electric dams which provide a large part of the North Island's electricity requirements. The Waikato is the main dairy farming region in New Zealand. The Coromandel Peninsula in the northeast corner of the region is a centre for forestry production. The Coromandel is a popular holiday destination and many families own second homes there. Its rugged bush-clad mountains protect almost deserted beaches. Other attractions include the thermal regions around Wairakei, where steam is harnessed to drive turbines producing electricity, and the limestone caves at Waitomo.

Hamilton, the largest city, has a population of 169,000 people but the atmosphere of a small town. It is home to one of the more dynamic universities in the country.

The Waikato is also the headquarters of the King movement, one of the Maori cultural and political movements responsible for the renaissance of Maoridom in the 20th century. The King movement is based at Turangawaewae marae (Maori meeting place and cultural centre) at Ngaruawahia, the home of the Maori king.

Bay of Plenty

Visitor Information: Tauranga Information & Visitor Centre, 95 Willow Street, Tauranga; ☎(07) 578 8103; fax: (07) 577 7020; e-mail: trgvin@tauranga.govt.nz; internet: www.tauranga.govt.nz.
Main Towns: Tauranga, Rotorua.

The Bay of Plenty is one of the main horticultural regions in the country and has a population of 129,138. It is located on the East Coast of the North Island above East Cape. The area around Te Puke is the kiwifruit growing capital of the country. If you are fond of the small, furry, brown fruit, you can find them on sale at roadside stalls at ridiculously cheap prices during the season; sometimes when export cargoes are held up for any reason, growers practically give them away. The Bay of Plenty region is a good place for finding casual fruit picking work in season, although students increasingly snap up such jobs. Rotorua is famous for its geysers, mudpools, steam rising from the street drains, and distinctive sulphuric smell of the thermal activity, reminiscent of rotten eggs. Tauranga has a population of around 90,000, and, along with Hawke's Bay, is a popular retirement place, due to its mild and pleasant climate. The beaches around Tauranga and Mount Maunganui are very picturesque and attract crowds (by New Zealand standards) of families and young people during the summer months.

Hawke's Bay/Gisborne

Visitor Information: Napier Visitor Information Centre, 100 Marine Parade, PO Box 722, Napier; ☎(06) 834 1911, fax: (06) 835 7219; e-mail: info@napiervic.co.nz; internet: www.venues.co.nz/napiervic.
Eastland and Gisborne District Information Centre, 209 Grey St, PO Box 170, Gisborne; ☎(06) 868 6139, fax (06) 868 6138; e-mail: info@gisbornenz.com; internet: www.gisbornenz.com.
Main towns: Napier, Hastings, Gisborne.

The East Cape region is very sparsely populated, and over three-quarters of the inhabitants live in the main town of Gisborne. Dairy and sheep farming are the dominant industries, although winemaking is small but growing activity. The East Cape is quite remote, Maori influences are strong and the lifestyle of local Maori is relatively unaffected by European culture. Hawke's Bay, located south of the East Cape, is another primarily agricultural and horticultural region and has a population of 80,253. It has a mild climate with long sunshine hours and low rainfall. The area around Napier and Hastings is particularly known for its vineyards, producing a number of excellent wines, particularly Chardonnay and Sauvignon Blanc. Napier boasts some of the most striking architecture in New Zealand. Totally flattened by an earthquake in 1931, the city was rebuilt in the art deco style then fashionable around the world. Most of the original buildings survive undwarfed by modern tower blocks.

Taranaki

Visitor Information: New Plymouth Information Centre, New Plymouth District Council, Civic Centre, Liardet Street, Private Bag 2025, New Plymouth; ☎(06) 759 6080; e-mail: info@newplymouth.govt.nz. Useful website: www.newplymouthnz.com.
Main town: New Plymouth.

According to Maori legend, the North Island of New Zealand was originally a giant fish which the hero Maui hooked from his canoe, the South Island. If you consider the shape of the North Island as a flattish sort of fish, with a fin on each side, Taranaki occupies the western fin. The dominant feature of the Taranaki landscape is Mt Taranaki, a perfect volcanic cone, topped year round with snow. Taranaki is dairy country and is also the centre of the petrochemical industry. Off the coast of New Plymouth are the Maui natural gas field and a number of small oil fields. The region around Mt Taranaki is a national park and there are a number of tramping paths on the mountain and surrounding area.

Manawatu/Wanganui

Visitor Information: Manawatu Visitor Centre, PO Box 474, Palmerston North; ☎(06) 354 6593; fax: (06) 356 9841; e-mail: manawatu.visitor-info@xtra.co.nz; internet: www.manawatu.co.nz.
Wanganui Information Centre, 101 Guyton Street, PO Box 637, Wanganui 5015; ☎(06) 349 0508; fax: (06) 349 0509; e-mail: info@wanganui.govt.nz. Useful websites: www.wanganui.govt.nz and www.wanganui.com.
Main towns: Palmerston North, Wanganui.

The Manawatu-Wanganui region stretches from just above Wellington up into the centre of the North Island to the central volcanic plateau. The main river in the region is the Wanganui, which is the same name as the town situated on its banks. They should both correctly be known as Whanganui, but established usage prevails. According to Maori myth, the Wanganui was first explored by the great navigator Kupe. The town was one of the earliest established by European settlers who recognised the navigable properties of the river. While other cities have expanded, Wanganui has retained the atmosphere of a quiet country town. Tourist attractions include jet boat rides on the Wanganui river. The main industry is sheep and dairy farming. Tongariro National Park, in the north of the region has within its bounds the highest points in the North Island, the snow-capped volcanoes, Mt Ruapehu (2,797 metres), Mt Ngaruahoe (2,287 metres) and the shortest of the three, Mt Tongariro (1,967 metres). Mt Ruapehu is the main North Island skiing destination, although the eruptions that occurred inconveniently in the winters of 1995 and 1996 wrecked havoc on following ski seasons. It was feared for some time that some ski-fields would have to close, as they had lost so much income, but during recent seasons the snow and business have improved. The whole area is a popular centre for outdoor activities, from climbing to fly-fishing. In the thermal region nearby there are hot springs, and a dip in a naturally heated pool is a popular end to a day's skiing. The largest town, Palmerston North, is towards the south of the region. It has a population of 76,000, and is the home of Massey University, originally one of two specialist agricultural colleges in the country.

Wellington

Visitor Information: Totally Wellington Visitor Centre, Civic Square, 101 Wakefield Street, PO Box 11007, Wellington; ☎(04) 802 4860; fax: (04) 802 4863; e-mail: info@WellingtonNZ.com; internet: www.wellingtonnz.com, and the New Zealand Tourism Board, (Wellington); ☎(04) 917 5400; fax: (04) 915 3817.
Main City: Wellington.

The Wellington region covers the southern tip of the North Island and has a population of 423,765. It is named for its largest city, Wellington, which is the capital of New Zealand and is home to 163,824 people. Parliament is usually housed in the distinctive circular building nicknamed 'the Beehive'. The city spreads across steep hills overlooking a harbour shaped like a natural amphitheatre. Wellington is infamous for its winds, which must easily rival those of that other windy city, Chicago. A favourite cheap thrill amongst inhabitants is watching airplanes battle their way into Wellington airport on a blustery day. Being a passenger on a plane trying to land at Wellington is less fun, as the landing strip is situated on a narrow strip between the harbour and the sea, and often planes abort their takeoff or landing due to high winds and fly to nearby Palmerston North. The city itself is quite small, but despite its size it is surprisingly lively. There are a host of late night cafés and bars, many of which feature local bands and DJs, a thriving theatre scene and several independent cinemas. Wellington hosts a biannual arts festival, and this attracts international musicians and performing artists as well as local performers. There is also a newly completed stadium, clearly visible as you enter the city along the motorway, and this was built to host concerts as well as sporting events. Most of the other towns in the region provide commuter fodder for Wellington, and as such lack much personality of their own. The exceptions perhaps are towns along the edge of the harbour opposite Wellington. Most of these are scarcely more than villages as the steep hills drop almost into the sea at this point leaving only a narrow strip of land to build on. A regular ferry service takes about 25 minutes to cross the harbour to Wellington from Days Bay.

Marlborough/Tasman

Visitor Information: Nelson Visitor Centre, Cnr Trafalgar & Halifax Street, PO Box 194, Nelson; ☎(03) 548 2304; fax: (03) 546 7393; e-mail: Vin@NelsonNZ.com. Useful websites: www.nelsonnz.com and www.webnz.com/nelson/tourism.
Main Cities: Nelson, Blenheim.

The Marlborough and Tasman districts cover the top of the South Island. It is the largest wine making region in the country. The climate is pleasant, hot without being as humid as northern parts, with more sunny days and less rain than Auckland. The area around Nelson is a centre for artisans and craftspeople, particularly potters, which may account for the slightly alternative feel to the town. It is a relaxed, laid-back place (as are most South Island towns) with easy access to some beautiful wilderness areas and beaches. Over the Takaka hills to the west lies the aptly named Golden

Bay. There are a number of national parks in the Tasman district. East of the city of Nelson lies the Marlborough district, which boasts the spectacular Marlborough Sounds, a popular yachting and holiday destination. In this area, along the water, there are many small houses accessible only by boat. Marlborough is also the largest wine-making area in the country. Blenheim is the main town in the region.

West Coast

Visitor Information: Greymouth Visitor and Information Centre, cnr Herbet and McKay Sts, Greymouth; ☎(03) 768 5101; fax: (03) 768 0317; e-mail: vingm@minidata.co.nz. Useful website: www.westcoast.org.nz.
Main Towns: Greymouth, Westport.

The West Coast is a wet and wild part of the South Island with its own distinctive breed of New Zealanders. It has the smallest population of the country, with just 7,776 permanent residents in the Westland District. The Coast is accessible by a few roads most of which climb up through the Alps in a series of hairpin bends through spectacular scenery. The routes through the centre of the island are occasionally cut off by weather, which may account for the remote feeling of the Coast. Or it may be the rugged independence of its inhabitants resulting from the area's historical legacy. Mining, gum digging and possum trapping were the main industries for much of the last two centuries - all fairly solitary occupations. Consequently 'West Coasters' are renowned for their 'man alone' strength of character and their sincere hospitality. There are so few cars on the road that, if driving, you end up waving to every car you pass! Popular tourist industries are as diverse as walking on the Fox and Franz Joseph Glaciers, eco-tourism and wildlife tours, to watching glass blowing and gem stone manufacture. The geography of this region is dramatic, from the 'Pancake Rocks' and blowholes on the coast in the north, to the spectacular glaciers and mountains in the south. Aoraki/Mt Cook, at 3,754 metres, is New Zealand's highest mountain, but its stature was reduced 10.5 metres in 1991 when the top of the mountain fell off in a landslide. It is a region of extremes; the rainfall is very high and the sandflies can be diabolical.

Canterbury

Visitor Information: Christchurch and Canterbury Information Centre, Old Chief Post Office, Cathedral Square West, PO Box 2600, Christchurch; ☎(03) 379 9629; fax: (03) 377 2424; e-mail: info@christchurchnz.net; internet: www.christchurchnz.net; and New Zealand Tourism Board (Christchurch), South Suite, 2nd Floor, 77 Heresford Street, PO Box 3182, Christchurch; ☎(03) 961 4830; fax: (03) 961 4835.
Main City: Christchurch.

The Canterbury region is mostly sheep farming country, miles of pasture land stretching from the foothills of the Southern Alps to the coast. The main city Christchurch is the largest in the South Island with a population of more than 342,000. Founded by an idealistic bunch of Oxford University graduates, it was named for their old college. These days it is known as the Garden City, for its botanic parks, trees and green spaces. It is set on the Avon river and is a popular destination for many tourists who like the slightly English flavour Christchurch retains. The skyline is dominated to the east by the Port Hills, and to the west by the Southern

Alps. Mt Hutt, a major ski resort, is only an hour's drive from the city. East of Christchurch is Banks Peninsula, a collection of bays and hills jutting out into the Pacific. Lyttleton Harbour is the deep water port for the city of Christchurch and is connected to the city by a 1.6 km tunnel running through the Port Hills. Akaroa, the main settlement on the Peninsula, was originally founded by the French, who had ambitions to colonise New Zealand but were beaten to it by the British. These days the French influence does not extend much beyond the street names and the architecture. The Canterbury plains are prime crop-growing land. Further west on the foothills of the Alps, the land is mostly used for sheep farming.

Otago

Visitor Information: Dunedin Visitor Information Centre, 48 The Octagon, PO Box 5457, Dunedin; ☎(03) 474 3300; fax: (03) 474 3311; e-mail: visitor.centre@ddc.govt.nz. Useful websites: www.CityofDunedin.com and www.atoz-nz.com.
Main city: Dunedin.

The Otago region covers the southeastern part of the South Island. Land is used mostly for dairy farming and crop growing. The central Otago basin enjoys surprisingly hot, dry summers despite its latitude, and is a centre for horticulture, particularly stone-fruit orchards. The southernmost city, Dunedin, was founded by Scottish settlers and now has a population of about 122,000. Perhaps the most characteristic buildings in Dunedin are those of Otago University, which reflect the importance of education to the early settlers; founded in 1869, it is the oldest university in New Zealand. The discovery of gold brought a temporary economic boom in the mid-1800s, and Dunedin grew to be one of biggest and most prosperous towns in colonial New Zealand. However, the gold largely ran out after the initial boom, and Dunedin's growth rate fell behind the northern cities. It has remained much the same size since the early days of the 20th century, and many of its historic buildings have been preserved as a result. It has also retained the somewhat austere character of its Presbyterian forefathers, although every year a new intake of students at Otago University tries to reverse this. It is the only truly 'student' town in the country, university life dominating the town during term time while the students (or 'scarfies' as they are known in this part of the country) provide much needed revenue for local businesses. Three and a half hours inland from Dunedin lies Queenstown, a major tourist area. Set on Lake Wakatipu against a spectacular mountain backdrop, it is close to ski resorts and the home of adrenaline activities. Try the 71 metre Skipper's Canyon bungy jump for measure.

Southland

Visitor Information: Invercargill Visitor Information Centre, 108 Gala Street, Queenspark, Invercargill; ☎(03) 214 9133; fax: (03) 218 4415; e-mail: tourismandtravel.invercargill@thenet.net.nz. Useful website: www.atoz-nz.com/ Invercargill.
Main towns: Invercargill, Gore.

Southland, as the name suggests, is the southernmost region of the South Island. Stewart Island at the very bottom of the South Island is the southernmost inhabited point of the country. It is off the coast of Southland, below Invercargill, the largest town in the region. At Bluff near Invercargill is the country's only aluminium smelter, powered by locally produced hydro-electricity. In the western part of the region is Fiordland National Park. It contains some truly awe-inspiring scenery, with fiords or sounds carved out by glaciers, cutting deep channels into the land. The surrounding cliffs are covered in bush and traced by waterfalls. One of the best known parts of Fiordland is Milford Sound, the destination of the Milford Track, a popular walking trip for tourists and Kiwis alike. On the eastern coast of Southland lies the Catlins area, which features abundant wildlife, (seals, sea lions, and Hector's dolphins), native forests, waterfalls and caves. The spectacular Cathedral Caves are only accessible at low tide. Most of Southland is beef and sheep farming country, with some dairy farming around Invercargill. The people of Southland can be gruff and down to earth, note the rolled 'rr' that can be found around the city of Gore - it's the only regional variation of the New Zealand accent.

GETTING THERE

Travel Agents

If you do not have a regular travel agent, it may be worthwhile considering the advantages of using an agency that specialises in long haul flights or in Australian and New Zealand destinations. They should be up to date with any discounted or cheaper fares that may be available, although the drawback of these deals is usually that the tickets have restrictions and can be very expensive to change once booked. Some antipodean travel agencies offer other services that may be useful, for example, organising temporary accommodation when you first arrive. The cheapest flights from Europe are via London, so if you are travelling from another European destination it may be worth checking if it makes sense to go via Heathrow or Gatwick. From London the trip is about 22,865 km (14,202 miles) long, and you can either fly east or west to get to New Zealand, with a refuelling stop either in Asia or the USA. From Los Angeles the flight covers 12,852 km (7,983 miles) and from New York you will travel 17,275 km (10,730 miles).

EXCESS BAGGAGE

Some airlines are much more generous with their baggage allowances than others. Allowances range from just 20 kg up to 64 kg, depending on which airline you fly, and whether you travel economy or business class. Some airlines may waive fees if your luggage is just a few kilograms overweight, but the tendency is to be quite strict and airlines are liable to charge you around £16/US$24 for each additional kilogram. If you overstep the baggage limit, there is no guarantee that any additional pieces of luggage will go on the flight with you. If you know in advance that your bags are going to be over the limit, you may be able to send them unaccompanied a week or so before you fly. This will cost around half the price of paying for additional kilograms to travel with you, and you will be able to collect the extra pieces when you arrive. You are entitled to carry on one piece of hand luggage, but usually this must weigh no more than 5 kg. Singapore Airlines currently has special reductions for migrants · if you can produce a migrant visa you will be allowed to take 40 kg of luggage with you. All

> airlines seem to have different policies (and different tolerance levels!) so it is worth checking with your travel agent well in advance of your flight.
>
> **Sports Equipment.** Many airlines offer extra weight allowances for 'sports equipment' and sometimes this can be as much as another 20 kg, but you should be sure to check with your airline well in advance to avoid any nasty surprises.

Should you arrive at the airport and discover that you are over the limit, the best option is unaccompanied baggage. Your luggage will go on the next available flight, and usually reaches your destination a couple of days after you do. You will have to clear it through Customs at the other end and there may be storage charges as well.

Jetlag and Other Effects of Long Flights

Flying west minimises jetlag somewhat, because you are following the path of the sun so your body clock is not so disoriented. There are other ways to minimise the effects of jetlag while on the flight. Drink plenty of water, avoid alcohol, and stretch your legs, arms and shoulders every so often. This may sound like boring advice but the jetlag after a 26-hour flight across twelve time zones can be considerable and may last several days. Avoiding the free airline alcohol is not such a big price to pay for being awake and alive your first few days in your new country. Another idea is to arrive in plenty of time for your flight so you can ask for bulkhead or exit row seats, which have extra leg room. Many airlines now recommend that you have a check-up with your doctor before you fly, to find out about the risks of Deep Vein Thrombosis (DVT) and for information about suitable precautions such as elasticated flight socks and exercises you can do in your seat.

Useful Addresses

ABTA (Association of British Travel Agents): 68-71 Newman Street, London W1T 3AH; ☎020-7637 2444; fax: 020-76370713, e-mail: informaton@abta.co.uk, internet: www.abta.com.

Air New Zealand (USA): Los Angeles area ☎310 615 1111; USA including Hawaii and Alaska ☎800 262 1234; internet: www.airnz.com or www.airnz.co.nz.

Air New Zealand (UK): Air NZ Travel Centre, Upper Ground Floor, New Zealand House, 80 Haymarket, London SW1Y 4TQ; ☎020-8600 7600 or 020-8741 2299; internet: www.airnz.co.uk or www.airnz.co.nz.

ASTA (American Society of Travel Agents): 1101 King Street, Suite 200, Alexandria, VA 22314; ☎703 739 2782; fax: 703 684 8319; e-mail: askasta@astahq.com; internet: www.astanet.com.

Austravel (UK): 50-51 Conduit Street, London W1R 9FB; ☎0870 055 0205; e-mail: westend@austravel.com; internet: www.austravel.com. Also has offices in Birmingham, Bournemouth, Bristol, Edinburgh, Leeds and Manchester (☎0870 166 2020 for specific contact details).

DownunderDirect (USA): 6 W Lancaster Ave, Ardmore, PA 19003; ☎800 642 6224 or 610 896 1741; fax: 610 896 1752; e-mail: info@downunderdirect.com; internet: www.downunderdirect.com.

Golden Wings Worldwide (UK): 51 Kent House, Second Floor, 87 Regent Street, London W1B 4EH; ☎020-7851 1150; fax 020-7851 1151; e-mail: sales@goldenwings.co.uk; internet: www.goldenwings.co.uk.

Trailfinders (UK): 194 Kensington High Street, Kensington, London W8 7RG; ☎020-7938 3939; internet: www.trailfinder.com. There are other *Trailfinder* offices in Belfast, Birmingham, Bristol, Cambridge, Dublin, Glasgow, Manchester and Newcastle, check the website for details.

Travel Agents' Association of New Zealand: Level 5, Paxus House, 79 Boulcott Street, PO Box 1888, Wellington; ☎(04) 499 0104; internet: www.taanz.org.nz.

World Connections Travel (USA): 1818 Independence Square, Suite D, Atlanta, GA 30338; ☎770-393 8892; fax: (770) 393 8882; e-mail: wctravel@mindspring.com; internet: www.mindspring.com/wctravel.

Insurance. Working travellers and those on speculative job searches in New Zealand are advised to take out comprehensive travel insurance.

Useful Addresses

Columbus Direct Travel Insurance (UK): 17 Devonshire Square, London EC2M 4SQ; ☎020-7375 0011; e-mail: administration@columbusdirect.com; internet: www.columbusdirect.net.

DownunderDirect (USA): 6 W Lancaster Ave, Ardmore, PA 19003; ☎800 642 6224 or 610 896 1741; fax: 610 896 1752; e-mail: info@downunderdirect.com; internet: www.downunderdirect.com/insurance.

Downunder Insurance (UK): 3 Spring Street, Paddington, London W2 3RA; ☎020-7402 9211 or freephone 0800 393 908; fax 020-7402 9272; internet: www.downunderinsurance.co.uk or www.duinsure.co.uk.

John Mahon: Visas Australia, PO Box 1, Nantwich, Cheshire CW5 7PB; ☎01270-626626; fax 01270-626226; www.newzealandvisas.com; john@visas-australia.com. Also in Dublin: 2nd Floor, 13 Aston Quay, Dublin 2; ☎01- 6795452; fax 01-6795459. Offers very competitive long-stay insurance for New Zealand that allows you to work.

TFG Global Travel Insurance (USA and Canada): 202-585 16th St, West Vancouver, BC V7V3R8, Canada; ☎604-913 1150 or USA tollfree: 800 232 9415; fax: 604-913 1153; e-mail: info@globalinsurance.com; internet: www.globaltravelinsurance.com.

Trailfinders (UK): 194 Kensington High Street, Kensington, London W8 7RG; ☎020-7938 3939; internet: www.trailfinder.com/insurance. There are other *Trailfinder* offices in Belfast, Birmingham, Bristol, Cambridge, Dublin, Glasgow, Manchester and Newcastle, check the website for details.

WorldTravelCenter.com: Global travel insurance on the internet; ☎1800 786 5566; e-mail: sales@worldtravelcentre.com; internet: www.worldtravelcentre.com.

RESIDENCE AND ENTRY REGULATIONS

The Current Position

Throughout New Zealand's history, population growth has been boosted at various points by government policies designed to attract immigrants. Britain was the main source of new arrivals for most of the first century of European settlement, and the other major source of European immigrants was the Netherlands. Sadly New Zealand missed out on achieving some of the ethnic diversity Australia enjoys by not actively encouraging immigration from other European countries in the post-Second World War period. The last major campaign to attract immigrants was during the 1950s. Those were the days when the New Zealand government paid for immigrants' passage on the condition that they stayed for at least two years. When this scheme ended, a more restrictive immigration policy was introduced, based on occupational quotas. Most potential immigrants were required to have a job waiting for them before they applied for residency.

In 1991 the Government changed the occupational quota scheme to a points-based migrant system that is similar to the Canadian and Australian schemes. Applicants for residency are ranked according to the number of points they score for attributes such as age, qualifications, work experience, family and finances. Those who reach the target number of points set by the New Zealand Government automatically receive provisional approval. At the time of print, the minimum number of points was 24 (see *Residence Categories* for more information).

Policy changes in 1995 caused a dramatic downturn in the number of migrants, and in the 1995-97 period these numbers were down by over 60% due to the difficulty of getting into the country. The Government has since realised that New Zealand needs migrants who will bring new ideas and skills, invest in business, create new opportunities and international contacts and who will help New Zealand compete on the global stage. New immigration policies covering entrepreneurs, investors and those on long-term business visas (temporary residence) were introduced in 1998. In November 1999, special provisions were made for IT specialists, and in October 2001 an extra 10,000 visas a year were allocated to the General Skills and Business immigration category. Immigration Minister Lianne Dalziel said that this increase reflected the 'desire to ensure that talent tops the list of residence approvals'. An entirely new category - the Talent Visa - will allow highly skilled temporary residents to apply for permanent residency. At the time of print, this visa had not yet been introduced but was in the process of being developed. For detailed information, contact the New Zealand Immigration Service (450 Queen Street, Private Bag, Wellesley Street, Auckland; ☎(09) 914 4100; fax: (09) 914 4119; internet: www.immigration.govt.nz).

Applying for New Zealand Residency

If you qualify for permanent New Zealand residency you will be entitled to work in New Zealand without any restrictions. You will be issued a residence visa if you apply outside New Zealand or a residence permit if you apply from within the country. A residence permit will expire if you leave the country; if you wish to leave temporarily after taking up residence, you must apply for a returning resident's visa.

IMMIGRATION STREAMS

There are three main streams of immigration, and only a restricted number of applications in each stream will be successful. From October 2001, new policy changes increased the total annual number of immigration approvals from 38,000 to 45,000. The General Skills and Business category will provide 60% of this total, which means that 27,000 people may immigrate under this category annually. (The 'Business' heading includes four subcategories: investors, entrepreneurs, long-term business visas and employees of relocating businesses.) There is a maximum of 14,500 visas available to applicants in the Family Sponsored stream (accounting for 32%), and a further 3,500 (8%) may qualify under the International/Humanitarian section. Within these major sections, there are around nineteen subcategories, and further sub-subcategories within these.

Bear in mind that the New Zealand Immigration Service operates from a weighty manual that is over 1000 pages long, and acceptance criteria are complex to say the very least, so what follows in this section is no more than a rough overview.

Immigration Refusal Criteria

Whatever category you are applying under, there is a lot of paperwork involved. You will be required to provide medical certificates and character references. In accordance with the Immigration Act of 1987, you will not be accepted if you have ever been convicted of a crime and served a sentence of five years or more, or a sentence of twelve months or more in the last ten years. You will not be accepted if you are subject to a current New Zealand removal order, or if you have ever been deported from any country. And it goes without saying that you will not be accepted if it is suspected that you constitute a likely danger to New Zealand security or public order, and/or if you are believed to be associated with any group or organisation with criminal objectives. These days, because of the sensitivity of race relations and concerns over the political affiliations of the growing number of South African immigrants, you will also be required to declare that you have never been a member of a white supremacist organisation. Like the American immigration requirement to declare that you have never participated in genocide, the point is not that anyone would declare themselves to be racist but that if you make a false declaration, it is an offence under the Immigration Act and you can be deported forthwith. None of this paperwork comes cheaply. New Zealand is the pioneer of charging for the privilege of filling out official forms. See the table below for costs of the different types of visa applications.

Immigration Consultants

You may consider employing the services of an immigration consultant. The number of organisations offering advice on emigrating to New Zealand has grown substantially since the new immigration policy was introduced in 1991. Most consultants offer help with all aspects of the immigration process. They will provide general information about New Zealand to help you decide whether you want to make the move. Some consultancies will organise special tour packages to New Zealand so you can visit the country before deciding whether to emigrate. As emigration is a major life step it may be worthwhile to consider a reconnaissance trip; you can make an application for permanent residency while in New Zealand on a visitor's visa or permit if you decide you like the place.

Once you have made the decision, an immigration consultant will guide you through the daunting maze of paperwork and residency regulations. Some immigration consultants say that candidates maximise their chances of qualifying by using a reputable consultancy, but no company can guarantee that you will be successful. Some consultancies charge a fee for a preliminary assessment (around NZ$170), which may save you wasting any further money if you are unlikely to succeed. Their final fees will vary widely depending on the services you require and the application you are making; charges may range from a few hundred to several thousand dollars. Consultancies cannot make the paperwork any easier, although they should make sure you do not omit any vital pieces of information such as previous job experience. You should be wary of any consultancy that appears to promise that they have a special relationship with the New Zealand Immigration Service. All applications are considered equally regardless of whether a consultant has been involved or not. The most useful service consultants provide is help with settling in New Zealand. Most good consultants should provide you with assistance in deciding where to live, looking for jobs, finding a house and other aspects of organising your new life. In choosing a consultant, the most important aspects to consider are the practical help they can offer. Do they have a job search branch in New Zealand? Do they have contacts that might be useful for promoting your employment chances? According to the New Zealand Immigration Service, the major consultancies they deal with regularly are all above board. If you are uncertain about whether a consultancy is bona fide, you can contact the Immigration Service to check them out. It is worth doing your research to make sure you get value for money.

Useful Addresses

Ambler Collins (UK): 59 Fulham High Street, London, SW3 3JJ; ☎020-7371 0213; fax: 020-7736 8841; e-mail: info@amblercollins.com; internet: www.amblercollins.com.

Ambler Collins (USA): Liebman-Mimbu, PLLC, 3228 3rd Ave S, Suite 200, Seattle, WA 38124-1910 USA; ☎206 381 3375; fax: 206 381 3376; e-mail: info@USA-immigration.com; internet: www.amblercollins.com.

The Emigration Group Ltd., 7 Herit-age Court, Lower Bridge Street, Chester, Cheshire CH1 1RD; ☎01244-321414; fax 01244-342288; e-mail: info@TEGltd.co.uk; www.jobfastrack.co.nz. Provides full assistance with applications for residence and/or work visas. Sister company, *Taylor and Associates,* (see entry below) matches job seekers with employers; together they provide an effective and total emigration service.

Four Corners Emigration, Strathblane

House, Ashfield Road, Cheadle SK8 1BB;☎0161-608 1608; fax 0161-608 1616; e-mail: info@4-corners.com; www.4-corners.com. Specialists in assisting with immigration and visas to New Zealand; full support with relocation and resettlement also given.

How2immigrate (Canada): 688-287 Broadway Ave, Winnipeg, Manitoba, Canada R3C OR9; ☎(204) 943 3303; e-mail: canada@how2immigrate.net; internet: www.how2immigrate.net.

Malcom Pacific (NZ): Level 12, 49 Symonds Street, PO Box 6219, Wellesley Street, Auckland, NZ; ☎09 309 4187; fax: 09 366 4739; e-mail: intel@malcolmpacific.com; internet: www.malcolmpacific.co.nz. Consultants from the Malcolm Pacific International Division regularly travel overseas to meet and assess potential migrants. Check the website or telephone the Auckland office for details.

Malcom Pacific (UK): 3rd Floor, Kingsgate House, 115 High Holburn, London WC1V 6JJ; ☎020-7404 0999; fax: 020-7831 3467; e-mail: lon@malcolmpacific.demon.co.uk.

New Zealand and Australia Migration Bureau, Argyll House, All Saints Passage, London SW18 1EP; ☎020-8875 5442; fax 020-8875 5443; For a free eligibility assessment visit www.migrationbureau.com or contact the office nearest you: *Europe* Migration Bureau: Oranje Nassaulaan 25, 1075 AJ Amsterdam, The Netherlands; ☎+31 (0)20-6717017.

South Africa Migration Bureau: Sandton Square, 2nd Floor, West Tower, Maude Street, P.O. Box 785553, Sandton, 2146 Johannesburg, South Africa; ☎+27 (0)11-881 5421.

Asia, The Americas & Australia Migration Bureau: Level 39, Citigroup Centre, 2 Park Street, Sydney, NSW 2000, Australia; ☎02-9004 7807.

New Zealand Migration Bureau, 366 Montreal Street, Christchurch 8001, New Zealand; ☎(+64) 03-3 77 44 11; fax (+64) 03 - 3 77 44 12.

OE Visas. 16 Forth Street, Edinburgh EH1 32H; ☎0131-625 6900; fax 0131-626 6907; www.overseas-emigration.co.uk. Scotland and the North's only Registered Migration Agent. Helping hundreds of people every day emigrate to Australia, New Zealand, Canada and the USA. Offices also in Cardiff, Ireland and London. Reg No. 990 5168

Protea Pacific Limited (NZ): PO Box 99606, Newmarket, Auckland; ☎+64 9 359 9319; fax: +64 9 359 9189; e-mail: info@proteapacific.co.nz; internet: www.proteapacific.co.nz.

Taylor & Associates, 27 Gillies Avenue, PO Box 9600, Newmarket, Auckland. New Zealand; tel (64) 0-9-520 5421; fax (64) 0-9-520 5487; e-mail nzjobs@jobfastrack.co.nz; www.jobfastrack.co.nz. Taylor & Associates link migrants to the New Zealand and Australian job markets, providing the *fast track way to a new job down under.*

All migration agents and consultants charge for their services.

Useful Publications

Destination New Zealand: a monthly magazine for people wanting to live, work and travel in New Zealand. ☎01352-4771 or email: outboundUK@aol.com for subscription details.

New Zealand Outlook published monthly by Consyl Publishing Ltd. (3 Buckhurst Road, Bexhill-on-Sea, East Sussex TN40 1QF; ☎01424-223111; fax: 01424-224992; internet: www.consylpublishing.co.uk). Aimed specifically at migrants, this publication is a useful way of keeping up with NZ migration policy and entry regulations. In the UK six issues cost £10.00 and twelve issues £14.75; in Europe six issues cost £12.00 and twelve issues £18.20; elsewhere six issues cost £15.00 and twelve cost £24.20.

Emigrate.com: a useful and free online magazine for people interested in emigration can be found at www.emigrate.com/newzealand.

Residence Categories

General Skills Category. The General Skills category accounts for 50% of all migrants. It operates as a points system based around education and qualifications, work experience and age, your spouse or partner's qualifications and work experience, family and educational links to New Zealand, and access to sufficient funds to establish yourself. The Government sets a pass mark each quarter and the highest-scoring applicants during that period will be selected.

To qualify in this category you must be under 55 years old and have sufficient understanding of English to conduct a conversation, and to read and respond to questions about yourself and your family. If your score is above the pass mark then your application is provisionally approved, subject to meeting normal immigration requirements such as a clean bill of health and not having a serious criminal record. You do not get your application fee refunded if you do not qualify.

The system favours young people with tertiary qualifications. However older people with work experience and qualifications can also gain enough points to pass. If you have work experience but no formal qualifications, then your experience only counts if your occupation is on the approved occupations list. Copies of the list can be obtained from the New Zealand Immigration Service. A job offer increases your chances but is not a prerequisite. It is also possible, in some circumstances, to apply for residency with less than a pass mark; if you are no more than five points short of the mark (the number awarded for a job offer) you may be invited to apply for a work visa. This allows you nine months from the date your points are confirmed to travel to New Zealand and find a job consistent with policy.

It makes no difference which country you apply from. The points system has the advantage of being completely neutral; if you have sufficient points to make the grade your application will be provisionally approved, it is not dependent on the discretion of any individual officer. You can check your eligibility in these areas by applying for a self-assessment guide from the New Zealand High Commission. To give you an idea of how the system works, see the sample points table below.

TABLE 16	SELF-ASSESSMENT POINTS TABLE	
Employability factors	**Factor**	**Points**
1.**Qualifications**	New Zealand base qualification: a degree, diploma or trade certificate of three years training, study or work experience	10
	New Zealand advanced qualification, or a minimum of one years' training, study or work experience which builds on the base qualification	11
	New Zealand masters degree or higher	12

You must score a minimum of 10 points for qualifications. Maximum points possible: 12

2. **Work Experience**	Two years	1
	Four years	2
	Six years	3
	Eight years	4
	Ten years	5
	Twelve years	6
	Fourteen years	7
	Sixteen years	8
	Eighteen years	9
	Twenty years	10
	One year work experience in NZ	1
	Two years work experience in NZ	2

You must score a minimum of 1 point for work experience.
A maximum of two extra points is available for work gained lawfully (i.e., with a work permit) in NZ.

3. **Offer of Employment**	Full time, permanent job offer	2 or 5

5 points if the job is relevant to qualifications or experience; 2 points if not.

4. **Age**	18-24 years	8
	25-29 years	10
	30-34 years	8
	35-39 years	6
	40-44 years	4
	45-49 years	2
	50-55 years	0

Maximum age limit: 55 years
Maximum points for age factor: 10
If you turn 25 while your claim is being processed you can claim maximum points.

5. **Settlement factors**	NZ $100,000 settlement funds	1
	NZ $200,000 settlement funds	2

Settlement funds must be owned wholly by principal applicant, or jointly by applicant and spouse.

	Family sponsorship	3

To qualify as your sponsor, your family member must be seventeen years of age or over, a NZ resident or citizen, and have lived in NZ for at least three years.

	Spouse/Partner's base qualification	1
	Spouse/Partner's advanced qualification or master's degree	2
	One year work experience in New Zealand	1
	Two years work experience in New Zealand	2

Maximum points for settlement factors: 7

PASS MARK:		25

POINTS TO WATCH OUT FOR

○ You can only claim points for your highest qualification.
○ Only one person in a family need qualify. Partners and dependent children under 20 will be granted residence as well.
○ You do not have to have a job offer although you will score more points if you do.
○ Years of work experience are rounded down, so if you have nine years and eight months of work experience that will only count as eight years or four points.
○ You can apply for residence under the general category if you are between 50 and 55 but you will receive no points for your age. You are not eligible if you are 55 years or older.
○ Medical requirements are not clearly spelled out anywhere but the assessment seems to be based on whether or not you would be a burden on the New Zealand health system. Chronic manageable syndromes such as epilepsy would not disqualify you, but having a terminal disease probably would.

If at any point a large number of applicants score over the pass mark and therefore automatically qualify, the Immigration Service will not draw any applicants from the pool. This was the case for most of 1993 and 1994. If you are unsuccessful in the pool after four months your application lapses. You will not receive a refund.

Sponsorship. If you are just below the pass mark, you should look carefully at the settlement factors to see if you can make up any critical extra points. Sponsorship is one area to investigate. Sponsorship imposes no formal obligations on the individual concerned. It is just an indication that you have some kind of support system when you arrive, a family member able to help you settle in. A family sponsor must be an adult brother, sister, parent or child of the principal applicant and must be a New Zealand citizen or resident who has been living in the country for the three years prior to your application.

Securing an offer of skilled full-time employment is worth five points. Skilled employment means that the job must be either relevant to your qualification or on the list of occupations approved by the Immigration Service.

Finding the extra points to raise you above the pass mark is an area where a good immigration consultant may be able to help. Most of them offer a job search service. You should consider visiting New Zealand and job-hunting in person, as most employers prefer to meet someone face to face before they make the offer of a job. Remember you can apply for permanent residency from within New Zealand. You will need enough money to finance your living costs while you are waiting for completion of the Immigration Service process, and this could be around six months. First hand experience of any country is still the best way to decide whether you want to live there.

Business Investment Category. This category is also a points system, based on age, experience and available investment funds. It is aimed at potential migrants who have professional or business skills and a minimum of $1 million to invest in New Zealand, although they may not wish to actively run a business.

- You gain maximum points for $6 million or more.
- The current pass mark is twelve points to qualify.
- Under this category you can apply for residency up to the age of 65.
- You will have to meet the same English language requirements as in the General category.
- If you meet the criteria and have the necessary funds to invest, provisional approval will be granted.
- The residence visa is not issued until after the investment is made.
- Once in New Zealand, the funds must remain there for at least two years, and are not for personal use during this time.

Entrepreneur Category. This category is open to those who have successfully established a New Zealand business while in New Zealand on an authorised work permit.

- The business must have been operating in New Zealand for a minimum of two years.
- The business must be benefiting New Zealand in some way.
- You must have a viable business plan, appropriate business skills and background, and sufficient funds for both business and personal use.

Long-Term Business Visa. The purpose of this visa is to encourage self-sufficient self-starters.

- You must intend to buy outright, buy into (minimum of 25%) or establish a business in New Zealand.
- You need to explain your idea, provide a realistic business plan, and prove that you have access to sufficient business and personal funds for a minimum of three years.
- You must have appropriate business skills and experience.
- It is not necessary for the business to employ anyone other than you, or to turn over an annual minimum.
- Your spouse or partner will be granted their own work permit, so they can work either for you or for another employer during the period your visa is valid.
- If there are no problems, in the first stage you will be granted an initial three-year visa. Following that period, if your business is successfully established and still trading, and assuming that no issues of health or character have arisen, you can apply for permanent residence.

Employees of Relocating Businesses. This category covers only key employees who would not otherwise qualify for residence.

Family Category. You are entitled to apply for residence under this category if you have a partner or close family member who is a New Zealand resident or citizen and who sponsors your application. Spouses, de facto and homosexual partners all qualify, but in the case of de facto or homosexual partners you have to go to greater lengths to convince the Immigration Service that the relationship is 'genuine and stable'. Approval is not automatic for any of these cases including spouses, and the Immigration Service will probably require an interview with both partners.

You can also qualify under family reunification if you have immediate family members who are residents/citizens and live permanently in New Zealand. Dependent children (now includes those aged up to 24 years, but they must be unmarried and childless) may qualify to be reunited with their parents if they were declared on their parents' residence application. Single adults may qualify for reunification with a New Zealand brother, sister or parent. Married and unmarried siblings, and dependent children, may now only apply for sponsorship if they have no other siblings or parents living in their own country and if they have an offer of employment in New Zealand. Under the 'centre of gravity' principle, parents may be reunited with adult children provided all their adult children live outside their country of origin, or, if they do not have dependent children, more of their adult children live in New Zealand than in any other country. If they do have dependent children, they may still apply if they have a greater or equal number of adult children living in New Zealand than in any other country. Children may sponsor parents who are alone in their home country. The definition of 'parents' has now been extended to include grandparents and legal guardians in cases where the parents are deceased.

To qualify under any of these categories you will need to provide evidence of your relationship to your family member and proof that they are New Zealand citizens or residents. The sponsor is responsible for accommodation and financial support of the applicant for the first year.

Family Quota. There is now an immigration lottery (similar to USA Green Card lotteries) which currently allows an additional number of persons to immigrate under the Family category every year.

- The quota size is announced each year – the most recent quota had 250 places.
- Registration takes place every April, and winners are given six months to file their residency applications.
- Normal health, character, and relationship requirements still apply.
- Applicants must be sponsored by a family member who is a New Zealand resident or citizen living there permanently and who is aged at least seventeen years.

Humanitarian Category. Applicants under the Humanitarian category have to be suffering some kind of persecution in their home country and must have a New Zealand sponsor who is a close family member.

The Application Process

If you are applying under the general category, you should be able to tell from having completed a self-assessment form whether you are likely to qualify automatically or go into the pool. Obtain an application for visa form from a New Zealand Embassy or High Commission and complete it along with the required documentation, then return it to the High Commission. A major cause of delay in processing applications is incorrect or insufficient documentation. Make sure, for example, that you send full birth certificates (not short birth certificates) for all family members included in an application for residency. Medical requirements include certain blood tests, and the results for these must be sent in. Once you have sent the correct documents, Immigration Service staff will check your eligibility. Processing time is often lengthy, although one family who applied recently had their visas returned to them within two weeks. However, to be on the safe side, you should begin the application process about a year before your intended date of migration.

Fees.			
Visitor's visa	£30/US$45	General Skills	£205/US$465
Business Investor	£725/US$1180	Entrepreneur	£725/US$1180
Family	£205/US$1180	Returning Resident's Visa	£30/US$70
Student Visa	£40/US$70	Work Visa	£50/US$100
Working Holiday Visa	£30/(Not available to US citizens.)		
Long-term Business Visa	£725/US$1180		

New Zealand Citizenship

Once you have resided legally in New Zealand for three years you can apply for New Zealand citizenship. This will entitle you to vote and to carry a New Zealand passport. You will no longer require a returning resident's visa when you travel outside New Zealand. Children born in New Zealand to non-New Zealanders are New Zealand citizens. They can have dual nationality and are entitled to a New Zealand passport.

For citizenship inquiries you should contact the Director of Citizenship (Department of Internal Affairs, PO Box 805, Wellington; ☎(04) 495 7200; fax: (04) 495 7222; e-mail: citizenship@dia.govt.nz; internet: www.dia.govt.nz).

Entry and Work Permits

If you want to visit New Zealand and you are not a citizen or permanent resident then you may need a visitor's visa or permit. You should apply for a visa from the New Zealand embassy in your home country before you travel. The initial period of a visa is usually three months but you can extend it by a further six months once you are in New Zealand by applying to local offices of the New Zealand Immigration Service. However, increasing numbers of travellers do not to need to obtain visas, as New Zealand has negotiated visa-free agreements with several countries. Tourists from the UK are entitled to stay for up to six months without a visa, and American, Canadian and European tourists can stay for three months without a visa. If you do not require a visa, you simply apply for a visitor's permit at the airport. You will be required to show that you have sufficient funds to support yourself while you are in New Zealand and a return or onward ticket. Like the visa, the visitor's permit is issued for three months initially and can be renewed by a further six months within New Zealand. Sufficient funding is deemed to be NZ$1000 for every month you intend to stay. If you have a friend or relative prepared to sponsor your visit, who can guarantee your accommodation, the amount is reduced to just $400. They will need to fill in a *Sponsoring a visitor* form, which they can get from New Zealand Immigration, and which must be sent to you so you can present it when required.

Australia. Australian citizens are free to travel to New Zealand without a visa and can work in New Zealand without requiring a work visa under the terms of the Closer Economic Relations agreement, which creates a free labour market across the Tasman.

Applying for a longer visa. If you know before you travel that you want to stay for longer than three months it is worth applying for a visa even if you are from a visa-waiver country. You can apply for a maximum of twelve months, and your application must be made before your current permit expires.

Studying in New Zealand. Any person wanting to travel to New Zealand for the principal reason of study or training must have a student visa before they travel. You will need to provide an acceptance letter from the New Zealand educational institution, receipt for the non-New Zealand student course fee, evidence of sufficient funds to support yourself, and an outward airline ticket. If you wish to work over the student holidays (November to February), you can apply for a 'Variation of Conditions' to your student permit. If you wish to work following the completion of your course, you can apply for a Work Permit, which will allow you to work a maximum of two years. Some tertiary students may work up to fifteen hours a week while studying. The student must be studying for a degree or diploma that would gain points under the General Skills immigration category: exchange students are not eligible. Information about New Zealand universities and polytechnics is available from the Trade Development Board of New Zealand, as well as from the universities themselves of course. You must be studying an approved course and must have sufficient funds to cover your tuition fees and maintenance (see the *Education* section of the *Daily Life* chapter for a general idea of the cost of New Zealand courses). Dependents of a work visa holder may be eligible for a student visa without already having a place arranged at a New Zealand school. They may also be exempt from overseas tuition fees. See listing below for John Mahon.

Working in New Zealand. If you wish to work in New Zealand for a short period and you are not a citizen or resident you will need to apply for a temporary work visa. You can apply for one before you travel if you already have a definite employment offer, or if you find a job while visiting New Zealand, you can apply for a visa there. Your prospective employer will need to provide details of your job title, responsibilities, qualifications required, conditions and duration of employment and pay, as well as proof that they have unsuccessfully tried to recruit a New Zealander to fill the position. You can apply for a work visa for up to three years if you have a job offer before you arrive in New Zealand. If you apply for a work visa in New Zealand, the maximum period you will be granted is nine months. The employer will be required to provide the local Immigration Service with the information outlined above. For further information you should contact the New Zealand Immigration Service.

Working Holiday Visa. New Zealand has a working holiday visa scheme for young visitors. British, Irish, French, German and Dutch citizens between the ages of eighteen and 30 inclusive can apply for the visa, which will enable them to take casual work without requiring a separate work visa while on holiday in New Zealand. The maximum period of the visa is twelve months and you must be resident in your home country at the time of application. When the scheme started in 1993 only 500 visas were issued; since then the quota has risen to 8,000 per year. You must apply to the New Zealand Immigration Service, showing evidence that you have at least NZ$4200 to support your visit, and a return travel ticket or enough money to purchase one. Sponsorship from a New Zealand citizen is not an acceptable substitute for proof of funds. Allocations are on a first come, first served basis and the quota opens on January 1st each year.

American students are eligible for a six-month work permit through Council (CIEE) to work in New Zealand between April 1st and October 21st. People between the ages of eighteen and 30 years may be eligible for a working holiday visa of up to twelve months through BUNAC USA. CCUSA runs a three-month work experience programme from June to September. A similar scheme operates in Canada through Travel CUTS branches.

Useful addresses

BUNAC USA: PO Box 430, Southbury, CT 06488, USA; ☎203-264 0901; fax: 203-264 0251; e-mail: enquiries@bunacusa.org; internet: www.bunacusa.org.

CIEE (Council) USA: 633 Third Avenue, 20th Floor, New York, NY 10017-6706; ☎tollfree: 1800 40 STUDY; fax: 1212 822 2779; internet: www.ciee.org.

John Mahon: New Zealand Visas, P.O. 1, Nantwich, Cheshire CW5 7PB; ☎01270-626626; fax 01270-626226; john@visas-australia.com. Also in Dublin: 2nd Floor, 13 Aston Quay, Dublin 2; ☎01- 6795452; fax 01-6795459. New Zealand Visas (www.newzealandvisas.com) can arrange a New Zealand working holiday visa for a service charge of £15 also a site (www.etavisas.com) that will issue and e-mail a copy of the visa for £5.

New Zealand Information, Immigration and Visa Inquiries in the USA and UK:

New Zealand Consulate General USA: Suite 1150, 12400 Wilshire Boulevard, Los Angeles, CA 90025; ☎310-207 1605; fax: 310-207 3605.

New Zealand Embassy USA: 37 Observatory Circle NW, Washington DC 20008; ☎202-328 4848; fax: 202-667 5227; internet: www.nzemb.org.

The New Zealand High Commission UK: 2nd Floor, New Zealand House, 80 Haymarket, London, SW1Y 4TQ; ☎020-7930 8422; fax: 020-7839 4580; e-mail: www.newzealandhc.org.uk; internet: www.nzembassy.com.

The New Zealand Immigration Service UK: 3rd Floor New Zealand House, 80 Haymarket, London, SW1Y 4TQ; ☎09069 100 100 (calls charged at £1.00 per minute); internet: (www.immigration.govt.nz).

The New Zealand Trade Development Board UK: 2nd Floor, New Zealand House, 80 Haymarket, London, SW1Y 4TQ; ☎020-7913 0380; fax: 020-7839 4580; internet: www.tradenz.govt.nz.

Information for British Citizens in New Zealand:

British High Commission: 44 Hill Street, PO Box 1812, Wellington; ☎(04) 472 6049; fax: (04) 471 1974; internet: www.brithighcomm.org.nz.

Information for American Citizens in New Zealand:

Consulate General of the United States of America: 3rd Floor, Citibank Building, 23 Custom Street, Private Bag 92022, Auckland; ☎(09) 303 2724; fax: (09) 316 0870.

Embassy of the United States of America: PO Box 1190, 29 Fitzherbert Terrace, Thorndon, Wellington; ☎(04) 462 6000; fax: (04) 478 1701.

John Mahon: New Zealand Visas, P O Box 1, Nantwich, Cheshire CW5 7PB; ☎01270-626626; fax 01270-626226; john@visas-australia.com. Also in Dublin: 2nd Floor, 13 Aston Quay, Dublin 2; ☎01- 6795452; fax 01-6795459. New Zealand Visas (www.newzealandvisas.com) can arrange a New Zealand working holiday visa; for a service charge of £15; also a site (www.etavisas.com) that will issue and e-mail a copy of the tourist visa for £5.

SETTING UP HOME

Typical New Zealand house prices can be ascertained from the property section of some New Zealand newspapers. The main newspapers can be read online, see www.nzherald.co.nz (Auckland), www.evpost.co.nz (Wellington), www.press.co.nz (Christchurch) and www.odt.co.nz (Otago). More detailed advertisements can be found in New Zealand real estate magazines. Information may also be obtained from the Real Estate Institute of New Zealand's website (www.reinz.org.nz).

Immigration consultants may also offer advice on buying properties. The property market in New Zealand's main cities is currently quite lively as a result of low interest rates and improving economic prospects. Auckland and Wellington are the most expensive places to buy houses, but outside the main cities property prices are considerably cheaper.

Most New Zealand houses are detached, single storey houses on individual plots of land known as 'sections' (the term 'bungalow' to describe such a house is not common). The average New Zealand home consists of three bedrooms, a living room and dining room, kitchen, laundry and bathroom. The standard size of the New Zealand section used to be a quarter of an acre, but as urban property prices have risen in recent years, subdivisions have become more common and new houses are being built on much smaller sites. The average size of new houses is now smaller and more compact at just under 170 square metres. Although the vast majority of houses are still separate units, in recent years multi-unit developments have become more common, particularly in the big cities.

For most people, the decision about where to live is influenced first and foremost by employment prospects. New immigrants are most likely to buy houses in either Auckland or Wellington. In both cities the residential areas are mostly suburban and it is most common for people to commute by car into the city centre to work. Each suburb has its own particular character and prices can also vary considerably between areas for reasons as diverse as mere fashion or, in the case of hilly areas, related to the amount of sunshine that different parts enjoy, or the view it affords. In Auckland, for example, your property is worth more if it has a view of the harbour or Rangitoto Island. It is worth looking at the less fashionable areas, where first homeowners and young families often buy. If you are aiming at the cheaper end of the market, you will get more house for your dollar.

If you have children, your choice may be influenced by proximity to schools. The location, however, does not make a lot of difference to the standard of education on offer. Inner city schools perform as well as suburban schools on the whole. Rural schools achieve slightly lower academic results than city schools but have the advantage of smaller class sizes and better pastoral care. The best idea is to visit schools in the area and see what you think of the atmosphere. Now that school zoning has been abolished, you are free to select the school of your preference.

How do New Zealanders Live?

New Zealand has a high level of home ownership, with nearly three-quarters of dwellings being owner-occupied. New Zealanders tend to be quite house-proud, and spend a lot of time on home improvements and gardening. The average standard of housing is high. Household services such as water, electricity and sewerage are almost universal. Over 98% of all homes have colour TVs, most have videos, and around a third have dishwashers.

Of those who are living in rented homes, a quarter live in state houses rented from Housing New Zealand, while the majority lease housing from private landlords or companies. Rental accommodation is usually provided unfurnished except for ovens, and sometimes fridges and washing machines. Local authorities do not play a major role in providing housing.

The majority of households are made up of just one family. Amongst Maori and Pacific Island communities, where extended kinship links are important and because average incomes amongst these groups tend to be lower, households are more likely to include more than one family or extended family members. Even amongst Maori and Pacific Island homes though, one-family households are the most common. The average number of occupants per dwelling is 2.7 people.

Levels of second home ownership are also quite high. Many New Zealand families own what is known as a 'bach' (pronounced 'batch' rather than after the composer) or 'crib'. Bach is the North Island term, while the word crib is only used in the South Island. These are usually small holiday cottages near a lake or by the sea. The bach is a great New Zealand institution. These mostly unpretentious and comfortable dwellings are often furnished with various items discarded from the family home, and provide the perfect way for families to 'get away from it all' with the minimum of planning.

Buying a House in New Zealand

Non-New Zealanders can buy property of less than one acre without any bureaucratic formalities, but property purchases over an acre require the permission of the District Land Registrar or the Land Valuation Tribunal. However as most immigrants buy a house once they have been granted permanent residency, this restriction is not normally relevant.

Finding a property

Most people begin either by approaching a local real estate agent or searching in free weekly property newspapers in their desired location. A good paper to try is the *Property Press* (PO Box 99772, Newmarket, Auckland; ☎(09) 524 0491) which is freely available in inner city areas. Daily newspapers also carry property advertisements.

There are many types of property on offer, although the variety is not as great as in countries where architecture of many periods co-exists. European style architecture only has a short history in New Zealand and the typical period house is a wooden Victorian villa. This type is very popular with the do-it-yourself set as a renovation project. Most older houses were made of wood because of the risk of earthquake. The standard New Zealand house of the post-war period is a three bedroom, brick single-storey building on a large section. Before this, houses were generally built with a northern hemisphere model in mind and thus did not always make the most of the New Zealand climate. Modern houses are designed to capture the sun and to make the most of outdoor living during the New Zealand summer, with decks and sliding doors to blur the indoor/outdoor distinction. Because of rising inner city land prices there is a growing trend towards building town houses and apartment blocks. Town houses are compact units, often multi-level, usually built as part of group on one site. In the suburbs, where land is cheaper, you can find modern mansions with swimming pools, en suite bathrooms, separate living rooms and dining rooms, all on a huge site. Often these homes also have separate living areas and bathrooms for the children. At the other end of the budget spectrum, you will find houses advertised as 'the handyman's dream' or 'needing TLC' (tender loving care), which is real estate speak for a dwelling in dire need of repair. This type of property brings a glint to the eye of the home handyman who seems to lurk under the skin of most New Zealand males and quite a few females. If your acquaintance with nails is confined to those on your digits, then you should probably avoid this type of thing and look for something a more immediately habitable. On the other hand, inner city Victorian villas can still be picked up relatively cheaply if you are prepared to spend the money and the time on renovations and, once 'done up', they make very desirable homes.

Useful Addresses

As there are such a large number of real estate agents operating in New Zealand it is impossible to list them all here. Many companies and offices are listed on the internet. To find one in your area try *Harcourts Real Estate* (www.harcourts.co.nz or e-mail: enquiries@harcourts.co.nz) or *L. J. Hooker* (www.ljh.co.nz or e-mail: enquiries@ljh.co.nz). Other useful websites include real estate agent listings on the internet at www.piperpat.co.nz and the Real Estate Institute of New Zealand online at www.reinz.org.nz.

New Zealand Real Estate Agents:

Auckland
Auckland City Real Estate Professionals: ANZ Bank Building, cnr Ponsonby Rd and Pompellier Tce, PO Box 47680, Ponsonby; ☎(09) 360 2333; e-mail: ross.brader@xtra.co.nz.

Hamilton
Hamilton City Real Estate: ☎(07) 854 1606; e-mail: sales@hamiltoncity.co.nz; internet: www.hamiltoncity.co.nz/realestate.

Waikato Real Estate Limited: ☎(07) 838 9988; fax: (07) 838 2437; e-mail: michael@waikatorealty.co.nz.

Wellington
Wellington Real Estate: freephone in NZ: 0800 427 794; e-mail: kevinmck@voyager.co.nz; internet: www.wellington-homes.co.nz.

Guardian First National Limited: 20 Johnsonville Road, Johnsonville, Wellington; ☎(04) 478 1620; fax: (04) 478 4612; e-mail: johnsonville@guardianfirst.co.nz; internet: www.guardianfirstnational.co.nz.

Christchurch
Gillman Group: ☎(03) 377 0419; fax: (03) 377 0511; e-mail: gillmans@gillmans.co.nz;

internet: www.realenz.net/gillmangroup.

Dunedin
Metro Realty: 308 Highgate, Roslyn, Dunedin; ☎(03) 477 6838; fax: (03) 477 6869; e-mail: metro-realty@xtra.co.nz; internet: www.metrorealty.co.nz.

Miscellaneous Useful Addresses
Directmoving.com (USA): ☎331-4215 7500 or 331-4215 7507; fax: 331-4215 7505; e-mail: expat@directmoving.com; internet: www.directmoving.com/expat.
Relocations International: 34 Douglas Street, Auckland; ☎(09) 378 9888; fax: (09) 378 8072; e-mail: gspeed@reloc.co.nz; internet: www.reloc.co.nz. Wellington office: 101-103 Molesworth Street, Wellington; ☎(04) 479 3765; fax: (04) 479 3769; e-mail: julia@reloc-wgtn.co.nz.

TABLE 17	AVERAGE HOUSE PRICES BY REGION
District	**House Price**
Northland	$135,000
Auckland	$249,000
Waikato/Bay of Plenty	$158,000
Hawke's Bay	$132,500
Manawatu/Wanganui	$107,000
Taranaki	$105,000
Wellington	$185,000
Nelson/Marlborough	$150,000
Canterbury/Westland	$142,000
Otago	$90,000
Southland	$85,000
Average for New Zealand	$175,000

Source: Real Estate Institute.

PURCHASING AND CONVEYANCING PROCEDURES

Buying a property is less complicated in New Zealand than in many other countries. Establishing clear title is generally straightforward because there are fewer complications like cross-leasing and leasehold properties. As a result you do not get chains of prospective buyers waiting for the next person in the chain to organise the sale of their house. Nor are there problems of establishing who actually owns the property in question.

When you wish to buy a property, you need to obtain the free copy of *Real Estate* magazine published by the combined local real estate firms. This has a photo of each property, relevant information, and details of the estate agents involved. You may attend an 'open home' (which means you turn up at that address at the time specified), or you can arrange a private visit with the estate agent. The agent is working for the seller, and receives a commission for the sale from them, but must present the property fairly to the buyer. It's possible to deal with several agents at once, as many estate agents have sharing arrangements over the commission for the sale.

It's sensible to have a solicitor check the title details when you come to sign the agreement to buy the property. A solicitor would also be useful in terms of arranging to get a Valuer's Report should you need it, or a Land Information Memorandum Report. A LIM report establishes the town planning requirements and anything that could affect the property, and is available from the local authority.

Most home-owners in New Zealand have a mortgage from a bank or financial institution. Most commercial and industrial properties are leased, as this provides an annual cost for taxation purposes. Your agreement to purchase a property can be subject to obtaining mortgage finance or the sale of your current New Zealand property. Your solicitor's charge may add as much as $1200 to the cost of the house but it could save you from making an expensive mistake. The market is not regulated so you can ask around for a reasonably priced solicitor. A useful magazine published by a network of independent legal firms is *Lawlink* (PO Box 6197, Wellesley Street, Auckland; ☎(09) 300 5470; fax: (09) 309 5113) which is also online (www.lawlink.co.nz/resources).

FINANCE

Borrowing Money to Buy a Property

Mortgages are the standard method of financing house purchasing in New Zealand. The majority of properties have a mortgage on them. If you wish to apply for a mortgage, or any other finance, it will be helpful to have records from your previous bank showing repayments, pay slips, references showing your work history, evidence of any other property that you own, etc. Your solicitor will help and this should be discussed before you make an offer to purchase a property. Interest rates are currently between 6.10% and 7.99%. Banks are the main lenders. Building societies used to be separate institutions from banks but since deregulation in the 1980s they have been allowed to provide the same services and most have now converted themselves to banks. The banks have responded to the competition to provide mortgages by offering more flexible repayment terms.

Up to 80-90% of the purchase price can be borrowed, but if you borrow more than 80% the bank may require some form of mortgage insurance (see below). The maximum amount you may borrow is not always directly related to your salary but you will be expected to provide information on your monthly income as part of a hypothetical budgeting exercise and repayments would not normally be expected to be more than 30% of your income. If you are borrowing more than 60% of the purchase price, the bank may require a Valuer's Report.

Mortgage and Associated Costs

Your bank will charge mortgage application costs of around 1% of the value of the mortgage. The Land Transfer Registration fee is $120, although if a lawyer acts on your behalf this fee will come out of general legal disbursements. There are two types of insurance. Mortgage protection insurance is more comprehensive, and it repays the mortgage in the event of your death. Mortgage risk insurance will pay the mortgage for a fixed period if you lose your regular income. There is no government benefit to help you pay the costs of a mortgage.

Repayment Conditions

Repayments are usually made on a monthly basis, but can be fortnightly. The usual term of mortgage used to be 25 years, but it is increasingly common for people to arrange shorter term mortgages with commensurably higher monthly repayments. Most banks will not approve of a mortgage arrangement that requires you to repay more than one third of your monthly income. Interest rates can be either fixed or floating. There are three main types of mortgage: table, straight-line or interest only. In a table mortgage you pay equal monthly (or fortnightly) payments of interest and capital over the whole term of the mortgage. In a straight-line mortgage, monthly payments start high because you pay fixed amounts of principal, plus the amount of interest you have accrued that month. At the beginning, there will be a lot of interest to pay off, but this will decrease as the principle is repaid resulting in decreasing monthly payments.

The third type is an interest-only mortgage, which is exactly what it sounds like. You pay a higher rate of interest on a monthly basis, which tends to add up to the same sum, more or less, as a repayment mortgage, but at the end of the whole term the original sum borrowed is effectively written off. The banks are quite flexible about changing the repayment conditions once you have entered into the mortgage, for example increasing or decreasing the size of monthly payments or switching to fortnightly payment intervals. You can even alter the type of mortgage or transfer it to another property.

RENTING PROPERTY

Most immigrants rent property while they look for a house. You can arrange to rent a furnished apartment before you arrive in New Zealand through an immigration consultant or through some of the newspapers for intending migrants : *New Zealand Outlook* and *Destination New Zealand*, see Chapter Two *Residence and Entry Regulations* for subscription details, or visit www.emigrate.com/newzealand online). Some travel agents will also provide assistance in finding a temporary place to stay. This type of arrangement tends to be more expensive than finding a rental house yourself, but it has the advantage of the accommodation being ready and waiting for you as soon as you step off the plane. It will certainly be cheaper than staying in a hotel while you are house hunting.

The cost of rented accommodation is quite moderate, although you can expect to pay more if you want something more than just a typical three-bedroom house. Rental properties are advertised in the daily newspapers - mostly on Saturdays, but some on Wednesdays as well. Cheaper houses can be hard to find in towns with a large student population. If you are looking for cheaper accommodation, February/ March is a bad time to look as it is the start of the university year and you will be competing with students looking for flats. However, many students leave their flats in mid to late November, so this can be a good time to find a bargain. You can also use a Real Estate letting agency, but you may have to pay as much as the equivalent of one month's rent as a fee for them to find you a suitable flat. The majority of privately let houses are unfurnished, although they may contain the odd piece of furniture. Real estate agents are good places to inquire about furnished properties.

Tenancy Agreements

There are two types of tenancy agreements, fixed term and periodic. With a periodic agreement, the tenancy continues until either side gives notice. In standard letting contracts, the tenant must give at least 21 days written notice that they want to end the tenancy, and the landlord must give 90 days notice. The landlord is allowed to give only 42 days notice if they or their family members are moving into the house themselves, or if they have sold the house. In a fixed term tenancy the duration is fixed at the start of the letting period and cannot be changed except by agreement of both parties. Most tenancy agreements are sorted out between the landlord and the tenant using a standard tenancy agreement available from the Tenancy Services section of the Ministry of Housing. It is not usually necessary to have a lawyer check the agreement. Tenancy Services are there to help in case of disputes between landlords and tenants and they will also give you information about your rights and responsibilities as tenants. The landlord is required to maintain the premises but tenants are responsible for any damage caused by misuse or abuse.

Rental Costs

Tenants are usually required to pay a bond or deposit to the landlord in case of damage to the property. A bond can be the equivalent of four weeks rent, but is more likely to be two weeks rental. These bonds used to be held by the landlord, but as a result of disputes between tenants and landlords over the withholding of bond money, the bond is now passed on to the Bond Processing Centre, part of Tenancy Services. At the end of the tenancy, the bond is refunded to you less any agreed unpaid rent or other amounts (such as bills or repairs) owing to the landlord. Tenancy Services act as arbitrators between tenants and landlords in disagreements over bonds and other disputes such as rental arrears and damage to property.

Useful Addresses

Tenancy Services, Advice/Mediation & Enquiries: ☎0800 836 262; e-mail: info@minhousing.govt.nz; internet: www.minhousing.govt.nz/tenancy/.

Citizens Advice Bureau (National Office): Level 7, 75 Ghuznee St, Wellington; ☎0800 367 222 (0800 FOR CAB) or (04) 382 8759; fax: (04) 382 8647; e-mail: admin@cab.org.nz; internet: www.cab.org.nz. Citizens Advice offers free confidential advice on housing, health, legal and consumer problems, employment and budgeting. It has over 90 offices throughout New Zealand.

Community Law Centres (National Office): 281 Madras Street, PO Box 2912, Christchurch; ☎(03) 366 6870; fax: (03) 366 6631; e-mail: admin@comlaw-chch.org.nz. Community Law Centres provides free confidential legal advice and is staffed by solicitors and law students. Contact the Christchurch office for details of your local branch.

Land Information New Zealand: internet: www.linz.govt.nz. Government department providing land and property information. Website includes government policy, maps, valuation rates, and a searchable database.

Rates

Each local council in New Zealand levies a tax based on the value of your property to fund local amenities and services. Road maintenance, sewage disposal, water supply, libraries, park maintenance and street lighting are all paid for by your council rates. The value of your property and hence the amount of rates you pay is decided by Valuation New Zealand. Rates are included in the rent of rental properties.

INSURANCE AND WILLS

Wills

If at the time of your death you have a permanent place of residence in New Zealand or you are living in New Zealand for more than half the year, you are considered by New Zealand law to be a resident. This means that any property you own in New Zealand is subject to New Zealand laws if you die intestate. It makes sense therefore to make a will after you have bought a house. Property disposed under a New Zealand will is not subject to inheritance tax. If you are retaining assets in your home country, you should check with your solicitor to see that your New Zealand will is recognised there. Property in other countries is normally subject to the inheritance laws of those countries.

You do not have to use a lawyer or trustee company to draw up a will in New Zealand but it does not cost much and may save problems later. Certain procedures must be followed for a will to be valid, and the testator must sign it in the presence of two non-beneficiary witnesses. Trustee companies (including the **Public Trust Office**: ☎0800 371471; e-mail: info@publictrust.co.nz; internet: www.publictrust.co.nz) will draw up a will for around $80.

Insurance

Taking out insurance on a new property is a sensible precaution. Most mortgage lenders will probably require you insure your new house. There are different types of cover available. Multi-risk policies (called accidental damage policies) provide blanket cover for all losses unless specifically excluded. Defined risk policies, as the name suggests, list what risks the policy provides cover for. This type of policy is less costly but accidental damage policies are probably a better option. Your house can either be insured for its indemnity value, or replacement value. The indemnity value is the depreciated or current market value of your house, excluding the value of the land. It does not replace with new, nor would it cover the cost of rebuilding, but you should be able to buy a similar house. The replacement value can be open-ended or fixed sum. The difference between this and indemnity value is that there is no deduction for depreciation. Open-ended replacement value means the insurer will pay the full cost of repairing or rebuilding as new. Fixed sum replacement value means that the insurer will pay up to the agreed sum. Typical premiums exclude the value of the land and can be reduced by increasing the excess, or installing burglar and fire alarms. Insurance for your home will cost anywhere between $350-$550, depending on where you live and the company you choose. Contents insurance varies according to what you wish to cover, but the average is around $250-$500. Premiums are cheaper outside the larger cities, and most expensive in the Auckland region.

It makes sense to take out household contents insurance with the same firm as you have your house insurance with. You should get a discount for having both types of insurance with the same company and it will save arguments over who is responsible for a claim. Again you can either get a multi-risk or a defined risk policy for either indemnity or replacement value. If you have an accidental damage policy you can sometimes buy an extension to cover your possessions outside of your house, for example, personal sports equipment.

One unique feature of buying household insurance in New Zealand is earthquake damage insurance. Because New Zealand is prone to earthquakes, a special government scheme exists to provide insurance cover against them. When you take out a household insurance policy that includes cover against fire (i.e., a total replacement policy) you also automatically gain cover in the case of earthquake, landslide, volcanic or tsunami damage. In fact, it is the New Zealand Government that underwrites the risk of earthquakes because the potential cost of a major earthquake in a big city is too great for commercial insurance companies to handle. Your insurance company will charge you a compulsory disaster insurance premium which they pass on to the Earthquake Commission (PO Box 311, Wellington; ☎0800 652 333; internet: www.eqc.govt.nz). The maximum amount the Commission will pay out is $100,000 or the amount for which you have insured your home, (whichever is lower) and $20,000 for personal belongings or the amount for which you have insured them. (Again they will pay out the lower amount). The coverage is fairly basic and does not extend, for example, to motor vehicles, boats, jewellery, or works of art. Nor will the Commission pay for any indirect costs arising out of an earthquake such as, for example, the cost of having to stay in rented accommodation. Top-up cover with an insurance company will cover the items noted above which EQCover does not include, and will also cover you for the value of your house above the $100,000 covered by the government. Earthquakes big enough to cause serious damage are rare.

UTILITIES

Services such as electricity, telephones, water and sewerage are just about universal in New Zealand. Holiday cottages in some of the remotest areas may not be on mainline electricity and commonly will have a septic tank rather than being on mainline sewerage, but the average family home comes provided with all services. People moving into a house or flat need to arrange for the electricity or gas and telephone to be connected. An agreement for the supply is signed between the supplier and the tenant, as utilities are not the responsibility of the landlord. Credit references from your previous power, gas and telephone companies will be helpful in setting up your New Zealand accounts. Most government departments providing commercial services were turned into State Owned Enterprises (SOEs) in the late 1980s. They were set up like commercial companies, although as the name suggests they remained publicly owned, and were given commercial targets. The change in performance between the new SOEs and the old government departments was dramatic. When telecommunications were run by the Post Office, average installation time was at least six weeks. Now it seldom takes more than two days. The creation of SOEs has also brought with it some competition in the utilities marketplace. Rival telephone companies are now offering price wars on toll calls, and a freer market exists for some utilities.

Electricity

Most of New Zealand's electricity supply is generated through hydro-electric schemes on the main rivers. Hydro-energy has the advantage of being cheap, clean and renewable. Most of the power is generated in the South Island on the rivers draining the mountains of the Southern Alps. Bills come once a month, and an average monthly bill for a three-bedroom house would be around $100-$150. There is usually an initial administration charge for setting up a new account, which is around $90.

New Zealand supplies alternating current at 240 volts, 50 hertz. Equipment designed for a 110 volt system will require a transformer, but bear in mind that some specialised equipment designed for a current other than 50 hertz may not work properly even with a transformer. Any appliances you bring with you may require new plugs. It is important to also consider the fact that you may not be able to find parts or repair services for certain electrical items if they are uncommon in New Zealand. Leave behind your telephones, faxes and telecommunications equipment - it may not work with the local network, and again you may not be able to find anyone to repair it if something goes wrong. New Zealand is a high-tech nation, and the latest electronic equipment will be readily available there.

The privatisation of electrical utilities in New Zealand has caused its own problems. The city of Auckland made international news in February 1998 when the electricity supply to the inner city was cut off for several weeks. The city's power supplier, Mercury Energy, did not sufficiently maintain its cables to the city, and, during the especially hot summer, the four 110 kilovolt cables melted simultaneously. Businesses were forced to close, and residents were evacuated. Although the city retailers claimed they were losing $10 million a day from the power cuts, Mercury Energy would not take responsibility for the disaster, and blamed the collapse of the cables on a freak of nature. The rest of the country, however, seemed to enjoy Auckland's plight, and Wellington and Dunedin tourist boards advertised the 'power' and 'energy' of their cities in Auckland newspapers.

Gas

Household gas supply is not universally available. Natural gas is produced off the Taranaki coast and piped to most areas of the North Island. It is available as far north of Auckland as Whangarei, in Wellington and on the East Coast in Gisborne, Napier and Hastings. In areas which do not have a household supply, bottled gas is available. In the South Island most gas is of the bottled variety except in Dunedin and parts of Christchurch. The local supply company can be found in the front of the *Yellow Pages*. Before they will connect your property, the gas company will require you to fill in an application for the supply of gas and to pay a bond of around $100.

Water

New Zealand water is clean and quite drinkable, although it tastes better in some areas of the country than others. In Auckland and Hamilton it can have an unpleasant chlorine taste. Most people seem to put up with it, although the bottled water market is growing. People building homes and renovating kitchens now often have a water filter installed with the kitchen taps. Water shortages are not normally a problem, although Canterbury and Auckland have suffered droughts in recent summers, and water conservation is often called for in other areas such as Hawke's Bay. In some

2

areas local councils charge for the water supply and your supply will be on a meter, in others the cost of water connection and supply is included in your annual rates bill.

Waste Services

Rubbish is disposed of in two ways; the local council collects everyone's rubbish bags once a week and residents can take their rubbish to the local 'tip'. Most local authorities charge for rubbish collection (meaning that only official rubbish bags, or bags bearing a correct sticker, will be collected) and for use of the local rubbish dump (usually depending on the size of the load you want to dispose of). In Auckland there is an inorganic rubbish collection once every month, when large unwanted household items, such as furniture, appliances and any other number of objects will be removed for your convenience. Contact your local council for information.

Telephone and Internet

There are many competing providers of telecommunications services in New Zealand, and the largest are Telecom New Zealand, Clear Communications and Telstra-Saturn. The 'local call' network is mainly operated by Telecom, although there are several competing firms in this market now, as well as in the area of toll calls, both national and international. Long distance or international services are provided to New Zealand by about twenty different telecommunications companies, and this number includes a number of 'callback operators' that usually connect calls through the USA. Pricing plans are often extremely competitive and it is a good idea to compare all your options before you make any decisions. There are often particularly good deals for off-peak international calls, including a flat charge for as long as you can talk which is sometimes as low as $8. It is also sometimes possible to nominate a country or overseas telephone numbers so that you can pay just a fixed fee (the amount depending on current promotions) for any off-peak call to that number or country.

Telephone books (White and Yellow pages) are supplied free by Telecom. There are several versions - each one covers a particular area or region. Most of the country is covered by both analogue and digital mobile communications networks, and 98% of New Zealand homes have a telephone.

An estimated 47% of New Zealanders have a computer at home, and over 25% have an internet connection. On most surveys New Zealand is ranked in the world's top five countries for internet connections. It is estimated that the New Zealand internet subscriber base will be around 1.5 million by 2004.

Telecom, the SOE that took over running telecommunications from the Post Office, was sold off in 1990 to a consortium of two US phone companies and two local companies. The investment programme was part of the process of revamping the company prior to selling it. As a result, New Zealand's rather antiquated phone system was given a much-needed overhaul. At the same time the industry was deregulated to allow competitors into domestic supply and provision of phone units. Deregulation has led to improvements in customer service.

The downside of telecommunications privatisation is that, despite being a private company, Telecom has an effective monopoly in many areas of telecommunications services, because it owns the network. There is no industry regulator to check that the prices Telecom charges consumers are fair. Despite competition in the long distance calling market, some industry commentators argue that toll calls are still too expensive.

In most areas you are obliged to hire your phone line from Telecom as they retain a monopoly on the provision of the network, and residential line rental costs $36.34 per month, which allows you unlimited local calls at no extra charge. It is anticipated that Telecom's line rental charges will shortly be raised, perhaps to around $39.95. Telecom no longer supplies rental telephones, but you can buy a telephone relatively cheaply at any number of retailers. To get your phone connected, Telecom will require proof of who you are, name, date of birth, postal address, physical address of the phone, previous addresses, your employment history and next of kin. It takes about 48 hours to connect a new number. The connection fee is $61.88 to reconnect an existing line, for both residential and business customers, and you can choose to have up to one week in between disconnection and connection. However, if you transfer to another property on the same day, the cost is only $30. If an installer is required to do the connection, as opposed to a remote connection, a further visit fee is charged, and the installer will quote this on the day.

Telecom has a free call number (called 'freephone') for businesses with a prefix of 0800. This enables customers to call free from anywhere in New Zealand. Freephone numbers for Clear Communications start with 0508.

Local calls are free for residential customers, but there is a small charge (50c) for telephoning directory enquiries on 018. You are entitled to two enquiries per call for this charge. However, Telecom's White Pages (alphabetical residents and companies listings) are on the internet at www.whitepages.co.nz, and the Yellow Pages at www.yellowpages.co.nz. The costs of toll calls are explained at the start of the phone directory. Peak time is 8am to noon Monday to Friday, and off-peak is 10pm to 8am weekdays and 10pm Fridays through to 8am Mondays. Long distance calls are slightly cheaper on Clear Communications. You do not require any special equipment or numbers to use Clear. Your phone company may be able to arrange special deals for your off-peak calls to frequently called international numbers if you ask them to.

Useful Contact Details

Clear Communications: ☎ 0508 888 800; fax: 0508 888 801; e-mail: question@clear.co.nz; internet: www.clear.co.nz.

Telecom New Zealand: ☎123; e-mail: customer-service@telecom.co.nz; internet: www.telecom.co.nz.

Telstra-Saturn: freephone: 0800 299 300 or 0800 949 000; internet: www.telstra.co.nz.

REMOVALS

Packing up your possessions and getting them to the other side of the world is an expensive business. There are basically two ways of shipping your household goods to New Zealand, depending on whether the removal consists of a small or large amount. Smaller removals are usually grouped with other people's small removal lots destined for the same port, so they can be shipped in shared containers. Be aware of this when choosing a mover - if you pick a company that does not regularly handle large numbers of this type of removal, your belongings could be delayed for quite some time while they wait for other consignments to fill up the container. Larger removals are usually shipped as whole container loads, which means that they are packed up and sent off immediately on the first vessel sailing to New Zealand. Transit time can take as long as twelve weeks if you are using a shared container. For a full-container removal it will probably take around six to eight weeks.

When deciding what to bring, remember that the New Zealand electricity supply will probably be different to what you are used to. New Zealand supplies alternating current at 240 volts, 50 hertz. Having your existing appliances adapted to suit New Zealand supply may work out more costly than replacing them in the end and not worth the trouble. Your removal company should be able to advise you on these points. On the other hand, good quality household furniture, fine china and glass will generally be worth bringing with you.

Most people who are planning to move overseas for the first time make the mistake of assuming that an international move is the same as a normal domestic one. You should use a specialist international mover. Representatives who will visit you to assess your removal requirements can offer advice regarding items you may be undecided about shifting. If you know of anyone who has shifted their household, ask them about their shipping company or, if you are dealing with an immigration consultancy, find out which companies other emigrants have used successfully. You should check whether they are members of an international removals trade association and if the association offers a payment guarantee scheme if the removals company goes bust while your goods are still in transit. Two well-known ones are the Association of International Removers and the British Association of Removers. When it comes to comparing quotes from different companies, be sure to get quotes in writing based on the same list of goods. Freighting cost quotes for a shared container will be based on the cubic volume of your goods, so it is essential to make sure the removals estimator knows exactly what you want to take as any last minute extras will cost more. In the case of a full container quote, the price per container is standard, but you should get a quote for the costs of any excess goods in case they do not all fit in one container. Make sure you know the type of container they are quoting, as volumes differ between insulated and non-insulated containers. If the quote is based on a shared container load, make sure it includes an estimate of total volume of your goods. If you have only a small amount of effects to move, it will probably be cheaper to pack them yourself. There are few important points:

- You should pack your possessions in stout containers, using a material such as polystyrene or paper.
- Most removals companies will provide suitable containers.
- Goods packed with straw or chaff will not pass New Zealand agricultural quarantine regulations.
- You should label baggage carefully, inside and out.

Always wait until you have received and checked a written estimate before booking your removal company. You should have written confirmation of several points, including the following:

- the list of items to be shipped;
- a cubic volume;
- special packing requirements for particular items;
- all door-to-door costs including customs and terminal charges, unloading etc.; and
- delivery instructions showing the name of your destination city or town in New Zealand.

Insurance for the Move

Insuring your possessions during the move is critical. Shipping firms will usually offer marine insurance as part of the service but you need to check the small print carefully. The cost of marine insurance may not be included in your initial estimate because this is assessed on the value of your possessions. Make sure that the policy is all risks and that it covers any storage period either in the UK or in New Zealand. If the insurance company has offices in New Zealand, any claims are likely to be settled much more quickly than if they have no New Zealand base. While rates quoted are often very similar, the level of cover can vary so make sure you obtain a copy of the terms and conditions and compare them carefully. Ask for a copy of the insurance company's proposal form well in advance so that you have plenty of time to ask any questions you may have and also to assess the values that you are planning to declare.

Useful Addresses

Abels International Moving Services: Wimbledon Avenue, Brandon, Suffolk IP27 0NZ; ☎01842-816600; fax: 01842-813613; e-mail: international@abels.co.uk; internet: www.abels.co.uk.

Air New Zealand Cargo (LA): 5721 West Imperial Highway, Los Angeles, CA 90045; ☎310-646 9891 or 800 421 5913; fax: 310-568 8620; internet: www.airnz.com.

Air New Zealand Cargo (Chicago): Building 517, Suite 400, O'Hare international Airport, Chicago, IL 60666; ☎847-671 6226; fax: 847-671 0071; internet: www.airnz.com.

Air New Zealand Cargo (New York): Building 15, East Hangar Road, JFK International Airport, Jamaica, NY 11430; ☎718-244 1333; fax: 718-244 1334; internet: www.airnz.com.

Air New Zealand Cargo (UK): London Heathrow; ☎020-8751 5000; fax: 020-8751 3333, internet: www.airnz.co.uk/cargo.

Allied International: specialists in international removals, check your local phone directory for an office near you, or find one online at www.alliedintl.com. The website for New Zealand is www.alliedpickfords.co.nz.

Avalon Overseas Movers: contact Noel Glavin; freephone: 08080 282 566; e-mail: avalon@transeuro.com; internet: www.avalon-overseas.com.

The Baggage Company: Galleon House, Kerry Avenue, Purfleet Industrial Park, Aveley, Essex RM15 4YA, England; ☎01708-867440; fax: 01708-680050; e-mail: the baggage.company@virgin.net; internet: www.thebaggagecompany.co.uk.

Crystal International: 1901 Camino Vida Roble Suite 206, Carlsbad, CA 92008; ☎800-307 8900 or 760-431 0266; e-mail:info@crystalinternational.com.

Directmoving.com: ☎331 4215 7500 or 331 4215 7507; fax: 331 4215 7505; e-mail: expat@directmoving.com; internet: www.directmoving.com/expat.

Excess International Movers: based in Auckland (☎(09) 275 7049), Wellington (☎(04) 499 8065) and Christchurch (☎(03) 357 9099). Freephone within New Zealand: 0800 500 599; e-mail: mail@worldwideremovals.com; internet: www.excess-bag.co.nz or www.worldwideremovals.com.

PSS International Removals: Head Office, 8 Redcross Way, London SE1 9HR; ☎020-7407 6606; fax: 020-7407 6704; e-mail: sales@p-s-s.co.uk; internet: www.pss.uk.com.

UTS/Unigroup Worldwide (USA): 1 United Drive, Fenton, MO 63026, St Louis, MO; ☎636-326 3100 or tollfree: 800 325 3924; fax: 636-305 2190; e-mail: david-gonzalez@unigroupworldwide.com; internet: www.unigroupworldwide.com or www.uts-international.com. Or contact the head of New Zealand removals, Rick Kehrman on ☎636-305 6032; e-mail: rick-kehrman@unigroupworldwide.com.

Customs Regulations

Information regarding the importation of household and personal effects and cars into New Zealand can be found in a series of leaflets from New Zealand Customs. New Zealand Embassies and High Commissions should have copies available, or you can obtain information on the internet (www.customs.govt.nz) or by e-mailing: feedback@customs.govt.nz. The basic principle is that if you are coming to New Zealand to take up permanent residence, you can import your household goods and car duty free. The goods must be used and not be intended for sale or commercial use. If you are a returning resident, coming back to New Zealand after an absence of more than 21 months, your household goods qualify for the duty free concession, but in the case of cars, you can only qualify for the duty free concession on the first occasion you arrive to take up residence. You are also entitled, like any visitor to New Zealand, to bring in personal effects duty free. The list of prohibited imports includes indecent articles and publications, ivory in any form, anything made from the bone of marine mammals, most weapons and some types of food. You may not bring plant material or fruit into New Zealand. The importation of firearms is strictly controlled and a Police permit is required.

Import Procedures

Provided that you qualify for the duty free exemption outlined above, importing your household goods ought to be straightforward. The complicating factor is that you and your possessions will most likely be travelling separately, you by plane and your worldly goods by sea, a process taking six weeks at minimum. You can either send off your goods well before your departure and hope that their arrival in New Zealand coincides with yours, or send them off when you leave and manage without for your first few weeks in your new country. You should make sure that your insurance policy covers any storage time, either before shipping or following delivery at the other end. If your car and possessions arrive in New Zealand before you do, you can avoid paying port storage charges by arranging for a nominee to clear them through Customs for you. The Collector of Customs at the port will require evidence of your nominee's authority to act for you and evidence that you are arriving in New Zealand for the first time to take up permanent residence. In the case of a car, additional documents proving that you have owned it for at least one year prior to departure will be required. Your nominee will be required to pay a deposit equivalent to the cost of duty on the vehicle and/or goods, which will be refunded in full once you arrive.

Whether you are picking up your goods yourself or have authorised a nominee, you need to provide Customs with an inventory of your belongings. You should be careful to thoroughly clean any garden tools or furniture, hiking boots, running shoes, or anything else that may have traces of mud or dirt on it. Your goods will be inspected by the Ministry of Agriculture and Forestry before being released to you, and they may require such items to be steam cleaned or fumigated to kill off any pests or diseases. MAF inspection charges vary depending on the consignment. If you have any queries about what types of goods you can import and the procedures contact the Collector of Customs at the port of destination (see addresses below).

New Zealand Customs; ☎*(09) 300 5399 or freephone within NZ: 0800 428 786; fax: (09) 359 6730; e-mail: feedback@customs.govt.nz; internet: www.customs.govt.nz.*
Auckland: Box 29; ☎(09) 359 6655; fax: (09) 359 6735.

Auckland International Airport: Box 73003; ☎(09) 275 9059; fax: (09) 275 5634.
Christchurch International Airport: Box 14086; ☎(03) 358 0600; fax: (03) 358 0606.
Dunedin: Private Bag 1928; ☎(03) 477 9251; fax: (03) 477 6773.
Invercargill: Box 840; ☎(03) 218 7329; fax: (03) 218 7328.
Napier: Box 440; ☎(06) 835 5799; fax: (06) 835 1298.
Nelson: Box 66; ☎(03) 548 1484; fax: (03) 546 9381.
New Plymouth: Box 136; ☎(06) 758 5721; fax: (06) 758 1441.
Tauranga: Box 5014, Mt Maunganui; ☎(07) 575 9699; fax: (07) 575 0522.
Timaru: Box 64; ☎(03) 688 9317; fax: (03) 688 4668.
Wellington: Box 2218; ☎(04) 473 6099; fax: (04) 473 7370.
Whangarei: Box 873; ☎(09) 438 2400; fax: (09) 438 2225.

Importing Pets

Getting your pets to New Zealand is going to cost as much as getting yourself there, and require every bit as much paperwork and many more vaccinations. Requirements for importing animals into New Zealand are extremely stringent, and nearly all animals except for cats and dogs are prohibited. However, if you fulfil all the pre-flight veterinary requirements, your animals may be able to go home with you when they arrive in New Zealand without requiring a quarantine period. Pets from Hawaii and the UK do not have to be quarantined, but they do need a series of tests. The length of the quarantine period required for animals arriving from other countries depends on where they have come from, but it will be at least 30 days. This is likely to cost around $1000. There are a number of firms who specialise in the air freighting of pets (for names and addresses see below) and some international removal companies also offer this service if they are shipping your household goods for you. As this involves organising an IATA approved air travel container, which must be sealed by a vet, as well as an examination immediately prior to departure, it is probably best to hand your pets over to the professionals. If you are using the services of a professional firm, it is best to contact them a few months in advance to avoid any unforeseen documentation delays. You will need to organise some of the veterinary procedures yourself, as some vaccinations have to be given six weeks prior to departure. There are a number of compulsory tests and the results of these must travel with the animals. Most firms will suggest that you leave your pets with them for the night prior to departure. An Import Health Permit must be obtained prior to the importation of dogs or cats; you must apply for this permit in writing from Import Management and Quarantine (see address below). New Zealand has quite strict laws governing the control of pets. The animals must not annoy or injure other people, and any dog which is found roaming freely can be impounded by the Dog Pound. There are laws to protect pets as well; the SPCA (Society for the Prevention of Cruelty to Animals) can take any person who has been cruel to an animal to court. You must also be aware that there are some areas, particularly near wildlife reserves, which have been designated cat-free zones due to the havoc that domestic cats have been wrecking on native bird populations. At present there are only a few of these areas, and the rules are enforced by general community consensus rather than the long arm of the law, but you should ensure that you do not unwittingly introduce a cat to such an area.

Useful Addresses

Airpets Oceanic: Willowslea Farm Kennels, Spout Lane North, Stanwell Moor, Staines, Middlesex, TW19 6BW; ☎01753-685571; fax: 01753-681655; internet: www.airpets.com.

Atwoods Pet Resorts Travel Agency: 25103 112th St E., Buckley, WA 98321, USA; ☎253-862 9454; fax: 253-862 3687.

Import Management and Quarantine: Ministry of Agriculture and Forestry, PO Box 2526, Wellington, NZ; ☎(04) 498 9624; fax: (04) 474 4312; e-mail: mulqueen@maf.govt.nz; internet: www.maf.govt.nz.

Independent Pet and Animal Transportation Association International (IPATA): Route 1, Box 747, Highway 2869, Big Sandy, Texas 75775, USA; e-mail: ipata@aol.com; internet: www.ipata.com.

Par Air Livestock Shipping Services: Stanway, Colchester, Essex CO3 5LN, UK; ☎01206-330332; fax: 01206 331277; e-mail: parair@btinternet.com; internet: www.parair.co.uk.

Pet Chauffeur: 135 East 32nd St, Suite 3G, NYC, NY 10016, USA; ☎212-696 9744; internet: www.petride.com.

Quarantine Addresses

Ministry of Agriculture and Forestry: Animal Quarantine Division, Box 2526 Wellington, NZ; ☎(04) 472 7171; fax: (04) 474 4132; e-mail: mclagganj@maf.govt.nz; internet: www.quarantine.co.nz.

Qualified Pet Services: 150 Airfield Road, Takanini, Auckland, NZ; ☎(09) 299 9539; fax: (09) 299 9539; e-mail: services@qualifiedpet.co.nz; internet: www.qualifiedpet.co.nz.

Canterbury Quarantine Services Ltd: Highfield Road, Aylesbury, PO Box 23158, Christchurch, NZ; ☎(03) 318 1279; fax: (03) 318 1289; e-mail: wumba@xtra.co.nz.

New Zealand Quarantine Stations:

Auckland: PO Box 39, Auckland; ☎(09) 303 3423; fax: (09) 303 3037.

Wellington: ASB Bank House, PO Box 12108, Wellington; ☎(04) 473 8996; fax: (04) 473 2975.

Christchurch: 14 Sir William Pickering Drive, Private Bag 4718, Christchurch; ☎(03) 358 1865; fax: (03) 358 1726.

Importing a Vehicle

If you are considering importing your car, you will obviously want to consider whether the original value of the car plus the cost of freight, port handling costs and insurance is lower than the replacement cost of the car in New Zealand. In general, European cars cost more to replace in New Zealand than their original value plus shipping costs, assuming the vehicle qualifies for duty free entry (see below for the conditions). Japanese and Asian cars are cheaper because of the commercial importation of second-hand vehicles from Japan. As a very rough guide, new cars can be purchased for between $15,000-$80,000, and second-hand cars for $2,000-$50,000. A good Japanese car will cost you around $5,000-$10,000. One source of information on second-hand car prices in New Zealand is the classified section of newspapers. You can order New Zealand motor trade magazines from *Destination New Zealand* and *New Zealand Outlook*. Some car shipping companies will also provide lists of recent New Zealand prices for common models of car.

If you are emigrating to New Zealand for the first time, you can import your car into New Zealand free of duty provided you satisfy Customs that you are importing the vehicle for your own use, that you have owned it for at least a year prior to your departure, and that you are arriving in New Zealand to take up permanent residence for the first time. You will be required to sign a deed of covenant agreeing that if you sell your car or boat within two years of importing it, you will be retrospectively liable for the duty and sales tax (GST). If your car does not qualify for duty-free entry, duty is levied at 20% of purchase price for UK made vehicles, and 30% of purchase price for other foreign cars, less depreciation. The exchange rate used in calculating the New Zealand dollar value of your car will be based on the current exchange rate at the time you clear your vehicle. The costs of shipping an average car vary depending on the size of the car and which port in New Zealand it is going to. It usually takes about six weeks. Some companies offer a cheaper option where the vehicle is not shipped in a container, but the risks of damage or theft in transit are higher. You should arrange insurance for your vehicle, whichever option you choose. Premiums are calculated on the New Zealand value of the car. Do not pack personal belongings in the car for the journey. There is a risk of pilferage, particularly if the car is not containerised during the journey, and the contents of the car will have to be declared to Customs by the shipping company or you will risk a fine.

Procedures for clearing your car through Customs in New Zealand are as follows. The vehicle will be inspected by the Ministry of Agriculture and Forestry (MAF). All used vehicles must be steam cleaned before MAF will pass them. You can have your car commercially steam cleaned before shipping but remember to keep the receipt to show to MAF in New Zealand. Some shipping companies will steam clean your car as part of the service. MAF's objective is to prevent any pests and diseases, which could endanger livestock, being brought into the country and their standards are therefore stringent. If inspectors are not satisfied that your vehicle has been thoroughly and properly cleaned, you will be required to have it done again. Your car will need to comply with New Zealand safety regulations, some of which differ from standards of other countries. Your vehicle must have front and rear seatbelts, and a high mounted rear stop light. It is a good idea to have these fitted before you leave because you will not be able to drive the car in New Zealand until it complies with local safety standards. Left-hand drive vehicles require special import permission. Apply to the Land Transport Safety Authority (7-27 Waterloo Quay, Box 2840, Wellington; ☎(04) 494 8600; internet: www.ltsa.govt.nz).

Next you will need to provide documentary evidence to the Collector of Customs that the car is yours and, if you are applying for a duty free entry, that you have owned it for at least one year prior to importing it. Such proof can include a dated receipt of purchase showing the date delivery was taken, registration papers, odometer details, evidence of the date on which you gave up the vehicle for shipping to New Zealand and your passport showing verification of permanent residency.

You cannot drive the car legally until it has a vehicle inspection certificate and is registered, so you will need to arrange for it to be transported from the port to the nearest vehicle inspection test centre. The VIC used to be called the Warrant of Fitness (WOF), and in some places testing centres still advertise them as Warrants. Once your car has passed, you take the certificate to a post office, along with the ownership documents and the importation documents, and obtain a registration certificate, sticker and number plates. All of this is likely to take a couple of days.

Useful Addresses

Anglo Pacific Shipping: ☎020-8838 8091; e-mail: info@anglopacific.co.uk; internet: www.acd73.dial.pipex.com.

Autoshippers UK: ☎0800 389 0784; internet: www.autoshippers.co.uk.

Autoshipping Co. of America: ☎800 551 2722; e-mail: info@carshipper.com; internet: www.carshipper.com or www.autotransportation.com.

PSS International Removals: Head Office, 8 Redcross Way, London SE1 9HR; ☎020-7407 6606; fax: 020-7407 6704;

e-mail: sales@p-s-s.co.uk; internet: www.pss.uk.com.

Seabridge International: Point Breeze Maritime Center II, 2310 Broening Highway, Suite 130, Baltimore, Maryland 21224; ☎410-633 0550; fax: 410- 633 0556; internet: www.seabrdge.com.

TnT AutoTransport: 6352 Corte del Abeto, Suite A, Carlsbad, CA 92009; ☎800 USA TNT1; fax: 800 800 3679; internet: www.tnt-inc.com.

BUYING A CAR

Having found out the cost of importing your car to New Zealand you may decide that the best option is to leave it behind. New cars are comparatively expensive but the second-hand market in Japanese and Asian cars is competitive. European cars tend to be quite pricey and parts can be difficult to obtain, as well as ridiculously expensive. Familiar models may go under slightly different names in New Zealand. There is no domestically owned brand, but most cars are locally assembled. The government is reducing tariffs resulting in fewer locally assembled cars and more new and second-hand imported vehicles. Two motor industry websites may be useful: www.autonet.co.nz and www.autovillage.co.nz.

Second Hand Cars. Buying second hand is a viable option. Cars have to be sold warranted as roadworthy. A second-hand vehicle dealer is required by law to inform the buyer honestly about the vehicle and its history, and the car must be of the model, year, and odometer mileage displayed. The Fair Trading Act operates to protect buyers, and under the Act it is not necessary to prove that a certain individual had been misled, only that a typical consumer could have been deceived. There are a number of companies offering pre-purchase vehicle checks, including the AA who will check a car without charge if you are a member. A second-hand vehicle can be repossessed if its previous owner used it as security for a loan, and the loan was not repaid. The Motor Vehicles Security Register (162-164 Grafton Road, Private Bag 92061, Auckland Mail Centre; freephone: 0800 909 777; fax: (09) 912 7787; internet: www.med.govt.nz) can check whether there is any money owing on your car for $2 an inquiry. MVSR 'Autocheck' allows callers to determine whether a security interest is registered against a particular vehicle for a charge of $5 a call plus GST (☎0900 909 777).

Car Hire. If you want to organise car hire before you arrive, your travel agency may arrange rental for you through a New Zealand firm. It is also possible to arrange your rental in advance through an international rental firm, such as Avis (www.avis.com), Hertz (www.hertz.com) or Budget (www.budgetrentacar.com). Hirers in New Zealand must be at least 21 years of age and will need a current international, UK or New Zealand driving licence.

Insurance

You are not legally required to get insurance in New Zealand, however it is sensible to get at least third party coverage. If you are involved in an accident and cause harm to another driver, you will not be personally liable for the injuries you cause them because of the no-faults compensation for personal injury provided by the Government through the Accident Compensation Corporation (See Chapter Four, *Daily Life*). But if you write off their car and you have no insurance then, like anywhere else in the world, you will be paying the bill. The premiums for full insurance coverage vary according to your age (under 25s pay a lot more), gender (some firms offer females a discount because they are statistically less likely to have accidents) and driving history. A no-claims record entitles you to discounted premiums. You should bring evidence of your claims record with you because a claim-free insurance record may qualify you for the bonus. Some firms may not be prepared to insure you until you have a New Zealand driver's licence (see Chapter Four *Daily Life* for requirements).

DAILY LIFE

CHAPTER SUMMARY

- **Languages.** New Zealand has two official languages, English and Maori.
  - Newcomers are usually only able to distinguish two vowel sounds in New Zealand English; New Zealanders can hear subtle variations.
  - The Maori language had no written form until the European settlers arrived.
- **Education.** New Zealand has a shortage of secondary school teachers.
  - A growing number of pre-school children, not only Maoris, attend Maori language 'nests' where they learn Maori language and culture.
- There is no television licence fee in New Zealand.
- **Shopping.** A 'dairy' in New Zealand is a corner shop.
- **Motoring.** Drivers in New Zealand have a reputation for being aggressive and inconsiderate.
  - New Zealand has one of the highest accident rates in the developed world.
- **Getting Around.** Major population centres are many miles apart and getting between them by road and rail is time consuming.
  - There are eight train routes and only a few trains a day.
  - Through a subsidiary, *Air New Zealand* runs a no frills service between Auckland, Wellington and Christchurch.
  - Coaches provide the most comprehensive service.
- **Accident Compensation.** New Zealand has a unique system of state protection in case of personal injury or accident.
  - On a case by case basis, the government provides financial and other assistance to anyone injured in the workplace, at home or while taking part in sports.

One of the disconcerting aspects of emigrating to a country where the locals speak the same language is that there is a tendency to underestimate the cultural differences. The New Zealand accent can be difficult to understand for a start, particularly as New Zealanders are not usually particularly expressive when they speak and can be quite tight-lipped. While you will usually find the locals fairly open and welcoming in their attitudes to new arrivals they become quickly defensive at any perceived slight towards their country. Just don't mention the sheep jokes (unless you are aiming them at Australia!).

THE LANGUAGES

New Zealanders speak their own distinctive version of English. Newcomers may be forgiven for thinking that New Zealanders use only two vowel sounds, although locals do not seem to have any problems distinguishing between words. 'New Zealand' as pronounced by New Zealanders may sound like 'Nu Zilind'. As well as the subtle distinctions between vowel sounds, further problems for the newcomer may arise from the rapid pace at which New Zealanders speak. Probably more of an obstacle than the accent to understanding New Zealanders is the use of uniquely Kiwi expressions. A 'dairy' is a corner store (open till late and selling most of the essentials), a 'crib' in the South Island or 'bach' in the North is a holiday home (generally on the coast or beside a lake). To 'bring a plate' to a party means you bring a plate of food along to share with others. BYO stands for 'Bring Your Own' alcohol - either to a party or to a restaurant. BYO restaurants have a licence to serve alcohol, but not to sell it. They are usually cheaper than 'licensed' restaurants, but they will generally charge a corkage fee per bottle (of about $2), or sometimes per person. To 'charge an arm and a leg' is to demand a high price for something. Some of the slang is similar to Australian, for example 'Pommy' for an English person, 'bush' for forest, 'shout' for buying a round in a pub or providing a special morning or afternoon tea for workmates (usually on birthdays or when someone is leaving). Additionally, a number of Maori expressions have become part of everyday New Zealand usage, for example *Pakeha* for a person of European descent. The *Dictionary of New Zealand English* (Oxford University Press), might prove useful to save you any confusion. This dictionary has been hailed as a celebration of the New Zealand language.

Maori is the other official language, although it is not widely used in everyday situations. Official signs are bilingual, as are many government documents. The number of Maori language speakers is growing and there is an active campaign to preserve this language (*Te Reo* in Maori). At least some knowledge of the language is a prerequisite for many jobs, especially those within public service. Pronunciation of Maori is not difficult to learn even if at first glance some of the place names seem impossibly long and complex. It is a good skill to master though, as correct pronunciation of Maori is a sign of courtesy and also indicates that, as a newcomer, you are prepared to integrate into the local community. The greeting 'Kia Ora' which extends good health to the other person, may be repeated back with the same words. Generally Maori words are spelt phonetically. The language had no written form before European settlement.

TABLE 18	MAORI VOWEL SOUNDS		

There are five Maori vowel sounds, each of which may be short or long:

short a:	like u in 'but'	long a:	like a in 'father'
short e:	like e in 'pet'	long e:	like ai in 'fairy'
short i	like i in 'pit'	long i	like ee in 'meet'
short o	like or in 'port'	long o	like ore in 'pore'
short u	like u in 'put'	long u	like oo in 'moon'

Diphthongs (double vowel sounds) retain the sound of the second vowel clearly.
Consonants are as in English with the following exceptions:

wh	is pronounced f; hence 'Whangarei' is pronounced 'Fong-a-ray'
ng	is like ng in the middle of 'singer, i.e. the g is never hard
r	is slightly rolled

Word stress is rather complicated and you would do better to learn by listening to a Maori speaker. It is worth noting that many Pakeha pronounce Maori words, particularly common place names, embarrassingly badly. There is however a general trend towards more accurate pronunciation and, in recent years, the standard has risen dramatically. Incorrect pronunciation is increasingly unacceptable, as it shows a lack of respect. This change has been perhaps most noticeable among radio and TV announcers, and, in general, their pronunciation is a reasonable guide.

SCHOOLS AND EDUCATION

The New Zealand education system is dominated by the state sector, which educates the vast majority of the population. Schooling is compulsory from ages six through to sixteen, although most New Zealand children start school at the age of five and many stay until they are around eighteen. The school year has four terms, beginning in late January and running through to mid-December with holidays in April and July. Most schooling is government-funded. Each state school is given a grant for operating costs and then it is the responsibility of the board of trustees to see that it is properly maintained. However, many state schools are beginning to charge 'optional' fees to cover development and maintenance of school property, and parents are still responsible for the purchase of textbooks, stationery and uniforms if required.

There is no tradition of streaming into academic and not-so-academic schools. Most schools have good cultural, academic and sporting facilities. Even inner city schools usually have extensive playing fields. There is a strong tradition of team sports, and not just rugby, although soccer used to be banned at some particularly strong rugby schools lest the boys be lured away from chasing the oval ball to 'inferior' versions of football. Many state schools offer outdoor activity programmes where pupils learn abseiling, canoeing, kayaking and go tramping (hiking) in national parks.

Like New Zealand society, its schools are becoming ethnically more diverse, particularly in Auckland with its significant and growing Pacific Island and Asian population. Japanese and other Asian languages are replacing foreign language instruction, which used to be predominantly in French and German. This reflects New Zealand's shift in trade focus, as Pacific Rim countries are now New Zealand's most important trading partners. The language of instruction, except in a few Maori language immersion schools, remains English.

In general, New Zealand state schools are safe and well-disciplined learning environments. Nevertheless, some parents choose alternatives to the state system for their children. Private schools are owned and run by independent boards, but they must meet certain standards. Integrated schools are those that used to be private and are now state schools. They follow state curriculum, but usually have their own individual beliefs, whether religious or ethical. They charge fees, but these are not as expensive as private schools. Like many private schools, integrated schools often offer boarding facilities. It is also possible to board at some state schools. Usually these are rural schools whose students come from a widely dispersed population so boarding is the only practical way of overcoming the problem of huge distances between home and school. However, not all state boarding schools are in the country. Nelson College and Christchurch Boys are city schools with a long tradition of providing a state boarding school education. As state schools, their boarding fees tend to be cheaper than the private sector.

At time of print, there is a fairly strong demand for overseas secondary school teachers, particularly of maths, science, technology, computing and graphics. The demand for primary teachers is subsiding. A department has been created in the Ministry of Education for teachers wanting to come to New Zealand to work. Contact TeachNZ for more information (TeachNZ, Ministry of Education, Private Box 1666, Wellington; ☎(04) 471 4413 or recruitment line (within NZ): 0800 832 246 (0800 TeachNZ); fax: (04) 471 4432; e-mail: TeachNZ@minedu.govt.nz; internet: www.TeachNZ.govt.nz).

The Structure of the Education System

Early Childhood. This includes childcare centres, playgroups, playcentres (which are usually run by volunteer groups of parents and cater for children from a young age), kindergartens (usually for the over-twos), home-based care, *Kohanga Reo* (Maori language and culture immersion), Pacific Islands language groups and private crèches. Kindergartens used to be free, but now often cost between $5-$10 a week, and there is also a small charge for playcentres. Crèches, on the other hand, can be quite expensive, although the government subsidises the running costs of all registered childcare centres with qualified staff. The majority of four-year-olds are in some kind of preschool programme. A growing number of children, not just Maori, attend *Kohanga Reo* (Maori language 'nests') where they learn *Taha Maori* (Maori language and culture).

Primary. Full primary schools cater for children aged from five to twelve years old (Year Zero to Year Eight). Contributing primary schools offer education for children from Year Zero to Year Six. These children usually then move on to an intermediate school. Primary curriculum includes reading, writing, science, mathematics, and social studies. Children are usually based in one classroom and each teacher covers all areas of the curriculum. Teaching standards are high. The teaching of reading skills is particularly strong and New Zealand reading programmes are copied in British and North American schools.

Intermediate: Most children spend two years (Years Seven and Eight) at intermediate school between primary and secondary (high) school. Intermediate schools were originally thought to provide a buffer zone to ease the transition between small primary schools and large secondary schools. However, some primary schools are beginning to keep their senior students for a further two years, as the interlude is now considered by some to be disruptive rather than helpful. In rural areas, state composite schools ('area' schools) have always included Years Six and Seven. At intermediate school, some pupils begin studying languages other than English (traditionally French, now increasingly Maori), and move between specialist teachers in different classrooms rather than being taught by one person for every subject.

Secondary: Secondary education covers Years Nine through to Thirteen. In pre-recession New Zealand, when jobs were easy to come by, it was quite common for students to leave school as soon as it was legal, at age fifteen. Since then, however, retention rates have improved. The core curriculum consists of seven essential learning areas: language and languages, mathematics, science, technology, social sciences, the arts and health and physical well being. Secondary school teachers have at least one specialist teaching area. Achievement objectives are based on a national curriculum statement for each area. Since 2001, all students work towards a new National Certificate of Educational Achievement (NCEA). The first level will take the place of School Certificate (at the end of the third year of secondary education), while the higher levels will replace Sixth Form Certificate and the University Bursary exams. Levels two and three of this certificate (for assessment during the students' final two years of secondary education) will be phased in during 2002 and 2003 respectively. NCEA will include a wider range of subjects and skills than did the earlier qualifications, and students will build on their achievements over the three year levels. Candidates for NCEA will also be able to work towards other qualifications and national certificates.

Further Education

Further education is divided into three main areas: universities, polytechnics and colleges of education (teacher training colleges).

Universities. University education was established in New Zealand in 1870, and the country now has eight universities, which offer degree programmes in a range of subjects. Most Bachelor degrees are three-year courses with an option of taking a four-year Honours programme. The universities are: the University of Auckland, the Auckland University of Technology, the University of Waikato (Hamilton), Massey University (Palmerston North), Victoria University of Wellington, the University of Canterbury (Christchurch), Lincoln University (Christchurch) and the University of Otago (Dunedin). Standards are uniform, and each university has its own specialist subjects, such as medicine at Auckland and Otago, and veterinary science at Palmerston North. Students looking for a campus environment head to Otago or Waikato. Teaching in arts subjects is mostly done in large lecture streams with weekly tutorials of about a dozen students. Admission procedures vary depending on the institution and the specific course. Some high-demand courses, such as medicine, law and business administration, have restricted entry usually based on University Bursary results. Other courses are open to anyone who meets the general university entrance requirement.

Polytechnics. There are 23 polytechnics in New Zealand. They offer a wide range of vocational, academic and professional courses. There is increasing crossover with universities in subject areas, although some programmes (such as business studies, marketing and accounting) can be studied either in a polytechnic (for a certificate or diploma) or in a longer degree programme at university. Many polytechnic students either study part-time while working or are on short full-time courses.

Colleges of Education. There are four colleges of education across the country, in Auckland, Wellington, Christchurch and Dunedin. Teacher training is also offered at both Waikato and Massey universities.

Student Fees. New Zealand students now contribute 25% of the cost of their tertiary education. Tuition, which used to be free, now costs New Zealand students between $2400-$20,000 for a full time year, depending on the course and the institution. Fees for foreign students are substantially higher, undergraduate course costs starting at around $6800. Reductions are available for New Zealand students from low-income families. Fees increase every year, and many students are taking more time to complete their tertiary education as they work to support themselves.

Student Allowances. Full time students from low-income families are eligible for means tested student maintenance grants, called student allowances. Students must be permanent residents to be eligible. For single students, the rate of allowance is dependent on age, whether the student lives at home with their parents and parental income (if the student is over 25). Students aged 25 and over are not subject to the family means test. There are different rates for those married to another student, and those with a dependent spouse and/or children. Each tertiary institution has student allowance officers available to help with inquiries.

Student Loans. Permanent resident students who do not qualify for allowances may borrow money through the government-run student loans scheme to pay for living costs and tuition. Each year eligible students may borrow the amount of their compulsory fees payable at enrolment, plus a maximum of $1000 for course-related costs and up to $150 per week to help cover living costs. Living costs are available only to full-time students. The living costs component used to be accessible as a lump sum, but is now paid out in regular instalments over the course of the year. Part-time students may borrow the amount of their compulsory fees plus the proportion of the $1000 course costs (the length of their course as a proportion of a full-time course). Applications are made through the institution at which the student will be enrolling. All loans incur a $50 administration fee each year. Students are now not charged interest on their loans until they have finished studying, and in 2000/2001 the rate of interest was 7%. You can pay the loan back at any stage until you earn $14,768 per annum, at which time repayment of the loan becomes compulsory as calculated instalments deducted from wages in the same manner as taxes are paid.

Foreigners at New Zealand Universities

Foreign students (that is, non-New Zealand residents) get hit even harder in the wallet than New Zealand students, as they have to pay full fees. Fees vary across courses and by university, from $6800 per annum for an undergraduate arts or humanities course, to $18,500-27,000 annually for medicine or dentistry. MBA courses cost between $18,000-24,500 per annum. For information on studying at New Zealand universities or polytechnics as a foreign student, see the Trade Development Board website (www.tradenz.govt.nz).

International Schools

There are no schools in New Zealand specifically set up for international students. However some secondary schools offer senior students preparation for the International Baccalaureate, which is an entrance qualification for most European universities. To find out more, contact the Trade Development Board (see above) or the Ministry of Education (45-47 Pipitea Street, Thorndon, Private Box 1666, Wellington; ☎(04) 471 4413; fax: (04) 471 4432).

MEDIA AND COMMUNICATIONS

Newspapers

For its size, New Zealand produces a large number of newspapers, with 28 published daily. Unfortunately the standard of the newspapers does not justify this dedication to newsprint. Regional papers were established last century when provincial government was more powerful than national government and communication networks between the scattered European settlements were poor. These regional papers have all survived and as a result New Zealand has a high number of daily newspapers, but there is no truly national paper. The apparently national *New Zealand Herald* is fairly Auckland focused and not widely circulated in the South Island. In Wellington, the *Dominion* is published in the morning, Monday to Saturday, and the *Evening Post*, as the name suggests, in the evenings. Sunday papers, such as the *Sunday Star Times* are more substantial, but still do not compare favourably in terms of size with their counterparts in either America or Britain. Most of the major papers are of the size and quality of a large provincial paper and betray their provincial loyalties by their selection of news stories. There is only one tabloid style newspaper, *The Truth*, which appears weekly and does not approach the shock, horror, or sheer awful appeal of tabloids in other countries.

Business news is provided by the *National Business Review*, also a weekly, which covers politics and international news as well. A growing trend is giveaway suburban and inner city newspapers, such as *City Voice* in Wellington, which includes community news and events, and extensive theatre, performance and exhibition listings and reviews.

Specialist newsagents in the main cities stock overseas newspapers, but they tend to be relatively expensive and usually arrive some days late, particularly European editions. Of course, the internet is probably the quickest and easiest way to access foreign news, with the added bonus that you don't have to wait for the papers to arrive by mail.

Main Newspapers

The New Zealand Herald: Conservative in tone and appearance, the Herald was founded well over 100 years ago. It is based in Auckland and the news content reflects this, despite its name. Circulation: 213,334; readership: 522,000; internet:

www.nzherald.co.nz.

The Dominion: It has a political focus, as might be expected of a newspaper based in the capital city. Used to be a liberal, unpartisan scrutineer of government, but has now become something of a convert to neo-liberal economic dogma. Circulation: 68,743; readership: 190,000.

The Evening Post: Also Wellington based, it contains more regional news than *The Dominion*, with worthwhile comment and good arts content. Circulation: 59,055; readership: 145,000; internet: www.evpost.co.nz.

The Christchurch Press: Distributed throughout top half of South Island. Good coverage of news from the Canterbury region, less so of national and international stories. Circulation: 92,992; readership: 231,000; internet: www.press.co.nz.

The Otago Daily Times: Dunedin based. Circulation: 44,093; readership: 106,000; internet: www.odt.co.nz.

There are two Sunday papers, the *Sunday Star Times* and *Sunday News*, which are published by Independent Newspapers Ltd and are distributed throughout the country.

Magazines

Over 2,300 magazines are available in New Zealand on a regular basis, but only 165 of these are published locally. The others include international newsmagazines such as *Time*, *The Economist*, and *Newsweek*. Local political comment is provided by the *New Zealand Listener* and the *Political Review*. The *Listener* also carries TV and radio listings, as does the *TV Guide*, which has the biggest circulation of any New Zealand magazine. Other very popular magazines are *Woman's Day* and the *New Zealand Women's Weekly*, dog-eared stacks of which can be found in nearly every doctor's surgery. *More* magazine is an upmarket women's magazine interesting and informative articles about a range of issues from health to business, and a no-nonsense practical feminist line. A number of glossy lifestyle magazines have sprung up in the last decade. Of particular note is *Metro*, the Auckland city magazine. Metro's stablemate, aimed at readers in the rest of the country, is *North and South*. Both are liberal on political issues, conservative on social welfare issues and support the economic liberalisation programme launched by the government in the 1980s. *New Zealand Cuisine* is dedicated to fine food and wine. There are a surprising number of literary magazines, apparently thriving, despite small circulation. The most well established of these is the Christchurch based *Landfall*, but the Wellington based *New Zealand Books* also provides excellent coverage of literary happenings and boasts some pillars of the literary community amongst its regular contributors. Both magazines provide a showcase for fresh writing talent, although *New Zealand Books* is mainly a vehicle for reviews.

Magazines exist for just about every sporting pursuit, including boating, horse riding and racing, surfing and skateboarding. Also popular are do-it-yourself, home improvement and interior design magazines, as well as magazines about arts and crafts. Many New Zealand magazines and newspapers can be ordered through Consyl Publishing Ltd. (3 Buckhurst Road, Bexhill-on-Sea, East Sussex, TN40 1QF; ☎01424 223 111; 24 hour credit card sales ☎01424 223 161). If you send a self-addressed envelope with four first-class stamps to Consyl, they will send you a copy of Outlook Express, which contains a list of New Zealand publications available.

Television

There are four free-to-air national TV channels in New Zealand, as well as regional stations and some other private specialist channels. TV1 broadcasts much sport and current affairs, and some serious drama, while TV2 shows more light entertainment. TV3 and Channel 4 are privately run, and broadcast both factual and entertainment programmes. All the terrestrial channels have advertising. Users pay for Sky (satellite) TV, which has channels showing movies, sport, CNN and BBC (and other international news), documentaries and educational and magazine programmes. There are a few regional TV channels, and the TAB channel, which broadcasts horse-racing. A number of local cable TV companies offer a variety of channels, some in different languages, but these come at a price and are only available in the larger cities. New Zealand TV news graphics and visual effects are sophisticated, but the news analysis and sometimes camerawork are not. Unsurprisingly, when the average item does not exceed a minute and half in length, in-depth analysis of stories is rare. On TV1, BBC News and other BBC programmes are screened during the night. The content of the four terrestrial channels provides a mixed diet of the best of the BBC, popular American sit-coms and Australian and home-grown dramas.

Television Licences. The national broadcasting company, New Zealand On Air does not charge a household licence fee.

Radio

Radio New Zealand runs a network of local stations, which are funded through advertising revenue and offer a mixed diet of middle of the road popular music, talk back, news and sports. It also runs two non-commercial nationally broadcast stations, the National Programme and Concert FM. The National Programme's morning news show from 9am to noon, *Morning Report*, is an excellent source of news and comment on political and economic issues. The Concert Programme broadcasts classical music and information programmes. There is a large local private radio sector, including student radio, Maori language radio and community access radio. Local and national radio stations in New Zealand broadcast on 110 AM and 332 FM frequencies, so there is a great choice of radio programmes. There is also a National Radio Sports Frequency. However many stations, especially FM radio, have a limited range due to the mountainous terrain of the country. An Auckland-based private radio station broadcasts the BBC World Service, with frequencies in Auckland and Wellington. Snippets from the World Service are also broadcast regularly on National Radio.

Post

Postal services are handled by New Zealand Post, which has a monopoly on letter delivery up to 80 grams in weight. Parcel delivery is also provided by private courier firms. Domestic delivery is once daily, usually mid-morning. There is a network of more than 1,000 Post Offices throughout the country, the majority of which are postal agencies and provide other services as well. Many other outlets also sell stamps, including book and stationery shops, newsagents and dairies.

There are two classes of mail, Fast Post, which promises next day delivery anywhere in the country, and ordinary post. The standard cost of a Fast Post letter is 80c and for an ordinary rate letter, 40c. The standard cost of a letter sent to the USA or the UK is $2. For customer enquiries and up to date charges, call NZ Post on freephone 0800 501 501, or email: csc@nzpost.co.nz.

Post Offices offer a *poste restante* service for letters and parcels at all locations throughout the country. Redirection service for *poste restante* costs $7. There is no storage fee for small packets (under 2 kg) and letters. There are storage fees for parcels over 2 kg after they have been held for seven days. Charges vary according to the length of time the parcel is held awaiting collection. Any mail uncollected after two months will be returned to sender.

Telephones

For information about having a telephone installed in your house, see *Setting Up Home*. New Zealand Telecom has been overhauling the phone system since 1990, introducing standard seven digit numbers throughout the country. Most of the chaos caused by the change is now over. The international code for New Zealand is 64. There are five area codes for the different regions of the country: 09 for Auckland and northwards; 07 for the Waikato and central North Island area; 06 for the southern half of the North Island; 04 for the Wellington region; and 03 for the South Island. Telecom's toll-free phone numbers start with 0800 and Clear freephone numbers start with 0508. Phone boxes are well distributed but most are now card phones, which can be irritating if you do not have a card handy. Phone cards come in $5, $10, $20, or $50 denominations and can be bought from bookshops, dairies or Post Offices. Local calls from a coin or card phone cost 50c. Very few coin phones can still be found, but you may find original model payphones, which have a button marked A on the front that you should press when the call is connected. In the cities, card and coin phones can usually be found cohabiting, and in some places, credit card phones as well.

To dial the UK from New Zealand dial 00 44 then drop the first zero from the area code. To dial the USA dial 00 1 . Fax numbers have the same prefix.

CARS AND MOTORING

It is common to see older model cars in New Zealand, this is a hangover from the days when new cars were very expensive so people drove their old car for a long time. Most of the older cars are British or American makes. Modern cars tend to be Japanese makes. Because of the absence of heavy traffic there is not much of a network of multi-lane motorways. Most state highways are single carriage ways and as a general rule there are no tolls. Multi-lane motorways carry traffic into and out of the four main cities and through parts of Auckland and Wellington. Congestion on these stretches during rush hour is often a problem, but nothing compared to traffic jams in European or North American cities. To relieve problems associated with rush hour, many larger firms operate on 'glide time', which means that, within reason, employees' daily work hours start when they arrive, rather than at an exact set time.

Driving outside the main cities is usually a pleasant experience. The roads are uncluttered and the scenery superb. The weather often provides more of an obstacle to reaching your destination than other drivers do. Flooding or heavy snowfalls only occasionally block main routes, particularly the roads through the volcanic plateau in the central North Island and the cross-alpine routes in South Island. There are signs at the start of tricky stretches of road indicating which routes are open. In general the signs indicating distances and routes on the highway system are less frequent than in other countries (although to be fair there is usually only one main route to any destination). Junctions are not as well designed, and roundabouts are less common and tend to be poorly sign posted. But then, there is less traffic on the roads.

New Zealand drivers have a reputation for being fast and rather aggressive, but the advent of speed cameras and other traffic safety programmes are tending to change this attitude. It is easy to see why you might be tempted to drive well over the speed limit when there is no other traffic in sight, let alone any sign of the law. City drivers are not particularly considerate. It is rare for people to give way to allow cars from side roads to join the main stream of traffic, again perhaps because there are usually fewer congestion problems. Nor do New Zealand drivers willingly move over into the slow lane to let faster traffic past. Unfortunately driving in New Zealand is not very safe. It has one of the worst accident records per head of population in the developed world. About 500 people die on the roads each year, and the 'road toll' often appears on the national TV news. The government is trying to improve the statistics by targeting the worst-offending group, specifically young men who drink and drive, so be aware that the blood-alcohol limits are strictly enforced. Increasingly there are official random roadblocks, particularly around the festive season, in which every passing driver may be stopped and breath-tested.

Driving Regulations

The maximum speed on highways and motorways is 100 km, and in built up areas 50 km. Speed cameras are being introduced at various places in cities and on country roads. New Zealanders drive on the left-hand side of the road, and the rules of the road are similar to British driving regulations. However, there are several important differences - at crossroads traffic turning left must give way to on-coming vehicles turning right, it is illegal to park facing the wrong way, and safety belts must be worn by the driver and all passengers. Traffic lights change straight from red to green, then amber followed by red again. Standard international road signs are being introduced. One sign that may be unfamiliar is LSZ enclosed by a red circle, indicating a Limited Speed Zone in which the motorist should slow down to allow for children, pedestrians or other traffic. This is frequently used when state highways pass through small towns.

As noted above, drink-driving regulations are strictly enforced. The limit is 80 mls per 100 mls of blood - less than two pints of beer for the average adult male. Drivers under twenty years old have a lower limit: 30 mls per 100 mls of blood. Police officers are able to stop motorists at random and breath test them. The maximum penalty is a $1,500 fine and six months in prison. Repeat offenders can lose their licence. Seat belts must be worn in the front of cars and in the back if they are fitted. Helmets are compulsory for motorcyclists as well as bicycle riders.

Breakdowns and Accidents

Over the last few years, the Government has made the driving test much more stringent and introduced restricted licences for the under 20s in an effort to improve road safety. If you are involved in an accident, you must contact the police. (The emergency number is 111). Unfortunately New Zealand highways are often not well provided with call boxes or emergency telephones.

Members can call the New Zealand Automobile Association (AA) at any time on freephone 0800 224 357 (0800 AA HELP) to assist with mechanical difficulties or breakdowns. Members of the international organisations AIT and FIA have reciprocal rights to use AA services. It costs $79 per year to join, or the same amount for a six-month visitor's subscription. For more information, visit the website at www.nzaa.co.nz.

Driving Licences

An International Drivers Licence is valid for 12 months after arrival in New Zealand. At the end of this period visitors must apply for a New Zealand licence which involves sitting a written and oral test, and then an interview with a police officer to obtain exemption from taking the practical test. Drivers under the age of twenty are eligible only for a restricted licence and are not allowed to drive after dark. See the Land Transport Safety Authority website (www.ltsa.govt.nz) for more information.

Car Registration and Insurance

Cars must be registered with the Post Office and have a current Vehicle Inspection Certificate (VIC) also known as a Warrant of Fitness (WOF). They must also have a Vehicle Identification Number (VIN), an identification scheme to try and cut down on vehicle theft. At the time of writing, the cost of registering an ordinary motorcar was $202.85 per year. First time registration for a new car costs approximately $300 including new numberplates. Cars can be registered at any Post Office shop. Re-registration forms are sent out automatically. Most garages offer VIC testing, which costs about $30. New cars need a warrant every year for the first six years and then every six months after that. The fee for registering change of ownership papers is $9.20. Further information may be obtained from the Transport Registry Centre Helpdesk (freephone: 0800 108 809; email: info@tregistry.co.nz). Of course, the price of car insurance varies depending on the value of the car, the area you live in and the age and driving record of the driver. The average cost of full insurance for one year, based on a car worth $7500, in a city area, with a 30 year old driver, would be about $630.

Useful Addresses

Land Transport Safety Authority Head Office: 4th Floor, 7-27 Waterloo Quay, Box 2840, Wellington; ☎(04) 494 8600; fax: (04) 494 8601. For information on vehicle warranties and vehicle and driver licensing, call freephone 0800 699 000 or visit the website: www.ltsa.govt.nz.

The New Zealand Automobile Association: 99 Albert St, Auckland City, Auckland; ☎(09) 377 4660; internet: www.nzaa.co.nz.

TRANSPORT

Air

As the major population centres are many miles apart, getting between cities by road or rail is fairly time consuming. It can take around ten hours to drive from Wellington to Auckland, and about four between Christchurch and Dunedin. Air travel is a popular alternative. Following the very recent and public collapse of Australian-owned Ansett, there is now only one main internal airline, the state-owned Air New Zealand. It operates out of sites in the main cities. Air New Zealand has expanded its services and now operates a 'no-frills' domestic service using subsidiary airline Freedom Air. Freedom Air began flying the main routes between Auckland, Wellington and Christchurch in May 2001.

Air New Zealand incorporates a number of smaller airlines, Eagle Air in the North Islands, Nelson Air, which covers the top of the South Island, and Mount Cook airlines (mostly tourist routes). A variety of discounted fares is available if you book ahead. Air New Zealand offers no-frills flights, called City Savers, on the main routes. There are also special deals on late night flights or flights during off-peak hours. Holders of the International Student Identity Card (ISIC) can get a 50% discount on standby travel. On the major routes this may entail waiting around in the airport until a flight has spare seats, but it rarely involves more than a couple of hours delay unless it is a particularly busy period such as the start of the school holidays or the festive season.

Auckland International Airport handles 75% of New Zealand's international arrivals and departures. 27 foreign airlines and three cargo airlines operate scheduled services to and from New Zealand. The website addresses for the three main airports are: www.auckland-airport.co.nz, www.wellington-airport.co.nz and www.christchurch-airport.co.nz.

Trains

The train network is not exactly comprehensive. There are eight train routes around the country and only a few trains to most major destinations each day. Trains cost about the same as the equivalent journey by bus, although there are some faster services that are more expensive. Many of the routes are chiefly designed with tourists in mind, such as the Transalpine Express from Christchurch to Greymouth across the Southern Alps. Reservations are advisable during the summer on popular tourist routes, and booking well in advance often enables you to buy tickets at reduced prices. The national reservations telephone number for Tranz Rail is 0800 802 802, and the enquiry line is 0800 801 070. Enquiries from outside the country can be made by phone (+64 4 498 3303) or fax (+64 4 498 3093). Bookings can also be made online using the website (www.tranzrail.co.nz) or by email (passengerservices@tra nzrail.co.nz). Bookings may be made by credit card and Tranz Rail will send your tickets by courier.

Coaches

Buses (usually called coaches) between major cities provide much more frequent services than the trains. There are three main companies: Newmans, Mt Cook, and InterCity. Mt Cook operates only in the South Island, and Newmans only in the North. InterCity is a subsidiary of Tranz Rail and provides the most comprehensive service. Reservations can be made by telephone or over the internet: Mt Cook ☎0800 800 287; Newmans ☎0800 733 500 or (09) 309 9738, internet: www.newmanscoach.co.nz; and InterCity ☎0800 468 372 or (09) 973 6100, or (03) 379 9020; internet: www.intercitycoach.co.nz. InterCity offers moneysaving coach passes for the whole of the country, or just the North or South Island, which are valid for three months. See the website for more information (www.travelpass.co.nz) or email: info@coachnet.co.nz.

City Transport

Public transport in most of the major cities does not provide a sufficiently comprehensive network to replace the private car as the major method of getting to work. Because urban population densities are low by world standards this does not yet produce enormous pollution and congestion problems, although it is best to avoid driving in central Auckland and Wellington during rush hour if at all possible. Inner city parking can be extremely expensive, both in metered street parks and in parking buildings, and parking wardens are vigilant. In Auckland and Wellington, commuter rail and bus networks replace the car for a small percentage of the working population.

Taxis. Taxis in New Zealand can be found at taxi stands or ordered by phone (check the Yellow Pages for local phone numbers). They do not drive around waiting to be hired, so there is no point trying to flag one down even if it looks empty. The fares are all metered so you do not need to agree a price with the driver before setting off. In many cities, mini-vans called 'airport shuttles' run a taxi service from the airport into any destination in the central city. Usually there is a flat fee per person for the ride. For an individual, this is almost always a cheaper option than a taxi, although slightly less convenient as you may not be the first person to be dropped off. If you need a shuttle to take you from the city to the airport, try to book at least one day early rather than just ten minutes before you would like to be collected. Because shuttles make more than one 'pick-up', the drivers need to plan their routes to the airport according to stops they have to make along the way. Company listings can be found in the Yellow Pages. Airport shuttles have their own stands outside terminals at most major airports.

The Inter-island Ferry

There are two types of ferry which cross Cook Strait to carry passengers between the North and South Islands: the Interislander ferry, and a high speed catamaran called The Lynx. The Interislander offers four to five ferry crossings a day, with a roll-on, roll-off service for cars. The trip takes about three hours. The standard cost for a small family car is $175, although there are discounts (between 15-50%) for travel during the off peak season (non-holiday periods) and for non-refundable tickets booked well in advance. You can also save up to 50% for a same day return ticket, and senior citizens may be entitled to a 30% discount. The fare for foot passengers is $49 standard one way. To check what special fares are available, visit the website at www.tranzrailtravel.co.nz/interislander. The North Island departure point is the Ferry Terminal on Aotea Quay in Wellington, and in the South Island the Picton Ferry Terminal. The ferries include such amenities as movie theatres, bars, children's play areas and cafeterias. If the crossing is bad though, food will probably be the last thing on your mind. The Cook Strait can be a particularly rough stretch of water, and travel may be delayed or cancelled during especially bad weather. On the upside however, the scenery as you enter the Sounds is spectacular and you may see dolphins swimming alongside or in front of the ferry.

The Lynx catamaran operates three crossings each way daily between December and March, and the crossing time is reduced to one hour 45 minutes. The single fare for adults is $63, and one way cost for cars is $199. The departure points are the same as for the Interislander.

Useful Addresses

Air New Zealand: cnr Customs and Albert Streets, Private Bag 92007, Auckland; ☎(09) 366 2400; fax: (09) 275 5927; internet: www.airnz.co.nz.

InterCity Coachlines: CPO Box 3625, Auckland; ☎0800 468 372, or (09) 639 0500; fax: (09) 639 0503; internet: www.intercitycoach.co.nz.

The Interislander: Tranz Rail Ltd, Private Bag, Wellington; ☎0800 802 802; fax: (04) 498 3721 or 0800 101 525; email: passengerservices@tranzrail.co.nz; internet: www.tranzrailtravel.co.nz.

The Lynx: Tranz Rail Ltd, Private Bag Wellington; ☎0800 802 802 or (04) 498 3000; fax: (04) 498 3090.

Mount Cook Line: Airline/Landline, PO Box 4644, Christchurch; ☎0800-800287 or (09) 309 5395; fax: (09) 275 9594; internet: www.clearfield.co.nz/mount–cook/mc–home for flights and www.mtcook.co.nz/landlines for coach trips.

Newmans Route Services: PO Box 90 821, Auckland; ☎(09)309 9738; fax: (09) 302 1614; internet: www.newmanscoach.co.nz.

Tranz Rail Ltd: Private Bag, Wellington, ☎0800-802 802; internet: www.tranzrail.co.nz.

BANKS AND FINANCE

New Zealand's banking system is amongst the most advanced in the world and is very convenient to use. A visit to the bank no longer need involve any paperwork as most transactions are done electronically using money cards with PINs (personal identification numbers) to access accounts. Banking hours are generally Monday to Friday, 9am to 5pm, although on Tuesdays some banks open at 9.30am because of staff training. You can use automatic tellers (cash machines) at any time to transfer money between accounts, and order statements or chequebooks. Your money card, known as an ATM (Automatic Teller Machine) card, also functions as a direct debit card for EFT-POS transactions, using your PIN. EFT-POS stands for Electronic Funds Transfer at the Point Of Sale. The amount you are charged is immediately removed from your account, meaning that if there are not sufficient funds available your transaction will be declined. Most retailers offer the EFT-POS service. Cheques are still accepted by many retailers and companies, but advances in electronic banking are fast rendering them obsolete.

New Zealand banks do not issue cheque guarantee cards. The onus is on the receiver of the cheque to make sure it is not fraudulent. Retailers usually require ID for cheques in the form of a credit or EFT-POS card, and often take your name and address as well. Some retailers refuse to accept cheques, and others may be at least unwilling to take them, particularly if you do not have a local address. Credit cards are popular in New Zealand, Mastercard and Visa being the most widely used. Most bills are paid through standing orders (called direct credit) and your wages will probably likewise be paid into your account directly. Most banks now offer telephone banking as a standard service to their clients, for a small charge per call. Telephone banking allows you to check balances, transfer funds, make bill payments, and hear a list of recent transactions, among other options.

Banking costs. Account holders pay bank fees for their accounts. There is a monthly transaction fee of around $3, but exemptions may apply for students and the elderly. There is also a fee for individual transactions on top of the monthly fee, but some banks exempt the first few entries each month. Electronic and telephone transactions usually cost between 25-50c, while manual transactions (carried out at the bank) may cost around 50c-$1. The government charges a resident withholding tax, currently 19.5% of your interest.

Bank Accounts

Most people open an account with one of the five main banks: the Bank of New Zealand (BNZ), the Australia New Zealand Banking Group (ANZ), the National Bank of New Zealand, WestpacTrust, (an amalgamation of Westpac Banking Corporation and Trustbank, which formerly operated as local district trusts), and ASB (formerly the Auckland Savings Bank, which now operates nationwide). Contact details are as follows:

ANZ: PO Box 1492, Wellington; tel; (04) 496 7000; fax: (04) 473 6919; internet: www.anz.co.nz.

ASB: PO Box 35, Auckland; ☎(09) 377 8930; fax: (09) 358 3511; internet: www.asbbank.co.nz.

BNZ: BNZ Centre, 1 Willis St, Wellington; ☎(04) 474 6000; fax: (04) 474 6531; internet: www.bnz.co.nz.

National Bank: PO Box 1791, Wellington; tel:(04) 494 4000; fax: (04) 473 6959; internet: www.nationalbank.co.nz.

Westpac Trust: 318-324 Lambton Quay, Wellington; ☎(04) 498 1000; fax: (04) 498 1350; internet: www.westpactrust.co.nz.

Branches of foreign banks also operate but the banks listed above have an extensive network of banking outlets developed as result of New Zealand's scattered population.

If you wish to open a bank account in New Zealand, it is recommended that you contact the head office of the bank involved to discuss any requirements before you leave for New Zealand. Your current bank may help you open a New Zealand account. There is a generally a fee for this service and a minimum deposit requirement. One advantage of opening an account before you arrive in New Zealand is that it solves the problem of transferring money; you simply arrange for a telexed transfer to your new account. The alternatives to telexing money directly to a New Zealand bank account are outlined in the section on *International Money Transfers* below. Opening an account once you arrive in New Zealand does not take long, but there are a few hitches for the new arrival. Some banks require proof of a regular income, such as a signed work contract, before allowing you to open a cheque account, even though you may have deposited money with them. You should be issued immediately with an ATM card, which will allow you to withdraw money from a bank or an automatic teller machine. To facilitate opening an account in New Zealand, it is a good idea to bring a letter of introduction from your bank at home. The government transaction duty on credit card accounts (5% of all purchases) was withdrawn on 1 April, 1998.

Banking Ombudsman

If you have a complaint about a bank in New Zealand your first step should be to contact the bank involved. If you can't resolve the problem through the bank's processes, you can contact the Banking Ombudsman. The Banking Ombudsman's Office can provide you with advice about how to make a complaint, although it will not hear the complaint until you have first approached the bank involved. The address is: Banking Ombudsman, PO Box 10573, The Terrace, Wellington; ☎(04) 471 0006; fax: (04) 471 0548.

International Money Transfers

There are no foreign exchange controls on shifting money out of New Zealand. Getting money to New Zealand is most quickly achieved through a money wire or a telegraphic transfer. You can either do this through a specialist money-wiring company such as American Express or Western Union, or through the banks. The specialist companies cost more but the process is much faster, less than 15 minutes. Through the banks it usually takes a couple of days but the cost is about half the amount charged by wiring companies.

Money

New Zealand has a decimal money system using dollars as the monetary unit, each dollar consisting of 100 cents. The abbreviation for the dollar is $ and c for cents which stand after the numbers. At the time of going to press the exchange rate was £1-$3.48 and US$1-$2.38.

Cost of Living

Living costs in New Zealand vary, as they do in every country, depending on where you live and how you spend your money. Generally, it is more expensive to live in Auckland and Wellington than the rest of the country, but then salaries are usually higher.

TABLE 19	AVERAGE WEEKLY LIVING COSTS PER HOUSEHOLD (2.7) PERSONS	
Food (groceries, takeaways)		$124.07
Housing (rent, mortgages, rates)		$128.89
Household operations (power, furniture, appliances)		$97.32
Apparel (clothing and footwear)		$28.31
Transport (public transport and road vehicles)		$134.16
Other goods (personal, alcohol, newspapers, etc.)		$92.59
Other services (health, savings, leisure etc.)		$126.59
Total		**$731.92**

Compiled by The New Zealand Institute of Economic Research.

TAXATION

The taxation system was extensively reformed as part of the economic liberalisation in the 1980s. A goods and services tax was introduced, called GST (a value-added tax), and the philosophy of a 'user pays' policy, resulted in a reduction in personal tax rates. GST and income tax are the main New Zealand taxes. Through the 'user pays' policy, government subsidies have been reduced for certain services like university education, and some medical costs. Some government departments have been sold off to become State Owned Enterprises, and these SOEs also charge out the cost of their services. The Inland Revenue Department (IRD) is the government agency responsible for implementing and enforcing New Zealand's tax policy, and there are IRD branches in all the cities and major towns. The income tax year runs from 1st April to 31st March of the following year. Paying income tax is now a lot simpler than it was, thanks to recent changes. If salary and wage earners ensure that they have the correct tax code, they no longer need to file tax returns.

Income Tax

TABLE 20	2001 PERSONAL TAX RATES
Annual Income	Tax Rate
$0-$38,000	graduated up to 19.5 cents in the dollar
$38,001-$60,000	33 cents in the dollar
over $60,001	39 cents in the dollar

There is a rebate system which means that low income earners may pay about 5% tax. It is then graduated up to 19.5% for $38,000 per annum. Most salary and wage earners have income tax automatically deducted from their wages under PAYE (Pay As You Earn). The employer pays the PAYE monthly to the Inland Revenue. Those who are PAYE and paying Resident Withholding Tax (on dividends or interest from a bank account) do not need to file a tax return. Self employed individuals, or those with income from a trust or rents pay three tax instalments throughout the financial year. They receive an IR3 form at the end of the tax year, which they may complete by 7th July, but even this is not compulsory.

Prior to 1st April 1988, aged beneficiaries who received National Superannuation had to pay a surcharge of 25% on other income they earned above a certain limit. Following a campaign of protest from the elderly, this surcharge has been wiped.

Banks charge a Resident Withholding Tax of 19.5% on interest and dividends, which is deducted by the financial institution before they send your payment. When you invest, you are required to provide your IRD number to the firm. You will need to apply for an IRD number before you earn money from any source. If you have a second job, you are taxed at a higher rate (called a secondary rate or SEC). An overall adjustment will take place when you file your annual return. Because most of your income is taxed at the source, some people no longer file tax returns. It is prudent to make your calculations, though, as you may be due a refund.

The IRD will help people complete their tax return at no cost, but the individual must provide all the necessary documents. Tax accountants charge a fee, but this fee can be deducted as an expense on the following year's return. All social security and health spending is financed through general taxation. For further details contact your local Inland Revenue Office or the National Office (Inland Revenue Department, PO Box 2198, Wellington; ☎(04) 472 1032 or (04) 473 0920; fax: (04) 473 2815; internet: www.ird.govt.nz).

Local Tax

Local authorities finance their activities by levying rates on land and property. Some local authorities charge separately for services such as rubbish collection and water supply. Rates are levied on the value of your land plus improvements (that is, the house). Rates vary around the country and depend on the value of the land and improvements. An annual bill of between $1000-2200 would be typical for a standard family house. Valuation New Zealand revalues property every five years.

Goods and Services Tax (GST)

GST is an indirect tax on most goods and services, uniformly applied at 12.5%. It is borne by the ultimate consumer but is payable at every stage of producing goods or services. GST is almost always included in the display price. It applies to most commodities, but exemptions include rental accommodation, donated goods and services and financial services. Exports are zero rated. Businesses with a net turnover of greater than $30,000 per annum must be GST registered and must complete a GST return every six months. They can claim back the GST content of the goods and services they purchase. However, visitors cannot claim a refund on this tax.

Other Taxes

There is no capital gains tax as such, or death duties in New Zealand. However, capital gains from disposal of personal property are taxed where:

- ⊙ the property is acquired for resale;
- ⊙ the taxpayer's business involves dealing in such property; or
- ⊙ there is an undertaking or scheme with the aim of making a profit.

Gift Duty. Gift duty is a charge on gifts worth over $27,000 made in any twelve month period which one person makes to another. The person who receives the gift is liable to pay any duty when nothing is received in return, or the value of the gift given in return is less in value than the gift. Subject to certain exemptions, duty is charged on a sliding scale from 5% of the value of a gift worth over $27,000 to $5,850 plus 25% for an amount exceeding $72,000.

HEALTH CARE, INSURANCE & HOSPITALS

Health Care

The health system is made up of public, private and voluntary sectors working together. More than three-quarters of health care is funded by taxes and prevailing public health care standards are generally high. Until recently, preventable diseases had been almost eradicated. However, one of the signs of the social distress caused by the economic restructuring of the 1980s is that diseases of poverty, such as rickets, scurvy and tuberculosis, are on the rise again.

The provision of health care has been a major political issue of recent years. Major reforms have been undertaken in an attempt to streamline administration and management in the health system. Apart from charges for doctors' fees and some prescription charges, for many years health services were provided free to the user. However, the increasing cost of specialist health services coupled with the reduction in the number of tax paying workers has brought about a partial user-pays service. Health spending follows social welfare as a major item of government expenditure. Government health expenditure amounted to approximately $7,113 million for the financial year ending in June 2001. This represented 6.3% of New Zealand's GDP, and was the equivalent of $1,850 per annum per head of the population. In addition, the life expectancy of New Zealanders is increasing; currently males are expected to live to age 74, and females to 80. This means that users need health care for longer, which also adds to costs.

The Ministry of Health, which gives the Government advice on health spending, monitors the Health Funding Authority (HFA). The HFA distributes funding for public health services, personal health and disability support. It also pays for maternity and laboratory services as well as hospital inpatient care. The general pattern of the public health system in New Zealand is that primary health care (GPs, prescriptions, out-patients' visits to hospitals) is paid for by the user, while secondary health care is provided free. Over a third of New Zealanders have supplementary private medical insurance to cover the additional costs of private health and surgical care in the public system and to enable them to afford the costs of private hospitals. Private health insurance can cost anything from $350 to $3800 per year, depending of course on the company and services you choose. Some costs of health care not covered by the state, although they are subsidised. You will pay between $35 and $45 for a visit to a doctor, although children between the ages of six and seventeen cost less, at $20, and children under six years old are entitled to free visits. Some doctors charge an extra $5 and $10 for weekend or evening appointments. Prescription charges are a maximum of $15 per item, and optometrists' (opticians) and dentists' charges are around $50 for a checkup. People on low incomes can get a Community Services Card that entitles them to cheaper primary care, but not dental care. GPs provide most basic health care. It is not necessary to register with just one doctor, although for obvious reasons most people tend to stay with the same doctor.

Hospitals

Through the HFA, the Government funds a national network of hospitals. Inpatient treatments, as well as outpatient and day services, are free of charge to all New Zealanders. 23 hospitals compete for the available funds on a regional basis. The population of each regional area has become a critical factor in this battle, and the more specialised and expensive surgical facilities are being concentrated in the higher populated areas. Even so, hospitals have huge deficits in their internal finance structure. The quality of care in the public hospital sector does not seem to have declined from its previous high standards but more services are being provided with user-charges, and waiting lists are growing. Public hospitals still provide no-charge operations but the waiting lists continue to grow and if your condition is non-emergency or life threatening, you will find there is a long wait for surgery. Additionally, a points system has been introduced so that people of high priority are dealt with first.

You are generally less likely than in many other countries to be a victim of medical misadventure at the hands of some young doctor at the end of 100 hour shift. Young doctors went on strike in the late 1980s and successfully negotiated better pay and conditions.

As a result of long waiting lists, a great number of people have taken out medical insurance and elect to go to a private hospital (there are no private beds in public hospitals). Private hospitals cater mainly for elective surgery and for those who prefer a private room and more choice of when they have their operation.

Dental Care. Dental care for adults is not subsidised by the government but is provided free for all primary school children through the school dental system. Most New Zealand primary schools will have a dental clinic on the premises. As a result of receiving free basic care nearly half of New Zealand school children have no fillings by the time they get to high school.

Abortion. Abortion is legal under certain strictly defined conditions. If it is judged that the continuation of the pregnancy would result in serious danger to the life or mental or physical health of the woman, or that there is substantial risk that the child would be born handicapped, then an abortion may be approved by two specially appointed consultants. The rate is about the same per 1000 of the population as the UK and roughly half that of the USA.

Reciprocal Agreements

New Zealand has reciprocal health care agreements with most Commonwealth countries, including the UK. Visitors from these countries are entitled to access to the New Zealand health care system on the same basis as New Zealand citizens and residents. Visitors from other countries will have to pay full price for health services. For further information see the Ministry of Health website at www.moh.govt.nz.

Private Medical Insurance

About 75% of New Zealanders have private medical insurance. The main reasons for buying private insurance seem to be to cover the additional costs of using the public system, such as doctors' fees and prescription charges, and to cover the costs of private hospital care. Getting insurance just to cover the costs of primary care is unlikely to be cost effective. The average annual costs for doctors' visits and prescriptions charges may be less than the premiums even for a budget insurance deal that only covers primary care. Premiums for this type of package are around $350 per year for an individual and between $450 to $1000 for a family. A comprehensive insurance deal which covers everything from routine primary care to major surgery in a private hospital will cost anything from $540 upwards annually or an individual or $1200 for a family. However policies vary widely depending on the amount of cover and the exclusions. The main advantages of private hospital care are greater choice over the timing of an operation, and private rooms. You can get hospital-only cover, which is usually cheaper than a comprehensive policy.

Remember, though, that the public hospital system still provides the full range of care. The advantages of having private insurance are mostly the convenience factor. It is not yet necessary to have private medical insurance in New Zealand. Check that there is a repatriation clause in your policy if this is important to you.

The Accident Compensation Corporation (ACC)

New Zealand has a unique system of state protection in the case of personal injury or accident, known as ACC. The government provides accident insurance cover for anyone who is injured due to accidents in the workplace, at home or on the sports field. This is a no-fault cover for residents of and visitors to New Zealand for accident, medical misadventure or certain behaviour for which criminal proceedings may be brought. Consequently, there is no right to sue for personal injury. Money for ACC comes from levies on vehicle owners, employers, the self-employed, workers and general taxes. This is another area of welfare provision that has suffered from retrenchment in recent years, and the original 1972 ACC system has been reduced. Lump-sum compensation according to a fixed scale depending on the injury has been abolished, and all assistance is made on a case by case basis. However assistance is available for a wide variety of costs including medical treatment, private hospital treatment, loss of earnings, loss of potential earnings, home help and child care, house modification in the case of permanent disability and training for independent living. The ACC places great emphasis on aiding people back to the workforce with rehabilitation treatment. The cost of non-work related accidents is met through the earner's premium which is collected through the tax system and the cost for work related accidents is collected through the employer's premium or levy. Firms are now allowed to take out accident insurance for their employees through private firms instead of ACC, if they wish.

ACC also covers visitors to New Zealand for certain personal accident injuries. Claims are started when you go to doctor or hospital, and ACC contributes towards treatment costs, transport (getting to the treatment) costs, and rehabilitation assistance. Visitors may only get this assistance while in New Zealand.

SOCIAL WELFARE & UNEMPLOYMENT BENEFITS

Work and Income New Zealand (WINZ) is the agency which combines employment and income support roles. It has offices throughout the country, and distributed over $9 billion in income support during the last year. Access to the social welfare system in New Zealand does not depend upon establishing a contribution record; benefits are available to all those who meet the residency and income criteria. Although entitlement criteria are generous, benefit rates are not: most benefits are worth considerably less than 50% of the average weekly wage (which is approximately $703). Increasingly prospective claimants face income and asset tests, for example high income earners who become unemployed may face a stand down period before they are entitled to an unemployment benefit and they may have to demonstrate that they have used up their own savings before qualifying for state aid. Benefits are available to those who fit the criteria and are legal residents of New Zealand, but in some cases applicants must have lived there for several years. There is a reciprocal social security agreement with the UK which entitles UK residents who move to New Zealand to qualify for New Zealand benefits under the same criteria as New Zealanders. Some UK benefits are payable in New Zealand and in some circumstances it may be advisable to keep paying British National Insurance contributions. Immigrants from other countries will have to satisfy residence criteria before they become eligible. Most benefits are taxed before payment and the net amount is paid to the beneficiary, usually directly into a bank account.

Unemployment benefit. Payments are not related to previous earnings and the weekly rate is very low. The single rate is currently ranges from \$121.21-\$181.84 per week, and for married couples, \$257.58 per week. Anyone under 25 years old is paid a lower rate. The unemployment benefit is payable to New Zealand citizens and residents only. The applicant must be actively looking and ready for work, or be involved in a training course. WINZ also helps people with finding work experience and seasonal jobs. Such work is usually in the tourist business, or in the farming, fishing, or horticulture industries. There is also a wage subsidy available to employers who offer the unemployed full time work. This is called 'Job Plus'.

Invalid benefit. Available to people aged sixteen or over who are severely restricted in their capacity for work due to accident, illness or congenital disability. It is not available to those who have enough money from other means to support themselves. The rates range from \$184.01-\$230.66 per week, depending on circumstances.

Sickness benefit. This is available those over 16 who are incapacitated for work through sickness or accident. It also includes women who are over 28 weeks pregnant. The level of the sickness benefit is the same rate as the dole, i.e., between \$121.21-\$181.84 per week.

Domestic purposes benefit (DPB): The DPB is available to a parent caring for a child without the support of a partner. The parent must be over eighteen years of age, (sixteen if married) and have a dependent child under eighteen. For a parent with one child the rate is \$266.34 weekly, with two or more children the rate is \$291.83. If the youngest child is over six years old, the beneficiary must be actively looking for part time work. People over sixteen caring for someone sick or frail who would ordinarily need hospital care can also be eligible for the DPB. The amount that someone receives depends on age and if they are married or have a partner, the number of children living with them and how much other income they have.

Family Support. Family support is cash assistance for low income families. The IRD calculates the amount due, based on the applicant's income and the number and age of children in the family. Family Support is paid to the main caregiver of the children, and children can be counted up to the age of 18.

Child Support. Parents who are not living with their children make payments to support those children through the Child Support Agency, a division of the IRD. The amount paid in child support is based on the income of the parent paying support. The IRD passes on the payment made to the parent or caregiver with whom the children are living.

Other benefits available include the transitional retirement benefit, War Pensions, Young Job Seekers Benefit, Training Benefit, Widows Benefit, Childcare Subsidy, Accommodation Supplement, and Emergency Benefit. For more details on any of these, enquire at the local Income Support Service office or call the Head Office (freephone 0800 559 009). For residents on low and middle incomes, Income Support provides a Community Services Card, which reduces the costs of health care. Permanent legal residents can apply to the National Community Services Card Centre (PO Box 5054, Wellington; freephone 0800 999 999).

CRIME AND THE POLICE

Although you should not have an unrealistically rosy picture of New Zealand society, it is generally a safe country. By world standards the police are corruption-free and for the most part are well respected in the community. The police carry out a wide range of duties; as well as enforcing criminal law, traffic patrols, carrying out investigations and search and rescue, they also perform Youth Education Services. Unfortunately the crime rate has been rising in recent years and the days when people would regularly go out without locking their front doors are over. However, violent crime is sufficiently uncommon as to be newsworthy. In general, New Zealand cities are safe places to walk around providing you use your common sense. Much of the crime in New Zealand is domestic violence. Police officers do not carry guns on normal duties, and for the most part it is illegal for ordinary citizens to carry or own hand guns or automatic weapons. Firearms are strictly controlled and gun carriers must have a special permit from the Police Arms Office. The emergency number, to access police, ambulance or fire brigade services, is 111. Cards or coins are not necessary to dial this number from a pay phone, and it will also connect from a toll-barred mobile phone.

LOCAL GOVERNMENT

Local government in New Zealand is very much subordinate to central government. Its powers and functions are set by parliament. There are two levels. Regional councils have broad responsibilities relating to the environment and land use, including control of pests and noxious plants. They also have some responsibilities over civil defence in the case of flood or earthquake. At the next level are territorial or local councils. Both are directly elected, and have the power to set rates. They mostly provide services such as rubbish collection and disposal, parks, swimming pools, cemeteries and libraries. They are responsible for a variety of regulatory measures, for example, building consent, health inspection and control of noise, pollution and parking.

Official Information

Information held by the government and its ministries, education and health institutions, State Owned Enterprises and local government is called official information. There is legislation governing the availability of this material, and members of the public can write in to the organisation concerned to find out certain facts and figures.

SOCIAL LIFE

Meeting People & Making Friends

New Zealanders are very easy to get to know. They are relaxed about opening up a conversation with complete strangers. In fact if you walk into a country pub and fail to say hello to the locals, it would be considered quite rude. People are welcoming in inviting you back to their homes. New Zealanders do not make such invitations out of politeness, they mean it, so never feel you are taking advantage. It is considered quite normal to call round without a specific invitation. Neighbours will often drop in and introduce themselves to new people moving in, and perhaps take them some baking. For all the immediate friendliness, New Zealanders can be quite reserved in some respects. They are not likely to tell you much about their feelings or values until you get to know them well.

Social Attitudes

Perhaps as a result of their pioneering forebears, New Zealanders are an independent people. There is a great tradition of self-reliance, whether it comes to building an extension on the back of the house, or cutting off ties with the rest of the Western alliance during the Cold War period by refusing American nuclear armed ships access to New Zealand ports. Innovation is respected. Finding an ingenious, low-cost solution to a problem was obviously an asset in pioneering days. There is even a phrase for it, 'Kiwi ingenuity', which describes a pragmatic, imaginative approach to problem solving.

Despite approving of innovative and non-traditional approaches to problem solving, rural New Zealand remains quite conservative in outlook. Innovative or alternative lifestyles are not widely approved of. However tolerance is also a New Zealand characteristic, perhaps because the independent streak in the average New Zealander leads them to respect the rights of others to live their lives as they choose. Urban New Zealand is more liberal in outlook. Green issues receive quite a lot of support, perhaps because New Zealanders are aware they live in one of the last largely unspoilt wilderness areas in the world and they have some responsibility to hand it on to their children without ruining it. There is strong support for biculturalism and multiculturalism in theory. However Pakeha New Zealanders can sometimes be heard complaining that government treats the Maori more favourably. In fact positive discrimination programmes of the type common in the USA are more perceived than actual. There are, however, special grants for Maori business and for educational purposes. Few institutions run a formal quota system although all are required to have an equal employment policy. Maori leaders acknowledge that Maori society is increasingly dependent on welfare benefits and Maori workers are more likely to be unemployed than Pakeha.

Like the Welsh and the Scots before them, New Zealanders feel the need to assert their own identity to prove that they are different from the English and the colonial power which shaped the early period of settlement, and hence became the original model for New Zealand culture. The need to assert themselves usually manifests itself as a fairly critical attitude towards English life, attitudes, culture and climate, on the part of those who have visited that country and even by some that have not. This criticism is usually not intended to be rude or offensive, rather it functions as a form of commiseration for the English for having had the misfortune to have been born there rather than in New Zealand. Reciprocal ruthless honesty about the drawbacks of living in New Zealand is unlikely to be welcomed however. In fact they tend to be defensive about New Zealand, even though they think its merits ought to be self-evident.

Smoking. Smoking is a lot less socially acceptable in New Zealand than it is in Europe. Public buildings, including shopping malls, are smoke-free zones by law. Most restaurants and cafés provide a smoke free area with some even banning smoking completely. Smoking is not banned in bars, pubs or nightclubs, however. If you are visiting a New Zealand home, it is perfectly acceptable for your host to request that you only smoke outside.

Entertainment and Culture

New Zealand may not be as well known overseas for its musicians and artists (pop band Crowded House and opera diva Dame Kiri Te Kanawa excepted) as it is for its sports men and women, but in fact there is a lively local cultural scene. Increasingly, performers from New Zealand are succeeding internationally. Kiri Te Kanawa is respected throughout New Zealand, not so much because every household worships opera, but because like the All Blacks she is a New Zealander succeeding internationally. She attracts huge audiences when she returns home to perform.

There are three fully professional orchestra companies, based in Auckland, Wellington and Christchurch, and there are a number of semi-professional and amateur regional orchestras. International soloists and chamber groups visit frequently, and every two years the Wellington Festival of the Performing Arts attracts some top rate orchestras and ensembles from all over the world.

Other types of performing arts thrive, particularly in Wellington where there are a number of professional theatres, the Royal New Zealand Ballet, several contemporary dance companies and the New Zealand Symphony Orchestra. The New Zealand film scene has enjoyed much success both at home and overseas. *The Piano,* made by New Zealander Jane Campion is one of line of internationally acclaimed films which includes *Heavenly Creatures, Once Were Warriors,* and *Angel at my Table.* There is much current international interest in New Zealand film makers, as the first of director Peter Jackson's trilogy of *The Lord of the Rings* was released in 2001 and the following two are due to follow at the end of 2002 and 2003 respectively. Location filming took place in New Zealand, and has significantly boosted New Zealand's profile as a holiday destination, resulting in an estimated 20% increase in tourism.

Eating Out

The traditional New Zealand European diet was mostly derived from the eating patterns of British immigrants, influenced by the relative abundance of dairy products and cheap mutton and beef. New Zealanders tend to consume too much cholesterol and saturated fat and as a result have one of the highest rates of heart disease in the western world. This is changing slowly as a result of government campaigns promoting healthier eating styles and a new interest in the diet and food of Asian countries. During the week the main meal is usually in the evening, which confusingly many New Zealanders call 'tea'.

Eating out isn't the letdown it once was, now that the country is no longer all that interested in 'traditional' British cooking. The quality of restaurants in the main cities is very high, as is the range of different international food styles on offer. Restaurants are constantly seeking to define a distinctive 'New Zealand cuisine', and come up with delicious combinations of fresh fruits, vegetables and meat.

The improvement in the domestic wine industry has helped to turn New Zealanders into more discerning gastronomes. There is a lot of interest in European food trends. Many New Zealand restaurants have what is called a BYO (BYO stands for Bring Your Own) licence. They are not allowed to sell alcoholic beverages, instead the customer brings their own wine, which the restaurant opens. They usually make a small charge called corkage for this. The advantage of BYO establishments is that you avoid the huge mark up restaurants usually put on wine and you have a much wider choice of what to drink. BYO restaurants tend to be cheaper than fully licensed places, at $25 to $45 a head for a three-course meal, not including what you paid for the wine. A three course meal at a licensed restaurant is more likely to be in the $45 to $60 range, not including the cost of wine. The cheapest and sometimes the most interesting food can be found at the fashionable espresso bars, which are mushrooming in the big cities. You can eat in these sorts of places for less than $20.

The situation in small towns can be grim. Chinese takeaways or fish and chips might be your best bet anywhere from north of Wellington to the Bombay Hills, and in the hinterlands of Canterbury and Otago. You will often see 'tea rooms' in the smaller towns as you pass through, but unless these look bustling and clean they are probably best avoided. Of course, there are many good local restaurants in small towns but unless a friend you trust (and who wants to keep your friendship) has recommended a restaurant, you might be better off with takeaways. Vineyards open to the public sometimes include a restaurant, particularly in areas such as Marlborough, Martinborough and Hawkes Bay. Indian restaurants are less common than in other countries, but other Asian food establishments, especially Japanese, Thai and Malaysian, are becoming more prolific. The fish and chips in takeaways are usually fresh and tasty, as instead of frying chips and other goodies in advance and letting them dry out under hot lamps, they fry your order up individually. Fish and chips still come wrapped in newspaper in most places too, with no European health regulations to interfere. No one has yet died in New Zealand of newsprint poisoning.

Tipping and Service Charges: gratuities are not necessary in New Zealand, and service charges are not added onto hotel or restaurant bills. However, a tip as recognition of extra service or consideration would be appreciated.

Sport

What can you say about a country where a former Prime Minister gets involved with the choice over the coach of the rugby team? New Zealanders are intensely nationalistic when it comes to identifying with the successes of their national teams, particularly the All Blacks rugby team. Losing a rugby match can cast a gloom over the entire nation. It is about more than just losing a game. New Zealand is such a small player in the international political and economic order, that the fact that the country's elite sports teams are capable of taking on the big guys and winning becomes a matter of national pride.

Cricket runs a close second in the interest of New Zealanders, although most New Zealanders bemoan the poor performance of their national team. However, test matches are followed closely on the television, even when broadcast from the other hemisphere in the middle of the night. In fact, television news bulletins always cover cricket and rugby - from watching New Zealand TV, you could be mistaken for thinking there are only two sports played in the country. Much less coverage is given to the Silver Ferns, the women's netball team, although they are more consistently successful on the world stage. For a brief and glorious period the soccer team (the 'All Whites') were in the limelight when they qualified for the World Cup.

New Zealanders are not just enthusiastic about watching sport. A large number of people participate in their spare time. Nearly 50% of the population belong to some kind of sport, fitness or leisure club. The most popular activities are aquatic sports such as swimming, diving, rowing, or water polo. As well as team sports such as hockey, netball, rugby and football (usually called soccer), an increasing number of New Zealanders are involved in individual sports like surfing, snowboarding, mountain biking, rock climbing, skateboarding, tramping, triathlon competitions, or motorcross. Adrenaline sports are on the increase in the country, as thrill seekers face the challenges presented by the mountains and rivers around them. From the birthplace of bungy jumping, adventures such as black water rafting (rafting in caves) rap jumping (abseiling face-down on a building) and river sledding (going down white water rapids on a boogie board) are on offer for large sums of money. New and more terrifying sports emerge each year. But if you do not count yourself among the adrenaline junkies there are plenty of more rational and relaxing sports and outdoor activities available including scuba diving, whale watching and swimming with dolphins in the open sea.

Recreational Fishing Restrictions. Fishing is a popular sport in New Zealand, and there is an abundance of clean rivers, lakes and fish life. However, there are regulations concerning New Zealand fishing in order to protect the resource. Amateur fishermen are not allowed to take more than the daily limit, sell or trade what they caught, or catch undersized fish. There are also restrictions on the minimum size of shellfish and lobsters. Fishermen who operate commercially are required to have a fishing permit. For more information, contact the Ministry of Agriculture and Forestry Information Bureau (101-103 The Terrace, PO Box 2526, Wellington; ☎(04) 474 4100; fax: (04) 474 4111; e-mail: info@maf.govt.nz; internet: www.maf.govt.nz).

MAORI CULTURE

The Maori have been in Aotearoa (New Zealand) for approximately 1000 years, a long time compared to the 150 years of Pakeha (European) settlement. Maori culture remains distinct from the rest of New Zealand culture, although each invariably influences the other.

Maori Social Customs

The Marae. The distinctive and central focus of Maori culture is the *marae* or meeting place. A *marae* consists of a *wharenui* (meeting house), a *wharekai* (eating house) and *wharepaku* (ablution block). To the Maori however, it is not the presence of the buildings that is significant, but the spiritual importance of the location, the discussions and exchanges between people and events ranging from marriages to funerals that take place on the *marae*. It is customary to welcome visitors onto the *marae* in a ceremony called a *powhiri* (welcome).

The Powhiri. Visitors (called the *manuhiri*) will gather outside the gate of the *marae*. It is considered improper to walk onto the *marae* uninvited. The visitors will be 'called on' by the host people (the *tangata whenua*). This is called the *karanga* and is usually performed by a woman from the host side. The *manuhiri* will proceed slowly onto the marae as one group. Usually the women are to the front of the group. One of these women will answer the welcoming call with a *karanga* of her own. The group will pause in silence to *tangi* (remember the dead) and then will move slowly to the seating provided. The front row of seating is reserved for those men who wish to *whaikorero* (speak). Traditionally, women do not have this right.

Whaikorero (speeches) are to welcome manuhiri, to remember those who have died, to thank *tangata whenua* and always mention the reason for the visit. Each speech is followed by a *waiata* (song), sung by the speaker's group to show their support of him. The final speaker for the *manuhiri* will lay down the *koha* (gift). Today *koha* are mostly monetary contributions towards the cost of the *hui* (gathering). The final speech is usually made by the host side.

At the conclusion of the *whaikorero* it is customary for the visitors and the hosts to *hongi* (press noses). This is usually done by shaking right hands, bracing your left hand on the other person's right arm and pressing your nose into theirs twice whilst looking them in the eye. Today some people will shake hands instead. It is best to follow the lead of the *tangata whenua*. After the formalities, hosts and guests share a meal together. It is at this point that the *manuhiri* become *tangata whenua* and the *powhiri* is concluded.

Points to Remember. The *wharenui* is for gatherings and for sleeping. You should always remove your shoes before entering the *wharenui*. Never walk on mattresses or sit on pillows. Certain places are reserved for the elders (*kaumatua*) to sit and sleep in. You should never eat in the *wharenui*.

In the *wharekai* (eating house) be careful not to put hair clips, scarves, combs, glasses or anything to do with the head on the table. This is because the head is sacred (tapu). Tables are also tapu, so you must never sit or put your feet on any tables. A *hangi* is a delicious feast of food that has been cooked in the ground. Rocks heated by fire are placed in a hole in the ground, and the food baskets are filled with vegetables and meat and placed on the rocks and are then covered over with earth. When serving yourself, it is polite to take small helpings (and quite acceptable to have several of them) rather than one large plateful. Before meals there will usually be grace. It is good manners to allow the *kaumatua* to eat first, and after the first meal, once you have become part of the tangata whenua, to offer to help with the dishes or preparation of the next meal.

Do not smoke in any of the buildings on the *marae* and do not use cameras or tape recorders unless given permission. Never be afraid to ask what protocol you should be following. Part of Maori culture emphasises the importance of welcoming guests and making them feel at home, so if you are prepared to be respectful of the culture and traditions, then nobody will mind explaining points of protocol to you. A useful book on Maori culture is *Te Marae-A Guide to Customs and Protocols* (Hiwi and Pat Tauroa, Heinemann Reed, 1986). If you want to find out more about Maori culture during a visit to New Zealand, the New Zealand Tourism Board publishes a leaflet called *New Zealand Maori Cultural Heritage Guide* which lists a number of tourism operators who provide visits to marae and other cultural experiences. The New Zealand Immigration Service publishes a leaflet called *The Treaty of Waitangi* which explains the relevance of the Treaty to new immigrants.

SHOPS AND SHOPPING

Most types of shops in New Zealand will be familiar to American and UK immigrants, and in some cases even the names are the same. In smaller towns, shops are open from 8.30 or 9am until 5pm or a little later, five days a week, and 8.30 or 9am until midday or later on Saturday. Sunday shopping began in 1989 and is now well established. Most shops also have one late night when they are open until 8 or 9pm, usually Thursday or Friday. However, with shops now opening during the weekend, late nights are no longer as important as they once were. In larger towns, many retail shops may be open the same hours on Saturdays as on weekdays, and will probably be open on Sunday as well, although perhaps not for a full day. In some larger towns suburban malls and superstores are drawing foot traffic and business out of the city centre. In some major cities, councils have made determined efforts to revive the town centres. Christchurch's Cathedral Square, Auckland's Aotea Square and Wanganui's Victoria Avenue are good examples.

Food and Drink Shopping

Most people buy their weekly groceries from supermarkets. The large supermarkets with the biggest range tend to be out-of-town, which makes access difficult for non-car owners. The four major grocery chains are fairly competitive: New World, Foodtown, Big Fresh and Woolworths. You will find the similar types of food to those you are used to, but most of the stock will be made in New Zealand as imported goods are expensive. There are definite distinctions between different types of supermarket chains in New Zealand. Some offer a cheap no-frills service with minimal overheads. These tend to be large warehouse style places where you pack your own bags and there is not a great range of goods, just all the basics sold very cheaply. Other chains are aiming at the high-income end of the market. They will offer a greater level of customer service, with a range of speciality departments in-store, including a bakery, butcher, delicatessen, seafood counter, etc. but they are comparatively expensive. Most supermarkets are open seven days a week and will usually have at least one late night when they are open until 9 or 10pm. In the larger cities, many supermarkets are open until 10pm daily.

Local Shops. Local shops have not yet disappeared, but they are threatened by the convenience and cheaper prices of supermarket shopping. Most city neighbourhoods have a convenience store (called a dairy). Dairies stock practically everything, from ice cream to batteries, and are usually open late (until 9pm or 10pm), but because they are small they charge higher prices than supermarkets. Some neighbourhoods still have their local butcher, greengrocers and bakery but these are becoming less common.

Delicatessens. Serious foodies will probably miss the range of speciality foods available in the USA, Europe and the UK. Delicatessens stock a range of imported foods but at a price. On the other hand, most staple foods are relatively cheap and high quality fresh foods are abundant. The good news is that many New Zealand companies are produce European style specialities locally. Many city bakeries now make Italian breads such as *foccacia* and *ciabatta* , and fresh pasta can be found in most towns. A New Plymouth company is producing French style cheeses, although they seem to cost nearly as much as the real thing. Local companies also make a variety of tempting cheeses.

New Zealand Specialities. New Zealand's varied climate provides suitable conditions for growing a wide range of fruit and vegetables, but you will find that what is available in the shops depends on the season, as it is mostly locally grown. Produce with a short shelf life cannot be imported to cover the off-season because the distances involved are too great. On the other hand you can buy exotic produce common to the area: Pacific Island specialities such as taro (a root vegetable), coconut and plantains are the type of imported produce that is commonly available in the bigger towns. Fresh fish and shellfish are another New Zealand speciality. Green-lipped mussels, Pacific oysters, and local salmon, smoked eel, whitebait and trout are all popular. Because export demand drives up the prices, seafood is not always cheap.

New Zealand Wines. Local wines are also generally of good quality. New Zealand white wines were 'discovered' by international wine writers in the late 1980s which had an enormous galvanising effect on the New Zealand industry. The number of vineyards multiplied, and everybody started producing Sauvignon Blanc as that was in demand. New Zealand wines are not much cheaper at home than they are overseas, but the range is greater. There are over 2000 labels produced every year. You can buy not just the ubiquitous Sauvignon Blanc but also some seriously good Chardonnay, and some excellent red wines - several New Zealand Pinot Noirs have won international acclaim.

Australian wines are readily available and are generally cheaper than New Zealand wines because their industry does not face the same crippling taxes that hit New Zealand producers.

Other Shopping

Most consumer goods are readily available in New Zealand. Imported goods are cheaper than they used to be as a result of tariffs being lowered in the 1980s. However it is probably not the shopping that attracts most visitors or immigrants. There is no equivalent to Regent Street or Fifth Avenue even in the big cities. Department store chains such as Farmers and K-Mart sell most of the essentials from clothing through to household goods and white goods in rather unimaginative surroundings. Basic clothing is comparatively cheap, although design and quality standards are not particularly high in the chain stores. Independent designers flourish in the larger cities selling well made and reasonably priced clothing, often through their own boutiques.

Hire Purchase. More expensive consumer durables are often available in New Zealand on hire purchase. Once the buyer signs a hire purchase agreement (subject to a credit check) and pays a deposit they can take the goods home to use, and pay the remainder of the price by regular instalments. If the instalment demands are not met, however, the goods can be repossessed.

TABLE 21	PUBLIC HOLIDAYS
1 January	New Year's Day
2 January	Day after New Year's Day
6 February	Waitangi Day (formerly New Zealand Day)
April	Good Friday
April	Easter Monday
25 April	Anzac Day
June	Queen's Birthday
October	Labour Day
25 December	Christmas Day
26 December	Boxing Day

However, the only days that almost all shops are closed on are Good Friday, Easter Sunday, Anzac Day and Christmas Day.

TIME

New Zealand is twelve hours ahead of Greenwich Mean Time. During Daylight Saving the clocks are put forward by one hour, from the first Sunday in October to the third Sunday of the following March.

METRICATION

New Zealand uses the metric measuring system for distances, weights and measures, with a few imperial hangovers. Beer, for example, is usually sold by the pint. People still talk about a pint of milk or a pound of butter, although these products are packaged in metric measurements. Road signs are all in kilometres, as are speed limits. To convert kilometres into miles, multiply by five and divide by eight. Temperatures are in degrees Celsius. As a rough guide, convert to Fahrenheit, double the degrees and add 30.

RETIREMENT

BACKGROUND INFORMATION

Around 12% of New Zealand's population is aged 65 or older, and a significant number were born in other countries. Undoubtedly for many older people, the chance to be reunited with children who have already migrated to New Zealand is a major attraction. Having adult children in New Zealand also makes it easier to get permanent residency. Otherwise migration may be difficult for people of retirement age, as New Zealand's immigration policy is aimed at attracting people into the workforce.

New Zealand offers many advantages for those considering a change of scenery for their retirement. The standard of living is high and the exchange rate is favourable, so your savings should go a long way. British and American retirees will not have to learn a new language and will find the culture reasonably familiar. The climate in most parts of New Zealand is warmer than Northern Europe. There are the attractions of living in a less crowded country, with, in general, fewer social problems and a lower crime rate. New Zealand's population is an ageing one, so there are many clubs and services that cater for older people's interests and needs.

Although doctors' visits cost about $35-45 per consultation, hospital care is still free for New Zealanders and immigrants from countries with reciprocal social security agreements. On the other hand, certain types of specialist medical care may be better provided in America, the UK and European countries, simply because New Zealand is too small to have the range of expertise in these areas.

The drawbacks of emigrating have to be considered as well. You will be far away from friends and family in the northern hemisphere and you may find life a little lonely at first. Many retirees mention that one of the hardest aspects of their new life is not being able to afford to return home for family events such as weddings. New Zealand is 26 hours away from London by plane, and around thirteen hours from the USA, and the trip is not cheap. Most migrants report that they find it easy to get to know New Zealanders, and although new friends are not a substitute for old, you need not fear being isolated for long in your new country.

The Decision to Leave

Making a permanent move to another country is a very different matter from just visiting it, particularly when you will be adjusting to all the lifestyle changes retirement brings as well. It may be a good idea therefore to spend a longer period in New Zealand before deciding whether to make a permanent move there. Many people make the decision to move after a visit to New Zealand to see family or friends. If you have a British passport you are entitled to visit New Zealand for up to six months without requiring a visa, and tourists from the USA, Canada and Europe are able to stay for three months without a visa. A visit may be a good opportunity to explore different parts of the country before deciding where you would most like to settle. A number of companies arrange coach and train tours with itineraries that cover most of New Zealand in a short period. One such company is Scenic Coach Tours, which arranges custom packaged vacations for senior citizens (internet: www.sceniccoachtours.co.nz/newzealand). Some companies will also arrange farm and home-stay tours, which will enable you to experience the lifestyle of New Zealand families. If you wish to arrange your own homestays or farmstays, contact New Zealand Homestay and Farmstays (80 Wairarapa Terrace, Merivale, Christchurch; tel/fax: (03) 355 6737; e-mail: info@nzhomestay.co.nz; internet: www.nzhomestay.co.nz).

As has been noted elsewhere, rental accommodation is generally easy to find, so you may like to try living in your prospective retirement locality for a while. It will also give you a chance to assess the real costs of living in New Zealand. Financial considerations are an important factor when you are living on a fixed income. You can use a visit to assess the property market in order to find out what kind of housing you will be able to afford. In general, if you have sold property in the UK or USA, you should be able to afford a New Zealand house of at least an equivalent if not better standard, particularly if you choose to live outside the main cities.

Residence and Entry Regulations

Because the general migration category is not open to people aged 55 or above, the most likely route to New Zealand residency for an older person is the family reunification or business development categories. Under the family reunification category, you are entitled to apply for residency if you have an adult child or children living in New Zealand and no adult children living in your own country. Alternatively, you can apply if you have children living in your home country but you have more children living in New Zealand than any other country including your own. If you are under the age of 65 and have sufficient capital you can apply under the business investment category. The minimum amount required is NZ$1 million, and you must meet the pass mark, which is currently 12 points. (See Chapter Two, *Residence and Entry*).

Applying for Residence

To qualify for residency under the family reunification category, you will need to provide evidence of your family relationships, and the citizenship or residency status of your New Zealand children, and of your children living in other countries. You will need to submit birth and marriage certificates and copies of residency permits. Additionally, you will have to satisfy the health and character requirements outlined in Chapter Two for general residency applications.

Possible Retirement Areas

Popular retirement areas are in the warmer regions on the East Coast of the North Island, and the north of the South Island. Many New Zealanders move to the coast when they retire, often to a beach house ('bach' or 'crib'). Some communities have a higher proportion of older people than others, which you may consider an advantage.

One consideration to bear in mind is that in remoter areas you will certainly need to own a car or to live close to local services as public transport may not be convenient enough to rely on. A popular retirement option for New Zealanders is the 'ten acre block' or 'lifestyle block', a house in the country on a large section of land. Ten acres may be the size of farm in Europe, but by the standards of New Zealand farms these are just hobby plots for city folk who want to try the rural lifestyle. Some people cultivate their land or keep animals, while others just enjoy the extra space.

Tauranga and the Bay of Plenty. On the east coast of the North Island, the Bay of Plenty has a pleasant climate and is one of the main horticultural regions as a result. In the summer time, the sun, white sandy beaches and gentle waves of the beach at Mt Manganui attract many families.

Hawke's Bay. Known for its subtropical climate and easy pace of life, Hawke's Bay is a popular retirement spot. There is a wealth of orchards and vineyards here, and Hawke's Bay is one of the premier winemaking regions in the country. Lovers of architecture will enjoy the buildings of Napier, the 'art deco capital of the world', which were built after the 1931 earthquake. A growing number of retired people live in Havelock North, a small town about twenty minutes from Napier. Hawke's Bay also boasts several beautiful beaches.

Kapiti Coast. Just north of Wellington, the west coast of the North Island is a popular retirement destination for locals. It is dotted with small towns, from Paraparaumu up to Otaki, many made up largely of holiday homes that Wellingtonians use to escape for the weekends. There are a large number of permanent residents as well, many of retirement age. Transport networks are good, there is a commuter train service into Wellington city, as well as a local bus network. The coast itself can be quite rough, but just down the coast Pirogue harbour provides more sheltered waters for boating or fishing.

Banks Peninsula. Over the Port Hills to the south of Christchurch, the peninsula was called Bank's Island on the first map of New Zealand after Captain Cook's navigator, Joseph Banks, who thought its deep inlets cut it off from the mainland. In contrast with the flat sweeping plains of Canterbury, the peninsula is all hills and valleys divided by deep harbours. Further east over the hills is Akaroa, with its echoes of the first French settlers. Streets are called 'Rues' and the building code specifies that new houses are to be built in the style of the homes of the original French settlers with steeply raked roofs. You would certainly need to be a car owner to live on the peninsula, as the bus service to Christchurch is infrequent and the remoter valleys lack local services.

Hobbies and interests

New Zealand offers many opportunities for using your new leisure time. The country is full of keen gardeners and the climate is well suited for those who like to spend time outdoors. If you are planning an active retirement, there is a lot of beautiful countryside to be explored. There are sporting opportunities to suit just about everybody. Golf is popular, and there are public golf courses outside most towns and cities. Lawn bowls and croquet are also popular with older people. If you are interested in cultural pursuits, you should consider settling near one of the main cities. Fortunately one of the advantages of living in New Zealand is that you can combine proximity to major cities with a semi-rural lifestyle if you so desire. Banks Peninsula, for example, is only 40 minutes away from the centre of Christchurch. Every town has a senior citizens club, equally open to the recent immigrant as to the native New Zealander. These provide a chance to meet other older people as well as to make use of social facilities. Many older people use their new leisure time to return to study, either through night classes, through correspondence courses (such as those offered by the Open Polytech) or by enrolling in university part-time. Most New Zealand universities exempt mature students from formal entrance qualifications and instead will assess your ability to study and will enrol you at the appropriate level. A pre-degree certificate in liberal arts, which has less rigorous assessment procedures, may help you to get into the swing of studying. Night classes are offered in a wide variety of subjects from foreign languages through to car maintenance and self-defence at local high schools or polytechnics. The following are just some of the groups available for European and American ex-pats.

Useful Addresses

American Club (Auckland): ☎(09) 815 5587 or (09) 631 0046.

Auckland Bowls: 1 Kimberley Road, Epsom, Auckland; ☎(09) 630 5770; fax: (09) 630 3093; internet: www.aucklandbowls.co.nz.

British Pensioners Association (NZ) Inc: 6a Taikata Road, Te Atatu Peninsula, Auckland 1008; ☎(09) 834 8559; fax: (09) 834 8885; e-mail: britishpensions nz@xtra.co.nz; internet: www.britishp ensioners.org.nz. Provides information about rights, pensions, taxation, Community Services cards, etc. for a yearly subscription fee of $8, which includes membership for your spouse as well.

Citizens Advice Bureau (National Office): PO Box 9777, Level 7, 75 Ghuznee Street, Wellington; ☎(04) 382 8759 or toll free: 0800 367 222; fax: (04) 382 8647; e-mail: cab.natnl@xtra.co.nz; internet: www.cab.org.nz. Citizens Advice have information about local social clubs and interest groups, and there are over 90 offices throughout New Zealand.

Lawn Bowls: PO Box 32 612, Devonport, Auckland; ☎0800 808 202; fax: (09) 445 7722; e-mail: info@sportingpulse.com; internet: www.sportingpulse.co.nz. See the website for a list of lawn bowls associations in different areas throughout the country.

NZ-American Association (Wellington): ☎(04) 232 6053.

NZ Communities Development Trust: ☎Chris Gaelic (chairman) (09) 577 1144; e-mail: chris@communities.co.nz; internet: www.communities.co.nz. Online magazine contains information about sports, gardens to visit, hobbies and interests.

NZ Golf Association: Level 1, Xacta Tower, PO Box 11842, Wellington; ☎(04) 385 4330; fax: (04) 385 4331; e-mail: info@nzga.co.nz; internet: www.nzga.co.nz.

SeniorNet: ☎toll free: 0800 SENIORNET (0800 736 467); internet: www.seniornet.org.nz. There are 77 SeniorNet learning centres throughout the country, teaching older people about communications and information technology. For those over the age of 55.

PENSIONS

New Zealand Pensions

Superannuation has been a fraught issue for the last 25 years, and pension levels have changed with nearly every government since 1975. In 2000, the superannuation rate was reinstated at 65% of the net average weekly wage, to be paid from the age of 65.

To qualify for the New Zealand state retirement pension, National Superannuation, a person must have lived in New Zealand for a total of at least ten years since the age of 20, including five years since the age of 50. National Superannuation currently pays a gross weekly rate of $282.78 for a single person living alone and $428.76 per week, before tax, for a married couple if both qualify. It is paid fortnightly. New Zealand currently has overseas social security arrangements with eight countries: the UK, Ireland, the Netherlands, Greece, Australia, the States of Jersey and Guernsey, Denmark and Canada. The general principal of these reciprocal arrangements is that people migrating from one country to the other are treated like citizens of their new country with regard to social security arrangements and are entitled to the same range of benefits. However, the particular arrangements differ between countries.

UK citizens, if entitled to receive a British retirement pension, can continue to receive it in New Zealand. The level of the British pension is frozen from the point you leave the UK, and is not inflation adjusted. If you become eligible for the pension while in New Zealand, it will be paid at the rate that applies in the UK when you are first entitled to a pension. Under the reciprocal agreement, if you qualify for National Superannuation, the New Zealand Government supplements the British pension so that it is at the same level as National Superannuation.

Emigrants who settle in New Zealand are entitled to a pension when they reach the qualifying age of 65. The amount of the pension is dependent on the number of years in paid employment, i.e., the amount you have contributed to the social security scheme in your country of origin. The pension can be directly credited to a New Zealand bank or building society account. When you become entitled to New Zealand National Superannuation, you will receive the full New Zealand pension, made up of the pension plus the balance being paid by the New Zealand government. To apply for the UK pension, write to the Contributions Agency International Services, (Overseas Benefits Directorate, Newcastle upon Tyne, NE98 1BA, United Kingdom).

The reciprocal agreements between New Zealand and other countries give equal treatment and protection of benefit rights when you move from one country to the other. The amount of the overseas pension you receive is taxable income in New Zealand.

Useful Addresses

Age Concern NZ *(Inc):* 3rd Floor, Riddiford House, 150 Featherston Street, PO Box 10 688, Wellington; ☎(04) 471 2709; fax: (04) 473 2504; e-mail: nationaloffice@age concern.org.nz; internet: www.ageconcern.org.nz. Promotes rights, quality of life and wellbeing for older people.

Citizens Advice Bureau (National Office): PO Box 9777, Level 7, 75 Ghuznee Street, Wellington; ☎(04) 382 8759 or toll free 0800 367 222; fax: (04) 382 8647; e-mail: cab.natnl@xtra.co.nz; internet: www.cab.org.nz.

Grey Power: PO Box 200-129, Papatoetoe Central, Auckland; ☎(09) 277 7954; fax: (09) 277 7958; e-mail: fed-office@xtra.co.nz; internet: www.greypower.co.nz. A lobby group and support network for people over 50. Not aligned with any political party, Grey Power provides information about political issues and policies, super-annuation, etc. See website or telephone for details of your local association.

Retirement Commission: PO Box 12 148, Wellington; ☎(04) 499 7396; internet: www.retirement.org.nz. This office is partly government funded, and has a range of activities aimed at raising public awareness and understanding of retirement income policies.

Receiving Your Pension Abroad

Pension arrangements for expatriates vary. In some countries if you have established entitlement in your own country then you can continue to receive your pension in New Zealand. As noted above, some countries have reciprocal agreements with New Zealand, which entitle you to the same range of benefits as a local. You should contact your local Department of Social Security for further information. One New Zealand company that specialises in completing necessary documentation and liaising with overseas agencies is Overseas Pension Transfers Ltd (Building 4, 106 Bush Road, Albany, Auckland; ☎0800 500 811 or (09) 414 4215; fax: (09) 414 4219; e-mail: al.opt@xtra.co.nz; internet: www.ukpensionstonz.com).

Taxation

Once you are a New Zealand resident, you pay New Zealand income tax on your worldwide income, including income from any overseas based pension schemes. Residency for taxation purposes has nothing to do with your immigration status. You are deemed to be New Zealand resident for tax purposes if you have a permanent place of abode in New Zealand, regardless of whether you also have one in another country. Having a permanent abode in New Zealand is not limited to owning a dwelling, the courts will also take into account social, personal, and financial ties as evidence of where your permanent abode is. If you are in New Zealand for more than 183 days in any twelve-month period, you are regarded as a New Zealand resident for taxation purposes whether or not you have a permanent abode in New Zealand. New Zealand has double tax treaties with 24 countries including the USA, Canada, the UK, France, Germany, and the Netherlands. These treaties limit the tax liability for citizens of one country resident in the other, so that an individual does not in theory pay tax twice on the same income.

Useful Address

Montfort International: Home Farm, Shere Road, Albury, Guildford, Surrey GU5 9BL; ☎01483-202072; fax 01483-203235. Provides expert tax planning and financial advice to New Zealand migrants to maximise on opportunities and minimise any potential tax liabilities.

New Zealand Health Care

One of the drawbacks of the New Zealand health care system for a retired person is that although hospital care is free, doctor's visits are not, nor are prescriptions. For those pensioners on low incomes from countries with reciprocal social security arrangements, the Community Services Card is available - this reduces the costs of health care. Permanent legal residents can apply to the National Community Services Card Centre (PO Box 5054, Wellington; ☎0800 999 999). Application forms can also be obtained from any Work and Income NZ (WINZ) centre, or your doctor or local pharmacy. There is a cap on the total amount you will be charged annually for prescriptions, so if you need a lot of medication, you do not pay more than a certain amount. Private medical insurance is one option to consider, to cover the additional costs of New Zealand health care. See the Heath Care section in Chapter Four, *Daily Life* for further details. Private insurance will cover the cost of treatment in private hospitals, which will give you more choice about the timing of operations. But, as is indicated in Chapter Four, the annual cost of premiums is likely to make full private insurance costly unless you are a frequent user of primary health care services.

Wills and Legal Considerations

You should draw up a will in New Zealand if you are considering buying property and settling there. Dying intestate complicates matters sufficiently for one's heirs, without doing so in a foreign country. In the event that a non-New Zealander dies intestate, the laws of their own country will apply. As it is more likely that you will be a New Zealand citizen or at least domiciled there in the eyes of the law, New Zealand intestate laws would apply. Under New Zealand intestate laws, your estate would be divided between a surviving spouse and your children, with your spouse getting the major share. This would be the case even if you had separated from but not divorced your spouse.

In New Zealand, a will does not have to be drawn up by a lawyer. However, there are obvious advantages to having your will drawn up by a lawyer or trust company. If there are any mistakes in the way the will is drawn up they can invalidate it, and the lawyer or trust company chosen to draw up your will can administer your estate. This may be a good idea, particularly if you have no close relatives in the country. In some countries, people often nominate a relative or friend(s) as executor of the will. However, it is better to have a trust company or solicitor as your executor, and this also saves problems if your nominated executor predeceases you. Many New Zealand lawyers do not charge for drawing up wills, and if you nominated the solicitor or trust company that drew up your will, you will either pay no fee or a minimal fee for the execution of the will.

A living will is separate from the will you make about your assets. It expresses your wishes about your care and welfare before your death, in the event that you are unable to express such wishes yourself at the time. It contains directives for medical decisions, including how much care you wish to receive should you develop any terminal illness, and how vigorous such care should be. There is no legal basis for living wills, but Age Concern advises that they are viewed sympathetically. For further information contact your lawyer or a Community Law Centre.

SECTION II

WORKING IN NEW ZEALAND

EMPLOYMENT

BUSINESS AND INDUSTRY REPORT

REGIONAL EMPLOYMENT GUIDE

STARTING A BUSINESS

EMPLOYMENT

CHAPTER SUMMARY

O **Job Opportunities:** British and Canadian people are often recruited by the health, education and legal sectors.

  O Many skilled people from India are recruited to work in IT.

O **Unemployment.** A decade ago, New Zealand unemployment was over 10%; it is now down to about half that.

  O 65% of jobs are in service industries, compared with 10% in agriculture.

O **Skills Shortage Lists.** New Zealand Immigration has a Labour Market Skills Shortage List which is updated every three months.

  O Secondary school teachers of maths, computing, technology and sports are needed in New Zealand.

O **Salaries.** New Zealand salaries are below those in Europe and the USA; living costs are however also lower in New Zealand.

O **Parental Leave.** This can last up to 52 weeks and can be shared between both parents.

  O If you take more than four weeks maternity leave your employer can offer your job to someone else, but is obliged to offer you a job substantially similar.

O **Unions.** Any group of employees can set up and register a trade union.

  O A trade union must have a minimum of 15 members.

O **Women.** About 65% of women over the age of 15 have jobs.

  O About a third of the female workforce works part-time.

The Employment Scene

Although New Zealand is a small country, it is a modern economy with a growing range of employment and business opportunities. With less than 0.1% of the world's population, New Zealand is never likely to compete with top international salary levels in the world's biggest businesses; however, the lifestyle attracts many skilled workers every year. Small population size and the country's relative isolation mean that it will always need migrants to fill the gaps in its economy. The Kiwi tradition of gaining overseas experience means that demand for employees often exceeds supply, and at the moment the new high-growth industries (software, wine, education services, etc.) offer a great number of employment opportunities to new migrants with the right skills. Demand for specific talent often leads employers to recruit overseas workers - last year, for example, boat builders recruited 100 people from South Africa. British and Canadian people in particular are often recruited by the legal and health sectors, and many skilled people come from India to work in the New Zealand IT industry every year.

In the past, the country enjoyed very low unemployment with the average level in the 1970s being less than 2%. However, throughout the 1980s unemployment increased rapidly. A large number of jobs were lost in manufacturing industries during the radical economic reforms of the 1980s. Some of the job losses can be attributed to long term trends in the labour market and reflect the same kinds of changes that have occurred in other western countries where manufacturing industries have been unable to compete with cheaper labour costs in the newly industrialised countries of Asia. There has been a shift in New Zealand's industrial structure from manufacturing to service industries. Other job losses can be traced to the lowering of tariff barriers as a result of New Zealand's conversion to neo-liberal economic policies. Tight monetary policy aimed at squeezing inflationary pressures out of the economy also contributed to the economic downturn.

In September 1991, unemployment reached 10.9%, following a recession and the period of restructuring in the public sector. However, aside from a brief period of increase during the Asian crisis, unemployment has fallen steadily over the last ten years. At 5.2%, it is now the lowest it has been since March 1988, when it was just 4.8%. The number of unemployed is currently around 100,000.

Labour market conditions are steady, and continue to improve. Overall, levels of employment have increased to an estimated 1,825,000 people, up from 1,621,500 in 1995. There has been 1.4% growth in full-time employment, and part-time employment is up 4.4%. The labour force participation rate is currently 65.9%. Within the labour force, around 65% are employed in services (including transport, accommodation, trade, communication, finance, software, educational and scientific services), 25% in industry and 10% in agriculture. Agriculture contributes 8% to GDP, while industry and services are responsible for 23% and 69% respectively.

According to the *National Bank Business Outlook Report* (December 2001), employment intentions remain positive in all sectors except manufacturing. Confidence in building activity is increasing - building completions have risen 4.3% and even more construction is expected in the year to come, as the number of building permits issued continues to increase. It is expected that retail activity will improve during the coming year, as lower petrol prices and low interest rates are encouraging consumers to spend.

Real GDP growth is currently 4.4%, and real wages rose 1.0% in the last year; annual wage growth was 3.4% compared to 1.3% the previous year. Rising wages may discourage employment growth to an extent, and the total number of filled jobs has decreased slightly (0.1% over the last quarter) but firms are increasing wages in the face of tight labour supply conditions. According to the New Zealand Institute of Economic Research, it is expected that this tightness in the labour market will ease somewhat over the next year or so. In the area of demand, firms will be a little cautious as trading partner growth and business confidence are somewhat uncertain due to recent developments in the world economy. However, in terms of supply, the pool of labour is expected to continue to increase with net migration inflows.

There are several useful websites containing up to date information about current trends and predictions, including those of the New Zealand Institute of Economic Research (www.nzier.org.nz), Statistics New Zealand (www.stats.govt.nz), TradeNZ (www.tradenz.govt.nz) and the Immigration Service (www.business-migrants.govt.nz and www.immigration.govt.nz). An annual guide to the employment environment and opportunities in New Zealand, entitled *Working In New Zealand*, is available from Working In Ltd (PO Box 3394, Shortland Street, Auckland; ☎(09) 631 0412; fax: (09) 623 7490; e-mail: info@workingin.com; internet: www.workingin.com).

Residence and Work Regulations

New Zealand requires that foreign nationals working in New Zealand, whether for local or foreign companies, obtain work permits for the period of employment. In most cases this may not exceed three years. Permission from the New Zealand Immigration Service must be sought prior to arrival and it must be shown that the worker has skills not readily available in New Zealand.

If you are visiting New Zealand and have found a job, you may apply for a work permit within the country, but the maximum period for which it will be granted is nine months. The same restrictions regarding skills apply. For further details about work permits see *Residence and Entry* chapter.

Skills

Due to demand for specific skills in certain areas of the country, the New Zealand Immigration Service has developed a Labour Market Skills Shortage List. This is designed to streamline the processing of work permits and approvals in principle for work permits or visas where there is a known regional labour shortage. The list is revised every three months. You can access it on the Immigration Service website (www.immigration.govt.nz/work/) or can request details through the 24 hour service at the National Contact Information Service Centre ☎(09) 914 4100; fax: (09) 914 4119).

Qualifications

In general, American and British qualifications are recognised and well regarded in New Zealand. New Zealand's university education system derives its structure from British, particularly Scottish, universities so the types of qualifications available from universities are similar in title and content to UK ones. Trade and vocational qualifications have different titles. You can apply to the *New Zealand Qualifications Authority* (the government agency that oversees the qualifications system) to have your qualifications assessed before you arrive in New Zealand. They will be assessed in comparison with current New Zealand qualifications. There is a fee for this service, and it will take around eight to ten weeks. In some cases you may be required to do this as part of the application for residency under the General Category. The necessary forms can be obtained from the New Zealand Immigration Service (internet: www.immigration.govt.nz), or you can contact the Qualifications Authority directly (New Zealand Qualifications Authority, PO Box 160, Wellington; ☎+64 4 802 3000; internet: www.nzqa.govt.nz).

Details of entry requirements for New Zealand universities are available from the Trade Development Board (NZ House, 80 Haymarket, London SW1Y 4TQ; ☎020-7973 0380; fax: 020-7839 4580; e-mail: email@newzealandhc.org.uk; internet: www.tradenz.govt.nz), and of course from the universities themselves.

Professional Qualifications

The relevant professional bodies regulate professional employment in New Zealand. In order to work in these areas you must register with these organisations. In most cases this will involve an assessment of qualifications and experience and you may be required to take further examinations. In some professions you can arrange to sit these exams in your own country. It is important to contact the relevant professional body in good time because they usually take several months to consider applications and qualifying exams are held only once or twice a year in foreign countries. As an example of the type of procedure you have to go through, the following are the requirements for foreign lawyers intending to practice in New Zealand.

Legal Practitioners seeking assessment should write to:

The Executive Director, Attn: Secretary, Admissions and Credentials Committee, New Zealand Law Society (PO Box 5041, Wellington; ☎+64 4 472 7837; fax: +64 4 915 1284; e-mail: admissions@nz-lawsoc.org.nz; internet: www.nz-lawsoc.org.nz). You will be required to include the following information:

- Documentary evidence of tertiary educational standing and attainment, including academic record, showing courses completed and grades.
- Documentary evidence of admission as a lawyer in your own country.
- A curriculum vitae giving names, dates, and places of practice.
- A copy of your law school's handbook showing the structure of the degree and the content and length of each course.
- A statutory declaration verifying identity and certifying the accuracy of the above information.
- Where applicable, a demonstration of proficiency in the English language.
- Two bank drafts in payment of application fees: one for NZ $100 payable to the New Zealand Law Society and one for NZ $720 payable to the Council for Legal Education. If you are applying from inside New Zealand, the bank drafts must be increased by 12.5% to cover GST. Applications normally take two or three months to consider.

Not all professional bodies have such complex registration procedures. Membership of the New Zealand Society of Accountants is automatically granted to any member of the three British Associations of Chartered Accountants, that is, the Institute of Chartered Accountants of England and Wales, the Institute of Chartered Accountants of Scotland, and the Chartered Association of Certified Accountants. However, any person in New Zealand is able to call themselves 'an accountant'. It is only when they want to call themselves 'chartered' that they will need to join the New Zealand body.

Teachers do not have to join a professional body, but overseas qualified teachers must have their qualifications assessed by the Teacher Registration Board.

Addresses of Professional Bodies

The Dental Council of New Zealand: PO Box 10448, Wellington; ☎(04) 4 499 4820; fax: (04) 499 1668; e-mail: enq uiries@dentalcouncil.org.nz; internet: www.dentalcouncil.org.nz.

Horticulture and Food Research Institute of NZ Ltd (Hortresearch): Private Bag 11 030, Palmerston North; ☎(06) 356 8080; fax: (06) 354 6731; internet: www.hortresearch.co.nz.

Hospitality Association of New Zealand: PO Box 503, Wellington; ☎(04) 385 1369; fax: (04) 384 8044; e-mail: nsc@hanz.org.nz.

Institute of Chartered Accountants of New Zealand: Level 2, Cigna House, 40 Mercer Street, PO Box 11-342, Wellington; ☎(04) 474 7840 or (04) 460 0606; fax: (04) 473 6303; e-mail: registry@icanz.co.nz; internet: www.icanz.co.nz.

Institute of Professional Engineers NZ: 101 Molesworth Street, PO Box 12 241, Wellington; ☎(04) 473 9444; fax: (04) 474 8933; e-mail: ero@ipenz.org.nz; internet: www.ipenz.org.nz.

The Medical Council of New Zealand: PO Box 11-649, Wellington; ☎(04) 384 7635; fax: (04) 385 8902; e-mail: mcnz@mcnz.org.nz; internet: www.mcnz.org.nz.

New Zealand Institute of Architects: Suite 1.5, D72 Building, Dominion Road, PO Box 2516, Auckland; ☎(09) 623 6080; fax: (09) 623 6081; e-mail: info@nzia.co.nz; internet: www.nzia.co.nz.

New Zealand Law Society: PO Box 5041, Wellington; ☎(04) 472 7837; fax: (04) 473 7909; e-mail: enquiries@nz-lawsoc.org.nz; internet: www.nz-lawsoc.org.nz.

The Nursing Council: PO Box 9644, Wellington; ☎(04) 385 9589; fax: (04) 801 8502; e-mail: admin@nursingcouncil.org.nz; internet: www.nursingcouncil.org.nz.

Physiotherapists Board: PO Box 3287, Wellington; ☎(04) 471 2610; fax: (04) 471 2613; internet: www.physioboard.org.nz.

Teacher Registration Board: Level 7, 93 The Terrace, PO Box 5326, Wellington; ☎(04) 471 0852; fax (04) 471 0870; e-mail: mail@trb.govt.nz; internet: www.trb.govt.nz.

New Zealand Veterinary Association: 69-71 Boulcott Street, PO Box 11 212, Manners Street, Wellington; ☎(04) 471 0484; fax: (04) 471 0494; internet: www.vets.org.nz.

SOURCES OF JOBS

Newspapers

Many New Zealand jobs are advertised in newspapers, most of which have a daily Situations Vacant section that tends to be larger on one particular day of the week; usually Saturdays and sometimes Wednesdays. Some professional jobs will be advertised in specialist publications and at executive level jobs are usually filled through recruitment agencies, sometimes without being advertised.

The starting place for your job-hunt, therefore, is the major New Zealand newspapers. A small number of jobs are advertised overseas. The types of jobs that tend to be advertised directly are in areas where there is a shortage of skills locally, for example in computers and information technology, teaching, medicine or accountancy.

The major daily newspapers can be read online, or at your local New Zealand Embassy or High Commission. For subscriptions to New Zealand newspapers it may be cheaper to contact the newspapers directly. Alternatively you could try going through the media companies that produce the major newspapers. Try Wilson and Horton's website (www.wilsonandhorton.co.nz) or contact Independent Newspapers Limited (NZI House, 25-33 Victoria Street, PO Box 2595, Wellington; ☎(04) 496 9800; fax: (04) 496 9841; internet: www.stuff.co.nz). Consyl Publishing Ltd in the UK can obtain New Zealand newspapers as well as magazines (☎01424-223111 or 01424-223161 for 24 hour credit card sales).

Addresses – Main New Zealand Newspapers

The New Zealand Herald: PO Box 32, Auckland; ☎(09) 379 5050; internet: www.nzherald.co.nz. Distributed throughout the North Island. Circulation: 213,334; readership: 522,000.

The Dominion: Press House, 40 Boulcott Street, PO Box 1297, Wellington; ☎(04) 474 0000; internet: www.stuff.co.nz. Distributed in lower North Island. Circulation: 68,743; readership: 190,000.

The Evening Post: PO Box 3740, Wellington; ☎(04) 474 0444; internet: www.evpost.co.nz. Distributed in lower North Island. Circulation: 59,055; readership: 145,000.

The Press: Private Bag 4722, Christchurch; ☎(03) 379 0940; fax: (03) 364 8492; internet: www.press.co.nz. Distributed in Canterbury and Nelson/Tasman region; Circulation: 92,992; readership: 231,000.

The Otago Daily Times: PO Box 181 or PO Box 517, Dunedin; ☎(03) 477 4760; fax: (03) 474 7424; internet: www.odt.co.nz. Distributed in lower South Island. Circulation: 44,093; readership: 106,000.

Specialist Publications

Some types of jobs tend to be advertised in specialist magazines. These publications are also useful sources of information about the current job scene in their particular field. It might be worthwhile placing an employment-wanted advertisement with them. Many New Zealand magazines can be purchased online from the New Zealand Magazine Shop (internet: www.nzmagazineshop.co.nz).

Addresses – Specialist Publications

AdMedia: Profile Publishing Limited, PO Box 5544, Wellesley Street, Auckland; ☎(09) 630 8940 or 0800 800 939; e-mail: subs@profile.co.nz; internet: www.profile.co.nz.

Architecture New Zealand: PO Box 2516, Auckland 1031; ☎(09) 846 4068; fax:

(09) 846 8742; e-mail: info@nzia.co.nz; internet: www.nzia.co.nz.

Commercial Horticulture Magazine: Reference Publishing Company; fax: (09) 358 2714; internet: www.nursery.net.nz.

Horticulture News: PO Box 4233, Auckland; ☎(09) 520 9451; fax: (09) 520 9459.

Hospitality Magazine: PO Box 9596, Newmarket, Auckland; ☎(09) 529 3000; fax: (09) 529 3001; e-mail: susand@tplmedia.co.nz; internet: www.tplmedia.co.nz.

Management: Profile Publishing Limited, PO Box 5544, Wellesley Street, Auckland; ☎(09) 630 8940 or 0800 800 939; e-mail: subs@profile.co.nz; internet: www.profile.co.nz.

Manufacturers Federation Magazine: Published by the New Zealand Manufacturers Federation Inc., PO Box 1925, Wellington; internet: www.businessnz.org.nz.

Marketing Magazine: Profile Publishing Limited, PO Box 5544, Wellesley Street, Auckland; ☎(09) 630 8940 or 0800 800 939; e-mail: subs@profile.co.nz; internet: www.profile.co.nz.

Mercantile Gazette: Freepost 5003, PO Box 20 034, Bishopdale, Christchurch; ☎(03) 358 3219; fax: (03) 358 4490; e-mail: susan.rees@tenders-gazette.co.nz; internet: www.tenders-gazette.co.nz.

National Business Review: PO Box 1734, Auckland; ☎(09) 307 1629; fax: (09) 307 5129; e-mail: bfrost@nbr.co.nz; internet: www.nbr.co.nz.

New Zealand Business: Profile Publishing Limited, PO Box 5544, Wellesley Street, Auckland; ☎(09) 630 8940 or 0800 800 939; e-mail: subs@profile.co.nz; internet: www.profile.co.nz or www.nzbusinessmag.co.nz.

New Zealand Forest: Profile Publishing Limited, PO Box 5544, Wellesley Street, Auckland; ☎(09) 630 8940 or 0800 800 939; e-mail: subs@profile.co.nz or andrewm@forest.co.nz; internet: www.profile.co.nz.

NZGP: Adis International Ltd, 41 Centorian Drive, Mairangi Bay, Auckland; ☎(09) 479 8100; fax: (09) 479 8066.

OnFilm: Profile Publishing Limited, PO Box 554, Wellesley Street, Auckland; ☎(09) 630 8940 or 0800 800 939; e-mail: subs@profile.co.nz or stacey@profile.co.nz; internet: www.profile.co.nz.

The Southern Doctor: e-mail: postmaster@southerndoctor.co.nz; internet: www.southerndoctor.co.nz.

Professional Associations

Many professional vacancies are carried in specialist magazines, which are usually published by the relevant professional associations. In some cases all vacancies appear in these publications, for example all permanent teaching jobs are advertised in the *Education Gazette.* They will also usually carry employment wanted adverts. Sometimes it is possible to subscribe just to the employment wanted pages. You can contact the professional bodies listed above for further information. Jobs with the New Zealand Government appear on the internet at (www.jobs.govt.nz). The Association of Commonwealth Universities advertises positions at New Zealand universities on its website (www.acu.ac.uk/cgi-bin/vacancies.pl).

Useful Addresses

Chartered Accountants Journal of New Zealand: PO Box 11 342, Wellington; ☎(04) 474 7840; fax: (04) 499 8033; e-mail: registry@icanz.co.nz; internet: www.icanz.co.nz.

Education Gazette: PO Box 249, Wellington; ☎(04) 917 3990; fax: (04) 917 3991; internet: www.edgazette.govt.nz.

Law Talk: New Zealand Law Society, PO Box 5041, Wellington; ☎(04) 472 7837; fax: (04) 473 7909; e-mail: lawtalk@nz-lawsoc.org.nz.

New Zealand Engineering: 101 Molesworth Street, Wellington; ☎0800 103 903; e-mail: editor@ipenz.org.nz; internet: www.ipenz.org.nz/ipenz/publications.

The New Zealand Medical Journal: The New Zealand Medical Association, 26 The Terrace, PO Box 156, Wellington; ☎(04) 472 4741; fax: (04) 471 0838; e-mail: nzma@nzma.org.nz; internet: www.nzma.org.nz/journal.

Trades and Skilled Craftspeople

As is the case with the professional associations, in order to work in New Zealand as a trades or craftsperson, you must join the relevant association or society. If you have qualifications and experience in your own country you will not normally be required to fulfil any additional requirements. You should contact the organisations listed below for further details. Most of these organisations publish a trade magazine, which may be a useful source of information about job prospects. The New Zealand Trades Directory provides online access to contact details for many trade associations on its website (http://nztrades.com).

Useful Addresses

Master Plumbers, Gasfitters and Drainlayers Inc: ☎Auckland (09) 415 0101, Wellington (04) 801 2015 or Canterbury (03) 348 1238; e-mail: info@masterplumbers.org.nz; internet: www.masterplumbers.org.nz. Also publishes *The New Zealand Plumbers Journal:* ☎0800 502 102; internet: www.masterplumbers.org.nz/plumbers – journal.

Plumbers, Gasfitters and Drainlayers Board: PO Box 30229, Lower Hutt; ☎(04) 589 5310; fax: (04) 589 5390; e-mail: enquiries@pgdb.co.nz; internet: www.pgdb.co.nz.

Registered Master Builders Federation: Level 6, 234 Wakefield Street, Wellington; ☎(04) 382 8999; fax: (04) 385 8995; e-mail: enquiries@masterbuilder@org.nz; internet: www.masterbuilder.org.nz. Also publishes:

BuildOnline: ☎(07) 856 6660; fax: (07) 858 3974; e-mail: info@buildonline.co.nz; internet: www.buildonline.co.nz.

New Zealand Institute of Surveyors: PO Box 831, Wellington 6015; ☎(04) 471 1774; fax: (04) 471 1907; e-mail: nzis@clear.net.nz; internet: www.surveyors.org.nz. Also publishes *Survey Quarterly* and *Newslink:* address as above and see website: www.surveyors.org.nz/publications.

Master Painters Association: 63 Mirimar Avenue, Mirimar, PO Box 15 190, Wellington; tel/fax: (04) 388 1516; e-mail: nzpainting@xtra.co.nz; internet: www.masterpaintersnz.org.nz.

New Zealand Property Institute: PO Box 27 340, Wellington; ☎(04) 384 7094; fax: (04) 384 8473; e-mail: national@property.org.nz; internet: www.property.org.nz. Also publishes: *New Zealand Property Journal:* address as above.

International Newspapers and Directories

As noted above, the trend for the international advertising of jobs has not generally caught on with New Zealand employers because of the obvious difficulties with labour mobility to such a remote country. Only a small percentage of jobs are advertised directly overseas. The fortnightly publication *Overseas Jobs Express* advertises full time jobs in a variety of areas for many countries including New Zealand. As well, there are two newspapers available in the UK for intending migrants to New

Zealand, *Destination New Zealand* and *New Zealand Outlook*. These occasionally carry advertisements for jobs and usually carry advertisements for job-search agencies based in the UK that will help you look in New Zealand. The weekly paper for New Zealanders in London, *New Zealand News UK*, is a good source of job advertisements for positions in New Zealand. *New Zealand News UK* is distributed free in London outside central city tube stations and all three papers are available from New Zealand House in London, or can be obtained on subscription from the addresses below. By far your best option, however, is to search for jobs online. One particularly useful website is www.access.co.nz, which provides quick and easy access to a wide range of employment sites, including recruitment agencies. The website for the New Zealand Embassy in Washington DC (www.nzemb.org; e-mail: nz@nzemb.org) also contains a long list of online contacts and references for those seeking employment in New Zealand, as well as a large amount of information about many aspects of living in New Zealand.

Useful Addresses

Destination New Zealand: Outbound Newspapers, 1 Commercial Road, Eastbourne, East Sussex, BN21 3XQ; ☎01323 726040; e-mail: outbounduk@aol.com; internet: www.outbound-newspapers.com. 12 issues cost £18.50 or £29.50 outside the UK.
New Zealand News UK: 3rd Floor New Zealand House, 80 Haymarket, London SW1Y 4TE; ☎0207 747 9200; fax: 0207 747 9223; e-mail: info@southernlink.co.uk; internet: www.nznewsuk.co.uk. Free weekly found in most London tube stations.
TNT Magazine: 14-15 Child's Place, Earls Court, London SW5 9RX; ☎0207 373 3377; fax: 0207 341 6600; e-mail: enquiries@tntmag.co.uk; internet: www.tntmagazine.com. Another free weekly distributed throughout London.
New Zealand Outlook: Consyl Publishing Ltd, 3 Buckhurst Road, Bexhill-on-Sea, Sussex TN40 1QF; ☎01424-223111. Published monthly.
Overseas Jobs Express: Randstad 22-117, 1316 BW Almere, The Netherlands; ☎+31 36 547 1450; fax: +31 36 547 1451; e-mail: info@overseasjobsexpress.co.uk; internet: www.overseasjobsexpress.co.uk.

Approaching Employers Direct

Advertising and screening applicants is lengthy and expensive. A well-written CV which lands on the personnel manager's desk at the right time could save them time and money, and find you the type of job you want. It is estimated that around 70% of jobs in New Zealand are filled without actually being advertised, so it is worth researching companies and contacting employers that interest you, whether or not they are currently advertising vacancies. It is also worthwhile asking friends, people in the community and also in job centres if they know of any jobs in your field. English language skills are obviously very important, and the biggest hindrance for immigrants in New Zealand trying to find employment, so the fact that you speak English is a good start. You can begin your research by finding contact details for New Zealand companies working in your area of expertise. One place to start is the Yellow Pages, which you can consult at the New Zealand Embassies and High Commissions, or over the internet (www.yellowpages.co.nz). The Information Office on the Second Floor of New Zealand House in London has business directories but is not a job search service. You can obtain a copy of *Working In New Zealand* from New Zealand high commissions or from the internet (www.workingin.com). There is a list of major New Zealand employers at the end of this chapter. A useful book is *Getting a Job in New Zealand* by Joy Muirhead (£10.99), which can be ordered through Destination New Zealand (☎+44 (0)1323-726040; e-mail: outboundUK@aol.com.

Chambers of Commerce & Professional Institutes

Chambers of Commerce promote the interests of their members, local businesses, not as job search agencies, but they are usually prepared to help with information. Local chambers of commerce should provide you with a list of their members for a small fee. A list of Chambers of Commerce in the main cities can be found in the *Regional Employment Guide* below. Other organisations that will have details of member companies are the professional institutes. Also listed below are the Australia-NZ-UK Chamber of Commerce and the American Chamber of Commerce, which publish directories of British and American companies respectively with branches, affiliates or subsidiaries in New Zealand.

Useful Addresses

Chambers of Commerce

American Chamber of Commerce: PO Box 106 002, Auckland; ☎(09) 309 9140; fax: (09) 309 1090; e-mail: amcham@amcham.co.nz.

New Zealand Chambers of Commerce: Level 9, 109 Featherston Street, Wellington; ☎(04) 914 6500; internet: www.chamber.co.nz or www.nzchamber.co.nz.

Australia-New Zealand-UK Chamber of Commerce: 393 The Strand, London WC2R 0JQ; ☎0207 379 0720; fax: 0207 379 0721; internet: www.anzcc.org.uk.

Professional Institutes and Registration Bodies:

Architects Education and Registration Board: PO Box 1106, Wellington; ☎(04) 801 8972; fax: (04) 801 7010; e-mail: registrar@aerb.org.nz; internet: www.aerb.org.nz.

Australia and New Zealand Institute of Insurance and Finance: PO Box 344, Auckland; ☎(09) 379 7128; fax: (09) 367 0639; e-mail: kdivehall@theinstitute.com.au; internet: www.theinstitute.com.au.

Electrical Contractors Association of New Zealand: PO Box 12 434, Wellington; ☎(04) 494 1540; fax: (04) 494 1549.

Engineers Registration Board: PO Box 12241, Wellington; ☎(04) 474 8937; fax: (04) 473 2324; e-mail: ero@ipenz.org.nz.

Medical Council of New Zealand: PO Box 11-649, Wellington; ☎(04) 384 7635; fax: (04) 385 8902; e-mail: mcnz@mcnz.org.nz; internet: www.mcnz.org.nz.

New Zealand Bankers Association: PO Box 3043, Wellington; ☎(04) 472 8838; fax: (04) 473 1698.

New Zealand Institute of Management: PO Box 1178, Wellington; ☎0800 373 700 or (04) 495 8300; fax: (04) 495 8301; e-mail: nzim@central.co.nz; internet: www.nzim.co.nz.

Nursing Council of New Zealand: PO Box 9644, Wellington; ☎(04) 385 9589; fax: (04) 801 8502; e-mail: oseas@nursingcouncil.org.nz; internet: www.nursingcouncil.org.nz.

Pharmaceutical Society of New Zealand: 112 Dixon Street, PO Box 11640, Wellington; ☎(04) 802 0030; fax: (04) 382 9297; e-mail: p.society@pharmacy-house.org.nz; internet: www.psnz.org.nz.

Plumbers, Gasfitters and Drainlayers Board: PO Box 30229, Lower Hutt; ☎(04) 589 5310; fax: (04) 589 5390; e-mail: enquiries@pgdb.co.nz; internet: www.pgdb.co.nz.

Real Estate Agents Licensing Board: PO Box

11270, Wellington; ☎(04) 520 6949; fax: (04) 520 6995.

Teachers Registration Board: PO Box 5326, Wellington; ☎(04) 471 0852; fax: (04) 471 0870; e-mail: mail@trb.govt.nz; internet: www.trb.govt.nz.

Veterinary Council of New Zealand: PO Box 10 563, Wellington; ☎(04) 473 9600; fax: (04) 473 8869; e-mail: vet@vetcouncil.org.nz; internet: www.vetcouncil.org.nz.

Placing Employment Wanted Adverts

Another approach is placing an employment wanted advert with the newspapers and specialist publications listed above. You can contact the newspaper and magazine publishers directly for current advertising rates.

EMPLOYMENT AGENCIES

International Organisations

There are a number of organisations that can help you find a job in New Zealand. Some companies specialise in finding jobs for intending migrants, others recruit on behalf of employers and sometimes have New Zealand assignments. The latter type operate on behalf of employers and do not search on behalf of prospective workers, however they will fill some vacancies from people they have on their books so it may be worthwhile sending them a CV and a speculative application. As has been mentioned elsewhere, help with job seeking is one of the services immigration consultancies usually provide.

Recruitment and Job Search Agencies for Intending Emigrants:

Carlisle Group Staffing Services: Albany Place, Hyde Way, Welwyn Garden City, Hertfordshire, AL7 3BQ; ☎01707-323000; fax: 01707-395085; ww.carlislestaffing.co.uk.

Contractor UK: ☎NZ: (04) 904 1110; e-mail: editor@contractoruk.co.uk or cutting@paradise.net.nz; internet: www.contractor uk.co.uk/nz.

Geneva Health International: 128-129 Cheapside, London EC2 V6LL; ☎020-7600 0859; fax: 020-7600 0944; e-mail: info@genevahealth.com; internet: www.genevahealth.com. NZ: PO Box 106 339, Auckland; ☎(09) 916 0200; fax: (09) 916 0201.

Global IT Recruitment: e-mail: enquiries@globalitrecruitment.com; internet: www.globalitrecruitment.com.

Headhunter.net: USA customer service ☎800 891 8880; internet: www.headhunter.net/JobSeeker/Jobs.

JobCafé International: internet: www.jobcafe.co.nz/entrees/international.

Parker Bridge Recruitment Ltd: 1st Floor, Marlborough Court, 14-16 Holborn, London EC1N 2LE; ☎020-7464 1550; fax: 020-7464 1999. Auckland branch ☎(09) 377 3727; fax: (09) 303 1496; internet: www.parkerbridge.com. Financial sector.

Prime Recruitment Contracts: 37 Locks Heath Centre, Locks Heath, Southampton, SO31 6DX; ☎01489-559 090; fax: 01489-559995; e-mail: contracts@prime-recruitment.co.uk; internet: www.prime-recruitment.co.uk.

Psych Recruitment: UK tel/fax: 020-7900 2974; USA fax: 070-7336 4714; e-mail: doug.mccall@psych-recruitment.com; internet: www.psych-recruitment.com. Psychologists recruitment agency.

Taylor & Associates, 27 Gillies Avenue, PO Box 9600, Newmarket, Auckland, New Zealand; ☎(64) 0-9-520 5421; fax (64) 0-9-520 5487; e-mail nzjobs@jobfastrack. co.nz; www.jobfastrack.co.nz. Enquiries are best addressed to the UK representative office; te; 01244-321414; fax 01244-342288; e-mail info@tegltd.co.uk.

TMP Worldwide Inc: 622 Third Avenue, 39th Floor, New York, NY 10017; ☎1212-351 7000; fax: 1646-658 0540; e-mail: corporate.communications@tmp.com; internet: www.tmp.com.

Other useful websites. For job listings try: www.nzjobs.co.nz, www.apl.co.nz, www.monster.com, www.seek.co.nz and www.sheffield.co.nz/CareerZone. Bear in mind though that these do not necessarily represent the entire job market, particularly towards the senior executive end.

New Zealand Employment Service

The Department of Labour in New Zealand provides job-search assistance through the New Zealand Employment Service, a national network of offices advertising local vacancies. They carry a wide range of vacancies for casual, skilled and unskilled work, and offer advice and information on training for job seekers. There is no fee to use the Employment Service, but you have to be a New Zealand resident or citizen. Contact the *New Zealand Employment Service* (☎0800 808 222) for an office near you. The New Zealand Department of Labour website may also prove useful (www.dol.govt.nz).

Employment Agencies in New Zealand

Increasingly, the global talent shortage means that employers rely on agency databases to supplement responses to their vacancy advertisements. There are a large number of private employment agencies in New Zealand, and they tend to be generalist rather than specialist by nature. Most cover all sectors of the economy, both public and private. Within the consultancies, however, there are often specialists who focus on specific areas. These agencies charge the employer when they make a successful placement and are usually free for the job seeker, although they will offer other services such as career assessment and advice on preparation of CVs for which there may be a charge.

Useful Addresses

Computing/Information Technology

Aacorn International Ltd: PO Box 105-355, Auckland Central; ☎(09) 309 7862; fax: (09) 309 9034; e-mail: aacorn@aacorn.co.nz; internet: www.aacorn.co.nz.

Candle IT&T Recruitment: PO Box 10-234, Wellington; ☎(04) 473 9149; fax: (04) 460 8676; PO Box 5044, Auckland; ☎(09) 309 6534; fax: (09) 309 3525; e-mail: global@candle.co.nz; internet: www.candle.co.nz.

Diversiti: Wellington; internet: www.diversiti.co.nz.

Enterprise Staff Consultants Ltd: 3rd Floor, Ferry Building, 99 Quay Street, Auckland, PO Box 1799, Auckland; ☎(09) 306 2160; fax: (09) 307 1285; e-mail: office@enterprise.co.nz; internet: www.enterprise.co.nz.

Icon: Auckland ☎(09) 377 3848; e-mail: resauck@iconrec.co.nz; Wellington ☎(04) 472 1566; e-mail: reswgtn@iconrec.co.nz.

Information Technology Recruitment (ITEC): PO Box 6798, Wellesley Street, Auckland; ☎(09) 302 5304; fax: (09) 373 2968; e-mail: suzan@itec.co.nz; internet: www.itec.co.nz.

IT Futures: PO Box 5405, Wellesley Street, Auckland; ☎(09) 379 1180; fax: (09) 379 8114; e-mail: theteam@itfutures.co.nz; internet: www.itfutures.co.nz.

LaceyLee Recruitment: PO Box 3427, Shortland Street, Auckland; ☎(09) 302 0347; fax: (09) 303 4216; e-mail: info.auckland@laceylee.co.nz; PO Box 27-144, Wellington; ☎(04) 382 9974; fax: (04) 385 0578; e-mail: info .wellington@laceylee.co.nz; internet: www.laceylee.co.nz.

Mercury Consulting Group: PO Box 10-605, Wellington; ☎(04) 499 2624; fax: (04) 499 6880; e-mail: inquire@mercuryrecruit.co.nz; internet: www.mercuryrecruit.co.nz.

Qube Associates Ltd: PO Box 1849, Auckland; ☎(09) 307 3852; fax: (09) 366 7171; e-mail: careers@qube.co.nz; internet: www.qube.co.nz.

Engineering

TAD Technical Careers and Contracts: PO Box 5341, Wellesley Street, Auckland; ☎(09) 309 9316; fax: (09) 309 0212; e-mail: cmarsh@tad.co.nz; internet: www.tad.co.au.

Farming

Agfirst Consultants NZ Ltd: PO Box 1261, Hastings; ☎(06) 876 9200; fax: (06) 876 9225; e-mail: enquiries@agfirst.co.nz; internet: www.agfirst.co.nz.

Marvin Farm Services: 95 Awara Street, PO Box 248, Matamata, Waikato; ☎(07) 888 6025; fax: (07) 888 6023; e-mail: marvinfarms@xtra.co.nz; www.marvinfarms.co.nz.

Finance/Accountancy

Clayton Ford: PO Box 10 083, Wellington; ☎(04) 473 6223; fax: (04) 471 2100; e-mail: wnweb@claytonford.co.nz; PO Box 7697, Auckland; ☎(09) 379 9924; fax: (09) 379 7785; e-mail: akweb@claytonford.co.nz; internet: www.claytonford.co.nz.

DG&A Recruitment Consultants: PO Box 4006, Auckland; ☎(09) 358 0888; fax: (09) 303 0254; e-mail: debbie.graham@dgal.co.nz or resume@dgal.co.nz; internet: www.debbiegraham.co.nz.

Opal Consulting Group: PO Box 7067, Auckland; ☎(09) 379 0200; fax: (09) 377 4127; e-mail: cv@opal.co.nz; internet: www.opal.co.nz.

Food Technology

Foodie Finders Ltd: PO Box 272 1297, Papakura, Auckland; ☎(09) 374 2128; e-mail: cathy@foodiefinders.co.nz; internet: www.foodiefinders.co.nz.

Hotel/Catering

Artisan International NZ: internet: www.artisan-recruitment.co.nz.

HHES Hospitality Recruitment: ☎(09) 379 7532; fax: (09) 379 4966; e-mail: info@hhes.co.nz; internet: www.hhes.co.nz.

Medical/Health

Auckland Medical Bureau: PO Box 37 753, Auckland; ☎(09) 377 5903; fax: (09) 377 5902; e-mail: doctors-amb@xtra.co.nz; internet: www.doctorjobs.co.nz.

eNZed Paramedical: 65 MacDonald Road, Glenview, Hamilton 2001; ☎(07) 843 0080; fax: (07) 843 0081; internet: www.enzedparamedical.co.nz.

Health Recruitment NZ Ltd: PO Box 205, Wellington; ☎(04) 499 1885; fax: (04) 499 1600; internet: www.healthrecruitment.com.

Medical Staffing International: 35 Kesteven Avenue, Glendowie, Auckland; ☎(09) 575 4258; fax: (09) 575 4259; e-mail: kirsten@medicalstaffing.co.nz; internet: www.medicalstaffing.co.nz.

Professional/Managerial/General

Advanced Personnel: PO Box 21 384,

Christchurch 8001; ☎(03) 365 4322; fax: (03) 365 7356; Auckland ☎(09) 263 4322; internet: www.advancedpersonnel.co.nz.

Drake International: Exchange Place, 5-7 Willeston Street, Wellington; ☎(04) 472 6972; fax: (04) 473 4930; internet: www.drake.co.nz.

IDPE Consulting Group: Level 13, St John House, 114 The Terrace, PO Box 5288, Wellington; ☎(04) 472 2212; fax: (04) 472 2211; e-mail: info@idpe-consulting.co.nz; internet: www.idpe-consulting.co.nz.

Kelly Staffing Services: Level 10, 119 Armagh Street, Christchurch 8001; ☎0800 4 KELLY; internet: www.kellyservices.co.nz.

Wheeler Campbell Consulting Ltd: PO Box 205, Wellington; ☎(04) 499 1500; fax: (04) 499 1600; e-mail: info@wheelercampbell.co.nz; PO Box 191, Shortland Street, Auckland; ☎(09) 303 4500; fax: (09) 303 4501; e-mail: best@wheelercampbell.co.nz; internet: www.wheelercampbell.co.nz.

Secretarial

Opal Consulting Group: Wellington ☎(04) 385 4011; fax: (04) 385 6704; PO Box 7067, Auckland; ☎(09) 379 0200; fax: (09) 308 9006; Christchurch ☎(03) 377 0030; fax: (03) 377 0027; e-mail: cv@opal.co.nz; internet: www.opal.co.nz.

TMP Worldwide: PO Box 2186, Wellington; ☎(04) 473 4073; fax: (04) 498 0548; e-mail: ernzinfo@tmp.com; internet: www.tmp.com.

Company or Organisation Transfers

One alternative to finding work straight away in New Zealand is to find work with a company with prospects of being transferred to New Zealand. Unfortunately few companies recruit staff with the promise of being posted to a particular country, however if you choose a New Zealand company to work for, your chances are obviously greater. Still this process is likely to be a long-term route into the country. The British/New Zealand Trade Council (PO Box 37162, Parnell, Auckland; tel/fax: (09) 522 0526; internet: www.brittrade.co.nz) publishes a trade directory of member companies, which might be useful if you are looking for New Zealand companies in the UK. The American Chamber of Commerce in New Zealand publishes a directory of American companies operating in New Zealand (see the address above). The big multinationals also have subsidiaries in New Zealand, sometimes under different names. For example, Levers trades in New Zealand as Unilever.

JOB APPLICATION

A typical job application will comprise of a letter of application or covering letter and a curriculum vita (CV). Companies short-list on the basis of CVs and interview the selected candidates before making a decision. Depending on the level of job you are applying for, and the company, you may be asked to attend more than one interview.

Application Letters and CVs.

If you are sending off speculative letters it is worth taking the time to ring up the company and find out who the personnel or relevant department manager is. A personally addressed letter is much more effective than one which is clearly a copy of one sent to a dozen other companies.

○ Letters, whether applying for a specific vacancy or inquiring about possible future vacancies, should be formal in tone, brief (one side of an A4 sheet), and should outline why you are particularly qualified to work for the company.

○ Curriculum Vitae are expected to cover education, qualifications, work experience, skills, professional goals and some personal details. In New Zealand CVs list jobs and qualifications in reverse chronological order, i.e., the most recent job first and the earliest last.

○ Try to keep your CV to two pages and make sure it is clearly laid out. This is particularly important if you are faxing applications to New Zealand as fax machines blur copy slightly and, if the typeface on your CV is too small, some important details may be lost.

○ These days, most companies prefer you to e-mail your CV to them if you are applying from overseas, so make the effort to ensure that any files you send are well-formatted, clearly laid out, and can be opened in standard programs with a minimum of fuss.

○ It is worthwhile getting some professional advice on the preparation of your CV; services that assist with CVs can be found under Employment Agencies in the Yellow Pages. Do not send original documents with applications.

Interview Procedure

If you are applying for a job in New Zealand from overseas, and a company wishes to interview you, in most cases they will not be prepared to pay your travel costs. Some companies will arrange interviews by video link or telephone. Another option to consider is arranging a number of job interviews to coincide with a visit to New Zealand, or your arrival if your residency has been approved. There are international job search companies that specialise in lining up job interviews before you set off for New Zealand. If you are using an agency to assist you with your residency application, they may have an employment-search facility or should at least be able to point you in the right direction by recommending recruitment agencies in your field.

Job interviews in New Zealand tend to be quite formal and you should dress appropriately for a work situation. If you are concerned about brushing up your job search and interview skills, most bookshops stock 'how to' guides for finding work.

It is illegal for employers to discriminate on the basis of gender, race, colour, marital status or sexual orientation. Firms will usually have an Equal Employment Opportunity (EEO) policy in their Mission Statement and will have a quota set of the proportion of their workers who are from minority groups.

ASPECTS OF EMPLOYMENT

Salaries

You should not expect a New Zealand salary to be the same as a salary in your home country once the exchange rate is taken into account. Salaries in New Zealand are lower than those for equivalent positions in the USA, the UK and Europe. However, living costs are considerably lower too. Primary produce, fruit and vegetables, and clothing are all quite cheap. It is difficult to make a direct comparison of living standards because so many factors are difficult to compare. For example, going overseas for an annual holiday becomes very expensive when the nearest country is three hours away, and that is only Australia. On the other hand, you have easy access to great beaches and can enjoy much better climate than northern Europeans, year round. As a generalisation, it would be fair to say that living standards are equivalent for most middle income earners. The minimum legal wage is $5.40 per hour for workers aged 16-17 and $7.70 an hour for those over 18 years old. Despite New Zealand's egalitarian attitudes and equal employment policies, there is still some pay disparity between men and women. The Statistics New Zealand lists average ordinary time hourly earnings as $19.81 for males and $16.75 for females.

TABLE 22	AVERAGE WEEKLY EARNINGS IN DIFFERENT JOB SECTORS
Electricity, gas and water:	$1,027
Finance and insurance:	$925
Government administration and defence:	$906
Property and business services:	$795
Wholesale trade:	$787
Forestry and mining:	$762
Education:	$762
Transport, storage and communications:	$731
Manufacturing:	$721
Construction:	$708
Health and community services:	$685
Cultural and recreational activities:	$652
Personal and other services:	$634
Retail trade:	$467
Accommodation, cafés and restaurants:	$449
Average weekly earning, before tax and including overtime:	$703
(based on the Statistics New Zealand Employment Survey at the end of 2001).	

Working Conditions

Standard conditions of employment are still generally 40-hour weeks, 8.30am-5pm, five days a week. However, with flexible working arrangements under the industrial relations legislation, variations on this theme, such as glide time, have become increasingly common. For example Fisher & Paykel, New Zealand's largest manufacturer of kitchen and laundry appliances has shifted to ten hour shifts, four days a week, in some of their divisions. Rates for overtime are another area changing due to the impact of new legislation. In most industries, overtime was one and half times the standard rates, but in many sectors now, particularly for casual workers and in the service sector, overtime rates are being cut back or disappearing entirely. You are more likely now to be awarded a day or hours off in lieu of extra hours worked, rather than actually being paid for them. In areas such as retail you may be paid overtime if you are required to work a public holiday. Longer working hours are also becoming a feature of many industries. Holiday provision is still protected by law under the Holidays Act. After twelve months' continuous employment, the employee is entitled to three weeks paid leave. In addition, there are eleven paid public holidays annually. Employees do not have to work on public holidays unless they agree or their contract provides for this. Remember that these will only be paid holidays if they actually fall on a day on which you would normally work. There is no compulsory retirement age anymore, although entitlement to National Superannuation is assessed from the age of 65.

Parental Leave

Parental leave is available to employees (both women and men) who have worked for twelve months or more with the same employer, either part-time (for more than ten hours per week) or full time. Employees adopting a child under five years old are also entitled to parental leave. It is not automatic, you must apply for it. The period of leave is the same for adoptive parents, but there are differences in the advanced notice you are required to give. The types of leave are all unpaid and the conditions are as follows:

Special Leave. Up to ten days during pregnancy for women to have ante-natal checks.

Maternity Leave. Up to fourteen continuous weeks for the mother, which can start up to six weeks before the expected date of birth or adoption.

Paternity Leave: Up to two continuous weeks for the father around the expected date of birth or adoption. A man can only apply for this leave if he is living with the woman with whom he will be sharing childcare responsibilities.

Extended Leave. Up to 52 continuous weeks, excluding any maternity leave taken in the twelve months after the birth. Extended leave may be shared by both parents but may not exceed 52 weeks in total.

Job Protection. If you take less than four weeks parental leave, your job must be kept open. If you take more than four weeks, the employer may decide that the job cannot be kept open, but you have a right to challenge that decision. If you accept this decision then you are entitled to a preference period of six months when the employer must offer you a job substantially similar to the one you have left. You may not be dismissed for becoming pregnant or for applying for parental leave. The Parental Leave and Employment Protection Act (1987) sets out minimum conditions. Your employment contract may contain special provisions. For further information, contact the Employment Relations Service (☎0800 800 863; internet: www.ers.dol.govt.nz).

Trade Unions

Prior to the Employment Contracts Act of 1991, New Zealand unions enjoyed a monopoly over workplace representation and union membership in many industries was compulsory. The resulting system of wage determination was highly centralised and inflexible. If unions and employers negotiating in each industry at a national level could not agree, the dispute would be settled through compulsory arbitration by a tribunal made up of members from both sides. As a result of this system, employment conditions were guaranteed at some minimum level in just about all industries, and the disparity between the high paid and the low paid was not very great.

The Employment Contracts Act of 1991 removed union monopolies over bargaining in the workplace, abolished compulsory membership, and the Arbitration Tribunals. Wage fixing is now in theory completely decentralised, although some of the bigger unions still negotiate at national level. Employers and employees negotiate employment contracts, which may be either collective or individual. Employees may nominate someone to act as their bargaining agent. Employers are obliged to recognise whomever an employee nominates as their bargaining agent, although this does not mean they must negotiate or settle with that agent. Trade unions no longer have a protected legal status, and total membership fell from approximately 683,000 in 1985 to approximately 339,000 in 1996, and is currently around 250,000. The number of employees on collective agreements has also fallen sharply; the majority of the workforce are now employed on individual contracts. Flexibility has brought benefits to some employees and industries but has weakened the position of others. Part time workers, those in workplaces with only a few employees and the service sector generally all have less job security, fewer employment protections and in some cases have seen a real reduction in pay.

The Employment Relations Act (2000) inserts into all collective agreements a requirement to deduct union fees where the employee consents. Unions and employers may vary these arrangements in a collective agreement. Employers must allow union representatives to come into the workplace and union officials must exercise their access rights in a reasonable way. Union members are entitled to attend two union meetings (of up to two hours each) each year. Employers must pay union members who attend these meetings during their normal working hours. Under this Act, any group of employees can set up and register as a union, provided they first become an incorporated society (under the Incorporated Societies Act, 1908) and then register as a union under the 2000 Act. Such groups must have a minimum of fifteen members, be independent of employers, and have a set of union rules.

Most New Zealand unions belong to the national body: The New Zealand Council of Trade Unions (PO Box 6645, Wellington; ☎(04) 385 1334; fax: (04) 385 6051; internet: www.union.org.nz or www.ctu.org.nz). The NZCTU publishes a comprehensive directory of all trade unions in the country. The Employment Relations Service can also provide information (☎0800 800 863; internet: www.ers.dol.govt.nz).

Employment Contracts

At the beginning of your employment you will negotiate an employment contract with your employer. You can be covered under an existing collective contract if it provides for new workers to join and if your employer agrees. Otherwise you will negotiate an individual contract. Individual contracts can be either written or oral but it is desirable to have a written contract. If you wish to have a bargaining agent represent you, you have a choice between joining a union or employing a private bargaining agent. Remember that though your employer must recognise your bargaining agent they are not obliged to settle with them. An employment contract must by law have certain provisions. There must be an effective personal grievance procedure and disputes procedure. The minimum conditions outlined above - wages and holiday provision and the parental leave provisions - cannot be overridden, although they can be improved upon. A good checklist for individual employment contracts can be obtained from the magazine published by a network of independent legal firms called *Lawlink* (PO Box 6197, Wellesley Street, Auckland; ☎(09) 300 5470; fax: (09) 309 5113), or found on their website (www.lawlink.co.nz).

Employment Tribunal & Employment Court

Two institutions for resolving disputes were set up under the Act - the Tribunal, which mostly mediates in disputes, either personal disputes or grievances arising from breach of employment contracts, and the Employment Court which deals with matters referred on by the Tribunal, and more serious issues such as disputes involving strikes and lockouts. There is no right to strike while an employment contract is still current.

Women in Work

Around 60% of New Zealand women over the age of 15 work in either full or part time jobs. This figure has been steadily increasing since the 1960s, although it seems to have reached a plateau in recent years after it dropped off slightly in the late 1980s, which may reflect the effects of the economic downturn. The participation rates for women are considerably lower than the corresponding figures for men across all age groups, and particularly in the 25-34 age group, reflecting the fact that women are still the primary care givers for children. According to figures from the Ministry of Women's Affairs, 31% of women's time is spent on unpaid work, as opposed to around 12% of men's time. About a third of the female workforce (about 283,000) work part time, while only about 106,000 men are in part-time employment.

Despite still bearing more family responsibilities than men, New Zealand women are moving into previously male dominated areas, particularly the professions. Female students outnumber men in areas such as medicine and law, although this is a recent development and men still dominate at senior levels in these professions. Women represent 48% of all salary and wage earners, 28% of employers, and 31.8% of all self-employed. Maori, Pacific Island, and women from other ethnic groups are less well represented in the labour force than Pakeha/European women.

Equal pay for the same work was established under the Equal Pay Act of 1972, and other forms of discrimination in the workplace based on gender, race or any other non-relevant factor is illegal under the Human Rights Commission Act of 1972. If you believe you have been discriminated against unlawfully, you can either use the personal grievance procedures in your employment contract or you can make a complaint to the Human Rights Commission. Despite the effects of the Equal Pay Act, women's ordinary time earnings are currently 84.6% of male earnings, compared with 83.7% one year ago. Women are still concentrated in a narrower range of occupations, which, in general, pay less well. Equal pay claims are also harder to establish in the new environment of individual contracts. Discrimination in individual cases is much harder to prove than in a situation where everyone receives the same rate of pay for a job. However, the attitude towards women in employment in New Zealand is generally positive. Childcare is becoming more affordable now that the government subsidises pre-school care centres. Some of these advances have been achieved through the efforts of women politicians. Women have a high profile in New Zealand public life. A third of the members of parliament are women and Helen Clark is New Zealand's second female Prime Minister.

For more information about women in New Zealand contact the Ministry of Women's Affairs (PO Box 10 049, Wellington; ☎(04) 473 4112; fax: (04) 472 0961; e-mail: mwa@mwa.govt.nz; internet: www.mwa.govt.nz) or see the Statistics New Zealand website (www.stats.govt.nz).

PERMANENT WORK

Executive Employment Prospects

Prospects are good for executive employment as the local labour market is unable to provide enough suitably skilled applicants for the growing demand. However, the executive vacancies are for people with a high level of technical and interpersonal skills.

Information Technology

There is always a demand for skilled programmers, particularly those with university level qualifications. New Zealanders qualified in these areas tend to be attracted overseas by the comparatively higher salaries, for a time at least. Currently IT is the second fastest growing occupational category; it saw a 10% increase in employment over the past year.

Medical

Doctors. The numbers of foreign doctors registering with the Medical Council has increased in recent years and there is some concern that this may lead to an oversupply of medical personnel. The increase in numbers seems to be the result of an increase in numbers of skilled immigrants, particularly from South Africa, which has resulted in a reverse 'brain-drain'. The situation in New Zealand has usually been the opposite with trained New Zealanders going abroad leaving opportunities for qualified migrants. You should contact the Medical Council for an accurate assessment of employment opportunities. As has been noted already, you must register with the Medical Council in order to practice as a doctor in New Zealand. Doctors from Australia, Britain, Ireland and South Africa, who have been registered in their own country, are usually accepted for registration without requiring further qualifications. Doctors from other countries will usually have to sit registration exams.

Nurses. Nurses must apply to be registered with the Nursing Council of New Zealand. There is a current demand for general nurses, and especially for experienced nurses and midwives with specialist skills.

Useful Addresses

Heartbeat Nurses: 12 Pitt Street, Parranatta, New South Wales 2150, Australia. ☎02-9891 2255; fax 02-9806 9731; www.heartbeatnursing.com.au.

Teaching

There are excellent work opportunities within the New Zealand education system. At the time of print, there is a particular demand for secondary school teachers of mathematics, computing, technology and physical education. Since January 2000, applications for work permits from overseas teachers have been subject to a work test requirement. This has recently been waived for overseas secondary teachers taking up positions in state or state-integrated schools. The requirement is also waived for overseas teachers taking up positions in intermediate or middle schools in South Auckland, Manukau City or Northland. A department has been created in the Ministry of Education to encourage teachers to come to New Zealand to work. Contact TeachNZ for more information (TeachNZ, Ministry of Education, PO Box 1666, Wellington; ☎(04) 473 5544; fax: (04) 471 4432; internet: www.TeachNZ.govt.nz).

As noted earlier in this section, immigrants intending to teach must have their qualifications verified and checked for comparability with New Zealand qualifications by the Teacher Registration Board. Teacher registration is compulsory for all teachers in New Zealand. The TeachNZ website has details and you can electronically request the relevant forms. The *Education Gazette* is published fortnightly and advertises all permanent teaching positions in state and independent schools. You can read the *Gazette* online, where it is constantly updated (www.edgazette.govt.nz), or by subscribing directly to PO Box 249, Wellington.

SHORT-TERM EMPLOYMENT

Short-term employment prospects are improving as the economy picks up after some rather lean years. However, as already noted in Chapter Two, *Residence and Entry* unless you are a New Zealander or have residency you will have to get a work visa to work while in New Zealand, even for a short period. One of the conditions of these visas is that you are doing jobs for which there are no appropriately qualified New Zealanders. Given that the types of jobs most people obtain while travelling are unskilled labouring jobs, your chances of working legitimately are not great. There is a lot of paperwork for your employer to get through (see Chapter Two) just to hire a fruit picker.

Alternatively, if you are a British, Dutch, French, German or Irish citizen aged between 18 and 30 you can apply for a working holiday visa before you leave for New Zealand (see the *Residence and Entry* chapter for details). If you do not have a work permit, some farmers may not be too concerned if they have short term jobs, particularly seasonal jobs in rural areas, and cannot find locals interested in doing them. Under these circumstances you may find that employers are more interested in whether you are hard working than legal. But be careful, because in recent years the Immigration Service has been doing sweeps of picking gangs in remote areas to check whether they have work permits. You may endanger your chances of staying in New Zealand if you try to bend the rules on working.

Useful Address

John Mahon, New Zealand Visas, P.O. 1, Nantwich, Cheshire CW5 7PB; ☎01270-626626; fax 01270-626226; john@visas-australia.com. Also in Dublin: 2nd Floor, 13 Aston Quay, Dublin 2; ☎01- 6795452; fax 01-6795459. On-line site (www.newzealandvisas.com) that arranges a working holiday visa for £10; also a site (www.etavisas.com) that will issue and e-mail the copy of the tourist visa for £5.

Horticulture and Agriculture

There are many opportunities for keen workers in orchards, even if you have little or no experience. However, since the work is unskilled you will find that pay rates are far from high. Fruit picking tends to be paid at what is called piece rates (rates per kilo or bin filled). Obviously as you get better at the work your pay rates will improve, but it can be discouraging at first, as well as backbreaking depending on the crop; asparagus picking is reputed to be the worst. It is possible to follow the different harvests around the country as each type of produce comes into season and to find work virtually year round. In the main horticultural areas during the harvest, work will not be hard to find. Farmers advertise locally, sometimes contacting local youth hostels or backpackers' accommodation, or simply putting a sign up at the gate. There is occasionally accommodation available, albeit of a rather basic kind, and you may be provided with some food, such as fresh fruit and vegetables or dairy products. Generally the remoter the area, the more difficulty the farmers have in attracting local labour, so the better your chances. However this is no guarantee that they will be able to pay more, they are just more likely to provide non-wage perks such as accommodation or food in order to get the workers. For details of the timing and locations of various harvests see *Work Your Way Around the World* available from Vacation Work Publications (9 Park End Street, Oxford OX1 1HJ; ☎01865-241978; fax: 01865-790 885; internet: www.vacationwork.co.uk).

Unlike fruit picking, working on farms usually requires some experience. For example, you will see almost daily advertisements in the Waikato papers for milkers, but they require people who are already skilled. Some unskilled work is available in shearing sheds, for example the job of rousie (the person who picks up the shorn fleeces), which does not require much beyond a strong pair of arms. If you have some practical farming experience under your belt and want work on a New Zealand farm, you can look for vacancies on the Farm News website (www.farmnews.co.nz) or advertise your skills on the Agrijobs website (www.agrisupportonline.com).

Wine production is one of New Zealand's fastest growing industries - there are now nearly 11,000 hectares of wine grapes and 376 licenced wine producers in the country. Innovative sustainable and environmentally friendly vineyard and industry practices are ensuring that New Zealand meets the international demand for wine produced in a 'clean, green' environment. Further expansion is expected as the number of vineyards continues to increase. Often there is casual work available on vineyards tying up the vines, and also during the grape harvest, particularly in the Marlborough and Hawke's Bay regions. For information about seasonal work see the WINZ website (www.winz.govt.nz).

Au Pair/Nannying

There is some demand for nannies and au pairs in New Zealand - the generic term child-carer is more usual. With the growing number of training courses available in New Zealand, you probably stand a better chance at these jobs if you actually have a child-care qualification. Posts are advertised in the daily papers or on community notice boards. There are several specialist agencies that can be found in the Yellow Pages or on the internet. Wages are quite low, but such jobs sometimes involve 'living in', so you may avoid food and accommodation expenses.

Useful Addresses

Aupair - the Kiwi Connection: internet: www.kiwiaupair.com.
NZ Professional Nanny Service: ☎(03) 382 6417; fax: (03) 385 6418; e-mail: amy@nznanny.co.nz; internet: www.nznanny.co.nz.
PORSE Nanny Childcare Network: PO Box 200, Hastings; ☎(06) 873 0033 or 0800 276 773; fax: (06) 870 6273; e-mail: childcare@porsenz.com; internet: www.nannynet.co.nz.

Teaching English

New Zealand is a popular destination for Asian students wanting to learn English, because of its reputation as a safe and friendly country. As an employment prospect you will almost certainly need the appropriate TEFL or ESL qualifications or experience in order to get a work permit, because as has already been noted above, the Immigration Service has to be satisfied that you have skills not possessed by New Zealand job seekers. Speaking English as your first language is not enough to qualify you. There are many public and private English-language schools, mainly based in Auckland, Wellington and Christchurch.

Useful Addresses

Aspiring Language Institute: 242 Papanui Road, Merivale, Christchurch; ☎(03) 355 3231; fax: (03) 355 3236; internet: www.aspiring.co.nz.
Capital Language Academy: 49-51 Courtenay Place, PO Box 1100, Wellington; ☎(04) 801 6010; fax: (04) 385 6655; e-mail: enquiries@cla.co.nz; internet: www.cla.co.nz.
Dominion English Schools: 67 Customs St, Auckland, PO Box 4217, Auckland; ☎(09) 377 3280; fax: (09) 377 3473; e-mail: andrew@dominion.co.nz; internet: www.dominion.school.nz.
Dominion English Schools: 4th Floor, 116 Worcester Street, PO Box 3908, Christchurch; ☎(03) 365 3370; fax: (03) 365 5215; e-mail: andrew@dominion.school.nz.
Garden City English School: cnr Hereford Street and Oxford Terrace, PO Box 2851, Christchurch; ☎(03) 377 0091; fax: (03) 377 1251; e-mail: info@EnglishLanguage.school.nz; internet: http://webnz.com/englishlanguage/.
International Language Academies: Head Office, 116 Worcester St, PO Box 25170, Christchurch; ☎(03) 379 5452; fax: (03) 379 5373; e-mail: ilachch@ila.co.nz; internet: www.ila.co.nz.
Languages International: 27 Princes St, PO Box 5293, Auckland 1036; ☎(09) 309 0615; fax: (09) 377 2806; e-mail: info@languages.ac.nz; internet: www.langsint.co.nz.

Seafield School of English: 71 Beresford St, PO Box 18516, New Brighton, Christchurch; ☎(03) 388 3850; internet: www.seafield.co.nz.

Southern English Schools: 69 Worcester Bvd, PO Box 1300, Christchurch; ☎(03) 365 6022; fax: (03) 365 6135; e-mail: info@ses.co.nz; internet: www.ses.ac.nz .

Tourism/ Hospitality

It is predicted that interest sparked by *The Lord of the Rings* trilogy which was shot in New Zealand, will boost the country's tourism industry by close to a third over the next three years. Tourism sales soared in the two weeks immediately following the first film's release, and tourist numbers are expected to double by the end of 2002. There are a lot of opportunities for casual workers in the tourist regions. Tourist destinations are a good place to start looking for hotel, bar and catering staff positions. It is usually easy to find café work in the main cities, and knowing your way around an espresso machine gives you a definite advantage. Kitchen hand and table waiting jobs are often advertised in local newspapers by the restaurants of large hotels. Working hours are long and the pay relatively low, but on the other hand, the location may make up for the working conditions. Tourists tip better than locals do, as New Zealanders traditionally do not tip serving staff. If you can ski and have the relevant qualification, there are many opportunities on New Zealand ski fields for ski instructors or ski patrol personnel. Other types of skills that may help you find employment include aquatic sports skills such as scuba diving, water skiing, or life saving skills. New Zealand beaches are patrolled mostly by volunteer surf life savers who are well trained and experienced in rescuing people from the often turbulent and dangerous waters, so you are more likely to find employment looking after hotel or private pools. Qualified aerobics instructors and personal trainers should find opportunities at the many private gyms around the country.

Voluntary Work

If you want to avoid work permit hassles and still be legal, there are voluntary schemes whereby you can work in exchange for food and lodgings. The most well known scheme goes under the name of WWOOF, which stands for Willing Workers On Organic Farms. There are many organic farms in New Zealand so there is the possibility that you could see quite a lot of the country without actually paying for your own keep. Usually you do about half a day's work in exchange for board. The work can be quite varied and you will usually be supplied with strictly vegetarian rations. To join the UK branch of WWOOF, send a s.a.e. to PO Box 2675, Lewes, East Sussex BN7 1RB; ☎01273-476286. You will receive a membership application form - membership costs £15 per year. Alternatively you can contact Jane and Andrew Strange directly in New Zealand (PO Box 1172, Nelson; tel/fax: (03) 544 9890; e-mail: andrew@wwoof.co.nz) to join for a fee of NZ$35/US$20/£10. See the WWOOF websites for further information (www.wwoof.co.nz and www.organicvolunteers.com).

Some members of the BioDynamic Farming and Gardening Association (NZ) Inc offer food and board in exchange for work at certain times of the year. For further information and a list of members, contact the Executive Secretary (PO Box 39045, Wellington; ☎(04) 589 5366; fax: (04) 589 5365) or see the website (www.organicpathways.co.nz).

The NZ Trust for Conservation Volunteers Inc. is another organisation that offers volunteer work. Projects include such activities as beach clean-ups and planting native forest. Lists of upcoming projects, and contact details for organisers, can be found on the website (http://nztcv.massey.ac.nz/projects). Project lengths vary, and so does the provision of accommodation and food depending on where, when and for how long you will be going.

BUSINESS AND INDUSTRY REPORT

New Zealand has now completed more than a decade of radical economic restructuring and the economy is now well-prepared for international competitiveness with a strong domestic currency, free movement of capital, no subsidies, deregulation and a modernised infrastructure. The GDP is growing steadily, and real GDP growth is currently 4.4%. With low inflation, falling debt and one of the world's lowest tariff rates, business confidence is beginning to pick up. The *Economic Freedom of the World: 2001 Annual Report*, published by the Fraser Institute, ranked New Zealand as the third most economically free country in the world. It is still uncertain how flow-on from recent developments in the world economy will affect New Zealand, but a number of factors (including interest rate cuts, the low New Zealand dollar and solid income growth to date) suggest that the country may evade the worst of a global slowdown.

Agriculture

Agriculture is New Zealand's largest industry and largest economic earner. It makes up nearly half of New Zealand's total exports, and contributes $11 billion to the GDP. The New Zealand agricultural industry is highly mechanised and is a low employer of labour as a result. However, over 205,000 people, or 11.4% of the labour force, are estimated to be employed in the agriculture industry. This includes 60,000 people on beef, sheep and dairy farms. In addition, around 25,000 family members work unpaid on farms. The average family farm employs the farmer, spouse and perhaps one farmhand.

New Zealand's is one of the most efficient agricultural sectors in the world and farmers receive no government subsidy. The removal of supplementary minimum payments in 1984 was predicted by many in the farming sector to be a disaster. Instead, although some farmers were forced to sell up, the sector responded by becoming more efficient and although farmland prices have not yet recovered to their pre-SMP prices, farm profitability is once again favourable. Farmers are now vulnerable to world prices in agricultural commodities and as a result many have diversified in order to spread their risk. Reliance upon traditional production areas has declined: sheep numbers dropped in response to low wool prices, but New Zealand is still the second largest wool exporter in the world, with 28% of the market. New production areas such as venison are being developed - deer farming is a comparatively small industry, but it has grown 80% during the last ten years. Other growing sectors include poultry farming and farm forestry. Despite the uncertainty of trading at world prices, the removal of subsidies seems to have done the industry good. The diversity of output has helped the country expand its export markets.

The main products are still sheep meat (55% of world trade comes from NZ), dairy products (31% of world trade), wool and beef. New Zealand has a natural advantage in agriculture due to its climate, which is ideal for grassland farming. The land itself was not originally suited for this purpose, being heavily forested and quite hilly. It has been brought under cultivation by lot of effort and the application of grassland management techniques developed in New Zealand's specialist agricultural research stations. Some of this agricultural expertise is being exported overseas in the form of sales of farm machinery developed in New Zealand, agricultural consulting services, and New Zealand breeding animals. New Zealand is a world leader in animal and plant breeding technology. There were hopes some years ago that 'agri-tech' might double its contribution to export earnings, but this seems to have been an optimistic assessment. On the other hand this sector is primarily responsive to local demand and as farm profitability improves, it is likely investment in agricultural production techniques will increase.

The impact of the 1995 GATT agreement improved market access for New Zealand's agricultural exports. The European Union has lifted the restrictive quotas, which prevented access for New Zealand butter and lamb into European markets. The most important export markets are the USA, Japan, Australia, Korea and the UK, and 80% of total farming output is sent overseas. The industry is good at reacting to world market demand by changing land use to suit demand, moving to more profitable areas, and specialising and developing products for niche market areas, as it has done with manuka honey and fine merino wool. It is expected that animal diseases around the world (such as foot and mouth and BSE) will add to increasing world demand for organic products. New Zealand's isolation and image put it in an excellent position to take advantage of this.

Finance and Insurance

The fast growth in employment in this sector between 1986 and 1991 was, in part, due to deregulation of the financial sector as part of the programme of economic reform instituted by the Labour government in the 1980s. As a result of deregulation there was a rapid growth in money market activity, particularly in the areas of foreign exchange, where all restrictions over transfers were lifted. New Zealand's relatively undeveloped financial industry enjoyed a boom. A range of new financial instruments was introduced such as forward contracts, options and exchange rate futures and secondary markets such as in government securities grew. The share market soared due to the increase in money supply resulting from deregulation. The boom was short-lived however and the inevitable collapse came in October 1987 when the main share price index, the Barclays share index, dropped to below its 1984 level. It has not recovered to pre-crash levels.

The second stage of deregulation in the financial sector occurred in the late 1980s. The regulations governing the supervision and registration of banks was relaxed under the Reserve Bank of New Zealand Act of 1986, and as result most building societies registered as banks and a number of foreign banks established New Zealand subsidiaries. Two further acts in 1987 and 1988 further removed distinctions between trading banks, trustee banks and building societies. The increase in the number of financial institutions and the range of activities they were involved in resulted in a rapid growth of employment in this area. Over the past few years many finance, insurance and services companies have merged – in some cases the resulting restructuring and centralisation of business functions has led to head offices relocating offshore. There has been a drop in the number of bank branches (639 closed since 1994, although this has now stabilised) and a rise in electronic banking methods. The overall future of this sector looks relatively positive, although possible mergers and control of New Zealand companies by overseas firms makes it hard to predict change. The insurance industry accounts for around 1% of GDP and employs roughly 8,100 full-time equivalent workers. Technological advances are having a major impact, with customer services and call centres being the main areas of growth. New Zealanders currently spend around NZ$2 billion annually on insurance, and it is expected that the amount of business available to the industry will grow slowly.

Construction

Construction currently employs 6.7% of New Zealand's employed workforce, and contributes around 4% of the GDP. The highest proportion of building construction enterprises are in Auckland, Wellington and Christchurch. There are three main parts to the industry - residential (homes), non-residential (offices, etc.) and civil construction (bridges, roads, hospitals, etc.). Growth has been slow for the past few years, but a rise in domestic demand for buildings is a key factor affecting the upturn in growth at present. New Zealand construction companies have particular expertise in earthquake proof standards in specialist areas, such as hydro and geothermal power station design and construction. When looking for employment, generally it is easier for skilled tradespeople - carpenters, fitters, welders and joiners - to find work in this sector.

Energy, Coal and Petrochemicals

Coal is New Zealand's largest energy resource, and just under three million tons of coal are produced annually, mainly sub-bitumous coal from North Island fields. The West Coast of the South Island is the biggest source of bitumous coal, most of which is exported to Japan, India and China. The quality of New Zealand coal makes it ideal for use in the chemical and steel industries. Industrial usage consumes nearly three-quarters of the remaining production. Coal is no longer a feed stock for thermal power stations as gas is becoming more competitive. In the future dual process stations such as the power station at Huntly, north of Hamilton, which can use either gas or coal, may go back to using coal as domestic gas supplies decline. The petrochemical industry is concentrated around the natural gas and oil fields off the coast of Taranaki. Six fields produce crude oil, condensate and natural gas, which provide about 50% of New Zealand's energy needs. Gas from the Maui and Kapuni offshore fields provides 95% of total gas production. Maui is expected to last until 2006 and Kapuni until 2014. Around a third of the natural gas produced is used to make synthetic petrol at a processing plant near Motonui.

Hydroelectric generators on major rivers, mostly in the South Island, produce 80% of New Zealand's electricity supply. The generating authority until 1999 was the Electricity Corporation of New Zealand (ECNZ), a state owned enterprise. It has now been split and its operating assets transferred to three new generation SOEs - Mighty River Power (MRP), Meridian Energy and Genesis Power. ECNZ is managing down its remaining activities with an eventual view to winding up completely. The main assets of Genesis are New Zealand's largest power station, at Huntly, and the Tongariro and Waikaremoana power schemes. Meridian's core assets are the South Island hydroelectric generators at Manapouri and Waitaki river, which have an average annual generation capacity of 12,500 gigawatt hours (GWh), 26% of New Zealand's total electricity generation. Meridian also has three-quarters of New

Zealand's total hydro-storage capacity. MRP generates electricity primarily from the Waikato River hydro power station, and from Mokai and Rotokawa geothermal.

Major Companies. MRP, Meridian Energy, Genesis Power, BP New Zealand, Fletcher Challenge, Dominion Oil Refining, Mobil Oil New Zealand, Caltex NZ.

Forestry

Forests cover 7.8 million hectares, or 29% of New Zealand's land area. The bulk of this is native rainforest which is no longer a major source of timber for export. Pressure from conservation groups and the increasing profitability of other plantation species has restricted the harvesting of native forests. Native forest covers 23% of New Zealand's land area, or 6.4 million hectares. Just under 2% of native forests are harvested commercially, and under strict conditions. Commercial forests cover 1.7 million hectares (6% of New Zealand's land area) and are a renewable resource. The bulk of these forests are planted in introduced species, mainly radiata pine, which reach maturity in 25-28 years in New Zealand conditions. A small percentage of commercial forest is made up of Douglas fir and a few other species. 98% of New Zealand wood is harvested from renewable resources, which means the land is immediately replanted. The forestry industry is concentrated in the central North Island where the main production forests are located. There are smaller plantation forests in the South Island, mainly in the Tasman area and on the West Coast. The forestry industry is New Zealand's third largest export earning sector after the meat and dairy industries, contributing around 4% to GDP. Future prospects for growth are encouraging as restrictions on the importing of tropical hardwoods spread. Although export volumes are predicted to keep growing, prices have proved volatile. In the future competition from radiata pine suppliers in other southern hemisphere countries may depress prices.

The state used to own half the total area of commercial forests but as part of the privatisation move in the last decade, management and cutting rights were sold to the private sector. The private sector now manages 80% of plantations. Major companies involved in the buying of state forestry assets were Carter Holt Harvey, Fletcher Challenge and Rayonier New Zealand who now own half the planted forest resource. Several other overseas companies made significant investments. The wood and pulp and paper industries do not seem to have suffered from the economic crises in Asia.

Major Companies. TT Rayonier, Juken Nissho, Ernslaw One, Forestry Corporation of New Zealand, Carter Holt Harvey, Fletcher Challenge, New Zealand Forest Products, Weyerhaeuser.

Horticulture

The horticulture industry in New Zealand is notable for its diverse range of products, including kiwifruit, pipfruit, stonefruit, grapes, berries, avocado, citrus, and exotic fruits, and vegetables such as buttercup squash, onions, tomatoes, potatoes, greenleaf and sweetcorn, as well as flowers. Kiwifruit is one particularly well-known product of the industry. For a brief period in the 1990s, land prices in the chief kiwifruit growing areas soared. However the entrance of new growers caused a glut on the market and competition from other countries reduced profits to lower levels. Kiwifruit has now taken its place again as the most valuable horticultural export, last year making up 30.6% of all horticultural exports and worth $588 million. Apple exports were worth $369 million (19.2% of horticultural exports). Organic growers contribute

$50 million a year to export earnings. Horticulture is a key economic producer and employs around 44,000 people throughout the country. In the last ten years, the area of land used for horticulture has increased 46%, to over 128,000 hectares. Exports have increased about 50%. Last year, horticultural exports had a value of around $1,921 million, forming 6.6% of all New Zealand exports.

The majority of grapes produced in New Zealand are used to make wine. Wine production is one of New Zealand's fastest growing industries - since 1990 the area used for grape growing and wine production has more than doubled, now totalling around 12,665 hectares. Most growth has been in the Hawke's Bay and Marlborough regions. New Zealand wine is exported to 60 countries, and the major export market for New Zealand wine is the UK, which bought $84 million worth of wine last year. The USA and Australia are the other main New Zealand wine-buying countries. New Zealand has sought a wine agreement with the European Union to gain access to valuable European markets. Further expansion in the industry is expected also because the number of vineyards continues to increase.

Fishing and Aquaculture

New Zealand's clean waters provide fish of exceptional quality. Seafood is the country's fifth largest primary industry, provides 5.5% of all exports and is the fourth largest export earner. This industry directly employs over 10,000 people. Major export markets are Japan, the USA and Europe, as well as Australia and Hong Kong. Annual seafood harvests bring in between $1.2 and $1.5 billion. These figures are predicted to reach $2 billion by 2010. New Zealand's exclusive economic zone (EEZ), wherein the Ministry of Agriculture and Fisheries controls all fishing, extends for 200 nautical miles from the coastline and is the fourth largest in the world, covering a total of 1.2 million square miles. MAF runs a system of transferable quotas which has been in place since 1986, and more recent legislation has further tightened the procedures operated by the 'Quota Management System' (QMS). Quotas cover most major commercial species. Assessments are made about the size of the fishstock and the sustainable commercial catch for each species is estimated. The total catch is allocated between fishing companies through individual quotas which companies can buy or sell. 80% of the quotas are held by ten organisations (listed below). 20% of quotas for new species are allocated to the Maori under a deal between the tribes and the government settled in 1992, and Maori stakeholders control one-third of the total quota.

There is a small but growing crustacia and shellfish farming industry, which includes rock lobsters, scallops, oysters, clams, cockles and crabs. The main export products are Pacific oysters and green-lipped mussels. Increased diversity is expected in the next decade. Paua (a large New Zealand shellfish) farms and seaweed trial projects have already been established. This industry, like much of New Zealand's agricultural and horticultural output, is vulnerable to disease which can wipe out an entire season's crop, as happened in the summer of 1992/93 when toxic algae bloom resulted in shellfish harvesting being suspended. The other major threat to the seafood industry comes from trade barriers. About 85% of industry revenues come from exports, but most of the markets New Zealand trades with have volume restrictions (quotas) on imports. New Zealand currently has less than 2% of world seafood trade and could expand this if the quotas were increased. One target is increasing sales to Europe, which currently takes about 14% of New Zealand exports. However the EU usually negotiates market liberalisation in return for access to fishing grounds. This would be difficult to grant directly in the case of the New Zealand industry because of the system of transferable fishing quotas described above. Given the current fierce competition over EU fishing grounds, and the charges being levelled at various countries of over-fishing, leasing the rights to fish in New Zealand waters could be a possible opening to European markets.

Major Companies. Sealord Group, Sanford Group, Treaty of Waitangi Fisheries, Amaltal Corporation, the Independent Fisheries Group, Vela Limited, Ruakura Moana Fisheries Limited, Ngai Tahu Fisheries, Moana Pacific, Talleys Group.

Manufacturing

The government has been encouraging competition and efficiency in the manufacturing sector with a programme of tariffs on imported goods. Tariffs have lowered the cost of imported materials, as well as increasing competition by opening up the country to more imported goods. After a period of instability and threatened jobs, companies in the industry have become more streamlined and innovative. Manufacturing sales (both international and domestic) are growing, with nine out of ten industries recording increases in the past year. There is significant optimism, as sales growth has now returned to levels not seen since the early 1990s, however most growth until now has been due to the US market and impacts of recent events cannot yet be predicted. Business confidence remains somewhat volatile, but there has recently been a slight improvement in profit expectations.

Automotive. There is no New Zealand owned car manufacturing industry. The majority of vehicles are imported unassembled, mainly from Japan, and assembled locally. The industry suffered a major decline with the lowering of tariffs between 1988-90 resulting in the introduction of used Japanese vehicles, as well as domestic and international recessions, which reduced the demand for new cars. Business and consumer confidence have improved, and there have been moves in the industry to rationalise production across the Tasman with Australia. New Zealand motor assembling plants have developed successful production of vehicle componentry totalling $400 million, of which roughly $150 million comes from exports.
Major Companies. Ford NZ, General Motors NZ, Toyota NZ.

Textiles, Clothing, Footwear and Leather Goods. This industry accounts for 5% of total manufacturing and just under 1% of GDP. With the decrease in tariffs and increased competition many businesses were forced to close or move offshore, resulting in a reduction in employment numbers. It was initially planned that all tariffs be eliminated by 2010; however, in April 2000 the Government announced that tariffs would be frozen until July 2005. Much of the industry is made up of small, owner-operated companies creating high-quality products for small niche export markets. Exports have grown from $49 million in 1989 to around $998 million in 2001; the low value of the New Zealand dollar has meant that exporters have gained good returns. 70% of exports are destined for Australia, but other important markets include Germany, Japan, the USA, South Korea and the UK.

Steel and non-ferrous metals. Steel and aluminium are the only metals produced in any quantity in New Zealand. The ironsands on the west coast of the North Island are the largest reserves of iron ore in the country, and were noted as far back as 1769, by Captain James Cook. The New Zealand steel works at Glenbrook produces steel from these sands by a unique direct reduction process. BHP New Zealand Steel remains the world's only producer of steel from ironsand, with a total production of around 700,000 tonnes. Unwrought aluminium from the Comalco smelter near Bluff is a major export earner using raw bauxite imported from Australia. Employment opportunities in this sector have decreased because of capital upgrades by firms to increase efficiency, and decreased demand from Asian countries cut export prices.

Major Companies. BHP New Zealand Steel, Pacific Steel, Comalco-CHH Aluminium, Steel and Tube Holdings Limited, Superior Industries Ltd.

Electronics. Electronics is one of the success stories of the restructured New Zealand economy. Under the old regime of protected domestic industries the sector was predominantly involved in the manufacture of consumer electronics. Now most of these goods (TVs, videos, etc.) are imported from Asia where costs are cheaper. The major exception is the domestic whiteware industry (the local term for fridges, dishwashers, ovens, etc.) where New Zealanders show a strong preference for long established local brands such as Fisher and Paykel. The electronics industry, instead of declining with the reduction in tariffs, has diversified and found niche markets in high tech commercial and industrial products. For example, one Christchurch based company, Dynamic Controls, is the world's leading supplier of mobility control systems for power wheelchairs and scooters. Software is another area where New Zealand firms have developed specialist markets. Big international firms such as Ericsson and IBM have introduced technological advancements and teamed up with companies like Synergy to develop cell phone and mobile internet software in New Zealand. Information technology is the second-fastest growing occupational category, and saw a 10% increase in staff last year. Job prospects for skilled workers in the industry are good. There is currently a skills shortage from assembly workers through to engineers and software designers. The size of the New Zealand industry has limited the numbers being trained so that it has been unable to keep up with the current leap in demand for its products.

Major Companies: AWA New Zealand, Dynamic Controls, Ericsson, Fisher and Paykel Electronics, IBM New Zealand.

Food and Beverages. The major destination for food manufacturing exports is the Australian market. Food and beverages enterprises employ just over a quarter of the total manufacturing workforce. Large enterprises dominate the industry and employ the majority of the workforce, but there are a number of small businesses producing high quality luxury goods such as smoked seafood, speciality cheeses and wines. Due to a low intake of students into Food Technology courses there is a shortage of food technologists, but there is a high demand as the industry is growing rapidly.

Major Companies: Bluebird Foods, DB Group, Cerebos Gregg, Goodman Fielder, Kraft General Foods, Nestle New Zealand, Lion Nathan, Abels, Montana Wines, Villa Maria Wines.

Tourism and Hospitality

Almost every aspect of the industry is growing and this looks likely to continue, especially with the new interest generated by Peter Jackson's *The Lord of the Rings* trilogy. It is estimated that these films will boost New Zealand's tourist industry by as much as one third over the next three years. Most visitors come from Japan, Australia, the USA, the UK and South Korea. During the 1990s international arrivals increased by 85% and domestic travel by 40%. Overseas and domestic tourism currently contributes 4.8% to the GDP. Last year, 1.8 million tourists visited from overseas, bringing in $4.9 billion for the New Zealand economy. Overseas visitor numbers are expected to increase to 3.2 million by 2010, which means that an additional 100,000 jobs will be created in various areas.

The New Zealand Tourism Board, which co-ordinates the Visitor Information Centre network, promotes New Zealand to overseas visitors. The main attractions for most are the clean environment and beautiful scenery, but a growing number of tourists are after more active holidays, skiing trips, jet-boat rides, white water rafting, black water rafting, even bungy jumping. This has lead to the growth of a new type of tourism, called 'adventure tourism'. Another area that is beginning to take off is 'green tourism' or 'eco-tourism'. Often thought to be a contradiction in terms because the impact of visitors upon the environment is usually harmful, green tourism aims to combine sharing the environment with tourists and protecting it. Activities such as whale watching off the Kaikoura coast above Christchurch, and visiting bird sanctuary islands already attract many tourists and Kiwis alike.

Transport

As a small exporting economy at great distances from many of its markets, New Zealand is highly dependent on maintaining its external transportation links. Internal transportation networks are also important as its small population is spread over two islands nearly 2,000 kilometres in combined length. Early transport developments were largely the result of government investment. The rail network, harbours, and road building were all extensively developed under a programme of major public works during the 1870s. State ownership and investment was the pattern for transportation development over the next century. The government owned and ran the railways, a shipping line, and eventually the national airline. State ownership of transportation links diminished under the programme of state asset sales begun by the Labour government in the 1980s. Now private sector investment is behind most new transport projects, with the exception of road building, which remains the responsibility of Transit New Zealand, a government authority. Road transportation was deregulated during the 1980s as was public transport in most cities. New Zealand Rail was sold to a consortium made up of a Canadian, an American and a New Zealand company in 1993. Port authorities were set up as companies, largely owned by local authorities, with two partly privately owned.

Transport is very dependent on other areas of the economy, such as agriculture. Recent growth in logging, tourism and dairy, as well as production industry centralisation, means that there is currently increased demand for transport services and this is likely to continue. Bulk freight, such as steel, coal, and cargo including dairy products, is mainly transported by rail. The highest proportions of rail transport enterprises are in Wellington, Canterbury and Manawatu-Wanganui regions. International trade relies heavily on water transport, as almost 99% of all exports are carried by sea. The main ports are at Auckland, Wellington, Tauranga and Lyttleton. There are three main international airports - at Auckland, Wellington and Christchurch. There are two New Zealand airlines operating international flights; Air New Zealand and its subsidiary Freedom Air. Qantas NZ was another major carrier, but this franchise was recently closed, resulting in many job losses. Qantas Australia plans to enter the market, as does Virgin Blue. Such expansion would create many more employment opportunities.

REGIONAL EMPLOYMENT GUIDE

THE UPPER NORTH ISLAND

Northland and Auckland

Major Cities: Auckland (pop. 1,158,891), Whangarei (pop. 68,094).
Newspapers: *The New Zealand Herald* (www.nzhearld.co.nz), *Northern Advocate* (PO Box 210, Whangarei).
Chambers of Commerce: Auckland Regional Chamber of Commerce and Industry: 100 Mayoral Drive, PO Box 47, Auckland; ☎(09) 309 6100; fax: (09) 309 0081; e-mail: akl@chamber.co.nz. Northland Chamber of Commerce: 3-5 Hunt St, PO Box 1703, Whangarei; ☎(09) 438 4771; fax: (09) 4384770; e-mail: northchamber@clear.net.nz.
Industry/Other Comments. The Auckland region is the main business and industrial centre and employs nearly one third of the total workforce. Around half are employed in the services sector, comprising wholesale, retail, community, social and personal services and also including tourism, film, television and sport. The Auckland region provides a wide range of job opportunities in manufacturing and distribution, boat building, construction, and business and financial services. Auckland has a container port and an international airport. Employment prospects in the area are good and continue to improve. The region is predicted to remain the leader in economic growth over the next few years and this is reflected in the number of businesses looking to expand their workforce. Numbers of job advertisements continue to increase, and growth industries in the future are likely to be construction and information technology and telecommunications. North of the greater Auckland area, job prospects are likely to be associated with the growth of tourism and the expected improvement in agricultural export volumes. There are opportunities to work in areas such as boat building, tourism, forestry (exotic forest) and acquaculture for coastal shellfish farming. New Zealand's only crude oil refinery is located at Marsden Point, near Whangarei, on the East Coast. South of Auckland, at Glenbrook, is the BHP New Zealand Steel factory that uses a unique production process based on the reduction of local ironsand. West Coast beaches in New Zealand are characterised by the high proportion of iron ore in the sand, which results in black coloration.

THE CENTRAL NORTH ISLAND

Waikato, Bay of Plenty, Gisborne and Hawke's Bay

Major Cities: Hamilton (pop. 114,921), Tauranga (pop. 90,906), Rotorua (pop. 52,000) New Plymouth (pop. 66,603) Hastings (pop. 67,425), Napier (pop. 54,300).
Newspapers: *The Waikato Times* (Private Bag 3086, Hamilton), *Bay of Plenty Times* (108 Durham Street, Tauranga), *Hawke's Bay Today* (PO Box 180, Hastings).
Chambers of Commerce: Waikato Chamber of Commerce: 554 Victoria Street, PO Box 1122, Hamilton; ☎(07) 839 5895; fax: (07) 839 4581; e-mail: admin@waikatoc

hamber.co.nz. Chamber of Commerce Tauranga Region: 51 Willow St, PO Box 414, Tauranga, ☎(07) 577 9823; fax: (07) 577 9823; e-mail: chamber@tauranga.org.nz. Hawke's Bay Chamber of Commerce: PO Box 144, Hastings; ☎(06) 876 5938; fax: (06) 876 3748; e-mail: hb.chamber@xtra.co.nz.

Industry/Other Comments. The Waikato is one of the main dairy farming regions in the country. Horticulture, particularly citrus fruit and kiwifruit, is the predominant industry in the Bay of Plenty on the East Coast. There are also opportunities for expansion within the tourism, forestry and food processing industries. Hawke's Bay is a premium wine-making district, and has some of the oldest established wineries in the country; the Mission Vineyard, run by Catholic monks, first began producing wine last century. It is also a significant farming and fruit-growing region and there are many job and investment opportunities in agriculture, food processing and tourism. Hamilton is home to a number of manufacturing enterprises, a university, and a large wholesale and retail sector. Most industry in the Waikato region is based on the processing of agricultural and forestry raw products, as well as dairy, technology, bloodstock, and education and research. The central region of the North Island is the main centre for the pulp and paper-making industry. Large plantation forests of radiata pine provide the raw materials for the production of newsprint, wood pulp, paper and paperboard. The Waikato is the largest coal-producing region in the country, with seventeen mainly open cast mines producing over half the total annual sub-bitumous coal output of the country. Main industries on the East Coast and in Gisborne are tourism, wine making and forestry (there are large exotic forests with opportunities for further expansion). Gas is main product of the petro-chemical industry based on the Taranaki coast near New Plymouth. The Taranaki region supports many energy related industries, including specialised engineering, and is a major dairy area with value-added food processing opportunities. The region is also a tourist destination. Major attractions include the thermal region around Rotorua and the network of limestone caves near Waitomo. Economic prospects in the region are favourable particularly for horticulture and forestry, and associated industries.

THE LOWER NORTH ISLAND

Taranaki, Manawatu-Wanganui and Wellington

Major Cities: Wellington (pop. 423,765), Palmerston North (pop. 76,000), Wanganui (pop. 40,000).

Newspapers: *The Dominion* (PO Box 1297, Wellington), *Manawatu Evening Standard* (PO Box 3, Palmerston North) *Wanganui Chronicle* (59 Taupo Quay, Wanganui).

Chambers of Commerce: Wellington Chamber of Commerce: Level 9, 109 Featherston St, Wellington; ☎(04) 914 6500; fax: (04) 914 6524; e-mail: info@wgtn-chamber.co.nz. Wanganui Chamber of Commerce: Enterprise House, 187 Victoria Ave, PO Box 88, Wanganui; ☎(06) 345 0080; fax: (06) 348 8210; e-mail: wanganui.chamber@clear.net.nz; Taranaki Chamber of Commerce: 49-55 Powderham St, PO Box 2, New Plymouth; ☎(06) 759 9080; fax: (06) 759 9145; e-mail: taranaki.chamber@xtra.co.nz.

Industry/Other Comments. The capital city Wellington is the headquarters of central government. Most major law firms, accountants and management firms have their base in Wellington as well, although some firms prefer to have their head office in Auckland, reflecting that city's commercial dominance. Wellington is the centre of the performing arts, as the national orchestra and ballet are based there, and there is an abundance of dance companies, opera groups and professional theatres in the city. Wellington also hosts a biannual International Festival of the Performing Arts. Business, government and retail enterprises dominate the main urban area. Manufacturing industry is concentrated in the outlying suburbs and on the Petone seafront at the northern end of the Wellington harbour. Growth industries in the Wellington region are information, communications, education and film. There are secondary processing opportunities in forestry, agriculture, horticulture and wine making. Outside the urban area, to the north, the Wairarapa district is dairy and sheep farming country. The main industries in the Manawatu-Wanganui area are forestry, dairy, food processing, specialised engineering, intensive horticultural activities, education and agriculture technology, and research based on tertiary institutions and the area's strong farming base. Martinborough, north of Wellington, is a newly emerging major player in wine production.

THE UPPER SOUTH ISLAND

Nelson-Marlborough, West Coast and Canterbury

Major Cities: Christchurch (pop. 316,227), Nelson (pop. 52,000).
Newspapers: *The Christchurch Press* (Private Bag 4722, Christchurch), *The Nelson Mail* (15 Bridge Street, PO Box 244, Nelson).
Chambers of Commerce: Canterbury Employers Chamber of Commerce: 57 Kilmore St, PO Box 359, Christchurch; ☎(03) 366 5096; fax: (03) 379 5454; e-mail: info@cecc.co.nz. Nelson Chamber of Commerce, 54 Montgomery Square, PO Box 1121, Nelson; ☎(03) 548 1363; fax: (03) 546 8373; e-mail: commerce.nelson@clear .net.nz.
Industry/Other Comments. Marlborough is the largest wine-making region in New Zealand, and opportunities for expansion include wine making, tourism, forestry and food processing. The Canterbury region is the largest sheep-farming region in the country. It has a container port nearby at Lyttleton and the second busiest international airport in the country. As well as agricultural industry, Christchurch is the largest region for manufacturing employment after Auckland. Canterbury has a number of high-tech electronic manufacturing and software firms, as well as wine making, horticulture, floriculture, food processing businesses. Tourism is a major source of economic activity in the region, thanks to the scenery and the skiing. Christchurch is only an hour away from the ski fields of Mt Hutt. Other important services here include education and research. The country's first legal casino opened in the former Christchurch railway station in 1994. Nelson is an important deep-sea fishing base and seafood processing location. West Coast industry is traditionally based on resource extraction - gold mining, coal mining and timber. This area is benefitting from its new deep water port, and the development of three new coal mines, which are expected to boost its already healthy coal exports. The strongest opportunities for expansion on the West Coast lie in tourism.

THE LOWER SOUTH ISLAND

Southland and Otago

Major Cities: Dunedin (pop. 114,342), Invercargill (pop. 46,000).
Newspapers: *The Otago Daily Times* (31 Clyde St, Dunedin) *The Southland Times* (67 Esk Street, Invercargill).
Chambers of Commerce: Otago Chamber of Commerce and Industry Incorporated: Level 7, 106 George Street, Dunedin; ☎(03) 479 0181; fax: (03) 477 0341; e-mail: office@otagochamber.co.nz. Chamber of Commerce Southland Inc.: PO Box 856, Invercargill; ☎(03) 218 7188; fax: (03) 218 7189; e-mail: information@commerceso uth.com.
Industry/Other Comments. The strong agricultural base of the rural economy in Otago and Southland is mainly concentrated on sheep farming with smaller numbers of dairy and beef farms. Other important activities include food processing and tourism, as well as horticulture, particularly stonefruit. Vineyards are relatively new to the region. Until recently the climate was thought to be too cold for grape growing, but several local wineries have established an enviable reputation. Main industries in Dunedin are education, tourism, food processing and niche manufacturing. Apart from Dunedin, manufacturing in the region is concentrated around Invercargill with the exception of the Comalco Aluminium smelter, which is located at Tiwai point near Bluff. Bluff is also known for its production of oysters.

DIRECTORY OF MAJOR EMPLOYERS

Accommodation and Hospitality
CDL Hotels NZ Ltd: Level 13, 280 Centre, 280 Queen St, Auckland; ☎(09) 309 4411; fax: (09) 309 3244; internet: www.cdlhotels.co.nz.
Restaurant Brands NZ Ltd: 60 Hugo Johnston Ave, Penrose, Auckland; ☎(09) 525 8700; fax: (09) 525 8711; internet: www.restaurantbrands.co.nz.

Accountancy
Advantage Group: PO Box 68-281, Auckland; ☎(09) 361 0500; fax: (09) 361 0666; e-mail: jobs@advantagegroup.co.nz; internet: www.advantagegroup.co.nz.
Gosling Chapman Chartered Accountants: Human Resources Manager, PO Box 158, Auckland; ☎(09) 303 4586; fax: (09) 309 1198; e-mail: caroleba@gosling.co.nz; internet: www.gosling.co.nz.

Agriculture and Forestry
Landcorp Farming Ltd: Landcorp House, 101 Lambton Quay, Wellington; ☎(04) 471 0400; fax: (04) 473 4966; internet: www.landcorp.co.nz.
Sanford Ltd: 22 Jellicoe St, Freemans Bay, Auckland; ☎(09) 379 4720; fax: (09) 309 1190; internet: www.sanford.co.nz.

Banking, Insurance and Financial Services
ACC: Shamrock House, 81-83 Molesworth St, Wellington; ☎(04) 918 7700; fax: (04) 918 7701; internet: www.acc.co.nz.
AMP Financial Services: Human Resources Consultant, PO Box 1290, Wellington; ☎(04) 498 8000; fax: (04) 498 8632; e-mail: helen – davey@amp.co.nz; internet: www.amp.co.nz.
ASB Bank: Manager Recruitment,

PO Box 35, Auckland; ☎(09) 374 8412; fax: (09) 306 0095; e-mail: roy.ball@asbbank.co.nz; internet: www.asbbank.co.nz.

Bank of New Zealand: Human Resources, PO Box 995, Auckland; ☎(09) 302 4973; fax: (09) 375 1277; e-mail: allison – fisher@bnz.co.nz; internet: www.bnz.co.nz.

Deutsche Bank: Human Resources Manager, PO Box 6900, Wellesley Street, Auckland; ☎(09) 351 1015; fax: (09) 351 1859; e-mail: kathryn.gilchrist@db.com; internet: www.deutschebank.co.nz.

KPMG: National Human Resources Manager, KPMG Centre, PO Box 1584, Auckland; ☎(09) 367 5800; e-mail: clgoodall@kpmg.co.nz; internet: www.kpmg.co.nz.

Meritec: HR Development Manager, PO Box 4241, Auckland; ☎(09) 379 1206; fax: (09) 379 1201; e-mail: opportunities@meritec.org; internet: www.meritec.org.

Reserve Bank of New Zealand: HR, PO Box 2498, Wellington; ☎(04) 472 2029; fax: (04) 471 3759; e-mail: recruitment@rbnz.govt.nz; internet: www.rbnz.govt.nz.

Tower Limited: Level 5, 50-64 Customhouse Quay, Wellington; ☎(04) 472 6059; fax: (04) 498 7903; internet: www.towerfin.co.nz.

The Treasury: HR and Recruitment Advisor, PO Box 3724, Wellington; ☎(04) 471 5276; fax: (04) 471 5978; e-mail: human.resources@treasury.govt.nz; internet: www.treasury.govt.nz.

Business and Management Services

AMP: Level 5, City Tower, 95 Customhouse Quay, Wellington; ☎(04) 494 2200; fax: (04) 494 2128; internet: www.amp.co.nz.

Ernst & Young: Recruitment and Retention Manager, PO Box 2146, Auckland ; ☎(09) 377 4790; fax: (09) 373 5607; e-mail: yourfuture@nz.eyi.com; internet: www.ey.com.

Construction and Engineering

Beca Carter Hollings & Ferner Ltd: Human Resources, PO Box 6345, Auckland; ☎(09) 300 9000; fax: (09) 300 9300; e-mail: hr@beca.co.nz; internet: www.becagroup.com.

Delta: Contract Services Manager, PO Box 1404, Dunedin; ☎(03) 479 6693; fax: (03) 479 6694; e-mail: rossp@del.co.nz; internet: www.4delta.co.nz.

Fulton Hogan Limited: General Manager Southern, PO Box 16-064, Hornby, Christchurch; ☎(03) 344 0941; fax: (03) 344 0987; e-mail: Roger.nuttall@fh.co.nz; internet: www.fh.co.nz.

Meritec: HR Development Manager, PO Box 4241, Auckland; ☎(09) 379 1206; fax: (09) 379 1201; e-mail: opportunities@meritec.org; internet: www.meritec.org.

Montgomery Watson: Staffing Specialist, PO Box 13-052, Christchurch; ☎(03) 366 8825; fax: (03) 366 8876; e-mail: nzstaffing@mw.com; internet: www.mw.com/jobs.

Opus: HR Advisor, PO Box 12343, Wellington; ☎(04) 471 7000; fax: (04) 473 3017; e-mail: hr.workingin@opus.co.nz; internet: www.opus.co.nz.

Cultural and Recreational Services

NZ Lotteries Commission: 54-56 Cambridge Terrace, Wellington; ☎(04) 802 7000; fax: (04) 385 2787.

NZ Totaliser Agency Board: 106-110 Jackson St, Petone; ☎(04) 576 6999; fax: (04) 576 6942.

Sky City Limited: Level 6 Federal House, 86 Federal St, Auckland; ☎(09) 363 6141; fax: (09) 363 6140; internet: www.skycity.co.nz.

Sky Network Television Limited: 10 Panorama Rd, Mt Wellington, Auckland; ☎(09) 579 9999; fax: (09) 579 0910; internet: www.skytelevision.co.nz.

Television New Zealand Limited: Television Centre, 100 Victoria St West, Auckland; ☎(09) 916 7000; fax: (09) 916 7934; internet: www.tvnz.co.nz.

Education

Open Polytechnic: The People Team, Private Bag 31 914, Lower Hutt; ☎(04) 560 5715; fax: (04) 560 5639; e-mail: recruit@topnz.ac.nz; internet: www.topnz.ac.nz.

Richina Pacific Ltd: Level 11, 385 Queen St, Auckland; ☎(09) 375 2120; fax: (09) 375 2104; internet: www.richina pacific.co.nz.

SES (Specialist Education Services): internet: www.ses.org.nz.

TeachNZ: internet: www.TeachNZ.govt.nz.

Health

Auckland District Health Board: Staffing Manager, Private Bag 92 189, Green Lane West, Auckland; ☎(09) 630 9943 (xtn 4582); fax: (09) 623 6477; e-mail: jackieb@ahsl.co.nz; internet: www.akhealth.co.nz.

MidCentral District Health Board: Employee Relations Consultant, PO Box 2056, Palmerston North; ☎(06) 350 8850; fax: (06) 350 8982; e-mail: anne.am oore@midcentral.co.nz; internet: www.MidCentral.co.nz.

Southern Cross Healthcare: Private Bag 999 34, Auckland; ☎(09) 356 0925 extn 8709; fax: (09) 377 5695; e-mail: kimm@sxhealth.co.nz; internet: www.southerncross.co.nz.

South Auckland Health: HR, Middlemore Hospital, PO Box 93311, Otahuhu, Auckland; ☎(09) 276 0044 extn 8083; fax: (09) 276 0127; e-mail: recr uitment@middlemore.co.nz; internet: www.jobpulse.co.nz.

Taranaki Health: HR Advisor, Private Bag 2016, New Plymouth; ☎(06) 753 6139 extn 8870; fax: (06) 753 7860; e-mail: bronwen.davies@thcl.co.nz; internet: www.thcl.co.nz.

Waitemata District Health Board: HR Recruitment Co-ordinator, Private Bag 93-503, Takapuna, Auckland; ☎(09) 486 1491; fax: (09) 489 0533;

e-mail: recruitment@whl.co.nz; internet: www.waitematahealth.co.nz.

Waikato District Health Board: PO Box 934, Hamilton; ☎(07) 839 8949; fax: (07) 839 8758; e-mail: recruit@hwl.co.nz; internet: www.waikatodhb.govt.nz.

West Coast District Health Board: Recruitment Co-ordinator, PO Box 387, Greymouth; ☎(03) 768 0499; fax: (03) 768 2791; e-mail: amartin@westcoast dhb.org.nz.

Information Technology and Telecommunications

Brocker Technology Group: HR Manager, PO Box 99-222, Newmarket, Auckland; ☎(09) 481 9999; fax: (09) 481 9989; e-mail: gcooper@brocker.co.nz; internet: www.brockergroup.com.

Cap Gemini Ernst & Young: Recruitment Manager, PO Box 1943, Auckland; ☎(09) 377 1440; fax: (09) 358 1018; e-mail: careers@nz.cgeyc.com; internet: www.nz.cgey.com.

Commsoft Group Ltd: Chief Technology Officer, 90 Symonds Street, Auckland; ☎(09) 358 5900; fax: (09) 358 5901; e-mail: hr@commsoftgroup.com; internet: www.commsoftgroup.com.

Computerland: Human Resources Consultant; ☎(09) 460 6045; fax: (09) 460 6002; e-mail: suzanne.riddle @computerland.co.nz; internet: www.computerland.co.nz.

Deltec Telesystems International Ltd: PO Box 50-691, Tawa, Wellington; ☎(04) 238 0700; fax: (04) 238 0701; e-mail: careers@deltec-telesystems.com; internet: www.deltec-telesystems.com.

Ericsson: GM Organisational Development, PO Box 14-616, Ellerslie, Auckland; ☎(09) 355 5460; fax: (09) 355 5501; e-mail: christine.sum merville@ericsson.co.nz; internet: www.ericsson.co.nz.

Inland Revenue (IT Dept): PO Box 2198, Wellington; ☎(04) 382 7007; fax: (04) 382 7054; e-mail: hr.it@ird.govt.nz; internet: www.ird.govt.nz.

ITC (IT Capital Limited): ☎(09) 307 2710;

internet: www.itcapital.net.

JADE: Staff Development Manager, PO Box 20 152, Christchurch; ☎(03) 365 2500; fax: (03) 358 6050; e-mail: ejullrich@discoverjade.com; internet: www.discoverjade.com.

[hi*Meritec:* HR Development Manager, PO Box 4241, Auckland; ☎(09) 379 1206; fax: (09) 379 1201; e-mail: opportunities@meritec.org; internet: www.meritec.org.

Microsoft NZ: HR Manager, PO Box 8070, Symonds Street, Auckland; ☎(09) 357 5815; fax: (09) 358 5558; e-mail: elizam@microsoft.com; internet: www.microsoft.com/nz/jobs.

Oracle: HR, Oracle Tower, 56 Wakefield Street, Auckland; ☎(09) 309 1946; fax: (09) 377 8847; e-mail: jobs – nz@oracle.com; internet: www.oracle.com or http:// jobs.oracle.com.

Powerlan: NZ Country Manager, PO Box 11-827, Wellington; ☎(04) 471 2112; fax: (04) 471 1300; e-mail: dm anderson@powerlan.co.nz; internet: www.powerlan.co.nz.

Solnet Ltd: HR, PO Box 397, Wellington; ☎(04) 62 0700; fax: (04) 462 0775; e-mail: info@solnet.co.nz; internet: www.solnet.co.nz.

Sungard Treasury Systems: HR Manager, PO Box 8956, Christchurch; ☎(03) 343 7350; fax: (03) 343 7359; e-mail: Chri stchurch.jobs@treasury.sungard.com; internet: www.sungardtreasury.com.

Synergy International Limited: e-mail: bestpeople@synergy.co.nz; internet: www.synergy.co.nz.

Telecom New Zealand: Manager Capability, PO Box 570, Wellington; ☎(04) 498 9352; fax: (04) 473 2576; e-mail: crispin.webster@telecom.co.nz; internet: www.telecom.co.nz.

TelstraSaturn Ltd: HR, PO Box 38 600, Wellington; ☎(04) 939 5000; fax: (04) 939 5108; e-mail: jobs@telstrasaturn.co .nz; internet: www.telstrasaturn.co.nz.

Turnstone NZ: HR, PO Box 30449, Lower Hutt; ☎(04) 570 3899; fax: (04) 570 3888; e-mail: hr@turnstone.co.nz; internet: www.turnstone.co.nz.

Vodafone: internet: www.vodafone.co.nz or www.vizzavi.net.nz.

Wireless Data: Recruitment Manager, PO Box 37-866, Parnell, Auckland; ☎(09) 379 4710; fax: (09) 379 7360; e-mail: jobs@wirelessdatanz.com.

Law Firms

Andersen Legal: Human Capital, PO Box 1523, Auckland 1015; ☎(09) 980 6100; fax: (09) 980 6111; internet: www.andersenlegal.com.

Russell McVeagh: National HR Manager, PO Box 8, Auckland; ☎(09) 367 8293; fax: (09) 367 8598; e-mail: jackie .stead@russellmcveagh.com; internet: www.russellmcveagh.com.

Manufacturing and Marketing

AFFCO Holdings Ltd: AFFCO House, 12-26 Swanson St, Auckland; ☎(09) 355 5700; fax: (09) 355 5722; internet: www.affco-usa.com/home/home.

Alliance Group Ltd: 51 Don St, Invercargill; ☎(03) 214 2700; fax: (03) 214 2708; internet: www.alliance.co.nz.

Bendon Group Ltd: 33 Birmingham Road, East Tamaki, Auckland; ☎(09) 273 0850; fax: (09) 273 0851; internet: www.bendon.co.nz.

Carter Holt Harvey Ltd: 640 Great South Road, Manukau City, Auckland; ☎(09) 262 6000; fax: (09) 262 6099; internet: www.chh.co.nz.

Cavalier Corporation Limited: 7 Grayson Avenue, Papatoetoe Auckland; ☎(09) 277 6000; fax: (09) 279 4756; internet: www.cavcorp.co.nz.

DB Group Ltd: Level 8 Citibank Centre, 23 Customs St East, Auckland; ☎(09) 377 8990; fax: (09) 309 9422; internet: www.db.co.nz.

Dynamic Controls: Human Resource Team, PO Box 1866, Christchurch; ☎(03) 338 0016; fax: (03) 338 3283; e-mail: careers@dynamic-controls.co.nz; internet: www.Dynamic/ Mobility.co.nz.

Fisher & Paykel Healthcare Ltd: PO Box 14-348, Panmure, Auckland; ☎(09) 574 0100; fax: (09) 574 0136; e-mail: recruit@fphcare.fp.co.nz; internet: www.fphcare.com/careers.

Fisher & Paykel Whiteware Ltd: PO Box 14917, Panmure, Auckland; ☎(09) 273 0600; fax: (09) 273 0609; e-mail: F&P.Opportunities@fp.co.nz; internet: www.fphcare.com.

Frucor Beverages Group Ltd: 97 Plunket Avenue, Wiri, Auckland; ☎(09) 250 0100; fax: (09) 250 0150; internet: www.frucor.com.

Goodman Fielder NZ: HR Services, Private Bag 76 903, Manukau City, Auckland; ☎(09) 262 8556; fax: (09) 262 8557; e-mail: gfcareers@bluebird.co.nz; internet: www.goodmanfielder.com.au.

Independent Newspapers Ltd: Level 5, NZI House, 25-33 Victoria St, Wellington; ☎(04) 496 9800; fax: (04) 496 6841; internet: www.inl.co.nz.

Invensys Energy Systems (NZ) Limited: 39 Princess Street, PO Box 111-88, Christchurch; ☎(03) 343 3314 or (03) 343 7442; fax: (03) 348 8871; e-mail: Lynne.Parker@energy.invensys.com; internet: www.invensys-energy.co.nz.

Montana Group (NZ) Ltd: Level 15, Tower 2, Shortland Centre, 55-65 Shortland St, Auckland; ☎(09) 307 2660; fax: (09) 366 1579; internet: www.montanawines.com.

Methanex NZ Ltd: HR Advisor, Private Bag 2011, New Plymouth; ☎(06) 754 9700; fax: (06) 754 9809; e-mail: Jobsnp@methanex.com; internet: www.methanex.com.

NZ Refining Company Ltd: Marsden Point Road, Ruakaka; ☎(09) 432 8311; fax: (09) 432 8035.

Nuplex Industries Ltd: 12 Industry Road, Penrose, Auckland; ☎(09) 579 2029; fax: (09) 571 0542.

PDL Holdings Ltd: 14 Hazeldean Road, Christchurch; ☎(03) 338 9059; fax: (03) 338 9828; internet: www.pdl-elec.co.nz.

Pulse Data: HR Manager, PO Box 3044, Christchurch; ☎(03) 384 4555; fax: (03) 384 4933; e-mail: pdi-career@pulsedata.com; internet: www.pulsedata.com.

Steel and Tube Holdings Ltd: 15-17 Kings Crescent, Lower Hutt; ☎(04) 570 5000; fax: (04) 569 4218; internet: www.steelandtube.co.nz.

Tait Radio Communications: Technical Recruitment Officer, 558 Wairakei Road, Christchurch; ☎(03) 358 6638; fax: (03) 358 3903; e-mail: richard.copeland@tait.co.nz; internet: www.taitworld.com.

ZESPRI International Limited: HR, PO Box 9906, Auckland; ☎(09) 367 7500; fax: (09) 367 0254; e-mail: recruitment@zespri.co.nz; internet: www.zespri.com.

Mining

Otter Gold Mines Ltd: Level 7, Tower 2, Shortland Centre, 55-65 Shortland St, Auckland; ☎(09) 300 5490; fax: (09) 300 5494.

Solid Energy NZ Ltd: Level 6, Nat College House, 51 Kilmore St, Christchurch; ☎(03) 353 0100; fax: (03) 353 0116; internet: www.solidenergy.co.nz.

Science, Research and Development

ESR (Institute of Environmental Science and Research Limited): HR Manager, PO Box 29-181, Christchurch; ☎(03) 351 6019; fax: (03) 351 0010; e-mail: kim.o'keefe@esr.cri.nz; internet: www.esr.cri.nz.

Hortresearch: Human Resources, Mt Albert, Private Bag 92 169, Auckland; ☎(09) 815 4200; fax: (09) 815 4224; e-mail: cjensen@hortresearch.co.nz.

Industrial Research Limited: HR Operations Executive, PO Box 31-310, Lower Hutt, Wellington; ☎(04) 569 0209; fax: (04) 569 0019; e-mail: p.morrissey@irl.cri.nz; internet: www.irl.cri.nz.

Transport

Air New Zealand: Shared Services Recruitment Centre, Private Bag 920007, Auckland 1; ☎(09) 336 2400; fax: (09) 336 3600; e-mail: recruitment2@airnz.co.nz; internet: www.airnz.co.nz.

Owens Group Ltd: 1st Floor, Owen House, 6 Harrison Rd, Mt Wellington, Auckland; ☎(09) 580 4200; fax: (09) 525 1689; internet: www.owens.co.nz.

Transit New Zealand: HR Manager, PO Box 5084, Lambton Quay, Wellington; ☎(04) 496 6651; fax: (04) 496 6666; e-mail: gbalmain@transitnz.govt.nz.

Utilities

Contact Energy Ltd: Level 1, Harbour City Tower, 29 Brandon St, Wellington; ☎(04) 499 4001; fax: (04) 499 4003; internet: www.contactenergy.com.

Genesis Power Ltd: Level 3, 3 Osterley Way, PO Box 76-555; Manukau City, Auckland; ☎(09) 262 2094; fax: (09) 262 7495; e-mail: Jobvacancy@genesispower.co.nz; internet: www.genesispower.co.nz.

Meridian Energy Ltd: Level 2, 15 Allen St, Wellington; ☎(04) 381 1200; fax: (04) 381 1207; internet: www.meridianenergy.co.nz.

Mighty River Power Limited: 22 Fanshawe St, Auckland; ☎(09) 308 8200; fax: (09) 308 8209; internet: www.mightyriverpower.com.

Natural Gas Corporation Holdings Ltd: 22 The Terrace, Wellington; ☎(04) 499 0136; fax: (04) 499 6973.

Orion NZ Ltd: 218 Manchester St, Christchurch; ☎(03) 363 9898; fax: (03) 363 9899; internet: www.orion.co.nz.

Transpower NZ Ltd: Level 11, Unisys House, 56 The Terrace, Wellington; ☎(04) 495 7000; fax: (04) 495 7100; internet: www.transpower.co.nz.

Trustpower Ltd: Trustpower Building, Truman Lane, Te Maunga; ☎(07) 574 4825; fax: (07) 574 4825; internet: www.trustpower.co.nz.

United Networks Limited: 44 Taharoto Road, Takapuna, Auckland; ☎(09) 919 4000; fax: (09) 919 4266; internet: www.unitednetworks.co.nz.

STARTING A BUSINESS

New Zealand is a very straightforward place to do business. It has an efficient market-oriented economy, stable and reasonably secure business environment and is relatively free from corruption. The workforce is, for the most part, highly educated and skilled, and the labour market is flexible and deregulated. With one of the lowest tariff rates in the world, New Zealand companies are naturally competitive exporters. Comparative costs also make it a feasible place to set up a business - in cost-critical industries like call centres and back office business staffing costs will be up to 30% less than in Australia and up to 50% less than the USA. This is because there is no payroll tax, no social services tax and no superannuation tax. There is just a small levy for accident compensation. Property costs are another plus - good quality commercial premises will cost as little as $160-300 per square metre. Energy costs are relatively low, particularly electricity - typical office power charges are around 8c/kwh.

In principle, it is quite feasible for foreigners to set up a business or to buy part or all of an existing business in New Zealand. The prevailing attitude towards business ventures, whether started by New Zealanders or immigrants, is positive and helpful. To make a success of the venture requires, of course, the same blend of careful planning, energy and luck that you need in any country. More than anything, you need to research your chosen potential market or markets to ensure that the products or services you offer are geared to meet a real demand at an appropriate price. Much of your groundwork can be done in advance, but there is no substitute for visiting and seeing for yourself the environment in which you wish to try the venture. It may well be worth considering spending a reasonable amount of time living and working in New Zealand before making a final commitment to a particular enterprise.

In most cases, therefore, it is likely that you will have obtained New Zealand residency before setting up a business on your own. Most New Zealand investment does not require approval. Only proposals involving international investment equity of a company of 25% or more, which have a value of NZ$50 million or more, or are related to fishing quota or particular land purchases require the permission of the Overseas Investment Commission (*OIC:* Level 9, 2 The Terrace, PO Box 2498, Wellington; ☎(04) 471 3838; fax: (04) 471 3655; e-mail: oic@oic.govt.nz; internet: www.oic.govt.nz). Permission is dependent on the extent to which the projected business will contribute to the economy. However these restrictions will not affect most immigrants considering setting up a small business in New Zealand.

If you are organising your application for New Zealand residency with the intention of setting up a business there, you should note that a special scheme exists to attract business investors. (See the *Residence and Entry* Chapter). The sums required to qualify for the Business Investment category are substantial. If you do not have the necessary capital to qualify under this category, then you will need to apply under the General Skills or Family categories.

In recent years, regulations governing setting up business in New Zealand have been relaxed. The Companies Act was substantially amended in 1994 to make the process of incorporating a company simpler. There are a number of government agencies set up to help small businesses and the attitude towards entrepreneurs is positive. As part of encouraging individual initiative and competitive economic environment, the government is trying to cut down on the amount of red tape involved in doing business, and to encourage small businesses to set up. The result is that it is a good time to be starting up a new business in New Zealand. This chapter will look at what is involved in buying a business in New Zealand or in starting your own.

PREPARATION

Choosing a Business

Since in broad terms, New Zealanders engage in similar business, cultural and social activities to Europeans, there are similar potential markets for anyone contemplating setting up a new enterprise. The differences need to be borne in mind, however, not the least of which is that the comparatively small total population and its distribution will have a significant effect on the structure of potential markets. For example if you are considering setting up in the hospitality industry you will find that in the larger cities restaurants, cafés and wine bars abound; the market is pretty well saturated and thus very competitive. Such businesses are stretched to find some new competitive advantage and that is often manifested as gimmickry, which of course has a short-lived novelty appeal. In the rural areas, there are fewer restaurants and wine-bars, however there is less population to support them as New Zealand is not particularly densely populated. This may provide an opportunity, yes, but maybe one that requires a lot of 'up front' investment in marketing and publicity. Given that moving to a new country is going to be pretty challenging in itself, it may be wise to opt for a safer bet such as selecting an enterprise for which there is a known or an established market, or one in which you have particular skills and experience. Obviously there is an advantage in buying an already established business in this respect, however before you buy you should research the track record of your chosen enterprise. Remember that the majority of businesses succeed not on the uniqueness of the concept but on the application of sound and careful management techniques.

Researching Your Business

New Zealand business is characterised by the prevalence of small firms; the country has a high rate of entrepreneurship. Recently released results from the Global Entrepreneurship Monitor (GEM) showed that, in 2001, there were 234,000 New Zealand firms employing a total of 1,380,000 people - an average of fewer than six people per firm. 85% of firms employ five or fewer people, and less than 2% have 50 or more employees. The research also shows that most small firms either stay small or expire - few grow to significant sizes, so it is important to find a solid starting point for your business.

Whether it is your intention to buy a business or to set up from scratch, researching the potential market for your business is essential. The specific information that you need to determine whether there is a viable market will depend greatly upon the type of business, the services or the products you have in mind. There are companies specialising in market research in the major cities in New Zealand, which would be able to provide data on most aspects of the market or would offer to conduct specific enquiries, for a fee, in areas of the market which were less well researched. This type of service is usually beyond the budget of those setting up a small business. There are some companies offering research services specifically tailored for small businesses and you can do some of the research work yourself.

One of the first places to start looking for information is the local public library. Most public libraries run an information service for local businesses and for those intending to set up a business. They will have information on market trends, local suppliers, possible competitors, planning and development strategies. Some libraries offer a contract research service and will do a lot of the legwork by investigating the feasibility of a project for you. This may be a cost-effective option simply because they will be familiar with the sources of information and will be able to find out quickly what you need to know. Information on businesses and commerce in specific regions can be obtained from the local Chamber of Commerce. Chambers of Commerce in the main cities are listed below. Statistics New Zealand runs a professional consultancy service for data on imports, prices, population, etc. They publish the *Quarterly Economic Survey* of various sectors of the economy. Predominantly this is income and expenditure data, although they also collect investment data. Each year this is gathered into the more detailed *Annual Enterprise Survey*. More general data on the New Zealand economy is published in the monthly *Key Statistics*. They also publish the *New Zealand Year Book*, and have a detailed business and economy information menu on their website as well as several useful links (see below). If your business is involved in the export market, the Ministry of Foreign Affairs and Trade can help with economic and political information about your target markets. The government has set up a website, linked to the New Zealand Immigration Service, to provide information for people coming to New Zealand to set up businesses (www.business-migrants.govt.nz).

Researching market opportunities in New Zealand from overseas is naturally more difficult than doing the groundwork once you arrive. There are companies that offer an information gathering service specifically for intending immigrants, in areas ranging from business opportunities to education prospects. (see 'Business and Market Research Organisations' listed below). Another source of information is the *New Zealand Yearbook*, which provides a highly detailed picture of social, demographic, and economic trends in New Zealand. It is a useful introduction to the structure of the economy and the main business sectors. The disadvantage of the Yearbook is that the information is based on five yearly census data, so while it is very detailed, it is not always up to date. The last census was at the end of 2001. Copies of the Yearbook can be found in some libraries or bought at the Kiwifruits New Zealand Shop, which specialises in New Zealand products (7 Royal Opera Arcade, London SW1Y 4UY; ☎0207 930 4587; e-mail: theteam@kiwifruitsnzshop.com; internet: www.kiwifru itsnzshop.com). New Zealand High Commissions and Embassies also have copies of the Yearbook as well as individual chapters on specific topics. Another excellent source of information is the New Zealand Institute of Economic Research (☎(04) 472 1880; internet: www.nzier.org.nz), which is a primary source of information about economics in New Zealand and provides independent consulting services to the public sector, industry and businesses. It also publishes the *Quarterly Survey of Business Opinion*, which surveys private sector enterprises with at least six employees in the manufacturing, building, distribution and services industries.

Useful Addresses

Chambers of Commerce

New Zealand Chambers of Commerce: Level 9, 109 Featherston St, Wellington; ☎(04) 914 6500; internet: www.chamber.co.nz or www.nzchamber.co.nz.

Auckland Regional Chamber of Commerce and Industry: 100 Mayoral Drive, PO Box 47, Auckland; ☎(09) 309 6100; fax: (09) 309 0081; e-mail: akl@chamber.co.nz.

Wellington Chamber of Commerce: Level 9, 109 Featherston St, Wellington; ☎(04) 914 6500; fax: (04) 914 6524; e-mail: info@wgtn-chamber.co.nz.

Canterbury Employers Chamber of Commerce: 57 Kilmore St, PO Box 359, Christchurch; ☎(03) 366 5096; fax: (03) 379 5454; e-mail: info@ecc.co.nz.

Otago Chamber of Commerce and Industry Incorporated: Level 7, 106 George St, Dunedin; ☎(03) 479 0181; fax: (03) 477 0341; e-mail: office@otagochamber.co.nz.

Business and Market Research Organisations

BERL (Business and Economic Research Ltd): Level 5, 108 The Terrace, PO Box 10277, Wellington; ☎(04) 470 5550; fax: (04) 473 3276; e-mail: innovate@berl.co.nz.

Business Research Centre: Level 7, Forsyth Barr House, 45 Johnson Street, PO Box 10617, Wellington; ☎(04) 4993088; fax: (04) 499 3414.

Business Research Service: Auckland City Library; ☎(09) 307 7790; e-mail: BIS@akcity.govt.nz; internet: www.akcity.govt.nz/library/bis/bisinfo. Fee-based information service, annual membership subscription costs $180 excluding GST.

New Zealand Institute of Economic Research: 8 Halswell Street, Thorndon, PO Box 3479, Wellington; ☎(04) 472 1880; fax: (04) 472 1211; e-mail: econ@nzier.org.nz.

New Zealand Institute of Economic Research: Suite 6, Level 6, Albert Plaza Building, 87-89 Albert Street, Auckland; ☎(09) 358 1305; e-mail: econ@nzier.org.nz; internet: www.nzier.org.nz.

Government Departments

Ministry of Foreign Affairs and Trade: Stafford House, 40 The Terrace, Private Bag 18901, Wellington; ☎(04) 494 8500; fax: (04) 494 8511; internet: www.mft.govt.nz.

Statistics New Zealand (Head Office): Aorangi House, 85 Molesworth Street, PO Box 2922, Wellington; ☎(04) 495 4600; fax: (04) 495 4610; e-mail: info@stats.govt.nz or publications@stats.govt.nz; internet: www.stats.govt.nz.

Statistics New Zealand: Information Consultancy Groups:

Auckland: Compag Building, 70 Symonds Street, Private Bag, 920003, Auckland; ☎(09) 357 2100; fax: (09) 379 0859.

Christchurch: Dollan House, 401 Madras Street, Private Bag 4741, Christchurch; ☎(03) 374 8700; fax: (03) 374 8864.

Choosing an Area

Having decided on your line of business, the next logical step is to decide where to locate it. Obviously the type of business will determine this in many cases; for example choosing where to site a horticultural enterprise will largely be determined by climate. The tourism industry was once concentrated in the geothermal area around Rotorua, and the South Island more generally, with most visitors staying in Christchurch or Queenstown. Auckland and areas to the north, such as the Bay of Islands, are attracting visitors for longer stays and are growing tourism areas. Another growing sector is adventure tourism, with the south of the Waikato region around

Waitomo caves, Nelson and the West Coast likely to benefit. Export manufacturing is strongest in Auckland and Christchurch. Forestry, another export sector predicted to grow is likely to benefit the region around the central North Island. Overall Auckland is likely to continue to enjoy the highest economic growth over the next few years, but the outlook is also positive for Canterbury and the Bay of Plenty.

USEFUL BOOKS & PERIODICALS

New Zealand Books is a company that sells New Zealand published books over the internet and ships them worldwide (www.newzealandbooks.co.nz). You should also be able to order any titles you want through most bookshops.

Accounting for Small Business: Sari Hodgson, Tandem Press, 2000.

Australia and New Zealand Small Business Manual (3rd ed): Janek Ratnatunga, CCH Australia Ltd., 1992.

8 Secrets of Investment Success: M. Hawes, Penguin.

New Zealand Small Business Guide: Penguin, 1999.

Small and Medium Enterprises: a New Zealand perspective: Alan Cameron and Claire Massey, Longman, 1995.

Small Business Survival Tactics: Glen Senior and Ian McBride, Enterprise Pub., 2000.

The Small Business Book: Bridget Williams Books, 1997.

Your Successful Small Business: A New Zealand Guide to Starting Out and Staying In Business: Judith Ashton, Viking Pacific, 1992.

Periodicals

Business Development News: Ministry of Economic Development, PO Box 1473, Wellington; ☎ (04) 472 0030; fax: (04) 471 2658; internet: www.med.govt.nz.

The National Business Review: Level 26, BNZ Tower, 125 Queen Street, PO Box 1734, Auckland; ☎ (09) 307 1629; fax: (09) 307 5129; internet: www.nbr.co.nz.

Small and Medium Enterprises

Specific assistance for people wanting to set up their own business is available from the Small Business Agency Ltd. (8 Cheshire St, Wilton, Wellington; ☎(04) 475 3154). The agency provides advice to individuals as well as running more general courses on how to set up a small business. There are a number of community based enterprise and employment centres involved with developing new employment and small business initiatives, contact your regional council for details. The Small Business Company also provides assistance, information and contacts (PO Box 25 159, Christchurch; ☎(03) 365 4242; e-mail: info@tsbc.co.nz; internet: www.tsbc.co.nz). The Inland Revenue Department runs a small business advisory service, which provides help with working out your tax obligations. They can be contacted at local IRD offices. BIZinfo is a business information and referral service for individuals and small and medium enterprises, with 34 centres nationwide (☎0800 424 946; internet:

www.bizinfo.co.nz). It produces several useful publications, including *Small Business Assistance Directory*, which lists around 400 organisations, and *Planning for Success*. Staff will provide contacts and information, and can help you identify services, people and organisations who might benefit your company. They also provide information about free management training and business assistance programmes.

Buying a Business v Setting up from Scratch

The decision between buying a business or setting up your own is basically about the degree of risk you are prepared to take and what kind of capital you can raise. Buying a business requires much more money, but on the other hand, you will be buying a going concern that will provide an immediate source of income. Setting up from scratch can be done on a shoestring, but if you underestimate your financial needs at the beginning, your enterprise may not last long. Your first years in business may be difficult in terms of cash flow and unanticipated expenses, so it is important not to miscalculate the size of the budget you can realistically manage on. You may also find that the stress of changing your country of abode is enough to cope with during your first years in New Zealand, and the move to set up your own operation may be easier after you have acclimatised to New Zealand in other ways. If you do decide to go ahead and buy an existing business, the place to start looking is the daily newspapers classified sections. Specialist business estate agencies can be found in your local *Yellow Pages*.

RAISING FINANCE

Banks & Business Plans

There are various sources of loans available for small businesses, the most common being the banks. However, any lender or giver of grants will expect some reassurance of serious commitment from the person or persons asking for help. This means, in most cases, evidence that they are committing a significant amount of their own capital to the venture. As was noted above, the major reason for small business failure is bad financial planning so in order to convince a bank that you are a worthwhile investment you need to produce a business plan. Some organisations, such as The Small Business Company and BIZinfo, may be able to offer you some assistance (see contact details above). Without going into too much detail here, your business plan should include:

- A summary containing a broad outline of your vision of the business.
- A brief CV of each person involved in the business, highlighting skills, experience and expertise relevant to the scheme.
- A description of the main services or products that you intend to offer.
- Evidence that a viable market exists for your services or products.
- An outline of your marketing communication strategy (how you intend to contact your potential customers).

It should also include financial information:
Expenditure
- Start-up costs

- Cash flow projections
- Salaries
- Running (operating) costs including materials, production, utilities, premises (rent), etc.
- and other expenses (remember to make a generous allowance for contingencies).
- **Projected income** – income from sales.

Remember that you are trying to present a positive case to your audience; the more professional and credible the plan, the more chance you have of success. Clarity and a realistic, rather than optimistic, view will enhance your proposal. If the realistic approach suggests that the idea is not sound, then you must review it or even come up with another idea.

A final comment on business plans: there are people who can offer advice on how to write your plan, and you should listen to that advice. There are also people who will write it for you, but if you prepare it yourself, then you will be that much closer to an understanding of your projected business.

Investment Incentives

There are several investment incentive schemes available directly from central government. The Ministry of Economic Development (www.med.govt.nz) provides some funding through Industry New Zealand. These schemes offer grants and incentive funds to attract businesses into specific regions. You should contact your local district council for details, or see the IndustryNZ website, as this is where new programme launches are announced (www.industrynz.govt.nz). IndustryNZ also offers a Specialist Support Service and Specialist Support Grants Programme. BIZinfo provides free access to information about assistance available to businesses, including BIZ courses (☎0800 424 946; internet: www.bizinfo.co.nz). There are several Industry and Regional Assistance Programme schemes currently in place. These include:

- the Enterprise Awards Scheme, which could entitle you to up to $10,000 to fund 50% of a project;
- the Investment Ready Scheme; and
- the Regional Partnership Programme, which provides funding for well-thought-out strategies to find local solutions to local problems.

Application forms are available on the IndustryNZ website or from BIZinfo. If your idea involves environmental protection, the Ministry for the Environment Sustainable Management Fund may be a possible source of funding. Contact the Ministry for further details (PO Box 10362, Wellington; ☎(04) 917 7400; fax: (04) 917 7523; internet: www.mfe.govt.nz). Technology NZ is a government-funded agency that provides a range of programmes to assist businesses with technology-based development projects (☎0800 832 449; internet: www.technz.co.nz). If your business concept has an arts focus, Creative NZ is a worthwhile place to ask about funding possibilities (Old Public Trust Building, 131 Lambton Quay, PO Box 3806, Wellington; ☎(04) 473 0880; fax: (04) 471 2865; internet: www.creativenz.govt.nz). For businesses with a community focus, the NZ Lotteries Commission's Lottery Grants Board offers grants to community organisations (54-56 Cambridge Tce, PO

Box 3145, Wellington; ☎(04) 802 7000; fax: (04) 385 2787).

Addresses of BIZinfo Offices

Business Services (Northland) Ltd.: PO Box 221, Whangarei; ☎0800 10 22 79; fax: (09) 438 1394; e-mail: businessservices @atrix.gen.nz.

Auckland New Ventures (North Shore) Inc.: PO Boc 5079, Wellesley St, Auckland; ☎(09) 366 0860; fax: (09) 366 0883; e-mail: johnm@anvi.org.nz.

BIZ Central (Auckland): c/- Gosling Chapman, PO Box 158, Auckland; ☎(09) 303 4586; fax: (09) 914 7882; e-mail: email@bizcentral.co.nz; internet: www.bizcentral.co.nz.

Enterprise Waitakere & Te Whanau O Waipareira Joint Venture (Auckland West and Rodney): PO Box 21 848, Henderson, Waitakere City, Auckland; ☎(09) 837 1855; fax: (09) 837 1877; e-mail: lee.carr@enterprisewaitakere.co.nz; internet: www.BIZ-waitakere.co.nz.

Auckland South Lead Provider Group: PO Box 76 565, Manukau City, Auckland; ☎(09) 277 7646; fax: (09) 262 2285; e-mail: biz@enterprisingmanukau.c o.nz.

Enterprise Central Network (Waikato and Bay of Plenty): PO Box 11 241, Papamoa 3003, Tauranga; ☎0800 42 49 43; fax: (07) 572 0412; e-mail: jennis@actrix.gen.nz.

Te Runanga O Turanganui A Kiwa (Turanga Ararau) (Gisborne): PO Box 1342, Gisborne; ☎0800 74 88 72; fax: (06) 868 1061; e-mail: biz@ta-pte.org.nz; internet: www.trotak.iwi.nz.

Workforce Consultants Ltd (Hawke's Bay) : PO Box 37, Napier; ☎0800 835 1014; fax: (06) 835 7014; e-mail:

BIZ@workforce.ac.nz.

Venture Taranaki: PO Box 670, New Plymouth; ☎0800 48 36 88; fax: (06) 759 5154; e-mail: vickyd@venture.org.nz; internet: www.venture.org.nz.

Enterprise MidWest Ltd (Manawatu/ Wanganui): PO Box 12 025; Palmerston North; ☎0800 24 96 93; fax: (06) 350 1814; e-mail: admin@enterprisemidw est.org.nz; internet: www.enterprisem idwest.co.nz.

Wellington Regional Chamber of Commerce: PO Box 1590, Wellington; ☎0800 24 26 23; fax: (04) 914 6524; e-mail: cynthism@wgtn-chamber.co.nz; internet: www.wgtn-chamber.co.nz.

BIZ Marlborough: PO Box 658, Blenheim; ☎(03) 577 7347; fax: (03) 577 7400; e-mail: mcoc@clear.net.nz.

BIZ Nelson Bays (Nelson and Tasman): PO Box 1121, Nelson; ☎0800 11 18 87; fax: (03) 546 8373; e-mail: sandra.cro ne@clear.net.nz.

Canterbury Development Corporation: PO Box 2962, Christchurch; ☎0800 24 92 32; fax: (03) 379 5554; e-mail: biz@cdc.org.nz; internet: www.cdc.org.nz.

BIZ Otago: PO Box 5713, Dunedin; ☎0800 42 49 68; fax: (03) 477 0341; e-mail: biz@otagochamber.co.nz; internet: www.otagochamber.co.nz.

Venture Southland: PO Box 1306, Invercargill; ☎0800 25 52 88; fax: (03) 214 4949; e-mail: ross.grey@venturesouth land.co.nz; internet: www.venturesout hland.co.nz.

BUSINESS STRUCTURES AND REGISTRATION

Businesses in New Zealand can take various forms: Public Limited Company, Partnership, Joint Venture, Trust, or Sole Trader. The three most common forms for small businesses are sole trader, partnership or public limited company. The form of your business determines who benefits from it but also who is liable should something go wrong. It is not uncommon for businesses to start up in one form then change into another as they expand so you don't have to make a once-and-for-all decision before you start.

Sole Trader. In this structure, you are the sole owner and controller of your business. This is the simplest form of business structure to start up: you simply tell the IRD you are becoming self-employed. If your business has an annual turnover greater than $40,000 you will also need to register for Goods and Services Tax (GST), but these are the only legal formalities required. The disadvantage of the simple structure is that as a sole trader you are personally responsible for any debts incurred by your business and your personal assets can be taken as payment.

Partnership. Partnerships are formed by private agreement between the partners and their form is quite flexible, dependent upon the terms of that agreement. It is a good idea, although not legally necessary, to have a lawyer draw up or check the agreement. Juliet Ashton, in her book *Your Successful Small Business*, suggests that the agreement should cover the following:

- the name of the partnership and the business;
- the date of the agreement;
- an indication of how long the partnership is intended to last;
- the amount of capital invested by each partner in the firm and the interest on it;
- how the profits will be split;
- who is responsible for management and control of the business;
- arrangements about holidays, illness, division of responsibilities; and
- what will happen if one of the partners dies.

There is a tendency to assume you will work things out as you go along, particularly if you are going into business with a friend. However, there are many potential pitfalls in this approach, and although it may seem legalistic it is a better idea to have written clearly who is responsible for what aspect of the business rather than put your partnership under strain by not having a clear understanding from the beginning. You should in any case think twice before going into business with a friend. You need to assess objectively their strengths and weaknesses as a potential businessperson, as well as how you will get along with them under pressure. As with a sole trader structure you are personally responsible for any debts incurred by your business, even if your partner made the decisions that led the business into difficulties.

Limited Companies. As distinct from partnerships and sole-trading operations, if you own a company you are not personally responsible for its debts. The company has a separate legal existence and your liability is limited to the extent of your share ownership. However it is worth noting that if you have to borrow money to set up your company, banks will commonly require personal guarantees from the directors, so you will not be protected by the company's legal status. You can either buy a company off the shelf from one of the businesses that specialise in selling shelf companies (advertised in the *Yellow Pages*) or you can set one up yourself. Company incorporation in New Zealand was simplified under the *Companies Act* of 1993. There is now only one type of company and there is no longer any minimum or maximum number of directors or shareholders required. To set up a company you require the following:

- a name;
- at least one shareholder;
- at least one director;
- at least one share;
- a registered office; and
- an address.

The director and shareholder can be one and the same so in fact it only needs one person to set up a company. You begin by registering the name you have chosen with the Registrar of Companies. Obviously you have to pick a name that no-one else has used already. Once the name has been approved you can apply to have your company registered. Along with your application (which must state the company's name, registered office and address) you must include consents from all directors to act as such and certificates stating that they are not disqualified from acting, consents by shareholders to take the stated number of shares, notice from the Registrar reserving the company's name, and the constitution of the company if there is one.

> It is now possible to incorporate a company over the internet, by lodging incorporation documentation with the Companies Office (www.companies.govt.nz), which is a Business Unit in the Ministry of Economic Development (www.med.govt.nz). This process has made registering a company significantly cheaper and easier, as, theoretically, it can be done in a matter of minutes. The first step is to reserve your company's name online, which costs $10. The second step is registering the company, which costs $50. You will receive an electronic response from the Registrar of Companies and a certificate of incorporation, which you can print out.

Local Companies Offices are listed below:

Auckland: Level 5, District Court Building, 3 Kingston Street, Private Bag 92 061 Auckland Mail Centre, Auckland; ☎0508 266 726; fax: (09) 916 4559.

Hamilton: Level 1, ASB Building, 500 Victoria Street, Private Bag 3090, Hamilton; ☎0508 266 726; fax: (07) 957 5562.

Wellington: Level 7, Boulcott House, 47 Boulcott Street, Private Bag 5901, Lambton Quay, Wellington; ☎0508 266 726; fax: (04) 495 1254.

Christchurch: Level 4, Cardinal House, cnr Gloucester Street and Oxford Terrace, Private Bag 4714, Christchurch; ☎0508 266 726; fax: (03) 371 7001.

Dunedin: Level 1, Moray Place, Private Bag 1927, Dunedin; ☎0508 266 726; fax: (03) 955 2508.

IDEAS FOR NEW BUSINESSES

Most new immigrants will need a chance to look around once they arrive in New Zealand before deciding what line of business to take up. There are a lot of established avenues for the first time businessperson, as you will see when looking at the 'Businesses For Sale' section in the papers. Should you want to consider trying something different, the following suggestions may give you some ideas.

Accommodation. As long as the tourist boom continues, providing accommodation is likely to be a reasonably safe bet. B&Bs are not as common in New Zealand as they are in the UK although the idea is beginning to catch on, as an inexpensive accommodation option. However you will need to research the potential market carefully. Many tourists arrive on package deals with accommodation organised through the large hotel chains. Another relatively undeveloped type of accommodation in New Zealand is the country house hotel. While there are a number of luxury country lodges at top prices, the market is by no means oversupplied at the high end.

Publications. The main cities (apart from Wellington) lack a quality weekly arts and events magazine. There are a number of give-away newspapers and flyers providing a listings service, but they are usually aimed at the youth market. There is an opportunity for a well produced magazine covering the music scene, arts, leisure and general listings.

IT Personnel. The current expansion of the New Zealand IT&T industry means that many businesses are crying out for qualified and/or experienced IT staff. Although there are several large specialist recruitment agencies in the IT area, there is still room for expansion, particularly if you target your business towards providing an avenue for employers to access a selection of IT specialists looking to emigrate to New Zealand.

Tourism. The most recent development in tourism is so-called adventure tourism, not just taking pictures of the scenery but actively getting into the environment, through, for example, jet boat rides, white water rafting, bungy jumping, big game fishing, and helicopter or balloon rides. Some of these areas are already well catered for and in some cases, where the rides take place in Department of Conservation lands for example, only a few operators may be licensed. Other areas could be developed, for example, the increasingly popular eco-tourism, horse trekking, or even *Lord of the Rings* tours.

RUNNING A BUSINESS

Employing Staff

You must register as an employer before you actually employ anyone. To register, you must fill in an IRD form, which you can do online (www.ird.govt.nz). You will need an IRD number to do this (see below).

As an employer you may negotiate individual contracts of employment with your staff, or a collective contract with some or all of your employees. Employees can either nominate a bargaining agent in the negotiations or represent themselves directly. While there is a lot of flexibility over negotiating terms and conditions relevant to your workplace, certain statutory protections remain for workers.

- There is a legal minimum hourly wage of $7.70 for a person over the age of 18. This does not apply to people under the age of 18, apprentices and other trainees.
- There are eleven paid public holidays.
- After twelve months employment, employees are entitled to three weeks paid annual leave.
- Annual leave accrues after one year of service and two weeks leave should be made available within the next six months.
- Annual leave is paid at the rate of average weekly earnings or not less than the ordinary rate of pay when leave began, whichever is greater.
- Anyone employed on a part-time basis may agree with the employer that holiday pay will be included in the hourly rate, although it must be shown as a separate amount.
- Untaken annual leave and lieu days must be paid out when employment terminates.
- There are provisions for special leave in the case of bereavement, sickness (of partners, children or dependent parents) and parental leave (both maternity and paternity, although new dads get less time off than new mums).

See *Working Conditions* in the *Employment* chapter for further details. For more information, contact the NZ Employers Federation (PO Box 1786, Wellington; ☎(04) 499 4111; fax: (04) 499 4112; e-mail: nzef@nzef.org.nz).

Contracts. Employment contracts must contain a section on dispute settlement, and there are standard procedures for dealing with personal grievance cases against employers for unjustified dismissal.

Wages & Time Record. You are required to keep a wages and time record for each employee. Wages must be paid in cash unless there is an agreement to payment by cheque or direct credit. All deductions must be agreed, unless required by law. Employees or their representatives are entitled to see their own wage and time record and to claim back any arrears or wrongly made deductions.

Taxes. Your other legal obligations as an employer concern taxation. You are required to deduct payroll taxes (known as PAYE) from your employees' wages and make returns of the same to the Inland Revenue Department. Legally required taxes include: PAYE (including ACC earner premiums); levies; child support payments; and student loan repayments. Other tax deductions may include withholding tax (from payments to people who work for you on a contract-for-service basis), superannuation scheme contributions, etc. If you provide any perks for staff as part of their employment package, then you have to pay fringe benefit taxes on them. (See *Taxation* below for more details.) For more information about your tax obligations as an employer, contact the IRD (☎0800 377 772; internet: www.ird.govt.nz/employers/).

Accountants

As has been noted, the major reason for small business failure is poor management, usually poor financial control. You would be well advised to consult an accountant who specialises in dealing with small businesses to help you look after this important area. You can find a list of local accountants through BIZinfo or in your local Yellow Pages. In the case of companies there are certain statutory requirements you must fulfill with regard to financial reporting. Every company is required to keep a full, true and complete record of its affairs and transactions, including providing a Profit and Loss Account and a Balance Sheet. Accounting practice is regulated by the Institute of Chartered Accountants of New Zealand (Level 2, Cigna House, 40 Mercer Street, PO Box 11-342, Wellington; ☎(04) 474 7840; fax: (04) 473 6303; internet: www.icanz.co.nz) which provides mandatory standards for company financial reporting called Statements of Standard Accounting Practice (SSAPs). Any material departure from these has to be disclosed in financial statements. The standards are intended for use by other types of business, though not compulsory.

Taxation

The Inland Revenue Department publishes a guide for small businesses on their tax obligations. You can obtain copies from any IRD office or see the website (www.ird.govt.nz). They also run the Small Business Advisory Service which advises beginning business people on taxes they need to know about, what records to keep, how to complete tax returns and when to file returns and make payments. To get in touch with the service, you simply indicate when you register for GST or as a new employer that you would like an advisory consultation. You can either go into an IRD office for an appointment or an advisor will come and visit your office. They also run regular seminars.

Applying for an IRD number. One of the first requirements of any type of business operation is an Inland Revenue Department (IRD) number. If you already have a personal IRD number and you are a sole trader, then you can continue to use this number. If your business location is different from your home address and you are registering for GST or as an employer then you may obtain another number for your business. Companies and partnerships must have their own numbers. You apply by contacting the nearest IRD office and filling in a form. You will need a passport or birth certificate as identification for a personal IRD number. In the case of a partnership, you must provide the IRD numbers of the partners, and for a company IRD, a copy of the certificate of incorporation. If you are an individual in business you will need to fill in an IR595 form, or an IR596 if you are a partnership, trust, company or other organisation.

Types of Taxes. There are four major types of taxes which you will have to deal with when doing business in New Zealand; income tax and company tax, Goods and Services Tax (GST), Accident Compensation Levies and Fringe Benefit Tax.

Income Tax and Company Tax: Income tax is payable by all persons or business entities. Individuals are taxed on a progressive rate system whereby 19.5% is payable on earnings up to $38,000, 33% over $38,001 and 39% over $60,001. Resident companies are taxed at a flat rate of 33% on income earned, whereas non-resident companies are taxed at 38%. If your gross annual PAYE deductions are less than $100,000 then you are classed as a small employer. PAYE deductions must be paid to the IRD monthly, by the 20th of the month following the payment they were deducted from.

Goods and Services Tax (GST): All businesses with an anticipated turnover greater than $40,000 per annum are required to register for GST. GST is not a tax on your own business, it is a tax on sales to your customers (called 'taxable supplies') which you collect on behalf of the IRD. You must charge and account for GST of 12.5% on these supplies. Under the $40,000 threshold you can choose whether or not to register. If you deal with other registered businesses it may be worthwhile because they will be charging you GST which you will not be able to claim back. You pay GST on all your business inputs, supplies, etc. You then add GST to all the sales you make. You make GST returns every six months. For more GST information contact the IRD (☎ 0800 377 776).

Fringe Benefit Tax and Accident Compensation: If you provide any extra benefits to your employees, such as a company car, then you must pay fringe benefit tax. This includes benefits provided through someone other than an employer. Even if you do not provide any perks, you must send in a yearly return. ACC is a fixed levy on each member of your workforce, however, from June 1998, there is a provision for work place accident insurance to be arranged through private insurance firms. ACC earner premiums are included in PAYE deductions.

Tax Returns. Different returns will be required depending on whether you are a sole trader, a company or a partnership. The tax year runs from 1st April to 31 March, and although businesses can use different year-end dates for reporting purposes, the balance date will be related to the nearest 31st March for tax purposes. Sole traders, partnerships and companies must all complete different returns. Each company shareholder must also file an individual return. Included with each return must be a copy of the accounts. It is now possible to file monthly payroll details to the IRD online, using the ir-File Service. Large employers are obliged to do this, but small employers are encouraged to do so as well. For an interactive demonstration and registration instructions see the website (http://ir-file.ird.govt.nz) or telephone 0800 473 829. For more information about any aspect of taxation, contact your local Inland Revenue Office, see the website (www.ird.govt.nz) or phone the IRD General Inquiries line (0800 377 774).

APPENDIX

PERSONAL CASE HISTORIES

NATHAN MALES (AUSTRALIA)

Nathan's parents taught Gypsy children for a number of years from a mobile school parked by the side of the road. As a result, Nathan's earliest memories are of falling off the backs of donkeys and of knocking about in hedgerows and scrap yards with assorted tangle-haired kids. This early nomadic, outdoor experience of life led to the wanderlust that eventually took Nathan to Australia. It also laid the foundations for his interest in the environment – Nathan now works for Bush Heritage, an Australian national organisation dedicated to protecting bio-diversity through protecting the bush and the creation of reserves on private land.

Of his life – pre-Australia – Nathan remembers: 'When I was still young we settled down in the north of England and it all seems lush, green and idyllic now after all this time living in Tasmania. At the time it was wellies and raincoats, rope swings, cuts and bruises. My parents were teaching and renovating houses so our holidays were short and close to hand, largely spent on the midge-infested West Coast of Scotland. After school and university, I chose to train as a teacher, and later, discovering it to be one of the least romantic jobs there is, I fell in love, in a bookshop, with an Australian traveller. She chose to stay a few days, then "just a little while longer" which turned out to be a long hot summer and more. Then in 1997, a few days after my final exams, I found myself on a plane to Australia.'

What were your first impressions of Australia?
I flew directly to Tasmania, to Hobart, a small city nestled between the banks of a big river and the slopes of a big mountain; an outpost of the world overlooked by development. I loved it instantly. Having no plans, I wandered for a day or two, and checked out the boats in the harbour. It wasn't long before one of the owners came along and by the next day I was employed sanding woodwork, scraping off old paint and varnishing decks. I was in a heaven full of wooden yachts. I was quickly to learn that Australians are opportunists, quick to judge, laugh and take advantage of a brand new pom for less than the minimum wage. I didn't mind; I was enjoying myself. Work was easy to find; when it dried up at the boat yard I became a waiter and then made coffee in a bar. By the end of my first year, I was living with the girl from the bookshop and I had to make a serious choice. On the one hand I had an offer to join the crew of a tall ship and sail to America; on the other a job offer in an Art's Centre.

It was 'a real job' and would mean staying in Hobart. I chose to stay.

What is your visa status? Is it easy to change the status once you are in the country?

I had arrived with a year's Working Holiday visa allowing me to work for each employer for three months. The department of immigration has a reputation for being very strict about not letting people extend their stay as a tourist. Many friends with similar visas have had to go to New Zealand to apply for a new tourist visa so they could return. I was lucky as the only visa (to my knowledge) that lets people stay during the application process is one for couples where one party is Australian. I applied, was granted a bridging visa, and stayed and waited.

The department didn't seem to regard my application as being a priority, which I suppose it wasn't, and the process dragged on for almost 18 months. During this time, we were interviewed by the department and had our relationship examined with a fine-tooth comb, to the extent of having to submit exchanged letters (none of them written with the expectation that a third party in a suit would ever read them). We both survived the embarrassment and the visa arrived. I was a permanent resident.

What is Australian bureaucracy like? How does it compare with Britain?

Australian bureaucracy seems much the same as bureaucracy everywhere, everything goes along fine until you upset someone or want something that is outside of procedure and then it all gets complicated. My experience is that it is generally fair and I have never experienced anything dishonest. The police are armed, but friendly and fair.

What sort of place do you live in?

We live in a rented weather-board house on the outskirts of Hobart. As Hobart is small, getting from the edge to the city centre for work takes only ten minutes by bike. The toilet and laundry are separate, and you have to go outside to access them. There are trees all around us and a creek that runs past the end of the garden. It costs $130 a fortnight, which is about £45.

We are also building a weekend house on a little island south of Hobart. Its waterfront position looks out onto a sheltered bay – very scenic. I am always amazed that with our salaries, we can afford two houses. Land and houses are relatively cheap in Tasmania, as there is no population growth and, consequently a low demand.

Did it take long to acclimatise?

I acclimatised to Hobart instantly. The climate is something like the best of English weather most of the time. I imagine it would be different if I had moved to tropical or arid Australia. Australia has a whole range of climatic conditions and it is impossible to generalise. Hobart's architecture is distinctly Australian with many buildings dating from the settlement and convict era in the 1800s. They are based on English styles and I felt at home with them quickly.

The one thing that took me a long time to appreciate was the bushland. Most forest and woodland here is eucalyptus trees. They are dry-looking scraggy things with long ribbons of loose bark hanging down and a dusty, grey appearance. For a few years I would look at it and think, 'what a mess'. I remember the day when I first looked at a bit of bush and thought, 'that is beautiful'. Now I love it.

What's the social life like?

The Australian social life is fantastic. There is a great outdoor culture and a great tradition of a couple of cold beers after work. A regular social event in Hobart is an outdoor band that plays Latin jazz in a courtyard every Friday after work. People pour out of their offices and come along. There is a total cross section of society ranging from suits to scruffy-types, all drinking and dancing together. There is much less snobbery here. It still exists but it doesn't pervade society.

Another great favourite is coffee at the markets. Sitting at the outdoor tables of the cafés with the craft and vegetable markets going on all around, you always run into friends and a quick coffee becomes a whole morning affair, a feast. The coffee is excellent.

How does the standard of living compare with Britain?

I can put my hand on my heart and say that the standard of living you can achieve for the same money is far, far higher in Hobart than in England. Rent and housing is inexpensive, cars and fuel are cheaper. Life is outdoors and the best things are free.

There is something about the values system and attitudes here that make life simpler and rather more enjoyable. It is acceptable to drive a shabby car, nearly everyone does, and the dirt roads make new cars into shabby ones quickly anyway. The sense of sprinting to keep up with the Joneses just isn't so strong here and it gives you time to relax, go to barbecues and play cricket with the lads in the paddock.

The combination of the relaxed lifestyle, fresh seafood, which you can buy at the wharf, lots of vineyards producing superb local wine, clean air, clean water and thousands of acres of world heritage wilderness only an hour's drive away are a potent lifestyle combination. Cultural life is also strong; Hobart is alive with music and theatre. There is a symphony orchestra. Summers are busy with music festivals, arts festivals, food and wine festivals, outdoor cinema, and many events are free. One could live a full and interesting life in Hobart on a shoestring. I know lots of people who do.

What do you like best about Australia?

For me, the exciting thing about Australia is the sense of extremes. Rural and outback Australia has a heady sense of frontier. The land is harsh, dry and hot and there is a sense of being out there, humans against the elements. In the outback people wear big hats and drive pick-ups. I've seen men on horseback driving huge herds of cattle along wide dusty roads, a cloud of red dust kicked up by the hooves. In stark contrast, the big cities, especially Sydney, are ultra-modern.

What do you like least about Australia?

If I think of anything I'll let you know.

Do you think you will stay in Australia?

I haven't decided whether to stay yet, that's not to say I've decided to go either. We both have jobs that would benefit from our moving either to mainland Australia or overseas. Tasmania and Hobart are microcosms of Australia. The population is small and as a result specialist work is scarce. As you move through a career and get more specialised, you end up forced to move away or to do something different. It's a tough decision which we are postponing as long as possible.

Do you have any regrets about leaving Britain?
My main regret about leaving Britain is leaving friends behind. I keep in touch with a handful of close friends, but e-mail and telephone doesn't replace being there to help repaint the lounge room or defrost the fridge. Most of my friends and family have visited, but it's too far to see each other often. I miss the mundane things – they are irreplaceable in relationships.

What advice would you give someone thinking of coming to live and work in Australia?
Australia isn't a place for wimps or whingers. It's a bold, brash culture in a bold, harsh climate. You have to give as good as you get in order to fit in. If you love life and, if you are prepared to grab it with both hands, Australia isn't bad.

DANNY JONES (AUSTRALIA)

Danny trained as a mechanical technician in the UK and worked for various companies before eventually ending up in London employed by a fuel injection development company. Several of his workmates were Australian which, he believes, was responsible for re-kindling 'an interest I'd had in Australia since my early childhood. I am fairly sure that *Skippy the Kangaroo* sparked off my initial interest in Australia.'

Danny visited Australia on a Working Holiday visa, travelled around as much as possible and remembers that, 'my first impression of Australia was how difficult it was to appreciate the sheer size of it.' He returned to the UK determined to migrate and is now an Australian citizen, having entered the country as a permanent resident under the witness protection act and taken the Oath after the minimum two years. He now lives in a fairly large house on a quarter acre block of land in one of Melbourne's older suburbs.

Accommodation in the major cities can be difficult to find he says, 'especially when you're from overseas, as it's not so easy for agents to check your history. Leases are normally for one year so choosing the right area is important. However, the standard of living is higher than in the UK, and you get paid more while being taxed less. And houses, fuel and food are all far cheaper – although the gap does seem to be narrowing.

'It takes a lot longer to acclimatise than you think, and even after five years here we still don't quite fit in. Work is relatively easy to find, especially for mechanical trades, and by far the best way of finding work here is to just turn up and sell yourself. It's amazing how many people will give you a job despite not having advertised a vacancy. Its rare for references to be taken, and most small employers have the 'give 'em a fair go' approach.

'By far the best thing about Australia is the open space and wildlife. You never forget the first time you see a large 'roo in the wild, or a snake.' Danny's greatest dislike of Australia is its obsession with sport and the hero worship of sporting people and he gets the impression that education doesn't seem to be valued as it is in the UK. As for the famed Australian stereotypical view of the Brits, 'believe me, Australians can out whinge the British ten to one. Not that I'm whinging about it, its just an observation!'

Danny has few regrets about relocating to Australia but says, 'you miss people. And whilst they're only ever a phone call away it's difficult to talk to somebody who's sitting by the phone on a cold winter's morning when you're in your best evening mood on a hot summer night on the other side of the world. I think there's a certain amount of truth in the aboriginal belief that you belong *to* the land, not it to you, and so you will always miss the country that you were born in.'

As for the advantages of moving to Australia, 'It is the age-old scheme of life that if you work hard here you will eventually get somewhere good. My only advice to any one coming to live and work in Australia is don't fall into the trap of comparing it to home. It's not better, it's not worse, but it is certainly different!'

KATIE DA GAMA (AUSTRALIA)

Katie Da Gama, in her twenties, decided to take a working holiday in Australia after completing a demanding law degree at Cambridge University. She wanted a 'gap year' between her finals and the commencement of the her year in bar school. Katie saw the trip as an opportunity to widen her experience of the world and eventually spent a whole year in Australia.

Katie applied for a Working Holiday visa at Australia House, opting not to apply by post, and was surprised by how quick and easy it was. She made sure that she took all the appropriate supporting documentation and waited only half an hour before she was granted her visa. She applied in December for a planned February departure on a charter airline on a one-way ticket. Katie was fortunate in having family connections in Perth, and arranged to fly to Western Australia where she was met by her godmother. 'I was glad that I had somewhere to go,' she says, 'and would advise anyone undertaking this trip to have accommodation arranged. It can be very daunting arriving in a completely strange environment after such a long flight'.

Katie decided to look for temporary work in the field of office administration and registered with as many agencies as she could. She took multiple copies of her CV with her to Australia, and found that being prepared in this way made the whole process less stressful. 'It would have been helpful if I had made sure that I had references as well, though,' Katie adds. 'Almost every employer wants evidence that you are reliable and of good character, and references from previous employers, tutors or landlords are invaluable.' Katie found work within two weeks at the University of Western Australia, which she loved, and after that was never without work during the period of her stay. She also found that the contacts she made helped her with accommodation; eventually she ended up house-sitting which enabled her to save more money for her travels.

After spending approximately nine months working in Perth, Katie set off on a round-Australia trip, taking in Uluru and other outback regions. She also travelled to New Zealand and Fiji. The highlights of the trip she considers too numerous to mention, but summarises its essential quality as one of welcome. 'I was amazed by the hospitality,' she said. 'Everywhere I went people welcomed me and went out of their way to help me. I couldn't believe the level of genuine friendliness and know that I have made lifelong friends.'

Katie recommends that anyone planning a working holiday in Australia should join the Youth Hostel Association before leaving and, if possible, obtain an International Student Identity Card (ISIC). These are cheaper to organise in your home country and offer very favourable discounts. She also suggests setting up a web-based e-mail address, such as Hotmail, which can be accessed from Internet terminals anywhere you travel. 'The State Libraries in every state in Australia have free Internet access.'

Katie says, 'and if you have an email address organised you can keep in touch instantly and for free.'

On returning to the UK in February, Katie worked for a few months before starting bar school. She enjoyed her Australian experience so much that both she and her brother have now applied to emigrate there.

SALLY STARLING (AUSTRALIA)

Sally is a part of history, as she went to Australia in 1971 as a 'ten pound pom' – one of the thousands of UK immigrants lured down-under by promises of sunshine and prosperity. 'In those days,' Sally remembers, 'they *paid* you to go. I was living in London at the time, and was fed up with the cold and endless minor winter illnesses. When I saw a poster in the tube advertising the £10 scheme, I made up my mind to go on the spot, and within weeks I was on my way.' Sally arrived in Melbourne and soon moved to Sydney where she quickly found work as a secretary. She remembers that the difference in her health and general wellbeing improved very rapidly after she arrived, and her overwhelming impression was one of good fortune.

Sally lived in Sydney for four years, during which time she saved money to travel abroad. Unfortunately, whilst living in Canada, she let her immigrant status lapse, and when she decided it was time to go back to Australia she found herself having to apply anew to emigrate. 'Luckily, it was still relatively easy at that time to move to Australia, and I was absolutely convinced, after spending a few years travelling, that Australia was the country where I wanted to spend the rest of my life. To me, it had become home.' Her application was accepted and she returned to Perth where she has since made a permanent home.

When asked to describe any difficulties in adjusting to her new environment, Sally mentioned the language barrier! 'When I first arrived I just couldn't understand what people were saying,' she said. 'I found it quite intimidating when I was out in a group of people, and it took me a while to feel comfortable socially.'

Sally now owns her own highly successful business which she established, and enjoys a relaxed and prosperous lifestyle. She and her husband have recently successfully sponsored her mother-in-law's application to migrate as a retiree, and they have also attempted to sponsor Sally's brother, although this application was turned down on age grounds under the points system. Sally maintains strong links with the UK and returns for holidays and family visits regularly.

PETE AND SALLY PLIMMER (NEW ZEALAND)

Pete and Sally Plimmer were both born in Birmingham, UK, but spent the last 40 years living in the United States.

Why did you decide to relocate to New Zealand (from the USA)?

I retired, and Sally agreed with my wish to start the next stage of our lives in the most user-friendly environment we could find. Since we had vacationed in New Zealand three or four times, and had failed to agree on a location within the United States, it was an easy decision. The major components of the decision making process were: the absence of extreme swings in the weather, the friendly NZ people, the opportunity to see some of the most attractive scenery in the world, the access to other attractive South Pacific regions and the favourable exchange rate.

Where in New Zealand do you live and why?
We live in Browns Bay, about twenty minutes (on a good day) from the centre of Auckland. We enjoy a panoramic view from the back deck of our house over the Hauraki Gulf. We have access to local shopping areas, excellent local restaurants, and a series of great beaches. It is also relatively easy to get to Auckland airport.

How did you go about finding work?
I have been lecturing at Auckland University (a graduate course in Polymer Technology) and consulting with the packaging and compounding industry. This happened through a Dupont (USA) colleague, a Kiwi, who had retired and taken a position at Auckland University. He introduced me to the Chemistry Department at a time they were desperately looking for a polymer chemist!

How does the quality of life compare to other countries you have lived in?
During the 24 years that I lived in the UK I was so impoverished that my quality of life was miserable. We enjoyed a relatively, astonishingly good quality of life over the next 40 years in the USA, but I now realise that 'prosperity' and 'quality' are not necessarily related. I am now convinced that the quality of life in New Zealand exceeds that of the UK or the USA because in New Zealand there is a unique combination of components that make up the 'quality' spectrum. (1) Weather - there are no huge temperature swings, violent hurricanes or tornadoes. (2) Low crime rate. (3) Relatively clean urban areas. (4) Access to a fantastic range of year-round activities - sport, music and plays. (5) Access to the outdoors - from walking up Rangitoto to a bus tour of Abel Tasman Park, all within easy reach. (6) Access to excellent medical services. (7) A political system that is as entertaining as Gilbert and Sullivan. (8) A great suburban transportation system. (9) Great people. (10) Good value for money.

Do you have NZ residency?
We do have NZ permanent resident's status - but it took a lot of time and trouble to get it because we were both over the magic 45-year age limit when we applied. The Immigration Department granted me an exemption once I showed that I could actually make a contribution to the NZ economy (University teaching, and consulting), and would not represent a burden to society (with a US pension and private health insurance). In 1998 and 1999 we had to live for six-months in NZ in order to get the 'unlimited' returning residents visa.

How did you go about arranging initial accommodation when you first arrived?
Sally's brother has lived here since 1970, so we used his hospitality. During subsequent visits he arranged rental accommodation for us.

Did you find it easy to make friends? And what is your general impression of New Zealanders?
Since we are both avid tennis and golf players we made some good friends with people who shared these interests. In general New Zealanders are easygoing and it isn't hard to make friends. Unlike the UK (and to some extent the US) people here

are not 'hung up' about status, and accept you without question. I do notice, however, that (a) there is a level of animosity between immigrants from the UK and native New Zealanders, and (b) New Zealanders are forever harping on the fact that because NZ is so small it cannot afford things like a second Harbour Bridge or a Rapid Transit System. I do not understand this!

What do you miss, and what do you feel you are giving up by choosing to live in New Zealand?
We miss our friends in the US (including our son, who still lives in Delaware), but we have the ability to travel back to the US each year to enjoy the good summer weather there. We really haven't 'given up' anything - in fact our lives are so much fuller by being able to live here and travel as we wish.

What do you feel you are gaining?
The major thing we gain is a stable, peaceful environment in which to live - good weather, excellent and varied food and the absence of daily drug-related crime.

What advice would you offer other people considering making a permanent move to New Zealand?
I would urge them not to judge the pace of life here, or the local and national politics, against their own previous experience. They should not be fooled by the fact that English is spoken here, and should accept that things are done differently (sometimes better). This is a remote foreign country where a newcomer must be prepared to accept the fact that people can seem at first a bit naïve.

LAURENCE MOSS (NEW ZEALAND)

Originally from the UK, Laurence and his partner Holly have also lived and worked in Germany.

How did you go about getting work and residence permits? Did you run into any problems or was it relatively smooth sailing through the bureaucracy?
After offering me a job, CLEAR Communications enlisted an immigration consultancy to help me get a work permit and this went fairly smoothly. However, we used the same consultancy to get residency for Holly, and they handled that very badly. Not only did they charge exorbitantly (I subsequently applied for residency for myself, and only then realised just how inexpensive, quick and easy it could be) but they actually lost Holly's papers and tried to blame her for the delay!

Where do you live, and why? What is your commute like to work?
We are renting a house in Brown's Bay (Auckland) and before that we rented a house in Takapuna. Living by the beach and sea is still a novelty for us and we like having great views. We work in Takapuna but our commute from Brown's Bay can be unpredictable - anything from 20 to 45 minutes.

Have you managed to see much of the rest of the country?
We have travelled quite a lot but plan to do more. We've been on the Great Walks in the South Island (Fiordland, Abel Tasman and Queen Charlotte) and have visited

most of the major cities in the country. We also regularly visit Rotorua, Taupo and the Coromandel Peninsula.

What kinds of things are you doing in your spare time?
We do a lot of tramping and walking along beaches. We generally spent a lot more time outdoors getting fresh air and exercise than we did living in other countries.

How do you find the people in New Zealand?
We have found Kiwis to be generally very friendly, very relaxed and very helpful. It's been easy to make friends.

Are you planning to stay on in NZ? How often do you leave the country?
We are planning to stay in NZ for the foreseeable future but are still undecided about long term. So far, we have left NZ on average every six months to visit the UK or go on holiday elsewhere (e.g. Australia).

How would you compare the NZ work ethic and work environment to other places you have worked? New Zealanders tend to think of themselves as relatively hard-working - do you think this is true?
Our impression is that they have a positive attitude, are very commercially aware and get stuck into the job at hand. However, we have observed that people generally work fewer hours than in the UK and Germany, and people quite often disappear during working time to go sailing!

Apart from Immigration, how easy have you found it to deal with other bureaucratic aspects of life in NZ?
Things have been fairly easy, although the banks and utility companies do not seem very customer focused and don't seem to provide especially good value for money. Holly has had problems with getting the IRD to update their address records and got exasperated by their inability to send things to the correct address.

Do you know many other new residents? Is there any general feeling about NZ among such a group?
We know several UK expats and they generally consider NZ a better place to be than the UK. They do sometimes feel, however, that they are missing out financially by earning NZ dollars.

JONATHAN YOUNG AND GILLIAN WEBSTER (NEW ZEALAND)

Jonathan Young is 37 and met New Zealander Gillian Webster, 28 in London. They settled in Auckland in 1995. After spending two years working in London, Gillian wanted to return home to enjoy a quality of life she felt she could not attain in England. Jonathan was working as an equity analyst in an investment bank in London, but enjoyed playing a lot of sport and wanted to spend less time commuting and more time on his windsurfer.

Why did you decide to move to New Zealand?

My partner was homesick and wanted to be near her parents in Auckland as they got older. I wasn't enjoying the treadmill of working in London and decided it was time for a change. I travelled home with Gillian for a couple of Christmases and really like the country and the lifestyle. After London, I really appreciate leaving my job at 5.30 and being at the beach in twenty minutes.

How did you go about preparing for the move?

First of all we bought airline tickets to New Zealand which went through the US, as the luggage allowance is much more generous – you are allowed 64kg of luggage rather than only 20kg when you fly via Asia. Also, a couple of Gillian's friends were at the end of their OE (overseas experience) in London and were shipping all their belongings home, so we decided to send all our belongings in the same consignment. It lowered the cost for all of us because the first box is the most expensive. It was lucky they were going to the same city, as only one person's address can go on the shipment.

Was it difficult to get New Zealand Residency?

I contacted a recruitment agency in London and had a job lined up which gave me more points. But I found that with my degree and all my years of work experience it wasn't hard to meet the criteria for qualifying successfully. It was actually harder to fill out all the forms and get all the necessary documentation together. The actual application process is the difficult bit.

Where did you live when you first arrived?

We had no problem as we could stay with Gillian's parents for as long as we liked. But I was anxious to be independent and make a go of it so we rented accommodation until we found the kind of Victorian villa we were looking for.

What were the houses like?

The house that we rented was with some other people – they call house sharing 'flatting' but it was a five bedroomed house. The place was quite basic and cheap, but quite adequate for a couple of months. The house we eventually bought needed a lot of work done on it, and so the price was quite reasonable. We're in the middle of suburbia and on Saturday afternoon every garden proud man gets his lawn mower out – it sounds like bees!

How do you find New Zealanders?

They are very open and down to earth, but some of their brutal honesty and tactlessness took me aback. Their sense of humour is quite different, and they like to poke fun at the English and mimic the British accent by trying to say 'Oh by George'. However, they don't like it if you mimic them or point out humourous things about New Zealanders. I think they are quite patriotic. A lot of people make a big issue of Britain entering the EU, and say we 'deserted' them.

What did you miss about the UK?

The nightlife is really limited and I miss the range of theatre. There is just so much going on in London. There are also fewer Indian restaurants and not much public transport in the larger cities so you really need a car. I think most of the differences come from New Zealand being such a small population and so far away from other countries.

What are the main differences between New Zealand and the UK?
There are lots of advertisements for fencing and sheep dips on television! I think the culture is not so developed, the quality of some television programmes for instance is just awful. The television news and newspapers mostly highlight what's going on in New Zealand politics and economy and you hear very little about what is happening in the rest of the world. I also think some people in New Zealand complain about things which seem ridiculous compared to Britain – like being caught in traffic for ten minutes, being asked to work late (until 6.30pm!) or hospital waiting lists.

What advice would you give intending emigrants to New Zealand?
Find out as much as you can about the country. A good place to start is the Public Affairs office of New Zealand House in London, where the people are really helpful and friendly. And try to meet a lot of New Zealanders in London – they think quite differently to British people. And there are so many of them in the city, especially in the Aussie and Kiwi pubs.

SARAH AND NEVILLE HARRISON (NEW ZEALAND)

Thirty-two-year-old Sarah moved with her husband Neville and young daughter Emily to New Zealand last year. Before having Emily, Sarah worked as an accountant, and wanted to get back into the workforce. Neville is a trained classical musician and was working freelance.

What were our reasons for moving?
Mainly for the lifestyle, and for Emily. We were a bit tired of living in Bristol and my husband was sick of driving all over southern England for work. Basically we wanted a change. My best friend was living there, and she used to rave about the place and how relaxed it was. She sent us calendars of the place every year! And New Zealand is a great place to bring up kids. It is safe and clean and there is so much room for them to play. New Zealand children seem to be much less sophisticated and urbanised that their British equivalents. They grow up slower. I also think they are more active and play more outdoor games, and there are lots of beaches and rivers around.

How did you go about finding work?
I contacted a New Zealand recruitment company for accountancy on the web and sent my CV to them. They found me a job in Christchurch, which was OK, and useful as a bridge, but I have since found a better job once I had networked a few contacts. Any British experience seems to be held in such high regard and people seemed to be impressed that I worked in a London firm. However, my husband is a musician and found it a lot more difficult to find work. In the Arts there seems to be a lot of amateur productions around which are at the standard that would have been professional back home.

Did you encounter many problems?
Not really. We wanted to import our car but once we worked out how much it was going to cost, we found it was cheaper to buy a Japanese import once we arrived. And the pound wasn't as strong as it is now – when I came over the exchange rate was 2.35, and now it is three to one, so it would have been a lot cheaper to move if we had left it a year.

How did you first find accommodation?

We stayed in a motel for the first couple of days until we could sort out a house to rent, which was advertised in the Christchurch Press. We have since bought a house we like. Housing prices are minimal compared with the UK, we found we could buy a lot more with the pound. Most homes come with a garden, and we are living on the outskirts of Christchurch and have a quarter acre block – something we could never have afforded in Britain.

What is the New Zealand accommodation like?

I had a Kiwi friend in Bristol who used to complain all the time that the British houses looked the same, but I think that's true for New Zealand! Everyone seems to live in wooden, single-storey houses. I like that all the houses are separated and all have gardens out the back, but it does make some of the cities sprawling. Cities can look really large and then you find out they only have thirty thousand people rather than a million. Its a really different mindset.

How do you find New Zealanders?

In formal situations they are very helpful and their concept of service is very important – if they do not know the answer to an enquiry, they will go and find out and get back to you. It's quite impressive, really. Personality wise, we find them a bit parochial and introverted. Many people have asked us what we think of their country and then go on about how beautiful it is – they call it 'God's Own Country'. But they don't want to hear about what it's like overseas.

What are the main differences between New Zealand and the UK?

Travel is much more expensive as you don't have the kind of competition that exists in the UK, and you don't get the variety in clothes shopping. But the food is so fresh and tastes so strong. And I'm worried about getting sunburned all the time – it is a really big issue over here. A lot of children wear swimsuits at the beach which look like wetsuits and cover the shoulders. Also, it's strange to say, but the colours are so vivid in New Zealand. The sky for example is really deep blue, rather than the pastel shades of Britain.

Vacation Work publish:

	Paperback	Hardback
Summer Jobs Abroad	£9.99	£15.95
Summer Jobs in Britain	£9.99	£15.95
Supplement to Summer Jobs in Britain and Abroad *published in May*	£6.00	–
Work Your Way Around the World	£12.95	–
Taking a Gap Year	£11.95	–
Taking a Career Break	£11.95	–
Working in Tourism – The UK, Europe & Beyond	£11.95	–
Kibbutz Volunteer	£10.99	–
Working on Cruise Ships	£10.99	–
Teaching English Abroad	£12.95	–
The Au Pair & Nanny's Guide to Working Abroad	£12.95	–
The Good Cook's Guide to Working Worldwide	£11.95	–
Working in Ski Resorts – Europe & North America	£10.99	–
Working with Animals – The UK, Europe & Worldwide	£11.95	–
Live & Work Abroad - a Guide for Modern Nomads	£11.95	–
Working with the Environment	£11.95	–
Health Professionals Abroad	£11.95	–
Accounting Jobs Worldwide	£11.95	–
The Directory of Jobs & Careers Abroad	£12.95	–
The International Directory of Voluntary Work	£12.95	–
Live & Work in Australia & New Zealand	£10.99	–
Live & Work in Belgium, The Netherlands & Luxembourg	£10.99	–
Live & Work in France	£10.99	–
Live & Work in Germany	£10.99	–
Live & Work in Italy	£10.99	–
Live & Work in Japan	£10.99	–
Live & Work in Russia & Eastern Europe	£10.99	–
Live & Work in Saudi & the Gulf	£10.99	–
Live & Work in Scandinavia	£10.99	–
Live & Work in Scotland	£10.99	–
Live & Work in Spain & Portugal	£10.99	–
Live & Work in the USA & Canada	£10.99	–
Drive USA	£10.99	–
Hand Made in Britain - The Visitors Guide	£10.99	–
Scottish Islands - The Western Isles	£12.95	–
Scottish Islands - Orkney & Shetland	£11.95	–
The Panamericana: On the Road through Mexico and Central America	£12.95	–
Travellers Survival Kit: Australia & New Zealand	£11.95	–
Travellers Survival Kit: Cuba	£10.99	–
Travellers Survival Kit: India	£10.99	–
Travellers Survival Kit: Lebanon	£10.99	–
Travellers Survival Kit: Madagascar, Mayotte & Comoros	£10.99	–
Travellers Survival Kit: Mauritius, Seychelles & Réunion	£10.99	–
Travellers Survival Kit: Mozambique	£10.99	–
Travellers Survival Kit: Oman & the Arabian Gulf	£11.95	–
Travellers Survival Kit: South Africa	£10.99	–
Travellers Survival Kit: South America	£15.95	–
Travellers Survival Kit: Sri Lanka	£10.99	–
Travellers Survival Kit: USA & Canada	£10.99	–

Distributors of:

Summer Jobs USA	£12.95	–
Internships (On-the-Job Training Opportunities in the USA)	£18.95	–
How to Become a US Citizen	£11.95	–
World Volunteers	£10.99	–
Green Volunteers	£10.99	–

Plus 27 titles from Peterson's, the leading American academic publisher, on college education and careers in the USA. Separate catalogue available on request.

 Vacation Work Publications, 9 Park End Street, Oxford OX1 1HJ
Tel 01865–241978   Fax 01865–790885

Visit us online for more information on our unrivalled range of titles for work, travel and gap years, readers' feedback and regular updates:
www.vacationwork.co.uk